The Regulation of Psychotherapists
Volume III

Series on The Regulation of Psychotherapists

Daniel B. Hogan
with a Series Foreword by Ralph Slovenko

- **Volume I. A Study in the Philosophy and Practice of Professional Regulation.**

  A concise history of psychotherapy, including an analysis of its effectiveness, dangers, and the skills needed for therapeutic competence. Using the findings of social science research, the author argues that traditional forms of regulation, such as licensure, have not protected the public and may have had significant negative impact. He proposes a comprehensive, alternative framework for professional regulation.

- **Volume II. A Handbook of State Licensure Laws.**

  A comprehensive analysis of all laws potentially regulating psychotherapists, including physicians, psychologists, social workers, and marriage and family counselors.

- **Volume III. A Review of Malpractice Suits in the United States.**

  A description of malpractice law, followed by an examination of the impact of malpractice suits on professional practice generally and psychotherapy in particular. 300 decisions involving psychotherapeutic diagnosis, treatment, and care are analysed.

- **Volume IV. A Resource Bibliography.**

  More than 3,000 references on professional regulation, the development of the professions in society, and the nature of the psychotherapeutic process. Each area is divided into detailed subcategories preceded by an introductory discussion. The author provides a list of journals and other sources of information useful to those conducting research.

The Regulation of Psychotherapists Volume III

A Review of Malpractice Suits in the United States

Daniel B. Hogan
Harvard University

Ballinger Publishing Company • Cambridge, Massachusetts
A Subsidiary of Harper & Row, Publishers, Inc.

This book is printed on recycled paper.

Publication of this book was made possible by a grant from the Maurice Falk Medical Fund, Pittsburgh, Pennsylvania.

International Standard Book Number: 0-88410-524-5

Library of Congress Catalog Card Number: 78-23778

Printed in the United States of America

Library of Congress Cataloging in Publication Data

Hogan, Daniel B
A review of malpractice suits in the United States.

(His The regulation of psychotherapists ; v. 3)
Bibliography: p.
1. Psychotherapists—Malpractice—United States—Cases. I. Title. II. Series.
KF2910.P75H63 vol. 3 [KF2910.P753] 344'.73'017618914s
ISBN 0-88410-524-5 [344'.73'017618914] 78-23778

To David and Barrie.

Contents in Brief

Table of Contents

List of Tables

Series Foreword

The most critical issue facing the professions today is how they should be regulated. Various alternatives have been proposed. Professional associations have argued that self-regulation is the only appropriate method, reasoning that the public does not have the ability to judge professional competence. The result has been a regulatory framework dominated by the professions, with little public input or control. In the licensing field administrative boards are composed almost solely of members of the profession regulated. In the judicial sphere, malpractice law is based on a standard of care very much determined by what professionals consider acceptable practice. More important, professional associations wield tremendous power through their direct and indirect influence on nearly all aspects of regulation.

A regulated trade is a guarantee against unwanted competition, a closed shop sanctioned by the state. The pursuit of monopoly is an old one. As far back as medieval times, barbers and butchers, the only professions with ready access to sharp instruments, clashed for the exclusive right to perform surgery. (The barbers triumphed, and the blood-stained sheets they hung outside after their ministrations evolved into the barber pole.) In the mental health field a number of professional associations are attempting to achieve the type of control that the American Medical Association and American Bar Association possess in their respective fields. Thus, the American Psychological Association and the National Association of Social Workers have urged the enactment of licensing laws granting them the nearly exclusive right to practice psychotherapy. At the same time, the American Psychiatric Association argues that even these groups, should only be allowed to practice psychotherapy under appropriate medical supervision. Other professions, such as marriage and family counseling, worried about their own right to practice, have begun to lobby for additional licensing laws of their own.

According to theory, in return for a monopolistic right of practice, there is a reciprocal commitment to admit only individuals of proven competence, to insist on the observance of an ethical code of conduct, and to protect the public against bungling and extortion. In virtually every profession, however, disciplinary enforcement is virtually nonexistent. The little enforcement that there is does not act as a deterrent and is often done to protect the reputation or the economic interest of the group rather than to protect the public from harm.

The public is growing increasingly dissatisfied with the quality and cost of professional services. Malpractice suits against physicians, psychiatrists, psychologists, lawyers, and other professionals have multiplied in the last decade. Jury verdicts have escalated in size. In addition, the public has begun to demand a role on licensing boards and in the formulation and implementation of regulations involving the professions.

The question, of course, is whether any of these proposed methods of regulation are likely to prove effective. In the mental health field the problems are especially complex. The process of psychotherapy is notoriously difficult to define, the standard of competent practice is open to serious dispute, and methods of training and selection are only in their infant stages of development. It is problematic whether traditional legislative methods such as licensing or judicial methods such as the malpractice suit will prove fruitful.

What is most needed at this juncture, especially in the field of psychotherapy, is a thoughtful analysis of the impact of current efforts to regulate professional practice, along with constructive recommendations. As a first step in this process, data are necessary on the extent and impact of current regulatory efforts, including the degree to which state licensing or certification laws cover therapeutic practice and the extent to which malpractice suits have been used against psychotherapists. Such data have been almost impossible to obtain until the publication of this series, which provides the first comprehensive review of psychotherapeutic regulation.

In Volume I Daniel Hogan has constructed his recommendations for the regulation of psychotherapists. He has provided a compelling analysis of the psychotherapeutic process, documenting the extreme difficulties involved in defining and measuring therapeutic competence. He has demonstrated that academic credentials bear little if any relationship to that competence. His arguments are provocative and persuasive. The evidence marshalled by Hogan strongly suggests that licensing laws, malpractice suits, and the activities of the major professional associations have not done much to protect the public. Indeed, he suggests that the quality of services provided by licensed practitioners is no better than would be provided if there were no licensing laws.

Volumes II–IV constitute invaluable reference tools for those interested in licensing, malpractice, or regulation in general. These volumes serve as the informational base on which Hogan has constructed his recommendations for the regulation of psychotherapists.

While many have criticized current regulatory efforts, Hogan is one of the first to propose a well-thought-out and systematic alternative. I especially appreciate his emphasis on education of the public, his recommendation to require therapists to fully disclose all relevant information to clients, his view of the regulatory process as one of facilitating interaction rather than controlling behavior, and his insistence on the inclusion of the public in the formulation and implementation of any set of regulations. His analysis of how professionals develop and the evidence that psychotherapy is still a very young field of organized practice provides strong support for his ideas.

For those who are in fundamental agreement with Hogan's views, these four volumes provide excellent evidence and argument in support of their position. For those who do not, Hogan's work should encourage a sharper understanding of the issues and an examination of previously unquestioned assumptions. This latter point needs emphasis. One cannot help but be deeply impressed with the tone in which this book was written. Instead of a polemic, Hogan has chosen to present his views as one way of looking at the problem—he recognizes its limitations, and his writing reflects a respect for those with opposing points of view. Since the problem of professional regulation requires a great deal of thought and is likely to be with us for some time, it is essential that all those concerned continue to engage in constructive, dialectical discussion.

Dan Hogan has contributed an impressive study on the regulation of professions. He is to be congratulated.

Ralph Slovenko
Professor of Law & Psychiatry
Wayne State University
Detroit, Michigan
October, 1978

Acknowledgments

The review of malpractice suits contained in this volume contains some of the first fruits of a long-term research project on psychotherapeutic regulation. It would not have been possible without the support of a variety of individuals and institutions.

My greatest debt is to the Maurice Falk Medical Fund and its president, Philip Hallen. The Falk Fund originally provided a grant for nine months to conduct research on the regulation of encounter group leaders, a project that had grown out of my third-year legal thesis at the Harvard Law School.

The scope of my work expanded rapidly, however, and soon encompassed the field of psychotherapy as well.

Perhaps more important, my interest began to focus on the problem of professional regulation in general, using psychotherapy as an illustrative example.

Obviously, research on a project of this scope required considerably more time and effort than the more limited research I had originally begun. The Falk Fund continued to provide the grant support to enable this project to see the light of day, and Philip Hallen's constant belief in its importance has been of significant moral support. The Falk Fund, of course, should not be understood as endorsing any statement made or expressed herein.

Equally deserving of thanks is the Ballinger Publishing Company, which at long last has received a manuscript to be published more than four years after the original contract based on this project was signed. It involved a seemingly simple six-month rewrite of my legal thesis. That has since stretched into four years and the publication of this review as part of a four-volume series on *The Regulation of Psychotherapists.* The staff at Ballinger has provided tremendous moral support, in addition to its skilled editorial assistance. Carol Franco and Sid Seamans, in particular, have given patient guidance in the fine art of writing, as has Geoffrey Gunn. Both Sid and Gerry Galvin also provided sound advice on the design necessary for the computer printout reproduced in portions of the text.

A third institution that has provided invaluable help in the preparation of this manuscript is Harvard University, where I have been a Research Fellow in the Department of Psychology and Social Relations for the past three years. Among the faculty, David McClelland, Freed Bales, Herbert Kelman, Brendan Maher, and Pat Patullo have given support that has been greatly appreciated. Among the student body, several undergraduates and graduates did painstaking and often tedious legal research to track down the many cases reported here, to conduct the initial analysis of each case, and in the writing of their brief descriptions. Dorit Schutzengel was responsible for developing part of the initial list of cases, and helped considerably in establishing what aspects of the cases were worthy of attention. Further case writing, analysis, and checking of cases was ably done by Chris Moylan, Chris Rutkowski, Lou Cozolino, and Richard Bashner. The final job of proofing was made considerably easier by the efforts of each of the above, along with Eric Larson, Tom Tweed, and Richard Ismach.

A most important person in this process was Hal Chapel, who designed and implemented the computer programs that allowed the analysis presented herein and was responsible for the actual design of many of the pages of this book, which are photocopies of the printout from Harvard's new IBM 3800 printer. Hal worked tirelessly, well beyond the call of duty, and he amazed me with his solutions to design or theoretical problems in inputting the data. Also worthy of mention in this regard were the staff at Harvard's Office of Information Technology and the Computation Facility at the Center for the Behavioral Sciences, who were generous and helpful with their advice.

My particular gratitude goes to Jennifer Lyons for her outstanding administrative and typing assistance. Her willingness to spend long hours preparing tables and lists, and her ability to decipher my sometimes unintelligible scribbles, have significantly eased the task of completing this manuscript.

Most of us were involved at one time or another in key-punching operations, but only Connie Dionne and Gay Ann Cooney could be considered experts in this regard, and they were of considerable help.

Unfortunately, a complete list of those who deserve recognition is impossible in the space provided. Others who must be mentioned, however, include Dick Hopkins, for his recommendation of Ballinger as a publisher; Alan Stone, for his advice and guidance on my initial research on encounter group regulation and his continued support since then; the Foundation for Applied Social Science, which has administered the grants from the Maurice Falk Medical Fund; and Ken Benne and Malcolm Knowles, both formerly of Boston University, whose wisdom has helped me understand the therapeutic process.

Finally, the encouragement and faith of family and friends, especially Ann Coles, Robert Fischelis, Kent Nelson, Horace Seldon, and Barbara Westman, have been especially important to me as I labored over this book. Most of all, the love and faith of Jean Haley has made this long enterprise most rewarding and fulfilling.

Chapter 1

Introduction

In recent years the medical field has been experiencing a crisis in malpractice. The number of suits and sizes of recovery against physicians, especially surgeons, has risen exponentially. The same trend is occurring in the mental health field, where psychotherapists and mental hospitals are finding their patients more willing to sue than ever before. The highly publicized case of *Roy v. Hartogs* (1976), involving allegations of sex between therapist and patient, and the controversial decision in *O'Connor v. Donaldson* (1975), concerning a mental patient's constitutional right to treatment, illustrate the wide range of suits that are emerging.

What this trend implies about the general level of therapeutic practice, and more important, what impact these suits will have on the mental health field as a whole, are crucial issues that require careful thought. The psychotherapeutic process seems to lend itself to abuse. Reports of nude encounter groups, sexual relations between therapist and patient, and suicides caused by negligently administered treatment or care, as well as documentation of economic fraud and charlatanry, make it important to determine whether professional liability suits are an effective vehicle for preventing incompetent, unethical, or harmful practices.

Essential to such an undertaking is a thorough examination of those suits that have been brought to date. The many law review articles on the subject, however, tend to focus on a relatively narrow set of cases, while the only full-length book (Dawidoff 1973) is an attempt at theory-building, not data presentation. Thus it became necessary to conduct an original search and analysis of the literature. When initially conceived, the purpose of this research lay in documenting the points made in Volume I concerning the effectiveness of judicial regulation of professional practice. There was no intention of publishing details on each case or analyzing the information, except where directly relevant to the arguments being made about the effectiveness of judicial regulation.

As the case list expanded, however, and when it became apparent that the total number of cases represented a nearly complete collection of all reported decisions handed down, the value of presenting this information in organized form for those who might find it useful became apparent. So this book will hopefully prove of value to policymakers in the mental health field, malpractice attorneys, judges, mental hospitals, insurance companies, employers of psychotherapists, and others interested in comprehensive data concerning therapeutic malpractice.

For the purposes of this review, psychotherapy has been broadly defined. It includes what is traditionally thought of as psychotherapy, including those types of influence exerted by a practitioner on a person who is suffering and seeking relief. Generally this influence is exerted through a circumscribed series of contacts in which the healer, often with the aid of a group, attempts to induce changes in the patient's emotional state, attitude, or behavior. Although the healing influence is mainly achieved through verbal communication, acts, and rituals (*see* Frank 1973: 2–3), physical and chemical methods may be employed, such as electro-convulsive therapy and the prescription of drugs.

Psychotherapy also is taken to include many of the newer humanistic and existential psychotherapies, which focus on self-actualization and which do not necessarily define a receiver of therapy as sick or otherwise ill. At the outer limits of the definition are encounter groups, including transactional-analysis, Erhard Seminars Training (EST), sensitivity groups, and T-groups. All are included within the scope of this review.

If this review were limited to the treatment process alone, the number of cases would be reduced by a third. Because diagnosis and care are a legitimate part of the therapeutic process, suits involving them are included. This means that the wide variety of cases involving wrongful commitment or inadequate custodial care in public mental institutions are dealt with.

One of the reasons a comprehensive review of suits against therapists has not been previously conducted is the difficulty of obtaining information. Insurance companies rarely reveal information on suits brought against their policyholders, which rules out the possibility of reexamining cases settled out of court. Most suits decided at the trial level are also impossible to discover, since state and regional reporters publish few cases below the supreme court level. Even reported decisions are difficult to track down, since the legal digests and encyclopedias do not conveniently index psychotherapeutic malpractice.

Comprehensiveness was thus difficult to achieve.

The initial list of cases for this book was drawn from the relevant law review articles, which were located through the *Index to Legal Periodicals* and the *Index to Periodical Articles Related to Law* under the following headings: Malpractice, Medical Jurisprudence, Mental Health, Paraprofessionals, Physicians and Surgeons, Psychiatry, Psychology, and Psychologists. In addition *Corpus Juris Secundum*, *American Jurisprudence*, *American Law Review Digest*, and all *West Decennial Digests* were examined for relevant cases listed under the decriptive words "Physicians and Surgeons" and "Negligence." These cases were examined for relevance and for citations to other cases. Shepard's citations were used to provide further suits.

Finally, a "Lexis" search was conducted. Among other capacities, this computerized search allows all recorded decisions to be examined for the occurrence of combinations of words within a certain number of words of each other. The computer was asked to list all cases in which "mental," "electro-convulsive," "psychologist," "psychiatrist," "sanity," "wrongful commitment," "psychotherapy," "social worker," "mental institution," "mental hospital," "insane," or any root of "insane," occurred within fifteen words of "malpractice" or "negligence." The printout, which covered all federal courts and twelve states (including New York and California), provided a further list of cases, which were then examined for relevance.

The final product of this search process was a list of 300 cases involving therapeutic malpractice, either in treatment, diagnosis, or care. These 300 cases amount to more than four times the number of malpractice suits against psychotherapists previously collected and reported in one review.[1] Despite this comprehensiveness, the findings and generalizations may not be applicable to those cases that remain unreported or are settled out of court.[2] The actual number of claims that are settled is quite high.

Sandor (1957) estimates that only 1 in 100 suits ever reaches an appellate court, although Mechanic (1977) put the figure at 1 in 10 for suits brought against physicians generally. Over a three-year period, Ficarra (1968: 509) found that more than 400 suits were filed against psychiatrists insured by the group malpractice insurance policy of the American Psychiatric Association. Although the number of suits filed is far higher than decisions eventually reported, the overall incidence of suits is still relatively small, and is smaller than for physicians generally (Trent undated: 4; see also Brook et al. 1977).

Slawson (1970), for instance, conducted a regional incidence study of psychiatric malpractice in the southern California area. He reviewed all claims brought against the principal insurer for the period 1958-1967. The number of psychiatrists insured grew from 169 to 388 during this time, representing nearly half of all psychiatrists working in the area. During the ten years in question only thirty-seven claims arose—a rate of 0.014 per psychiatrist per year, or a little less than 1.5 claims per 100 psychiatrists per year. Twenty-five of these claims were resolved by the time Slawson's study was published. Of these twelve were settled before trial and seven were dismissed. Six went to trial, where the psychiatrist won a decision in four instances, lost a judgment in one case, and negotiated a settlement during trial in the final case. Twelve cases were still pending. Slawson concluded that suits against psychiatrists were infrequent, unpredictable, and not increasing.[3]

For psychologists the number of suits filed is also extremely small. Brownfain (1971), for instance, reviewed the claims file of the Interstate Fire and Casualty Company, which underwrites the Professional Liability Program of the American Psychological Association. In 1971 nearly 5,000 psychologists were enrolled in the program, which had grown considerably since the early sixties, when the membership was nearer 1,000. According to Brownfain (1971: 650), as of 1970 not a single negligence suit involving enrollees in the program had gone to trial. Since 1961 approximately ten cases per year have been dealt with by the carrier, but the total number of cases on file is less than a hundred for the fifteen-year period since the program's inception. Between 1965 and 1975 the Jury Verdict Research Company was able to find data on only two suits against psychologists in the United States (White and Gross, 1975: 267).[4]

A wide range of negligent activities are considered within the scope of this review. Under the rubric of treatment, perhaps the most disturbing negligence involves sex between therapist and patient or the disturbance of a person's marital relationship as a result of therapist intervention. The *Zipkin* case is probably most galling in this regard. There, the therapist not only engaged in sexual intercourse with his client, but recommended nude bathing, divorce, and stealing from her husband as part of the therapeutic process. In *Anclote Manor Foundation v. Wilkinson* the therapist promised plaintiff's wife that he would divorce his own wife and marry her, but did not, and the patient committed suicide a year later. Other examples of sexual abuse are not uncommon.[5]

The faddishness of many therapies, the rise of encounter groups, and the radical experimentation that many therapists seem willing to engage in has brought about a rash of cases involving rather unusual therapeutic techniques. These range from the "rage-reduction therapy" in *Abraham v. Zaslow*, wherein the therapist induces repressed anger to escape by tieing patients down and poking, beating, and otherwise torturing them, to John Rosen's treatment of schizophrenics through "direct analysis," which also involves physical beating of the patient (*see Hammer v. Rosen*).[6] Related to these cases are several involving the use of experimental drugs on patients (*see, e.g., Blauer v. State* and *Saron v. State*).

Equally disturbing are the many cases involving violent death or severe injury to a patient resulting from negligent diagnosis or custodial care. Some of these deaths are the direct result of the intervention of the therapist. In *Bellandi v. Park Sanitarium Association*, for instance, the director of a mental hospital virtually murdered a patient by administering almost a full can of ether and placing a tourniquet tightly around the patient's neck in an effort to subdue him. In *Brown v. Moore* a patient died from a broken neck and other injuries after a fall down a flight of stairs. The doctor in charge refused to perform any diagnostic tests and chose to interpret the patient's physical symptoms as hysterical paralysis.

In other cases, patients have died from falling into a vat of boiling soap (*Daley v. State*), from asphyxiation after being force fed (*People v. McCaughan*), or from the misdiagnosis of a staphylococcal infection as an hysterical reaction to a sore throat (*Weinshenk v. Kaiser*). Several other cases involve patients in mental institutions who were sexually abused by other patients.[7]

A significant number of suits concern the death or serious injury of a person attacked by an improperly restrained mental patient.[8] The most horrifying of these is *Freach v. Commonwealth*, in which a former mental patient was alleged to have sexually assaulted and killed two young boys. He performed these acts after having been released from a mental hospital and after receiving employment by the city of Scranton as a special policeman. He was released and hired, despite the fact that he allegedly had bludgeoned his great aunt to death when he was sixteen, had killed a four-year-old boy he was attempting to molest by shoving a toy rifle down his throat, and had assaulted an eleven-year-old girl with the intent to ravish her.

A number of negligence suits are significant for the serious injustices they reveal.[9] In *Dennison v. State*, for instance, a sixteen-year-old boy was institutionalized following conviction of third-degree burglary for stealing five dollars' worth of candy. During his confinement he was classified as a "low-grade moron." His efforts at obtaining release and his assertions that he was being unjustly confined were interpreted by the hospital staff as evidence of his paranoia and proof of his insanity. More than thirty years later he was finally released after the intervention of his brother-in-law. Independent tests proved that he was of normal intelligence. Despite appeal to the U.S. Supreme Court, the plaintiff lost his case, since the defendants were considered immune from suit.[10]

Finally, several suits are worthy of mention for their dramatic quality and unusualness. In *Roasario v. State*, for instance, the plaintiff had been committed to Matteawan State Hospital in New York. He maintained that his wife had a lover who cut his (the plaintiff's) arm, let the blood flow into a glass, and then drank the blood. Although the hospital staff believed these allegations to be delusional, they were discovered to be true. In *Vassolo v. County of Westchester Halcyon Rest Hospital* a patient at a mental hospital actually bit the nose off a lawyer during a meeting with the patient's wife to work out the terms of support payments. And in *Whaley v. Kirby* the plaintiff was committed after publicly protesting the denial of his driver's license and parading around the streets with a sign that contained a series of slanderous statements, including the imputation of unchastity and wanton sexual activity on the part of several state employees.

Apart from instances of sexual abuse,

physical assault, wrongful commitment, inadequate supervision, and premature release, the cases include a wide range of other forms of negligence. For instance, cases involving the incorrect diagnosis of a physical illness, when the patient was actually suffering from mental illness, or vice versa, have been included. In the area of custodial care, typical cases involve failure to protect a person from a dangerous patient, failure to bar windows to prevent suicide attempts, and carelessly releasing a dangerous and violent patient. The line is drawn with negligence unrelated to the provision of direct patient care. Thus, a suit brought by the estate of a patient who died because a cook accidentally dropped poison in hospital food would be ignored. On the other hand, a case involving a patient falling into a vat of boiling soap, where work in the soap room was part of the patient's rehabilitative program, would be considered relevant.

More than 95 percent of the 300 cases are officially reported decisions. A majority of these are appellate level or above, although the many New York cases include a significant number of trial-level decisions. The thirteen unreported suits include four cases settled out of court that were found through newspaper clippings or personal correspondence with the involved parties. Three other unreported cases have not yet been decided, and the remainder involve court decisions cited in newspapers or other media sources. Except for three suits involving the revocation by a licensing board of a therapist's right to practice, and three cases involving criminal proceedings initiated by the state, all suits are civil actions brought by private individuals against the allegedly negligent party.

The organization of this review is relatively straightforward. Following this introduction, Chapter 2 presents a brief description of the elements involved in a malpractice suit. Chapter 3 analyzes the trends and implications of the 300 cases, drawing heavily on the correlations presented in Tables 1-46 of Appendix C. Appendix A contains a brief synopsis of each case, beginning with an explanation of the study variables, abbreviations, and symbols. Appendix B lists cases involving each variable. These variables include setting of the case, year and state in which the negligent act occurred, years in which court decisions were handed down, type of court in which suit was brought, who brought suit, who was sued, what type of negligent activity was involved, what harm was caused, what legal action was brought, what special doctrines were invoked, who tried the case, what was decided, what recovery was granted, and what defenses were successful. Appendix C contains the above-mentioned correlation tables, which give the correlations of different variables with the year of suit and whom the verdict was for, among other things. This provides important information for analyzing trends and determining what variables correlate highly with success in a suit. Appendix D contains the full legal citations to all cases, and in addition includes a list of foreign cases, recent cases found too late for inclusion, additional citations for information on specific cases, and a table of cases for defendants. The remainder of the book consists of a bibliography, organized by subject area; a list of references cited in the text; and a glossary with a complete list of abbreviations used in both text and appendixes.

NOTES

1. For instance, Bellamy's (1962) review of appellate court cases from 1946 to 1961 found only eighteen cases. A follow-up three years later added five more decisions (Bel-

lamy, 1965). In their textbooks on medical malpractice, Louisell and Williams (1975; 1973) report only ten cases prior to 1950, nine decisions between 1951 and 1960, twenty-four in the sixties, and fourteen suits from 1971 to 1975. Their complete list is less than seventy-five. Perhaps the most extensive collection of cases is that of Dawidoff (1973), but his total is still less than a fourth of the cases reported here.

2. Trent (undated) has recently analyzed all claims brought against psychiatrists insured by the American Psychiatric Association's Professional Liability Program. Of the 100 claims filed since the program's inception in October 1972 through April 1976, 65 have still not been settled. These represent the more difficult suits in which the plaintiff either has a strong case or is suing for a large award. Of the claims that were closed, only 4 involved a settlement, 1 went to trial and was decided for the defendant, and the balance resulted only in legal expenses. Interestingly, the two main types of claims were for wrongful commitment (9 instances) and negligent custodial care (8 instances), which corresponds with the two most frequently occurring suits in this review. Other claims were for drug reactions (3 times), negligent electro-convulsive therapy (2), improper treatment (2), and unauthorized release of confidential information (2). There were 5 suits brought by patients who refused to pay their fees, and another 5 in which a psychiatrist was subpoenaed to testify. Neither of these is represented in the cases described in this review.

3. In an earlier study of all professional liability claims in the entire state of California, Sadusk and Waterson (1957) found that only 12 of 700 claims filed against physicians were filed against psychiatrists, with another 8 being against general practitioners because of injuries classified as psychiatric.

4. Despite the relative lack of suits against psychologists, the underwriter of the American Psychological Association's program did not intend to renew its policy at the close of the 1976 policy year (Dörkin et al. 1976: 120-21).

5. *See Colorado State Board of Medical Examiners v. Weiler, Cooper v. Board of Medical Examiners, Crocco v. Harris, Morra v. State Board of Examiners of Psychologists, Nicholson v. Han, People v. Bernstein, Ross v. Leonard, Roy v. Hartogs, Salters v. Grant, Seymour v. Lofgreen*, and *Whitesell v. Green*, as summarized herein.

6. *See Also Annis v. Donahue* (physical injury suffered in an encounter group), *Borker v. NTL Institute* (suicide allegedly resulting from encounter group), and *Grant v. NTL Institute* (physical injury resulting from encounter group).

7. *See A.A. v. State* (sodomy), *Boykin v. State* (sexual assault), *McCandless v. State* (sexual intercourse resulting in pregnancy and abortion performed without consent), and *Williams v. State* (patient raped in hospital, resulting in birth of illegitimate child).

8. *See Fair v. United States, Hicks v. United States, Johnson v. United States, Merchants National Bank v. United States, St. George v. State, Semler v. Psychiatric Institute of Washington, Taylor v. State*, and *Underwood v. United States.*

9. *See Dyzynski v. Nosal* (neighbors allegedly had immigrants committed and then took most of their money), *Groce v. Myers* (broken arm of woman, caused during scuffle with doctor, left untreated because physician claimed woman resisted treatment), *Jobson v. Henne* (plaintiff allegedly required to work eight hours a night, six nights a week in boiler house of Newark State School, while also working eight hours a day at assigned jobs in the village of Newark), *Schwartz v. Thiele* (plaintiff allegedly committed on basis of psychiatric examination of less than three minutes made in a restaurant parking lot after breakfast).

10. There are numerous cases involving wrongful commitment or the provision of inadequate treatment during confinement. Some of the more dramatic are *O'Connor v. Donaldson, Stowers v. Ardmore Acres Hospital*, and *Whitree v. State.*

Chapter 2

Malpractice Law: A Brief Description

The major form of court suits that have a direct impact on the professions are malpractice suits and other forms of civil actions. Criminal suits against practitioners for unethical activities are relatively rare, as are cases involving judicial review of decisions of administrative agencies, such as licensing boards.

The most frequent form of civil suit is based on tort or contract law. In such suits the plaintiff seeks redress for injuries sustained. These injuries may be economic (for instance, the loss of money used to pay for psychotherapeutic services), physical (broken bones or physical illnesses suffered as the result of poorly rendered services), or mental (anxiety, depression, emotional distress, and other mental upset). In addition, a plaintiff may allege denial of constitutional rights (such as the right to liberty or due process).

Decisions in a civil suit are made by a judge or jury based on the common law. The common law, or case law, as it is frequently referred to, is created by prior judicial decisions. It is the fundamental source of authority for the courts of all states but Louisiana (which is based on a civil code). Under the common law a judge determines whether a particular case falls within the rule of a prior case (*stare decisis*), or generates a new law based on the case at hand (precedent).

Tort law is by far the most important type of civil action to be considered, with more than 90 percent of all actions against psychotherapists being brought as torts, and because the partial purpose of tort law is to have an impact on professional practice.[1] The different varieties of civil suits, either in tort or contract, which may be brought against a therapist, are considerable. In the 300 cases collected here, more than twenty-five types of actions were brought, including involuntary serviture, false arrest, trespass, malicious infliction of emotional distress, abuse of process, loss of liberty, misrepresentation, libel, assault and battery, malicious prosecution, and false imprisonment. Outnumbering all actions put together, however, is the simple negligence or malpractice suit, which occurs in more than two-thirds of the cases. Because of its frequency, a brief elaboration of its history and elements is advisable.

The malpractice suit has its origins in early English common law. Sandor (1957: 459) states that the earliest mention of professional liability for physicians is to be found near the end of the thirteenth century. In 1534 the English jurist Sir

Anthony Fitzherbert provided one of the first expositions on the law of malpractice, stating: "It is the duty of every artificer to exercise his art right and truly as he ought" (*cited in* Sandor, 1957: 459).

Over the centuries the doctrine of malpractice became more fully articulated. In 1767 in the case of *Slater v. Baker & Stapleton*, the King's Bench formulated the law as follows:

> He who acts rashly acts ignorantly; and although the defendants in general may be as skilful in their respective professions as any two gentlemen in England, yet the Court cannot help saying that in this particular case they have acted ignorantly and unskilfully, contrary to the known rule and usage of surgeons. [95 English Reports 860, at 863, 2 Wils. 359, at 362.]

The first reported malpractice case in the United States was *Cross v. Guthry* in 1794. There, a physician was found liable for negligence in performing surgery on a woman, who died. Her husband was awarded damages of £40. Since this first case, thousands have followed, and U.S. malpractice law has developed its own distinct set of principles.

The essential elements necessary to support a malpractice action are fourfold. Ordinarily, a plaintiff must demonstrate that: (1) a legal duty existed between the practitioner and the injured party; (2) the practitioner was derelict in that duty (either through an act that should have occurred or through an omission); (3) the patient or client suffered harm or injury of some sort; and (4) the harm or injury was directly and proximately caused by the professional's dereliction of duty.

The first element required—existence of a legal duty—does not usually create problems for a plaintiff, since evidence of this is generally clear. The fact that a practitioner is not a physician is of no great import, since malpractice suits may be brought against any profession. Where a professional-client relationship is not alleged, however, a lawsuit will be dismissed (*see, e.g., Hammer v. Polsky*, 1962). In determining whether a professional was derelict in her or his duty, the courts will ask whether the practitioner conformed to the standard of care required, measured by the degree of ability or skill possessed by other practitioners; the degree of care, attention, diligence, or vigilance ordinarily exercised by those practitioners in the application of their skills; and the special or extraordinary skill of specialists, if the practitioner has represented himself or herself as such (U.S. DHEW, 1973a: 123).[2]

For psychiatrists this duty has been defined as bringing "to their relationship the skill and the care of a professionally qualified psychiatrist practicing in that community. . . . The concept of skill is one of technical proficiency: knowledge of and the ability to apply the medically appropriate therapy. Care on the other hand, imports a mode of execution, the guidance which the will gives to skill" (Dawidoff, 1966: 700–1). More specifically, Saxe (1969: 191) has argued that "The psychiatrist should have some degree of insight into his own motivation in order to control the countertransference. . . . [The patient's interest] may be impeded by a lack of insight by the psychiatrist into his own unconscious motivations."[3]

In determining standard of care, courts until recently would only compare a practitioner's actions with those of professionals from the same community (Holder, 1975: 53–55). This so-called "locality rule" was designed to protect rural practitioners, who would have difficulty keeping abreast of recent developments in the field. This placed an inordinate burden of proof on claimants, since practitioners from the same community were not sanguine about testifying against their fellow professionals (*Minnesota Law Review* 1961).[4] Because of improved communications, better systems of transportation, and the increase in available professional journals and postgraduate courses, however, the locality rule has been overturned in many jurisdictions, either by judicial decision or legislative action (*see, e.g.*, *Brune v. Belinkoff*, and Mass. Ann. Laws, ch. 233, § 79C [1956]). As a result, courts are increasingly allowing out-of-state physicians to testify as expert witnesses, and judges are allowing the introduction of medical tests as evidence of acceptable professional practice.

One of the more difficult tasks confronting an injured patient is to determine what school of therapy a practitioner adheres to and what standards of care are appropriate for that school. The idea that different standards are permissible developed from nineteenth-century medicine, when physicians adhered to many different schools (Kett, 1968). Each school had its own standards of practice, its own theories as to the causes and cures of disease, and its own modes of treatment. The judiciary refused to accept any one school as necessarily best. Instead, the judicial doctrine developed that where different schools of thought existed, a doctor would ordinarily be judged by the school she or he professed to follow (Prosser, 1964: 166; *see also* Pope, "Who Shall Decide When Doctors Disagree?" in *Moral Essays*, 1732, Epistle III, Line 1; *Force v. Gregory*, 63 Conn. 167, 27 A. 1116 [1893]; *Nelson v. Dahl*, 174 Minn. 574, 219 N.W. 941 [1928]).

To constitute a school, Prosser (1964: 166) has said that it "must be a recognized one with definite principles, and it must be the line of thought of at least a respectable minority of the profession." Schools of psychotherapy such as behaviorism, client-centered therapy, and psychoanalysis meet these criteria. Newer schools, such as Gestalt therapy, transactional analysis, and rational-emotive therapy, probably do as well.

Whether some of the more esoteric therapies qualify as schools, such as the "rage-reduction therapy" advocated by Robert Zaslow (see *Abraham v. Zaslow*, 1972), is a matter of judicial judgment. Stone (1970: 226) argues that the field might reduce itself to radical experimentation unless the newer therapies attempt to validate what works and what does not. On the other hand, the courts do not want to hinder necessary experimentation in an evolving profession.[5] In actually deciding a particular case, a judge may look at whether the particular school in question has developed a professional association, clearly articulated standards of practice, and ethical guidelines.

In determining the standard of care to which a practitioner will be held, two other doctrines must be taken into account. The first has to do with the psychotherapist as specialist. Generally, a practitioner will only be held to the level of performance of the ordinary practitioner in the field. However, when therapists represent themselves as experts in a particular field, they must then meet the standard of care required in that area. Thus, physicians who refer to themselves as psychiatrists will be held to a standard of care different from that of physicians who make no such claim. Similarly, clinical psychologists will probably be held to higher standards than those who do not profess to have special expertise. Where nonmedical practitioners perform psychotherapy, the courts will not require them to meet the standards of physicians or psychiatrists (*see, e.g.*, *Bogust v. Iverson*, 1960).

In some cases, where a negligent act is so glaring as to constitute sufficient evidence in itself of negligence, the requirement of expert testimony is dispensed with. This doctrine, known as *res ipsa loquitur*, originated from an early English case in which a customs officer walking near a warehouse was hit on the head by several sacks of sugar that had fallen from the window above. The judges reasoned that someone must have been negligent for these sacks to have fallen on the street (*see Scott v. London & St. Katherine*

Docks Co., 1865). According to Wigmore (1961: vol. 4, § 2509), three elements are essential before the doctrine can be invoked:

1. The apparatus must be such that in the ordinary instance no injurious operation is to be expected unless from a careless construction, inspection, or user;
2. Both inspection and user must have been at the time of the injury in the control of the party charged;
3. The injurious occurrence or condition must have happened irrespective of any voluntary action at the time by the party injured.

In the past this doctrine has had only limited applicability in malpractice suits. It is generally applied when a foreign object is left in a patient's body after surgery or after burns or other injuries are suffered while a patient is under anesthesia (U.S. DHEW, 1973: 28). In California the doctrine has been extended to situations where a rare accident occurs and some evidence of negligence exists. In the field of psychotherapy the doctrine has not been widely used. Public mental hospitals that place suicidal patients on the fourth story of a building without window bars may find the doctrine invoked against them, as may therapists who engage in unusual and obviously dangerous techniques, such as physically beating patients (*see Abraham v. Zaslow*, 1972; *Hammer v. Rosen*, 1960).

After the standard of care required has been established by expert testimony or medical treatise, the plaintiff must demonstrate that the psychotherapist deviated from this standard. Expert testimony is not necessary, and the plaintiff may demonstrate negligence through written memoranda, letters, and the statements of witnesses (Cassidy, 1974: 133–34). Unfortunately, since most treatment consists of one-to-one contact between therapist and client, evidence of negligence is difficult to substantiate. Even allegations of sexual abuse can be denied or explained as the neurotic or psychotic fantasies of a patient.

Where the therapist has simply made a mistake in judgment or has employed less skill than others in utilizing a specific method of treatment, the courts will not generally grant a verdict for the plaintiff (Rothblatt and Leroy, 1973: 263). Thus, the court in *Taig v. State* (1963) stated:

> The decision to release the patient from the hospital and place him on convalescent status was a medical judgment and the decision to continue him on convalescent out-patient status after February, 1955 and to discharge him in June were also matters of professional medical judgment. Although another physician might disagree as to the form and period of treatment to be followed, a liability would not arise; nor would it arise if the professional judgment to discharge him was in fact erroneous. [241 N.Y.S.2d 495, at 496.]

Even where negligent activity occurred, recovery is dependent upon the existence of compensable damages. This does not pose an insuperable hurdle in those suits involving physical injuries or where there has been physical contact of some sort between therapist and client. Historically, however, the judiciary has hesitated to allow an action where the only damages sought are for emotional distress or other impairment of mental functioning, including such factors as loss of self-esteem (Cassidy, 1974: 134). The basis for this position was that determining whether injury had occurred and what dollar value was to be attached to it was too difficult.[6] Today, far less hesitation exists in this regard.[7]

Where it has been demonstrated that a psychotherapist did deviate from the requisite standard of care, and the client has indeed suffered an actionable injury, it still has to be proved that the injury was proximately caused by the negligent activity. This is frequently not an easy matter. Declines in mental health may be attributable to other factors, such as loss of job, divorce, or other life changes. Where the plaintiff alleges that his or her job was lost as a result of negligent treatment, the courts may find that other precipitating factors account for the injuries equally well. In addition, the injury must not be too remotely related to the negligent act and it must be foreseeable. As Dawidoff 1973: 72) has said, "In short, the injury must be within the risk exposed by the breach, and the person who is injured must be among the group protected by the duty." In most cases it will be expert testimony that determines whether the plaintiff's injury resulted from the defendant's carelessness, except for instances that are clearly within the reach of the average person and where the negligence is so gross and readily apparent that the injury must have been caused by it (Cassidy, 1974: 135).

The end result is extreme difficulty in proving proximate causation,[8] for proving each of the necessary elements of a malpractice suit is not an easy matter. This situation is unlikely to change in the future. An analysis of the 300 suits that follow provides a picture of the circumstances that most and least frequently result in victory for the plaintiff or defendant.

NOTES

1. Although the primary purpose of tort law has been to strike an equitable settlement between plaintiff and defendant and to protect society from various kinds of harms (Prosser 1964: 14 and 634), the tort action is increasingly responding to a notion of "public policy." This involves the recognition of the public's interest in a particular case stemming from the fact that the law as decided will affect future litigants. Thus, tort law now must attempt to achieve desirable social results (Prosser 1964: 14–15).

2. This standard of care was long ago concisely summarized by Chief Justice Tindal in *Lanphier v. Phipos* (8 Carr. & Payne's 475, at 479, 173 Eng. Rep. 581, at 583 [1832]):

> Every person who enters into a learned profession undertakes to bring to the exercise of it a reasonable degree of care and skill. He does not undertake, if he is an attorney, that at all events you shall gain your case, nor does a surgeon undertake that he will perform a cure nor does he undertake to use the highest possible degree of skill. There may be persons who have higher education and greater advantages than he has, but he undertakes to bring a fair, reasonable, and competent degree of skill, and you will say whether, in this case, the injury was occasioned by the want of such skill in the defendant. The question is, whether this injury must be referred to the want of a proper degree of skill and care in the defendant or not.

3. Dawidoff (1966: 711) supports this position:

> The question in each case should be whether the doctor has taken undue advantage of the relationship for the pursuit of personal gain; whether he has demonstrated a control of his own motives which falls below the standard of the relevant psychiatric community, not alone whether his treatment was an expression of his unconscious hostility toward the patient.

4. Where the courts have adopted the "locality rule" psychiatrists are afraid that such testimony will result in ostracism from the profession. William Bellamy (*cited in* Dawidoff 1973: 62) has written that:

> Too many physicians believe that it is unethical to testify against a colleague. If more physicians would only read the Code of Ethics of the American Medical Asso-

> ciation—as adopted, too, by the American Psychiatric Association—they would see that a professional man is expected to speak up in the face of wrong.

Dawidoff (1973: 62) has offered other reasons why expert testimony is difficult to come by: "Time, financial deprivation, fear of reprisal and compromise of a reticence to come forth from a realm of privacy and confidence may loom among the motivations contributing to the 'conspiracy of silence.'"

5. William Curran (1959: 541) argues as follows:

> One might say that any practice starts out as experimental, then becomes a new procedure, and then becomes commonly accepted. At what stage in this development does its user cease to apply it at his own peril? I would think it is part of legally accepted practice while it is still a "new procedure," as long as a significant number of the profession is now using it in ordinary practice (not with experimental patients or clients). Otherwise, the law would be penalizing intelligent advances in the professions.

6. Although this represented the prevailing opinion, even as long ago as 1936 MaGruder (1936: 1067) wrote that "the courts have already given extensive protection to feelings and emotions. . . . No longer is it even approximately true that the law does not pretend to redress mental pain and anguish 'when the unlawful act complained of causes that alone.'"

7. Dawidoff (1973: 75) argues that the courts must be quite careful in allowing recovery:

> This raises an important point about any injury dealt a psychiatric patient. In the myriad of psychiatric judgments, not every palpable decline in health is actionable. Perhaps only a congeries of setbacks or the kind of serious reaction which makes further improvement more difficult and costly is or should be the occasion for successful legal recompense. There are declines of even a psychotic nature which will not and should not be compensated for, since they may be unavoidable pitfalls in working through the tangled terrain of one's mental complexion. Research in the traditional therapies as in the encounter therapy may be sparse and the unavoidable concomitants of many treatments may be psychiatric ups and downs multiplied by intensity when compared to the usual struggles of living. Thus temporary psychosis should be separated from chronic schizophrenia in the phenomena being advanced as injury. Similarly, while some psychiatrists may interpret every act of living as being a result of the psychiatrist-patient interaction, car accidents, job or marital failures and even suicide may be difficult of causal link to acts in the therapy, or at least until more ample evidence makes the psychopathology of everyday life of more universal acceptance.

8. Cassidy (1974: 135) has concluded, "It is quite likely that a psychiatrist will be liable only where the injury is substantial and explainable by nothing other than the psychiatrist's negligence."

Chapter 3

Findings

Appearing below are the major findings resulting from an analysis of the tables presented in Appendix C. These findings are generally organized in the same order as the tables. They attempt to determine what factors influence whether a final verdict will be for the plaintiff or defendant, whether trends have appeared in those variables that influence outcome, and whether the size of recovery is related to specific variables. In several instances other factors are examined, such as how initial verdicts at the trial level compare with the final outcome of trial after appeal.

Results of Suits Generally (See Tables 1 and 2)

Overall, plaintiffs won roughly 30 percent of all suits. This compares with a figure of 45 percent for defendants. Of the remaining suits, 20 percent were nonfinal for plaintiff, 3 percent were nonfinal for defendant, and 1 percent had not yet been decided. A nonfinal decision indicates that the verdict did not reach the issue of defendants' negligence, but consisted of an interim order regarding such matters as the right to examine court records or the need for a retrial. Thus, if one adds in the nonfinal decisions, plaintiffs fare as well as defendants.

The total number of suits is rising exponentially, with a third of all decisions occurring in the ten-year period from 1960-1969, and another third in the last seven years. More recently, plaintiffs are finding it easier to win, with decisions in their favor rising to nearly 40 percent of all decisions in the seventies, while the percentage of decisions in favor of defendants decreased slightly to 42 percent.

If one looks at the initial verdict before appeal, the statistics are somewhat different, because of the jury's increased tendency to decide for plaintiff, the plaintiff wins 36.3 percent of the time, as opposed to the overall average of 31.0 percent. Verdicts for defendants also increase at the trial level, however (52.7 percent to 45 percent). In the last seven years plaintiffs have won more than half of all initial decisions, while the share of verdicts for defendants decreases to roughly a quarter. Because information on the year of initial decision is frequently unavailable from the published report, more than half of all cases are listed as unspecified. Interestingly, more than 60 percent of these were decided for defendant.

Region (See Tables 3, 4, and 46)

Perhaps the most surprising finding is that New York State, with 121 cases, is the venue for 40 percent of all suits reported herein. California is next with 26 suits

(8.7 percent), Texas has 11 cases (3.7 percent), and no other state has more than 9 suits. More than half of all states have less than 2 suits each, and the following 11 have none: Alaska, Arizona, Delaware, Montana, Nebraska, Nevada, North Dakota, Rhode Island, Vermont, West Virginia, and Wyoming. The District of Columbia, Missouri, and Pennsylvania each have 9 cases.

The large number of cases reported in California, Texas, and New York is partially due to their active reporting of lower court decisions, especially New York's inclusion of trial court decisions in the Court of Claims. A number of other factors may also be involved. First, California and New York have a high concentration of therapists and mental institutions in comparison with other states. Second, their residents may be more conscious of the possibility of suing, and hence more likely to sue. Third, the quality of services, especially in the larger institutions, may be inferior to other states. Finally, both states have reputations for radical therapies with an orientation to sex and physical contact.

Plaintiffs have a better chance of winning in New York (34.7 percent) in comparison with California (23.1 percent) and other parts of the country (29.4 percent). Similarly, defendants do not win as frequently in New York (42.1 percent), as they do in California (53.8 percent) and other places (45.8 percent). At the trial level both New York and California have an even higher percentage of verdicts for the plaintiff, with a proportionate decrease in verdicts for the defendant, indicating that appeals are generally resolved in favor of the defendant. This trend does not occur in other states, where the plaintiff wins approximately 30 percent of the time, whether at trial or on appeal.

Setting of the Case (See Tables 5 and 6)

Nearly two thirds of all cases occur in hospitals, of which most are mental hospitals and two-thirds are public hospitals. Judicial proceedings, which are almost inevitably commitment proceedings, are involved 21.7 percent of the time. Suits against practitioners in private practice account for only 6.9 percent of all cases, with the remaining cases split among a variety of settings.

In all the major categories the absolute number of suits is increasing each year. The relative composition of suits has been fairly stable, however, except for the following: suits involving a mental hospital, which decreased from 60 percent of all suits in the fifties to 44.4 percent in the sixties; suits involving private hospitals, which decreased from 27.5 percent of all suits from 1850-1949 to only 9.1 percent of all suits in the seventies; and private practice, which has shown a gradual but consistent rise to its current level of 8.1 percent.

The best chance for plaintiff appears to be in suits involving encounter groups, but these statistics are misleading since the number of cases is small, and all involve out-of-court settlements. If the suit involves private practice the plaintiff's chances are distinctly better than average (42.9 percent versus 31.0 percent), while the defendant's chances of winning an outright verdict are substantially decreased (14.3 percent versus 45.0 percent). This finding is somewhat surprising, given the difficulties of proof involved, but is partially accounted for by the nature of the acts frequently alleged in this setting (sexual abuse or physical assault—both of which are considered serious moral wrongs by our society). Suits involving a hospital fare about average, although the chances for plaintiff winning are almost double in a mental hospital case versus a general hospital case (37.3 percent versus 19.4 percent). By far the least advantageous setting in which to institute a case is a judicial proceeding, where the plaintiff stands less than a one-in-five chance, while the defendant's chances are more than six in ten.

Plaintiffs (See Tables 7-10)

Approximately three-fourths of all suits are brought by patients or their representatives. In another 11.4 percent of the cases the suit is initiated by a third party injured by harm to the patient, while 10.1 percent involve a third party injured by the patient. The remaining cases involve criminal proceedings instituted by the state, or license revocation proceedings instituted by a state licensing board.

Males or their representatives brought a larger number of suits than females (54 percent to 39 percent), but the percentage of males bringing suit is decreasing. Women who are harmed stand a slightly better chance of winning than men (33.3 percent to 27.8 percent), although this difference is eliminated when nonfinal decisions are included. All types of plaintiffs are bringing more suits each year.

One's chances of winning are somewhat increased if the patient does not bring suit, although the defendant's chances of winning are also increased. This incongruity is accounted for by the fact that the nonfinal decisions for plaintiff are greater when the plaintiff is a patient.

Defendants (See Tables 11 and 12)

Three classes of defendants account for more than 90 percent of all defendants sued: (1) practitioners, who are involved in more than 30 percent of all suits; (2) the government (including officials), which accounts for a third of all suits; and (3) hospitals, which are involved as defendants a fifth of the time. Other classes of defendants make up the remainder, including the judiciary, educational institutions, paraprofessionals, and relatives of the plaintiff.

Each category of defendant is having more suits initiated against it, except for the federal government, where the number of suits has remained stable from the sixties to the seventies at about a third of all suits. In the seventies the total percentage of suits against practitioners has decreased from previous decades to less than 30 percent, while suits against the judiciary and educational institutions have risen.

The plaintiff has the best chance of winning if the suit involves the government as defendant (36.4 percent for plaintiff with another 13.6 percent nonfinal for plaintiff). Suits against the state are the most successful of any branch of government (40.0 percent). On the other hand, plaintiff does not have as good a chance where the judiciary is involved (20.0 percent for plaintiff versus 53.3 percent for defendant), or a private practitioner (21.4 percent for plaintiff versus 48.4 percent for defendant).

Negligent Treatment (See Tables 13 and 14)

Negligent treatment is involved in 32 percent of all suits, and the number of suits is increasing. Of these, thirty-three of the negligence suits have involved the question of inadequate treatment or allegations of no treatment. On the whole, such cases tend to be class-action suits involving the constitutional rights of patients in federal or state facilities.

The next most frequent type of negligent treatment is electro-convulsive therapy, of which there are seventeen reported instances. Most of these occurred in the fifties and sixties before the introduction of muscle-relaxant drugs, which have since virtually eliminated the risks of physical injury involved in this type of treatment. Related to these cases are those involving the negligent administration of drugs, which are on the increase and constitute more than 10 percent of all cases. Sexual involvement occurs in twelve cases, most of which have occurred recently. Failure to obtain consent is alleged in ten instances. Suits involving some form of physical assault as a treatment technique were found in only five instances, and are spread out in time.

Overall, suits involving negligent treatment are successful 38.5 percent of the time, with another 23.9 percent of the verdicts being nonfinal for plaintiff, and only 27.4 percent decided in favor of defendant. This compares favorably with the 31 percent figure for all 300 cases, and is significantly better than suits involving negligent diagnosis or care. The most likely suit to succeed is one involving physical assault (80.0 percent for plaintiff, 20.0 percent nonfinal for plaintiff), while suits involving sexual abuse are nearly as successful (66.7 percent for plaintiff; only 25.0 percent for defendant). Where the negligent activity is simply not providing adequate treatment or providing no treatment at all, plaintiffs win nearly half the time, with another 30 percent of the cases resulting in nonfinal decisions in their favor. The least advantageous suit for plaintiff involves negligent electroconvulsive therapy or the failure to obtain an informed consent, which succeeds about 10 percent of the time, and which results in a verdict for the defendant approximately 40 percent of the time.

Negligent Diagnosis (See Tables 15-18)

Negligent diagnosis is involved in exactly half of all suits, and its frequency is increasing. By far the most common allegation is negligently diagnosing mental illness instead of sanity, which involves 41 percent of all cases. Of these cases, 14 percent saw the plaintiff allege that the defendant wrongly concluded that a patient was not dangerous, when the reverse was alleged to be true. The only other frequently occurring allegation was failure to recognize a patient's suicidal tendencies, which was alleged in eleven cases (6.3 percent). Very rarely was suit brought for diagnosing sanity when a person was mentally ill; for diagnosing dangerousness when a person was not; or for diagnosing suicidal tendencies when a person did not have them. This is not surprising since demonstration of significant harm, apart from loss of liberty, is difficult. When the diagnosis concerned the type of treatment or care needed, suits were also infrequent.

What action was taken about a patient as a result of the particular diagnosis varies considerably. Improper commitment (41 percent) was alleged more than three times as frequently as any other allegation, which coincides with the frequency of negligently diagnosing mental illness. Tied for the second most common result were improper care and improper release, both of which occurred in twenty-six instances (15.2 percent). Other frequent results included improper treatment (10.5 percent), improper failure to release (8.8 percent), and improper prescription of drugs (5.8 percent). Interestingly, only one reported case exists of negligently failing to commit a person.

Nearly all types of allegations of negligent diagnosis are increasing. The only marked exception is the claim of lack of suicidal tendencies, more than half of which occurred in the sixties. The proportion of each type of suit within a given period has remained fairly stable, except for cases involving a diagnosis of lack of suicidal tendencies, which decreased from roughly 10 percent of all cases in the fifties and sixties to 2.7 percent in the seventies. Trends in the result of diagnosis are more variable. Nearly half of all instances allegedly resulting in improper care occurred in the sixties, which constituted roughly 20 percent of all suits brought for negligent diagnosis in that time period. In the seventies this latter figure had dropped to 7 percent. Exhibiting a steady decline is improper release, while negligent failure to release has risen to its current level of 16 percent of all cases in the seventies.

Plaintiff's chances of succeeding in a suit involving negligent diagnosis are not good. Overall, plaintiff wins less than 25 percent of all suits, while the defendants win nearly 60 percent of the time. The best chances for the suing party are an allegation that dangerousness was diagnosed, instead of harmlessness, or that the wrong type of care was prescribed. Even so, the rate of success in each case is based on a fairly small sample size. Clearly one of the least successful routes is to argue that the defendant should have diagnosed sanity instead of mental illness, since plaintiff wins only 15 percent of the time, and the defendant is victorious roughly six out of ten times. Even worse is alleging that the defendant should have found a person mentally ill, instead of sane. This will result in a verdict for the defendant in more than three-fourths of all cases.

Negligent Care (See Tables 19 and 20)

Negligent care is alleged in nearly half of all suits (47.0 percent). By far the most typical allegation is the claim that defendant did not provide adequate supervision (65.4 percent). Accounting for more than half of the remaining cases is the general allegation of failing to provide proper care (18.5 percent), followed by the claim of negligent release (5.6 percent) and failing to warn third parties or improperly giving confidential information to others (3.7 percent each). Overall the number of suits in this category are leveling off, which may be a result of the decline in the population of mental institutions or the increasing use of tranquilizing drugs to control violent and destructive behavior.

Allegations of inadequate supervision have declined from 82.8 percent of all cases prior to 1950 to only 56.1 percent in the seventies, which may again reflect the decline in numbers of institutionalized patients. Alternatively, supervisory techniques may have become more sophisticated. On the other hand, suits involving failure to provide proper care are increasing both absolutely (more than 400 percent since the fifties) and as a percentage of all suits within each decade, having more than doubled since the fifties.

The successfulness of suits involving negligent care are about average. The best chance for the plaintiff occurs in suits for improper care, which will succeed almost half the time, and where 20 percent of the cases will result in at least a nonfinal verdict for the plaintiff. Premature release, on the other hand, has only a one-in-ten chance of winning, but stands to lose outright more than three-fourths of the time.

Harm Caused (See Tables 21 and 22)

In any individual suit more than one type of harm may have occurred, and it may have happened to more than one individual. Accidental injuries are the most frequently reported, involving approximately a fifth of all cases. Suicide, accidental death, loss of liberty, and deprivation of constitutional rights are each alleged in 10 percent of the cases. Sexual or marital harm occurs in only 4.4 percent of all cases, and economic loss is alleged only 5.7 percent of the time.

Many of the types of harm alleged vary widely and do not lend themselves to easy categorization. Most types are increasing, due in part to the rapid rise in the number of suits. Suicide, however, has decreased from an average level of 10–12 percent of all cases before 1970 to 5.5 percent in the seventies. This is also true for accidental death (from more than 10 percent to 5 percent) and accidental injuries (from 34 percent to 14 percent in the seventies). Similarly, nearly half of all suicides reported herein occurred in the sixties, with only a fifth taking place in the seventies; and more than half of all suits involving economic loss took place in the sixties, while the seventies account for less than a third.

Not surprisingly, the type of harm that elicits the largest likelihood of success in court is sexual abuse or disruption of the marital relationship. This yields a favorable result 60 percent of the time, with defendants winning fewer than 30 percent of all cases (the remainder are nonfinal decisions). Despite difficulties of proof (and perhaps because other injuries are alleged as well), suits involving emotional distress will be resolved in plaintiff's favor more than half the time. The successfulness of suits involving exacerbation of one's previous condition, self-inflicted injury, and deprivation of one's constitutional rights is also above average, although self-inflicted injuries show a high rate of victory for the defendant. Suits other than those mentioned do not fare particularly well, with economic loss offering one of the poorest chances (26.1 percent for plaintiff and 65.2 percent for defendant).

Type of Action Brought (See Tables 23-26)

Despite the myriad actions available, the simple negligence or malpractice suit is by far the most preferred by plaintiffs, occurring in more than half of all cases, and more than five times as frequently as the next most common legal action, which is deprivation of one's constitutional rights (11.3 percent). After these two, an assortment of actions exists, ranging from false imprisonment (8.0 percent) to administrative law (less than 1 percent). Occasionally suits are brought for false arrest, trespass, malicious infliction of emotional distress, abuse of process, and misrepresentation. Although negligence suits are the most common, they are showing a gradual decline in relation to other suits. Most of this decline is accounted for by the rise in suits involving constitutional rights. Otherwise the relative composition of suits has not changed significantly, and there has been a consistent increase in all types of suits each decade.

The types of suits that fare best do not involve tort law. Instead, criminal suits, administrative actions, and suits involving constitutional rights are the most successful. This is especially true of suits for equitable relief and class actions, both of which recently have risen dramatically in frequency. This fact may be somewhat misleading in the case of criminal suits and administrative actions, since the number of cases involved is small, and it is unlikely that an administrative decision in favor of the defendant would ever be appealed to a court of law.

They very worst suits from the plaintiff's point of view are those for malicious prosecution and false imprisonment. The former has a success rate of less than 10 percent, while the latter percentage is less than one in four. In both cases the defendants win more than half of all cases brought. Defamation of character is also unlikely to succeed (18.2 percent for plaintiff; 45.5 percent for defendant), although the nonfinals in favor of plaintiff are relatively high (36.4 percent). Suits brought in negligence are about average in their success rate (31.4 percent for plaintiff, 46.3 percent for defendant, 18.3 percent nonfinal for plaintiff, and 3.1 percent nonfinal for defendant).

State versus Federal Suits (See Tables 27 and 28)

State suits outnumber federal suits by a margin of four to one. The absolute number of suits for either category doubled from the fifties to sixties, but federal suits are increasing at a faster rate and now represent nearly 30 percent of all suits. Suit in a federal court offers a slightly better chance of success for the plaintiff, although the margin is probably not statistically significant and is most likely accounted for by the right-to-treatment cases.

Trier of Fact (See Tables 29 and 30)

Surprisingly, a jury is known to be involved in a decision only one out of every five cases. In virtually all other instances a judge is responsible for the final decision, either because no jury was involved or because summary judgment, judgment notwithstanding the verdict, or some other similar judgment led to the jury being overruled or not looked toward. Given the nature of malpractice suits and the tendency of a jury to be more favorable to the plaintiff, one would expect a higher percentage of cases involving juries to be won by plaintiff. One possible explanation for their relatively low use in these cases is the high percentage of cases involving suits against New York State that were decided in the New York Court of Claims, which has no provision for a jury.

The percentage of cases involving a jury is gradually increasing, and nearly doubled from 1950 to 1960 (17.7 percent to 32.3 percent). On the other hand, the number of instances in which a judge decides a case in which the jury is present has declined from 40.0 percent prior to 1950 to 9.1 percent in the seventies.

In terms of results, the data clearly support the contention that a jury is a more favorable forum for the plaintiff than a judge. Judges decided in favor of the plaintiff only 26.0 percent of the time, compared with 43.5 percent for a jury, although judges tended to award plaintiffs a higher percentage of nonfinal decisions. From the defendant's point of view, judges awarded verdicts for the defendant in more than half of all suits, while juries did so less than a third of the time.

Level of Court (See Tables 31-34)

Virtually all suits discussed in this review have been at the trial level. The only exceptions are the four suits settled out of court, three suits that have not yet been decided, and two suits that were heard directly by a state supreme court. Two suits have been at the trial level twice (as opposed to retrial) because of a rehearing or further order of the trial court. One case (*Pettis*) went through six different judicial decisions. More than half of all cases involved an appeal to an intermediate court, and more than a third saw either direct appeal from a trial court decision or appeal from an intermediate court to a state supreme court or the U.S. Supreme Court. Unfortunately the number of decisions in which the date of decision is not known is extremely high (29.1 percent of all decisions). This is due to the fact that reported decisions at the appellate level or above frequently do not provide the date of decision for the court of first instance.

Considering decisions that may have been appealed from, as well as those that were not, the plaintiff's best chance appears to be on remand, where verdict is for the plaintiff in nearly half of all cases. The defendant fares best if a verdict is appealed to the United States Supreme Court from a state court (16.7 percent for plaintiff; 66.7 percent for defendant) or if it is otherwise appealed to a state or federal appellate or supreme court, where the plaintiff has only a one-in-four chance of winning and a one-in-two chance of losing. For all trial decisions the plaintiff fares slightly better than the average for all final decisions. This means that plaintiffs do better than average at the trial level, fare less well on initial appeals, but do well on remand if they are persistent.

If one looks at decisions that are not subsequently appealed, but where there has been at least one previous appeal (see Table 34), and if one compares those results with unappealed decisions (see Table 33: "Trial Court"), certain interesting trends appear. An unappealed trial court decision is decided in favor of plaintiff nearly half the time, as compared with the average of 31 percent. Such decisions have a 10 percent less chance of being decided in favor of defendant. As before, decisions decided by the United States Supreme Court on appeal from a state court, or final decisions at the appellate or supreme court level, whether federal or state, much more strongly favor the defendant. The clear message is that plaintiffs do not fare well on appeal, unless they are willing to fight through three or four court decisions to have their case eventually remanded for a final decision by a lower court.

Reason Suit Failed (See Tables 35 and 36)

When a plaintiff loses, the typical reason is failure to demonstrate negligence, which is the case more than half the time. Another quarter of all failures result from some form of judicial or governmental immunity. Most states have recently begun to relax this doctrine, either through judicial decision or legislative amendment, which means that immunity should play a smaller role in the future. The only other frequently mentioned ground for defeat is failure to state a cause of action (11.6 percent), which means that even if true, the facts as stated by plaintiff would not be grounds for relief. The reasons why suits have failed have remained fairly stable over time.

Recovery (See Tables 37-40)[1]

Of the ninety-three suits won by the plaintiff, the amount of recovery granted is known in fifty-seven cases. Of the remainder: (1) the suit did not ask for damages, demanding equitable relief or criminal penalties instead; (2) the amount of recovery was not stated; or (3) the amount was to be determined by subsequent trial.

The mean recovery for all suits was $45,504, although the median was somewhat lower at $20,000. Thirteen suits involved awards of $50,000 or more, with another twelve granting recoveries between $25,000 and $50,000. Most of these occurred recently. These rather large figures are undoubtedly not representative of the typical suit, since smaller awards are probably seldom appealed and go unreported.

Reported versus Unreported Decisions. Unreported decisions constitute more than half of all decisions at the $50,000 level or above, with a median of $85,111. The number of other unreported but large decisions is probably not great, since these would most likely receive considerable attention in the press, and therefore come to the attention of researchers in the field.

Region. The number of recoveries in New York State is distinctly above average—it has slightly more than half of all recoveries, though only 40 percent of all suits were in New York. California, while granting fewer monetary awards, gives extremely large recoveries (mean = $121,250). The remaining states grant fewer awards and their average size is slightly less than the mean for all cases.

Setting. Plaintiffs have a better chance of receiving an award if the setting of their case is a hospital, especially for verdicts of $25,000 or more. Mental hospitals offer the best chance for a large recovery (72 percent of all $25,000-plus recoveries occurred in such a setting, although mental hospitals were involved in only half of all cases). Where the suit involves private practice, the chances of recovery are about average, although the size of recovery is more then $8,000 above the mean. Judicial proceedings offer the worst odds, recoveries being nonexistent at the $25,000-plus level, and the mean recovery rate being only $5,800. Otherwise, the setting of the case does not affect the chance or size of recovery to any great extent.

Plaintiff. Interestingly, a patient injured by psychotherapy or in a hospital has less chance of recovering than a person who is injured by harm to the patient (such as the husband of a woman whose earning power is lost) or a person injured by the patient. In fact, persons injured by patients had nearly a third of all $50,000-plus recoveries. These recoveries also tended to be the largest of any plaintiff type, with a mean of $76,722.

Defendant. When one of the defendants involved in a suit is a hospital, the chances of recovery are about normal. Hospitals are involved more than 50 percent of the time in suits granting recoveries at the $25,000 to $50,000 level. Suits against state governments grant recoveries in a higher percentage of cases than normal, except for extremely large awards. In the case of practitioners, both the chance and size of recovery are about normal. The average level of recovery for suits against the federal government is an extremely large $150,000, but this is based on only two decisions. At the opposite end of the spectrum, when an educational institution is involved, the level of recovery is a meagre $1,750, but again this is based on only two cases.

Negligent Treatment. The mean amount of recovery for all cases involving negligent treatment ($64,352; N = 25) is roughly $20,000 above the mean for all cases. Perhaps the most surprising finding is that the chance of recovery for a suit involving sexual abuse is not much greater than normal, and the mean size of recovery ($25,320) is distinctly below the mean for all cases. On the other hand, awards for physical assaults ($131,250) are three times the mean for all cases, while allegations of negligent administration of drugs or the provision of inadequate treatment yields a mean recovery rate approximately four times the mean for all cases ($170,000 and $160,000, respectively), but again these mean figures are based on only two cases each.

Negligent Diagnosis. Twenty cases alleging negligent diagnosis awarded recovery to the plaintiff, with a mean level of $82,275. This high level is largely accounted for by those cases involving the negligent diagnosis of lack of dangerousness, with three recoveries at the $50,000-plus level. Diagnosing mental or physical illness instead of its opposite, or sanity instead of mental illness, leads to an average recovery of more than $100,000, although the number of cases involved is small (5 cases). As would be expected, diagnosing somebody as mentally ill when she or he was allegedly sane offers a reduced chance of the plaintiff winning as well as a below-average level of recovery for cases won by plaintiff. These suits generally involve wrongful commitment, which offers very little chance of the plaintiff winning. Of interest is the fact that diagnosing somebody as not having suicidal tendencies, although occurring eleven times, did not result in one verdict for the plaintiff, much less one recovery. Any other result, whether improper care, improper release, or negligent treatment, offers an above-average chance of a large recovery, with a mean more than twice the average.

Negligent Care. While suits involving negligent treatment or diagnosis offer a mean recovery rate well above average, negligent care is about normal ($47,044; N = 38). Perhaps the best chance for the plaintiff occurs when failure to provide proper care is alleged, since the number of large recoveries is higher than expected. Inadequate supervision accounts for a high number of the smaller recoveries (below $25,000).

Harm Caused. Where accidental death will be rewarded with an average verdict of $63,439, suicide is not so highly regarded, with a mean level of recovery of only $27,126. This would appear to involve some form of moral judgment on the part of the judge or jury, but such a theory is contradicted by the data for non-self-inflicted and self-inflicted injuries. For these two categories the size of recovery is reversed: self-inflicted injuries have a mean level of recovery of $111,839, while the mean for non-self-inflicted injuries is only $47,332.

Cases involving sexual or marital harm (which are almost coincident with allegations of sexual abuse as a treatment technique) are more likely to have some form of recovery for the plaintiff, but the average size of recovery is approximately one-third the mean. Economic loss, although offering less chance of winning for the plaintiff, does offer a good chance at a high recovery, with a mean of nearly $100,000 (based on six cases).

Type of Legal Action Brought. For all levels of recovery, an action in negligence offers a distinctly better chance of being rewarded, although the average level of recovery is not extraordinary. Corresponding to this is the fact that a nonnegligence suit has an inferior chance of recovery, with a mean level roughly half the overall average. This may be a consequence of the type of wrong over which suit is brought—where a standard negligence suit is somewhat inappropriate, as in some wrongful commitment cases, the type of wrong may not be one that has much chance of winning, no matter what the basis of suit.

State versus Federal Court. Whether suit is brought in state or federal court does not make a great deal of difference, except that federal courts grant more than their share of large verdicts, with four at the $50,000-plus level.

Trier of Fact. As might be expected, the chance of winning and size of recovery are significantly increased for the plaintiff if a jury decides a case. Although judges are involved in nearly three-fourths of all decisions, less than half the cases with a recovery involve a judge. Those suits settled out of court are generally settled for amounts significantly below the mean for all cases, which may reflect the savings to both plaintiff and defendant of time plus court costs. The thirteen suits in which it is unknown whether a judge or jury decided the case have a very high level of recovery. Why this is so is unknown.

Number of Appeals and Year from Negligent Act to Final Decision. The average duration of all 300 cases from the time the negligent act occurred to the last court decision was 4.8 years, and the average case involved 2.1 appeals. For recoveries of $50,000-plus, however, fully one more year was required, despite the fact that such decisions were appealed less than half the time. Several hypotheses may explain this fact. Where a large recovery is sought, the defendants may be willing to put up a long and arduous fight at the trial level to avoid an initial adverse decision. If the recovery is extremely large, the case may involve a fact situation, making reversal at the appellate level unlikely. In addition, if the defendants threaten a long appeal, the plaintiffs may be willing to settle for immediate payment of a considerably reduced sum, rather than go through a lengthy appeal process.

At all other recovery levels the length of time required exceeds the average by a considerable amount, although the number of court decisions is no greater than normal. One interesting fact, which is difficult to explain, is that the greater the average time from negligent act to final decision, the less mean number of court decisions are involved.

Years from Negligent Act to Trial to Final Decision (See Tables 41-45)

The mean length of time for a case to reach a final decision is 4.8 years, with the modal (most frequently occurring) number of years being 5. In two instances more than 15 years was required, and in fifteen cases 10 or more years was necessary. This length of time probably operates as a discouraging factor to potential plaintiffs. How much of this time is due to the appeal process is unclear. The mean time from negligent act to trial is 3.6 years, but the mode is only two years. On the other hand, the time from trial to final decision requires a mean period of 1.8 years, with a mode of one year.

Modal Cases

In examining all 300 cases, several fact situations were found that were consistently repeated. There were 27 cases in which patients or their representatives sued the state of New York for negligence in a state court for injuries or death allegedly resulting from inadequate supervision. In comparison with the overall success rate of 31 percent, plaintiffs in this situation won more than half of the 27 decisions and were granted recovery nearly two-thirds of the time. In 6 other cases the exact same fact situation occurred, except that the negligence alleged involved the failure to provide proper care. The defendants did not win any of these cases, the plaintiffs won 5 outright, and the sixth decision was a nonfinal verdict in favor of plaintiff. Recoveries were awarded in 4 of the 5 decisions for the plaintiff.

Limitations

The conclusions and findings in this review should prove generalizable to future reported decisions. The cases analyzed probably constitute more than 90 percent of all reported decisions through 1977. Whether the findings are generalizable to unreported decisions, decisions that are not appealed, or to out-of-court settlements is difficult to answer. Of the reported decisions that were not appealed, the plaintiff fared much better than the overall success rate of 31 percent, winning nearly half of the time, while the defendant won slightly more than a third of the time (in comparison with a nearly 50 percent chance of success on appeal).

It is reasonable to expect that unreported and unappealed trial decisions will also follow this pattern. Of those suits settled out of court, one may expect that settlements will be made in cases likely to be decided in plaintiff's favor to avoid publicity and to eliminate the costs of a lengthy trial. Thus, fact situations moderately similar to those where the plaintiff is victorious in a reported decision probably stand an excellent chance of being settled out of court.

NOTES

1. In interpreting Table 38, several points should be noted. By comparing the percentages given in the first, second, fourth, and sixth columns, one can determine whether there is an increase or decrease in the percentage of cases at that level of recovery for a particular variable as compared with all cases at that level. Thus, New York has 38.5 percent of all recoveries greater than $50,000, but more than half of the recoveries between $25,000 and $50,000, more than half of those between $1 and $25,000, but only 36.1 percent of the cases in which there is no recovery.

If one looks at the first, third, fifth, and seventh columns of percentages, the overall total for a particular level of recovery is revealed. Thus, column five for New York indicates that 50.9 percent of all recoveries were awarded for cases occurring in New York. On a thoroughly random basis these figures should match the percentage in the last column (all cases in which the variable occurs as a percentage of all cases). Thus one sees that New York has more than its share of recoveries (50 percent of all recoveries, whereas New York is the locus of only 40.3 percent of all cases).

The second percentage given in the next-to-last column of percentages gives the number of cases for plaintiff for that variable as a percentage of all cases in which that variable occurs. The law of averages says that this percentage should be the same as the overall percentage of verdicts for plaintiff (31.0 percent). Therefore, in the case of New York the percentage of all verdicts for plaintiff is slightly higher (34.7 percent).

Chapter 4

Conclusions

Judicial regulation of psychotherapeutic practice through professional liability suits obviously has potential for great impact. In the medical field this has certainly been true. The question remains, however, whether that impact will be positive or negative. The purpose of this review has not been to resolve this problem, but to gather the necessary data to begin that process. Nonetheless, some concluding hypotheses and comments are warranted.

Perhaps the most obvious fact is that suits against psychotherapists, hospitals, and others responsible for the diagnosis, treatment, and care of the mentally ill are increasing exponentially. In addition, plaintiff's chances of winning are also increasing, at least for the decisions reported here. Despite this, the total number of suits involving psychotherapy is much smaller than the corresponding number against physicians and surgeons involved in ordinary medicine.

The probability is that suits against therapists will continue to rise in the near future. The publicity being given to cases involving sex between therapist and patient, the growing awareness of the possibility of suing practitioners, the erosion of the myth of physician infallibility, the extremely high cost of professional services, the demand by consumers for accountability, the growing willingness of U.S. citizens to use the court system to resolve disputes, the fact that many of the doctrines that formerly made it difficult to win a malpractice suit against a professional no longer have force, and the increasing belief that the quality of care provided by professionals is less than adequate—each of these factors should ensure that malpractice suits continue to proliferate.

Plaintiff will, however, continue to have difficulty winning psychotherapeutic malpractice suits. A variety of reasons accounts for this. An important one has to do with the nature of the therapeutic relationship. One of the many explanations posited for the rise in suits against physicians has been the deterioration in the physician-patient relationship. The decreasing amount of face-to-face contact and the emphasis on seeing specialists has resulted in the decline of the family physician and the increasing depersonalization of medical practice. This has not occurred to nearly the same extent in psychotherapy, and in addition, the psychotherapist generally has well-developed skills in handling hostility and other negative feelings (Dawidoff, 1966: 696; Heller, 1957: 401). Since patients often come into therapy with negative self-images, if dissatisfaction exists with their therapists, patients are likely to blame themselves and neglect the fact that the therapist might have been at fault. Patients who have been harmed are often loath to disclose the details surrounding the incident in a court of law (Cassidy, 1974: 131; Dawidoff, 1966: 696; and Slovenko in Dawidoff, 1973: vii), where this is probably much less true for physical injuries resulting from medical malpractice.

Additionally, the difficult technical problems of effectively establishing a case against a psychotherapist make liability suits a chancy proposition. Very often the patient does not have any physical injuries as evidence of the damage done. In such cases the courts will tend to look for extreme outrage or wanton or reckless conduct on the part of the therapist before granting recovery (Prosser, 1964: 52).

The problems of proof involved are little short of monumental, except in instances of negligent custodial care, physical assault, and several other categories of negligence. Where the particular act complained of consists of words spoken by a therapist in private session with a client, it may be impossible to prove deeds actually took place (Cassidy, 1974: 134; Dawidoff, 1973: 6 and 67). Where the particular acts are not in question, proof that these acts were the proximate cause of the plaintiff's distress are enormous (Dawidoff, 1973: 75 et seq.).

Establishing the amount of damages is also a task of considerable difficulty, especially where the injuries complained of are emotional distress. The fact that courts will rarely award damages for an honest error in judgment compounds the problems of the prospective plaintiff (Cassidy, 1974: 134; Dawidoff, 1973: 61), since most of what a therapist does may be so viewed. In the mental health field the tendency to excuse such mistakes will be especially common since the courts recognize that diagnosis and treatment of mental illness is not an exact science (*see Baker v. United States*).

Finally, the existence of so many diverse, yet legitimate, schools of therapy poses significant hurdles for any plaintiff, since it is not a difficult matter for a therapist to find support for virtually any technique short of violence. In fact, Fink (1973: 708) has made a strong case in favor of the court's refraining from developing strict standards of what constitutes a psychotherapeutic school:

> Psychiatry is not yet at the stage where it can provide the courts with such standards. Unless the psychiatrist's behavior is so exceptional that the court is willing to waive the requirement of expert testimony to establish negligence, a patient injured by psychiatric negligence in the execution of psychotherapy would most likely be without recourse. If courts were to relax the traditional standard of proof for malpractice cases when dealing with psychotherapy, they would, in effect, be shaping the future course of psychotherapy. Before courts will be able to deal effectively with psychiatric negligence, psychiatry will have to develop its theories and procedures so that courts will have some guidelines in setting standards of care. For a court to take a more active role at this point the court would have to be willing to pretend that there is more "order" in psychiatry than there actually exists, or the court would have to disregard psychiatric practice and treat the psychiatrist as it would treat any lay defendant in a negligence case.

Although the difficulties of proof will not diminish significantly, it is clear from the data that this has not and probably will not deter an increase in the number of suits being brought. The question remains whether such suits will have a salutary impact on the field. Many commentators have aruged that current judicial trends are having a decidedly adverse impact on the therapeutic profession. Stone (1975) argues that the right to treatment cases may be counterproductive unless carefully thought through, and he makes a thought-provoking case against recent decisions involving therapeutic confidentiality (Stone, 1976), involuntary confinement, the right to refuse treatment, and the least-restrictive-alternative theory (Stone, 1977).

As an example of how the data presented in this review may assist others in further understanding some of the unintended consequences of therapeutic malpractice suits, one possible implication will be explored. It seems probable from the available information that the best policy for mental hospitals to follow is to err on the side of keeping patients institutionalized once they have been committed. This is so because the premature release of a person who turns out to be dangerous may lead to large recoveries against defendants. The outcome of such a policy will be the continuing commitment of many patients who are not insane or dangerous—a choice that may not represent wise social policy, but which mental hospitals ignore at their peril.

Apart from unintended side effects of recent decisions, it is true that certain types of abuses will probably be deterred. The current play given by the media to suits against therapists who engage in sexual activity with their clients or who subject them to physical attack and injury will reduce the extent to which these activities take place. Judicial regulation has played a role in ensuring fully informed consent to electro-shock or insulin treatment, and has probably improved the degree of supervision and the type of custodial care provided in some public and private mental institutions.

Unfortunately, it is still the case that virtually no reported decisions exist in which a psychotherapist has been successfully sued for negligence in what was said to a client during the therapeutic process. As long as therapists restrict their practice to talk, interpretations, and advice, they will remain nearly immune from suit, no matter how poor their advice, how damaging their comments, or how incorrect their interpretations. Even unsuccessful suits in this realm are difficult to come by. Since the bulk of psychotherapeutic treatment consists of just such verbal communications, judicial regulation of the psychotherapy field may ultimately be unable to reach the heart of the therapeutic process, thus calling into question the potential value of such regulation for the future development of the profession.

Appendix A

Brief Synopses of Each Case

The 300 cases used in this study are presented here in synopsis form. After an opening description of the circumstances surrounding the negligent activity and the harm caused, each synopsis contains the most important aspects of each case. This includes the time and setting of the negligence, who the plaintiffs and defendants were, what the negligent activity consisted of, what harm was caused, what type of action was brought, and the history of the case in the judicial system.

Before examining the synopses themselves, a review of the variables, abbreviations and symbols used in them will be useful. This explanation is organized in the order that the variables fall in the synopses.

EXPLANATION OF VARIABLES, ABBREVIATIONS, AND SYMBOLS

Because of programming considerations and space allocations in the Statistical Program for the Social Sciences (SPSS), it was frequently necessary to abbreviate headings and cases to keep them within the twenty- or forty-character limits. Appearing below are explanations of these abbreviations along with a discussion of what is included within each particular category.

Year of Negligent Act

Information on the year when the negligent act occurred is frequently unavailable in the reported decisions. When known, it is provided. The year given is when the negligence occurred, which may be different from the time when harm was caused. For example, where a mental hospital negligently releases a patient, who injures a third party several years later, the negligence is dated to the time of release, not the year in which the injury occurred.

State in which Negligent Act Occurred

The state in which the negligent act occurred is listed, and this is not necessarily the state in which the harm occurred. For instance, where a patient of a therapist in state *A* travels to state *B* and injures a third party, if that party sues and alleges that the therapist was negligent, the state is listed as *A* where the therapist practices.

Setting of the Case

An attempt has been made to identify the actual setting in which the negligent act occurred. Where wrongful commitment has been alleged, the setting is generally considered to be a judicial proceeding, although commitment to a state mental hospital is the result. Occasionally both are involved, as when a plaintiff argues that he or she was illegally committed *and* illegally detained after the initial commitment. In the case of hospitals, as much precision is given in describing their type as allowed by the available information. Thus, where a setting is described as a "mental hospital," this means that further information on its public or private status is absent in the reported decision. Where a suit involves negligence in a university hospital or school clinic, the case is described as occurring in a hospital. Clinics, infirmaries, and nursing homes are considered hospitals, and veterans administration facilities have been categorized as public mental hospitals.

Pub. Ment. Hosp.	Public Mental Hospital
Priv. Ment. Hosp.	Private Mental Hospital
Pub. Gen. Hosp.	Public General Hospital
Priv. Gen. Hosp.	Private General Hospital
Jud. Pcdg. & Pub. Hosp.	Judicial Proceeding and Public Hospital
Pub. & Priv. Men. Hosp.	Public and Private Mental Hospital

Plaintiffs

Plaintiffs are placed in three broad categories. More than 90 percent of all suits involve a patient or third party injured by the negligence of a therapist or hospital. The second category of plaintiff consists of administrative agencies such as licensing boards, which sue to revoke a therapist's license. The third class is the state as prosecutor of criminal suits. Where patients are involved as plaintiffs, no distinction has been made between suits brought by the patients themselves or those brought by administrators of the patients' estate or the patients' legal guardian. Where the administrator of an estate of a deceased patient is also the patient's spouse, he or she may bring suit both individually on his or her own behalf and on behalf of the patient, and this is noted.

Patient(s) or Rep.	Patient(s) or Representative(s)
3rd Party, I	Third Party Injured by Harm to Patient
3rd Party, II	Third Party Injured by Patient
Pat. & 3rd Pty., I	Patient and Third Party Injured by Harm to Patient
3rd Party, I & II	Third Party Injured by Patient and Third Party Injured by Harm to Patient

Defendants

The list of defendants sued represents only those defendants mentioned by the courts in their reported decisions. Others may have been sued as well, but they were either dropped from suit at an early stage or simply not mentioned in the court's opinion. In many of the suits for wrongful commitment the defendant is described as a physician and information on whether that person is a psychiatrist is not available. Such defendants have been listed with those physicians who are known *not* to be psychiatrists.

The paraprofessional category includes hospital attendants, nonprofessional staff, assistants, and other employees, but does not include nurses, social workers, or laypeople. Practitioners (see Tables 11 and 12) include psychiatrists, physicians, psychologists, paraprofessionals, pharmacists, lawyers, encounter group leaders, nurses, educators, and social workers.

Where a suit has been brought against individuals in their capacity as owners, board members, directors, or administrators of a hospital, the defendant is listed as the hospital, not the individual involved. The same applies for suits against individuals in their capacity as a state official (for instance, the suit against Nelson Rockefeller by the New York State Association for Retarded Children).

Suits against various state agencies are simply listed as suits against the state, except in the case of correctional institutions, judiciary, hospitals, and the police. This is also true for suits against federal, municipal, or county governments, and for suits against deans, presidents, and other staff of educational institutions. Suits involving institutes for encounter groups, sensitivity training, or other forms of human relations are listed as "growth centers."

Nonpsychiat. or Unknown Type Physician(s)	Nonpsychiatrist(s) or Unknown Type of Physician(s)
Encounter. Grp. Leader	Encounter Group Leader
Pl's. Spouse &/ Moth.	Plaintiff's Spouse and/or Mother
Correctional Inst.	Correctional Institution
Commit. Pcdgs. Init.	Initiator of Mental Hospital Commitment Proceedings
Patient(s) or Rep.	Patient(s) or Representative(s)
Nonprof. Org. Pat., Ins.	Nonprofit Organization, Patient, and Correctional Institution

Negligent Activity

Negligent Activities are divided according to whether treatment, diagnosis, or care was involved. In any particular suit more than one negligent activity may occur.

Treatment. Although not always designed as "treatment," sexual activity between patient and therapist or physical assaults upon a patient are placed in the treatment category. This is also true where lack of informed consent is involved, or the therapist fails to consult another practitioner.

Sexual Abuse or Disturb of Marital Rel.	Sexual Abuse or Disturbance of the Marital Relationship
Neg. Transfer. or Ctrt.	Negligent Handling of the Transference or Countertransference Relationship
Unspec. Neg. Treat	The Type of Negligent Treatment was Unspecified
? Whether Treat. Inv.	A Question Exists as to Whether Negligent Treatment was Involved
Neg. Admin. of Drugs	Negligent Administration of Drugs
Failure to Consult	Failure to Properly Consult Another Therapist
Neg. Appl. of Wetpack	Negligent Application of Wetpacks

Diagnosis. Diagnosis has been broken down into two variables. The first examines what was actually diagnosed and includes, either expressly or implicitly, what should have been diagnosed. The second lists the consequence of diagnosis.

What Was Diagnosed. Most categories are self-explanatory. "Type of mental illness" means the therapist was allegedly negligent in diagnosing the type of mental illness, resulting in harm to the patient. "Unfitness for duty" concerns the determination made by the armed services about a person's psychological state.

The diagnosis involved is not always of a person's state of mind. Occasionally suits are brought for prescribing the wrong type of treatment, care, or type of drug. In some cases the negligent activity involves a failure to make a diagnosis when it is called for. In a few instances the activity consists of an allegedly negligent recommendation that a psychiatric examination be administered, when it is not called for. Finally, there are several instances in which the diagnosis is alleged to be inadequate or in which a question exists as to whether diagnosis was involved.

Ment. Ill, Instead of Physical Illness	Mental Illness, Instead of Physical Illness
Phys. Ill, Instead of Ment. Illness	Physical Illness, Instead of Mental Illness
Neg. Rec. to take Psychiatric Exam	Negligent Recommendation to take a Psychiatric Examination
? Whether Diag. Inv.	A Question Exists as to Whether Diagnosis Is Involved

Result of Diagnosis. This category does not include the type of harm caused to the patient or other person involved in the suit. It does indicate what happened to the patient as a result of the diagnosis. For instance, where a male patient is diagnosed as nondangerous, the result may be his premature release from a mental institution. Another result may be that improper treatment or custodial care is prescribed.

Neg. Determ. of Competence to Stand Trial	Negligent Determination of a Person's Competence to Stand Trial
Neg. Determ. of Type of Sentence	Negligent Determination of Type of Sentence
Neg. Determ. of Unfitness for Duty	Negligent Determination that Person Was Unfit for Duty

Care. The final category of negligent activity involves the care provided to the patient. Generally this occurs in a mental institution, and a typical problem is the adequacy of supervision provided. Where premature release is not only due tc negligent diagnosis, but also occurs because a member of the hospital staff may have misread an order from a superior, such negligent activity is classified as a problem in care. Where the plaintiff alleges that the defendant should have provided better protection from fellow patients or bars on windows to prevent suicides, such suits are classified under the general category of "failure to provide proper custodial care."

? Whether Care Inv.	A Question Exists as to Whether Care is Involved

Harm Caused

Harm caused to the plaintiff and/or patient may vary from suicide to loss of liberty to alienation of affection. The categories labeled "nonsuicidal death" and "non-self-inflicted injuries" apply to those cases where a person does not intentionally hurt herself or himself. Both these categories may include injuries inflicted intentionally by another person, as where a mental patient escapes from a hospital and murders a third party. An attempt has been made to list only those injuries that form the basis for suit, even though other injuries may be involved.

Exacerb of Prev. Condition	Exacerbation of a Person's Previous Condition
Self-infl. or Acc. Inj.	Self-inflicted Injuries or Accidental Injuries, But Unknown Which One
Suic. or Accid. Death	Suicide or Accidental Death, But Unknown Which One
No Chance for Impr.	No Chance for Improvement
Preg. & Abortion	Pregnancy and Abortion
Loss of Compnship	Loss of Companionship

Type of Legal Action Brought

The four main types of legal actions brought against defendants are torts, contract actions, criminal proceedings, and administrative actions. Less frequent, but rapidly increasing in number, are injunctive suits and actions seeking declaratory or other equitable relief. By far the most frequent suit is for negligence, which includes all suits brought for malpractice, most of those for wrongful commitment or wrongful death, since these are basically suits for negligence (malpractice is professional negligence; suits for wrongful death or commitment are negligence suits based on statutory law).

Another broad category of tort suit is for intentional interference with the person. Included within this area are suits for assault, assault and battery, false imprisonment, and malicious prosecution.

Defamation of character includes both libel and slander. One of the more recent developments has been tort suits for deprivation of one's constitutional rights including loss of liberty, the right to treatment, and the right to refuse treatment. Positions for habeas corpus and class-action suits are listed as legal actions. Unfortunately, reported decisions frequently do not furnish a complete description of the grounds for suit, so that the actions listed are by no means complete. All actions are listed that are reported, however, including those that failed.

Const. Rts. in Gen.	Constitutional Rights in General
Rt. to Refuse Treat.	Right to Refuse Treatment
Mal. Infl. of Emot. Dis	Malicious Infliction of Emotional Distress
Fail. to do Stat. Duty	Failure to Do One's Statutory Duty
Involunt. Servitude	Involuntary Servitude, Peonage, and/or Slavery
Consc. Pain & Suffer.	Conscious Pain and Suffering
Priv. Inv.-Proc. Abuse	Invasion of Privacy and Abuse of Process
Ins. Claim Payment	Insurance Claim Payment
Fraud-Breach of Con.	Fraud and Breach of Contract
Mot. to Dism. Indict.	Motion to Dismiss Indictment
Lic. Rev. Pcdg.	License Revocation Proceeding
Race Discr-Cl. Act	Racial Discrimination Suit and Class Action

Type of Court

Whether suit was brought in federal or state court is the concern of his section. Suits appealed from state courts to the U.S. Supreme Court are classified as suits in a state court. Suits that originated in municipal or county courts, and which are appealed to state courts, are also classified as a state suit.

Trier of Fact

This heading includes information on whether a suit was tried before a judge or jury. Where a jury was present, but the judge did not allow the case to go to the jury (e.g., summary judgment) or overturned by a jury decision (e.g., judgment notwithstanding the verdict), this is noted. In some cases it is important to determine whether a jury was present or whether a decision was made by the judge or the jury.

Judge, no jury	Decision Made by Judge with No Jury Present
Judge, Uninv. Jury	Decision Made by Judge, Although Jury Was Present
Judge; Jury Present ?	Decision Made by judge, But Unknown whether Jury Was Present
Jury	Decision Made by Jury
?, Judge or Jury	A Question Exists as to Whether the Decision Was Made by a Judge or Jury

Level of Court

The history of each individual case in the judicial system can become quite complex. Over the course of appeals and remands a case may be heard in six or more courts. Many suits are not reported, however, because they are settled at the trial level or are not worth reporting. From a careful reading of the reported decisions an attempt has been made to piece together the history of each case from trial to final decision. The level of court is reported as appellate or supreme based on its function, not name. Thus, the supreme courts of New York are classified as trial level, while the court of appeals is listed as the supreme court, since no higher level of court exists in New York.

Cases Never at Trial Level	Includes cases settled out of court, those not yet decided, and those begun at the Supreme Court level.
US Sup. Ct. fr. State	Includes only those U.S. Court cases on appeal from state courts.
Reappeal to App.	Includes all cases remanded to a lower court and reappealed to the appellate court level.
Reappeal to S.C.	Includes all cases remanded to a lower court and reappealed to a supreme court either directly or after reappeal to an appellate-level court.

Remanded to App. Ct.	Includes cases remanded from a supreme court to an appellate court.

Result of Suit

A decision is considered final for the plaintiff or defendant if no further appeals are reported and if the court's decision reached the issue of whether the defendant was negligent. It is considered nonfinal where an appeal has been taken, where the decision has been remanded for retrial, or where the court's decision does not reach the issue of negligence. An example of the latter occurs when the plaintiff has brought a negligence suit, but the court's decision concerns only the right of the plaintiff to obtain information in hospital records, or the court denies the defendant's motion for dismissal of the suit.

A decision is considered nonfinal for the plaintiff if an appellate court reverses a trial court's verdict for the defendant and remands the case for retrial. A further example occurs when the court rules in favor of a plaintiff's request for hospital records.

A decision is considered nonfinal for the defendant when a higher court overturns a lower court's decision for plaintiff, either final or nonfinal, and orders the case retried or remanded. Another instance consists of ruling in favor of the defendant on an intermediate issue, such as denying the plaintiff the right to examine the records of the defendant.

Special Doctrines

Although incomplete, examples of cases involving special judicial doctrines related to the issue of negligence are provided in the list of cases involving various variables. Of special interest are *res ipsa loquitur*, governmental and other forms of immunity, the locality rule, whether the therapist guaranteed cure, *respondeat superior*, whether the plaintiff gave informed consent, the statute of limitations bar, the concept of privileged information, and whether the plaintiff was contributorily negligent.

Govern. Immunity	Governmental Immunity as a Bar to Suit
Doc-Pat. Priv. Prevented Info. Disclosure	The Doctor-Patient Relationship as Establishing a Privilege Preventing Information Disclosure
Statute of Limitations	The Statute of Limitations Operating as a Bar to Suit
Respondeat Superior	The doctrine that those responsible for another's behavior are equally liable for that person's acts
Hosp. Infor. is Priv.	Hospital Information is Privileged

Recovery or Other Relief Granted

In those cases where the plaintiff was successful, the type of recovery is described. Relief may range from a monetary award for damages, interest, attorney fees, and court costs, to nonmonetary relief in the form of an injunction, declaratory relief, loss of license, or criminal sentence. Occasionally the amount of recovery is not specified or is to be determined on retrial. Whether the plaintiff actually receives the amount awarded depends on subsequent negotiations between plaintiff and defendant.

To be Determ. on Retr	Damages to Be Determined on Retrial

Reason Suit Failed

In those cases where the defendant was exonerated, the reason suit failed is described. Some of the more frequent reasons include failure to prove one's case, not stating a cause of action, and the operation of governmental or judicial immunity.

No bad faith or Mal.	No bad faith or malice demonstrated
Govern. Immunity	Governmental Immunity Barred Suit

1. A.A. V. STATE

AFTER BEING DIAGNOSED AS SCHIZOPHRENIC, THE PLAINTIFF, A TWELVE-YEAR-OLD BOY, WAS SENT TO ROCKLAND STATE HOSPITAL IN ORANGEBURG, NEW YORK. BECAUSE OF HIS VIOLENT EXCEPTIONS TO BEING PLACED WITH CHILDREN, "A.A." WAS PLACED IN AN ADULT WARD, CONTAINING A RANGE OF MENTALLY ILL PATIENTS. HE WAS ORDERED TO A CLOTHING CLOSET BY ONE OF THE PATIENTS, WHERE A KNIFE WAS HELD AT HIS THROAT AND ANOTHER PATIENT COMMITTED AN ACT OF BUGGERY, CAUSING BOTH PHYSICAL AND EMOTIONAL INJURY. THE ATTENDANT ON DUTY HAD LEFT THE WARD WITHOUT PERMISSION, AND A SECOND ATTENDANT, COVERING FOR THE FIRST, DID NOT HAVE THE KEY TO THE CLOTHING CLOSET. MANY OF THE PATIENTS ON THE WARD WERE KNOWN TO HAVE ASSAULTIVE TENDENCIES.

YEAR OF NEGLIGENT ACT: 1959

STATE IN WHICH NEGLIGENT ACT OCCURRED: NEW YORK

SETTING OF THE CASE: PUB. MENT. HOSP.

PLAINTIFF(S): PATIENT(S) OR REP.

DEFENDANT(S):
1. STATE GOV. &/OR OFFICIALS, ETC.

NEGLIGENT ACTIVITY:

TREATMENT: NOT APPLICABLE

DIAGNOSIS:

WHAT WAS DIAGNOSED: NOT APPLICABLE

RESULT OF DIAGNOSIS: NOT APPLICABLE

CARE:
1. INADEQUATE SUPERVISION
2. FAILURE TO PROVIDE PROPER CUSTODIAL CARE

HARM CAUSED TO PLAINTIFF &/OR PATIENT:
1. EMOTIONAL DISTRESS
2. EXACERB.OF PREV.CONDITION
3. SEXUAL OR MARITAL HARM

TYPE OF ACTION BROUGHT:
1. NEGLIGENCE

HISTORY OF THE CASE:

TYPE OF COURT: STATE

TRIER OF FACT: JUDGE,NO JURY

COURT DECISION(S):

TRIAL COURT: FOR PLAINTIFF
YEAR: 1964

VERDICT AGAINST WHICH DEFENDANTS:
1. STATE GOV. &/OR OFFICIALS, ETC.

RECOVERY OR OTHER RELIEF GRANTED:
1. $ 90000

2. ABRAHAM V. ZASLOW

THE DEFENDANT, A PSYCHOLOGIST, HAD DEVELOPED A NEW FORM OF TREATMENT KNOWN AS "RAGE REDUCTION THERAPY" OR "Z-THERAPY." THE PURPOSE OF THE THERAPY WAS TO BREAK DOWN A PATIENT'S RESISTANCE THROUGH EXTENSIVE USE OF TACTILE STIMULATION WHILE THE PATIENT WAS IMMOBILIZED. THIS INDUCED REPRESSED ANGER TO ESCAPE. THE PLAINTIFF, UNAWARE OF THE NATURE OF THE TECHNIQUE, VOLUNTARILY ENTERED THE $400 TREATMENT, AFTER BEING REFERRED TO THE PSYCHOLOGIST FOR AN ADVERSE DRUG REACTION TO MARIJUANA AND/OR OTHER DRUGS. HE DIAGNOSED HER AS AN INCIPIENT SCHIZOPHRENIC AND TREATED HER WITH MORE THAN TEN HOURS OF HIS NEWLY DEVELOPED THERAPY. THE PLAINTIFF ALLEGED SHE WAS POKED, BEATEN, AND TORTURED DURING THIS TIME, AND THAT AS A RESULT SHE SUFFERED SEVERE BRUISING OF THE UPPER HALF OF HER BODY, COMPLETE KIDNEY FAILURE, AS WELL AS AGGRAVATION OF HER PRE-EXISTING MENTAL CONDITION.

YEAR OF NEGLIGENT ACT: NOT SPECIFIED

STATE IN WHICH NEGLIGENT ACT OCCURRED: CALIFORNIA

SETTING OF THE CASE: PRIVATE PRACTICE

PLAINTIFF(S): PATIENT(S) OR REP.

DEFENDANT(S):
1. PSYCHOLOGIST(S)

NEGLIGENT ACTIVITY:

TREATMENT:
1. NEGLIGENCE IN USE OF TECHNIQUE
2. PHYSICAL ASSAULT

DIAGNOSIS:

WHAT WAS DIAGNOSED: NOT APPLICABLE

RESULT OF DIAGNOSIS: NOT APPLICABLE

CARE: NOT APPLICABLE

HARM CAUSED TO PLAINTIFF &/OR PATIENT:
1. NONSELF-INFLICTED INJURIES
2. EXACERB.OF PREV.CONDITION

TYPE OF ACTION BROUGHT:
1. NEGLIGENCE

HISTORY OF THE CASE:

TYPE OF COURT: STATE

TRIER OF FACT: JURY

COURT DECISION(S):

TRIAL COURT: FOR PLAINTIFF
YEAR: 1972

VERDICT AGAINST WHICH DEFENDANTS:
1. PSYCHOLOGIST(S)

RECOVERY OR OTHER RELIEF GRANTED:
1. $170000

3. ADAMS V. RICKS

THE PLAINTIFF RICKS HAD VOLUNTARILY ENTERED PEACHTREE SANITARIUM FOR A SERIES OF SHOCK TREATMENTS. AFTER THE SIXTH ADMINISTRATION HE SUFFERED A CONVULSION, AND WHILE IN A SEMI-CONSCIOUS STATE FELL OFF HIS BED. AS A RESULT HE SUFFERED TWO BROKEN HIPS. FOUR OPERATIONS WERE TOTALLY UNSUCCESSFUL, AND RICKS LOST THE USE OF HIS LEGS AND INCURRED SUBSTANTIAL PAIN AND SUFFERING, AS WELL AS LOSS OF EARNING POWER. HE ALLEGED THAT THE HOSPITAL WAS NEGLIGENT IN FAILING TO PROVIDE GUARD RAILS FOR HIS BED, IN LEAVING THE ROOM UNATTENDED, AND IN NOT PROVIDING A CALL BUTTON.

YEAR OF NEGLIGENT ACT: NOT SPECIFIED

STATE IN WHICH NEGLIGENT ACT OCCURRED: GEORGIA

SETTING OF THE CASE: PRIV. MENT. HOSP.

PLAINTIFF(S): PATIENT(S) OR REP.

DEFENDANT(S):
1. HOSPITAL &/OR OWNERS, ETC.

NEGLIGENT ACTIVITY:

TREATMENT:
1. NEGLIGENT ELECTROCONVULSIVE THERAPY

DIAGNOSIS:

WHAT WAS DIAGNOSED: NOT APPLICABLE

RESULT OF DIAGNOSIS: NOT APPLICABLE

CARE:
1. INADEQUATE SUPERVISION

HARM CAUSED TO PLAINTIFF &/OR PATIENT:
1. NONSELF-INFLICTED INJURIES
2. EMOTIONAL DISTRESS

TYPE OF ACTION BROUGHT:
1. NEGLIGENCE

HISTORY OF THE CASE:

TYPE OF COURT: STATE

TRIER OF FACT: JUDGE;JURY PRESENT ?

COURT DECISION(S):

TRIAL COURT: NONFINAL FOR PL.
YEAR: NOT SPECIFIED
APPELLATE COURT: NONFINAL FOR PL.
YEAR: 1955

DEFENDANTS STILL INVOLVED IN SUIT:
1. HOSPITAL &/OR OWNERS, ETC.

4. ADAMS V. STATE

MAUDE ADAMS, THE PLAINTIFF, VOLUNTARILY BECAME A PATIENT AT THE WESTERN STATE HOSPITAL IN STEILACOOM, WASHINGTON. HER PROBLEMS STEMMED FROM WORRY OVER THE ILLNESS OF HER ADOPTED CHILD AND FINANCIAL CONCERNS SINCE HER HUSBAND HAD BEEN OUT OF WORK FOR FIVE MONTHS. UPON THE BIRTH OF HER THIRD CHILD SHE BECAME QUITE DEPRESSED AND ATTEMPTED SUICIDE. PSYCHIATRIC COUNSELING AND ELECTRO-SHOCK TREATMENTS HELPED TEMPORARILY, BUT THE PLAINTIFF THEN ATTEMPTED A SECOND SUICIDE AND WAS READMITTED. ALLEGEDLY BECAUSE OF THE NEGLIGENCE OF STAFF IN FAILING TO SUPERVISE HER, SHE WAS ABLE TO ESCAPE FROM THE HOSPITAL AND JUMPED IN FRONT OF AN AUTOMOBILE, SUFFERING EXTENSIVE AND PERMANENT INJURIES, INCLUDING BRAIN DAMAGE AND MULTIPLE FRACTURES OF THE SKULL, JAW, RIBS, AND PELVIS.

YEAR OF NEGLIGENT ACT: 1965

STATE IN WHICH NEGLIGENT ACT OCCURRED: WASHINGTON

SETTING OF THE CASE: PUB. MENT. HOSP.

PLAINTIFF(S): 3RD PARTY, I

DEFENDANT(S):
1. STATE GOV. &/OR OFFICIALS, ETC.

NEGLIGENT ACTIVITY:

TREATMENT: NOT APPLICABLE

DIAGNOSIS:

WHAT WAS DIAGNOSED: NOT APPLICABLE

RESULT OF DIAGNOSIS: NOT APPLICABLE

CARE:
1. INADEQUATE SUPERVISION

HARM CAUSED TO PLAINTIFF &/OR PATIENT:
1. SELF-INFLICTED INJURIES
2. LOSS OF CONSORTIUM

TYPE OF ACTION BROUGHT:
1. NEGLIGENCE

HISTORY OF THE CASE:

TYPE OF COURT: STATE

TRIER OF FACT: JURY

COURT DECISION(S):

TRIAL COURT: FOR PLAINTIFF
YEAR: 1965
SUPREME COURT: FOR PLAINTIFF
YEAR: 1967

VERDICT AGAINST WHICH DEFENDANTS:
1. STATE GOV. &/OR OFFICIALS, ETC.

RECOVERY OR OTHER RELIEF GRANTED:
1. $275000

5. AIKEN V. CLARY

IN THIS CASE AIKEN ALLEGED HE HAD NOT GIVEN INFORMED CONSENT TO THE COURSE OF INSULIN THERAPY RECOMMENDED BY CLARY. AS A RESULT OF THE TREATMENT, GIVEN AT ST. JOHN'S HOSPITAL IN SPRINGFIELD, MISSOURI, THE PLAINTIFF SUFFERED IRREPARABLE BRAIN DAMAGE AND WAS PERMANENTLY AND TOTALLY INCAPACITATED. HIS GUARDIAN AND CURATOR IN THE SUIT ARGUED THAT THE DEFENDANT HAD NOT PROPERLY EXPLAINED THE DANGERS INVOLVED, EVEN THOUGH A CONSENT FORM HAD BEEN SIGNED. SPECIFICALLY, HE HAD NOT MENTIONED THE POSSIBILITY OF DEATH OR BRAIN DAMAGE.

YEAR OF NEGLIGENT ACT: 1961

STATE IN WHICH NEGLIGENT ACT OCCURRED: MISSOURI

SETTING OF THE CASE: PRIVATE PRACTICE

PLAINTIFF(S): PATIENT(S) OR REP.

DEFENDANT(S):
1. PSYCHIATRIST(S)

NEGLIGENT ACTIVITY:

TREATMENT:
1. FAILURE TO OBTAIN -OR LACK OF- CONSENT

DIAGNOSIS:

WHAT WAS DIAGNOSED: NOT APPLICABLE

RESULT OF DIAGNOSIS: NOT APPLICABLE

CARE: NOT APPLICABLE

HARM CAUSED TO PLAINTIFF &/OR PATIENT:
1. NONSELF-INFLICTED INJURIES

TYPE OF ACTION BROUGHT:
1. NEGLIGENCE

HISTORY OF THE CASE:

TYPE OF COURT: STATE

TRIER OF FACT: JURY

COURT DECISION(S):

TRIAL COURT: FOR DEFENDANT
YEAR: NOT SPECIFIED
SUPREME COURT: NONFINAL FOR PL.
YEAR: 1965

DEFENDANTS STILL INVOLVED IN SUIT:
1. PSYCHIATRIST(S)

6. ANCLOTE MANOR FOUNDATION V. WILKINSON

WILKINSON BROUGHT THIS SUIT AGAINST THE ANCLOTE MANOR FOUNDATION AS A RESULT OF THE SUICIDE OF HIS WIFE, WHICH HE ALLEGED RESULTED FROM THE NEGLIGENCE OF A PSYCHIATRIST IN THE FULL-TIME EMPLOY OF THE FOUNDATION. THE PLAINTIFF'S WIFE HAD BEEN A PATIENT AT THE DEFENDANT'S HOSPITAL FOR APPROXIMATELY TWO YEARS AT A COST OF MORE THAN $25,000. DURING THIS TIME THE PSYCHIATRIST TOLD WILKINSON'S WIFE THAT HE WAS GOING TO DIVORCE HIS OWN WIFE AND MARRY HER. AFTER SHE WAS DISCHARGED FROM THE HOSPITAL, WILKINSON GRANTED HIS WIFE A DIVORCE, AND THE FOLLOWING YEAR SHE COMMITTED SUICIDE. IN THE INTERVENING TIME HER BROTHER HAD BEEN KILLED IN VIET NAM AND A GRANDMOTHER HAD PASSED AWAY, BOTH OF WHICH MAY ALSO HAVE BEEN CONTRIBUTING FACTORS TO THE SUICIDE.

YEAR OF NEGLIGENT ACT: 1966

STATE IN WHICH NEGLIGENT ACT OCCURRED: FLORIDA

SETTING OF THE CASE: PRIV. MENT. HOSP.

PLAINTIFF(S): 3RD PARTY, I

DEFENDANT(S):
1. HOSPITAL &/OR OWNERS, ETC.

NEGLIGENT ACTIVITY:

TREATMENT:
1. SEXUAL ABUSE OR DISTURB.OF MARITAL REL.
2. NEG.TRANSFER.OR CTRT

DIAGNOSIS:

WHAT WAS DIAGNOSED: NOT APPLICABLE

RESULT OF DIAGNOSIS: NOT APPLICABLE

CARE: NOT APPLICABLE

HARM CAUSED TO PLAINTIFF &/OR PATIENT:
1. SUICIDE
2. EMOTIONAL DISTRESS
3. ECONOMIC LOSS
4. SEXUAL OR MARITAL HARM

TYPE OF ACTION BROUGHT:
1. NEGLIGENCE
2. CONTRACT LAW: BREACH OF CONTRACT

HISTORY OF THE CASE:

TYPE OF COURT: STATE

TRIER OF FACT: JURY

COURT DECISION(S):

TRIAL COURT: FOR PLAINTIFF
YEAR: NOT SPECIFIED
APPELLATE COURT: FOR PLAINTIFF
YEAR: 1972

VERDICT AGAINST WHICH DEFENDANTS:
1. HOSPITAL &/OR OWNERS, ETC.

RECOVERY OR OTHER RELIEF GRANTED:
1. $ 28600

7. ANNIS V. DONAHUE

IN ONE OF THE FEW CASES AGAINST AN ENCOUNTER GROUP LEADER, THE DEFENDANT, DONAHUE, RAN A HUMAN-RELATIONS GROUP FOR THE LEADERSHIP CONSULTING SERVICE, A TRAINING ORGANIZATION OPERATING UNDER THE AUSPICES OF BOSTON UNIVERSITY. THE PLAINTIFF CLAIMED THAT THE LEADER PHYSICALLY GRABBED HER BY THE ARMS, RAISED HER FROM A SEATED POSITION, THREW HER OVER HIS SHOULDER AND THEN ONTO THE FLOOR, WHERE HE SLAPPED HER. THE RESULT WAS A CONTUSION OF THE HIP, PAINS IN THE NECK, SHOULDER AND BACK, HEADACHES, DISCOMFORT AND NERVOUS UPSET.

YEAR OF NEGLIGENT ACT: 1968

STATE IN WHICH NEGLIGENT ACT OCCURRED: MASSACHUSETTS

SETTING OF THE CASE: ENCOUNTER GROUP

PLAINTIFF(S): PATIENT(S) OR REP.

DEFENDANT(S):
1. EDUCATIONAL INST. &/OR DEANS, ETC.
2. ENCOUNT.GRP.LEADER

NEGLIGENT ACTIVITY:

TREATMENT:
1. NEGLIGENCE IN USE OF TECHNIQUE

DIAGNOSIS:

WHAT WAS DIAGNOSED: NOT APPLICABLE

RESULT OF DIAGNOSIS: NOT APPLICABLE

CARE: NOT APPLICABLE

HARM CAUSED TO PLAINTIFF &/OR PATIENT:
1. NONSELF-INFLICTED INJURIES

TYPE OF ACTION BROUGHT:
1. NEGLIGENCE
2. ASSAULT AND BATTERY

HISTORY OF THE CASE:

TYPE OF COURT: STATE

TRIER OF FACT: SETTLED OUT OF COURT

COURT DECISION(S):

SETTLED OUT OF COURT
YEAR: 1970

VERDICT AGAINST WHICH DEFENDANTS:
1. EDUCATIONAL INST. &/OR DEANS, ETC.

RECOVERY OR OTHER RELIEF GRANTED:
1. $ 2500

8. ANONYMOUS V. STATE

AT THE INSISTENCE OF HIS FATHER, THE PLAINTIFF--A THIRTY-FOUR-YEAR-OLD MALE--WAS COMMITTED TO KINGS COUNTY HOSPITAL, WHERE HE WAS ADJUDGED AS SUFFERING FROM DEMENTIA PRAECOX, MIXED TYPE, FEATURED BY CATATONIC AND PARANOID SCHIZOPHRENIA. HE WAS TREATED WITH INSULIN COMA THERAPY OVER A PERIOD OF THREE MONTHS, AND EVENTUALLY RELEASED FROM THE HOSPITAL. THE PLAINTIFF BROUGHT SUIT, ALLEGING THAT CONSENT SHOULD HAVE BEEN OBTAINED FROM A COURT-APPOINTED GUARDIAN OR FROM BOTH PARENTS.

YEAR OF NEGLIGENT ACT: 1955

STATE IN WHICH NEGLIGENT ACT OCCURRED: NEW YORK

SETTING OF THE CASE: PUB. MENT. HOSP.

PLAINTIFF(S): PATIENT(S) OR REP.

DEFENDANT(S):
1. STATE GOV. &/OR OFFICIALS, ETC.

NEGLIGENT ACTIVITY:

TREATMENT:
1. FAILURE TO OBTAIN -OR LACK OF- CONSENT

DIAGNOSIS:

WHAT WAS DIAGNOSED: NOT APPLICABLE

RESULT OF DIAGNOSIS: NOT APPLICABLE

CARE: NOT APPLICABLE

HARM CAUSED TO PLAINTIFF &/OR PATIENT:
1. NOT SPECIFIED

TYPE OF ACTION BROUGHT:
1. ASSAULT AND BATTERY

HISTORY OF THE CASE:

TYPE OF COURT: STATE

TRIER OF FACT: JUDGE,NO JURY

COURT DECISION(S):

TRIAL COURT: FOR DEFENDANT
YEAR: NOT SPECIFIED
APPELLATE COURT: FOR DEFENDANT
YEAR: 1963

REASON SUIT FAILED:
1. PATIENT HAD GIVEN INFORMED CONSENT

9. ARLINGTON HEIGHTS SANITARIUM V. DEADERICK

THE PLAINTIFFS IN THIS SUIT WERE THE MOTHER AND DAUGHTER OF A PATIENT WHO HAD ESCAPED FROM THE SANITARIUM AND WAS FOUND DEAD ON A RAILROAD TRACK IN THE YARDS OF THE TEXAS AND PACIFIC RAILWAY COMPANY IN FORT WORTH, TEXAS. HE HAD ESCAPED FROM THE SANITARIUM EARLY IN THE MORNING AT A TIME WHEN HE WAS WALKING ABOUT WITHOUT RESTRAINT OR SUPERVISION. THE PLAINTIFFS ALLEGED NEGLIGENCE IN LACK OF SUPERVISION, IN FAILING TO PLACE THE PATIENT IN A WARD WITH GREATER SECURITY, AND IN MISLEADING THEM BY STATING THAT THE PATIENT WAS NOT SERIOUSLY ILL.

YEAR OF NEGLIGENT ACT: 1920

STATE IN WHICH NEGLIGENT ACT OCCURRED: TEXAS

SETTING OF THE CASE: PRIV. MENT. HOSP.

PLAINTIFF(S): 3RD PARTY, I

DEFENDANT(S):
1. HOSPITAL &/OR OWNERS, ETC.

NEGLIGENT ACTIVITY:

TREATMENT: NOT APPLICABLE

DIAGNOSIS:

WHAT WAS DIAGNOSED:
1. TYPE OF CUSTODIAL CARE

RESULT OF DIAGNOSIS:
1. IMPROPER CUSTODIAL CARE

CARE:
1. INADEQUATE SUPERVISION

HARM CAUSED TO PLAINTIFF &/OR PATIENT:
1. NONSUICIDAL DEATH

TYPE OF ACTION BROUGHT:
1. NEGLIGENCE

HISTORY OF THE CASE:

TYPE OF COURT: STATE

TRIER OF FACT: JURY

COURT DECISION(S):

TRIAL COURT: FOR PLAINTIFF
YEAR: NOT SPECIFIED
APPELLATE COURT: FOR PLAINTIFF
YEAR: 1925

VERDICT AGAINST WHICH DEFENDANTS:
1. HOSPITAL &/OR OWNERS, ETC.

RECOVERY OR OTHER RELIEF GRANTED:
1. $ 5000

10. AVEY V. ST. FRANCIS HOSPITAL

BEN AVEY SUFFERED FROM RECURRING PERIODS OF NERVOUSNESS, WORRY, IMAGINARY ILLNESS, AND INSOMNIA. HE WAS REHOSPITALIZED AT THE ST. FRANCIS HOSPITAL AND SCHOOL OF NURSING, WHERE PSYCHIATRIC OBSERVATION REVEALED HE WAS SUFFERING FROM INVOLUTIONAL DEPRESSION AND A PROSTATE CONDITION. THE LATTER WAS OPERATED UPON IMMEDIATELY. DURING THE RECOVERY PERIOD, PLAINTIFF JUMPED OUT OF A BATHROOM WINDOW, SUSTAINING SERIOUS INJURIES, INCLUDING SEVERAL FRACTURED BONES. AVEY ALLEGED THAT THE DEFENDANT WAS NEGLIGENT IN FAILING TO HAVE NURSES EXPERIENCED IN PSYCHIATRIC CARE ON HAND AND IN FAILING TO PROPERLY SUPERVISE HIM. ON APPEAL THE CRITICAL ISSUE WAS WHETHER AN OUT-OF-STATE DOCTOR COULD TESTIFY ABOUT WHAT CONSTITUTED PROPER STANDARDS OF CARE IN THAT COMMUNITY.

YEAR OF NEGLIGENT ACT: 1962

STATE IN WHICH NEGLIGENT ACT OCCURRED: KANSAS

SETTING OF THE CASE: PRIV. GEN. HOSP.

PLAINTIFF(S): PATIENT(S) OR REP.

DEFENDANT(S):
1. HOSPITAL &/OR OWNERS, ETC.

NEGLIGENT ACTIVITY:

TREATMENT: NOT APPLICABLE

DIAGNOSIS:

WHAT WAS DIAGNOSED: NOT APPLICABLE

RESULT OF DIAGNOSIS: NOT APPLICABLE

CARE:
1. INADEQUATE SUPERVISION

HARM CAUSED TO PLAINTIFF &/OR PATIENT:
1. SELF-INFL.OR ACC.INJ

TYPE OF ACTION BROUGHT:
1. NEGLIGENCE

HISTORY OF THE CASE:

TYPE OF COURT: STATE

TRIER OF FACT: JURY

COURT DECISION(S):

TRIAL COURT: FOR DEFENDANT
YEAR: NOT SPECIFIED
SUPREME COURT: NONFINAL FOR PL.
YEAR: 1968

DEFENDANTS STILL INVOLVED IN SUIT:
1. HOSPITAL &/OR OWNERS, ETC.

11. AYERS V. RUSSELL

THIS IS ONE OF THE EARLIEST WRONGFUL COMMITMENT CASES. PLAINTIFF AYERS WAS TEMPORARILY CONFINED AS A LUNATIC ON THE BASIS OF TESTIMONY BY TWO PHYSICIANS AND WITH THE SIGNATURE OF THE RECORDER OF THE CITY OF ALBANY. IN A CONCURRING OPINION JUDGE LEARNED STATED THAT NO EVIDENCE EXISTED THAT PLAINTIFF WAS NOT OF SUFFICIENT MEANS, NOR WAS FURIOUSLY MAD, NOR SO DISORDERED IN HIS SENSES AS TO ENDANGER HIS OWN PERSON.

YEAR OF NEGLIGENT ACT: 1887

STATE IN WHICH NEGLIGENT ACT OCCURRED: NEW YORK

SETTING OF THE CASE: JUDICIAL PROCEEDING

PLAINTIFF(S): PATIENT(S) OR REP.

DEFENDANT(S):
1. NONPSYCHIAT.OR UNKNOWN TYPE PHYSICIAN(S)
2. MUNICIPAL GOV. &/OR OFFICIALS, ETC.

NEGLIGENT ACTIVITY:

TREATMENT: NOT APPLICABLE

DIAGNOSIS:

WHAT WAS DIAGNOSED:
1. MENTAL ILLNESS, INSTEAD OF SANITY

RESULT OF DIAGNOSIS:
1. IMPROPER COMMITMENT

CARE: NOT APPLICABLE

HARM CAUSED TO PLAINTIFF &/OR PATIENT:
1. NOT SPECIFIED

TYPE OF ACTION BROUGHT:
1. NEGLIGENCE

HISTORY OF THE CASE:

TYPE OF COURT: STATE

TRIER OF FACT: JUDGE;JURY PRESENT ?

COURT DECISION(S):

TRIAL COURT: FOR DEFENDANT
YEAR: NOT SPECIFIED
APPELLATE COURT: NONFINAL FOR PL.
YEAR: 1888

DEFENDANTS STILL INVOLVED IN SUIT:
1. NONPSYCHIAT.OR UNKNOWN TYPE PHYSICIAN(S)
2. MUNICIPAL GOV. &/OR OFFICIALS, ETC.

12. BACON V. BACON

IN ANOTHER VERY EARLY COMMITMENT CASE THE PLAINTIFF MARY KATE BACON WAS COMMITTED TO AN ASYLUM ON THE BASIS OF SIGNED STATEMENTS BY TWO PHYSICIANS WHO HAD ONLY OBSERVED HER IN A MOST CASUAL WAY: ONE IN A SHOE STORE WHILE WAITING FOR THE SERVICES OF AN ATTENDANT; THE OTHER IN A HALLWAY WHERE SHE WAS OBSERVED AS SAD, SILENT, AND INATTENTIVE TO WHAT WAS HAPPENING AROUND HER.

YEAR OF NEGLIGENT ACT: NOT SPECIFIED

STATE IN WHICH NEGLIGENT ACT OCCURRED: MISSISSIPPI

SETTING OF THE CASE: JUDICIAL PROCEEDING

PLAINTIFF(S): PATIENT(S) OR REP.

DEFENDANT(S):
1. NONPSYCHIAT.OR UNKNOWN TYPE PHYSICIAN(S)

NEGLIGENT ACTIVITY:

TREATMENT: NOT APPLICABLE

DIAGNOSIS:

WHAT WAS DIAGNOSED:
1. MENTAL ILLNESS, INSTEAD OF SANITY

RESULT OF DIAGNOSIS:
1. IMPROPER COMMITMENT

CARE: NOT APPLICABLE

HARM CAUSED TO PLAINTIFF &/OR PATIENT:
1. EMOTIONAL DISTRESS
2. INJURY TO REPUTATION

TYPE OF ACTION BROUGHT:
1. FALSE IMPRISONMENT
2. MALICIOUS PROSECUTION
3. DEFAMATION OF CHARACTER: TYPE NOT SPECIFIED

HISTORY OF THE CASE:

TYPE OF COURT: STATE

TRIER OF FACT: JURY

COURT DECISION(S):

TRIAL COURT: FOR PLAINTIFF
YEAR: NOT SPECIFIED
SUPREME COURT: FOR PLAINTIFF
YEAR: 1899

VERDICT AGAINST WHICH DEFENDANTS:
1. NONPSYCHIAT.OR UNKNOWN TYPE PHYSICIAN(S)

RECOVERY OR OTHER RELIEF GRANTED:
1. $ 1500

13. BAKER V. ORLOWSKY

IN THIS CASE FOR WRONGFUL COMMITMENT THE PLAINTIFF ALLEGED THAT THE DEFENDANT HAD MADE FRAUDULENT REPRESENTATIONS TO THE PROBATE COURT CONCERNING THE PLAINTIFF'S SANITY, WHICH RESULTED IN HIS BEING PLACED IN A MENTAL INSTITUTION.

YEAR OF NEGLIGENT ACT: 1965

STATE IN WHICH NEGLIGENT ACT OCCURRED: OHIO

SETTING OF THE CASE: JUDICIAL PROCEEDING

PLAINTIFF(S): PATIENT(S) OR REP.

DEFENDANT(S):
1. NONPSYCHIAT.OR UNKNOWN TYPE PHYSICIAN(S)

NEGLIGENT ACTIVITY:

TREATMENT: NOT APPLICABLE

DIAGNOSIS:

WHAT WAS DIAGNOSED:
1. MENTAL ILLNESS, INSTEAD OF SANITY

RESULT OF DIAGNOSIS:
1. IMPROPER COMMITMENT

CARE: NOT APPLICABLE

HARM CAUSED TO PLAINTIFF &/OR PATIENT:
1. NOT SPECIFIED

TYPE OF ACTION BROUGHT:
1. OTHER TORT(S): WRONGFUL COMMITMENT

HISTORY OF THE CASE:

TYPE OF COURT: STATE

TRIER OF FACT: JUDGE,NO JURY

COURT DECISION(S):

TRIAL COURT: FOR DEFENDANT
YEAR: NOT SPECIFIED
APPELLATE COURT: FOR DEFENDANT
YEAR: 1971

REASON SUIT FAILED:
1. DEFENDANT(S) CANNOT BE SUED DUE TO: JUDICIAL IMMUNITY

14. BAKER V. UNITED STATES

KENNETH BAKER, SIXTY-ONE YEARS OLD, AND A PATIENT AT THE VETERANS ADMINISTRATION HOSPITAL IN IOWA CITY, ATTEMPTED TO COMMIT SUICIDE BY JUMPING INTO A WINDOW WELL THIRTEEN FEET DEEP. HE SUFFERED SCALP WOUNDS, FRACTURES, AN OCCLUSION OF THE LEFT CAROTID ARTERY AND SUBSEQUENTLY UNDERWENT A COMPLETE PARALYSIS OF HIS RIGHT SIDE. DURING THE NEXT YEAR HE WAS REMOVED TO A PRIVATE NURSING HOME. HE WAS COMPLETELY AND PERMANENTLY DISABLED BOTH MENTALLY AND PHYSICALLY. THE PATIENT'S WIFE BROUGHT SUIT, ALLEGING THAT THE HOSPITAL WAS NEGLIGENT IN ITS SUPERVISION OF THE PATIENT, IN FAILING TO DIAGNOSE HIS MENTAL CONDITION, AND IN FAILING TO HEED THE ADVICE OF PATIENT'S ATTENDING PHYSICIAN, WHO HAD NOTED HIS SUICIDAL TENDENCIES.

YEAR OF NEGLIGENT ACT: 1960

STATE IN WHICH NEGLIGENT ACT OCCURRED: IOWA

SETTING OF THE CASE: PUB. GEN. HOSP.

PLAINTIFF(S): PAT. & 3RD PTY., I

DEFENDANT(S):
1. FEDERAL GOV. &/OR OFFICIALS, ETC.

NEGLIGENT ACTIVITY:

TREATMENT: NOT APPLICABLE

DIAGNOSIS:

WHAT WAS DIAGNOSED:
1. LACK OF SUICIDAL TENDENCIES

RESULT OF DIAGNOSIS:
1. IMPROPER CUSTODIAL CARE

CARE:
1. INADEQUATE SUPERVISION

HARM CAUSED TO PLAINTIFF &/OR PATIENT:
1. SELF-INFLICTED INJURIES

TYPE OF ACTION BROUGHT:
1. NEGLIGENCE

HISTORY OF THE CASE:

TYPE OF COURT: FEDERAL

TRIER OF FACT: JUDGE,NO JURY

COURT DECISION(S):

TRIAL COURT: FOR DEFENDANT
YEAR: 1964
APPELLATE COURT: FOR DEFENDANT
YEAR: 1965

REASON SUIT FAILED:
1. NEGLIGENCE OR CASE NOT PROVEN

15. BANGS V. STATE

THE PLAINTIFF SUED THE STATE OF NEW YORK FOR HER COMMITMENT TO MATTEAWAN STATE HOSPITAL FROM WHERE SHE WAS RELEASED AFTER SEVEN AND ONE-HALF YEARS. THE ORDER OF COMMITMENT WAS BASED ON THE REPORT OF AN EXAMINING PSYCHIATRIST, FOLLOWING AN INCIDENT IN WHICH THE PLAINTIFF FIRED A GUN AT AN AUTOMOBILE CONTAINING ANOTHER WOMAN AND SOME OF HER CHILDREN. SHE MAINTAINED THAT THE DRIVER OF THE VEHICLE HAD ATTEMPTED TO RUN OVER HER.

YEAR OF NEGLIGENT ACT: NOT SPECIFIED

STATE IN WHICH NEGLIGENT ACT OCCURRED: NEW YORK

SETTING OF THE CASE: JUDICIAL PROCEEDING

PLAINTIFF(S): PATIENT(S) OR REP.

DEFENDANT(S):
1. STATE GOV. &/OR OFFICIALS, ETC.

NEGLIGENT ACTIVITY:

TREATMENT:
1. UNSPEC.NEG.TREAT

DIAGNOSIS:

WHAT WAS DIAGNOSED:
1. MENTAL ILLNESS, INSTEAD OF SANITY

RESULT OF DIAGNOSIS:
1. IMPROPER COMMITMENT

CARE: NOT APPLICABLE

HARM CAUSED TO PLAINTIFF &/OR PATIENT:
1. NOT SPECIFIED

TYPE OF ACTION BROUGHT:
1. NEGLIGENCE
2. FALSE IMPRISONMENT
3. MALICIOUS PROSECUTION
4. OTHER TORT(S): WRONGFUL COMMITMENT

HISTORY OF THE CASE:

TYPE OF COURT: STATE

TRIER OF FACT: JUDGE,NO JURY

COURT DECISION(S):

TRIAL COURT: FOR DEFENDANT
YEAR: 1966
APPELLATE COURT: FOR DEFENDANT
YEAR: 1973

REASON SUIT FAILED:
1. NEGLIGENCE OR CASE NOT PROVEN

16. BARTLETT V. WEIMER

SUBSEQUENT TO AN ORDER OF A PROBATE COURT OF THE STATE OF OHIO, THE PLAINTIFF WAS COMMITTED TO A STATE MENTAL INSTITUTION FOR FOURTEEN MONTHS. THE ORDER FOR HIS COMMITMENT WAS SUBSEQUENTLY VACATED FOR FAILURE TO COMPLY WITH THE NOTICE PROVISIONS OF THE RELEVANT OHIO LAWS. BARTLETT THEN SUED DR. WEIMER, CHARGING THAT THE MANNER IN WHICH THE EXAMINATION WAS CONDUCTED AND THE NATURE OF THE FINDINGS AMOUNTED TO A DEPRIVATION OF HIS CONSTITUTIONAL RIGHTS.

YEAR OF NEGLIGENT ACT: NOT SPECIFIED

STATE IN WHICH NEGLIGENT ACT OCCURRED: OHIO

SETTING OF THE CASE: JUDICIAL PROCEEDING

PLAINTIFF(S): PATIENT(S) OR REP.

DEFENDANT(S):
1. NONPSYCHIAT.OR UNKNOWN TYPE PHYSICIAN(S)

NEGLIGENT ACTIVITY:

TREATMENT: NOT APPLICABLE

DIAGNOSIS:

WHAT WAS DIAGNOSED:
1. MENTAL ILLNESS, INSTEAD OF SANITY

RESULT OF DIAGNOSIS:
1. IMPROPER COMMITMENT

CARE: NOT APPLICABLE

HARM CAUSED TO PLAINTIFF &/OR PATIENT:
1. LOSS OF LIBERTY

TYPE OF ACTION BROUGHT:
1. MALICIOUS PROSECUTION
2. DEFAMATION OF CHARACTER: LIBEL AND SLANDER
3. DEPRIVATION OF CONSTITUTIONAL RIGHTS: LOSS OF LIBERTY
4. OTHER TORT(S): WRONGFUL COMMITMENT

HISTORY OF THE CASE:

TYPE OF COURT: FEDERAL

TRIER OF FACT: JUDGE;JURY PRESENT ?

COURT DECISION(S):

TRIAL COURT: FOR DEFENDANT
YEAR: NOT SPECIFIED
APPELLATE COURT: FOR DEFENDANT
YEAR: 1959

REASON SUIT FAILED:
1. DEFENDANT(S) CANNOT BE SUED DUE TO: JUDICIAL IMMUNITY

17. BEAUMONT V. MORGAN

THE PLAINTIFF, SUSAN BEAUMONT, WAS A FORTY-SIX-YEAR-OLD DIVORCED WOMAN, TEMPORARILY UNEMPLOYED, ALONE IN BOSTON, WITHOUT FAMILY. ON THE DAY BEFORE THE FOURTH OF JULY SHE FAINTED ON A SIDEWALK AFTER THREE MANHATTANS IN A CAMBRIDGE TAVERN. HER NEXT MEMORY IS WAKING UP STRAPPED TO AN EXAMINING TABLE AT CAMBRIDGE CITY HOSPITAL. POLICE TESTIFIED THAT SHE WAS ABUSIVE, STRUCK THEM REPEATEDLY WITH HER PURSE AND CANE, AND THREATENED SUICIDE. ON THE BASIS OF THIS REPORT AND HIS OWN OBSERVATIONS OF PLAINTIFF'S VIOLENT BEHAVIOR, THE INTERN ON DUTY AT CAMBRIDGE CITY HOSPITAL CONCLUDED THAT PLAINTIFF SUFFERED FROM "ACUTE PSYCHOSIS WITH ALCOHOLISM" AND EXECUTED A REQUEST FOR TEMPORARY ADMISSION TO WESTBOROUGH STATE HOSPITAL. ON ARRIVAL AT WESTBOROUGH SHE WAS OBSERVED AS UNDER THE INFLUENCE OF ALCOHOL AND THE EXAMINING PSYCHIATRIST TENTATIVELY CONCLUDED THAT HER PSYCHOSIS WAS DUE TO EXCESS ALCOHOL IN A PARANOID PERSONALITY. A LATER CONSENSUS WAS THAT PLAINTIFF SUFFERED FROM "PATHOLOGICAL INTOXICATION IN A SOCIOPATHIC PERSONALITY." AFTER A TWO-WEEK STAY AT WESTBOROUGH THE PLAINTIFF WAS RELEASED. SHE BROUGHT SUIT IN BOTH FEDERAL AND STATE COURTS FOR WRONGFUL COMMITMENT.

YEAR OF NEGLIGENT ACT: 1967

STATE IN WHICH NEGLIGENT ACT OCCURRED: MASSACHUSETTS

SETTING OF THE CASE: JUDICIAL PROCEEDING

PLAINTIFF(S): PATIENT(S) OR REP.

DEFENDANT(S):
1. PSYCHIATRIST(S)
2. NONPSYCHIAT.OR UNKNOWN TYPE PHYSICIAN(S)

NEGLIGENT ACTIVITY:

TREATMENT: NOT APPLICABLE

DIAGNOSIS:

WHAT WAS DIAGNOSED:
1. MENTAL ILLNESS, INSTEAD OF SANITY

RESULT OF DIAGNOSIS:
1. IMPROPER COMMITMENT
2. IMPROPER FAILURE TO RELEASE

CARE: NOT APPLICABLE

HARM CAUSED TO PLAINTIFF &/OR PATIENT:
1. LOSS OF LIBERTY

TYPE OF ACTION BROUGHT:
1. DEPRIVATION OF CONSTITUTIONAL RIGHTS: LOSS OF LIBERTY

HISTORY OF THE CASE:

TYPE OF COURT: FEDERAL

TRIER OF FACT: JURY

COURT DECISION(S):

TRIAL COURT: FOR DEFENDANT
YEAR: NOT SPECIFIED
APPELLATE COURT: FOR DEFENDANT
YEAR: 1970
SUPREME COURT: FOR DEFENDANT
YEAR: 1970

REASON SUIT FAILED:
1. NEGLIGENCE OR CASE NOT PROVEN

18. BECKHAM V. CLINE

FIVE PERSONS PETITIONED THE COUNTY JUDGE OF POLK COUNTY, ALLEGING THAT VIRGINIA BECKHAM WAS INSANE. THE JUDGE APPOINTED TWO PHYSICIANS TO EXAMINE HER. ALTHOUGH THEY ALLEGEDLY DID NOT MAKE ANY EXAMINATION, THEY DULY CERTIFIED THAT SHE WAS IN FACT INSANE, AND SHE WAS SUBSEQUENTLY COMMITTED TO FLORIDA STATE HOSPITAL. SHE BROUGHT SUIT FOR THE ALLEGED FAILURE TO COMPLY WITH THE STATUTORY PROVISIONS REQUIRING AN EXAMINATION.

YEAR OF NEGLIGENT ACT: 1941

STATE IN WHICH NEGLIGENT ACT OCCURRED: FLORIDA

SETTING OF THE CASE: JUDICIAL PROCEEDING

PLAINTIFF(S): PATIENT(S) OR REP.

DEFENDANT(S):
1. NONPSYCHIAT.OR UNKNOWN TYPE PHYSICIAN(S)

NEGLIGENT ACTIVITY:

TREATMENT: NOT APPLICABLE

DIAGNOSIS:

WHAT WAS DIAGNOSED:
1. MENTAL ILLNESS, INSTEAD OF SANITY

RESULT OF DIAGNOSIS:
1. IMPROPER COMMITMENT

CARE: NOT APPLICABLE

HARM CAUSED TO PLAINTIFF &/OR PATIENT:
1. LOSS OF LIBERTY

TYPE OF ACTION BROUGHT:
1. NEGLIGENCE
2. FALSE IMPRISONMENT

HISTORY OF THE CASE:

TYPE OF COURT: STATE

TRIER OF FACT: JUDGE;JURY PRESENT ?

COURT DECISION(S):

TRIAL COURT: FOR DEFENDANT
YEAR: NOT SPECIFIED
SUPREME COURT: NONFINAL FOR PL.
YEAR: 1942

DEFENDANTS STILL INVOLVED IN SUIT:
1. NONPSYCHIAT.OR UNKNOWN TYPE PHYSICIAN(S)

19. BELLANDI V. PARK SANITARIUM ASSOCIATION

ENRICO BELLANDI BROUGHT THIS SUIT ON BEHALF OF HIS DECEASED BROTHER ANTONIO. AT THE TIME OF HIS DEATH ANTONIO WAS THIRTY-THREE, SPOKE VERY LITTLE ENGLISH, AND WAS ABOUT TO EMBARK ON A TRIP TO ITALY TO VISIT HIS MOTHER. HIS EXCITEMENT ABOUT HIS IMPENDING DEPARTURE CAUSED ENRICO TO TAKE HIM TO THE DEFENDANT SANITARIUM, WHERE THE ADMITTING NURSE WAS INFORMED OF HIS EXTREME DIFFIDENCE AND SHYNESS WITH RESPECT TO WOMEN. HIS CLOTHING WAS REMOVED. EARLY IN THE MORNING ON HIS WAY TO THE BATHROOM, WRAPPED ONLY IN A SHEET, HE TOLD A FEMALE NURSE NOT TO TOUCH HIM OR HE WOULD KILL HER. HE WAS THEREUPON PLACED IN A BARRED ROOM, FROM WHICH HE ESCAPED AND ATTEMPTED TO RECOVER HIS CLOTHES. AT NO TIME DID HE MAKE ANY FURTHER THREATS. SHORTLY THEREAFTER HE WAS SEEN BEING PURSUED BY THE MEDICAL DIRECTOR OF THE SANITARIUM, WHO CHASED HIM UP AND DOWN THE HALL WITH AN UPRAISED CHAIR. ANTONIO WAS EVENTUALLY SUBDUED BY THE DIRECTOR AND FIVE OR SIX NURSES. THE METHOD OF SUBMISSION CONSISTED OF PLACING A TOURNIQUET TIGHTLY AROUND HIS NECK AND ADMINISTERING ALMOST A FULL CAN OF ETHER. WHEN THE DIRECTOR'S ATTENTION WAS CALLED TO THE FACT THAT THE PATIENT WAS TURNING BLUE AND NEEDED AIR, HE RESPONDED THAT HE WOULD GIVE HIM NOTHING. ANTONIO DIED SHORTLY THEREAFTER.

YEAR OF NEGLIGENT ACT: 1923

STATE IN WHICH NEGLIGENT ACT OCCURRED: CALIFORNIA

SETTING OF THE CASE: PRIV. MENT. HOSP.

PLAINTIFF(S): 3RD PARTY, I

DEFENDANT(S):
1. NONPSYCHIAT.OR UNKNOWN TYPE PHYSICIAN(S)
2. HOSPITAL &/OR OWNERS, ETC.
3. NURSE(S)

NEGLIGENT ACTIVITY:

TREATMENT:
1. NEGLIGENCE IN USE OF TECHNIQUE
2. PHYSICAL ASSAULT

DIAGNOSIS:

WHAT WAS DIAGNOSED: NOT APPLICABLE

RESULT OF DIAGNOSIS: NOT APPLICABLE

CARE: NOT APPLICABLE

HARM CAUSED TO PLAINTIFF &/OR PATIENT:
1. NONSUICIDAL DEATH

TYPE OF ACTION BROUGHT:
1. NEGLIGENCE

HISTORY OF THE CASE:

TYPE OF COURT: STATE

TRIER OF FACT: JURY

COURT DECISION(S):

TRIAL COURT: FOR PLAINTIFF
YEAR: NOT SPECIFIED
SUPREME COURT: FOR PLAINTIFF
YEAR: 1931

VERDICT AGAINST WHICH DEFENDANTS:
1. HOSPITAL &/OR OWNERS, ETC.

RECOVERY OR OTHER RELIEF GRANTED:
1. $ 15000

20. BELLOWS V. STATE

BERNARD BELLOWS WAS SENTENCED TO AN INDETERMINATE TERM OF ONE-DAY-TO-LIFE FOLLOWING HIS GUILTY PLEA TO AN INDICTMENT CHARGING HIM WITH CARNAL ABUSE OF A CHILD, SECOND DEGREE ASSAULT WITH INTENT TO COMMIT SODOMY, FIRST DEGREE SODOMY, AND ENDANGERING THE LIFE AND HEALTH OF A CHILD. HE WAS INCARCERATED FROM 1951 TO 1969. AFTER HIS RELEASE HE BROUGHT SUIT CLAIMING THAT THE STATE FAILED TO FURNISH HIM WITH SUFFICIENT PSYCHIATRIC AND MEDICAL DIAGNOSIS AND CARE.

YEAR OF NEGLIGENT ACT: OCCURRED OVER A SERIES OF YEARS, ENDING IN 1969

STATE IN WHICH NEGLIGENT ACT OCCURRED: NEW YORK

SETTING OF THE CASE: CORRECTIONAL INST.

PLAINTIFF(S): PATIENT(S) OR REP.

DEFENDANT(S):
1. STATE GOV. &/OR OFFICIALS, ETC.

NEGLIGENT ACTIVITY:

TREATMENT:
1. NO TREATMENT OR INADEQUATE TREATMENT

DIAGNOSIS:

WHAT WAS DIAGNOSED:
1. FAILURE TO MAKE A DIAGNOSIS

RESULT OF DIAGNOSIS:
1. IMPROPER FAILURE TO RELEASE

CARE: NOT APPLICABLE

HARM CAUSED TO PLAINTIFF &/OR PATIENT:
1. DEPRIVATION OF CONSTITUTIONAL RIGHTS

TYPE OF ACTION BROUGHT:
1. NEGLIGENCE

HISTORY OF THE CASE:

TYPE OF COURT: STATE

TRIER OF FACT: JUDGE,NO JURY

COURT DECISION(S):

TRIAL COURT: NONFINAL FOR PL.
YEAR: 1970
APPELLATE COURT: FOR DEFENDANT
YEAR: 1971

REASON SUIT FAILED:
1. DEFENDANT(S) CANNOT BE SUED DUE TO: GOVERN. IMMUNITY

21. BENCOMO V. MORGAN

PLAINTIFF'S HUSBAND FILED A PETITION IN THE COUNTY JUDGES' COURT TO HAVE PLAINTIFF DECLARED INCOMPETENT. THE PETITION WAS SUPPORTED BY A LETTER OF THE DEFENDANT, WHO HAD TREATED HER TEN YEARS BEFORE, AND WHO STATED THAT SHE WAS BADLY IN NEED OF A PSYCHIATRIC EXAMINATION. AT THE COMPETENCY HEARING HE REITERATED HIS TESTIMONY, BUT THE COURT-APPOINTED COMMITTEE DISMISSED THE PETITION AND UPHELD HER COMPETENCY. SHE BROUGHT SUIT AGAINST HIM, ALLEGING DEFAMATION OF CHARACTER AND VARIOUS OTHER WRONGS.

YEAR OF NEGLIGENT ACT: NOT SPECIFIED

STATE IN WHICH NEGLIGENT ACT OCCURRED: FLORIDA

SETTING OF THE CASE: JUDICIAL PROCEEDING

PLAINTIFF(S): PATIENT(S) OR REP.

DEFENDANT(S):
1. NONPSYCHIAT.OR UNKNOWN TYPE PHYSICIAN(S)

NEGLIGENT ACTIVITY:

TREATMENT: NOT APPLICABLE

DIAGNOSIS:

WHAT WAS DIAGNOSED:
1. MENTAL ILLNESS, INSTEAD OF SANITY
2. NEG.REC.TO TAKE PSYCHIATRIC EXAM

RESULT OF DIAGNOSIS:
1. IMPROPER COMMITMENT

CARE: NOT APPLICABLE

HARM CAUSED TO PLAINTIFF &/OR PATIENT:
1. EMOTIONAL DISTRESS

TYPE OF ACTION BROUGHT:
1. MALICIOUS PROSECUTION
2. DEFAMATION OF CHARACTER: LIBEL AND SLANDER
3. OTHER TORT(S): MAL.INFL.OF EMOT.DIS

HISTORY OF THE CASE:

TYPE OF COURT: STATE

TRIER OF FACT: JUDGE;JURY PRESENT ?

COURT DECISION(S):

TRIAL COURT: FOR DEFENDANT
YEAR: NOT SPECIFIED
APPELLATE COURT: FOR DEFENDANT
YEAR: 1968

REASON SUIT FAILED:
1. NEGLIGENCE OR CASE NOT PROVEN
2. DEFENDANT(S) CANNOT BE SUED DUE TO: JUDICIAL IMMUNITY

22. BENJAMIN V. HAVENS, INC.

A PSYCHIATRIST, TO WHOM IRENE BENJAMIN HAD BEEN REFERRED, RECOMMENDED IMMEDIATE HOSPITALIZATION IN THE DEFENDANT HOSPITAL, TOGETHER WITH ELECTRIC SHOCK TREATMENTS. THE PLAINTIFF WAS PLACED ON AN OPEN WARD AND RECEIVED FIVE ELECTRIC SHOCK TREATMENTS BETWEEN CHRISTMAS AND NEW YEARS, 1957. ON THE EVENING OF JANUARY 1 SHE FLED THROUGH AN UNLOCKED OUTER DOOR AND FELL ONTO A CEMENT PATIO, SUSTAINING VARIOUS INJURIES. SHE AND HER HUSBAND SUED THE HOSPITAL, ALLEGING THAT IT DID NOT PROVIDE ADEQUATE SUPERVISION OF THE PATIENT. THEY ALSO SUED THE REFERRING PSYCHIATRIST, CLAIMING THAT HE KNEW OF HER SELF-DESTRUCTIVE TENDENCIES BUT FAILED TO SELECT A SUITABLE HOSPITAL AND DID NOT PRESCRIBE THE NECESSARY RESTRAINTS.

YEAR OF NEGLIGENT ACT: 1957

STATE IN WHICH NEGLIGENT ACT OCCURRED: WASHINGTON

SETTING OF THE CASE: PRIV. GEN. HOSP.

PLAINTIFF(S): PAT. & 3RD PTY., I

DEFENDANT(S):
1. PSYCHIATRIST(S)
2. HOSPITAL &/OR OWNERS, ETC.
3. DEFENDANT'S SPOUSE

NEGLIGENT ACTIVITY:

TREATMENT: NOT APPLICABLE

DIAGNOSIS:

WHAT WAS DIAGNOSED:
1. TYPE OF CUSTODIAL CARE

RESULT OF DIAGNOSIS:
1. IMPROPER CUSTODIAL CARE

CARE:
1. INADEQUATE SUPERVISION

HARM CAUSED TO PLAINTIFF &/OR PATIENT:
1. NONSELF-INFLICTED INJURIES

TYPE OF ACTION BROUGHT:
1. NEGLIGENCE

HISTORY OF THE CASE:

TYPE OF COURT: STATE

TRIER OF FACT: JURY

COURT DECISION(S):

TRIAL COURT: FOR DEFENDANT
YEAR: NOT SPECIFIED
SUPREME COURT: NONFINAL FOR PL.
YEAR: 1962

DEFENDANTS STILL INVOLVED IN SUIT:
1. HOSPITAL &/OR OWNERS, ETC.

23. BENNETT V. STATE

IN THIS SUIT THE PLAINTIFF, TWENTY-TWO-YEAR-OLD JOHN BENNETT, WAS BEING TRANSFERRED FROM QUEENS GENERAL HOSPITAL TO CREEDMOOR STATE HOSPITAL IN NEW YORK. HE WAS ASSIGNED TO AN ELEVENTH-FLOOR WARD. DURING THE ELEVATOR RIDE HE WAS VERBALLY ABUSIVE TO THE ATTENDANTS, ONE OF WHOM STRUCK HIM IN THE FACE AND BROKE HIS JAW. THE ADMITTING PSYCHIATRIST AT CREEDMOOR STATED THAT BENNETT WAS RESTLESS, INSULTING AND NOT COOPERATIVE. DURING THE ENTIRE TIME, BENNETT'S HANDS WERE HANDCUFFED BEHIND HIS BACK.

YEAR OF NEGLIGENT ACT: 1966

STATE IN WHICH NEGLIGENT ACT OCCURRED: NEW YORK

SETTING OF THE CASE: PUB. MENT. HOSP.

PLAINTIFF(S): PATIENT(S) OR REP.

DEFENDANT(S):
1. STATE GOV. &/OR OFFICIALS, ETC.

NEGLIGENT ACTIVITY:

TREATMENT: NOT APPLICABLE

DIAGNOSIS:

WHAT WAS DIAGNOSED: NOT APPLICABLE

RESULT OF DIAGNOSIS: NOT APPLICABLE

CARE:
1. FAILURE TO PROVIDE PROPER CUSTODIAL CARE

HARM CAUSED TO PLAINTIFF &/OR PATIENT:
1. NONSELF-INFLICTED INJURIES

TYPE OF ACTION BROUGHT:
1. NEGLIGENCE

HISTORY OF THE CASE:

TYPE OF COURT: STATE

TRIER OF FACT: JUDGE,NO JURY

COURT DECISION(S):

TRIAL COURT: FOR PLAINTIFF
YEAR: 1969

VERDICT AGAINST WHICH DEFENDANTS:
1. STATE GOV. &/OR OFFICIALS, ETC.

RECOVERY OR OTHER RELIEF GRANTED:
1. $ 10000

24. BERRY V. MOENCH

A DOCTOR IN WYOMING REQUESTED INFORMATION CONCERNING THE PLAINTIFF, WHICH WAS FURNISHED BY THE DEFENDANT PSYCHIATRIST. IN HIS LETTER DR. MOENCH STATED THAT HE HAD TREATED THE DEFENDANT SEVEN YEARS BEFORE AND HAD DIAGNOSED HIM AS A MANIC DEPRESSIVE IN A PSYCHOPATHIC PERSONALITY. HE MADE OTHER DEROGATORY STATEMENTS, CLAIMING THE PATIENT DID NOT PAY HIS BILLS, WAS IN CONSTANT TROUBLE, AND DID NOT GIVE PROPER SUPPORT TO HIS WIFE AND CHILDREN. THESE STATEMENTS WERE BASED ON THE TESTIMONY OF HIS ESTRANGED WIFE AND SISTER-IN-LAW. HE RECOMMENDED THAT THE WOMAN THE PLAINTIFF WAS CURRENTLY SEEING SHOULD BE TOLD TO RUN AWAY AS FAST AS POSSIBLE. THIS LETTER WAS GIVEN TO THE WOMAN'S PARENTS, WHO BECAME VIOLENTLY OPPOSED TO THEIR DAUGHTER SEEING THE PLAINTIFF. SHE NEVERTHELESS MARRIED HIM, AND THEY DISOWNED HER. THE BASIC ISSUE IN THE SUIT WAS THE PROPRIETY OF DISCLOSING SUCH INFORMATION, WHICH HAD BEEN GATHERED IN A DOCTOR-PATIENT RELATIONSHIP.

YEAR OF NEGLIGENT ACT: 1956

STATE IN WHICH NEGLIGENT ACT OCCURRED: UTAH

SETTING OF THE CASE: PRIVATE PRACTICE

PLAINTIFF(S): PATIENT(S) OR REP.

DEFENDANT(S):
1. PSYCHIATRIST(S)

NEGLIGENT ACTIVITY:

TREATMENT: NOT APPLICABLE

DIAGNOSIS:

WHAT WAS DIAGNOSED: NOT APPLICABLE

RESULT OF DIAGNOSIS: NOT APPLICABLE

CARE:
1. IMPROPER GIVING OF INFORMATION TO OTHERS

HARM CAUSED TO PLAINTIFF &/OR PATIENT:
1. INJURY TO REPUTATION

TYPE OF ACTION BROUGHT:
1. DEFAMATION OF CHARACTER: LIBEL

HISTORY OF THE CASE:

TYPE OF COURT: STATE

TRIER OF FACT: JURY

COURT DECISION(S):

TRIAL COURT: FOR DEFENDANT
YEAR: NOT SPECIFIED
SUPREME COURT: NONFINAL FOR PL.
YEAR: 1958

DEFENDANTS STILL INVOLVED IN SUIT:
1. PSYCHIATRIST(S)

25. BETTS V. STATE

THIS SUIT WAS BROUGHT ON BEHALF OF EARL D. ENGLE, AN EPILEPTIC, WHO WAS COMMITTED TO BINGHAMTON STATE HOSPITAL PURSUANT TO AN ORDER OF THE SCHOHARIE COUNTY COURT. WHILE AT BINGHAMTON ENGLE WAS OBSERVED LIMPING AND AN EXAMINATION REVEALED A BLISTER ON THE BOTTOM OF HIS RIGHT FOOT, WHICH TURNED OUT TO BE A SECOND-DEGREE BURN. NEGLIGENCE WAS ALLEGED, ALTHOUGH NO PROOF WAS ADDUCED TO SHOW HOW THE INJURY WAS SUSTAINED.

YEAR OF NEGLIGENT ACT: 1943

STATE IN WHICH NEGLIGENT ACT OCCURRED: NEW YORK

SETTING OF THE CASE: PUB. MENT. HOSP.

PLAINTIFF(S): PATIENT(S) OR REP.

DEFENDANT(S):
1. STATE GOV. &/OR OFFICIALS, ETC.

NEGLIGENT ACTIVITY:

TREATMENT: NOT APPLICABLE

DIAGNOSIS:

WHAT WAS DIAGNOSED: NOT APPLICABLE

RESULT OF DIAGNOSIS: NOT APPLICABLE

CARE:
1. INADEQUATE SUPERVISION

HARM CAUSED TO PLAINTIFF &/OR PATIENT:
1. NONSELF-INFLICTED INJURIES

TYPE OF ACTION BROUGHT:
1. NEGLIGENCE

HISTORY OF THE CASE:

TYPE OF COURT: STATE

TRIER OF FACT: JUDGE,NO JURY

COURT DECISION(S):

TRIAL COURT: FOR DEFENDANT
YEAR: 1945

REASON SUIT FAILED:
1. NEGLIGENCE OR CASE NOT PROVEN

26. BLAUER V. STATE

HAROLD BLAUER DIED ON JANUARY 8, 1953 AT THE NEW YORK STATE PSYCHIATRIC INSTITUTE. HIS WIFE BROUGHT SUIT, ALLEGING THAT HER HUSBAND HAD BEEN ADMINISTERED A TOXIC AND DANGEROUS SUBSTANCE, DYING LESS THAN THREE HOURS LATER. THE PLAINTIFF RECOVERED THE SUM OF $18,000. MORE THAN TWENTY YEARS LATER THE UNITED STATES ARMY DISCLOSED THAT HAROLD BLAUER HAD ACTUALLY DIED DURING A DRUG EXPERIMENT PROGRAM CARRIED OUT BY THE PSYCHIATRIC INSTITUTE PURSUANT TO A CONTRACT IT HAD ENTERED WITH THE CHEMICAL CORPS PROCUREMENT AGENCY, ARMY CHEMICAL CENTER.

YEAR OF NEGLIGENT ACT: 1953

STATE IN WHICH NEGLIGENT ACT OCCURRED: NEW YORK

SETTING OF THE CASE: PUB. MENT. HOSP.

PLAINTIFF(S): PATIENT(S) OR REP.

DEFENDANT(S):
1. STATE GOV. &/OR OFFICIALS, ETC.

NEGLIGENT ACTIVITY:

TREATMENT:
1. NEGLIGENCE IN USE OF TECHNIQUE

DIAGNOSIS:

WHAT WAS DIAGNOSED: NOT APPLICABLE

RESULT OF DIAGNOSIS: NOT APPLICABLE

CARE: NOT APPLICABLE

HARM CAUSED TO PLAINTIFF &/OR PATIENT:
1. NONSUICIDAL DEATH

TYPE OF ACTION BROUGHT:
1. NEGLIGENCE

HISTORY OF THE CASE:

TYPE OF COURT: STATE

TRIER OF FACT: JUDGE,NO JURY

COURT DECISION(S):

TRIAL COURT: FOR PLAINTIFF
YEAR: 1955

VERDICT AGAINST WHICH DEFENDANTS:
1. STATE GOV. &/OR OFFICIALS, ETC.

RECOVERY OR OTHER RELIEF GRANTED:
1. $ 18000

27. BLITZ V. BOOG

THE PLAINTIFF, JULIE BLITZ, SOUGHT TREATMENT AT THE 24TH STREET VETERANS ADMINISTRATION HOSPITAL IN NEW YORK CITY FOR EMOTIONAL PROBLEMS RELATING BACK TO WORLD WAR II. SHE ALLEGED THAT THE STAFF AT THE HOSPITAL REFUSED TO BELIEVE SHE WAS A VETERAN, BUT NONETHELESS GAVE HER AN INJECTION, PREVENTED HER FROM LEAVING, AND THEN FORCEFULLY REMOVED HER TO BELLEVUE HOSPITAL, WHERE SHE REMAINED FOR EIGHT DAYS, SUFFERING BEATINGS AND RECEIVING IMPROPER TREATMENT. SHE BROUGHT SUIT AGAINST DR. BOOG, A RESIDENT IN PSYCHIATRY AT THE V.A., WHO SUPERVISED THE FOUR MEN RESPONSIBLE FOR PHYSICALLY OVERPOWERING HER DURING THE TRANSFER TO BELLEVUE.

YEAR OF NEGLIGENT ACT: 1960

STATE IN WHICH NEGLIGENT ACT OCCURRED: NEW YORK

SETTING OF THE CASE: PUB. GEN. HOSP.

PLAINTIFF(S): PATIENT(S) OR REP.

DEFENDANT(S):
1. PSYCHIATRIST(S)
2. FEDERAL GOV. &/OR OFFICIALS, ETC.

NEGLIGENT ACTIVITY:

TREATMENT:
1. FAILURE TO OBTAIN -OR LACK OF- CONSENT

DIAGNOSIS:

WHAT WAS DIAGNOSED:
1. MENT.ILL, INSTEAD OF PHYSICAL ILLNESS

RESULT OF DIAGNOSIS:
1. IMPROPER TREATMENT PRESCRIBED

CARE: NOT APPLICABLE

HARM CAUSED TO PLAINTIFF &/OR PATIENT:
1. LOSS OF LIBERTY

TYPE OF ACTION BROUGHT:
1. NEGLIGENCE
2. FALSE IMPRISONMENT

HISTORY OF THE CASE:

TYPE OF COURT: FEDERAL

TRIER OF FACT: JUDGE;JURY PRESENT ?

COURT DECISION(S):

TRIAL COURT: FOR DEFENDANT
YEAR: 1964
APPELLATE COURT: FOR DEFENDANT
YEAR: 1964
SUPREME COURT: FOR DEFENDANT
YEAR: 1964

REASON SUIT FAILED:
1. DEFENDANT(S) CANNOT BE SUED DUE TO: GOVERN. IMMUNITY

28. BOGUST V. IVERSON

JEANNIE BOGUST WAS A STUDENT AT STOUT STATE COLLEGE, WHERE RALPH IVERSON, A PH.D. PROFESSOR OF EDUCATION, ACTED AS DIRECTOR OF STUDENT PERSONNEL SERVICES. IN NOVEMBER, 1957 JEANNIE CAME UNDER THE DIRECT GUIDANCE OF THE DEFENDANT, WHO GAVE HER A SERIES OF APTITUDE AND PERSONALITY TESTS AND PROVIDED HER WITH GUIDANCE COUNSELING. IN APRIL OF THE FOLLOWING YEAR HE SUGGESTED TERMINATION OF FUTURE INTERVIEWS. ONE MONTH LATER SHE COMMITTED SUICIDE. HER PARENTS BROUGHT SUIT AGAINST IVERSON, ALLEGING THAT HE WAS FAMILIAR WITH HER EMOTIONAL AND SCHOLASTIC PROBLEMS, AND THAT AS A RESULT OF IMPROPER GUIDANCE, IMPROPERLY RECOMMENDING TERMINATION OF THE INTERVIEWS, AND FAILING TO RECOMMEND PSYCHIATRIC CONSULTATION HE WAS NEGLIGENT. THE COURT CONCLUDED THAT THE DEFENDANT COULD NOT BE CONSIDERED AN EXPERT IN MEDICINE OR PSYCHIATRY AND THEREFORE SHOULD NOT BE HELD TO THE SAME STANDARD OF CARE AS THOSE PRACTICING IN THOSE FIELDS.

YEAR OF NEGLIGENT ACT: 1958

STATE IN WHICH NEGLIGENT ACT OCCURRED: WISCONSIN

SETTING OF THE CASE: EDUCATIONAL INST.

PLAINTIFF(S): 3RD PARTY, I

DEFENDANT(S):
1. EDUCATIONAL INST. &/OR DEANS, ETC.

NEGLIGENT ACTIVITY:

TREATMENT: NOT APPLICABLE

DIAGNOSIS:

WHAT WAS DIAGNOSED:
1. LACK OF SUICIDAL TENDENCIES

RESULT OF DIAGNOSIS:
1. IMPROPER TREATMENT PRESCRIBED
2. IMPROPER CUSTODIAL CARE

CARE:
1. INADEQUATE SUPERVISION
2. FAILURE TO WARN THIRD PARTIES

HARM CAUSED TO PLAINTIFF &/OR PATIENT:
1. SUICIDE

TYPE OF ACTION BROUGHT:
1. NEGLIGENCE

HISTORY OF THE CASE:

TYPE OF COURT: STATE

TRIER OF FACT: JUDGE;JURY PRESENT ?

COURT DECISION(S):

TRIAL COURT: FOR DEFENDANT
YEAR: NOT SPECIFIED
SUPREME COURT: FOR DEFENDANT
YEAR: 1960

REASON SUIT FAILED:
1. NEGLIGENCE OR CASE NOT PROVEN

29. BOLAND V. STATE

ON NOVEMBER 8, 1965 THE PLAINTIFF, MARIE BOLAND, WAS ADMITTED TO CENTRAL ISLIP HOSPITAL PURSUANT TO COURT ORDER. FIVE MONTHS LATER SHE SIGNED A PAPER DESIGNATED AS "APPLICATION FOR HOSPITALIZATION," WHICH THE STATE CLAIMED MADE HER A VOLUNTARY PATIENT. ON JUNE 9, 1966 THE PLAINTIFF WAS RELEASED FROM THE HOSPITAL, BUT NOT DISCHARGED. SHE WAS PLACED UNDER CONVALESCENT STATUS WITH A DIAGNOSIS OF "SCHIZOPHRENIA, PARANOID; IMPROVED." SHE BROUGHT SUIT AGAINST THE STATE FOR WRONGFUL COMMITMENT AND NEGLIGENCE IN THE DIAGNOSIS AND TREATMENT OF HER MENTAL ILLNESS. THE STATE ARGUED THAT THE CLAIM WAS NOT TIMELY FILED.

YEAR OF NEGLIGENT ACT: 1965

STATE IN WHICH NEGLIGENT ACT OCCURRED: NEW YORK

SETTING OF THE CASE: JUDICIAL PROCEEDING

PLAINTIFF(S): PATIENT(S) OR REP.

DEFENDANT(S):
1. STATE GOV. &/OR OFFICIALS, ETC.

NEGLIGENT ACTIVITY:

TREATMENT:
1. UNSPEC.NEG.TREAT

DIAGNOSIS:

WHAT WAS DIAGNOSED:
1. MENTAL ILLNESS, INSTEAD OF SANITY

RESULT OF DIAGNOSIS:
1. IMPROPER COMMITMENT

CARE: NOT APPLICABLE

HARM CAUSED TO PLAINTIFF &/OR PATIENT:
1. NOT SPECIFIED

TYPE OF ACTION BROUGHT:
1. NEGLIGENCE
2. FALSE IMPRISONMENT

HISTORY OF THE CASE:

TYPE OF COURT: STATE

TRIER OF FACT: JUDGE,NO JURY

COURT DECISION(S):

TRIAL COURT: NONFINAL FOR PL.
YEAR: 1969
APPELLATE COURT: FOR DEFENDANT
YEAR: 1970
SUPREME COURT: NONFINAL FOR PL.
YEAR: 1972

DEFENDANTS STILL INVOLVED IN SUIT:
1. STATE GOV. &/OR OFFICIALS, ETC.

30. BOOE V. HALL

THE PLAINTIFF, CARLYLE BOOE, SUFFERED FROM THROMBOPHLEBITIS, WHICH REQUIRED PERIODIC HOSPITALIZATION AND RESULTED IN MARITAL DISHARMONY. HE ALLEGED THAT HIS WIFE MALICIOUSLY HAD HIM COMMITTED, ARGUING THAT HE SUFFERED FROM MENTAL ILLNESS OR INEBRIETY. HE ALSO ALLEGED THAT THE TWO PHYSICIANS WHO EXAMINED HIM DID NOT DO SO FOR MORE THAN FIVE MINUTES EACH. HE WAS COMMITTED TO JOHN UMSTEAD HOSPITAL AT BUTNER, NORTH CAROLINA ON MARCH 15, 1972. A MONTH LATER HE WAS TRANSFERRED TO MEDICAL PARK HOSPITAL IN WINSTON-SALEM, NORTH CAROLINA, WHERE HE WAS TREATED FOR A PHYSICAL AILMENT, AND AFTER WHICH HE WAS DISCHARGED.

YEAR OF NEGLIGENT ACT: 1972

STATE IN WHICH NEGLIGENT ACT OCCURRED: NORTH CAROLINA

SETTING OF THE CASE: JUDICIAL PROCEEDING

PLAINTIFF(S): PATIENT(S) OR REP.

DEFENDANT(S):
1. NONPSYCHIAT.OR UNKNOWN TYPE PHYSICIAN(S)
2. COUNTY GOV. &/OR OFFICIALS, ETC.
3. JUDICIARY &/OR CLERKS, ETC.
4. PL'S.SPOUSE &/ MOTH.

NEGLIGENT ACTIVITY:

TREATMENT: NOT APPLICABLE

DIAGNOSIS:

WHAT WAS DIAGNOSED:
1. MENTAL ILLNESS, INSTEAD OF SANITY

RESULT OF DIAGNOSIS:
1. IMPROPER COMMITMENT

CARE: NOT APPLICABLE

HARM CAUSED TO PLAINTIFF &/OR PATIENT:
1. NOT SPECIFIED

TYPE OF ACTION BROUGHT:
1. FALSE IMPRISONMENT
2. MALICIOUS PROSECUTION
3. OTHER TORT(S): ABUSE OF PROCESS

HISTORY OF THE CASE:

TYPE OF COURT: STATE

TRIER OF FACT: JUDGE;JURY PRESENT ?

COURT DECISION(S):

TRIAL COURT: FOR DEFENDANT
YEAR: NOT SPECIFIED
APPELLATE COURT: NONFINAL FOR PL.
YEAR: 1974

DEFENDANTS STILL INVOLVED IN SUIT:
1. PL'S.SPOUSE &/ MOTH.

31. BORKER V. NTL INSTITUTE

PLAINTIFF BROUGHT SUIT AGAINST NTL INSTITUTE CLAIMING THAT THE DECEDENT'S SUICIDE WAS ATTRIBUTABLE TO PARTICIPATION IN ONE OF DEFENDANT'S HUMAN RELATIONS TRAINING PROGRAMS. THE DECEASED HAD EXPERIENCED A PSYCHOTIC EPISODE DURING THE TENTH DAY OF A TWO-WEEK T-GROUP. THE GROUP LEADERS BROUGHT HIM TO A PHYSICIAN WHO RECOMMENDED PSYCHIATRIC HOSPITALIZATION. THE PARTICIPANT REMAINED HOSPITALIZED FOR THE DURATION OF THE PROGRAM AND WAS THEN BROUGHT HOME BY THE GROUP LEADERS. THREE MONTHS LATER HE COMMITTED SUICIDE.

YEAR OF NEGLIGENT ACT: NOT SPECIFIED

STATE IN WHICH NEGLIGENT ACT OCCURRED: NEW YORK

SETTING OF THE CASE: ENCOUNTER GROUP

PLAINTIFF(S): PATIENT(S) OR REP.

DEFENDANT(S):
1. GROWTH CENTER

NEGLIGENT ACTIVITY:

TREATMENT:
1. UNSPEC.NEG.TREAT

DIAGNOSIS:

WHAT WAS DIAGNOSED: NOT APPLICABLE

RESULT OF DIAGNOSIS: NOT APPLICABLE

CARE: NOT APPLICABLE

HARM CAUSED TO PLAINTIFF &/OR PATIENT:
1. SUICIDE

TYPE OF ACTION BROUGHT:
1. NEGLIGENCE

HISTORY OF THE CASE:

TYPE OF COURT: FEDERAL

TRIER OF FACT: SETTLED OUT OF COURT

COURT DECISION(S):

SETTLED OUT OF COURT
YEAR: NOT SPECIFIED

VERDICT AGAINST WHICH DEFENDANTS:
1. GROWTH CENTER

RECOVERY OR OTHER RELIEF GRANTED:
1. $ 50000

32. BOYKIN V. STATE

THE INFANT CLAIMANT WAS SEXUALLY ASSAULTED BY A FELLOW INMATE AT THE ROCKLAND STATE HOSPITAL. THE SUIT, BROUGHT BY THE CHILD'S FATHER, ATTEMPTED TO OBTAIN HOSPITAL RECORDS ON THE INMATE WHO ASSAULTED HIS SON. MORE DETAILED INFORMATION ON THE CASE IS UNAVAILABLE.

YEAR OF NEGLIGENT ACT: 1956

STATE IN WHICH NEGLIGENT ACT OCCURRED: NEW YORK

SETTING OF THE CASE: PUB. MENT. HOSP.

PLAINTIFF(S): PATIENT(S) OR REP.

DEFENDANT(S):
1. HOSPITAL &/OR OWNERS, ETC.

NEGLIGENT ACTIVITY:

TREATMENT: NOT APPLICABLE

DIAGNOSIS:

WHAT WAS DIAGNOSED: NOT APPLICABLE

RESULT OF DIAGNOSIS: NOT APPLICABLE

CARE:
1. INADEQUATE SUPERVISION

HARM CAUSED TO PLAINTIFF &/OR PATIENT:
1. NONSELF-INFLICTED INJURIES

TYPE OF ACTION BROUGHT:
1. NEGLIGENCE

HISTORY OF THE CASE:

TYPE OF COURT: STATE

TRIER OF FACT: JUDGE,NO JURY

COURT DECISION(S):

TRIAL COURT: NONFINAL FOR PL.
YEAR: 1958
APPELLATE COURT: NONFINAL FOR PL.
YEAR: 1958

DEFENDANTS STILL INVOLVED IN SUIT:
1. HOSPITAL &/OR OWNERS, ETC.

33. BRADSHAW V. STATE

THE PLAINTIFF APPEALED A LOWER COURT'S RESTRICTIONS PLACED ON THE EXAMINATION AND INSPECTION OF CERTAIN CREEDMOOR STATE HOSPITAL RECORDS. THE PLAINTIFF HAD BEEN DENIED THE RIGHT TO MAKE NOTES OR TO OBTAIN COPIES OF THE RECORDS. SHE ARGUED THAT THESE RECORDS WERE NEEDED TO DETERMINE WHETHER A CAUSE OF ACTION AGAINST THE STATE EXISTED FOR INJURIES SUFFERED BY HER IN AN ALLEGED ACCIDENT AT THE HOSPITAL.

YEAR OF NEGLIGENT ACT: NOT SPECIFIED

STATE IN WHICH NEGLIGENT ACT OCCURRED: NEW YORK

SETTING OF THE CASE: PUB. MENT. HOSP.

PLAINTIFF(S): PATIENT(S) OR REP.

DEFENDANT(S):
1. STATE GOV. &/OR OFFICIALS, ETC.

NEGLIGENT ACTIVITY:

TREATMENT:
1. ? WHETHER TREAT.INV.

DIAGNOSIS:

WHAT WAS DIAGNOSED:
1. ? WHETHER DIAG.INV.

RESULT OF DIAGNOSIS: NOT APPLICABLE

CARE:
1. ? WHETHER CARE INV.

HARM CAUSED TO PLAINTIFF &/OR PATIENT:
1. NOT SPECIFIED

TYPE OF ACTION BROUGHT:
1. OTHER ACTION, EXCLUDING TORT LAW: ACT.NOT YET BROUGHT

HISTORY OF THE CASE:

TYPE OF COURT: STATE

TRIER OF FACT: JUDGE,NO JURY

COURT DECISION(S):

TRIAL COURT: NONFINAL FOR PL.
YEAR: 1957
APPELLATE COURT: NONFINAL FOR PL.
YEAR: 1958

DEFENDANTS STILL INVOLVED IN SUIT:
1. STATE GOV. &/OR OFFICIALS, ETC.

34. BRANDT V. BRANDT

IN 1926 AND 1927 ROSE BRANDT'S HUSBAND HAD HER COMMITTED TO THE COUNTY PSYCHOPATHIC HOSPITAL FOR PERIODS OF ABOUT EIGHT DAYS EACH. DURING 1927 SHE WAS GRANTED A DIVORCE FROM HER HUSBAND AND AWARDED CUSTODY OF THEIR TWO CHILDREN. ACCORDING TO THE TERMS OF THE DECREE HE WAS TO PAY HER $9,500, IN INTERVALS, FOR THE SUPPORT OF THE CHILDREN. THESE PAYMENTS WERE NEVER MADE, AND SHORTLY THEREAFTER HER HUSBAND INITIATED FURTHER COMMITMENT PROCEEDINGS. BASED ON THE TESTIMONY OF I. VAL. FREEDMAN, A PRACTICING PHYSICIAN, WHO DIAGNOSED HER AS SUFFERING FROM "IMPROPER HALLUCINATIONS," WHICH HE ATTRIBUTED TO A "PERSECUTORY DEMENTIA," SHE WAS COMMITTED. THIS CONCLUSION WAS BASED ON FREEDMAN'S OBSERVATION OF HER IN A COURTROOM AND ON SEVERAL HOUSE VISITS, ALLEGEDLY INSTIGATED BY HER HUSBAND, WHERE THE PHYSICIAN DESCRIBED HER AS "AGITATED," "UNKEPT," "FIDGETY," AND THE LIKE. SEVERAL FRIENDS AND NEIGHBORS, HOWEVER, TESTIFIED THAT SHE WAS A GOOD MOTHER AND NOT INSANE. AFTER HER RELEASE SHE BROUGHT SUIT AGAINST HER HUSBAND AND FREEDMAN FOR UNLAWFULLY CONSPIRING TO HAVE HER ARRESTED AND COMMITTED TO THE COUNTY PSYCHOPATHIC HOSPITAL.

YEAR OF NEGLIGENT ACT: OCCURRED OVER A SERIES OF YEARS, ENDING IN 1931

STATE IN WHICH NEGLIGENT ACT OCCURRED: ILLINOIS

SETTING OF THE CASE: PUB. MENT. HOSP.

PLAINTIFF(S): PATIENT(S) OR REP.

DEFENDANT(S):
1. NONPSYCHIAT.OR UNKNOWN TYPE PHYSICIAN(S)
2. PL'S.SPOUSE &/ MOTH.

NEGLIGENT ACTIVITY:

TREATMENT: NOT APPLICABLE

DIAGNOSIS:

WHAT WAS DIAGNOSED:
1. MENTAL ILLNESS, INSTEAD OF SANITY

RESULT OF DIAGNOSIS:
1. IMPROPER COMMITMENT

CARE: NOT APPLICABLE

HARM CAUSED TO PLAINTIFF &/OR PATIENT:
1. NOT SPECIFIED

TYPE OF ACTION BROUGHT:
1. MALICIOUS PROSECUTION
2. OTHER TORT(S): WRONGFUL COMMITMENT

HISTORY OF THE CASE:

TYPE OF COURT: STATE

TRIER OF FACT: JUDGE,UNINV.JURY

COURT DECISION(S):

TRIAL COURT: FOR DEFENDANT
YEAR: NOT SPECIFIED
APPELLATE COURT: FOR DEFENDANT
YEAR: 1936

REASON SUIT FAILED:
1. NO CAUSE OF ACTION STATED

35. BRIGANTE V. STATE

MARGARET BRIGANTE WAS COMMITTED TO BROOKLYN STATE HOSPITAL IN 1939. AFTER COMPLAINTS FROM HER FAMILY ABOUT LACK OF PROPER TREATMENT AND ADEQUATE SUPERVISION, MARGARET WAS MOVED TO WARD 12, WHERE SHE REQUESTED TO HELP WITH POLISHING THE FLOOR. THIS MARKED HER FIRST REQUEST FOR A WORK ASSIGNMENT. WITHIN TWO MINUTES OF RECEIVING THE POLISHER, HOWEVER, AND IN VIEW OF THE ATTENDANT FOR PART OF THAT TIME, MARGARET SET HERSELF ON FIRE. SHE DIED OF SHOCK WITHIN NINETEEN HOURS. THE MANNER IN WHICH THE FIRE STARTED REMAINED UNKNOWN, ALTHOUGH THE ATTENDANT ON DUTY TESTIFIED THAT MARGARET HAD SAID SHE WANTED TO DIE AND HAD REQUESTED POISON AS THE FIRE WAS BEING PUT OUT. HER FATHER CHARGED THE HOSPITAL WITH NEGLIGENCE IN PROVIDING ONLY ONE ATTENDANT FOR EVERY SEVENTY-NINE INMATES.

YEAR OF NEGLIGENT ACT: 1940

STATE IN WHICH NEGLIGENT ACT OCCURRED: NEW YORK

SETTING OF THE CASE: PUB. MENT. HOSP.

PLAINTIFF(S): PATIENT(S) OR REP.

DEFENDANT(S):
1. STATE GOV. &/OR OFFICIALS, ETC.

NEGLIGENT ACTIVITY:

TREATMENT: NOT APPLICABLE

DIAGNOSIS:

WHAT WAS DIAGNOSED: NOT APPLICABLE

RESULT OF DIAGNOSIS: NOT APPLICABLE

CARE:
1. INADEQUATE SUPERVISION

HARM CAUSED TO PLAINTIFF &/OR PATIENT:
1. SUIC.OR ACCID.DEATH

TYPE OF ACTION BROUGHT:
1. NEGLIGENCE

, ISTORY OF THE CASE:

TYPE OF COURT: STATE

TRIER OF FACT: JUDGE,NO JURY

COURT DECISION(S):

TRIAL COURT: FOR DEFENDANT
YEAR: 1942

REASON SUIT FAILED:
1. NEGLIGENCE OR CASE NOT PROVEN

36. BROWN V. MOORE

GEORGE R. BROWN WAS NEUROTIC AND BELIEVED HE WAS SUFFERING FROM CANCER. HIS NEURO-PSYCHIATRIST, DR. FINKELHOR, SUGGESTED REST AT THE MERCER SANITARIUM, WHERE BROWN RECEIVED ELECTRO-SHOCK TREATMENTS. SEVEN HOURS AFTER ONE SUCH TREATMENT, IN WHICH HE EXPERIENCED GRAND MAL SEIZURES, BROWN WAS ALLOWED TO WALK UNATTENDED TO A MASSAGE ON THE SECOND FLOOR. RETURNING TWENTY MINUTES LATER, HE FELL DOWN A FLIGHT OF STAIRS UNOBSERVED. NURSES FOUND HIM AT THE BOTTOM OF THE STAIRS, WHERE HE COMPLAINED OF A BROKEN NECK AND SAID HE WAS DYING. AT LEAST FOUR NURSES CARRIED HIM TO A BED BY HIS EXTREMITIES WITH HIS HEAD SPLAYED BACK. NO NEUROLOGICAL TESTS, SPINAL TAPS, OR X-RAYS WERE TAKEN. DR. KELLY OF THE SANITARIUM DISREGARDED THE POSSIBILITY OF NECK INJURY AND INSTEAD DIAGNOSED HYSTERICAL PARALYSIS. DURING THE NEXT FEW DAYS, OTHER SYMPTOMS INDICATING A BROKEN NECK APPEARED. BROWN DIED FOUR DAYS AFTER THE FALL. HIS WIFE FILED SUIT AGAINST THE OWNERS OF THE SANITARIUM, CHARGING NEGLIGENCE.

YEAR OF NEGLIGENT ACT: 1949

STATE IN WHICH NEGLIGENT ACT OCCURRED: PENNSYLVANIA

SETTING OF THE CASE: PRIV. MENT. HOSP.

PLAINTIFF(S): PATIENT(S) OR REP.

DEFENDANT(S):
1. NONPSYCHIAT.OR UNKNOWN TYPE PHYSICIAN(S)
2. HOSPITAL &/OR OWNERS, ETC.
3. NURSE(S)

NEGLIGENT ACTIVITY:

TREATMENT:
1. NEGLIGENCE IN USE OF TECHNIQUE

DIAGNOSIS:

WHAT WAS DIAGNOSED:
1. MENT.ILL, INSTEAD OF PHYSICAL ILLNESS

RESULT OF DIAGNOSIS:
1. IMPROPER TREATMENT PRESCRIBED
2. IMPROPER CUSTODIAL CARE

CARE:
1. INADEQUATE SUPERVISION

HARM CAUSED TO PLAINTIFF &/OR PATIENT:
1. NONSUICIDAL DEATH

TYPE OF ACTION BROUGHT:
1. NEGLIGENCE

HISTORY OF THE CASE:

TYPE OF COURT: FEDERAL

TRIER OF FACT: JURY

COURT DECISION(S):

TRIAL COURT: FOR DEFENDANT
YEAR: 1956
APPELLATE COURT: FOR PLAINTIFF
YEAR: 1957

VERDICT AGAINST WHICH DEFENDANTS:
1. NONPSYCHIAT.OR UNKNOWN TYPE PHYSICIAN(S)
2. NURSE(S)

RECOVERY OR OTHER RELIEF GRANTED:
1. $ 60000

37. BURKES V. CALLION

NORMAN BURKES, JR. ALLEGED THAT HE WAS IMPROPERLY SENTENCED TO STATE PRISON FOR A HOMICIDE OFFENSE INSTEAD OF BEING GRANTED PROBATION. HE ATTRIBUTED RESPONSIBILITY TO LUTHER CALLION, DEPUTY PROBATION OFFICER FOR LOS ANGELES COUNTY, AND DR. GEORGE ABE AND DR. ALVIN DAVIS, COURT-APPOINTED MEDICAL EXAMINERS, WHOM HE CLAIMED MADE FALSE STATEMENTS AND OMITTED MATERIAL FACTS IN MAKING THEIR REPORTS TO THE COURT.

YEAR OF NEGLIGENT ACT: NOT SPECIFIED

STATE IN WHICH NEGLIGENT ACT OCCURRED: CALIFORNIA

SETTING OF THE CASE: JUDICIAL PROCEEDING

PLAINTIFF(S): PATIENT(S) OR REP.

DEFENDANT(S):
1. PSYCHIATRIST(S)
2. JUDICIARY &/OR CLERKS, ETC.

NEGLIGENT ACTIVITY:

TREATMENT: NOT APPLICABLE

DIAGNOSIS:

WHAT WAS DIAGNOSED:
1. SANITY, INSTEAD OF MENTAL ILLNESS

RESULT OF DIAGNOSIS:
1. IMPROPER COMMITMENT

CARE: NOT APPLICABLE

HARM CAUSED TO PLAINTIFF &/OR PATIENT:
1. DEPRIVATION OF CONSTITUTIONAL RIGHTS
2. LOSS OF LIBERTY

TYPE OF ACTION BROUGHT:
1. DEPRIVATION OF CONSTITUTIONAL RIGHTS: LOSS OF LIBERTY

HISTORY OF THE CASE:

TYPE OF COURT: FEDERAL

TRIER OF FACT: JUDGE;JURY PRESENT ?

COURT DECISION(S):

TRIAL COURT: FOR DEFENDANT
YEAR: NOT SPECIFIED
APPELLATE COURT: FOR DEFENDANT
YEAR: 1970
SUPREME COURT: FOR DEFENDANT
YEAR: 1971

REASON SUIT FAILED:
1. DEFENDANT(S) CANNOT BE SUED DUE TO: JUDICIAL IMMUNITY

38. BURKS V. ROSS

THE PROBATE COURT OF GENESEE COUNTY COMMITTED RICHARD BURKS TO THE V.A. HOSPITAL AT ANN ARBOR AS A CLOSED WARD PATIENT. THE COURT PSYCHIATRISTS HAD DIAGNOSED HIM AS OVERLY DEPRESSED, PSYCHOTIC, AND SUICIDAL. BURKS WAS TAKEN WITH FELLOW PATIENTS TO SEE MOVIES IN THE HOSPITAL AUDITORIUM. HE DISAPPEARED AND WAS NOT MISSED FOR TWO HOURS. ABOUT THREE HOURS LATER HE WAS FOUND LYING NEAR THE RAILROAD TRACKS OF THE NEW YORK CENTRAL, HAVING BEEN HIT BY A TRAIN. BURKS DIED TWO DAYS LATER, AND HIS WIFE BROUGHT SUIT AGAINST ROSS, WHO WAS THE ADMINISTRATOR OF THE HOSPITAL, AND OTHERS FOR NEGLIGENCE.

YEAR OF NEGLIGENT ACT: 1961

STATE IN WHICH NEGLIGENT ACT OCCURRED: MICHIGAN

SETTING OF THE CASE: PUB. GEN. HOSP.

PLAINTIFF(S): PATIENT(S) OR REP.

DEFENDANT(S):
1. PSYCHIATRIST(S)
2. NONPSYCHIAT.OR UNKNOWN TYPE PHYSICIAN(S)
3. PARAPROFESSIONAL, NONPRO.EMPLOYEE, ETC.
4. HOSPITAL &/OR OWNERS, ETC.
5. NURSE(S)

NEGLIGENT ACTIVITY:

TREATMENT: NOT APPLICABLE

DIAGNOSIS:

WHAT WAS DIAGNOSED: NOT APPLICABLE

RESULT OF DIAGNOSIS: NOT APPLICABLE

CARE:
1. INADEQUATE SUPERVISION

HARM CAUSED TO PLAINTIFF &/OR PATIENT:
1. NONSUICIDAL DEATH

TYPE OF ACTION BROUGHT:
1. NEGLIGENCE

HISTORY OF THE CASE:

TYPE OF COURT: FEDERAL

TRIER OF FACT: JUDGE;JURY PRESENT ?

COURT DECISION(S):

TRIAL COURT: FOR DEFENDANT
YEAR: NOT SPECIFIED
APPELLATE COURT: NONFINAL FOR PL.
YEAR: 1971

DEFENDANTS STILL INVOLVED IN SUIT:
1. PARAPROFESSIONAL,NONPRO.EMPLOYEE, ETC.
2. NURSE(S)

39. BURNHAM V. DEPARTMENT OF PUBLIC HEALTH

THE PLAINTIFFS, CURRENT AND/OR FORMER PATIENTS IN VARIOUS MENTAL INSTITUTIONS RUN BY THE DEPARTMENT OF HEALTH OF THE STATE OF GEORGIA, CLAIMED THAT PATIENTS WERE CONSTITUTIONALLY ENTITLED TO ADEQUATE DIAGNOSIS, CARE, AND TREATMENT. FEW DETAILS ON ACTUAL CONDITIONS IN THE VARIOUS GEORGIA INSTITUTIONS WERE PROVIDED IN THE COURT'S OPINION. IT DID MENTION THAT LEGISLATION PASSED IN 1969 HAD BEEN HERALDED AS ONE OF THE MOST ADVANCED STATUTORY TREATMENTS OF THE PROBLEM IN THE NATION, AND COMMENTED ON THE FACT THAT A NEARLY SEVEN-FOLD INCREASE IN LEGISLATIVE FUNDS FOR THE MENTALLY ILL HAD TAKEN PLACE BETWEEN 1960 AND 1972.

YEAR OF NEGLIGENT ACT: OCCURRED OVER A SERIES OF YEARS, ENDING IN 1972

STATE IN WHICH NEGLIGENT ACT OCCURRED: GEORGIA

SETTING OF THE CASE: PUB. MENT. HOSP.

PLAINTIFF(S): PATIENT(S) OR REP.

DEFENDANT(S):
1. STATE GOV. &/OR OFFICIALS, ETC.

NEGLIGENT ACTIVITY:

TREATMENT:
1. NO TREATMENT OR INADEQUATE TREATMENT

DIAGNOSIS:

WHAT WAS DIAGNOSED:
1. INADEQUATE DIAGNOSIS

RESULT OF DIAGNOSIS:
1. IMPROPER TREATMENT PRESCRIBED

CARE:
1. FAILURE TO PROVIDE PROPER CUSTODIAL CARE

HARM CAUSED TO PLAINTIFF &/OR PATIENT:
1. DEPRIVATION OF CONSTITUTIONAL RIGHTS

TYPE OF ACTION BROUGHT:
1. DEPRIVATION OF CONSTITUTIONAL RIGHTS: RIGHT TO TREATMENT
2. NONMONETARY RELIEF
3. OTHER ACTION, EXCLUDING TORT LAW: CLASS ACTION SUIT

HISTORY OF THE CASE:

TYPE OF COURT: FEDERAL

TRIER OF FACT: JUDGE,NO JURY

COURT DECISION(S):

TRIAL COURT: FOR DEFENDANT
YEAR: 1972
APPELLATE COURT: FOR PLAINTIFF
YEAR: 1974

VERDICT AGAINST WHICH DEFENDANTS:

RECOVERY OR OTHER RELIEF GRANTED:
1. NONMONETARY RELIEF: INJ.OR OTHER EQ.REL.

40. BYRNE V. KYSAR

PAUL V. BYRNE, JR. WAS COMMITTED BY A COURT-APPOINTED COMMITTEE, BUT HE CLAIMED THAT HE NEVER SUFFERED FROM MENTAL ILLNESS OR REQUIRED ANY CARE OR TREATMENT. BYRNE SUED THOSE INVOLVED FOR DEPRIVING HIM OF HIS CONSTITUTIONAL RIGHTS IN WRONGFULLY COMMITTING HIM. THE COURT'S OPINION IS SILENT AS TO OTHER SALIENT FACTS.

YEAR OF NEGLIGENT ACT: NOT SPECIFIED

STATE IN WHICH NEGLIGENT ACT OCCURRED: ILLINOIS

SETTING OF THE CASE: JUDICIAL PROCEEDING

PLAINTIFF(S): PATIENT(S) OR REP.

DEFENDANT(S):
1. NONPSYCHIAT.OR UNKNOWN TYPE PHYSICIAN(S)
2. LAWYER(S)
3. JUDICIARY &/OR CLERKS, ETC.

NEGLIGENT ACTIVITY:

TREATMENT: NOT APPLICABLE

DIAGNOSIS:

WHAT WAS DIAGNOSED:
1. MENTAL ILLNESS, INSTEAD OF SANITY

RESULT OF DIAGNOSIS:
1. IMPROPER COMMITMENT

CARE: NOT APPLICABLE

HARM CAUSED TO PLAINTIFF &/OR PATIENT:
1. DEPRIVATION OF CONSTITUTIONAL RIGHTS

TYPE OF ACTION BROUGHT:
1. DEPRIVATION OF CONSTITUTIONAL RIGHTS: LOSS OF LIBERTY

HISTORY OF THE CASE:

TYPE OF COURT: FEDERAL

TRIER OF FACT: JUDGE;JURY PRESENT ?

COURT DECISION(S):

TRIAL COURT: FOR DEFENDANT
YEAR: NOT SPECIFIED
APPELLATE COURT: FOR DEFENDANT
YEAR: 1965
SUPREME COURT: FOR DEFENDANT
YEAR: 1966

REASON SUIT FAILED:
1. NEGLIGENCE OR CASE NOT PROVEN
2. DEFENDANT(S) CANNOT BE SUED DUE TO: JUDICIAL IMMUNITY

41. CALLAHAN V. STATE

MISS KATHERINE CALLAHAN, DIAGNOSED AS MANIC DEPRESSIVE, MANIC TYPE, WAS CONFINED AT UTICA STATE HOSPITAL. AFTER ONE ESCAPE HER OPEN WARD STATUS WAS REVOKED, BUT LATER RESTORED ON NOVEMBER 6, 1941. ON NOVEMBER 8 SHE ESCAPED A SECOND TIME, ATTEMPTING SUICIDE BY JUMPING INTO A WAIST-HIGH POND. WHEN THIS FAILED, SHE WANDERED, COLD AND WET, TO AN UNHEATED GARAGE WHERE SHE LAY FOR SIX DAYS AND NIGHTS UNTIL DISCOVERED BY THE OWNER. THE RESULT OF HER EXPOSURE TO THE ELEMENTS WAS THE AMPUTATION OF BOTH LEGS AT THE KNEE.

YEAR OF NEGLIGENT ACT: 1941

STATE IN WHICH NEGLIGENT ACT OCCURRED: NEW YORK

SETTING OF THE CASE: PUB. MENT. HOSP.

PLAINTIFF(S): PATIENT(S) OR REP.

DEFENDANT(S):
1. STATE GOV. &/OR OFFICIALS, ETC.

NEGLIGENT ACTIVITY:

TREATMENT: NOT APPLICABLE

DIAGNOSIS:

WHAT WAS DIAGNOSED: NOT APPLICABLE

RESULT OF DIAGNOSIS: NOT APPLICABLE

CARE:
1. INADEQUATE SUPERVISION
2. FAILURE TO PROVIDE PROPER CUSTODIAL CARE

HARM CAUSED TO PLAINTIFF &/OR PATIENT:
1. NONSELF-INFLICTED INJURIES

TYPE OF ACTION BROUGHT:
1. NEGLIGENCE

HISTORY OF THE CASE:

TYPE OF COURT: STATE

TRIER OF FACT: JUDGE,NO JURY

COURT DECISION(S):

TRIAL COURT: FOR PLAINTIFF
YEAR: 1943
APPELLATE COURT: FOR PLAINTIFF
YEAR: 1943

VERDICT AGAINST WHICH DEFENDANTS:
1. STATE GOV. &/OR OFFICIALS, ETC.

RECOVERY OR OTHER RELIEF GRANTED:
1. $ 25220

42. CAMERON V. STATE

IN AND OUT OF HOSPITALS AND INSTITUTIONS SINCE NOVEMBER OF 1965, DENNIS BUTHY HAD A HISTORY OF SEXUALLY RELATED ASSAULTS ON WOMEN, INCLUDING HIS MOTHER AND SISTERS, AND HAD BEEN DIAGNOSED AS "EXTREMELY DANGEROUS." ON JUNE 15, 1967 HE WAS ADMITTED TO BUFFALO STATE HOSPITAL AFTER AN ATTEMPTED SUICIDE, BUT WAS RELEASED ON JUNE 20 AT HIS MOTHER'S REQUEST, IN SPITE OF THE FACT THAT HE HAD BEEN DIAGNOSED AS HAVING A COMPULSION TO ASSAULT WOMEN AS A SYMBOLIC ATTACK AGAINST LIFE. ON AUGUST 4, ARMED WITH A MEAT CLEAVER AND BUTCHER KNIFE, HE ATTACKED AND SEVERLY INJURED PATRICIA CAMERON, AGE NINETEEN.

YEAR OF NEGLIGENT ACT: 1967

STATE IN WHICH NEGLIGENT ACT OCCURRED: NEW YORK

SETTING OF THE CASE: PUB. MENT. HOSP.

PLAINTIFF(S): 3RD PARTY, II

DEFENDANT(S):
1. STATE GOV. &/OR OFFICIALS, ETC.

NEGLIGENT ACTIVITY:

TREATMENT: NOT APPLICABLE

DIAGNOSIS:

WHAT WAS DIAGNOSED:
1. SANITY, INSTEAD OF MENTAL ILLNESS

RESULT OF DIAGNOSIS:
1. IMPROPER RELEASE

CARE:
1. PREMATURE RELEASE

HARM CAUSED TO PLAINTIFF &/OR PATIENT:
1. NONSELF-INFLICTED INJURIES

TYPE OF ACTION BROUGHT:
1. NEGLIGENCE

HISTORY OF THE CASE:

TYPE OF COURT: STATE

TRIER OF FACT: JUDGE,NO JURY

COURT DECISION(S):

TRIAL COURT: FOR PLAINTIFF
YEAR: NOT SPECIFIED
APPELLATE COURT: FOR DEFENDANT
YEAR: 1971
SUPREME COURT: FOR DEFENDANT
YEAR: 1972

REASON SUIT FAILED:
1. NEGLIGENCE OR CASE NOT PROVEN

43. CAMPBELL V. GLENWOOD HILLS HOSPITAL

THE HENNEPIN COUNTY PROBATE COURT RECEIVED A PETITION FROM HELEN CAMPBELL ON FEBRUARY 13, 1962 TO INVESTIGATE THE MENTAL STATUS OF HER HUSBAND GEORGE. THE PETITION, ACCOMPANIED BY A LETTER FROM THEIR FAMILY DOCTOR, DR. THOMPSON, TOLD OF ATTACKS OF TEMPER AND PHYSICAL ABUSE AIMED AT MRS. CAMPBELL AS WELL AS THE HOUSEHOLD FURNITURE. IT ALSO REPORTED THAT MR. CAMPBELL HAD BEEN PARKING IN FRONT OF HOSPITALS AT NIGHT, WHERE HE SPENT ENTIRE EVENINGS CRYING AND SLEEPING IN HIS CAR. THE FAMILY PHYSICIAN RECOMMENDED PSYCHIATRIC CONSULTATION AND CARE. THE PROBATE COURT ORDERED THE SHERIFF TO TAKE MR. CAMPBELL INTO CUSTODY AND TO DELIVER HIM TO GLENWOOD HILLS HOSPITAL TO BE CONFINED FOR OBSERVATION AND EXAMINATION. HE BROUGHT SUIT AGAINST THE HOSPITAL AND AN ATTENDING PHYSICIAN FOR DENYING HIM HIS RIGHT TO COUNSEL AND OTHER CONSTITUTIONAL RIGHTS.

YEAR OF NEGLIGENT ACT: NOT SPECIFIED

STATE IN WHICH NEGLIGENT ACT OCCURRED: MINNESOTA

SETTING OF THE CASE: PRIV. MENT. HOSP.

PLAINTIFF(S): PATIENT(S) OR REP.

DEFENDANT(S):
1. NONPSYCHIAT.OR UNKNOWN TYPE PHYSICIAN(S)
2. HOSPITAL &/OR OWNERS, ETC.

NEGLIGENT ACTIVITY:

TREATMENT: NOT APPLICABLE

DIAGNOSIS:

WHAT WAS DIAGNOSED:
1. IMPROPER DRUG PRESCRIPTION
2. TYPE OF CUSTODIAL CARE

RESULT OF DIAGNOSIS:
1. IMPROPER DRUG PRESCRIPTION
2. IMPROPER CUSTODIAL CARE

CARE:
1. FAILURE TO PROVIDE PROPER CUSTODIAL CARE

HARM CAUSED TO PLAINTIFF &/OR PATIENT:
1. DEPRIVATION OF CONSTITUTIONAL RIGHTS

TYPE OF ACTION BROUGHT:
1. ASSAULT AND BATTERY
2. FALSE IMPRISONMENT
3. DEPRIVATION OF CONSTITUTIONAL RIGHTS: CONST.RTS.IN GEN.

HISTORY OF THE CASE:

TYPE OF COURT: FEDERAL

TRIER OF FACT: JUDGE;JURY PRESENT ?

COURT DECISION(S):

TRIAL COURT: FOR DEFENDANT
YEAR: 1963

REASON SUIT FAILED:
1. DEFENDANT(S) CANNOT BE SUED DUE TO: JUDICIAL IMMUNITY

44. CARLINO V. STATE

ANNA CARLINO, A PATIENT IN THE PILGRIM STATE HOSPITAL, HAD BEEN DIAGNOSED AS SCHIZOPHRENIC, CATATONIC TYPE. EPILEPSY HAD ALSO BEEN SUSPECTED, BUT HAD NOT BEEN FIRMLY DIAGNOSED. SHE WAS AN OPEN WARD PATIENT RECEIVING DAILY DOSAGES OF MELARIL FOR TRANQUILIZING PURPOSES AND DILANTIN FOR THE PREVENTION OF CONVULSIONS. ON THE MORNING OF JULY 31, 1963, ANNA FELL THROUGH AN OPEN, UNBARRED, SECOND-STORY WINDOW. ALTHOUGH ANNA CLAIMED THAT HER FALL WAS ACCIDENTAL, THE COURT ACCEPTED DR. STEINMENTZ'S TESTIMONY THAT IT WAS A SUICIDE ATTEMPT. NONETHELESS, THE COURT RULED THAT THE STATE WAS NOT GUILTY OF NEGLIGENCE BECAUSE ANNA HAD SHOWN NO PREVIOUS SIGNS OF SUICIDAL TENDENCIES.

YEAR OF NEGLIGENT ACT: 1963

STATE IN WHICH NEGLIGENT ACT OCCURRED: NEW YORK

SETTING OF THE CASE: PUB. MENT. HOSP.

PLAINTIFF(S): PATIENT(S) OR REP.

DEFENDANT(S):
1. STATE GOV. &/OR OFFICIALS, ETC.

NEGLIGENT ACTIVITY:

TREATMENT: NOT APPLICABLE

DIAGNOSIS:

WHAT WAS DIAGNOSED: NOT APPLICABLE

RESULT OF DIAGNOSIS: NOT APPLICABLE

CARE:
1. INADEQUATE SUPERVISION

HARM CAUSED TO PLAINTIFF &/OR PATIENT:
1. SELF-INFL.OR ACC.INJ

TYPE OF ACTION BROUGHT:
1. NEGLIGENCE

HISTORY OF THE CASE:

TYPE OF COURT: STATE

TRIER OF FACT: JUDGE,NO JURY

COURT DECISION(S):

TRIAL COURT: FOR DEFENDANT
YEAR: NOT SPECIFIED
APPELLATE COURT: FOR DEFENDANT
YEAR: 1968

REASON SUIT FAILED:
1. NEGLIGENCE OR CASE NOT PROVEN

45. CASTIGLIONE V. STATE

ALBERT VINCENT CASTIGLIONE WAS AN INMATE IN A SECURITY WARD OF THE KINGS PARK STATE HOSPITAL. ON MAY 18, 1953, HE TRIED TO ESCAPE WITH SEVERAL OTHER INMATES BY USING THE IRON HANDLE OF A MOP-WRINGER TO SHEAR THE PIN HOLDING ONE OF THE WINDOWS SHUT. HE WAS INJURED DURING THIS ESCAPE, AND HIS WIFE SUED, ARGUING THAT THE STATE WAS NEGLIGENT IN NOT USING IRON BARS ON THE WINDOWS AND IN FAILING TO DISCOVER THAT THE HANDLE TO THE MOP-WRINGER WAS MISSING. THE STATE COUNTERED THAT ADEQUATE SUPERVISION HAD BEEN PROVIDED AND THAT 1,800 WINDOWS HAD BEEN INSTALLED WITHOUT BARS SINCE 1939 WITH NO ONE ATTEMPTING TO ESCAPE THROUGH THEM.

YEAR OF NEGLIGENT ACT: 1953

STATE IN WHICH NEGLIGENT ACT OCCURRED: NEW YORK

SETTING OF THE CASE: PUB. MENT. HOSP.

PLAINTIFF(S): PATIENT(S) OR REP.

DEFENDANT(S):
1. STATE GOV. &/OR OFFICIALS, ETC.

NEGLIGENT ACTIVITY:

TREATMENT: NOT APPLICABLE

DIAGNOSIS:

WHAT WAS DIAGNOSED: NOT APPLICABLE

RESULT OF DIAGNOSIS: NOT APPLICABLE

CARE:
1. INADEQUATE SUPERVISION

HARM CAUSED TO PLAINTIFF &/OR PATIENT:
1. NONSELF-INFLICTED INJURIES

TYPE OF ACTION BROUGHT:
1. NEGLIGENCE

HISTORY OF THE CASE:

TYPE OF COURT: STATE

TRIER OF FACT: JUDGE,NO JURY

COURT DECISION(S):

TRIAL COURT: FOR DEFENDANT
YEAR: NOT SPECIFIED
APPELLATE COURT: FOR DEFENDANT
YEAR: 1966

REASON SUIT FAILED:
1. NEGLIGENCE OR CASE NOT PROVEN

46. CASTILLO V. UNITED STATES

RICHARD MONTOYA HAD BEEN VOLUNTARILY HOSPITALIZED IN THE PSYCHIATRIC WARD OF THE ALBUQUERQUE V.A. HOSPITAL NINE TIMES BETWEEN 1970 AND 1972. THE HOSPITAL STAFF HAD DIAGNOSED HIS CONDITION AS "CHRONIC UNDIFFERENTIATED SCHIZOPHRENIA." ALTHOUGH RICHARD HAD HAD EPISODES OF PHYSICALLY AGGRESSIVE BEHAVIOR, ACUTELY PSYCHOTIC PERIODS, AND VISUAL AND AUDITORY HALLUCINATIONS DURING HIS PERIODS OF HOSPITALIZATION, HE HAD BEEN DIAGNOSED AS RECENTLY AS OCTOBER 1972 AS NOT BEING A DANGER TO HIMSELF OR OTHERS. ON OCTOBER 18 RICHARD ESCAPED FROM THE HOSPITAL, AS HE HAD DONE FOUR TIMES IN THE PAST. ABOUT THREE HOURS LATER RICHARD WAS RUN OVER WHILE ATTEMPTING TO BOARD A TRAIN IN THE SANTE FE RAILROAD YARDS NEAR BELEN.

YEAR OF NEGLIGENT ACT: 1972

STATE IN WHICH NEGLIGENT ACT OCCURRED: NEW MEXICO

SETTING OF THE CASE: PUB. GEN. HOSP.

PLAINTIFF(S): PATIENT(S) OR REP.

DEFENDANT(S):
1. FEDERAL GOV. &/OR OFFICIALS, ETC.

NEGLIGENT ACTIVITY:

TREATMENT: NOT APPLICABLE

DIAGNOSIS:

WHAT WAS DIAGNOSED:
1. TYPE OF TREATMENT NEEDED

RESULT OF DIAGNOSIS:
1. IMPROPER TREATMENT PRESCRIBED

CARE:
1. INADEQUATE SUPERVISION

HARM CAUSED TO PLAINTIFF &/OR PATIENT:
1. NONSUICIDAL DEATH

TYPE OF ACTION BROUGHT:
1. NEGLIGENCE

HISTORY OF THE CASE:

TYPE OF COURT: FEDERAL

TRIER OF FACT: JUDGE,NO JURY

COURT DECISION(S):

TRIAL COURT: FOR DEFENDANT
YEAR: NOT SPECIFIED
APPELLATE COURT: FOR DEFENDANT
YEAR: 1977

REASON SUIT FAILED:
1. NEGLIGENCE OR CASE NOT PROVEN

47. CAWTHON V. COFFER

EDWARD HARLEY CAWTHON WAS JUDGED INCOMPETENT ON THE BASIS OF A COURT-ASSIGNED REPORT BY TWO PSYCHIATRISTS, INCLUDING COFFER, AND A LAYPERSON. CAWTHON CHARGED THAT THE PSYCHIATRIC EXAM WAS SUPERFICIAL AND UNSPECIFIC.

YEAR OF NEGLIGENT ACT: NOT SPECIFIED

STATE IN WHICH NEGLIGENT ACT OCCURRED: FLORIDA

SETTING OF THE CASE: JUDICIAL PROCEEDING

PLAINTIFF(S): PATIENT(S) OR REP.

DEFENDANT(S):
1. PSYCHIATRIST(S)
2. LAYPERSON

NEGLIGENT ACTIVITY:

TREATMENT: NOT APPLICABLE

DIAGNOSIS:

WHAT WAS DIAGNOSED:
1. MENTAL ILLNESS, INSTEAD OF SANITY

RESULT OF DIAGNOSIS:
1. IMPROPER COMMITMENT

CARE: NOT APPLICABLE

HARM CAUSED TO PLAINTIFF &/OR PATIENT:
1. EMOTIONAL DISTRESS
2. ECONOMIC LOSS
3. LOSS OF HEALTH

TYPE OF ACTION BROUGHT:
1. NEGLIGENCE

HISTORY OF THE CASE:

TYPE OF COURT: STATE

TRIER OF FACT: JUDGE;JURY PRESENT ?

COURT DECISION(S):

TRIAL COURT: FOR DEFENDANT
YEAR: NOT SPECIFIED
APPELLATE COURT: FOR DEFENDANT
YEAR: 1972

REASON SUIT FAILED:
1. NO CAUSE OF ACTION STATED
2. DEFENDANT(S) CANNOT BE SUED DUE TO: JUDICIAL IMMUNITY

48. CENTENO V. CITY OF NEW YORK

ABRAHAM CENTENO WAS A PATIENT AT BELLEVUE HOSPITAL. THE ATTENDING PSYCHIATRIST DECIDED THAT ABRAHAM WOULD DO BETTER IF PLACED ON CONVALESCENT STATUS. HE WAS THEREFORE RETURNED TO HIS FAMILY TO CONTINUE TREATMENT ON AN OUTPATIENT BASIS, DESPITE HAVING SHOWN PSYCHOTIC SYMPTOMS AND VIOLENT BEHAVIOR THREE DAYS BEFORE DISCHARGE. AFTER HIS RELEASE, ABRAHAM COMMITTED SUICIDE. MRS. CENTENO, SUPPORTED BY EXPERT TESTIMONY, CHARGED THAT HER HUSBAND WAS RELEASED PREMATURELY.

YEAR OF NEGLIGENT ACT: 1955

STATE IN WHICH NEGLIGENT ACT OCCURRED: NEW YORK

SETTING OF THE CASE: PUB. MENT. HOSP.

PLAINTIFF(S): PATIENT(S) OR REP.

DEFENDANT(S):
1. MUNICIPAL GOV. &/OR OFFICIALS, ETC.

NEGLIGENT ACTIVITY:

TREATMENT: NOT APPLICABLE

DIAGNOSIS:

WHAT WAS DIAGNOSED:
1. LACK OF DANGEROUSNESS
2. TYPE OF TREATMENT NEEDED

RESULT OF DIAGNOSIS:
1. IMPROPER TREATMENT PRESCRIBED
2. IMPROPER RELEASE

CARE: NOT APPLICABLE

HARM CAUSED TO PLAINTIFF &/OR PATIENT:
1. SUICIDE

TYPE OF ACTION BROUGHT:
1. NEGLIGENCE

HISTORY OF THE CASE:

TYPE OF COURT: STATE

TRIER OF FACT: JUDGE,UNINV.JURY

COURT DECISION(S):

TRIAL COURT: FOR DEFENDANT
YEAR: 1974
APPELLATE COURT: FOR DEFENDANT
YEAR: 1975
SUPREME COURT: FOR DEFENDANT
YEAR: 1976

REASON SUIT FAILED:
1. NEGLIGENCE OR CASE NOT PROVEN

49. CHRISTY V. SALITERMAN

CHARLES LAWRENCE CHRISTY HAD A HISTORY OF INTEMPERATE USE OF ALCOHOL AND MEDICATIONS. AFTER A HIATUS HERNIA OPERATION, HE WENT THROUGH A SERIES OF DEPRESSIONS AND WAS PERIODICALLY ADMITTED TO THE PSYCHIATRIC WARD OF THE GLENWOOD HILLS HOSPITAL. HIS TREATMENT WAS STOPPED, HOWEVER, WHEN DR. CRANSTON NOTIFIED THE HOSPITAL THAT CHARLES'S CREDIT WAS TERMINATED. HE WAS DISCHARGED BY TELEPHONE, AND THAT AFTERNOON DR. CRANSTON TOLD MRS. CHRISTY TO CONTINUE THE MEDICATION CHARLES HAD BEEN RECEIVING AT THE HOSPITAL: PARALDEHYDE, A FAST-ACTING, SLEEP-INDUCING HYPNOTIC, AND MELLARIL. HE DID NOT DISCUSS THE MEDICATION IN DETAIL WITH MRS. CHRISTY. THAT EVENING, AFTER RECEIVING THE MEDICATION, CHARLES FELL ASLEEP IN A CHAIR. A CIGARETTE IGNITED THE CHAIR AND CHARLES, WHO SUFFERED SECOND- AND THIRD-DEGREE BURNS OVER 30 PERCENT OF HIS BODY. CHRISTY SUBSEQUENTLY UNDERWENT TEN OPERATIONS AND PERMANENTLY LOST USE OF HIS RIGHT ELBOW. HE FILED FOR DAMAGES AGAINST HIS ATTORNEY, SAMUEL SALITERMAN, FOR LEGAL MALPRACTICE IN NOT FILING A MEDICAL MALPRACTICE SUIT BEFORE THE TWO-YEAR STATUTE OF LIMITATIONS HAD EXPIRED.

YEAR OF NEGLIGENT ACT: 1961

STATE IN WHICH NEGLIGENT ACT OCCURRED: MINNESOTA

SETTING OF THE CASE: PRIV. MENT. HOSP.

PLAINTIFF(S): PATIENT(S) OR REP.

DEFENDANT(S):
1. LAWYER(S)

NEGLIGENT ACTIVITY:

TREATMENT: NOT APPLICABLE

DIAGNOSIS:

WHAT WAS DIAGNOSED:
1. SANITY, INSTEAD OF MENTAL ILLNESS
2. TYPE OF TREATMENT NEEDED
3. IMPROPER DRUG PRESCRIPTION
4. TYPE OF CUSTODIAL CARE

RESULT OF DIAGNOSIS:
1. IMPROPER TREATMENT PRESCRIBED
2. IMPROPER DRUG PRESCRIPTION
3. IMPROPER CUSTODIAL CARE
4. IMPROPER RELEASE

CARE: NOT APPLICABLE

HARM CAUSED TO PLAINTIFF &/OR PATIENT:
1. NONSELF-INFLICTED INJURIES
2. EMOTIONAL DISTRESS

TYPE OF ACTION BROUGHT:
1. NEGLIGENCE
2. CONTRACT LAW: BREACH OF CONTRACT

HISTORY OF THE CASE:

TYPE OF COURT: STATE

TRIER OF FACT: JURY

COURT DECISION(S):

TRIAL COURT: FOR PLAINTIFF
YEAR: NOT SPECIFIED
SUPREME COURT: FOR PLAINTIFF
YEAR: 1970

VERDICT AGAINST WHICH DEFENDANTS:
1. LAWYER(S)

RECOVERY OR OTHER RELIEF GRANTED:
1. $103530

50. CHUDY V. CHUDY

ON AUGUST 19, 1965, MRS. CAROLYN E. CHUDY FILED SUIT FOR DIVORCE AGAINST HER HUSBAND, BRUNAN S. CHUDY. ON AUGUST 30, BRUNAN'S BROTHER, DR. AMAIL CHUDY, SIGNED A CERTIFICATE STATING THAT CAROLYN NEEDED PSYCHIATRIC CARE EVEN THOUGH DR. CHUDY ALLEGEDLY KNEW THAT MRS. CHUDY WAS SANE AND NOT IN NEED OF MENTAL CARE. AS A RESULT OF THIS ALLEGEDLY FALSE STATEMENT, CAROLYN WAS TAKEN FROM HER HOME ON AUGUST 31 BY TWO DEPUTY SHERIFFS. SHE WAS COMMITTED TO THE ARKANSAS STATE HOSPITAL FOR NERVOUS DISEASES, WHERE SHE REMAINED UNTIL RELEASED THE NEXT DAY BY A PULASKI CHANCERY COURT ORDER. CAROLYN CHARGED THAT DR. CHUDY HAD CONSPIRED WITH HER HUSBAND TO HAVE HER WRONGFULLY COMMITTED.

YEAR OF NEGLIGENT ACT: 1965

STATE IN WHICH NEGLIGENT ACT OCCURRED: ARKANSAS

SETTING OF THE CASE: JUDICIAL PROCEEDING

PLAINTIFF(S): PATIENT(S) OR REP.

DEFENDANT(S):
1. NONPSYCHIAT.OR UNKNOWN TYPE PHYSICIAN(S)

NEGLIGENT ACTIVITY:

TREATMENT: NOT APPLICABLE

DIAGNOSIS:

WHAT WAS DIAGNOSED:
1. MENTAL ILLNESS, INSTEAD OF SANITY

RESULT OF DIAGNOSIS:
1. IMPROPER COMMITMENT

CARE: NOT APPLICABLE

HARM CAUSED TO PLAINTIFF &/OR PATIENT:
1. EMOTIONAL DISTRESS
2. LOSS OF LIBERTY
3. INJURY TO REPUTATION

TYPE OF ACTION BROUGHT:
1. MALICIOUS PROSECUTION

HISTORY OF THE CASE:

TYPE OF COURT: STATE

TRIER OF FACT: JUDGE;JURY PRESENT ?

COURT DECISION(S):

TRIAL COURT: FOR DEFENDANT
YEAR: NOT SPECIFIED
SUPREME COURT: NONFINAL FOR PL.
YEAR: 1967

DEFENDANTS STILL INVOLVED IN SUIT:
1. NONPSYCHIAT.OR UNKNOWN TYPE PHYSICIAN(S)

51. CLARK V. GERACI

ROBERT S. CLARK, A CIVILIAN EMPLOYEE OF THE U.S. AIR FORCE, WAS AN ALCOHOLIC, WHOSE DRINKING CAUSED RESPIRATORY AND BRONCHIAL ILLNESS. THESE LATTER CONDITIONS CREATED PROBLEMS IN WORK ATTENDANCE. IN INITIALLY REPORTING TO THE AIR FORCE ON CLARK'S CONDITION, HIS PHYSICIAN, DR. VINCENT J. GERACI, DID NOT MENTION HIS ALCOHOLISM. EVENTUALLY, HOWEVER, DR. GERACI DID DO SO, BELIEVING THAT HIS DUTY TO A MILITARY ARM OF THE GOVERNMENT OVERRODE HIS DUTY OF CONFIDENTIALITY IN THE DOCTOR-PATIENT RELATIONSHIP. ROBERT SUBSEQUENTLY LOST HIS JOB AND CHARGED THAT DR. GERACI HAD VIOLATED HIS RIGHT TO CONFIDENTIALITY, LEADING TO HIS INABILITY TO OBTAIN WORK.

YEAR OF NEGLIGENT ACT: NOT SPECIFIED

STATE IN WHICH NEGLIGENT ACT OCCURRED: NEW YORK

SETTING OF THE CASE: PRIVATE PRACTICE

PLAINTIFF(S): PATIENT(S) OR REP.

DEFENDANT(S):
1. NONPSYCHIAT.OR UNKNOWN TYPE PHYSICIAN(S)

NEGLIGENT ACTIVITY:

TREATMENT: NOT APPLICABLE

DIAGNOSIS:

WHAT WAS DIAGNOSED: NOT APPLICABLE

RESULT OF DIAGNOSIS: NOT APPLICABLE

CARE:
1. IMPROPER GIVING OF INFORMATION TO OTHERS

HARM CAUSED TO PLAINTIFF &/OR PATIENT:
1. ECONOMIC LOSS

TYPE OF ACTION BROUGHT:
1. NEGLIGENCE
2. OTHER TORT(S): PRIMA FACIE TORT

HISTORY OF THE CASE:

TYPE OF COURT: STATE

TRIER OF FACT: JUDGE;JURY PRESENT ?

COURT DECISION(S):

TRIAL COURT: FOR DEFENDANT
YEAR: 1960

REASON SUIT FAILED:
1. NEGLIGENCE OR CASE NOT PROVEN

52. COLLINS V. BENSINGER

DONNA MICHELLE COLLINS WAS DECLARED A MINOR IN NEED OF SUPERVISION BY THE STATE OF ILLINOIS. SHE WAS SENT TO THE ILLINOIS STATE TRAINING SCHOOL FOR GIRLS AT GENEVA BY COURT ORDER WHERE SHE SPENT THE NEXT THREE YEARS SHUTTLING IN AND OUT OF THE SCHOOL ON PAROLE VIOLATIONS, AND WAS THEREBY INSTITUTIONALIZED FOR A TOTAL OF 611 DAYS. AFTER HER RELEASE, DONNA FILED SUIT ASKING FOR PUNITIVE AND COMPENSATORY DAMAGES, CHARGING THAT HER CONSTITUTIONAL RIGHT TO ADEQUATE TREATMENT, WHICH HAD BEEN STATUTORILY AFFIRMED ONLY AFTER HER RELEASE, HAD BEEN VIOLATED. AMONG HER SPECIFIC ALLEGATIONS WERE THE SCHOOL'S FAILURE TO DEVISE OR IMPLEMENT AN ADEQUATE INDIVIDUALIZED TREATMENT PLAN AND TO PROVIDE SUFFICIENT QUALIFIED THERAPEUTIC PERSONNEL.

YEAR OF NEGLIGENT ACT: OCCURRED OVER A SERIES OF YEARS, ENDING IN 1973

STATE IN WHICH NEGLIGENT ACT OCCURRED: ILLINOIS

SETTING OF THE CASE: CORRECTIONAL INST.

PLAINTIFF(S): PATIENT(S) OR REP.

DEFENDANT(S):
1. CORRECTIONAL INST.

NEGLIGENT ACTIVITY:

TREATMENT:
1. NO TREATMENT OR INADEQUATE TREATMENT

DIAGNOSIS:

WHAT WAS DIAGNOSED: NOT APPLICABLE

RESULT OF DIAGNOSIS: NOT APPLICABLE

CARE: NOT APPLICABLE

HARM CAUSED TO PLAINTIFF &/OR PATIENT:
1. DEPRIVATION OF CONSTITUTIONAL RIGHTS

TYPE OF ACTION BROUGHT:
1. NEGLIGENCE
2. DEPRIVATION OF CONSTITUTIONAL RIGHTS: RIGHT TO TREATMENT
3. OTHER TORT(S): FAIL.TO DO STAT.DUTY

HISTORY OF THE CASE:

TYPE OF COURT: FEDERAL

TRIER OF FACT: JUDGE,NO JURY

COURT DECISION(S):

TRIAL COURT: FOR DEFENDANT
YEAR: 1974
APPELLATE COURT: FOR DEFENDANT
YEAR: 1974
SUPREME COURT: FOR DEFENDANT
YEAR: 1975

REASON SUIT FAILED:
1. NO CAUSE OF ACTION STATED

53. COLLINS V. HAND

SUFFERING FROM EXTREME NERVOUSNESS, JULIA COLLINS, AGE SEVENTY-FOUR, ENTERED HAHNEMANN HOSPITAL IN PHILADELPHIA ON THE ADVICE OF HER PHYSICIAN, WHO HAD DECIDED SHE NEEDED PSYCHIATRIC CARE. HE REFERRED HER TO DR. B. MARVIN HAND, A PSYCHIATRIST AND NEUROLOGIST, WHO DIAGNOSED HER AS A MANIC DEPRESSIVE IN A STATE OF AGITATED DEPRESSION AND RECOMMENDED ELECTROSHOCK THERAPY. SINCE HAHNEMANN WAS UNEQUIPPED FOR ELECTROSHOCK, JULIA WAS SENT TO EUGENIA MEMORIAL, INC., A PRIVATE PSYCHIATRIC HOSPITAL. DURING THE SECOND ELECTROSHOCK TREATMENT, JULIA FRACTURED BOTH ACETABULAE, RESULTING IN LIMITED HIP MOVEMENT AND NECESSITATING THE USE OF A CANE. JULIA CHARGED THAT DR. HAND WAS NEGLIGENT IN NOT READING X-RAYS FROM HAHNEMANN OR TAKING HIS OWN. HAD HE DONE SO HE WOULD HAVE DISCOVERED THAT SHE WAS SUFFERING FROM OSTEOPOROSIS, A BONE DEMINERALIZATION RESULTING IN WEAKENING OF THE BONE STRUCTURE AND FREQUENTLY FOUND IN THE ELDERLY.

YEAR OF NEGLIGENT ACT: 1959

STATE IN WHICH NEGLIGENT ACT OCCURRED: PENNSYLVANIA

SETTING OF THE CASE: PRIV. MENT. HOSP.

PLAINTIFF(S): PATIENT(S) OR REP.

DEFENDANT(S):
1. PSYCHIATRIST(S)

NEGLIGENT ACTIVITY:

TREATMENT:
1. NEGLIGENT ELECTROCONVULSIVE THERAPY

DIAGNOSIS:

WHAT WAS DIAGNOSED:
1. TYPE OF TREATMENT NEEDED

RESULT OF DIAGNOSIS:
1. IMPROPER TREATMENT PRESCRIBED

CARE: NOT APPLICABLE

HARM CAUSED TO PLAINTIFF &/OR PATIENT:
1. NONSELF-INFLICTED INJURIES

TYPE OF ACTION BROUGHT:
1. NEGLIGENCE

HISTORY OF THE CASE:

TYPE OF COURT: STATE

TRIER OF FACT: JURY

COURT DECISION(S):

TRIAL COURT: FOR PLAINTIFF
YEAR: 1961
SUPREME COURT: FOR DEFENDANT
YEAR: 1968

REASON SUIT FAILED:
1. NEGLIGENCE OR CASE NOT PROVEN

54. COLLINS V. STATE

MR. COLLINS BECAME DEPRESSED AND WAS VOLUNTARILY ADMITTED TO BELLEVUE HOSPITAL, FROM WHICH HE WAS TRANSFERRED TO ROCKLAND STATE HOSPITAL. ABOUT FIVE MONTHS LATER COLLINS WAS RELEASED, ONLY TO BE READMITTED IN ANOTHER FOUR MONTHS AFTER A REPORT BY HIS SISTER THAT HE HAD ATTEMPTED SUICIDE BY TAKING THORAZINE TABLETS. IN HIS HOSPITAL RECORD THE SUICIDE ATTEMPT AND HIS PREVIOUS CONDITION WERE REPORTED. IN ADDITION, NOTE WAS MADE THAT COLLINS WAS A POTENTIAL SUICIDE WHO MIGHT HOARD MEDICINE. HIS CONDITION WAS DIAGNOSED AS DEMENTIA PRAECOX, PARANOID TYPE. COLLINS WAS ASSIGNED TO A GENERAL WARD; WHICH ASSIGNMENT WAS NOT CHANGED DESPITE AN ESCAPE. HE WAS FOUND SLUMPED AGAINST THE RADIATOR UNDER THE WINDOW, HANGING BY HIS NECK FROM A SHOWLACE ATTACHED TO THE WINDOW CORD. THE GENERAL WARD SUPERVISOR HAD NEVER SEEN THE NOTE DESCRIBING COLLINS AS A POTENTIAL SUICIDE AND THOSE IN CHARGE OF COLLINS ON A DAILY BASIS WERE ALSO UNAWARE OF THIS. MR. COLLINS'S MOTHER FILED SUIT, CHARGING THE STATE WITH NEGLIGENCE.

YEAR OF NEGLIGENT ACT: 1959

STATE IN WHICH NEGLIGENT ACT OCCURRED: NEW YORK

SETTING OF THE CASE: PUB. MENT. HOSP.

PLAINTIFF(S): 3RD PARTY, II

DEFENDANT(S):
1. STATE GOV. &/OR OFFICIALS, ETC.

NEGLIGENT ACTIVITY:

TREATMENT: NOT APPLICABLE

DIAGNOSIS:

WHAT WAS DIAGNOSED: NOT APPLICABLE

RESULT OF DIAGNOSIS: NOT APPLICABLE

CARE:
1. INADEQUATE SUPERVISION

HARM CAUSED TO PLAINTIFF &/OR PATIENT:
1. SUICIDE

TYPE OF ACTION BROUGHT:
1. NEGLIGENCE

HISTORY OF THE CASE:

TYPE OF COURT: STATE

TRIER OF FACT: JUDGE,NO JURY

COURT DECISION(S):

TRIAL COURT: FOR PLAINTIFF
YEAR: NOT SPECIFIED
APPELLATE COURT: FOR PLAINTIFF
YEAR: 1965
SUPREME COURT: FOR PLAINTIFF
YEAR: 1966

VERDICT AGAINST WHICH DEFENDANTS:
1. STATE GOV. &/OR OFFICIALS, ETC.

RECOVERY OR OTHER RELIEF GRANTED:
1. $ 8492

55. COLORADO STATE BOARD OF MEDICAL EXAMINERS V. WEILER

DR. WEILER ALLEGEDLY PRESCRIBED EXTRA-MARITAL SEXUAL INTERCOURSE FOR A PATIENT SUFFERING FROM A PSYCHOLOGICAL DISORDER AND THEN ALLEGEDLY PROCEEDED TO FILL THE PRESCRIPTION HIMSELF. THE STATE BOARD OF MEDICAL EXAMINERS ATTEMPTED TO REVOKE WEILER'S LICENSE ON THE BASIS OF A NUMBER OF CHARGES, INCLUDING CONDUCT DETRIMENTAL TO THE BEST INTERESTS OF THE PUBLIC, AIDING OR ABETTING ONE NOT ELIGIBLE TO PRACTICE MEDICINE AND RECEIVING A FEE ON THE REPRESENTATION THAT HE WOULD BE ABLE TO CURE A MANIFESTLY INCURABLE DISEASE, CONDITION, OR INJURY.

YEAR OF NEGLIGENT ACT: NOT SPECIFIED

STATE IN WHICH NEGLIGENT ACT OCCURRED: COLORADO

SETTING OF THE CASE: PRIVATE PRACTICE

PLAINTIFF(S): LICENSING BOARD

DEFENDANT(S):
1. NONPSYCHIAT.OR UNKNOWN TYPE PHYSICIAN(S)

NEGLIGENT ACTIVITY:

TREATMENT:
1. SEXUAL ABUSE OR DISTURB.OF MARITAL REL.

DIAGNOSIS:

WHAT WAS DIAGNOSED: NOT APPLICABLE

RESULT OF DIAGNOSIS: NOT APPLICABLE

CARE: NOT APPLICABLE

HARM CAUSED TO PLAINTIFF &/OR PATIENT:
1. SEXUAL OR MARITAL HARM

TYPE OF ACTION BROUGHT:
1. ADMINISTRATIVE LAW: LIC.REV.PCDG.

HISTORY OF THE CASE:

TYPE OF COURT: STATE

TRIER OF FACT: JUDGE;JURY PRESENT ?

COURT DECISION(S):

TRIAL COURT: FOR DEFENDANT
YEAR: NOT SPECIFIED
SUPREME COURT: FOR DEFENDANT
YEAR: 1965

REASON SUIT FAILED:
1. NEGLIGENCE OR CASE NOT PROVEN

56. COMMONWEALTH V. PAGE

UNDER THE SEXUALLY DANGEROUS PERSONS LAW A TREATMENT CENTER FOR SEX OFFENDERS WAS ESTABLISHED AT THE MASSACHUSETTS CORRECTIONAL INSTITUTION IN CONCORD. ARTHUR A. PAGE WAS COMMITTED TO THE CENTER UPON DISCHARGE FROM A PRISON TERM AT THE CORRECTIONAL INSTITUTE. HE ALLEGED THAT THIS WAS A DENIAL OF DUE PROCESS OF LAW, SINCE THE CENTER HAD INADEQUATE FACILITIES TO PROVIDE MEANINGFUL TREATMENT. THE FACILITIES CONSISTED OF TWELVE BEDS AND WAS USED ONLY FOR DIAGNOSTIC PURPOSES. PATIENTS COMMITTED FOR OBSERVATION AND/OR TREATMENT WERE HOUSED WITH THE GENERAL PRISON POPULATION. IN ADDITION, THE CENTER DID NOT HAVE ITS OWN STAFF, AND ONCE DIAGNOSED, THE ONLY THERAPY AVAILABLE FOR SEX OFFENDERS WAS THE PRISON'S GROUP AND INDIVIDUAL THERAPY PROGRAM. PAGE CLAIMED THAT THIS WAS THE EQUIVALENT OF BEING RETURNED TO PRISON WITH AN INDEFINITE SENTENCE, SINCE THE CENTER WAS NOT INDEPENDENT.

YEAR OF NEGLIGENT ACT: 1957

STATE IN WHICH NEGLIGENT ACT OCCURRED: MASSACHUSETTS

SETTING OF THE CASE: JUDICIAL PROCEEDING

PLAINTIFF(S): PATIENT(S) OR REP.

DEFENDANT(S):
1. STATE GOV. &/OR OFFICIALS, ETC.

NEGLIGENT ACTIVITY:

TREATMENT:
1. NO TREATMENT OR INADEQUATE TREATMENT

DIAGNOSIS:

WHAT WAS DIAGNOSED:
1. DANGEROUSNESS

RESULT OF DIAGNOSIS:
1. IMPROPER COMMITMENT

CARE: NOT APPLICABLE

HARM CAUSED TO PLAINTIFF &/OR PATIENT:
1. DEPRIVATION OF CONSTITUTIONAL RIGHTS
2. LOSS OF LIBERTY

TYPE OF ACTION BROUGHT:
1. DEPRIVATION OF CONSTITUTIONAL RIGHTS: RIGHT TO TREATMENT

HISTORY OF THE CASE:

TYPE OF COURT: STATE

TRIER OF FACT: JUDGE,NO JURY

COURT DECISION(S):

SUPREME COURT: FOR PLAINTIFF
YEAR: 1959

VERDICT AGAINST WHICH DEFENDANTS:
1. STATE GOV. &/OR OFFICIALS, ETC.

RECOVERY OR OTHER RELIEF GRANTED:
1. NONMONETARY RELIEF: INJ.OR OTHER EQ.REL.

57. CONSTANT V. HOWE

MRS. ESTELLE HOWE ENTERED THE CITIZENS MEMORIAL HOSPITAL OF VICTORIA, TEXAS, AT THE URGING OF HER DOCTOR, DR. GEORGE A. CONSTANT. ESTELLE SUFFERED FROM A SCHIZO-AFFECTIVE DISORDER AND ATTENDING DEPRESSION. DR. CONSTANT PRESCRIBED DAILY ELECTROCHOCK THERAPY AND BED RESTRAINT WITH A TIED GLISSANDO SHEET. ALTHOUGH THE SHEET WAS SECURELY TIED, ESTELLE ESCAPED, FALLING TO THE FLOOR. ADDITIONAL RESTRAINTS WERE EMPLOYED, BUT ESTELLE ESCAPED AGAIN, THIS TIME FALLING AND BREAKING HER HIP. ESTELLE CHARGED NEGLIGENCE FOR THE FAILURE TO USE SUFFICIENT RESTRAINING DEVICES, SUCH AS BEDRAILS.

YEAR OF NEGLIGENT ACT: 1963

STATE IN WHICH NEGLIGENT ACT OCCURRED: TEXAS

SETTING OF THE CASE: PUB. MENT. HOSP.

PLAINTIFF(S): PATIENT(S) OR REP.

DEFENDANT(S):
1. NONPSYCHIAT.OR UNKNOWN TYPE PHYSICIAN(S)
2. HOSPITAL &/OR OWNERS, ETC.
3. COUNTY GOV. &/OR OFFICIALS, ETC.

NEGLIGENT ACTIVITY:

TREATMENT: NOT APPLICABLE

DIAGNOSIS:

WHAT WAS DIAGNOSED: NOT APPLICABLE

RESULT OF DIAGNOSIS: NOT APPLICABLE

CARE:
1. INADEQUATE SUPERVISION

HARM CAUSED TO PLAINTIFF &/OR PATIENT:
1. NONSELF-INFLICTED INJURIES

TYPE OF ACTION BROUGHT:
1. NEGLIGENCE

HISTORY OF THE CASE:

TYPE OF COURT: STATE

TRIER OF FACT: JURY

COURT DECISION(S):

TRIAL COURT: FOR DEFENDANT
YEAR: NOT SPECIFIED
APPELLATE COURT: NONFINAL FOR PL.
YEAR: NOT SPECIFIED
SUPREME COURT: FOR DEFENDANT
YEAR: 1968

REASON SUIT FAILED:
1. NEGLIGENCE OR CASE NOT PROVEN

58. COOPER V. BOARD OF MEDICAL EXAMINERS

JOHN R. COOPER, PH.D., WAS A PRACTICING PSYCHOLOGIST WHOSE LICENSE WAS REVOKED BY THE BOARD OF MEDICAL EXAMINERS OF THE STATE OF CALIFORNIA ON THE RECOMMENDATIONS OF THE PSYCHOLOGY EXAMINING COMMITTEE. COOPER WAS CHARGED WITH ILLEGAL PRESCRIPTION OF DRUGS AND UNPROFESSIONAL BEHAVIOR. SPECIFICALLY IT WAS ALLEGED THAT HE ENGAGED IN PHYSICAL INTIMACIES WITH THREE FEMALE PATIENTS. THE COMMITTEE STATED THAT AT LEAST ONE OF THESE PATIENTS SUFFERED GREAT EMOTIONAL DISTRESS FROM HIS ACTIONS. COOPER CLAIMED THAT NO EVIDENCE EXISTED THAT ANYONE WAS HARMED BY HIS TREATMENT AND ASSERTED THAT POSITIVE BENEFITS MIGHT POSSIBLY HAVE BEEN ACHIEVED. FURTHERMORE, HE CLAIMED THAT EXPERT OPINION EXISTED THAT WOULD CONSIDER HIS TREATMENT ACCEPTABLE. COOPER FILED FOR JUDICIAL REVIEW OF HIS CASE.

YEAR OF NEGLIGENT ACT: NOT SPECIFIED

STATE IN WHICH NEGLIGENT ACT OCCURRED: CALIFORNIA

SETTING OF THE CASE: PRIVATE PRACTICE

PLAINTIFF(S): LICENSING BOARD

DEFENDANT(S):
1. PSYCHOLOGIST(S)

NEGLIGENT ACTIVITY:

TREATMENT:
1. SEXUAL ABUSE OR DISTURB.OF MARITAL REL.

DIAGNOSIS:

WHAT WAS DIAGNOSED:
1. IMPROPER DRUG PRESCRIPTION

RESULT OF DIAGNOSIS:
1. IMPROPER DRUG PRESCRIPTION

CARE: NOT APPLICABLE

HARM CAUSED TO PLAINTIFF &/OR PATIENT:
1. SEXUAL OR MARITAL HARM

TYPE OF ACTION BROUGHT:
1. ADMINISTRATIVE LAW: LIC.REV.PCDG.

HISTORY OF THE CASE:

TYPE OF COURT: STATE

TRIER OF FACT: JUDGE,NO JURY

COURT DECISION(S):

TRIAL COURT: FOR PLAINTIFF
YEAR: 1973
APPELLATE COURT: FOR PLAINTIFF
YEAR: 1975

VERDICT AGAINST WHICH DEFENDANTS:
1. PSYCHOLOGIST(S)

RECOVERY OR OTHER RELIEF GRANTED:
1. NONMONETARY RELIEF: LOSS OF LICENSE

59. CORCORAN V. JERREL

DANIEL CORCORAN SENT A LETTER TO THE COMMISSIONERS OF INSANITY OF MAHASKA COUNTY, IOWA, STATING THAT HIS SISTER WAS INSANE AND A FIT SUBJECT FOR TREATMENT AND CUSTODY IN ONE OF THE STATE'S HOSPITALS. DR. JERREL, HER PHYSICIAN, WAS CALLED TO TESTIFY. AS A RESULT OF HIS, AND OTHER CORROBORATING TESTIMONY, MS. CORCORAN WAS TAKEN BY THE SHERIFF TO THE HOSPITAL AT MT. PLEASANT. SHE REMAINED ABOUT FIVE MONTHS AND WAS THEN RELEASED IN HER MOTHER'S CUSTODY. SHE WAS LATER DISCHARGED AS CURED, AND BROUGHT SUIT AGAINST DR. JERREL FOR LIBEL IN MAKING AN INCORRECT DIAGNOSIS.

YEAR OF NEGLIGENT ACT: 1914

STATE IN WHICH NEGLIGENT ACT OCCURRED: IOWA

SETTING OF THE CASE: JUDICIAL PROCEEDING

PLAINTIFF(S): PATIENT(S) OR REP.

DEFENDANT(S):
1. NONPSYCHIAT.OR UNKNOWN TYPE PHYSICIAN(S)

NEGLIGENT ACTIVITY:

TREATMENT: NOT APPLICABLE

DIAGNOSIS:

WHAT WAS DIAGNOSED:
1. MENTAL ILLNESS, INSTEAD OF SANITY

RESULT OF DIAGNOSIS:
1. IMPROPER COMMITMENT

CARE: NOT APPLICABLE

HARM CAUSED TO PLAINTIFF &/OR PATIENT:
1. NOT SPECIFIED

TYPE OF ACTION BROUGHT:
1. DEFAMATION OF CHARACTER: LIBEL

HISTORY OF THE CASE:

TYPE OF COURT: STATE

TRIER OF FACT: JUDGE;JURY PRESENT ?

COURT DECISION(S):

TRIAL COURT: FOR DEFENDANT
YEAR: NOT SPECIFIED
SUPREME COURT: FOR DEFENDANT
YEAR: 1919

REASON SUIT FAILED:
1. DEFENDANT(S) CANNOT BE SUED DUE TO: JUDICIAL IMMUNITY

60. COUNTY OF LOS ANGELES V. SUPERIOR COURT

MRS. SHIRLEY M. HAWLEY WAS ADMITTED TO THE LOS ANGELES COUNTY HOSPITAL FOR ALCOHOLISM AND BARBITURATE INTOXICATION. SHE WAS PLACED IN SOFT RESTRAINTS, AT THE REQUEST OF AN ATTENDING PHYSICIAN. A STAFF PSYCHIATRIST EXAMINED HER, TENTATIVELY DIAGNOSING AN INFANTILE PERSONALITY AND RECOMMENDING TRANSFER TO THE PSYCHIATRIC UNIT. UPON TRANSFER, WHILE IN THE ADMITTING ROOM OF THE PSYCHIATRIC UNIT, SHE FELL FROM BED, ALLEGEDLY SUFFERING SERIOUS BRAIN INJURIES. HER HUSBAND BROUGHT SUIT ON HER BEHALF AGAINST L.A. COUNTY FOR FAILING TO PROVIDE ADEQUATE SUPERVISION.

YEAR OF NEGLIGENT ACT: 1960

STATE IN WHICH NEGLIGENT ACT OCCURRED: CALIFORNIA

SETTING OF THE CASE: PUB. GEN. HOSP.

PLAINTIFF(S): PATIENT(S) OR REP.

DEFENDANT(S):
1. COUNTY GOV. &/OR OFFICIALS, ETC.

NEGLIGENT ACTIVITY:

TREATMENT: NOT APPLICABLE

DIAGNOSIS:

WHAT WAS DIAGNOSED: NOT APPLICABLE

RESULT OF DIAGNOSIS: NOT APPLICABLE

CARE:
1. INADEQUATE SUPERVISION

HARM CAUSED TO PLAINTIFF &/OR PATIENT:
1. NONSELF-INFLICTED INJURIES

TYPE OF ACTION BROUGHT:
1. NEGLIGENCE

HISTORY OF THE CASE:

TYPE OF COURT: STATE

TRIER OF FACT: JUDGE;JURY PRESENT ?

COURT DECISION(S):

TRIAL COURT: NONFINAL FOR PL.
YEAR: 1964
APPELLATE COURT: NONFINAL FOR PL.
YEAR: 1965
SUPREME COURT: FOR DEFENDANT
YEAR: 1965

REASON SUIT FAILED:
1. DEFENDANT(S) CANNOT BE SUED DUE TO: GOVERN. IMMUNITY

61. COX V. STATE

MRS. MARY MCGRATH WAS ADMITTED TO THE HUDSON RIVER STATE HOSPITAL AT AGE SIXTY-TWO SUFFERING FROM A PSYCHOSIS DUE TO METABOLIC DISEASE AND HYPEROSTOSIS OF THE INTERNAL TABLE OF THE FRONTAL SKULL BONE. HER HOSPITAL RECORDS STATED THAT SHE SHOULD BE WATCHED, SINCE HER BEHAVIOR WAS ANTAGONISTIC AND CONFLICT-PROVOKING TO OTHER PATIENTS. SUBSEQUENTLY, MARY ANNOYED A FELLOW PATIENT, HELEN LANTZ, WHO PUSHED HER AND CAUSED HER TO FALL. MARY SUSTAINED INJURIES FROM THE FALL WHICH CAUSED HER TO REMAIN BEDRIDDEN UNTIL HER DEATH SIXTEEN MONTHS LATER. SHE DIED FROM UNCONNECTED CAUSES. CATHERINE COX, THE EXECUTOR OF MARY'S HUSBAND'S ESTATE, BROUGHT SUIT FOR INADEQUATE SUPERVISION.

YEAR OF NEGLIGENT ACT: 1949

STATE IN WHICH NEGLIGENT ACT OCCURRED: NEW YORK

SETTING OF THE CASE: PUB. MENT. HOSP.

PLAINTIFF(S): PATIENT(S) OR REP.

DEFENDANT(S):
1. STATE GOV. &/OR OFFICIALS, ETC.

NEGLIGENT ACTIVITY:

TREATMENT: NOT APPLICABLE

DIAGNOSIS:

WHAT WAS DIAGNOSED: NOT APPLICABLE

RESULT OF DIAGNOSIS: NOT APPLICABLE

CARE:
1. INADEQUATE SUPERVISION

HARM CAUSED TO PLAINTIFF &/OR PATIENT:
1. NONSELF-INFLICTED INJURIES

TYPE OF ACTION BROUGHT:
1. NEGLIGENCE

HISTORY OF THE CASE:

TYPE OF COURT: STATE

TRIER OF FACT: JUDGE,NO JURY

COURT DECISION(S):

TRIAL COURT: FOR PLAINTIFF
YEAR: 1952
APPELLATE COURT: NONFINAL FOR DEF.
YEAR: 1953
ON RETRIAL: FOR PLAINTIFF
YEAR: 1954

VERDICT AGAINST WHICH DEFENDANTS:
1. STATE GOV. &/OR OFFICIALS, ETC.

RECOVERY OR OTHER RELIEF GRANTED:
1. $ 9647

62. CROCCO V. HARRIS

IN THIS OUT OF COURT SETTLEMENT MS. CROCCO ALLEGED SHE BECAME A PATIENT OF DR. HARRIS IN 1965. SHE CLAIMED THAT HE KEPT HER AS A MISTRESS UNDER THE INFLUENCE OF DRUGS AND LIQUOR. SHE ALSO ALLEGED THAT SHE DIVORCED HER HUSBAND ON HIS ADVICE.

YEAR OF NEGLIGENT ACT: NOT SPECIFIED, BUT OCCURRED OVER A SERIES OF YEARS

STATE IN WHICH NEGLIGENT ACT OCCURRED: CALIFORNIA

SETTING OF THE CASE: PRIVATE PRACTICE

PLAINTIFF(S): PATIENT(S) OR REP.

DEFENDANT(S):
1. PSYCHIATRIST(S)

NEGLIGENT ACTIVITY:

TREATMENT:
1. SEXUAL ABUSE OR DISTURB.OF MARITAL REL.
2. NEG.ADMIN.OF DRUGS

DIAGNOSIS:

WHAT WAS DIAGNOSED: NOT APPLICABLE

RESULT OF DIAGNOSIS: NOT APPLICABLE

CARE: NOT APPLICABLE

HARM CAUSED TO PLAINTIFF &/OR PATIENT:
1. SEXUAL OR MARITAL HARM

TYPE OF ACTION BROUGHT:
1. OTHER ACTION, EXCLUDING TORT LAW: TYPE NOT SPECIFIED

HISTORY OF THE CASE:

TYPE OF COURT: STATE

TRIER OF FACT: SETTLED OUT OF COURT

COURT DECISION(S):

TRIAL COURT: FOR PLAINTIFF
YEAR: 1974

VERDICT AGAINST WHICH DEFENDANTS:
1. PSYCHIATRIST(S)

RECOVERY OR OTHER RELIEF GRANTED:
1. $ 50000

63. CURLEY V. STATE

THE PLAINTIFF, ANNA BRENNAN CURLEY, BROUGHT SUIT ON BEHALF OF HER SISTER MARIE, WHO HAD BEEN COMMITTED AS AN INSANE PERSON TO ST. LAWRENCE HOSPITAL IN NOVEMBER 1923. ON MARCH 18, 1929, MARIE WAS ASSAULTED BY ANOTHER PATIENT, ANNIE TINNEY, WHO SUDDENLY AND WITHOUT APPARENT PROVOCATION, RUSHED ACROSS A WARD ROOM AND PUSHED MARIE TO THE FLOOR, BREAKING HER LEFT HIP. AT THE TIME THERE WERE SIXTY-THREE PATIENTS ON THE WARD BEING WATCHED BY TWO ATTENDANTS. AS A RESULT OF HER INJURY, MARIE WAS PERMANENTLY CONFINED TO HER BED, UNABLE TO WALK.

YEAR OF NEGLIGENT ACT: 1927

STATE IN WHICH NEGLIGENT ACT OCCURRED: NEW YORK

SETTING OF THE CASE: PUB. MENT. HOSP.

PLAINTIFF(S): PATIENT(S) OR REP.

DEFENDANT(S):
1. STATE GOV. &/OR OFFICIALS, ETC.

NEGLIGENT ACTIVITY:

TREATMENT: NOT APPLICABLE

DIAGNOSIS:

WHAT WAS DIAGNOSED: NOT APPLICABLE

RESULT OF DIAGNOSIS: NOT APPLICABLE

CARE:
1. INADEQUATE SUPERVISION

HARM CAUSED TO PLAINTIFF &/OR PATIENT:
1. NONSELF-INFLICTED INJURIES

TYPE OF ACTION BROUGHT:
1. NEGLIGENCE

HISTORY OF THE CASE:

TYPE OF COURT: STATE

TRIER OF FACT: JUDGE,NO JURY

COURT DECISION(S):

TRIAL COURT: FOR PLAINTIFF
YEAR: 1933
APPELLATE COURT: FOR PLAINTIFF
YEAR: 1937

VERDICT AGAINST WHICH DEFENDANTS:
1. STATE GOV. &/OR OFFICIALS, ETC.

RECOVERY OR OTHER RELIEF GRANTED:
1. $ 6000

64. DABKOWSKI V. DAVIS

THE PLAINTIFF, THERESE DABKOWSKI, BROUGHT SUIT AS A RESULT OF HER HUSBAND'S ATTEMPTS TO HAVE HER COMMITTED TO KALAMAZOO STATE HOSPITAL. BASED ON A CONVERSATION BETWEEN THE HUSBAND AND A PROBATE JUDGE, TWO PHYSICIANS ISSUED A CERTIFICATE ORDERING COMMITMENT TO KENT COUNTY RECEIVING HOSPITAL, WHERE PLAINTIFF REMAINED FOR ELEVEN DAYS. DABKOWSKI ARGUED THAT THE DEFENDANT PHYSICIANS WERE NEGLIGENT IN NOT PERSONALLY EXAMINING HER.

YEAR OF NEGLIGENT ACT: NOT SPECIFIED

STATE IN WHICH NEGLIGENT ACT OCCURRED: MICHIGAN

SETTING OF THE CASE: JUDICIAL PROCEEDING

PLAINTIFF(S): PATIENT(S) OR REP.

DEFENDANT(S):
1. NONPSYCHIAT.OR UNKNOWN TYPE PHYSICIAN(S)

NEGLIGENT ACTIVITY:

TREATMENT: NOT APPLICABLE

DIAGNOSIS:

WHAT WAS DIAGNOSED:
1. MENTAL ILLNESS, INSTEAD OF SANITY

RESULT OF DIAGNOSIS:
1. IMPROPER COMMITMENT

CARE: NOT APPLICABLE

HARM CAUSED TO PLAINTIFF &/OR PATIENT:
1. NOT SPECIFIED

TYPE OF ACTION BROUGHT:
1. ASSAULT AND BATTERY
2. FALSE IMPRISONMENT

HISTORY OF THE CASE:

TYPE OF COURT: STATE

TRIER OF FACT: ?, JUDGE OR JURY

COURT DECISION(S):

TRIAL COURT: FOR DEFENDANT
YEAR: NOT SPECIFIED
SUPREME COURT: FOR DEFENDANT
YEAR: 1961

REASON SUIT FAILED:
1. DEFENDANT(S) CANNOT BE SUED DUE TO: JUDICIAL IMMUNITY

65. DALEY V. STATE

THIS SUIT WAS FILED BY THE FATHER OF JOHN E. DALEY, WHO WAS ADMITTED TO HUDSON RIVER STATE HOSPITAL IN 1941. AFTER HIS RELEASE HE ENTERED THE UNITED STATES NAVY, FROM WHICH HE WAS HONORABLY DISCHARGED. SUBSEQUENTLY, HE WAS RE-ADMITTED TO HUDSON RIVER, AND PLACED IN A SEMI-DISTURBED WARD, AND ASSIGNED TO WORK IN THE SORTING ROOM AT THE LAUNDRY. ON THE AFTERNOON OF APRIL 21, 1943, THE PATIENT FELL OR JUMPED INTO A VAT OF BOILING SOAP, FROM WHICH HE DIED OF SECOND- AND THIRD-DEGREE BURNS. THE PLAINTIFF CHARGED THE STATE WITH NEGLIGENCE IN HAVING NO ATTENDANT IN THE SOAP ROOM AT THE TIME OF THE INCIDENT.

YEAR OF NEGLIGENT ACT: 1943

STATE IN WHICH NEGLIGENT ACT OCCURRED: NEW YORK

SETTING OF THE CASE: PUB. MENT. HOSP.

PLAINTIFF(S): PATIENT(S) OR REP.

DEFENDANT(S):
1. STATE GOV. &/OR OFFICIALS, ETC.

NEGLIGENT ACTIVITY:

TREATMENT: NOT APPLICABLE

DIAGNOSIS:

WHAT WAS DIAGNOSED: NOT APPLICABLE

RESULT OF DIAGNOSIS: NOT APPLICABLE

CARE:
1. INADEQUATE SUPERVISION

HARM CAUSED TO PLAINTIFF &/OR PATIENT:
1. NONSUICIDAL DEATH

TYPE OF ACTION BROUGHT:
1. NEGLIGENCE

HISTORY OF THE CASE:

TYPE OF COURT: STATE

TRIER OF FACT: JUDGE,NO JURY

COURT DECISION(S):

TRIAL COURT: FOR DEFENDANT
YEAR: NOT SPECIFIED
APPELLATE COURT: FOR PLAINTIFF
YEAR: 1948
SUPREME COURT: FOR PLAINTIFF
YEAR: 1949

VERDICT AGAINST WHICH DEFENDANTS:
1. STATE GOV. &/OR OFFICIALS, ETC.

RECOVERY OR OTHER RELIEF GRANTED:
1. OTHER RECOVERY: TO BE DETERM.ON RETR

66. DANIELS V. FINNEY

LONNIE E. DANIELS BROUGHT SUIT AGAINST R. MILTON FINNEY, A PSYCHIATRIST, FOR HIS PART IN A COMMITMENT PROCEEDING. ON JUNE 7, 1951, THE PLAINTIFF'S THEN WIFE AND A MINISTER HAD TOLD FINNEY OF NUMEROUS THREATS AND BEATINGS THE WIFE HAD RECEIVED FROM THE PLAINTIFF AS THE RESULT OF A SEXUAL AFFAIR BETWEEN HER AND AN EMPLOYEE OF THE PLAINTIFF. CONVINCED THAT THE PLAINTIFF POSED A THREAT TO THE WIFE'S LIFE, THE PSYCHIATRIST WROTE A DIAGNOSIS OF SERIOUS MENTAL ILLNESS AND RECOMMENDED COMMITMENT.

YEAR OF NEGLIGENT ACT: 1951

STATE IN WHICH NEGLIGENT ACT OCCURRED: TEXAS

SETTING OF THE CASE: JUDICIAL PROCEEDING

PLAINTIFF(S): PATIENT(S) OR REP.

DEFENDANT(S):
1. PSYCHIATRIST(S)

NEGLIGENT ACTIVITY:

TREATMENT: NOT APPLICABLE

DIAGNOSIS:

WHAT WAS DIAGNOSED:
1. MENTAL ILLNESS, INSTEAD OF SANITY

RESULT OF DIAGNOSIS:
1. IMPROPER COMMITMENT

CARE: NOT APPLICABLE

HARM CAUSED TO PLAINTIFF &/OR PATIENT:
1. NOT SPECIFIED

TYPE OF ACTION BROUGHT:
1. NEGLIGENCE
2. MALICIOUS PROSECUTION

HISTORY OF THE CASE:

TYPE OF COURT: STATE

TRIER OF FACT: JUDGE,UNINV.JURY

COURT DECISION(S):

TRIAL COURT: FOR DEFENDANT
YEAR: NOT SPECIFIED
APPELLATE COURT: FOR DEFENDANT
YEAR: 1953

REASON SUIT FAILED:
1. NEGLIGENCE OR CASE NOT PROVEN

67. DARNELL V. CAMERON

IN 1959, THE PLAINTIFF, BASIL DARNELL, WAS CHARGED WITH INDECENT EXPOSURE BUT JUDGED NOT GUILTY BY REASON OF INSANITY. HE WAS COMMITTED TO ST. ELIZABETH'S HOSPITAL. IN 1961, THE PLAINTIFF WAS GIVEN A CONDITIONAL RELEASE WHICH ALLOWED HIM TO LIVE IN THE CITY OF WASHINGTON, PROVIDED HE REPORT TO THE HOSPITAL PERIODICALLY. TWO YEARS LATER DARNELL WAS ARRESTED IN ARLINGTON, VIRGINIA ON ANOTHER INDECENT EXPOSURE CHARGE. WITHOUT A NEW TRIAL ON THIS CHARGE AND WITHOUT SEEKING COURT APPROVAL FOR REVOCATION OF THE CONDITIONAL RELEASE, THE HOSPITAL TOOK THE PLAINTIFF INTO ITS CUSTODY. THE PLAINTIFF FILED FOR HABEAS CORPUS, ALLEGING THAT THE HOSPITAL DENIED HIM DUE PROCESS OF LAW.

YEAR OF NEGLIGENT ACT: 1963

STATE IN WHICH NEGLIGENT ACT OCCURRED: DISTRICT OF COLUMBIA

SETTING OF THE CASE: PUB. MENT. HOSP.

PLAINTIFF(S): PATIENT(S) OR REP.

DEFENDANT(S):
1. HOSPITAL &/OR OWNERS, ETC.

NEGLIGENT ACTIVITY:

TREATMENT: NOT APPLICABLE

DIAGNOSIS:

WHAT WAS DIAGNOSED:
1. MENTAL ILLNESS, INSTEAD OF SANITY
2. DANGEROUSNESS

RESULT OF DIAGNOSIS:
1. IMPROPER COMMITMENT
2. IMPROPER FAILURE TO RELEASE

CARE: NOT APPLICABLE

HARM CAUSED TO PLAINTIFF &/OR PATIENT:
1. NOT SPECIFIED

TYPE OF ACTION BROUGHT:
1. HABEAS CORPUS

HISTORY OF THE CASE:

TYPE OF COURT: FEDERAL

TRIER OF FACT: JUDGE,NO JURY

COURT DECISION(S):

TRIAL COURT: FOR DEFENDANT
YEAR: NOT SPECIFIED
APPELLATE COURT: NONFINAL FOR PL.
YEAR: 1965

DEFENDANTS STILL INVOLVED IN SUIT:
1. HOSPITAL &/OR OWNERS, ETC.

68. DAVIS V. WATKINS

JOHN DAVIS, A PATIENT OF LIMA STATE HOSPITAL IN OHIO, BROUGHT THIS CLASS ACTION SUIT TO SECURE FOR PRESENT AND FUTURE PATIENTS THE RIGHT TO INDIVIDUAL TREATMENT PLANS, AND THE RIGHT TO PERSONAL POSSESSIONS, PRIVACY, DIGNITY, AND PROPER PHYSICAL ACCOMMODATIONS.

YEAR OF NEGLIGENT ACT: OCCURRED OVER A SERIES OF YEARS, ENDING IN 1974

STATE IN WHICH NEGLIGENT ACT OCCURRED: OHIO

SETTING OF THE CASE: PUB. MENT. HOSP.

PLAINTIFF(S): PATIENT(S) OR REP.

DEFENDANT(S):
1. HOSPITAL &/OR OWNERS, ETC.

NEGLIGENT ACTIVITY:

TREATMENT:
1. NO TREATMENT OR INADEQUATE TREATMENT

DIAGNOSIS:

WHAT WAS DIAGNOSED: NOT APPLICABLE

RESULT OF DIAGNOSIS: NOT APPLICABLE

CARE: NOT APPLICABLE

HARM CAUSED TO PLAINTIFF &/OR PATIENT:
1. DEPRIVATION OF CONSTITUTIONAL RIGHTS

TYPE OF ACTION BROUGHT:
1. DEPRIVATION OF CONSTITUTIONAL RIGHTS: RIGHT TO TREATMENT
2. NONMONETARY RELIEF

HISTORY OF THE CASE:

TYPE OF COURT: FEDERAL

TRIER OF FACT: JUDGE,NO JURY

COURT DECISION(S):

TRIAL COURT: FOR PLAINTIFF
YEAR: 1974

VERDICT AGAINST WHICH DEFENDANTS:
1. HOSPITAL &/OR OWNERS, ETC.

RECOVERY OR OTHER RELIEF GRANTED:
1. NONMONETARY RELIEF: INJ.OR OTHER EQ.REL.

69. DEMARTINI V. ALEXANDER SANITARIUM

MR. DEMARTINI, A DENTIST FOR THIRTY YEARS, HAD BEEN MENTALLY DISTURBED FOR SOME TIME. FOR TREATMENT HE WAS SEEING PSYCHIATRISTS AND UNDERGOING ELECTRO-SHOCK THERAPY. DR. HARTER HAD DIAGNOSED HIM AS HAVING A "DEPRESSIVE REACTION WITH SOME QUESTION OF AN UNDERLYING SCHIZOPHRENIC REACTION" AND RECOMMENDED THE MINIMUM SECURITY FACILITY AT DEFENDANT'S HOSPITAL ALONG WITH FURTHER SHOCK TREATMENTS. AFTER INSPECTING AND APPROVING OF ALEXANDER SANITARIUM, DEMARTINI WAS VOLUNTARILY ADMITTED AND FREE TO SIGN HIMSELF OUT AT ANY TIME. ON HIS TENTH DAY AT THE HOSPITAL, THE PLAINTIFF AND SEVERAL OTHER PATIENTS WERE RELAXING ON A PATIO WITH A NURSE PRESENT. THE NURSE WENT INSIDE TO FIND SOME THERMOMETERS AND CAME OUT TO FIND THAT MR. DEMARTINI HAD CLIMBED UP ON THE SIX-FOOT WALL SURROUNDING THE GARDEN AND HAD FALLEN, FRACTURING HIS ANKLE. THE PLAINTIFF CLAIMED TO HAVE NO MEMORY OF THE INCIDENT. THE DOCTORS CLAIMED THAT THE SHOCK TREATMENT OF THE DAY BEFORE WOULD HAVE CAUSED ONLY TEMPORARY FORGETFULNESS AND WOULD HAVE BEEN MORE LIKELY TO CALM THE PATIENT THAN INDUCE HIM TO CLIMB A GARDEN WALL.

YEAR OF NEGLIGENT ACT: NOT SPECIFIED

STATE IN WHICH NEGLIGENT ACT OCCURRED: CALIFORNIA

SETTING OF THE CASE: PRIV. MENT. HOSP.

PLAINTIFF(S): PATIENT(S) OR REP.

DEFENDANT(S):
1. SOME OR ALL DEFENDANTS NOT SPECIFIED
2. HOSPITAL &/OR OWNERS, ETC.

NEGLIGENT ACTIVITY:

TREATMENT: NOT APPLICABLE

DIAGNOSIS:

WHAT WAS DIAGNOSED: NOT APPLICABLE

RESULT OF DIAGNOSIS: NOT APPLICABLE

CARE:
1. INADEQUATE SUPERVISION

HARM CAUSED TO PLAINTIFF &/OR PATIENT:
1. SELF-INFLICTED INJURIES

TYPE OF ACTION BROUGHT:
1. NEGLIGENCE

HISTORY OF THE CASE:

TYPE OF COURT: STATE

TRIER OF FACT: JURY

COURT DECISION(S):

TRIAL COURT: FOR DEFENDANT
YEAR: NOT SPECIFIED
APPELLATE COURT: FOR DEFENDANT
YEAR: 1961

REASON SUIT FAILED:
1. NEGLIGENCE OR CASE NOT PROVEN

70. DENNISON V. STATE

A NIGHTMARE WHICH LASTED FOR MORE THAN THIRTY-FOUR YEARS BEGAN FOR STEPHEN DENNISON ON OCTOBER 6, 1925, WHEN HE PLED GUILTY TO A CHARGE OF THIRD-DEGREE BURGLARY FOR THE THEFT OF $5.00 WORTH OF CANDY. DURING HIS SUSPENDED SENTENCE HE VIOLATED THE TERMS OF HIS PROBATION, AND ON AUGUST 14, 1926 HE WAS SENTENCED TO THE NEW YORK STATE REFORMATORY AT ELMIRA. AT ELMIRA HE WAS CLASSIFIED AS A "LOW GRADE MORON," AND IN SEPTEMBER OF 1927, HE WAS SENT TO THE INSTITUTION FOR MALE DEFECTIVE DELINQUENTS AT NAPANOCH, UNTIL MARCH 3, 1936. AT THIS TIME HE WAS GIVEN A "CERTIFICATE OF LUNACY" AND SENT ON TO DANNEMORA STATE HOSPITAL. ALTHOUGH HIS CRIMINAL SENTENCE WOULD HAVE EXPIRED ON SEPTEMBER 17, 1936, HE WAS STILL CONSIDERED INSANE AND RETAINED AT DANNEMORA. DENNISON'S HALF-BROTHER, FINALLY CONVINCED BY CORRESPONDENCE WITH HIM THAT HE WAS NOT INSANE, BEGAN TO PUSH FOR HIS RELEASE. INDEPENDENT TESTS PROVED THAT HE WAS OF NORMAL INTELLIGENCE, AND HE WAS FINALLY RELEASED IN 1959.

YEAR OF NEGLIGENT ACT: OCCURRED OVER A SERIES OF YEARS, ENDING IN 1960

STATE IN WHICH NEGLIGENT ACT OCCURRED: NEW YORK

SETTING OF THE CASE: PUB. MENT. HOSP.

PLAINTIFF(S): PATIENT(S) OR REP.

DEFENDANT(S):
1. STATE GOV. &/OR OFFICIALS, ETC.

NEGLIGENT ACTIVITY:

TREATMENT: NOT APPLICABLE

DIAGNOSIS:

WHAT WAS DIAGNOSED:
1. MENTAL ILLNESS, INSTEAD OF SANITY

RESULT OF DIAGNOSIS:
1. IMPROPER COMMITMENT
2. IMPROPER FAILURE TO RELEASE

CARE: NOT APPLICABLE

HARM CAUSED TO PLAINTIFF &/OR PATIENT:
1. ECONOMIC LOSS
2. DEPRIVATION OF CONSTITUTIONAL RIGHTS
3. LOSS OF LIBERTY

TYPE OF ACTION BROUGHT:
1. FALSE IMPRISONMENT
2. DEPRIVATION OF CONSTITUTIONAL RIGHTS: LOSS OF LIBERTY

HISTORY OF THE CASE:

TYPE OF COURT: STATE

TRIER OF FACT: JUDGE,NO JURY

COURT DECISION(S):

TRIAL COURT: FOR PLAINTIFF
YEAR: 1966
APPELLATE COURT: FOR DEFENDANT
YEAR: 1967
SUPREME COURT: FOR DEFENDANT
YEAR: 1969
U.S. SUPREME COURT (ON APPEAL FROM STATE COURT): FOR DEFENDANT
YEAR: 1970

REASON SUIT FAILED:
1. NEGLIGENCE OR CASE NOT PROVEN
2. DEFENDANT(S) CANNOT BE SUED DUE TO: JUDICIAL IMMUNITY

71. DI FIORE V. STATE

JOSEPH DI FIORE, AN INMATE OF BINGHAMTON STATE HOSPITAL, WAS AN EMOTIONALLY UNSTABLE, EXCITABLE, BOISTEROUS AND GRANDIOSE PERSON WHO ANNOYED THE OTHER PATIENTS WITH HIS PROFANITY AND IRRITATING LANGUAGE CONCERNING HIS ALLEGED WEALTH AND PROWESS. HE WAS ONE OF SEVENTEEN INMATES WHO WERE EMPLOYED IN HANDLING COAL AND ASHES IN THE YARD OF THE HOSPITAL UNDER THE SUPERVISION OF ONE ATTENDANT. A LONG TUNNEL WHICH THEY WOULD PASS THROUGH DAILY CONNECTED THEIR LIVING QUARTERS AND THE YARD. ON THE DAY OF THIS INCIDENT, WITH AN ATTENDANT EIGHT FEET AWAY, ANOTHER INMATE, PUGLISI, PUT OUT HIS HAND WHILE PASSING DI FIORE IN THE TUNNEL, HITTING HIM IN THE FACE. AS A RESULT DI FIORE LOST HIS EYE AND BROUGHT SUIT AGAINST THE STATE.

YEAR OF NEGLIGENT ACT: NOT SPECIFIED

STATE IN WHICH NEGLIGENT ACT OCCURRED: NEW YORK

SETTING OF THE CASE: PUB. MENT. HOSP.

PLAINTIFF(S): PATIENT(S) OR REP.

DEFENDANT(S):
1. STATE GOV. &/OR OFFICIALS, ETC.

NEGLIGENT ACTIVITY:

TREATMENT: NOT APPLICABLE

DIAGNOSIS:

WHAT WAS DIAGNOSED: NOT APPLICABLE

RESULT OF DIAGNOSIS: NOT APPLICABLE

CARE:
1. INADEQUATE SUPERVISION

HARM CAUSED TO PLAINTIFF &/OR PATIENT:
1. NONSELF-INFLICTED INJURIES

TYPE OF ACTION BROUGHT:
1. NEGLIGENCE

HISTORY OF THE CASE:

TYPE OF COURT: STATE

TRIER OF FACT: JUDGE,NO JURY

COURT DECISION(S):

TRIAL COURT: FOR DEFENDANT
YEAR: NOT SPECIFIED
APPELLATE COURT: FOR DEFENDANT
YEAR: 1949

REASON SUIT FAILED:
1. NEGLIGENCE OR CASE NOT PROVEN

72. DI GIOVANNI V. PESSEL

JOSEPHINE DI GIOVANNI WAS EXPERIENCING A WORSENING NERVOUS CONDITION WHICH WAS CAUSING HER TO BECOME VIOLENT AND IRRATIONAL. SHE VISITED DR. PESSEL FROM MAY 29, 1964, THROUGH MARCH 27, 1965. HEARING OF HER DECLINING CONDITION FROM HER FAMILY, DR. PESSEL RECOMMENDED COMMITMENT TO A STATE HOSPITAL IN JULY 1965. THE FAMILY PREFERRED PRIVATE INSTITUTIONALIZATION AND CAJOLED PESSEL INTO MAILING A LETTER TO THE CARRIER CLINIC WITHOUT EXAMINING THE PLAINTIFF. SHE WAS TEMPORARILY COMMITTED ON THE BASIS OF THIS LETTER AND LATER SIGNED A VOLUNTARY COMMITMENT FORM, REMAINING HOSPITALIZED UNTIL SEPTEMBER 15, 1965. THE SUIT WAS BROUGHT BECAUSE OF THE LACK OF EXAMINATION AND THE LACK OF A NOTARY SIGNATURE FOR COMMITMENT PAPERS SIGNED BY A DR. BORIAS AT THE CLINIC.

YEAR OF NEGLIGENT ACT: 1965

STATE IN WHICH NEGLIGENT ACT OCCURRED: NEW JERSEY

SETTING OF THE CASE: JUDICIAL PROCEEDING

PLAINTIFF(S): PATIENT(S) OR REP.

DEFENDANT(S):
1. NONPSYCHIAT.OR UNKNOWN TYPE PHYSICIAN(S)
2. HOSPITAL &/OR OWNERS, ETC.

NEGLIGENT ACTIVITY:

TREATMENT: NOT APPLICABLE

DIAGNOSIS:

WHAT WAS DIAGNOSED:
1. MENTAL ILLNESS, INSTEAD OF SANITY

RESULT OF DIAGNOSIS:
1. IMPROPER COMMITMENT

CARE: NOT APPLICABLE

HARM CAUSED TO PLAINTIFF &/OR PATIENT:
1. NOT SPECIFIED

TYPE OF ACTION BROUGHT:
1. NEGLIGENCE
2. FALSE IMPRISONMENT

HISTORY OF THE CASE:

TYPE OF COURT: STATE

TRIER OF FACT: JURY

COURT DECISION(S):

TRIAL COURT: FOR PLAINTIFF
YEAR: NOT SPECIFIED
APPELLATE COURT: FOR PLAINTIFF
YEAR: NOT SPECIFIED
SUPREME COURT: FOR DEFENDANT
YEAR: 1970

REASON SUIT FAILED:
1. NEGLIGENCE OR CASE NOT PROVEN

73. DILLMANN V. HELLMAN

FRANCES DILLMAN, NINE DAYS AFTER BEING ADMITTED AND CONFINED TO A HOSPITAL FOR A MENTAL DISORDER, WAS TRANSFERRED BY HER PSYCHIATRIST TO A MORE REHABILITATING AND LESS CONTROLLED SECTION OF THE SAME WING OF THE HOSPITAL. THE NEXT DAY SHE JUMPED FROM AN OPEN WINDOW, SUSTAINING VARIOUS PHYSICAL INJURIES.

YEAR OF NEGLIGENT ACT: NOT SPECIFIED

STATE IN WHICH NEGLIGENT ACT OCCURRED: FLORIDA

SETTING OF THE CASE: MENTAL HOSPITAL

PLAINTIFF(S): PATIENT(S) OR REP.

DEFENDANT(S):
1. PSYCHIATRIST(S)

NEGLIGENT ACTIVITY:

TREATMENT: NOT APPLICABLE

DIAGNOSIS:

WHAT WAS DIAGNOSED:
1. LACK OF SUICIDAL TENDENCIES

RESULT OF DIAGNOSIS:
1. IMPROPER CUSTODIAL CARE

CARE:
1. INADEQUATE SUPERVISION

HARM CAUSED TO PLAINTIFF &/OR PATIENT:
1. SELF-INFLICTED INJURIES

TYPE OF ACTION BROUGHT:
1. NEGLIGENCE

HISTORY OF THE CASE:

TYPE OF COURT: STATE

TRIER OF FACT: JUDGE;JURY PRESENT ?

COURT DECISION(S):

TRIAL COURT: FOR DEFENDANT
YEAR: NOT SPECIFIED
APPELLATE COURT: FOR DEFENDANT
YEAR: 1973

REASON SUIT FAILED:
1. NEGLIGENCE OR CASE NOT PROVEN

74. DIMITRIJEVIC V. CHICAGO WESLEY MEMORIAL HOSPITAL

DIMITRIJE DIMITRIJEVIC HAD BEEN SUFFERING FROM INCREASING DEPRESSION. ON THE ADVICE OF HIS FAMILY DOCTOR HE WENT TO THE DEFENDANT HOSPITAL FOR PSYCHIATRIC TREATMENT. A RESIDENT WHO SAW HIM ON ADMISSION STATED DIMITRIJEVIC HAD SUICIDAL THOUGHTS BUT ONLY PRESCRIBED A SLEEPING PILL, A SEDATIVE, AN ASPIRIN, AND NO RESTRAINTS. HE WAS PUT IN A DOUBLE ROOM ON THE ELEVENTH FLOOR NEXT TO AN UNGUARDED WINDOW. ACCORDING TO THE DIAGNOSIS OF ANOTHER HOSPITAL PSYCHIATRIST, WHO ALSO KNEW OF DIMITRIJEVIC'S SUICIDAL THOUGHTS, HIS DEFENSES WERE ADEQUATE TO SUSTAIN HIM THROUGH HIS DEPRESSION. UNFORTUNATELY, ON MARCH 5 HE LEAPED FROM THE UNGUARDED WINDOW TO HIS DEATH.

YEAR OF NEGLIGENT ACT: 1958

STATE IN WHICH NEGLIGENT ACT OCCURRED: ILLINOIS

SETTING OF THE CASE: HOSPITAL

PLAINTIFF(S): PATIENT(S) OR REP.

DEFENDANT(S):
1. NONPSYCHIAT.OR UNKNOWN TYPE PHYSICIAN(S)
2. HOSPITAL &/OR OWNERS, ETC.

NEGLIGENT ACTIVITY:

TREATMENT: NOT APPLICABLE

DIAGNOSIS:

WHAT WAS DIAGNOSED: NOT APPLICABLE

RESULT OF DIAGNOSIS: NOT APPLICABLE

CARE:
1. INADEQUATE SUPERVISION

HARM CAUSED TO PLAINTIFF &/OR PATIENT:
1. SUICIDE

TYPE OF ACTION BROUGHT:
1. NEGLIGENCE

HISTORY OF THE CASE:

TYPE OF COURT: STATE

TRIER OF FACT: JUDGE;JURY PRESENT ?

COURT DECISION(S):

TRIAL COURT: FOR DEFENDANT
YEAR: NOT SPECIFIED
APPELLATE COURT: FOR DEFENDANT
YEAR: 1968

REASON SUIT FAILED:
1. NEGLIGENCE OR CASE NOT PROVEN

75. DINNERSTEIN V. UNITED STATES

HOWARD DINNERSTEIN'S SUICIDE WAS PRECEDED BY A HISTORY OF DEPRESSION AND PSYCHIATRIC CARE. THIS INCLUDED AN ATTEMPTED SUICIDE IN JANUARY OF 1968 FOLLOWED BY A SHORT STAY IN THE V.A. HOSPITAL. IN THE FALL OF 1968, INCREASING DEPRESSION CAUSED HIS ADMISSION TO ST. RAPHAEL'S HOSPITAL, ONE REASON BEING TO PROTECT HIM FROM POSSIBLE SUICIDE. HE WAS RELEASED AT THE END OF NOVEMBER BUT READMITTED ON JANUARY 3, 1969. HE WAS DIAGNOSED AS "DEPRESSIVE REACTION" BUT NOT CONSIDERED A SUICIDE RISK. HE WAS TAKEN OFF ANTI-DEPRESSANT DRUGS DESPITE HIS KNOWN HISTORY. THE FOLLOWING DAY, DINNERSTEIN WALKED TO THE SEVENTH FLOOR LAVATORY AND LEAPED TO HIS DEATH THROUGH AN UNSECURED WINDOW.

YEAR OF NEGLIGENT ACT: 1969

STATE IN WHICH NEGLIGENT ACT OCCURRED: CONNECTICUT

SETTING OF THE CASE: PUB. GEN. HOSP.

PLAINTIFF(S): PATIENT(S) OR REP.

DEFENDANT(S):
1. FEDERAL GOV. &/OR OFFICIALS, ETC.

NEGLIGENT ACTIVITY:

TREATMENT: NOT APPLICABLE

DIAGNOSIS:

WHAT WAS DIAGNOSED: NOT APPLICABLE

RESULT OF DIAGNOSIS: NOT APPLICABLE

CARE:
1. INADEQUATE SUPERVISION

HARM CAUSED TO PLAINTIFF &/OR PATIENT:
1. SUICIDE

TYPE OF ACTION BROUGHT:
1. NEGLIGENCE

HISTORY OF THE CASE:

TYPE OF COURT: FEDERAL

TRIER OF FACT: ?, JUDGE OR JURY

COURT DECISION(S):

TRIAL COURT: FOR PLAINTIFF
YEAR: NOT SPECIFIED
APPELLATE COURT: FOR PLAINTIFF
YEAR: 1973

VERDICT AGAINST WHICH DEFENDANTS:
1. FEDERAL GOV. &/OR OFFICIALS, ETC.

RECOVERY OR OTHER RELIEF GRANTED:
1. OTHER RECOVERY: NOT SPECIFIED

76. DOE V. ROE

A FORMER MENTAL PATIENT BROUGHT SUIT AGAINST HER ANALYST TO RESTRAIN HER FROM PUBLISHING A BOOK CONTAINING THE CASE HISTORY OF THE PATIENT AND HER FAMILY.

YEAR OF NEGLIGENT ACT: 1973

STATE IN WHICH NEGLIGENT ACT OCCURRED: NEW YORK

SETTING OF THE CASE: PRIVATE PRACTICE

PLAINTIFF(S): PATIENT(S) OR REP.

DEFENDANT(S):
1. PSYCHIATRIST(S)

NEGLIGENT ACTIVITY:

TREATMENT: NOT APPLICABLE

DIAGNOSIS:

WHAT WAS DIAGNOSED: NOT APPLICABLE

RESULT OF DIAGNOSIS: NOT APPLICABLE

CARE:
1. IMPROPER GIVING OF INFORMATION TO OTHERS

HARM CAUSED TO PLAINTIFF &/OR PATIENT:
1. INVASION OF PRIVACY

TYPE OF ACTION BROUGHT:
1. OTHER TORT(S): INVASION OF PRIVACY
2. OTHER ACTION, EXCLUDING TORT LAW: BREACH OF CONFIDENCE

HISTORY OF THE CASE:

TYPE OF COURT: STATE

TRIER OF FACT: JUDGE,NO JURY

COURT DECISION(S):

TRIAL COURT: FOR PLAINTIFF
YEAR: NOT SPECIFIED
APPELLATE COURT: FOR PLAINTIFF
YEAR: 1973
SUPREME COURT: FOR PLAINTIFF
YEAR: 1974

VERDICT AGAINST WHICH DEFENDANTS:
1. PSYCHIATRIST(S)

RECOVERY OR OTHER RELIEF GRANTED:
1. NONMONETARY RELIEF: INJ.OR OTHER EQ.REL.

77. DOTY V. STATE

EDWARD DOTY, AN INMATE OF THE SYRACUSE STATE SCHOOL, AN INSTITUTION FOR MENTAL DEFECTIVES, HAD THE DUTY OF PREPARING VEGETABLES FOR COOKING. HE WAS ADMITTED TO SYRACUSE WHEN HE WAS EIGHT FOR HIS OBVIOUS MENTAL DEFICIENCIES: HIS IQ WAS BETWEEN FIFTY-TWO AND SEVENTY-SEVEN, DEPENDING ON THE TYPE OF TEST ADMINISTERED. ON APRIL 22, 1956, THE PLAINTIFF WAS IN THE BASEMENT PEELING POTATOES WITH A KNIFE FURNISHED HIM FOR THE TASK. ANOTHER INMATE TAUNTED HIM UNTIL HE THREW THE KNIFE AT HIS TORMENTOR WHO, IN TURN, THREW IT BACK CAUSING TWO INJURIES: A GASH ABOVE HIS LEFT EYE AND AN INCISION INTO THE EYEBALL ITSELF CAUSING ITS EVENTUAL ENUCLEATION.

YEAR OF NEGLIGENT ACT: 1956

STATE IN WHICH NEGLIGENT ACT OCCURRED: NEW YORK

SETTING OF THE CASE: PUB. MENT. HOSP.

PLAINTIFF(S): PATIENT(S) OR REP.

DEFENDANT(S):
1. STATE GOV. &/OR OFFICIALS, ETC.

NEGLIGENT ACTIVITY:

TREATMENT: NOT APPLICABLE

DIAGNOSIS:

WHAT WAS DIAGNOSED: NOT APPLICABLE

RESULT OF DIAGNOSIS: NOT APPLICABLE

CARE:
1. INADEQUATE SUPERVISION

HARM CAUSED TO PLAINTIFF &/OR PATIENT:
1. NONSELF-INFLICTED INJURIES

TYPE OF ACTION BROUGHT:
1. NEGLIGENCE

HISTORY OF THE CASE:

TYPE OF COURT: STATE

TRIER OF FACT: JUDGE,NO JURY

COURT DECISION(S):

TRIAL COURT: FOR PLAINTIFF
YEAR: 1961

VERDICT AGAINST WHICH DEFENDANTS:
1. STATE GOV. &/OR OFFICIALS, ETC.

RECOVERY OR OTHER RELIEF GRANTED:
1. $ 30000

78. DOUGHERTY V. SNYDER

THE PLAINTIFF, JOHN W. DOUGHERTY, HAD A HISTORY OF MENTAL ILLNESS AND HAD BEEN CONFINED IN A "LUNATIC ASYLUM." RECOVERING TO THE POINT OF BEING RELEASED AND STARTING HIS OWN BUSINESS, HE BECAME SUCCESSFUL AND OWNED A LARGE AMOUNT OF PROPERTY IN HIS COMMUNITY. THE DEFENDANT, ABRAHAM SNYDER, WAS INSTRUMENTAL IN HAVING A PROBATE JUDGE ISSUE A WARRANT FOR DOUGHERTY'S APPREHENSION AND RESTRAINT UNTIL HIS ALLEGATIONS COULD BE INQUIRED INTO BY A JURY. SNYDER'S FEELINGS WERE THAT DOUGHERTY WAS "SO FAR DISORDERED IN HIS MIND AS TO ENDANGER HIS OWN PERSON AND PERSONS AND PROPERTY OF OTHERS." SNYDER ALSO CLAIMED THAT DOUGHERTY THREATENED TO KILL HIM AND DESTROY HIS PROPERTY. A JURY, WHEN PRESENTED WITH THE EVIDENCE, DID NOT AGREE.

YEAR OF NEGLIGENT ACT: NOT SPECIFIED

STATE IN WHICH NEGLIGENT ACT OCCURRED: MISSOURI

SETTING OF THE CASE: JUDICIAL PROCEEDING

PLAINTIFF(S): PATIENT(S) OR REP.

DEFENDANT(S):
1. COMMIT.PCDGS.INIT.

NEGLIGENT ACTIVITY:

TREATMENT: NOT APPLICABLE

DIAGNOSIS:

WHAT WAS DIAGNOSED:
1. MENTAL ILLNESS, INSTEAD OF SANITY
2. DANGEROUSNESS

RESULT OF DIAGNOSIS:
1. IMPROPER COMMITMENT

CARE: NOT APPLICABLE

HARM CAUSED TO PLAINTIFF &/OR PATIENT:
1. NOT SPECIFIED

TYPE OF ACTION BROUGHT:
1. FALSE IMPRISONMENT

HISTORY OF THE CASE:

TYPE OF COURT: STATE

TRIER OF FACT: JURY

COURT DECISION(S):

TRIAL COURT: FOR PLAINTIFF
YEAR: NOT SPECIFIED
APPELLATE COURT: FOR DEFENDANT
YEAR: 1903

REASON SUIT FAILED:
1. NO BAD FAITH OR MAL.

79. DOWLY V. STATE

MR. KAREN DOWLY, DIAGNOSED AS A SCHIZOPHRENIC, HEBEPHRENIC TYPE, WAS ONE OF SIXTY PATIENTS IN A WARD FOR DISTURBED AND VIOLENT PATIENTS SUPERVISED BY THREE ATTENDANTS AT CREEDMOOR STATE HOSPITAL. FROM THE TIME OF HIS ADMITTANCE ON NOVEMBER 21, 1942 UNTIL HIS BATTLE WITH ANOTHER PATIENT ON FEBRUARY 21, 1943, THERE WAS NO RECORD OF VIOLENCE ON HIS PART. THE OTHER PATIENT, GILBERT HAMILTON, WAS A LONG-TIME PATIENT OF THE HOSPITAL AND HAD EXHIBITED A PREVIOUS PROCLIVITY TOWARD FISTICUFFS. AT THE TIME OF THEIR CONFRONTATION IN A CLOTHES CLOSET, THERE WERE ONLY TWO ATTENDANTS ON THE WARD, THE CLOSEST ONE BEING FORTY FEET FROM THE CLOSET. WHEN THE ATTENDANT ARRIVED, HE FOUND BOTH "SWINGING ARMS AND FISTS." DOWLY SUBSEQUENTLY DIED FROM THE INJURIES SUSTAINED AND HIS WIFE BROUGHT SUIT FOR INADEQUATE SUPERVISION.

YEAR OF NEGLIGENT ACT: 1943

STATE IN WHICH NEGLIGENT ACT OCCURRED: NEW YORK

SETTING OF THE CASE: PUB. MENT. HOSP.

PLAINTIFF(S): PATIENT(S) OR REP.

DEFENDANT(S):
1. STATE GOV. &/OR OFFICIALS, ETC.

NEGLIGENT ACTIVITY:

TREATMENT: NOT APPLICABLE

DIAGNOSIS:

WHAT WAS DIAGNOSED: NOT APPLICABLE

RESULT OF DIAGNOSIS: NOT APPLICABLE

CARE:
1. INADEQUATE SUPERVISION

HARM CAUSED TO PLAINTIFF &/OR PATIENT:
1. NONSUICIDAL DEATH

TYPE OF ACTION BROUGHT:
1. NEGLIGENCE

HISTORY OF THE CASE:

TYPE OF COURT: STATE

TRIER OF FACT: JUDGE,NO JURY

COURT DECISION(S):

TRIAL COURT: FOR PLAINTIFF
YEAR: 1947

VERDICT AGAINST WHICH DEFENDANTS:
1. STATE GOV. &/OR OFFICIALS, ETC.

RECOVERY OR OTHER RELIEF GRANTED:
1. OTHER RECOVERY: NOT SPECIFIED

80. DUGAN V. UNITED STATES

WHILE IN A LAVATORY ON A WARD FOR OBEDIENT, COOPERATIVE INMATES AT ST. ELIZABETH'S HOSPITAL IN D.C., ROBERT DUGAN WAS STRUCK ON THE CHEST BY ANOTHER PATIENT FROM WHICH HE SUSTAINED FRACTURED RIBS AND A PUNCTURED LUNG. DUGAN, IN ADDITION TO HIS MENTAL ILLNESS, WAS AFFLICTED WITH TUBERCULOSIS AND OTHER PHYSICAL PROBLEMS. DUE TO HIS FRAIL NATURE AND POOR HEALTH, THE IMMEDIATE MEDICAL ATTENTION HE RECEIVED WAS OF NO AVAIL AND SHORTLY AFTER THE INCIDENT HE DIED. HIS ASSAILANT, BRODSGAARD, HAD A HISTORY OF VIOLENCE WHICH HAD SUPPOSEDLY BEEN RECTIFIED BY A LOBOTOMY.

YEAR OF NEGLIGENT ACT: 1954

STATE IN WHICH NEGLIGENT ACT OCCURRED: DISTRICT OF COLUMBIA

SETTING OF THE CASE: PUB. MENT. HOSP.

PLAINTIFF(S): PATIENT(S) OR REP.

DEFENDANT(S):
1. FEDERAL GOV. &/OR OFFICIALS, ETC.

NEGLIGENT ACTIVITY:

TREATMENT: NOT APPLICABLE

DIAGNOSIS:

WHAT WAS DIAGNOSED: NOT APPLICABLE

RESULT OF DIAGNOSIS: NOT APPLICABLE

CARE:
1. INADEQUATE SUPERVISION

HARM CAUSED TO PLAINTIFF &/OR PATIENT:
1. NONSUICIDAL DEATH

TYPE OF ACTION BROUGHT:
1. NEGLIGENCE

HISTORY OF THE CASE:

TYPE OF COURT: FEDERAL

TRIER OF FACT: JUDGE;JURY PRESENT ?

COURT DECISION(S):

TRIAL COURT: FOR DEFENDANT
YEAR: 1956

REASON SUIT FAILED:
1. NEGLIGENCE OR CASE NOT PROVEN

81. DUNBAR V. GREENLAW

INFORMATION, OTHER THAN CONTAINED IN THE ANALYSIS BELOW, IS ABSENT.

YEAR OF NEGLIGENT ACT: NOT SPECIFIED

STATE IN WHICH NEGLIGENT ACT OCCURRED: MAINE

SETTING OF THE CASE: JUDICIAL PROCEEDING

PLAINTIFF(S): PATIENT(S) OR REP.

DEFENDANT(S):
1. NONPSYCHIAT.OR UNKNOWN TYPE PHYSICIAN(S)

NEGLIGENT ACTIVITY:

TREATMENT: NOT APPLICABLE

DIAGNOSIS:

WHAT WAS DIAGNOSED:
1. MENTAL ILLNESS, INSTEAD OF SANITY

RESULT OF DIAGNOSIS:
1. IMPROPER COMMITMENT

CARE: NOT APPLICABLE

HARM CAUSED TO PLAINTIFF &/OR PATIENT:
1. NOT SPECIFIED

TYPE OF ACTION BROUGHT:
1. NEGLIGENCE

HISTORY OF THE CASE:

TYPE OF COURT: STATE

TRIER OF FACT: ?, JUDGE OR JURY

COURT DECISION(S):

TRIAL COURT: NONFINAL FOR PL.
YEAR: NOT SPECIFIED
SUPREME COURT: FOR DEFENDANT
YEAR: 1956

REASON SUIT FAILED:
1. DEFENDANT(S) CANNOT BE SUED DUE TO: JUDICIAL IMMUNITY

82. DUNN V. STATE

ON AUGUST 25, 1961, SEVENTEEN-YEAR-OLD JACK PROPER WAS FOUND SLEEPING IN PENNSYLVANIA STATION AND BROUGHT TO BELLEVUE PSYCHIATRIC HOSPITAL BY NEW YORK CITY POLICEMEN. HE WAS DIAGNOSED AS HAVING A "PSYCHOSIS WITH MENTAL DEFICIENCY, SEVERE" AND COMMITTED TO CENTRAL ISLIP STATE HOSPITAL, FROM WHICH HE WAS TRANSFERRED TO HUDSON RIVER STATE HOSPITAL ON APRIL 17, 1962. IT WAS FOUND HE HAD A RECORD OF MINOR ILLEGAL ACTIVITIES AND HAD BECOME KNOWN AS AN AGITATOR WHILE AT HUDSON RIVER STATE HOSPITAL. A FIGHT ON JUNE 26 PUT HIM IN MAXIMUM SECURITY FROM WHERE HE ESCAPED ON JULY 6. ONLY ONE OF THE TWO ATTENDANTS WAS PRESENT TO GUARD THE THIRTY-SEVEN PATIENTS ON THIS WARD ON THE NIGHT OF THE ESCAPE. WITH THE HELP OF ANOTHER PATIENT, HE OVERPOWERED THE GUARD, STOLE HIS KEYS AND ESCAPED. GOING HIS SEPARATE WAY AFTER THE ESCAPE, PROPER STOLE A CAR AND HEADED NORTH ON ROUTE 9 NEAR RHINEBACK. AFTER A HIT AND RUN, THE POLICE WERE NOTIFIED AND THEY GAVE CHASE. PROPER RAN A LIGHT AND HIT THE CAR OF SPRINGHORN'S, RESULTING IN HIS DEATH. AS ADMINISTRATOR OF SPRINGHORN'S ESTATE, DUNN BROUGHT SUIT FOR NEGLIGENCE.

YEAR OF NEGLIGENT ACT: 1962

STATE IN WHICH NEGLIGENT ACT OCCURRED: NEW YORK

SETTING OF THE CASE: PUB. MENT. HOSP.

PLAINTIFF(S): 3RD PARTY, I

DEFENDANT(S):
1. STATE GOV. &/OR OFFICIALS, ETC.

NEGLIGENT ACTIVITY:

TREATMENT: NOT APPLICABLE

DIAGNOSIS:

WHAT WAS DIAGNOSED: NOT APPLICABLE

RESULT OF DIAGNOSIS: NOT APPLICABLE

CARE:
1. INADEQUATE SUPERVISION

HARM CAUSED TO PLAINTIFF &/OR PATIENT:
1. NONSUICIDAL DEATH

TYPE OF ACTION BROUGHT:
1. NEGLIGENCE

HISTORY OF THE CASE:

TYPE OF COURT: STATE

TRIER OF FACT: JUDGE,NO JURY

COURT DECISION(S):

TRIAL COURT: FOR DEFENDANT
YEAR: NOT SPECIFIED
APPELLATE COURT: FOR PLAINTIFF
YEAR: 1970
ON RETRIAL: FOR PLAINTIFF
YEAR: NOT SPECIFIED
ON REAPPEAL TO SUPREME COURT: FOR DEFENDANT
YEAR: 1971

REASON SUIT FAILED:
1. NEGLIGENCE OR CASE NOT PROVEN

83. DUZYNSKI V. NOSAL

ANNA DUZYNSKI CAME FROM GERMANY WITH HER HUSBAND MICHAEL IN 1957. THEY RESIDED IN CHICAGO, SPEAKING VERY LITTLE ENGLISH, AND RELYING ON A FEW FRIENDS FOR ADVICE AND GUIDANCE. ON OCTOBER 5, 1960, THEY FOUND A SUM OF MONEY MISSING FROM THEIR APARTMENT AND SUSPECTED THE DOWNSTAIRS NEIGHBOR, NOSAL, BUT SAID NOTHING. SEVERAL DAYS LATER, HOWEVER, THEY FOUND THE SAME PERSON IN THEIR APARTMENT. A CHASE ENSUED AND EITHER THE NEIGHBORS OR ONE OF THE DEFENDANTS CALLED THE POLICE. BOTH ANNA AND MICHAEL WERE TAKEN INTO CUSTODY AND EVENTUALLY DECLARED MENTALLY ILL AND INCAPABLE OF MANAGING THEIR OWN AFFAIRS. MICHAEL COMMITTED SUICIDE AND ANNA WAS EVENTUALLY RELEASED THROUGH THE EFFORTS OF THE MIKOLAZCZYKS, WHO IN RETURN MADE HER AGREE TO TURN HER SAVINGS OVER TO THEM. THIS MONEY PAID FOR HER HUSBAND'S FUNERAL EXPENSES AND SOME OTHER EXPENSES. THE REMAINDER WAS HELD BY THE MIKOLAZCZYKS, AND SHE BROUGHT SUIT FOR WRONGFUL COMMITMENT AND THE WRONGFUL TAKING OF HER MONEY.

YEAR OF NEGLIGENT ACT: 1960

STATE IN WHICH NEGLIGENT ACT OCCURRED: ILLINOIS

SETTING OF THE CASE: JUDICIAL PROCEEDING

PLAINTIFF(S): PATIENT(S) OR REP.

DEFENDANT(S):
1. NONPSYCHIAT.OR UNKNOWN TYPE PHYSICIAN(S)
2. JUDICIARY &/OR CLERKS, ETC.
3. LAYPERSON

NEGLIGENT ACTIVITY:

TREATMENT: NOT APPLICABLE

DIAGNOSIS:

WHAT WAS DIAGNOSED:
1. MENTAL ILLNESS, INSTEAD OF SANITY

RESULT OF DIAGNOSIS:
1. IMPROPER COMMITMENT

CARE: NOT APPLICABLE

HARM CAUSED TO PLAINTIFF &/OR PATIENT:
1. ECONOMIC LOSS

TYPE OF ACTION BROUGHT:
1. NEGLIGENCE
2. DEPRIVATION OF CONSTITUTIONAL RIGHTS: RIGHT TO TREATMENT
3. OTHER TORT(S): WRONGFUL COMMITMENT

HISTORY OF THE CASE:

TYPE OF COURT: FEDERAL

TRIER OF FACT: JUDGE;JURY PRESENT ?

COURT DECISION(S):

TRIAL COURT: FOR DEFENDANT
YEAR: NOT SPECIFIED
APPELLATE COURT: FOR DEFENDANT
YEAR: 1963

REASON SUIT FAILED:
1. NO CAUSE OF ACTION STATED
2. DEFENDANT(S) CANNOT BE SUED DUE TO: JUDICIAL IMMUNITY

84. EABY V. UNITED STATES

ALAN EABY, A MINOR, HAD JUST BEEN ADMITTED TO ST. ELIZABETH'S HOSPITAL IN WASHINGTON, D.C. WHILE AN ATTENDANT WAS TAKING HIM TO WARD ONE OF THE DIX PAVILLION, HE ESCAPED. HE RAN TO A GROCERY STORE FOLLOWED CLOSE BEHIND BY HOSPITAL EMPLOYEES. TO AVOID APPREHENSION HE TRIED TO RUN FROM THE STORE BUT INJURED HIMSELF WHEN HE RAN THROUGH A LOCKED GLASS DOOR. HE WAS PROMPTLY CAUGHT IN THE STREET BY HIS PURSUERS. SUIT WAS SUBSEQUENTLY BROUGHT ON HIS BEHALF FOR THE INJURIES HE SUFFERED.

YEAR OF NEGLIGENT ACT: NOT SPECIFIED

STATE IN WHICH NEGLIGENT ACT OCCURRED: DISTRICT OF COLUMBIA

SETTING OF THE CASE: PUB. MENT. HOSP.

PLAINTIFF(S): PATIENT(S) OR REP.

DEFENDANT(S):
1. FEDERAL GOV. &/OR OFFICIALS, ETC.

NEGLIGENT ACTIVITY:

TREATMENT: NOT APPLICABLE

DIAGNOSIS:

WHAT WAS DIAGNOSED: NOT APPLICABLE

RESULT OF DIAGNOSIS: NOT APPLICABLE

CARE:
1. INADEQUATE SUPERVISION

HARM CAUSED TO PLAINTIFF &/OR PATIENT:
1. NONSELF-INFLICTED INJURIES

TYPE OF ACTION BROUGHT:
1. NEGLIGENCE

HISTORY OF THE CASE:

TYPE OF COURT: FEDERAL

TRIER OF FACT: JUDGE,NO JURY

COURT DECISION(S):

TRIAL COURT: FOR DEFENDANT
YEAR: 1969

REASON SUIT FAILED:
1. NEGLIGENCE OR CASE NOT PROVEN

85. EANES V. UNITED STATES

IN AUGUST OF 1962, PAUL EANES WAS TREATED BY A GENERAL PRACTITIONER FOR "NERVOUSNESS, ANXIETY AND DEPRESSION." IN THE THIRTEEN-MONTH PERIOD FOLLOWING THIS EVENT, EANES WAS IN AND OUT OF THREE DIFFERENT HOSPITALS WITH A VARIETY OF MENTAL AND PHYSICAL MALADIES. IN JULY OF 1963 HE WAS DIAGNOSED AS "DEPRESSIVE REACTION, ACUTE" AND SUBSEQUENTLY FOUND TO HAVE "CHRONIC BRAIN SYNDROME ASSOCIATED WITH CEREBRAL ARTERIOSCLEROSIS." HE WAS UNDER TREATMENT AND MEDICATION BUT WAS ALLOWED TO VISIT HOME OCCASIONALLY. DURING ONE OF THESE PASSES HE ATTACKED HIS WIFE, VERA, WITH A CLAWHAMMER AND WAS COMMITTED TO SOUTHWESTERN STATE HOSPITAL WITH A DIAGNOSIS OF "SCHIZOPHRENIC REACTION, PARANOID TYPE." HIS WIFE BROUGHT SUIT AGAINST THE STATE FOR NEGLIGENCE.

YEAR OF NEGLIGENT ACT: 1963

STATE IN WHICH NEGLIGENT ACT OCCURRED: VIRGINIA

SETTING OF THE CASE: PUB. MENT. HOSP.

PLAINTIFF(S): 3RD PARTY, II

DEFENDANT(S):
1. FEDERAL GOV. &/OR OFFICIALS, ETC.

NEGLIGENT ACTIVITY:

TREATMENT: NOT APPLICABLE

DIAGNOSIS:

WHAT WAS DIAGNOSED:
1. LACK OF DANGEROUSNESS

RESULT OF DIAGNOSIS:
1. IMPROPER RELEASE

CARE: NOT APPLICABLE

HARM CAUSED TO PLAINTIFF &/OR PATIENT:
1. NONSELF-INFLICTED INJURIES

TYPE OF ACTION BROUGHT:
1. NEGLIGENCE

HISTORY OF THE CASE:

TYPE OF COURT: FEDERAL

TRIER OF FACT: JUDGE,NO JURY

COURT DECISION(S):

TRIAL COURT: FOR DEFENDANT
YEAR: 1968
APPELLATE COURT: FOR DEFENDANT
YEAR: 1969

REASON SUIT FAILED:
1. NEGLIGENCE OR CASE NOT PROVEN

86. EDDINGS V. PENNSYLVANIA

FEW FACTS ARE AVAILABLE FROM THE REPORTED CASE, EXCEPT THAT JACK EDDINGS, WHILE A CRIMINAL PRISONER, WAS DIAGNOSED AS MENTALLY ILL AND TRANSFERRED TO A MENTAL INSTITUTION.

YEAR OF NEGLIGENT ACT: NOT SPECIFIED

STATE IN WHICH NEGLIGENT ACT OCCURRED: PENNSYLVANIA

SETTING OF THE CASE: JUDICIAL PROCEEDING

PLAINTIFF(S): PATIENT(S) OR REP.

DEFENDANT(S):
1. NONPSYCHIAT.OR UNKNOWN TYPE PHYSICIAN(S)
2. STATE GOV. &/OR OFFICIALS, ETC.
3. MUNICIPAL GOV. &/OR OFFICIALS, ETC.

NEGLIGENT ACTIVITY:

TREATMENT: NOT APPLICABLE

DIAGNOSIS:

WHAT WAS DIAGNOSED:
1. MENTAL ILLNESS, INSTEAD OF SANITY

RESULT OF DIAGNOSIS:
1. IMPROPER COMMITMENT

CARE: NOT APPLICABLE

HARM CAUSED TO PLAINTIFF &/OR PATIENT:
1. DEPRIVATION OF CONSTITUTIONAL RIGHTS

TYPE OF ACTION BROUGHT:
1. NEGLIGENCE
2. DEPRIVATION OF CONSTITUTIONAL RIGHTS: CONST.RTS.IN GEN.

HISTORY OF THE CASE:

TYPE OF COURT: FEDERAL

TRIER OF FACT: JUDGE;JURY PRESENT ?

COURT DECISION(S):

TRIAL COURT: NONFINAL FOR PL.
YEAR: 1970

DEFENDANTS STILL INVOLVED IN SUIT:
1. NONPSYCHIAT.OR UNKNOWN TYPE PHYSICIAN(S)

87. EISELE V. MALONE

JOHN EISELE, A PATIENT AT LOUDEN-KNICKERBOCKER HALL INC., A PRIVATE SANITARIUM, WAS UNDERGOING ELECTRO-SHOCK TREATMENTS. DURING EIGHT SUCH TREATMENTS, MR. EISELE SUFFERED COMPRESSION FRACTURES OF FOUR SPINAL VERTEBRAE, WHICH LATER REQUIRED PAINFUL SURGERY. HE CLAIMED THAT FAILURE TO PROVIDE AN X-RAY AFTER INITIAL SHOCK TREATMENT ALLOWED TREATMENT TO CONTINUE AND THE FRACTURE TO SPREAD.

YEAR OF NEGLIGENT ACT: NOT SPECIFIED

STATE IN WHICH NEGLIGENT ACT OCCURRED: NEW YORK

SETTING OF THE CASE: PRIV. MENT. HOSP.

PLAINTIFF(S): PATIENT(S) OR REP.

DEFENDANT(S):
1. PSYCHIATRIST(S)
2. HOSPITAL &/OR OWNERS, ETC.

NEGLIGENT ACTIVITY:

TREATMENT:
1. NEGLIGENT ELECTROCONVULSIVE THERAPY

DIAGNOSIS:

WHAT WAS DIAGNOSED: NOT APPLICABLE

RESULT OF DIAGNOSIS: NOT APPLICABLE

CARE: NOT APPLICABLE

HARM CAUSED TO PLAINTIFF &/OR PATIENT:
1. NONSELF-INFLICTED INJURIES
2. EMOTIONAL DISTRESS

TYPE OF ACTION BROUGHT:
1. NEGLIGENCE

HISTORY OF THE CASE:

TYPE OF COURT: STATE

TRIER OF FACT: JURY

COURT DECISION(S):

TRIAL COURT: FOR PLAINTIFF
YEAR: NOT SPECIFIED
APPELLATE COURT: NONFINAL FOR DEF.
YEAR: 1956

DEFENDANTS STILL INVOLVED IN SUIT:
1. PSYCHIATRIST(S)
2. HOSPITAL &/OR OWNERS, ETC.

88. EVANUIK V. UNIVERSITY OF PITTSBURGH WESTERN PSYCHIATRIC INSTITUTE

ALTHOUGH HER SUICIDAL AND HOMICIDAL TENDENCIES WERE KNOWN, KAREN FISHELL MANAGED TO ESCAPE FROM WESTERN PSYCHIATRIC INSTITUTE AND CLINIC, A PSYCHIATRIC INSTITUTE CONNECTED TO THE UNIVERSITY OF PITTSBURGH. SHE WENT TO HER APARTMENT TO RETRIEVE A GUN PURCHASED BEFORE HER COMMITMENT AND PROCEEDED TO THE APARTMENT OF HER FORMER LOVER. UPON FINDING HIM THERE WITH DARLENE DOBRUSHIN, KAREN SHOT AND KILLED HER. DARLENE'S ADMINISTRATOR BROUGHT SUIT FOR INADEQUATE SUPERVISION.

YEAR OF NEGLIGENT ACT: NOT SPECIFIED

STATE IN WHICH NEGLIGENT ACT OCCURRED: PENNSYLVANIA

SETTING OF THE CASE: PRIV. MENT. HOSP.

PLAINTIFF(S): 3RD PARTY, II

DEFENDANT(S):
1. HOSPITAL &/OR OWNERS, ETC.
2. PATIENT(S) OR REP.

NEGLIGENT ACTIVITY:

TREATMENT: NOT APPLICABLE

DIAGNOSIS:

WHAT WAS DIAGNOSED: NOT APPLICABLE

RESULT OF DIAGNOSIS: NOT APPLICABLE

CARE:
1. INADEQUATE SUPERVISION

HARM CAUSED TO PLAINTIFF &/OR PATIENT:
1. NONSUICIDAL DEATH

TYPE OF ACTION BROUGHT:
1. NEGLIGENCE

HISTORY OF THE CASE:

TYPE OF COURT: STATE

TRIER OF FACT: JURY

COURT DECISION(S):

TRIAL COURT: FOR PLAINTIFF
YEAR: 1971
APPELLATE COURT: FOR PLAINTIFF
YEAR: 1975

VERDICT AGAINST WHICH DEFENDANTS:
1. PATIENT(S) OR REP.

RECOVERY OR OTHER RELIEF GRANTED:
1. OTHER RECOVERY: NOT SPECIFIED

89. EXCELSIOR INSURANCE CO. V. STATE

ON THE NIGHT OF FEBRUARY 19, 1936, FRANCIS FLOOD, A HIGH-GRADE MORON (IQ 66), ESCAPED FROM THE WASSAIC STATE SCHOOL THROUGH A BASEMENT WINDOW. HIS RECORD SHOWED THAT HE HAD ESCAPED MANY TIMES FROM VARIOUS OTHER INSTITUTIONS. ALTHOUGH HIS PROCLIVITIES WERE KNOWN BY THE ADMINISTRATORS OF THE SCHOOL, THE WINDOW WAS UNGUARDED AND THE ATTENDANT WAS UNAWARE OF HIS ESCAPE HISTORY. DURING THIS ESCAPE HE CAME UPON THE BARN OF MR. WETHLEY AND BUILT A FIRE TO KEEP WARM. THE FIRE SPREAD AND THREE BUILDINGS AND THEIR CONTENTS WERE DESTROYED. THE OWNER AND TWO INSURANCE COMPANIES SUED THE STATE FOR ACTIONABLE NEGLIGENCE.

YEAR OF NEGLIGENT ACT: 1936

STATE IN WHICH NEGLIGENT ACT OCCURRED: NEW YORK

SETTING OF THE CASE: PUB. MENT. HOSP.

PLAINTIFF(S): 3RD PARTY, II

DEFENDANT(S):
1. STATE GOV. &/OR OFFICIALS, ETC.

NEGLIGENT ACTIVITY:

TREATMENT: NOT APPLICABLE

DIAGNOSIS:

WHAT WAS DIAGNOSED: NOT APPLICABLE

RESULT OF DIAGNOSIS: NOT APPLICABLE

CARE:
1. INADEQUATE SUPERVISION

HARM CAUSED TO PLAINTIFF &/OR PATIENT:
1. ECONOMIC LOSS

TYPE OF ACTION BROUGHT:
1. NEGLIGENCE

HISTORY OF THE CASE:

TYPE OF COURT: STATE

TRIER OF FACT: JUDGE,NO JURY

COURT DECISION(S):

TRIAL COURT: FOR DEFENDANT
YEAR: 1942
APPELLATE COURT: FOR PLAINTIFF
YEAR: 1945
APPELLATE COURT: FOR PLAINTIFF
YEAR: 1946
SUPREME COURT: FOR DEFENDANT
YEAR: 1946

REASON SUIT FAILED:
1. NEGLIGENCE OR CASE NOT PROVEN

90. FAIR V. UNITED STATES

CAPTAIN R. F. HAYWOOD WAS DETAINED IN A HOSPITAL AT ELLINGTON AIR FORCE BASE FOR HIS MENTAL PROBLEMS. HE HAD PREVIOUSLY THREATENED TO KILL NURSE COOPER AND THE BASE COMMANDER. THE HOSPITAL MADE AN ARRANGEMENT WITH THE COMMANDER TO NOTIFY ALL INVOLVED, INCLUDING THE BURNS SECURITY GUARDS, OF HIS RELEASE. IN SPITE OF THIS, HAYWOOD WAS GIVEN A CURSORY PSYCHIATRIC EXAM AND RELEASED WITHOUT NOTIFICATION TO BURNS OR ANYONE ELSE. ON JULY 10, 1952, HE SHOT AND KILLED MS. COOPER AND TWO BURNS GUARDS. HE THEN TOOK HIS OWN LIFE IN THE SAME MANNER. THE BENEFICIARIES OF MS. COOPER AND THE TWO GUARDS BROUGHT SUIT FOR NEGLIGENCE.

YEAR OF NEGLIGENT ACT: 1952

STATE IN WHICH NEGLIGENT ACT OCCURRED: TEXAS

SETTING OF THE CASE: ARMED SERVICE

PLAINTIFF(S): 3RD PARTY, II

DEFENDANT(S):
1. FEDERAL GOV. &/OR OFFICIALS, ETC.

NEGLIGENT ACTIVITY:

TREATMENT: NOT APPLICABLE

DIAGNOSIS:

WHAT WAS DIAGNOSED:
1. LACK OF DANGEROUSNESS

RESULT OF DIAGNOSIS:
1. IMPROPER RELEASE

CARE:
1. PREMATURE RELEASE
2. FAILURE TO WARN THIRD PARTIES

HARM CAUSED TO PLAINTIFF &/OR PATIENT:
1. SUICIDE
2. NONSUICIDAL DEATH

TYPE OF ACTION BROUGHT:
1. NEGLIGENCE

HISTORY OF THE CASE:

TYPE OF COURT: FEDERAL

TRIER OF FACT: ?, JUDGE OR JURY

COURT DECISION(S):

TRIAL COURT: FOR DEFENDANT
YEAR: NOT SPECIFIED
APPELLATE COURT: NONFINAL FOR PL.
YEAR: 1956

DEFENDANTS STILL INVOLVED IN SUIT:
1. FEDERAL GOV. &/OR OFFICIALS, ETC.

91. FARBER V. OLKON

THE PLAINTIFF BECAME MENTALLY ILL AT THE AGE OF NINETEEN AND HAD SINCE SUFFERED FROM "SCHIZOPHRENIA WITH HEBEPHRENIC AND PARANOID FEATURES WITH PROGRESSIVE MENTAL DETERIORATION." FROM 1936 THROUGH 1948 HIS FATHER HAD TAKEN HIM TO MANY INSTITUTIONS AND HAD CARED FOR HIM AT HOME MUCH OF THE TIME. THE PATIENT HAD HAD SOME EIGHTY SHOCK TREATMENTS AND A LOBOTOMY, ALL TO NO AVAIL. ON SEPTEMBER 1, 1948, WHILE A PATIENT OF CAMARILLO STATE HOSPITAL, A DR. WAYNE ADMINISTERED A SHOCK TREATMENT TO HIM DURING WHICH "A SNAPPING OR CRUNCHING SOUND WAS HEARD." X-RAYS REVEALED TWO BROKEN FEMURS, WHICH RESULTED IN A PERMANENT DEFORMATION OF THE HIPS. THE PLAINTIFF, THROUGH HIS GUARDIAN AD LITEM, BROUGHT SUIT AGAINST OLKON AND WAYNE, AS OWNERS OF THE CORPORATION UNDER WHICH THEY CONDUCTED THEIR BUSINESS, AND SEVERAL NURSES WHO ADMINISTERED THE TREATMENT.

YEAR OF NEGLIGENT ACT: 1948

STATE IN WHICH NEGLIGENT ACT OCCURRED: CALIFORNIA

SETTING OF THE CASE: PUB. MENT. HOSP.

PLAINTIFF(S): PATIENT(S) OR REP.

DEFENDANT(S):
1. PSYCHIATRIST(S)
2. HOSPITAL &/OR OWNERS, ETC.
3. NURSE(S)

NEGLIGENT ACTIVITY:

TREATMENT:
1. NEGLIGENT ELECTROCONVULSIVE THERAPY

DIAGNOSIS:

WHAT WAS DIAGNOSED: NOT APPLICABLE

RESULT OF DIAGNOSIS: NOT APPLICABLE

CARE: NOT APPLICABLE

HARM CAUSED TO PLAINTIFF &/OR PATIENT:
1. NONSELF-INFLICTED INJURIES

TYPE OF ACTION BROUGHT:
1. NEGLIGENCE
2. ASSAULT AND BATTERY

HISTORY OF THE CASE:

TYPE OF COURT: STATE

TRIER OF FACT: JURY

COURT DECISION(S):

TRIAL COURT: FOR DEFENDANT
YEAR: NOT SPECIFIED
SUPREME COURT: FOR DEFENDANT
YEAR: 1953

REASON SUIT FAILED:
1. NEGLIGENCE OR CASE NOT PROVEN

92. FATUCK V. HILLSIDE HOSPITAL

THE DECEDENT HAD A FOURTEEN-YEAR HISTORY OF MENTAL ILLNESS DURING WHICH TIME HE HAD BEEN IN A NUMBER OF INSTITUTIONS AND HAD SEEN NUMEROUS DOCTORS. THERE WERE NO INDICATIONS OF EITHER ESCAPE OR SUICIDAL TENDENCIES. IN OCTOBER OF 1968, HE WAS ADMITTED TO HILLSIDE HOSPITAL AND IN HIS NINE DAYS THERE HE SHOWED A TENDENCY TO WANDER OFF AND EXPRESSED SUICIDAL THREATS. HE WAS PUT ON FIFTEEN-MINUTE CHECKS TWO DAYS AFTER HIS ADMITTANCE, BUT SEVEN DAYS LATER HE MANAGED TO ESCAPE. UPON HIS ESCAPE HE COMMITTED SUICIDE BY JUMPING OFF THE ROOF OF A BUILDING. HIS WIFE BROUGHT SUIT FOR HIS WRONGFUL DEATH.

YEAR OF NEGLIGENT ACT: 1968

STATE IN WHICH NEGLIGENT ACT OCCURRED: NEW YORK

SETTING OF THE CASE: HOSPITAL

PLAINTIFF(S): 3RD PARTY, I

DEFENDANT(S):
1. HOSPITAL &/OR OWNERS, ETC.

NEGLIGENT ACTIVITY:

TREATMENT: NOT APPLICABLE

DIAGNOSIS:

WHAT WAS DIAGNOSED: NOT APPLICABLE

RESULT OF DIAGNOSIS: NOT APPLICABLE

CARE:
1. INADEQUATE SUPERVISION

HARM CAUSED TO PLAINTIFF &/OR PATIENT:
1. SUICIDE

TYPE OF ACTION BROUGHT:
1. NEGLIGENCE

HISTORY OF THE CASE:

TYPE OF COURT: STATE

TRIER OF FACT: JURY

COURT DECISION(S):

TRIAL COURT: FOR DEFENDANT
YEAR: NOT SPECIFIED
APPELLATE COURT: FOR PLAINTIFF
YEAR: 1974
SUPREME COURT: FOR PLAINTIFF
YEAR: 1975

VERDICT AGAINST WHICH DEFENDANTS:
1. HOSPITAL &/OR OWNERS, ETC.

RECOVERY OR OTHER RELIEF GRANTED:
1. $ 30000

93. FEITELBERG V. STATE

ITALIA GOTTO WAS ONE OF FORTY-TWO PATIENTS ON A WARD FOR "ASSAULTIVE" PATIENTS WHO WERE IN THE CARE OF THREE ATTENDANTS AT ROCKLAND STATE HOSPITAL. SUIT WAS BROUGHT ON HER BEHALF BY ABRAHAM FEITELBERG WHEN SHE WAS ASSAULTED WHILE ONLY TWO ATTENDANTS WERE PRESENT. FURTHER INFORMATION IS UNAVAILABLE.

YEAR OF NEGLIGENT ACT: NOT SPECIFIED

STATE IN WHICH NEGLIGENT ACT OCCURRED: NEW YORK

SETTING OF THE CASE: PUB. MENT. HOSP.

PLAINTIFF(S): PATIENT(S) OR REP.

DEFENDANT(S):
1. STATE GOV. &/OR OFFICIALS, ETC.

NEGLIGENT ACTIVITY:

TREATMENT: NOT APPLICABLE

DIAGNOSIS:

WHAT WAS DIAGNOSED: NOT APPLICABLE

RESULT OF DIAGNOSIS: NOT APPLICABLE

CARE:
1. INADEQUATE SUPERVISION

HARM CAUSED TO PLAINTIFF &/OR PATIENT:
1. NONSELF-INFLICTED INJURIES

TYPE OF ACTION BROUGHT:
1. NEGLIGENCE

HISTORY OF THE CASE:

TYPE OF COURT: STATE

TRIER OF FACT: JUDGE,NO JURY

COURT DECISION(S):

TRIAL COURT: FOR DEFENDANT
YEAR: NOT SPECIFIED
APPELLATE COURT: FOR DEFENDANT
YEAR: 1954

REASON SUIT FAILED:
1. NEGLIGENCE OR CASE NOT PROVEN

94. FERNANDEZ V. BARUCH

FOR FOUR MONTHS PEDRO FERNANDEZ HAD BEEN SUFFERING FROM INSOMNIA AND FREQUENT HEADACHES. EVENTUALLY HE BECAME OVERLY DISTURBED BY LOUD NOISES. ON MAY 25, 1962, HE WAS ARRESTED ON THREE COUNTS OF ASSAULT AND BATTERY AFTER ATTACKING A FRIEND WITH A KNIFE AND THEN BITING AND ATTACKING TWO BYSTANDERS AT THE INCIDENT. HE WAS TAKEN BY POLICE TO THE HOSPITAL WHERE PSYCHIATRISTS ATTEMPTED TO HAVE HIS WIFE SIGN COMMITMENT PAPERS. SHE REFUSED BECAUSE THE STATE MENTAL HOSPITAL WAS TOO FAR AWAY AND SHE WOULD NOT BE ABLE TO VISIT HIM. THE DOCTORS DISCHARGED HIM TO THE POLICE ON JUNE 12. HE WAS ARRAIGNED THE NEXT DAY AND SENT ON TO THE UNION COUNTY JAIL, WHERE ON JUNE 16 HE HUNG HIMSELF WITH HIS SOCKS. HIS WIDOW BROUGHT AN ACTION FOR WRONGFUL DEATH, ALLEGING THAT HER HUSBAND DIED AS THE RESULT OF THE MALPRACTICE OF THE DEFENDANT PSYCHIATRISTS.

YEAR OF NEGLIGENT ACT: 1962

STATE IN WHICH NEGLIGENT ACT OCCURRED: NEW JERSEY

SETTING OF THE CASE: PUB. GEN. HOSP.

PLAINTIFF(S): PAT. & 3RD PTY., I

DEFENDANT(S):
1. PSYCHIATRIST(S)

NEGLIGENT ACTIVITY:

TREATMENT: NOT APPLICABLE

DIAGNOSIS:

WHAT WAS DIAGNOSED:
1. LACK OF SUICIDAL TENDENCIES

RESULT OF DIAGNOSIS:
1. IMPROPER RELEASE

CARE:
1. PREMATURE RELEASE
2. FAILURE TO WARN THIRD PARTIES

HARM CAUSED TO PLAINTIFF &/OR PATIENT:
1. SUICIDE

TYPE OF ACTION BROUGHT:
1. NEGLIGENCE

HISTORY OF THE CASE:

TYPE OF COURT: STATE

TRIER OF FACT: JURY

COURT DECISION(S):

TRIAL COURT: FOR PLAINTIFF
YEAR: NOT SPECIFIED
APPELLATE COURT: NONFINAL FOR DEF.
YEAR: 1967
SUPREME COURT: FOR DEFENDANT
YEAR: 1968

REASON SUIT FAILED:
1. NEGLIGENCE OR CASE NOT PROVEN

95. FINKEL V. STATE

A NEIGHBOR, HEARING SCREAMS FROM THE FINKEL HOME, ENTERED THE HOUSE TO FIND MRS. EVELYN FINKEL BEING BEATEN AND STABBED BY LEON THOMAS. THOMAS HAD ESCAPED FROM A DISTURBED WARD OF A STATE HOSPITAL THROUGH AN UNLOCKED DOOR EARLIER THAT DAY. THE POLICE ARRIVED SHORTLY BEFORE SHE DIED. THOMAS WAS LATER APPREHENDED AND WAS CONFINED AT MATTEAWAN STATE HOSPITAL FOR THE CRIMINALLY INSANE. THE ADMINISTRATOR OF EVELYN FINKEL'S ESTATE BROUGHT SUIT FOR NEGLIGENCE.

YEAR OF NEGLIGENT ACT: 1958

STATE IN WHICH NEGLIGENT ACT OCCURRED: NEW YORK

SETTING OF THE CASE: PUB. MENT. HOSP.

PLAINTIFF(S): 3RD PARTY, II

DEFENDANT(S):
1. STATE GOV. &/OR OFFICIALS, ETC.

NEGLIGENT ACTIVITY:

TREATMENT: NOT APPLICABLE

DIAGNOSIS:

WHAT WAS DIAGNOSED: NOT APPLICABLE

RESULT OF DIAGNOSIS: NOT APPLICABLE

CARE:
1. INADEQUATE SUPERVISION

HARM CAUSED TO PLAINTIFF &/OR PATIENT:
1. NONSUICIDAL DEATH

TYPE OF ACTION BROUGHT:
1. NEGLIGENCE

HISTORY OF THE CASE:

TYPE OF COURT: STATE

TRIER OF FACT: JUDGE,NO JURY

COURT DECISION(S):

TRIAL COURT: FOR PLAINTIFF
YEAR: 1962

VERDICT AGAINST WHICH DEFENDANTS:
1. STATE GOV. &/OR OFFICIALS, ETC.

RECOVERY OR OTHER RELIEF GRANTED:
1. $ 70997

96. FISCHER V. CITY OF ELMIRA

POLICE DETAINED GEORGE FISCHER IN THE ELMIRA COUNTY JAIL ON AUGUST 21, 1971. DURING HIS CONFINEMENT HE REQUESTED MEDICATION FOR HIS EPILEPTIC CONDITION. A DOCTOR, PROVIDED BY THE COUNTY, ALLEGEDLY EXAMINED HIM BUT FAILED TO GIVE HIM THE PROPER MEDICATION, RESULTING IN SERIOUS HARM.

YEAR OF NEGLIGENT ACT: 1971

STATE IN WHICH NEGLIGENT ACT OCCURRED: NEW YORK

SETTING OF THE CASE: CORRECTIONAL INST.

PLAINTIFF(S): PATIENT(S) OR REP.

DEFENDANT(S):
1. COUNTY GOV. &/OR OFFICIALS, ETC.
2. MUNICIPAL GOV. &/OR OFFICIALS, ETC.

NEGLIGENT ACTIVITY:

TREATMENT:
1. NEG.ADMIN.OF DRUGS

DIAGNOSIS:

WHAT WAS DIAGNOSED:
1. IMPROPER DRUG PRESCRIPTION

RESULT OF DIAGNOSIS:
1. IMPROPER DRUG PRESCRIPTION

CARE:
1. INADEQUATE SUPERVISION

HARM CAUSED TO PLAINTIFF &/OR PATIENT:
1. NONSELF-INFLICTED INJURIES

TYPE OF ACTION BROUGHT:
1. NEGLIGENCE

HISTORY OF THE CASE:

TYPE OF COURT: STATE

TRIER OF FACT: JUDGE;JURY PRESENT ?

COURT DECISION(S):

TRIAL COURT: NONFINAL FOR PL.
YEAR: 1973

DEFENDANTS STILL INVOLVED IN SUIT:
1. COUNTY GOV. &/OR OFFICIALS, ETC.
2. MUNICIPAL GOV. &/OR OFFICIALS, ETC.

97. FORDE V. COUNTY OF LOS ANGELES

SUFFERING FROM AN ACUTE PSYCHOTIC REACTION, MICHAEL FORDE WAS ADMITTED TO LOS ANGELES COUNTY HOSPITAL ON AUGUST 29, 1971. THE NEXT MORNING HE WAS TRANSFERRED TO A CLOSED WARD BECAUSE OF THE SERIOUSNESS OF HIS CONDITION AND THE POSSIBILITY OF SUICIDE. SUBSEQUENTLY HE WAS TRANSFERRED BACK TO AN OPEN WARD, AND AT THIS POINT HIS ORIGINAL INVOLUNTARY COMMITMENT BECAME VOLUNTARY. ON SEPTEMBER 6, THE PATIENT WAS PERMITTED TO GO TO THE LABOR DAY DANCE FROM WHICH HE "ELOPED." WITHIN A FEW HOURS, HE JUMPED OFF THE MACY STREET BRIDGE AND INJURED HIMSELF.

YEAR OF NEGLIGENT ACT: 1971

STATE IN WHICH NEGLIGENT ACT OCCURRED: CALIFORNIA

SETTING OF THE CASE: PUBLIC HOSPITAL

PLAINTIFF(S): PATIENT(S) OR REP.

DEFENDANT(S):
1. COUNTY GOV. &/OR OFFICIALS, ETC.

NEGLIGENT ACTIVITY:

TREATMENT: NOT APPLICABLE

DIAGNOSIS:

WHAT WAS DIAGNOSED:
1. TYPE OF CUSTODIAL CARE

RESULT OF DIAGNOSIS:
1. IMPROPER COMMITMENT

CARE:
1. INADEQUATE SUPERVISION

HARM CAUSED TO PLAINTIFF &/OR PATIENT:
1. SELF-INFLICTED INJURIES

TYPE OF ACTION BROUGHT:
1. NEGLIGENCE

HISTORY OF THE CASE:

TYPE OF COURT: STATE

TRIER OF FACT: JUDGE;JURY PRESENT ?

COURT DECISION(S):

TRIAL COURT: FOR DEFENDANT
YEAR: NOT SPECIFIED
APPELLATE COURT: FOR DEFENDANT
YEAR: 1976

REASON SUIT FAILED:
1. DEFENDANT(S) CANNOT BE SUED DUE TO: GOVERN. IMMUNITY

98. FOSTER V. STATE

STANLEY FOSTER, AN INMATE OF EDWARDS COLONY, A DIVISION OF THE SYRACUSE STATE SCHOOL, WAS A SIXTEEN-YEAR-OLD MENTAL DEFECTIVE. ON JULY 19, 1949, AFTER THEIR CHORES WERE DONE, STANLEY AND A FELLOW INMATE, MICKEY, SHARED A FORBIDDEN CIGARETTE BEHIND THE BARN. MICKEY THEN FETCHED SOME GASOLINE TO CLEAN A PAINT BRUSH, AND FOR AN UNKNOWN REASON LIT A MATCH WHICH IGNITED THE GASOLINE. STANLEY ATTEMPTED TO ESCAPE, BUT MICKEY PICKED UP THE CAN OF FLAMING GAS AND THREW IT AT HIM, HITTING HIS ARM AND CAUSING SEVERE BURNS. FOSTER SUED FOR NEGLIGENCE.

YEAR OF NEGLIGENT ACT: 1949

STATE IN WHICH NEGLIGENT ACT OCCURRED: NEW YORK

SETTING OF THE CASE: EDUCATIONAL INST.

PLAINTIFF(S): PATIENT(S) OR REP.

DEFENDANT(S):
1. STATE GOV. &/OR OFFICIALS, ETC.

NEGLIGENT ACTIVITY:

TREATMENT: NOT APPLICABLE

DIAGNOSIS:

WHAT WAS DIAGNOSED: NOT APPLICABLE

RESULT OF DIAGNOSIS: NOT APPLICABLE

CARE:
1. INADEQUATE SUPERVISION

HARM CAUSED TO PLAINTIFF &/OR PATIENT:
1. NONSELF-INFLICTED INJURIES

TYPE OF ACTION BROUGHT:
1. NEGLIGENCE

HISTORY OF THE CASE:

TYPE OF COURT: STATE

TRIER OF FACT: JUDGE,NO JURY

COURT DECISION(S):

TRIAL COURT: FOR PLAINTIFF
YEAR: 1961

VERDICT AGAINST WHICH DEFENDANTS:
1. STATE GOV. &/OR OFFICIALS, ETC.

RECOVERY OR OTHER RELIEF GRANTED:
1. $ 14000

99. FOWLE V. FOWLE

ON JANUARY 28, 1960, MR. WILLIS FOWLE INSTITUTED COMMITMENT PROCEEDINGS AGAINST HIS WIFE MARY. ALTHOUGH THE DOCTORS ALLEGEDLY DID NOT EXAMINE MRS. FOWLE, THEY SIGNED AFFIDAVITS STATING THEY HAD DONE SO AND FOUND HER SUFFERING FROM A MENTAL DISEASE. SHE WAS SOON AFTER COMMITTED TO UMSTEAD STATE HOSPITAL, WHERE SHE WAS CONFINED FOR TWENTY-FOUR DAYS. SHE WON HER RELEASE BY WRIT OF HABEAS CORPUS INSTITUTED BY A JUDGE WHO HAD LEARNED OF HER DETENTION.

YEAR OF NEGLIGENT ACT: 1960

STATE IN WHICH NEGLIGENT ACT OCCURRED: NORTH CAROLINA

SETTING OF THE CASE: JUDICIAL PROCEEDING

PLAINTIFF(S): PATIENT(S) OR REP.

DEFENDANT(S):
1. NONPSYCHIAT.OR UNKNOWN TYPE PHYSICIAN(S)

NEGLIGENT ACTIVITY:

TREATMENT: NOT APPLICABLE

DIAGNOSIS:

WHAT WAS DIAGNOSED:
1. MENTAL ILLNESS, INSTEAD OF SANITY

RESULT OF DIAGNOSIS:
1. IMPROPER COMMITMENT

CARE: NOT APPLICABLE

HARM CAUSED TO PLAINTIFF &/OR PATIENT:
1. NOT SPECIFIED

TYPE OF ACTION BROUGHT:
1. NEGLIGENCE
2. DEFAMATION OF CHARACTER: LIBEL
3. OTHER TORT(S): WRONGFUL COMMITMENT

HISTORY OF THE CASE:

TYPE OF COURT: STATE

TRIER OF FACT: JUDGE;JURY PRESENT ?

COURT DECISION(S):

TRIAL COURT: FOR DEFENDANT
YEAR: NOT SPECIFIED
SUPREME COURT: FOR DEFENDANT
YEAR: 1961

REASON SUIT FAILED:
1. DEFENDANT(S) CANNOT BE SUED DUE TO: JUDICIAL IMMUNITY

100. FOWLER V. NORWAYS SANITORIUM

PETER FOWLER, SUFFERING FROM A MENTAL DISORDER WITH SUICIDAL TENDENCIES, WAS ADMITTED TO NORWAYS SANITORIUM ON AUGUST 5, 1939. CARL JONES, A TWENTY-THREE-YEAR-OLD ATTENDANT, WAS PLACED ON TWENTY-ONE-HOUR DUTY WITH FOWLER AND INFORMED OF HIS SELF-DESTRUCTIVE TENDENCIES. ON AUGUST 8, JONES WAS INSTRUCTED TO TAKE FOWLER TO DR. BEELER, WHOSE OFFICE WAS ON THE SEVENTH FLOOR OF THE HUME-MANSUR BUILDING IN INDIANAPOLIS, FOR X-RAYS OF HIS CHEST AND TEETH. WHILE FOWLER WAS HAVING HIS TEETH X-RAYED AND WITH JONES SITTING CLOSE BY, FOWLER STOOD UP AS IF TO STRETCH. SUDDENLY, HE RAN OUT OF THE DOOR, CLOSING IT BEHIND HIM. WHEN THE ATTENDANT REACHED THE MIDDLE ROOM, FOWLER WAS ON HIS WAY OUT THE WINDOW. JONES GRABBED HIS CUFFS BUT COULD NOT HOLD ON AND FOWLER FELL TO HIS DEATH. MRS. FOWLER SUED THE SANITORIUM FOR WRONGFUL DEATH.

YEAR OF NEGLIGENT ACT: 1939

STATE IN WHICH NEGLIGENT ACT OCCURRED: INDIANA

SETTING OF THE CASE: PRIV. MENT. HOSP.

PLAINTIFF(S): PATIENT(S) OR REP.

DEFENDANT(S):
1. NONPSYCHIAT.OR UNKNOWN TYPE PHYSICIAN(S)
2. PARAPROFESSIONAL, NONPRO.EMPLOYEE, ETC.
3. HOSPITAL &/OR OWNERS, ETC.

NEGLIGENT ACTIVITY:

TREATMENT: NOT APPLICABLE

DIAGNOSIS:

WHAT WAS DIAGNOSED: NOT APPLICABLE

RESULT OF DIAGNOSIS: NOT APPLICABLE

CARE:
1. INADEQUATE SUPERVISION

HARM CAUSED TO PLAINTIFF &/OR PATIENT:
1. SUICIDE

TYPE OF ACTION BROUGHT:
1. NEGLIGENCE

HISTORY OF THE CASE:

TYPE OF COURT: STATE

TRIER OF FACT: JUDGE,UNINV.JURY

COURT DECISION(S):

TRIAL COURT: FOR DEFENDANT
YEAR: NOT SPECIFIED
APPELLATE COURT: NONFINAL FOR PL.
YEAR: 1942

DEFENDANTS STILL INVOLVED IN SUIT:
1. PARAPROFESSIONAL,NONPRO.EMPLOYEE, ETC.
2. HOSPITAL &/OR OWNERS, ETC.

101. FOXLUGER V. STATE

SUFFERING FROM INVOLUTIONAL PSYCHOSIS MELANCHOLIA, ETHEL FOXLUGER, AGED SIXTY-FIVE, WAS ADMITTED TO BINGHAMTON STATE HOSPITAL ON JUNE 4, 1956. ELECTROSHOCK THERAPY WAS RECOMMENDED AND TREATMENT BEGAN ON JUNE 29, CONTINUING WITH SIX TREATMENTS IN JULY. UPON THE FIRST ADMINISTRATION, A FRACTURE OF THE RIGHT HUMERAL NECK WAS SUFFERED AND ON THE LAST ADMINISTRATION, A SIMILAR FRACTURE ON THE LEFT SIDE OCCURRED. ALTHOUGH AN X-RAY ON JUNE 29 REVEALED NO FRACTURE, BOTH WERE DISCOVERED ON AUGUST 15. MRS. FOXLUGER CLAIMS THAT RELAXANT DRUGS SHOULD HAVE BEEN USED AND THAT THE STATE WAS NEGLIGENT IN THE ADMINISTRATION OF TREATMENT.

YEAR OF NEGLIGENT ACT: 1956

STATE IN WHICH NEGLIGENT ACT OCCURRED: NEW YORK

SETTING OF THE CASE: PUB. MENT. HOSP.

PLAINTIFF(S): PAT. & 3RD PTY., I

DEFENDANT(S):
1. STATE GOV. &/OR OFFICIALS, ETC.

NEGLIGENT ACTIVITY:

TREATMENT:
1. NEGLIGENT ELECTROCONVULSIVE THERAPY

DIAGNOSIS:

WHAT WAS DIAGNOSED: NOT APPLICABLE

RESULT OF DIAGNOSIS: NOT APPLICABLE

CARE: NOT APPLICABLE

HARM CAUSED TO PLAINTIFF &/OR PATIENT:
1. NONSELF-INFLICTED INJURIES

TYPE OF ACTION BROUGHT:
1. NEGLIGENCE

HISTORY OF THE CASE:

TYPE OF COURT: STATE

TRIER OF FACT: JUDGE,NO JURY

COURT DECISION(S):

TRIAL COURT: FOR DEFENDANT
YEAR: 1960

REASON SUIT FAILED:
1. NEGLIGENCE OR CASE NOT PROVEN

102. FREACH V. COMMONWEALTH

ON NOVEMBER 1, 1973 ONE MR. WRIGHT ALLEGEDLY SEXUALLY ASSAULTED AND KILLED PAUL FREACH AND EDMUND KEEN IN SCRANTON, PENNSYLVANIA. AN INVESTIGATION INTO WRIGHT'S PAST REVEALED A HISTORY OF ALLEGED PSYCHOPATHIC BEHAVIOR. ON MARCH 5, 1955, WHILE SIXTEEN YEARS OF AGE, HE WAS ALLEGED TO HAVE BEEN CONVICTED OF BLUDGEONING HIS GREAT AUNT TO DEATH AND SENTENCED TO TWENTY YEARS IN PRISON. AFTER PAROLE, HE WAS ALLEGEDLY ARRESTED FOR ASSAULT WITH INTENT TO RAVISH AN ELEVEN-YEAR-OLD GIRL. THIS CAUSED HIS COMMITMENT TO FARVIEW STATE HOSPITAL WHERE HE ALLEGEDLY CONFESSED TO MURDERING A YOUNG BOY WHILE ATTEMPTING TO SHOVE A TOY RIFLE DOWN HIS THROAT. WRIGHT WAS RELEASED FROM FARVIEW IN 1973, NEVER STANDING TRIAL FOR HIS OTHER OFFENSES, AND HIS TREATMENT WAS TERMINATED. WRIGHT WAS EMPLOYED BY THE CITY OF SCRANTON AND THE NORTHEAST VECTOR ASSOCIATION AS A SPECIAL POLICEMAN. PLAINTIFFS ALLEGED THAT HIS POSITION CREATED THE CIRCUMSTANCES WHICH ALLOWED HIM TO KILL THE MINOR CHILDREN, WHOSE PARENTS SUBSEQUENTLY SUED THE COMMONWEALTH.

YEAR OF NEGLIGENT ACT: 1973

STATE IN WHICH NEGLIGENT ACT OCCURRED: PENNSYLVANIA

SETTING OF THE CASE: PUB. MENT. HOSP.

PLAINTIFF(S): 3RD PARTY, II

DEFENDANT(S):
1. NONPSYCHIAT.OR UNKNOWN TYPE PHYSICIAN(S)
2. PARAPROFESSIONAL, NONPRO.EMPLOYEE, ETC.
3. HOSPITAL &/OR OWNERS, ETC.
4. STATE GOV. &/OR OFFICIALS, ETC.
5. MUNICIPAL GOV. &/OR OFFICIALS, ETC.
6. JUDICIARY &/OR CLERKS, ETC.
7. NOPRF.ORG.PAT.,INS.

NEGLIGENT ACTIVITY:

TREATMENT:
1. NO TREATMENT OR INADEQUATE TREATMENT

DIAGNOSIS:

WHAT WAS DIAGNOSED:
1. LACK OF DANGEROUSNESS

RESULT OF DIAGNOSIS:
1. IMPROPER RELEASE

CARE: NOT APPLICABLE

HARM CAUSED TO PLAINTIFF &/OR PATIENT:
1. NONSUICIDAL DEATH
2. SEXUAL OR MARITAL HARM

TYPE OF ACTION BROUGHT:
1. NEGLIGENCE
2. ASSAULT

HISTORY OF THE CASE:

TYPE OF COURT: STATE

TRIER OF FACT: JUDGE,NO JURY

COURT DECISION(S):

TRIAL COURT: FOR DEFENDANT
YEAR: 1976
SUPREME COURT: NONFINAL FOR PL.
YEAR: 1977

DEFENDANTS STILL INVOLVED IN SUIT:
1. NONPSYCHIAT.OR UNKNOWN TYPE PHYSICIAN(S)
2. STATE GOV. &/OR OFFICIALS, ETC.
3. JUDICIARY &/OR CLERKS, ETC.

103. FRIEDLAND V. UNITED STATES

LITTLE INFORMATION IS AVAILABLE FROM THE REPORTED CASE. WHILE AN INMATE AT THE V.A. HOSPITAL IN BROCKTON, MASS., WHERE HE WAS DIAGNOSED AS SCHIZOPHRENIC, RAYMOND POIRIER DIED FROM SELF-INFLICTED WOUNDS. HIS ADMINISTRATOR, SHELDON FRIEDLAND, SUED FOR DAMAGES FOR FAILURE TO PROPERLY SUPERVISE MR. POIRIER.

YEAR OF NEGLIGENT ACT: NOT SPECIFIED

STATE IN WHICH NEGLIGENT ACT OCCURRED: MASSACHUSETTS

SETTING OF THE CASE: PUB. GEN. HOSP.

PLAINTIFF(S): PATIENT(S) OR REP.

DEFENDANT(S):
1. FEDERAL GOV. &/OR OFFICIALS, ETC.

NEGLIGENT ACTIVITY:

TREATMENT: NOT APPLICABLE

DIAGNOSIS:

WHAT WAS DIAGNOSED: NOT APPLICABLE

RESULT OF DIAGNOSIS: NOT APPLICABLE

CARE:
1. INADEQUATE SUPERVISION

HARM CAUSED TO PLAINTIFF &/OR PATIENT:
1. SUICIDE

TYPE OF ACTION BROUGHT:
1. NEGLIGENCE

HISTORY OF THE CASE:

TYPE OF COURT: FEDERAL

TRIER OF FACT: JUDGE;JURY PRESENT ?

COURT DECISION(S):

TRIAL COURT: NONFINAL FOR PL.
YEAR: 1962

DEFENDANTS STILL INVOLVED IN SUIT:
1. FEDERAL GOV. &/OR OFFICIALS, ETC.

104. GASPERINI V. MANGINELLI

MR. GASPERINI, SENIOR CLAIMED THAT HE WAS LIBELED AND CHARGED EXCESSIVE FEES BECAUSE MANGINELLI, A PSYCHIATRIST, HAD PUBLISHED A HISTORY OF HIS SON'S CASE, BUT FAILED TO ADD THE SUFFIX "JR." AFTER HIS SON'S NAME. THE REPORTED DECISION CONTAINS LITTLE FURTHER INFORMATION.

YEAR OF NEGLIGENT ACT: NOT SPECIFIED

STATE IN WHICH NEGLIGENT ACT OCCURRED: NEW YORK

SETTING OF THE CASE: PRIVATE PRACTICE

PLAINTIFF(S): PAT. & 3RD PTY., I

DEFENDANT(S):
1. PSYCHIATRIST(S)

NEGLIGENT ACTIVITY:

TREATMENT:
1. NO TREATMENT OR INADEQUATE TREATMENT
2. FAILURE TO CONSULT

DIAGNOSIS:

WHAT WAS DIAGNOSED: NOT APPLICABLE

RESULT OF DIAGNOSIS: NOT APPLICABLE

CARE:
1. IMPROPER GIVING OF INFORMATION TO OTHERS

HARM CAUSED TO PLAINTIFF &/OR PATIENT:
1. ECONOMIC LOSS
2. INJURY TO REPUTATION

TYPE OF ACTION BROUGHT:
1. NEGLIGENCE
2. DEFAMATION OF CHARACTER: LIBEL
3. CONTRACT LAW: BREACH OF CONTRACT

HISTORY OF THE CASE:

TYPE OF COURT: STATE

TRIER OF FACT: JUDGE;JURY PRESENT ?

COURT DECISION(S):

TRIAL COURT: NONFINAL FOR PL.
YEAR: 1949

DEFENDANTS STILL INVOLVED IN SUIT:
1. PSYCHIATRIST(S)

105. GERBA V. NEUROLOGICAL HOSPITAL ASSOCIATION

ON JUNE 25, 1961 NANCY GERBA, SUFFERING FROM SEVERE MENTAL AND EMOTIONAL DERANGEMENT, WAS ADMITTED TO THE NEUROLOGICAL HOSPITAL ASSOCIATION FOR TREATMENT. WHILE SHE WAS LEFT UNATTENDED AND UNRESTRAINED SHE GOUGED OUT BOTH HER EYES, "RENDERING HERSELF TOTALLY AND PERMANENTLY BLIND." SHE BROUGHT SUIT FOR THE INJURIES SHE RECEIVED AND HER HUSBAND BROUGHT SUIT FOR ECONOMIC LOSS AND LOSS OF CONSORTIUM. THEY CLAIMED THAT THE HOSPITAL KNEW OF THE LIKELIHOOD OF MS. GERBA DOING INJURY TO HERSELF BUT FAILED TO FURNISH PROPER CARE AND SUPERVISION.

YEAR OF NEGLIGENT ACT: 1961

STATE IN WHICH NEGLIGENT ACT OCCURRED: MISSOURI

SETTING OF THE CASE: PRIV. GEN. HOSP.

PLAINTIFF(S): PAT. & 3RD PTY., I

DEFENDANT(S):
1. HOSPITAL &/OR OWNERS, ETC.

NEGLIGENT ACTIVITY:

TREATMENT: NOT APPLICABLE

DIAGNOSIS:

WHAT WAS DIAGNOSED: NOT APPLICABLE

RESULT OF DIAGNOSIS: NOT APPLICABLE

CARE:
1. INADEQUATE SUPERVISION

HARM CAUSED TO PLAINTIFF &/OR PATIENT:
1. SELF-INFLICTED INJURIES
2. ECONOMIC LOSS
3. LOSS OF CONSORTIUM

TYPE OF ACTION BROUGHT:
1. NEGLIGENCE

HISTORY OF THE CASE:

TYPE OF COURT: STATE

TRIER OF FACT: JUDGE;JURY PRESENT ?

COURT DECISION(S):

TRIAL COURT: FOR DEFENDANT
YEAR: NOT SPECIFIED
SUPREME COURT: FOR DEFENDANT
YEAR: 1967

REASON SUIT FAILED:
1. STATUTE OF LIMITATIONS BARRED SUIT

106. GIOIA V. STATE

AFTER SIX YEARS OF MARRIAGE JOSEPH GIOIA WAS ARRESTED FOR THE MURDER OF HIS WIFE, SURRENDERING WITHOUT RESISTANCE ON OCTOBER 17, 1958. HE WAS TAKEN TO THE STATE POLICE BARRACKS IN BATAVIA FOR QUESTIONING, WHERE HE JUMPED OUT OF A SECOND STORY-WINDOW, INJURING HIS ANKLE. AFTER TREATMENT AT ST. JEROME HOSPITAL, HE WAS TRANSFERRED TO ROCHESTER STATE HOSPITAL, AND, WHILE THERE, AN ACE BANDAGE WAS PUT ON HIS INJURED ANKLE. BETWEEN INTERVALS OF HIS FIFTEEN-MINUTE ROOM CHECK, GIOIA STRANGLED HIMSELF TO DEATH WITH THE ACE BANDAGE. HIS BROTHER BROUGHT SUIT, ALLEGING THAT THE HOSPITAL SHOULD HAVE REALIZED THE BANDAGE MIGHT HAVE BEEN USED IN A SUICIDE ATTEMPT.

YEAR OF NEGLIGENT ACT: NOT SPECIFIED

STATE IN WHICH NEGLIGENT ACT OCCURRED: NEW YORK

SETTING OF THE CASE: PUB. MENT. HOSP.

PLAINTIFF(S): PATIENT(S) OR REP.

DEFENDANT(S):
1. STATE GOV. &/OR OFFICIALS, ETC.

NEGLIGENT ACTIVITY:

TREATMENT: NOT APPLICABLE

DIAGNOSIS:

WHAT WAS DIAGNOSED: NOT APPLICABLE

RESULT OF DIAGNOSIS: NOT APPLICABLE

CARE:
1. INADEQUATE SUPERVISION

HARM CAUSED TO PLAINTIFF &/OR PATIENT:
1. SUICIDE

TYPE OF ACTION BROUGHT:
1. NEGLIGENCE

HISTORY OF THE CASE:

TYPE OF COURT: STATE

TRIER OF FACT: JUDGE,NO JURY

COURT DECISION(S):

TRIAL COURT: FOR PLAINTIFF
YEAR: 1961
APPELLATE COURT: NONFINAL FOR DEF.
YEAR: 1962
ON RETRIAL: FOR DEFENDANT
YEAR: 1963
ON REAPPEAL TO APPELLATE COURT: FOR PLAINTIFF
YEAR: 1964

VERDICT AGAINST WHICH DEFENDANTS:
1. STATE GOV. &/OR OFFICIALS, ETC.

RECOVERY OR OTHER RELIEF GRANTED:
1. $ 41124

107. GOULD V. STATE

SUFFERING FROM "MANIC DEPRESSIVE PSYCHOSIS, MANIC TYPE," MR. GOULD WAS ONE OF TWENTY-EIGHT INMATES, ALL OF WHOM WERE KNOWN TO BE OF AN ASSAULTIVE NATURE, IN A WARD OF ROCKLAND STATE HOSPITAL. PRIOR TO HIS LAST BATTLE, HE HAD BEEN INVOLVED IN SEVEN ASSAULTS OVER A FIVE-MONTH PERIOD. IN HIS LATEST FIGHT HE RECEIVED SEVERE BLOWS ABOUT THE FACE AND HEAD WITH A SHOE AND DIED THIRTY MINUTES LATER. THE SUIT BROUGHT BY HIS WIFE ALLEGED IN PART WRONGFUL DEATH IN PROVIDING INADEQUATE CUSTODIAL CARE AND FOR UNLAWFULLY PERFORMING AN AUTOPSY.

YEAR OF NEGLIGENT ACT: NOT SPECIFIED

STATE IN WHICH NEGLIGENT ACT OCCURRED: NEW YORK

SETTING OF THE CASE: PUB. MENT. HOSP.

PLAINTIFF(S): PATIENT(S) OR REP.

DEFENDANT(S):
1. STATE GOV. &/OR OFFICIALS, ETC.

NEGLIGENT ACTIVITY:

TREATMENT: NOT APPLICABLE

DIAGNOSIS:

WHAT WAS DIAGNOSED: NOT APPLICABLE

RESULT OF DIAGNOSIS: NOT APPLICABLE

CARE:
1. INADEQUATE SUPERVISION

HARM CAUSED TO PLAINTIFF &/OR PATIENT:
1. NONSUICIDAL DEATH
2. EMOTIONAL DISTRESS

TYPE OF ACTION BROUGHT:
1. NEGLIGENCE

HISTORY OF THE CASE:

TYPE OF COURT: STATE

TRIER OF FACT: JUDGE,NO JURY

COURT DECISION(S):

TRIAL COURT: FOR PLAINTIFF
YEAR: 1944

VERDICT AGAINST WHICH DEFENDANTS:
1. STATE GOV. &/OR OFFICIALS, ETC.

RECOVERY OR OTHER RELIEF GRANTED:
1. $ 6320

108. GRANT V. NTL INSTITUTE

WHILE ATTENDING A TWELVE-DAY NTL "TRAINING GROUP," CONSTANCE GRANT WAS DROPPED TO THE FLOOR BY A JUDO HOLD FROM FELLOW PARTICIPANT SANDRA PINE. THE ACCIDENT OCCURRED DURING AN AGGRESSION AND HOSTILITY EXERCISE. ACCORDING TO GRANT THE SUPERVISOR OF THE SESSION WAS NEGLIGENT IN FAILING TO PREVENT INJURY TO HER. THIS CASE WAS ONE OF THE FIRST CIVIL SUITS FILED AGAINST THE SENSITIVITY TRAINING MOVEMENT.

YEAR OF NEGLIGENT ACT: 1968

STATE IN WHICH NEGLIGENT ACT OCCURRED: NEW HAMPSHIRE

SETTING OF THE CASE: ENCOUNTER GROUP

PLAINTIFF(S): PATIENT(S) OR REP.

DEFENDANT(S):
1. GROWTH CENTER

NEGLIGENT ACTIVITY:

TREATMENT:
1. NEGLIGENCE IN USE OF TECHNIQUE

DIAGNOSIS:

WHAT WAS DIAGNOSED: NOT APPLICABLE

RESULT OF DIAGNOSIS: NOT APPLICABLE

CARE: NOT APPLICABLE

HARM CAUSED TO PLAINTIFF &/OR PATIENT:
1. NONSELF-INFLICTED INJURIES
2. EMOTIONAL DISTRESS

TYPE OF ACTION BROUGHT:
1. NEGLIGENCE
2. MISREPRESENTATION

HISTORY OF THE CASE:

TYPE OF COURT: FEDERAL

TRIER OF FACT: SETTLED OUT OF COURT

COURT DECISION(S):

SETTLED OUT OF COURT
YEAR: NOT SPECIFIED

VERDICT AGAINST WHICH DEFENDANTS:
1. GROWTH CENTER

RECOVERY OR OTHER RELIEF GRANTED:
1. $ 7500

109. GREGORY V. ROBINSON

THE PLAINTIFF, WHILE AN EMPLOYEE OF BENDIX AVIATION CORP. IN KANSAS CITY, BECAME DEPRESSED AND WORRIED AND WAS TAKEN TO THE HOSPITAL ON SEPTEMBER 15, 1955. HE WAS SEEN BY A CONSULTING PSYCHIATRIST WHO FOUND HIM SEVERELY DEPRESSED AND SUICIDAL. ON SEPTEMBER 18, HE WAS ADMITTED TO NEUROLOGICAL HOSPITAL AND PLACED ON THE THIRD FLOOR WHERE ACUTELY ILL PATIENTS WERE KEPT. HE RECEIVED THREE ELECTRO-SHOCK THERAPY TREATMENTS AND BEGAN SHOWING IMPROVEMENT. ON SEPTEMBER 22, GREGORY TOLD DR. HINES HE WAS BETTER AND WOULD LIKE TO GO HOME, REQUESTING TO CALL HIS WIFE SO THAT SHE MIGHT PICK HIM UP. DR. HINES REFUSED HIS REQUEST. GREGORY RETURNED TO HIS ROOM DIRECTLY ACROSS FROM THE STAIRWAY DOOR. AS DR. HINES ARRIVED AT THIS DOOR GREGORY BURST THROUGH, CLIMBED ON A RADIATOR AND JUMPED OUT AN OPEN WINDOW. THE INJURIES SUFFERED FROM THIS FALL FORMED THE BASIS FOR SUIT AGAINST THE HOSPITAL OWNERS, INCLUDING ROBINSON, AND TWO PHYSICIANS.

YEAR OF NEGLIGENT ACT: 1955

STATE IN WHICH NEGLIGENT ACT OCCURRED: MISSOURI

SETTING OF THE CASE: PRIV. MENT. HOSP.

PLAINTIFF(S): PATIENT(S) OR REP.

DEFENDANT(S):
1. NONPSYCHIAT.OR UNKNOWN TYPE PHYSICIAN(S)

NEGLIGENT ACTIVITY:

TREATMENT: NOT APPLICABLE

DIAGNOSIS:

WHAT WAS DIAGNOSED: NOT APPLICABLE

RESULT OF DIAGNOSIS: NOT APPLICABLE

CARE:
1. INADEQUATE SUPERVISION

HARM CAUSED TO PLAINTIFF &/OR PATIENT:
1. SELF-INFLICTED INJURIES

TYPE OF ACTION BROUGHT:
1. NEGLIGENCE

HISTORY OF THE CASE:

TYPE OF COURT: STATE

TRIER OF FACT: JUDGE,UNINV.JURY

COURT DECISION(S):

TRIAL COURT: FOR DEFENDANT
YEAR: NOT SPECIFIED
SUPREME COURT: FOR DEFENDANT
YEAR: 1960

REASON SUIT FAILED:
1. NEGLIGENCE OR CASE NOT PROVEN

110. GRIES V. LONG ISLAND HOME

FEW FACTS ARE AVAILABLE FROM THE REPORTED DECISION, EXCEPT THAT LAWRENCE GRIES COMMITTED SUICIDE WHILE LEFT UNATTENDED AS A PATIENT AT LONG ISLAND HOME. SUBSEQUENTLY HIS WIDOW BROUGHT SUIT FOR NEGLIGENCE.

YEAR OF NEGLIGENT ACT: NOT SPECIFIED

STATE IN WHICH NEGLIGENT ACT OCCURRED: NEW YORK

SETTING OF THE CASE: PRIV. MENT. HOSP.

PLAINTIFF(S): PATIENT(S) OR REP.

DEFENDANT(S):
1. HOSPITAL &/OR OWNERS, ETC.

NEGLIGENT ACTIVITY:

TREATMENT: NOT APPLICABLE

DIAGNOSIS:

WHAT WAS DIAGNOSED: NOT APPLICABLE

RESULT OF DIAGNOSIS: NOT APPLICABLE

CARE:
1. INADEQUATE SUPERVISION

HARM CAUSED TO PLAINTIFF &/OR PATIENT:
1. SUICIDE

TYPE OF ACTION BROUGHT:
1. NEGLIGENCE

HISTORY OF THE CASE:

TYPE OF COURT: STATE

TRIER OF FACT: JUDGE,UNINV.JURY

COURT DECISION(S):

TRIAL COURT: FOR DEFENDANT
YEAR: NOT SPECIFIED
APPELLATE COURT: NONFINAL FOR PL.
YEAR: 1948

DEFENDANTS STILL INVOLVED IN SUIT:
1. HOSPITAL &/OR OWNERS, ETC.

111. GROCE V. MYERS

FANNIE GROCE WAS CARRIED TO DR. MYERS' CLINIC ON JUNE 19, 1941 SUFFERING FROM DYSMENORRHEA AND DIFFICULT MENSTRUATION, WHICH HAD AFFLICTED HER SINCE PUBERTY. NOW THIRTY-THREE, THERE WAS EVIDENCE THAT SHE HAD EMOTIONAL PROBLEMS AS HER MENSTRUAL PERIOD APPROACHED, BUT WAS GENERALLY IN GOOD MENTAL HEALTH. MEMBERS OF HER FAMILY VISITED HER DURING HER EIGHT DAYS AT MYERS' AND INITIALLY FOUND HER IN GOOD SPIRITS. UPON THEIR LAST VISIT, HOWEVER, THEY FOUND HER HIGHLY DISTURBED, WITH BRUISES OVER HER ENTIRE BODY AND A BROKEN ARM DANGLING FROM HER SIDE. DR. MYERS CLAIMED THAT HE HAD BEEN TRYING TO PULL FANNIE OUT FROM UNDER HER BED WHEN HE BROKE HER ARM. HE LEFT THE ARM IN THAT CONDITION BECAUSE SHE RESISTED TREATMENT. THERE WAS NO EXPLANATION GIVEN AS TO THE BRUISES ON HER BODY. HER FAMILY TOOK HER TO A DOCTOR WHERE THE ARM WAS SET AND HER BRUISES TREATED. THEY LATER SUED MYERS FOR NEGLIGENCE.

YEAR OF NEGLIGENT ACT: 1941

STATE IN WHICH NEGLIGENT ACT OCCURRED: NORTH CAROLINA

SETTING OF THE CASE: PRIVATE HOSPITAL

PLAINTIFF(S): PATIENT(S) OR REP.

DEFENDANT(S):
1. NONPSYCHIAT.OR UNKNOWN TYPE PHYSICIAN(S)

NEGLIGENT ACTIVITY:

TREATMENT: NOT APPLICABLE

DIAGNOSIS:

WHAT WAS DIAGNOSED: NOT APPLICABLE

RESULT OF DIAGNOSIS: NOT APPLICABLE

CARE:
1. FAILURE TO PROVIDE PROPER CUSTODIAL CARE

HARM CAUSED TO PLAINTIFF &/OR PATIENT:
1. NONSELF-INFLICTED INJURIES

TYPE OF ACTION BROUGHT:
1. NEGLIGENCE

HISTORY OF THE CASE:

TYPE OF COURT: STATE

TRIER OF FACT: JUDGE,UNINV.JURY

COURT DECISION(S):

TRIAL COURT: FOR DEFENDANT
YEAR: NOT SPECIFIED
SUPREME COURT: NONFINAL FOR PL.
YEAR: 1944

DEFENDANTS STILL INVOLVED IN SUIT:
1. NONPSYCHIAT.OR UNKNOWN TYPE PHYSICIAN(S)

112. GUZY V. GUZY

FEW FACTS ARE CONTAINED IN THE REPORTED DECISION, EXCEPT THAT STEPHEN GUZY WAS COMMITTED FOR A PERIOD OF SIXTY DAYS FOR OBSERVATION AND TREATMENT BY HIS WIFE AND TWO PHYSICIANS.

YEAR OF NEGLIGENT ACT: NOT SPECIFIED

STATE IN WHICH NEGLIGENT ACT OCCURRED: NEW YORK

SETTING OF THE CASE: JUDICIAL PROCEEDING

PLAINTIFF(S): PATIENT(S) OR REP.

DEFENDANT(S):
1. NONPSYCHIAT.OR UNKNOWN TYPE PHYSICIAN(S)
2. PL'S.SPOUSE &/ MOTH.

NEGLIGENT ACTIVITY:

TREATMENT: NOT APPLICABLE

DIAGNOSIS:

WHAT WAS DIAGNOSED:
1. MENTAL ILLNESS, INSTEAD OF SANITY

RESULT OF DIAGNOSIS:
1. IMPROPER COMMITMENT

CARE: NOT APPLICABLE

HARM CAUSED TO PLAINTIFF &/OR PATIENT:
1. NOT SPECIFIED

TYPE OF ACTION BROUGHT:
1. FALSE IMPRISONMENT

HISTORY OF THE CASE:

TYPE OF COURT: STATE

TRIER OF FACT: JUDGE;JURY PRESENT ?

COURT DECISION(S):

TRIAL COURT: FOR DEFENDANT
YEAR: 1959
APPELLATE COURT: FOR DEFENDANT
YEAR: 1960

REASON SUIT FAILED:
1. NO CAUSE OF ACTION STATED

113. HAMMER V. POLSKY

PAUL D. HAMMER VISITED DR. MURRAY POLSKY A NUMBER OF TIMES, BOTH WITH AND WITHOUT MRS. HAMMER, TO AID IN HER TREATMENT. FROM THESE MEETINGS AND ON THE BASIS OF OTHER INFORMATION OBTAINED FROM PHYSICIANS AND PSYCHOLOGISTS, DR. POLSKY TESTIFIED IN THE CUSTODY PROCEEDING THAT PAUL WAS SUFFERING FROM PARANOID SCHIZOPHRENIA. MR. HAMMER SUED FOR MALPRACTICE IN MAKING A NEGLIGENT DIAGNOSIS.

YEAR OF NEGLIGENT ACT: NOT SPECIFIED

STATE IN WHICH NEGLIGENT ACT OCCURRED: NEW YORK

SETTING OF THE CASE: JUDICIAL PROCEEDING

PLAINTIFF(S): PATIENT(S) OR REP.

DEFENDANT(S):
1. NONPSYCHIAT.OR UNKNOWN TYPE PHYSICIAN(S)

NEGLIGENT ACTIVITY:

TREATMENT: NOT APPLICABLE

DIAGNOSIS:

WHAT WAS DIAGNOSED:
1. MENTAL ILLNESS, INSTEAD OF SANITY

RESULT OF DIAGNOSIS:
1. IMPROPER DETERMINATION OF CUSTODY

CARE:
1. IMPROPER GIVING OF INFORMATION TO OTHERS

HARM CAUSED TO PLAINTIFF &/OR PATIENT:
1. NOT SPECIFIED

TYPE OF ACTION BROUGHT:
1. NEGLIGENCE
2. DEFAMATION OF CHARACTER: LIBEL
3. OTHER TORT(S): PRIMA FACIE TORT

HISTORY OF THE CASE:

TYPE OF COURT: STATE

TRIER OF FACT: JUDGE;JURY PRESENT ?

COURT DECISION(S):

TRIAL COURT: NONFINAL FOR PL.
YEAR: 1962

DEFENDANTS STILL INVOLVED IN SUIT:
1. NONPSYCHIAT.OR UNKNOWN TYPE PHYSICIAN(S)

114. HAMMER V. ROSEN

IN 1945 DR. JOHN NATHANIEL ROSEN BEGAN HIS SPECIALIZATION IN PSYCHIATRY AFTER RESIDENCIES AT THE BROOKLYN STATE HOSPITAL AND NEW YORK PSYCHIATRIC INSTITUTE AND HOSPITAL. ATTRACTED BY CLAIMS OF A HIGH SUCCESS RATE IN THE TREATMENT OF SCHIZOPHRENIC PATIENTS, ALICE HAMMER'S FAMILY BROUGHT HER TO DR. ROSEN IN 1948, AFTER SHE HAD ALREADY HAD OVER 200 ELECTRO-SHOCK TREATMENTS. DR. ROSEN'S TREATMENT ALLEGEDLY INCLUDED PHYSICAL BEATING WHICH OCCASIONALLY LEFT ALICE WITH BRUISES AND TORN CLOTHING. SEVEN YEARS AND $55,000 LATER, ALICE'S CONDITION HAD NOT IMPROVED. THE FAMILY SUED FOR NEGLIGENCE AND BREACH OF CONTRACT.

YEAR OF NEGLIGENT ACT: OCCURRED OVER A SERIES OF YEARS, ENDING IN 1955

STATE IN WHICH NEGLIGENT ACT OCCURRED: NEW YORK

SETTING OF THE CASE: PRIVATE PRACTICE

PLAINTIFF(S): PAT. & 3RD PTY., I

DEFENDANT(S):
1. PSYCHIATRIST(S)

NEGLIGENT ACTIVITY:

TREATMENT:
1. NEGLIGENCE IN USE OF TECHNIQUE
2. PHYSICAL ASSAULT

DIAGNOSIS:

WHAT WAS DIAGNOSED: NOT APPLICABLE

RESULT OF DIAGNOSIS: NOT APPLICABLE

CARE: NOT APPLICABLE

HARM CAUSED TO PLAINTIFF &/OR PATIENT:
1. NONSELF-INFLICTED INJURIES
2. EMOTIONAL DISTRESS
3. ECONOMIC LOSS

TYPE OF ACTION BROUGHT:
1. NEGLIGENCE
2. CONTRACT LAW: FRAUD-BREACH OF CON.

HISTORY OF THE CASE:

TYPE OF COURT: STATE

TRIER OF FACT: JURY

COURT DECISION(S):

TRIAL COURT: FOR DEFENDANT
YEAR: 1957
APPELLATE COURT: FOR DEFENDANT
YEAR: 1959
SUPREME COURT: NONFINAL FOR PL.
YEAR: 1960

DEFENDANTS STILL INVOLVED IN SUIT:
1. PSYCHIATRIST(S)

115. HARRIS HOSPITAL V. POPE

MRS. BARBARA POPE AND HER HUSBAND WERE INVOLVED IN A CAR ACCIDENT. BARBARA'S JAW WAS BADLY FRACTURED AND SHE UNDERWENT A TRACHEOTOMY IN CLEBURNE, TEXAS. LATER SHE WAS ADMITTED TO THE INTENSIVE CARE UNIT OF HARRIS HOSPITAL OF FORT WORTH, TEXAS. AFTER FOUR DAYS IN WHICH SHE HAD SHOWN NO SIGNS OF IRRATIONAL BEHAVIOR, BARBARA CRAWLED OUT ONTO THE SECOND-FLOOR WINDOW LEDGE. A NURSE GRABBED AT HER FINGERS, BUT BARBARA FREED HERSELF AND EITHER JUMPED OR FELL TO THE GROUND, SUSTAINING SERIOUS INJURIES. AFTER THE FALL, MR. POPE TOLD THE DOCTOR THAT BARBARA HAD ATTEMPTED SUICIDE TWICE BEFORE, BUT THE DOCTOR HAD HAD NO PRIOR REASON TO SUSPECT SHE MIGHT TRY TO INJURE HERSELF.

YEAR OF NEGLIGENT ACT: 1970

STATE IN WHICH NEGLIGENT ACT OCCURRED: TEXAS

SETTING OF THE CASE: HOSPITAL

PLAINTIFF(S): PAT. & 3RD PTY., I

DEFENDANT(S):
1. HOSPITAL &/OR OWNERS, ETC.

NEGLIGENT ACTIVITY:

TREATMENT: NOT APPLICABLE

DIAGNOSIS:

WHAT WAS DIAGNOSED: NOT APPLICABLE

RESULT OF DIAGNOSIS: NOT APPLICABLE

CARE:
1. INADEQUATE SUPERVISION

HARM CAUSED TO PLAINTIFF &/OR PATIENT:
1. SELF-INFLICTED INJURIES

TYPE OF ACTION BROUGHT:
1. NEGLIGENCE

HISTORY OF THE CASE:

TYPE OF COURT: STATE

TRIER OF FACT: JURY

COURT DECISION(S):

TRIAL COURT: FOR PLAINTIFF
YEAR: NOT SPECIFIED
APPELLATE COURT: FOR DEFENDANT
YEAR: 1975

REASON SUIT FAILED:
1. NEGLIGENCE OR CASE NOT PROVEN

116. HAWLEY V. STATE

LAWRENCE HAWLEY WAS PLACED IN THE SYRACUSE STATE SCHOOL AT AGE THIRTEEN. AT AGE TWENTY-FIVE, LAWRENCE COULD NOT READ OR WRITE, HAD THE MENTALITY OF A NINE-YEAR-OLD, AND HAD AN I.Q. OF SIXTY-ONE. AT THAT TIME, AFTER TRAINING IN FARM WORK, LAWRENCE WAS ASSIGNED TO WORK FOR ROBERT THOMPSON ON A FARM IN PHOENIX, NEW YORK, MAKING $50 PER MONTH. ON SEPTEMBER 23, 1959, WHILE TOPPING OFF A SILO, HE WAS TOLD TO CLIMB UP FORTY FEET, STAND ON A NARROW, RAIL-LESS PLATFORM, AND HELP GUIDE A 200-POUND PIPE TO THE TOP OF THE SILO. THE PLATFORM COLLAPSED AND LAWRENCE SUSTAINED PAINFUL AND DISABLING FRACTURES TO BOTH ANKLES AND A COMPRESSION FRACTURE OF THE SECOND LUMBAR VERTEBRA; HE HEALED WELL, THOUGH, WITH THE EXCEPTION OF THE LEFT ANKLE WHERE THE JOINT THICKENED AND THE LEG WAS THEREBY SHORTENED. HIS GUARDIAN AD LITEM, LAWRENCE HAWLEY, SUED THE STATE FOR FAILING TO FULLY INFORM THOMPSON OF HAWLEY'S MENTAL CAPACITY AND NEED FOR CLOSE SUPERVISION.

YEAR OF NEGLIGENT ACT: 1959

STATE IN WHICH NEGLIGENT ACT OCCURRED: NEW YORK

SETTING OF THE CASE: FARM

PLAINTIFF(S): PATIENT(S) OR REP.

DEFENDANT(S):
1. STATE GOV. &/OR OFFICIALS, ETC.

NEGLIGENT ACTIVITY:

TREATMENT: NOT APPLICABLE

DIAGNOSIS:

WHAT WAS DIAGNOSED: NOT APPLICABLE

RESULT OF DIAGNOSIS: NOT APPLICABLE

CARE:
1. INADEQUATE SUPERVISION
2. FAILURE TO PROVIDE PROPER CUSTODIAL CARE

HARM CAUSED TO PLAINTIFF &/OR PATIENT:
1. NONSELF-INFLICTED INJURIES

TYPE OF ACTION BROUGHT:
1. NEGLIGENCE

HISTORY OF THE CASE:

TYPE OF COURT: STATE

TRIER OF FACT: JUDGE,NO JURY

COURT DECISION(S):

TRIAL COURT: FOR PLAINTIFF
YEAR: 1963
APPELLATE COURT: FOR PLAINTIFF
YEAR: 1965
SUPREME COURT: FOR DEFENDANT
YEAR: 1965

REASON SUIT FAILED:
1. DEFENDANT(S) CANNOT BE SUED DUE TO: GOVERN. IMMUNITY

117. HEBEL V. HINSDALE SANITARIUM

MS. HEBEL, A PATIENT AT THE HINSDALE SANITARIUM AND HOSPITAL, WAS ALLEGEDLY INCAPABLE OF EXERCISING SOUND JUDGMENT. SHE WANDERED AWAY FROM THE SANITARIUM AND ONTO A RAILROAD TRACK, WHERE SHE WAS HIT BY A TRAIN, SUFFERING INJURIES LEADING TO HER DEATH. HER HUSBAND SUED HINSDALE FOR PROVIDING INADEQUATE SUPERVISION.

YEAR OF NEGLIGENT ACT: NOT SPECIFIED

STATE IN WHICH NEGLIGENT ACT OCCURRED: ILLINOIS

SETTING OF THE CASE: PRIV. MENT. HOSP.

PLAINTIFF(S): PATIENT(S) OR REP.

DEFENDANT(S):
1. HOSPITAL &/OR OWNERS, ETC.

NEGLIGENT ACTIVITY:

TREATMENT: NOT APPLICABLE

DIAGNOSIS:

WHAT WAS DIAGNOSED: NOT APPLICABLE

RESULT OF DIAGNOSIS: NOT APPLICABLE

CARE:
1. INADEQUATE SUPERVISION

HARM CAUSED TO PLAINTIFF &/OR PATIENT:
1. NONSUICIDAL DEATH

TYPE OF ACTION BROUGHT:
1. NEGLIGENCE

HISTORY OF THE CASE:

TYPE OF COURT: STATE

TRIER OF FACT: JUDGE,UNINV.JURY

COURT DECISION(S):

TRIAL COURT: FOR DEFENDANT
YEAR: NOT SPECIFIED
APPELLATE COURT: FOR DEFENDANT
YEAR: 1954

REASON SUIT FAILED:
1. NO CAUSE OF ACTION STATED

118. HEIFETZ V. PHILADELPHIA STATE HOSPITAL

SONNY DAVES WAS CIVILLY COMMITTED TO THE PHILADELPHIA STATE HOSPITAL. AFTER ONE MONTH OF TREATMENT, HE WAS RELEASED. THE COMMODORE APARTMENTS HIRED HIM AS A MAINTENANCE PERSON, AFTER WHICH SONNY SEXUALLY ASSAULTED ONE OF THE TENANTS. SUIT WAS FILED AGAINST MELVIN HEIFETZ AND ARNOLD LEVIT FOR THE NEGLIGENT HIRING OF SONNY, WHOM THEY KNEW, OR SHOULD HAVE KNOWN, HAD PERVERTED INCLINATIONS AND WAS DANGEROUS. SUIT WAS ALSO BROUGHT AGAINST THE PHILADELPHIA STATE HOSPITAL FOR NEGLIGENCE IN PREMATURELY RELEASING SONNY.

YEAR OF NEGLIGENT ACT: NOT SPECIFIED

STATE IN WHICH NEGLIGENT ACT OCCURRED: PENNSYLVANIA

SETTING OF THE CASE: PUB. MENT. HOSP.

PLAINTIFF(S): 3RD PARTY, II

DEFENDANT(S):
1. PSYCHIATRIST(S)
2. HOSPITAL &/OR OWNERS, ETC.

NEGLIGENT ACTIVITY:

TREATMENT: NOT APPLICABLE

DIAGNOSIS:

WHAT WAS DIAGNOSED:
1. LACK OF DANGEROUSNESS

RESULT OF DIAGNOSIS:
1. IMPROPER RELEASE

CARE: NOT APPLICABLE

HARM CAUSED TO PLAINTIFF &/OR PATIENT:
1. ECONOMIC LOSS

TYPE OF ACTION BROUGHT:
1. NEGLIGENCE

HISTORY OF THE CASE:

TYPE OF COURT: STATE

TRIER OF FACT: JUDGE;JURY PRESENT ?

COURT DECISION(S):

TRIAL COURT: FOR DEFENDANT
YEAR: 1975

REASON SUIT FAILED:
1. DEFENDANT(S) CANNOT BE SUED DUE TO: GOVERN. IMMUNITY

119. HENDLER V. STATE

IN MAY, 1954 DAVID MICHEL WAS ADMITTED TO THE MIDDLETOWN STATE HOSPITAL IN MIDDLETOWN, NEW YORK, A STATE INSTITUTION UNDER THE SUPERVISION OF THE MENTAL HYGIENE DEPARTMENT. HE WAS DIAGNOSED AS SUFFERING FROM DEMENTIA PRAECOX, SIMPLE TYPE. IN JUNE, DAVID WAS PLACED WITH CLIVE FRANKS UNDER THE FAMILY CARE PROGRAM AT FRANKS' FARM IN HARVARD, NEW YORK. UNDER THAT PROGRAM, DAVID WAS ENCOURAGED TO DO WORK AROUND THE FARM; SOCIAL WORKERS FROM THE HOSPITAL PERIODICALLY CHECKED ON HIS PROGRESS. ON NOVEMBER 5, 1957, FRANKS ALLOWED DAVID TO SAW WOOD WITH A MOTOR-DRIVEN BUZZ SAW. DAVID HAD WATCHED FRANKS USE THE SAW IN THE PAST, BUT HAD NEVER BEEN TAUGHT HOW TO USE IT. AS HE BEGAN SAWING FOR THE FIRST TIME, A CHUNK OF WOOD HIT HIM IN THE FACE, NOSE, AND LEFT EYE. SUBSEQUENTLY, DAVID UNDERWENT OPERATIONS TO REPAIR HIS NOSE AND TO REPLACE HIS EYE WITH AN ARTIFICIAL ONE. AARON HENDLER BROUGHT SUIT ON BEHALF OF MICHEL, ALLEGING THAT THE STATE HAD FAILED TO PROVIDE ADEQUATE SUPERVISION.

YEAR OF NEGLIGENT ACT: 1957

STATE IN WHICH NEGLIGENT ACT OCCURRED: NEW YORK

SETTING OF THE CASE: FARM

PLAINTIFF(S): PATIENT(S) OR REP.

DEFENDANT(S):
1. STATE GOV. &/OR OFFICIALS, ETC.

NEGLIGENT ACTIVITY:

TREATMENT: NOT APPLICABLE

DIAGNOSIS:

WHAT WAS DIAGNOSED: NOT APPLICABLE

RESULT OF DIAGNOSIS: NOT APPLICABLE

CARE:
1. INADEQUATE SUPERVISION
2. FAILURE TO PROVIDE PROPER CUSTODIAL CARE

HARM CAUSED TO PLAINTIFF &/OR PATIENT:
1. NONSELF-INFLICTED INJURIES

TYPE OF ACTION BROUGHT:
1. NEGLIGENCE

HISTORY OF THE CASE:

TYPE OF COURT: STATE

TRIER OF FACT: JUDGE,NO JURY

COURT DECISION(S):

TRIAL COURT: FOR PLAINTIFF
YEAR: 1962

VERDICT AGAINST WHICH DEFENDANTS:
1. STATE GOV. &/OR OFFICIALS, ETC.

RECOVERY OR OTHER RELIEF GRANTED:
1. $ 15000

120. HENDRY V. UNITED STATES

ERNEST J. HENDRY WAS A LICENSED DESK OFFICER IN THE UNITED STATES MERCHANT MARINE. AFTER A HISTORY OF COMPLAINTS AGAINST FELLOW CREWMEN AND CAPTAIN, ERNEST COMPLAINED TO THE COAST GUARD IN PHILADELPHIA THAT HE HAD BEEN ASSAULTED BY THE CAPTAIN. THE COMPLAINT WAS INVESTIGATED AND FOUND TO BE UNTRUE. ERNEST WAS ASKED TO VOLUNTARILY SUSPEND HIMSELF FROM DUTY UNTIL A PSYCHIATRIC EXAMINATION COULD BE PERFORMED TO ASSURE THAT HE WAS FIT FOR DUTY. HE WAS EXAMINED BY DR. CARLOS RAMIREZ, WHO FOUND HIM SANE AND FIT FOR DUTY, ALTHOUGH HE ALSO SUSPECTED THAT ERNEST HAD A PSYCHIATRIC PROBLEM INVOLVING A PERSONALITY DISTURBANCE. HE WAS THEREFORE REFERRED TO A PSYCHOLOGIST. ON THE BASIS OF THIS SECOND DOCTOR'S REPORT, DR. RAMIREZ FOUND ERNEST TO BE A NON-PSYCHOTIC PARANOID SCHIZOPHRENIC. ERNEST COMPLAINED TO THE UNION, WHICH HIRED ANOTHER PSYCHIATRIST WHO FOUND HIM FIT FOR DUTY. THE COAST GUARD ORDERED STILL ANOTHER EXAMINATION WHICH REACHED THE SAME RESULT AND ERNEST'S SUSPENSION WAS ENDED. HENDRY SUED THE UNITED STATES FOR THE ALLEGEDLY NEGLIGENT DIAGNOSIS OF THE PSYCHIATRIST AND PSYCHOLOGIST.

YEAR OF NEGLIGENT ACT: 1962

STATE IN WHICH NEGLIGENT ACT OCCURRED: NEW YORK

SETTING OF THE CASE: ARMED SERVICE

PLAINTIFF(S): PATIENT(S) OR REP.

DEFENDANT(S):
1. FEDERAL GOV. &/OR OFFICIALS, ETC.

NEGLIGENT ACTIVITY:

TREATMENT: NOT APPLICABLE

DIAGNOSIS:

WHAT WAS DIAGNOSED:
1. TYPE OF MENTAL ILLNESS
2. UNFITNESS FOR DUTY

RESULT OF DIAGNOSIS:
1. NEG. DETERM.OF UNFITNESS FOR DUTY

CARE: NOT APPLICABLE

HARM CAUSED TO PLAINTIFF &/OR PATIENT:
1. EMOTIONAL DISTRESS
2. ECONOMIC LOSS

TYPE OF ACTION BROUGHT:
1. NEGLIGENCE

HISTORY OF THE CASE:

TYPE OF COURT: FEDERAL

TRIER OF FACT: JUDGE;JURY PRESENT ?

COURT DECISION(S):

TRIAL COURT: FOR DEFENDANT
YEAR: 1968
APPELLATE COURT: FOR DEFENDANT
YEAR: 1969

REASON SUIT FAILED:
1. NEGLIGENCE OR CASE NOT PROVEN
2. DEFENDANT(S) CANNOT BE SUED DUE TO: GOVERN. IMMUNITY

121. HERNANDEZ V. STATE OF CALIFORNIA

IN JUNE 1968, MR. HERNANDEZ WAS RELEASED FROM THE CAMARILLO STATE HOSPITAL, ALLEGEDLY IN A DANGEROUSLY DISTURBED CONDITION. TWO MONTHS LATER HE ASSAULTED AND KILLED HIS MOTHER, MRS. LUZ LEYBA HERNANDEZ. HER HEIRS CHARGED THE HOSPITAL WITH NEGLIGENCE IN RECORD-KEEPING LEADING TO THE IMPROPER RELEASE OF HERNANDEZ.

YEAR OF NEGLIGENT ACT: 1968

STATE IN WHICH NEGLIGENT ACT OCCURRED: CALIFORNIA

SETTING OF THE CASE: PUB. MENT. HOSP.

PLAINTIFF(S): 3RD PARTY, II

DEFENDANT(S):
1. STATE GOV. &/OR OFFICIALS, ETC.

NEGLIGENT ACTIVITY:

TREATMENT: NOT APPLICABLE

DIAGNOSIS:

WHAT WAS DIAGNOSED: NOT APPLICABLE

RESULT OF DIAGNOSIS: NOT APPLICABLE

CARE:
1. PREMATURE RELEASE
2. FAILURE TO PROVIDE PROPER CUSTODIAL CARE

HARM CAUSED TO PLAINTIFF &/OR PATIENT:
1. NONSUICIDAL DEATH

TYPE OF ACTION BROUGHT:
1. NEGLIGENCE

HISTORY OF THE CASE:

TYPE OF COURT: STATE

TRIER OF FACT: JUDGE;JURY PRESENT ?

COURT DECISION(S):

TRIAL COURT: FOR DEFENDANT
YEAR: NOT SPECIFIED
APPELLATE COURT: FOR DEFENDANT
YEAR: 1970

REASON SUIT FAILED:
1. DEFENDANT(S) CANNOT BE SUED DUE TO: GOVERN. IMMUNITY

122. HERNANDEZ V. STATE OF NEW YORK

ERNEST HERNANDEZ, AGE TWENTY, WAS A PATIENT AT MANHATTAN STATE HOSPITAL. ERNEST WAS IN A CLOSED WARD BECAUSE OF THREE ESCAPE ATTEMPTS AND HIS CONTINUED INTENTIONS OF ESCAPE. ON JUNE 29, 1969 HE TRIED AGAIN, THIS TIME BY TYING BEDSHEETS TO A RADIATOR PIPE AND LOWERING HIMSELF OUT THROUGH A WINDOW. HE FELL SEVERAL STORIES AND SUSTAINED SEVERE INJURIES; HIS FAMILY CHARGED THAT THE HOSPITAL HAD NOT TAKEN SUFFICIENT PRECAUTIONS IN PROTECTING ERNEST.

YEAR OF NEGLIGENT ACT: 1969

STATE IN WHICH NEGLIGENT ACT OCCURRED: NEW YORK

SETTING OF THE CASE: PUB. MENT. HOSP.

PLAINTIFF(S): PATIENT(S) OR REP.

DEFENDANT(S):
1. STATE GOV. &/OR OFFICIALS, ETC.

NEGLIGENT ACTIVITY:

TREATMENT: NOT APPLICABLE

DIAGNOSIS:

WHAT WAS DIAGNOSED: NOT APPLICABLE

RESULT OF DIAGNOSIS: NOT APPLICABLE

CARE:
1. INADEQUATE SUPERVISION

HARM CAUSED TO PLAINTIFF &/OR PATIENT:
1. NONSELF-INFLICTED INJURIES

TYPE OF ACTION BROUGHT:
1. NEGLIGENCE

HISTORY OF THE CASE:

TYPE OF COURT: STATE

TRIER OF FACT: JUDGE,NO JURY

COURT DECISION(S):

TRIAL COURT: FOR DEFENDANT
YEAR: 1972
APPELLATE COURT: FOR DEFENDANT
YEAR: 1974

REASON SUIT FAILED:
1. NEGLIGENCE OR CASE NOT PROVEN

123. HICKS V. UNITED STATES

JOSEPH MORGAN HAD BEATEN HIS WIFE AND DRUNK HEAVILY FOR MANY YEARS, AT TIMES THREATENING TO KILL HER. AFTER ONE EPISODE SHE CALLED THE POLICE, AS SHE HAD DONE MANY TIMES IN THE PAST. A PSYCHIATRIC EXAMINATION RESULTED IN JOSEPH'S COMMITMENT TO ST. ELIZABETH'S HOSPITAL, WHERE HE WAS DIAGNOSED AS HAVING A MODERATELY SEVERE ORGANIC BRAIN SYNDROME DUE TO BRAIN DAMAGE PROBABLY CAUSED BY PROLONGED, EXCESSIVE DRINKING. THE HOSPITAL DECLARED JOSEPH COMPETENT ENOUGH TO STAND TRIAL FOR ASSAULT, BUT THE CHARGES WERE DROPPED WHEN MRS. MORGAN, WHO WAS NOT AWARE THAT HE HAD BEEN RELEASED, MISSED THE TRIAL. JOSEPH WAS ARRESTED TWO DAYS LATER FOR INTOXICATION, BUT WAS RELEASED TO OUTPATIENT STATUS. LESS THAN A MONTH LATER, WHEN HE FINALLY WENT HOME, MRS. MORGAN TOLD HIM THAT HE COULD NOT STAY. JOSEPH THEN SHOT AND KILLED HER. HER FAMILY CHARGED THAT THE UNITED STATES WAS RESPONSIBLE FOR THE NEGLIGENCE OF ST. ELIZABETH'S IN NOT SUPPLYING THE COURT WITH ENOUGH DETAIL TO INTELLIGENTLY DECIDE WHAT TO DO WITH JOSEPH.

YEAR OF NEGLIGENT ACT: 1966

STATE IN WHICH NEGLIGENT ACT OCCURRED: DISTRICT OF COLUMBIA

SETTING OF THE CASE: PUB. MENT. HOSP.

PLAINTIFF(S): 3RD PARTY, I & II

DEFENDANT(S):
1. FEDERAL GOV. &/OR OFFICIALS, ETC.

NEGLIGENT ACTIVITY:

TREATMENT: NOT APPLICABLE

DIAGNOSIS:

WHAT WAS DIAGNOSED:
1. LACK OF DANGEROUSNESS

RESULT OF DIAGNOSIS:
1. IMPROPER RELEASE

CARE: NOT APPLICABLE

HARM CAUSED TO PLAINTIFF &/OR PATIENT:
1. NONSUICIDAL DEATH

TYPE OF ACTION BROUGHT:
1. NEGLIGENCE

HISTORY OF THE CASE:

TYPE OF COURT: FEDERAL

TRIER OF FACT: JUDGE;JURY PRESENT ?

COURT DECISION(S):

TRIAL COURT: FOR PLAINTIFF
YEAR: NOT SPECIFIED
APPELLATE COURT: FOR PLAINTIFF
YEAR: 1975

VERDICT AGAINST WHICH DEFENDANTS:
1. FEDERAL GOV. &/OR OFFICIALS, ETC.

RECOVERY OR OTHER RELIEF GRANTED:
1. $100000

124. HIGGINS V. STATE

ROBERT HIGGINS, JR., AN INFANT, WAS ASSAULTED IN A PARK IN BUFFALO, NEW YORK, BY A BUFFALO STATE HOSPITAL PATIENT. AFTER TWELVE YEARS IN THE HOSPITAL, THE PATIENT HAD BEEN PLACED ON OPEN WARD STATUS, WHICH ALLOWED HIM ACCESS TO THE AREA SURROUNDING THE HOSPITAL, INCLUDING THE PARK, ON HIS OWN RECOGNIZANCE. THE RECORD INDICATES NOTHING IN HIS PAST HISTORY WHICH WOULD HAVE ALLOWED THE PREDICTION OF THIS VIOLENT BEHAVIOR.

YEAR OF NEGLIGENT ACT: 1962

STATE IN WHICH NEGLIGENT ACT OCCURRED: NEW YORK

SETTING OF THE CASE: PUB. MENT. HOSP.

PLAINTIFF(S): 3RD PARTY, II

DEFENDANT(S):
1. STATE GOV. &/OR OFFICIALS, ETC.

NEGLIGENT ACTIVITY:

TREATMENT: NOT APPLICABLE

DIAGNOSIS:

WHAT WAS DIAGNOSED:
1. SANITY, INSTEAD OF MENTAL ILLNESS
2. LACK OF DANGEROUSNESS
3. FAILURE TO MAKE A DIAGNOSIS

RESULT OF DIAGNOSIS:
1. IMPROPER CUSTODIAL CARE

CARE:
1. INADEQUATE SUPERVISION

HARM CAUSED TO PLAINTIFF &/OR PATIENT:
1. NONSELF-INFLICTED INJURIES

TYPE OF ACTION BROUGHT:
1. ASSAULT

HISTORY OF THE CASE:

TYPE OF COURT: STATE

TRIER OF FACT: JUDGE,NO JURY

COURT DECISION(S):

TRIAL COURT: FOR PLAINTIFF
YEAR: NOT SPECIFIED
APPELLATE COURT: FOR DEFENDANT
YEAR: 1965

REASON SUIT FAILED:
1. DEFENDANT(S) CANNOT BE SUED DUE TO: GOVERN. IMMUNITY

125. HIRSH V. STATE

IRVING S. HIRSH, A RUSSIAN IMMIGRANT, SUFFERED FROM MENTAL ILLNESSES DIAGNOSED AT DIFFERENT TIMES AS MANIC-DEPRESSIVE-HYPOMANIC PHASE; DEMENTIA PRAECOX, PARANOID TYPE; AND DEMENTIA PRAECOX, CATATONIC TYPE. AFTER SEVEN YEARS OF ILLNESS AND TWO OF TREATMENT, IRVING WAS DECLARED TO HAVE RECOVERED. DURING THIS FIRST PHASE OF ILLNESS, IRVING OFTEN ESCAPED FROM THOSE HOSPITALS IN WHICH HE WAS COMMITTED. TWELVE YEARS LATER, IRVING WAS AGAIN DIAGNOSED AS PSYCHOTIC AND COMMITTED. AFTER HIS SECOND RELEASE HE BECAME DEPRESSED AND SPOKE OF SUICIDE. FOUR MONTHS LATER, HE WAS ADMITTED TO HIGH POINT HOSPITAL, WHERE HE UNDERWENT INTENSIVE PSYCHOTHERAPY. DURING THIS TIME HE ESCAPED ONCE AND ALSO ATTEMPTED SUICIDE TWICE, ONCE BY HANGING AND ONCE BY A BARBITURATE OVER-DOSE. HE WAS TRANSFERRED TO BROOKLYN STATE HOSPITAL, DIAGNOSED AS DEMENTIA PRAECOX, PARANOID TYPE, AND PLACED IN A SUICIDE WARD. IRVING, BY SOME UNKNOWN METHOD, OBTAINED AT LEAST TWELVE TO FIFTEEN SECONAL TABLETS AND COMMITTED SUICIDE. ALICE HIRSH, THE ADMINISTRATOR OF HIS ESTATE, BROUGHT SUIT.

YEAR OF NEGLIGENT ACT: 1953

STATE IN WHICH NEGLIGENT ACT OCCURRED: NEW YORK

SETTING OF THE CASE: PUB. MENT. HOSP.

PLAINTIFF(S): PATIENT(S) OR REP.

DEFENDANT(S):
1. STATE GOV. &/OR OFFICIALS, ETC.

NEGLIGENT ACTIVITY:

TREATMENT: NOT APPLICABLE

DIAGNOSIS:

WHAT WAS DIAGNOSED: NOT APPLICABLE

RESULT OF DIAGNOSIS: NOT APPLICABLE

CARE:
1. INADEQUATE SUPERVISION

HARM CAUSED TO PLAINTIFF &/OR PATIENT:
1. SUICIDE

TYPE OF ACTION BROUGHT:
1. NEGLIGENCE

HISTORY OF THE CASE:

TYPE OF COURT: STATE

TRIER OF FACT: JUDGE,NO JURY

COURT DECISION(S):

TRIAL COURT: FOR PLAINTIFF
YEAR: 1959
APPELLATE COURT: FOR PLAINTIFF
YEAR: 1959
SUPREME COURT: FOR DEFENDANT
YEAR: 1960

REASON SUIT FAILED:
1. NEGLIGENCE OR CASE NOT PROVEN

126. HOMERE V. STATE

MELVIN SAMUELS, AN UNEDUCATED, BORDERLINE MENTAL RETARDATE WITH A PAST HISTORY OF VIOLENT, UNPROVOKED ASSAULTS AGAINST FEMALES, WAS A VOLUNTARY PATIENT AT PILGRIM STATE HOSPITAL IN NEW YORK. ON FEBRUARY 7, 1972, A SPECIAL COMMISSION OF THREE PSYCHIATRISTS DECLARED MELVIN SAFE TO BE DISCHARGED. ABOUT TWO WEEKS LATER MELVIN BECAME VIOLENT AND WAS RECOMMITTED. HE WAS DISCHARGED ABOUT ONE MONTH LATER WITHOUT A FURTHER EVALUATION OF HIS CONDITION. HE WAS RELEASED AT THE AQUEDUCT SUBWAY STATION IN QUEENS AND TOLD TO GO TO MANHATTAN. THAT DAY MELVIN ASSAULTED FIVE WOMEN IN THE SUBWAY, PUSHING ONE OF THEM ONTO THE TRACKS AND SLAPPING ANOTHER IN THE HEAD. TWO OF THE WOMEN CHARGED THE HOSPITAL WITH NEGLIGENCE.

YEAR OF NEGLIGENT ACT: 1972

STATE IN WHICH NEGLIGENT ACT OCCURRED: NEW YORK

SETTING OF THE CASE: PUB. MENT. HOSP.

PLAINTIFF(S): 3RD PARTY, II

DEFENDANT(S):
1. STATE GOV. &/OR OFFICIALS, ETC.

NEGLIGENT ACTIVITY:

TREATMENT: NOT APPLICABLE

DIAGNOSIS:

WHAT WAS DIAGNOSED:
1. LACK OF DANGEROUSNESS

RESULT OF DIAGNOSIS:
1. IMPROPER RELEASE

CARE: NOT APPLICABLE

HARM CAUSED TO PLAINTIFF &/OR PATIENT:
1. NONSELF-INFLICTED INJURIES

TYPE OF ACTION BROUGHT:
1. NEGLIGENCE

HISTORY OF THE CASE:

TYPE OF COURT: STATE

TRIER OF FACT: JUDGE,NO JURY

COURT DECISION(S):

TRIAL COURT: FOR PLAINTIFF
YEAR: 1974
APPELLATE COURT: FOR PLAINTIFF
YEAR: 1975

VERDICT AGAINST WHICH DEFENDANTS:
1. STATE GOV. &/OR OFFICIALS, ETC.

RECOVERY OR OTHER RELIEF GRANTED:
1. OTHER RECOVERY: NOT SPECIFIED

127. HOUGH V. OGDEN

ESTHER E. HOUGH WAS TAKEN FROM THE BERGEN COUNTY JAIL TO THE STATE HOSPITAL FOR THE INSANE AT MORRIS PLAINS, NEW JERSEY, AND KEPT THERE FOR THREE WEEKS. ESTHER CHARGED THE PHYSICIANS UPON WHOSE SIGNED TESTIMONY SHE WAS DECLARED INSANE (INCLUDING DR. WILLIAM E. OGDEN) WITH CONSPIRACY AND WRONGFUL COMMITMENT. FURTHER INFORMATION DOES NOT APPEAR IN THE COURT RECORD.

YEAR OF NEGLIGENT ACT: 1918

STATE IN WHICH NEGLIGENT ACT OCCURRED: NEW JERSEY

SETTING OF THE CASE: JUDICIAL PROCEEDING

PLAINTIFF(S): PATIENT(S) OR REP.

DEFENDANT(S):
1. NONPSYCHIAT.OR UNKNOWN TYPE PHYSICIAN(S)

NEGLIGENT ACTIVITY:

TREATMENT: NOT APPLICABLE

DIAGNOSIS:

WHAT WAS DIAGNOSED:
1. MENTAL ILLNESS, INSTEAD OF SANITY

RESULT OF DIAGNOSIS:
1. IMPROPER COMMITMENT

CARE: NOT APPLICABLE

HARM CAUSED TO PLAINTIFF &/OR PATIENT:
1. NOT SPECIFIED

TYPE OF ACTION BROUGHT:
1. OTHER TORT(S): WRONGFUL COMMITMENT

HISTORY OF THE CASE:

TYPE OF COURT: STATE

TRIER OF FACT: JURY

COURT DECISION(S):

TRIAL COURT: FOR PLAINTIFF
YEAR: NOT SPECIFIED
SUPREME COURT: FOR PLAINTIFF
YEAR: 1926

VERDICT AGAINST WHICH DEFENDANTS:
1. NONPSYCHIAT.OR UNKNOWN TYPE PHYSICIAN(S)

RECOVERY OR OTHER RELIEF GRANTED:
1. $ 3000

128. HUNGERFORD V. UNITED STATES

VICTOR M. HUNGERFORD, JR., WAS DISHONORABLY DISCHARGED FROM THE UNITED STATES ARMY IN 1953 FOR BEING AWOL. IN 1950, WHILE SERVING IN KOREA, VICTOR HAD BEEN WOUNDED IN COMBAT AND SUBSEQUENTLY SUFFERED FROM BLACKOUTS, SEVERE HEAD PAINS, AND UNACCOUNTABLE FALLS. IN 1957 HE WENT TO THE BEACON HILL VETERANS ADMINISTRATION HOSPITAL IN SEATTLE, WASHINGTON, AND HIS CONDITION WAS DIAGNOSED AS PSYCHOSOMATIC. DURING THE NEXT TWO YEARS VICTOR WAS ARRESTED SEVERAL TIMES FOR PASSING FORGED CHECKS; ON TWO SUCH OCCASIONS, HE WAS SENT TO CALIFORNIA STATE HOSPITALS FOR OBSERVATION. FINALLY, ON MARCH 9, 1959, VICTOR WAS CONVICTED OF PASSING FORGED CHECKS AND COMMITTED TO THE CALIFORNIA MEDICAL FACILITY IN VACAVILLE, CALIFORNIA. AFTER TESTS THE DOCTORS DISCOVERED THAT VICTOR HAD AN ORGANIC BRAIN INJURY OF TRAUMATIC ORIGIN. SURGERY WAS SUCCESSFULLY PERFORMED AND HE WAS PAROLED ON APRIL 4, 1960. VICTOR CHARGED THE VETERANS HOSPITAL WITH NEGLIGENCE IN FAILING TO PERFORM THE PROPER DIAGNOSTIC TESTS TO DETECT HIS TRUE CONDITION.

YEAR OF NEGLIGENT ACT: 1957

STATE IN WHICH NEGLIGENT ACT OCCURRED: WASHINGTON

SETTING OF THE CASE: PUB. GEN. HOSP.

PLAINTIFF(S): PATIENT(S) OR REP.

DEFENDANT(S):
1. FEDERAL GOV. &/OR OFFICIALS, ETC.

NEGLIGENT ACTIVITY:

TREATMENT:
1. NO TREATMENT OR INADEQUATE TREATMENT

DIAGNOSIS:

WHAT WAS DIAGNOSED:
1. MENT.ILL, INSTEAD OF PHYSICAL ILLNESS

RESULT OF DIAGNOSIS:
1. IMPROPER TREATMENT PRESCRIBED

CARE: NOT APPLICABLE

HARM CAUSED TO PLAINTIFF &/OR PATIENT:
1. NOT SPECIFIED

TYPE OF ACTION BROUGHT:
1. NEGLIGENCE

HISTORY OF THE CASE:

TYPE OF COURT: FEDERAL

TRIER OF FACT: JUDGE;JURY PRESENT ?

COURT DECISION(S):

TRIAL COURT: FOR DEFENDANT
YEAR: NOT SPECIFIED
APPELLATE COURT: NONFINAL FOR PL.
YEAR: 1962

DEFENDANTS STILL INVOLVED IN SUIT:
1. FEDERAL GOV. &/OR OFFICIALS, ETC.

129. HUNT V. KING COUNTY

JEROME B. HUNT, AGE TWENTY, HAD A DRUG PROBLEM FOR WHICH DOCTORS RECOMMENDED COMMITMENT TO HARBORVIEW HOSPITAL IN SEATTLE, WASHINGTON. JEROME OBJECTED AND LOCKED HIMSELF IN THE BASEMENT OF HIS PARENTS' HOUSE, SUBSEQUENTLY DESTROYING WHAT WAS IN THE BASEMENT WITH A PICK. HIS FATHER CALLED THE POLICE, WHO SECURELY BOUND HIM AND FORCIBLY TOOK HIM TO HARBORVIEW HOSPITAL BY AMBULANCE. AT MR. HUNT'S URGINGS, JEROME WAS PLACED IN A CLOSED WARD. DOCTORS DIAGNOSED HIM AS SUFFERING FROM AN ACUTE SCHIZOPHRENIC BREAK. THREE DAYS LATER JEROME WENT INTO AN UNLOCKED UTILITY ROOM AND JUMPED OUT THE WINDOW. AFTER FALLING FIVE STORIES TO THE GROUND, JEROME WAS VERY CONSCIOUS, VERY HOSTILE, AND VERY BELLIGERENT. THE EXAMINING DOCTOR SAID THAT HE APPEARED TO BE PSYCHOTIC AND SUICIDAL. JEROME'S FAMILY BROUGHT SUIT, CHARGING THE HOSPITAL WITH NEGLIGENCE IN LEAVING THE UTILITY ROOM UNLOCKED.

YEAR OF NEGLIGENT ACT: 1967

STATE IN WHICH NEGLIGENT ACT OCCURRED: WASHINGTON

SETTING OF THE CASE: PUB. GEN. HOSP.

PLAINTIFF(S): PAT. & 3RD PTY., I

DEFENDANT(S):
1. MUNICIPAL GOV. &/OR OFFICIALS, ETC.

NEGLIGENT ACTIVITY:

TREATMENT: NOT APPLICABLE

DIAGNOSIS:

WHAT WAS DIAGNOSED: NOT APPLICABLE

RESULT OF DIAGNOSIS: NOT APPLICABLE

CARE:
1. INADEQUATE SUPERVISION

HARM CAUSED TO PLAINTIFF &/OR PATIENT:
1. SELF-INFLICTED INJURIES

TYPE OF ACTION BROUGHT:
1. NEGLIGENCE

HISTORY OF THE CASE:

TYPE OF COURT: STATE

TRIER OF FACT: JURY

COURT DECISION(S):

TRIAL COURT: FOR PLAINTIFF
YEAR: NOT SPECIFIED
APPELLATE COURT: FOR PLAINTIFF
YEAR: 1971

VERDICT AGAINST WHICH DEFENDANTS:
1. MUNICIPAL GOV. &/OR OFFICIALS, ETC.

RECOVERY OR OTHER RELIEF GRANTED:
1. OTHER RECOVERY: NOT SPECIFIED

130. IN RE ANONYMOUS

THIS CASE WAS BROUGHT TO DETERMINE THE CONSTITUTIONALITY OF SECTION 29.13 OF THE NEW YORK MENTAL HYGIENE LAW. ANONYMOUS WAS A PATIENT AT MANHATTAN STATE HOSPITAL WHO HAD COMMITTED SEVERAL ASSAULTS WHILE IN THE HOSPITAL. AS A RESULT HE HAD BEEN DEEMED "DANGEROUSLY MENTALLY ILL" UNDER THE STATUTE AND THE JUDGE ORDERED HIM HOSPITALIZED IN MATTEAWAN STATE HOSPITAL, A CORRECTIONAL FACILITY PRIMARILY FOR MENTALLY ILL CONVICTED CRIMINALS. ANONYMOUS HAD NEVER BEEN CONVICTED OF ANY CRIME AND OBJECTED TO HIS TRANSFER ON THE GROUNDS THAT HE WAS NOT "DANGEROUSLY MENTALLY ILL" AND, EVEN IF HE WERE, HIS TRANSFER WOULD BE A VIOLATION OF THE EQUAL PROTECTION AND DUE PROCESS CLAUSES OF THE STATE AND FEDERAL CONSTITUTIONS.

YEAR OF NEGLIGENT ACT: 1972

STATE IN WHICH NEGLIGENT ACT OCCURRED: NEW YORK

SETTING OF THE CASE: JUDICIAL PROCEEDING

PLAINTIFF(S): PATIENT(S) OR REP.

DEFENDANT(S):
1. HOSPITAL &/OR OWNERS, ETC.

NEGLIGENT ACTIVITY:

TREATMENT:
1. NO TREATMENT OR INADEQUATE TREATMENT

DIAGNOSIS:

WHAT WAS DIAGNOSED:
1. DANGEROUSNESS

RESULT OF DIAGNOSIS:
1. IMPROPER CUSTODIAL CARE

CARE: NOT APPLICABLE

HARM CAUSED TO PLAINTIFF &/OR PATIENT:
1. DEPRIVATION OF CONSTITUTIONAL RIGHTS

TYPE OF ACTION BROUGHT:
1. DEPRIVATION OF CONSTITUTIONAL RIGHTS: RIGHT TO TREATMENT
2. NONMONETARY RELIEF

HISTORY OF THE CASE:

TYPE OF COURT: STATE

TRIER OF FACT: JUDGE,NO JURY

COURT DECISION(S):

TRIAL COURT: FOR PLAINTIFF
YEAR: 1972
APPELLATE COURT: FOR DEFENDANT
YEAR: 1972
SUPREME COURT: FOR PLAINTIFF
YEAR: 1973

VERDICT AGAINST WHICH DEFENDANTS:
1. HOSPITAL &/OR OWNERS, ETC.

RECOVERY OR OTHER RELIEF GRANTED:
1. NONMONETARY RELIEF: INJ.OR OTHER EQ.REL.

131. IN RE MADDOX

EMBRA MADDOX CONTENDED THAT HIS CONVICTION UNDER THE MICH. SEXUAL PSYCHOPATH LAW AROSE OUT OF THE FACT THAT AS A BLACK MAN HE HAD MARRIED A WHITE WOMAN. AFTER HIS CONVICTION HE WAS PLACED IN IONIA STATE HOSPITAL FOR TREATMENT; HE WAS LATER TRANSFERRED TO THE STATE PRISON OF SOUTHERN MICHIGAN IN ORDER TO LEARN "SELF-DISCIPLINE." MADDOX CLAIMED THAT HE WAS HOUSED WITH CONVICTED CRIMINALS AND TREATED AS ONE WITHOUT BEING PROVIDED THERAPY. MADDOX ALSO CLAIMED THAT HIS CONFINEMENT WAS UNCONSTITUTIONAL BECAUSE HE WAS DENIED THE RIGHT OF TRIAL BEFORE CONFINEMENT IN A PENAL INSTITUTION.

YEAR OF NEGLIGENT ACT: NOT SPECIFIED

STATE IN WHICH NEGLIGENT ACT OCCURRED: MICHIGAN

SETTING OF THE CASE: JUDICIAL PROCEEDING

PLAINTIFF(S): PATIENT(S) OR REP.

DEFENDANT(S):
1. STATE GOV. &/OR OFFICIALS, ETC.

NEGLIGENT ACTIVITY:

TREATMENT:
1. NO TREATMENT OR INADEQUATE TREATMENT

DIAGNOSIS:

WHAT WAS DIAGNOSED:
1. DANGEROUSNESS

RESULT OF DIAGNOSIS:
1. IMPROPER CUSTODIAL CARE

CARE: NOT APPLICABLE

HARM CAUSED TO PLAINTIFF &/OR PATIENT:
1. DEPRIVATION OF CONSTITUTIONAL RIGHTS

TYPE OF ACTION BROUGHT:
1. DEPRIVATION OF CONSTITUTIONAL RIGHTS: RIGHT TO TREATMENT
2. HABEAS CORPUS

HISTORY OF THE CASE:

TYPE OF COURT: STATE

TRIER OF FACT: JUDGE,NO JURY

COURT DECISION(S):

TRIAL COURT: FOR DEFENDANT
YEAR: NOT SPECIFIED
SUPREME COURT: FOR PLAINTIFF
YEAR: 1958

VERDICT AGAINST WHICH DEFENDANTS:

RECOVERY OR OTHER RELIEF GRANTED:
1. NONMONETARY RELIEF: INJ.OR OTHER EQ.REL.

132. IN RE PIERRE'S ESTATE

PIERRE WAS A NATIVE OF TRINIDAD, CONFINED TO KINGS PARK STATE HOSPITAL WITH A DIAGNOSIS OF "SCHIZOPHRENIC, HEBEPHRENIC TYPE." AT THE BEGINNING OF HIS STAY PIERRE WAS UNCOOPERATIVE AND DEMANDED HIS RELEASE, BUT LATER MADE A SATISFACTORY ADJUSTMENT AND WORKED QUIETLY AT THE WARD. HIS VIOLENT TENDENCIES REAPPEARED, HOWEVER, WHEN HE WAS VISITED BY A U.S. INSPECTION OFFICER WHO ORDERED HIM DEPORTED TO TRINIDAD. PIERRE BECAME SCHIZOPHRENIC AND THE PSYCHIATRIST ON HIS WARD HAD HIM PUT UNDER CLOSE SUPERVISION. WHEN THIS PSYCHIATRIST WAS ABSENT, A SECOND ALLOWED PIERRE TO EAT WITH THE OTHER PATIENTS. PIERRE MANAGED TO BREAK AWAY AND WAS FOUND A FEW MINUTES LATER ON THE GROUND, HAVING FALLEN OR JUMPED OFF THE BUILDING. HE DIED WITHIN AN HOUR.

YEAR OF NEGLIGENT ACT: 1948

STATE IN WHICH NEGLIGENT ACT OCCURRED: NEW YORK

SETTING OF THE CASE: PUB. MENT. HOSP.

PLAINTIFF(S): PATIENT(S) OR REP.

DEFENDANT(S):
1. STATE GOV. &/OR OFFICIALS, ETC.

NEGLIGENT ACTIVITY:

TREATMENT: NOT APPLICABLE

DIAGNOSIS:

WHAT WAS DIAGNOSED:
1. LACK OF SUICIDAL TENDENCIES

RESULT OF DIAGNOSIS:
1. IMPROPER CUSTODIAL CARE

CARE:
1. INADEQUATE SUPERVISION

HARM CAUSED TO PLAINTIFF &/OR PATIENT:
1. SUICIDE

TYPE OF ACTION BROUGHT:
1. NEGLIGENCE

HISTORY OF THE CASE:

TYPE OF COURT: STATE

TRIER OF FACT: JUDGE,NO JURY

COURT DECISION(S):

TRIAL COURT: FOR PLAINTIFF
YEAR: 1955
APPELLATE COURT: FOR DEFENDANT
YEAR: 1955

REASON SUIT FAILED:
1. NEGLIGENCE OR CASE NOT PROVEN

133. IN RE WARRINGTON

THE DETAILS OF THE INCIDENT ARE NOT NOTED IN ANY OF THE REPORTED DECISIONS. THE PLAINTIFF BROUGHT SUIT ON BEHALF OF AN INCOMPETENT PERSON CONFINED AT KINGS PARK STATE HOSPITAL, WHO FELL TO THE GROUND FROM A FOURTH-FLOOR DOORWAY, SUFFERING PERMANENT INJURIES. IN THE INSTANT CASE, SUIT WAS BROUGHT OVER THE RIGHT OF PLAINTIFF TO EXAMINE HOSPITAL RECORDS UNDER THE MENTAL HYGIENE LAW OF NEW YORK.

YEAR OF NEGLIGENT ACT: 1945

STATE IN WHICH NEGLIGENT ACT OCCURRED: NEW YORK

SETTING OF THE CASE: PUB. MENT. HOSP.

PLAINTIFF(S): PATIENT(S) OR REP.

DEFENDANT(S):
1. HOSPITAL &/OR OWNERS, ETC.

NEGLIGENT ACTIVITY:

TREATMENT:
1. ? WHETHER TREAT.INV.

DIAGNOSIS:

WHAT WAS DIAGNOSED:
1. ? WHETHER DIAG.INV.

RESULT OF DIAGNOSIS: NOT APPLICABLE

CARE:
1. ? WHETHER CARE INV.

HARM CAUSED TO PLAINTIFF &/OR PATIENT:
1. NONSELF-INFLICTED INJURIES

TYPE OF ACTION BROUGHT:
1. NONMONETARY RELIEF

HISTORY OF THE CASE:

TYPE OF COURT: STATE

TRIER OF FACT: JUDGE,NO JURY

COURT DECISION(S):

TRIAL COURT: NONFINAL FOR PL.
YEAR: NOT SPECIFIED
APPELLATE COURT: NONFINAL FOR PL.
YEAR: 1950
SUPREME COURT: NONFINAL FOR PL.
YEAR: 1951

DEFENDANTS STILL INVOLVED IN SUIT:
1. HOSPITAL &/OR OWNERS, ETC.

134. JACKSON V. INDIANA

THEON JACKSON WAS A MENTALLY DEFECTIVE DEAF MUTE WITH THE MENTAL LEVEL OF A PRESCHOOL CHILD. HE COULD NOT READ, WRITE, OR COMMUNICATE, EXCEPT THROUGH A VERY LIMITED SIGN LANGUAGE. IN MAY 1968, HE WAS CHARGED WITH TWO ROBBERIES, WHICH NETTED HIM A TOTAL OF NINE DOLLARS. TWO STATE PSYCHIATRISTS DECIDED THAT JACKSON COULD NOT STAND TRIAL BECAUSE OF HIS MENTAL DEFICIENCY AND HIS LACK OF COMMUNICATION SKILLS. ALTHOUGH THE DOCTORS ADMITTED THAT THE STATE OF INDIANA HAD NO FACILITIES TO HELP SOMEONE LIKE JACKSON, THE TRIAL COURT ORDERED HIM COMMITTED TO THE INDIANA DEPARTMENT OF MENTAL HEALTH UNTIL THE DEPARTMENT COULD CERTIFY THAT JACKSON WAS SANE. THE PLAINTIFF'S COUNSEL ARGUED THAT NO EVIDENCE EXISTED THAT JACKSON WAS INSANE AND THAT COMMITMENT TO A FACILITY WHICH COULD NEVER MAKE HIM COMPETENT TO STAND TRIAL AMOUNTED TO A LIFE SENTENCE.

YEAR OF NEGLIGENT ACT: NOT SPECIFIED

STATE IN WHICH NEGLIGENT ACT OCCURRED: INDIANA

SETTING OF THE CASE: PUB. MENT. HOSP.

PLAINTIFF(S): PATIENT(S) OR REP.

DEFENDANT(S):
1. STATE GOV. &/OR OFFICIALS, ETC.

NEGLIGENT ACTIVITY:

TREATMENT:
1. NO TREATMENT OR INADEQUATE TREATMENT

DIAGNOSIS:

WHAT WAS DIAGNOSED:
1. MENTAL ILLNESS, INSTEAD OF SANITY

RESULT OF DIAGNOSIS:
1. IMPROPER COMMITMENT
2. IMPROPER FAILURE TO RELEASE

CARE: NOT APPLICABLE

HARM CAUSED TO PLAINTIFF &/OR PATIENT:
1. DEPRIVATION OF CONSTITUTIONAL RIGHTS
2. LOSS OF LIBERTY

TYPE OF ACTION BROUGHT:
1. DEPRIVATION OF CONSTITUTIONAL RIGHTS: RIGHT TO TREATMENT

HISTORY OF THE CASE:

TYPE OF COURT: STATE

TRIER OF FACT: JUDGE,NO JURY

COURT DECISION(S):

TRIAL COURT: FOR DEFENDANT
YEAR: NOT SPECIFIED
SUPREME COURT: FOR DEFENDANT
YEAR: 1970
U.S. SUPREME COURT (ON APPEAL FROM STATE COURT): NONFINAL FOR PL.
YEAR: 1972

DEFENDANTS STILL INVOLVED IN SUIT:
1. STATE GOV. &/OR OFFICIALS, ETC.

135. JAMES V. TURNER

ON SEPTEMBER 20, 1938, CLARENCE JAMES WAS PLACED IN THE TURNER-GOTTEN SANATORIUM BY HIS WIFE BECAUSE HE WAS SUFFERING FROM "CHRONIC ALCOHOLISM," AND HAD THREATENED TO TAKE HIS OWN LIFE. THE PATIENT'S CONDITION SEEMED TO IMPROVE MARKEDLY, AND ON SEPTEMBER 30 THE PATIENT WENT FOR A WALK WITH AN ATTENDANT. THE PATIENT ASKED THE ATTENDANT HOW MUCH WATER WAS IN A FIFTY-THREE-FOOT WATER TANK ON THE PROPERTY. WHEN THE GUARD ANSWERED THAT IT CONTAINED BETWEEN TWELVE AND FOURTEEN THOUSAND GALLONS, JAMES SUDDENLY BEGAN RUNNING AND CLIMBED THE LADDER TO THE TANK, THREW HIMSELF IN, AND DROWNED HIMSELF. HIS WIDOW BROUGHT SUIT FOR HIS WRONGFUL DEATH.

YEAR OF NEGLIGENT ACT: 1938

STATE IN WHICH NEGLIGENT ACT OCCURRED: TENNESSEE

SETTING OF THE CASE: PRIV. MENT. HOSP.

PLAINTIFF(S): 3RD PARTY, II

DEFENDANT(S):
1. NONPSYCHIAT.OR UNKNOWN TYPE PHYSICIAN(S)

NEGLIGENT ACTIVITY:

TREATMENT: NOT APPLICABLE

DIAGNOSIS:

WHAT WAS DIAGNOSED: NOT APPLICABLE

RESULT OF DIAGNOSIS: NOT APPLICABLE

CARE:
1. INADEQUATE SUPERVISION

HARM CAUSED TO PLAINTIFF &/OR PATIENT:
1. SUICIDE

TYPE OF ACTION BROUGHT:
1. NEGLIGENCE

HISTORY OF THE CASE:

TYPE OF COURT: STATE

TRIER OF FACT: JUDGE,UNINV.JURY

COURT DECISION(S):

TRIAL COURT: FOR DEFENDANT
YEAR: NOT SPECIFIED
APPELLATE COURT: FOR PLAINTIFF
YEAR: NOT SPECIFIED
SUPREME COURT: FOR DEFENDANT
YEAR: 1942

REASON SUIT FAILED:
1. NEGLIGENCE OR CASE NOT PROVEN

136. JOBSON V. HENNE

WARREN JOBSON HAD BEEN AN INMATE AT THE NEWARK STATE SCHOOL FOR MENTAL DEFECTIVES MOST OF HIS LIFE. HE WAS FIRST COMMITTED IN 1935 AT THE AGE OF TWELVE. HE WAS FINALLY DISCHARGED IN 1956 AND BECAME INVOLVED WITH A GROUP OF BOYS ENGAGED IN VARIOUS ILLEGAL ACTIVITIES. HE WAS ARRESTED AND CONVICTED OF LARCENY AND BURGLARY. PRIOR TO SENTENCING, THE CHARGES WERE DROPPED, AND JOBSON WAS RECERTIFIED TO NEWARK STATE SCHOOL. FOR LONG PERIODS JOBSON CLAIMED HE WAS REQUIRED TO WORK EIGHT HOURS A NIGHT, SIX NIGHTS A WEEK IN THE NEWARK STATE SCHOOL'S BOILER HOUSE. HE ALSO CLAIMED HE WORKED EIGHT HOURS A DAY AT ASSIGNED JOBS IN THE VILLAGE OF NEWARK. IN 1963 JOBSON FILED SUIT SEEKING A JUDGMENT OF $100,000 AND CHARGING THAT HE HAD BEEN "INTENTIONALLY AND MALICIOUSLY" HELD IN INVOLUNTARY SERVITUDE.

YEAR OF NEGLIGENT ACT: 1963

STATE IN WHICH NEGLIGENT ACT OCCURRED: NEW YORK

SETTING OF THE CASE: PUB. MENT. HOSP.

PLAINTIFF(S): PATIENT(S) OR REP.

DEFENDANT(S):
1. PSYCHIATRIST(S)
2. HOSPITAL &/OR OWNERS, ETC.

NEGLIGENT ACTIVITY:

TREATMENT:
1. NEGLIGENCE IN USE OF TECHNIQUE

DIAGNOSIS:

WHAT WAS DIAGNOSED: NOT APPLICABLE

RESULT OF DIAGNOSIS: NOT APPLICABLE

CARE: NOT APPLICABLE

HARM CAUSED TO PLAINTIFF &/OR PATIENT:
1. DEPRIVATION OF CONSTITUTIONAL RIGHTS

TYPE OF ACTION BROUGHT:
1. DEPRIVATION OF CONSTITUTIONAL RIGHTS: RIGHT TO TREATMENT
2. OTHER TORT(S): INVOLUNT. SERVITUDE

HISTORY OF THE CASE:

TYPE OF COURT: FEDERAL

TRIER OF FACT: JUDGE,UNINV.JURY

COURT DECISION(S):

TRIAL COURT: FOR DEFENDANT
YEAR: 1965
APPELLATE COURT: NONFINAL FOR PL.
YEAR: 1966

DEFENDANTS STILL INVOLVED IN SUIT:
1. PSYCHIATRIST(S)
2. HOSPITAL &/OR OWNERS, ETC.

137. JOHNSON V. GREER

AFTER IMAGINING THAT HE WAS BEING HOUNDED BY VOICES AND MUSIC, LEON JOHNSON EITHER VOLUNTEERED HIMSELF OR WAS TAKEN INTO CUSTODY BY THE POLICE. HE REQUESTED TO BE LOCKED UP WHERE HE WOULD NOT BE BOTHERED BY THE VOICES AND MUSIC. A PSYCHIATRIST DIAGNOSED HIM AS SUFFERING FROM "TOXIC DELIRIUM," AND AN EMERGENCY WARRANT WAS ISSUED TO PLACE HIM IN CUSTODY AT GREER'S CLINIC. THOUGH THE WARRANT STATED THAT JOHNSON COULD NOT BE DETAINED FOR MORE THAN TWENTY-FOUR HOURS, HE WAS KEPT IN THE CLINIC FOR APPROXIMATELY FIVE DAYS. NO ADDITIONAL COURT ORDERS WERE OBTAINED TO AUTHORIZE THIS DETENTION. JOHNSON SUED GREER FOR NEGLIGENT TREATMENT, DIAGNOSIS, AND CARE.

YEAR OF NEGLIGENT ACT: NOT SPECIFIED

STATE IN WHICH NEGLIGENT ACT OCCURRED: TEXAS

SETTING OF THE CASE: MENTAL HOSPITAL

PLAINTIFF(S): PATIENT(S) OR REP.

DEFENDANT(S):
1. HOSPITAL &/OR OWNERS, ETC.

NEGLIGENT ACTIVITY:

TREATMENT:
1. NEG.ADMIN.OF DRUGS

DIAGNOSIS:

WHAT WAS DIAGNOSED:
1. MENTAL ILLNESS, INSTEAD OF SANITY

RESULT OF DIAGNOSIS:
1. IMPROPER FAILURE TO RELEASE

CARE:
1. FAILURE TO RELEASE

HARM CAUSED TO PLAINTIFF &/OR PATIENT:
1. NONSELF-INFLICTED INJURIES
2. DEPRIVATION OF CONSTITUTIONAL RIGHTS
3. LOSS OF LIBERTY

TYPE OF ACTION BROUGHT:
1. FALSE IMPRISONMENT
2. DEPRIVATION OF CONSTITUTIONAL RIGHTS: CONST.RTS.IN GEN.

HISTORY OF THE CASE:

TYPE OF COURT: FEDERAL

TRIER OF FACT: JURY

COURT DECISION(S):

TRIAL COURT: FOR PLAINTIFF
YEAR: NOT SPECIFIED
APPELLATE COURT: NONFINAL FOR PL.
YEAR: 1973

DEFENDANTS STILL INVOLVED IN SUIT:
1. HOSPITAL &/OR OWNERS, ETC.

138. JOHNSON V. METHODIST HOSPITAL

THE DETAILS ABOUT THE ORIGINAL INCIDENT IN THE CASE RECORD ARE VERY SKETCHY. IN JANUARY OF 1951, THE PLAINTIFF SUFFERED DAMAGE TO HER BRAIN AND CENTRAL NERVOUS SYSTEM AND ALLEGED THAT SHE WAS MADE INSANE AS A RESULT OF ALLEGED IMPROPER CARE AND TREATMENT.

YEAR OF NEGLIGENT ACT: 1950

STATE IN WHICH NEGLIGENT ACT OCCURRED: NEW YORK

SETTING OF THE CASE: PRIVATE HOSPITAL

PLAINTIFF(S): PATIENT(S) OR REP.

DEFENDANT(S):
1. HOSPITAL &/OR OWNERS, ETC.

NEGLIGENT ACTIVITY:

TREATMENT:
1. UNSPEC.NEG.TREAT

DIAGNOSIS:

WHAT WAS DIAGNOSED: NOT APPLICABLE

RESULT OF DIAGNOSIS: NOT APPLICABLE

CARE:
1. FAILURE TO PROVIDE PROPER CUSTODIAL CARE

HARM CAUSED TO PLAINTIFF &/OR PATIENT:
1. NONSELF-INFLICTED INJURIES
2. INSANITY

TYPE OF ACTION BROUGHT:
1. NEGLIGENCE

HISTORY OF THE CASE:

TYPE OF COURT: STATE

TRIER OF FACT: JUDGE;JURY PRESENT ?

COURT DECISION(S):

TRIAL COURT: NONFINAL FOR PL.
YEAR: 1961
APPELLATE COURT: NONFINAL FOR PL.
YEAR: 1961

DEFENDANTS STILL INVOLVED IN SUIT:
1. HOSPITAL &/OR OWNERS, ETC.

139. JOHNSON V. UNITED STATES

JIMMY RAY JOHNSON WAS A SERGEANT IN THE U.S. ARMY. HE, HIS WIFE, AND THEIR TWO CHILDREN LIVED AT FORT STEWART. BECAUSE OF A MARITAL DISPUTE OVER DISCIPLINING THE CHILDREN, THE JOHNSONS WERE REFERRED TO THE MENTAL HYGIENE CLINIC AT THE BASE. IN AUGUST 1970 SERGEANT JOHNSON WAS DIAGNOSED AS PARANOID. BECAUSE OF HOMICIDAL AND SUICIDAL TENDENCIES HE WAS FIRST PLACED ON MEDICATION AND LATER HOSPITALIZED. AFTER DISCHARGE HE AGAIN BECAME ABUSIVE TO HIS FAMILY, WHO LEFT HIM ON CHRISTMAS EVE TO LIVE WITH HIS WIFE'S BROTHER. HIS WIFE REFUSED TO RETURN UNTIL HE SOUGHT TREATMENT, AND SEVERAL WEEKS LATER HE PROCEEDED TO RAPE HER, FOR WHICH HE WAS JAILED. HE WAS TRANSFERRED TO THE CLINIC BUT DISCHARGED TEN DAYS LATER. FOUR DAYS AFTER DISCHARGE HE TOOK A SHOTGUN TO HIS BROTHER-IN-LAW'S HOUSE AND PROCEEDED TO MURDER HIM, THEN WOUNDED HIS WIFE, BEFORE FINALLY KILLING HIMSELF WITH THE SAME WEAPON. SUIT WAS BROUGHT ALLEGING THAT THE GOVERNMENT FAILED TO TREAT THE SERGEANT'S ILLNESS PROPERLY AND IN ALLOWING HIM TO BE PREMATURELY DISCHARGED FROM THE CLINIC.

YEAR OF NEGLIGENT ACT: 1971

STATE IN WHICH NEGLIGENT ACT OCCURRED: GEORGIA

SETTING OF THE CASE: PUB. MENT. HOSP.

PLAINTIFF(S): 3RD PARTY, I & II

DEFENDANT(S):
1. FEDERAL GOV. &/OR OFFICIALS, ETC.

NEGLIGENT ACTIVITY:

TREATMENT:
1. NEGLIGENCE IN USE OF TECHNIQUE
2. NO TREATMENT OR INADEQUATE TREATMENT
3. NEG.ADMIN.OF DRUGS

DIAGNOSIS:

WHAT WAS DIAGNOSED:
1. LACK OF DANGEROUSNESS
2. LACK OF SUICIDAL TENDENCIES

RESULT OF DIAGNOSIS:
1. IMPROPER RELEASE

CARE:
1. INADEQUATE SUPERVISION
2. PREMATURE RELEASE

HARM CAUSED TO PLAINTIFF &/OR PATIENT:
1. SUICIDE
2. NONSELF-INFLICTED INJURIES

TYPE OF ACTION BROUGHT:
1. NEGLIGENCE

HISTORY OF THE CASE:

TYPE OF COURT: FEDERAL

TRIER OF FACT: JUDGE,NO JURY

COURT DECISION(S):

TRIAL COURT: FOR DEFENDANT
YEAR: 1976

REASON SUIT FAILED:
1. NEGLIGENCE OR CASE NOT PROVEN

140. JOHNSTON V. RODIS

THIS SUIT WAS BROUGHT BY JOHN AND KATHRYN JOHNSTON AGAINST ISADORE RODIS, A PSYCHIATRIST, FOR A FRACTURED ARM CLAIMED TO HAVE BEEN SUSTAINED BY KATHRYN IN ELECTRO-SHOCK TREATMENT. THE PLAINTIFFS CLAIMED THAT THE PSYCHIATRIST HAD PREVIOUSLY REPRESENTED THAT THE PROCEDURE WAS PERFECTLY SAFE. FURTHER DETAILS ARE UNAVAILABLE.

YEAR OF NEGLIGENT ACT: NOT SPECIFIED

STATE IN WHICH NEGLIGENT ACT OCCURRED: DISTRICT OF COLUMBIA

SETTING OF THE CASE: TYPE NOT SPECIFIED

PLAINTIFF(S): PATIENT(S) OR REP.

DEFENDANT(S):
1. PSYCHIATRIST(S)

NEGLIGENT ACTIVITY:

TREATMENT:
1. NEGLIGENT ELECTROCONVULSIVE THERAPY

DIAGNOSIS:

WHAT WAS DIAGNOSED: NOT APPLICABLE

RESULT OF DIAGNOSIS: NOT APPLICABLE

CARE: NOT APPLICABLE

HARM CAUSED TO PLAINTIFF &/OR PATIENT:
1. NONSELF-INFLICTED INJURIES

TYPE OF ACTION BROUGHT:
1. NEGLIGENCE
2. CONTRACT LAW: BREACH OF WARRANTY

HISTORY OF THE CASE:

TYPE OF COURT: FEDERAL

TRIER OF FACT: JUDGE,UNINV.JURY

COURT DECISION(S):

TRIAL COURT: FOR DEFENDANT
YEAR: 1957
APPELLATE COURT: NONFINAL FOR PL.
YEAR: 1958

DEFENDANTS STILL INVOLVED IN SUIT:
1. PSYCHIATRIST(S)

141. JOYCE V. FERRAZZI

RESPONDING TO INDEPENDENT TELEPHONE COMPLAINTS BY THE PLAINTIFF'S WIFE AND A NEIGHBOR, POLICE OFFICERS WENT TO THE PLAINTIFF'S HOME AND FOUND HIM STRUGGLING ON THE FLOOR WITH HIS SEVENTEEN-YEAR-OLD SON. SINCE THIS WAS NOT THE FIRST SUCH COMPLAINT AND SINCE THE OFFICERS BELIEVED THAT THE PLAINTIFF WAS NOT ACTING RATIONALLY, THEY TOOK JOYCE TO THE POLICE STATION, WHERE HE WAS SEARCHED, STRIPPED OF HIS OUTER CLOTHING, AND PLACED IN A CELL. THE PLAINTIFF'S WIFE ASKED THE OFFICER IN CHARGE TO CALL A DOCTOR WHO HAD TREATED VARIOUS MEMBERS OF THE FAMILY FOR YEARS. THE DOCTOR SPOKE WITH THE DEFENDANT AND PROCEEDED TO HAVE HIM COMMITTED. JOYCE WAS CONFINED FOR NINE OR TEN DAYS, AND BROUGHT SUIT AGAINST THE MAYOR, POLICE OFFICERS, A PRIVATE PHYSICIAN, AND THE SUPERINTENDENT OF THE INSTITUTION TO WHICH HE WAS COMMITTED FOR DEPRIVING HIM OF HIS CONSTITUTIONAL RIGHTS.

YEAR OF NEGLIGENT ACT: NOT SPECIFIED

STATE IN WHICH NEGLIGENT ACT OCCURRED: MASSACHUSETTS

SETTING OF THE CASE: JUDICIAL PROCEEDING

PLAINTIFF(S): PATIENT(S) OR REP.

DEFENDANT(S):
1. NONPSYCHIAT.OR UNKNOWN TYPE PHYSICIAN(S)
2. HOSPITAL &/OR OWNERS, ETC.
3. MUNICIPAL GOV. &/OR OFFICIALS, ETC.
4. POLICE

NEGLIGENT ACTIVITY:

TREATMENT: NOT APPLICABLE

DIAGNOSIS:

WHAT WAS DIAGNOSED:
1. MENTAL ILLNESS, INSTEAD OF SANITY

RESULT OF DIAGNOSIS:
1. IMPROPER COMMITMENT

CARE: NOT APPLICABLE

HARM CAUSED TO PLAINTIFF &/OR PATIENT:
1. DEPRIVATION OF CONSTITUTIONAL RIGHTS

TYPE OF ACTION BROUGHT:
1. DEPRIVATION OF CONSTITUTIONAL RIGHTS: CONST.RTS.IN GEN.

HISTORY OF THE CASE:

TYPE OF COURT: FEDERAL

TRIER OF FACT: JUDGE;JURY PRESENT ?

COURT DECISION(S):

TRIAL COURT: FOR DEFENDANT
YEAR: NOT SPECIFIED
APPELLATE COURT: FOR DEFENDANT
YEAR: 1963

REASON SUIT FAILED:
1. NO CAUSE OF ACTION STATED

142. KATZ V. STATE

SOLOMON KATZ HAD A HISTORY OF PHYSICAL PAIN AND SUFFERING, OPERATIONS FOR PHYSICAL AILMENTS, AND MENTAL DEPRESSIONS APPARENTLY BROUGHT ON BECAUSE OF HIS DETERIORATING PHYSICAL CONDITION. HE WAS FIRST ADMITTED TO THE NEW YORK STATE PSYCHIATRIC INSTITUTE FOR ONE MONTH IN MAY 1961. TWO MONTHS AFTER HIS DISCHARGE HE REVERTED TO HIS DEPRESSED MOOD AND SPOKE OF COMMITTING SUICIDE. HE WAS READMITTED TO THE HOSPITAL AND DIAGNOSED AS PSYCHONEUROTIC WITH A REACTIVE DEPRESSION. ALTHOUGH HIS WIFE HAD INFORMED THE DOCTORS THAT THE PATIENT HAD PREVIOUSLY TRIED TO COMMIT SUICIDE BY JUMPING OUT A WINDOW AND BY AN OVERDOSE OF PILLS, MR. KATZ WAS NOT JUDGED TO BE A SUICIDAL RISK. HE WAS THEREFORE PLACED IN A SEMI-OPEN WARD, WHICH HE LEFT BY ELEVATOR ON JULY 8, 1962. HE PROCEEDED TO THE SUBWAY AT 168TH STREET AND BROADWAY IN NEW YORK CITY AND KILLED HIMSELF BY JUMPING IN FRONT OF AN ONCOMING TRAIN.

YEAR OF NEGLIGENT ACT: 1962

STATE IN WHICH NEGLIGENT ACT OCCURRED: NEW YORK

SETTING OF THE CASE: PUB. MENT. HOSP.

PLAINTIFF(S): PATIENT(S) OR REP.

DEFENDANT(S):
1. STATE GOV. &/OR OFFICIALS, ETC.

NEGLIGENT ACTIVITY:

TREATMENT: NOT APPLICABLE

DIAGNOSIS:

WHAT WAS DIAGNOSED:
1. LACK OF SUICIDAL TENDENCIES

RESULT OF DIAGNOSIS:
1. IMPROPER CUSTODIAL CARE

CARE: NOT APPLICABLE

HARM CAUSED TO PLAINTIFF &/OR PATIENT:
1. SUICIDE

TYPE OF ACTION BROUGHT:
1. NEGLIGENCE

HISTORY OF THE CASE:

TYPE OF COURT: STATE

TRIER OF FACT: JUDGE,NO JURY

COURT DECISION(S):

TRIAL COURT: FOR DEFENDANT
YEAR: 1965

REASON SUIT FAILED:
1. NEGLIGENCE OR CASE NOT PROVEN

143. KEATING V. KELLER

ON FRIDAY, JUNE 25, 1965, THE PLAINTIFF'S WIFE SIGNED A STATEMENT THAT THE PLAINTIFF WAS "MENTALLY DERANGED." THE DEFENDANT, A CORONER, OBSERVED THE PLAINTIFF ON FRIDAY AFTERNOON. BELIEVING THAT THE PLAINTIFF'S BEHAVIOR AND APPARENT STATE OF MIND INDICATED THE NEED FOR IMMEDIATE CARE, HE EXECUTED A "CORONOR'S EMERGENCY DETENTION" FORM AND CAUSED THE PLAINTIFF TO BE TAKEN IMMEDIATELY TO THE HOSPITAL. THE PATIENT ENTERED THE HOSPITAL ON JUNE 25 AND WAS RELEASED ON JULY 16 ON CONVALESCENT LEAVE STATUS. THE PLAINTIFF ALLEGED THAT THE DEFENDANT HAD NEVER EXAMINED HIM.

YEAR OF NEGLIGENT ACT: 1965

STATE IN WHICH NEGLIGENT ACT OCCURRED: LOUISIANA

SETTING OF THE CASE: JUDICIAL PROCEEDING

PLAINTIFF(S): PATIENT(S) OR REP.

DEFENDANT(S):
1. NONPSYCHIAT.OR UNKNOWN TYPE PHYSICIAN(S)

NEGLIGENT ACTIVITY:

TREATMENT: NOT APPLICABLE

DIAGNOSIS:

WHAT WAS DIAGNOSED:
1. MENTAL ILLNESS, INSTEAD OF SANITY
2. FAILURE TO MAKE A DIAGNOSIS

RESULT OF DIAGNOSIS:
1. IMPROPER COMMITMENT

CARE: NOT APPLICABLE

HARM CAUSED TO PLAINTIFF &/OR PATIENT:
1. NOT SPECIFIED

TYPE OF ACTION BROUGHT:
1. NEGLIGENCE

HISTORY OF THE CASE:

TYPE OF COURT: STATE

TRIER OF FACT: ?, JUDGE OR JURY

COURT DECISION(S):

TRIAL COURT: FOR DEFENDANT
YEAR: NOT SPECIFIED
APPELLATE COURT: FOR PLAINTIFF
YEAR: 1970

VERDICT AGAINST WHICH DEFENDANTS:
1. NONPSYCHIAT.OR UNKNOWN TYPE PHYSICIAN(S)

RECOVERY OR OTHER RELIEF GRANTED:
1. $ 3500

144. KELLY V. STATE

MRS. MARY L. KELLY LEFT HER HOME AT APPROXIMATELY 5:00 P.M. ON THURSDAY, JANUARY 27, 1966, FOR THE EMERGENCY CLINIC OF THE QUEENS HOSPITAL CENTER. SHE TESTIFIED TO BEING NAUSEOUS AND HAVING PAINS IN HER STOMACH, WHICH SHE BELIEVED TO BE THE RESULT OF POISONING. MRS. KELLY TOLD A PSYCHIATRIST THAT HER HUSBAND AND "A GROUP" HAD DONE THIS. SHORTLY THEREAFTER, MR. KELLY ARRIVED STATING THAT HE WANTED TO TAKE HIS WIFE HOME. SHE REFUSED, STATING THAT SHE WANTED TO KNOW WHETHER SHE HAD BEEN POISONED. UPON THE CERTIFICATION OF THE QUEENS HOSPITAL CENTER PHYSICIANS, MRS. KELLY WAS COMMITTED TO CREEDMOOR STATE HOSPITAL, WHERE SHE WAS DIAGNOSED AS HAVING AN INVOLUTIONAL PSYCHOSIS, PARANOID TYPE. MRS. KELLY REMAINED AT CREEDMOOR FOR ONE WEEK. UPON HER RELEASE SHE AND HER HUSBAND BROUGHT SUIT AGAINST THE STATE FOR THE NEGLIGENCE OF ITS EMPLOYEES IN COMMITTING HER.

YEAR OF NEGLIGENT ACT: 1966

STATE IN WHICH NEGLIGENT ACT OCCURRED: NEW YORK

SETTING OF THE CASE: JUDICIAL PROCEEDING

PLAINTIFF(S): PATIENT(S) OR REP.

DEFENDANT(S):
1. STATE GOV. &/OR OFFICIALS, ETC.

NEGLIGENT ACTIVITY:

TREATMENT: NOT APPLICABLE

DIAGNOSIS:

WHAT WAS DIAGNOSED:
1. MENTAL ILLNESS, INSTEAD OF SANITY
2. DANGEROUSNESS

RESULT OF DIAGNOSIS:
1. IMPROPER COMMITMENT

CARE: NOT APPLICABLE

HARM CAUSED TO PLAINTIFF &/OR PATIENT:
1. EMOTIONAL DISTRESS
2. ECONOMIC LOSS

TYPE OF ACTION BROUGHT:
1. NEGLIGENCE
2. FALSE IMPRISONMENT
3. OTHER TORT(S): FALSE ARREST

HISTORY OF THE CASE:

TYPE OF COURT: STATE

TRIER OF FACT: JUDGE,NO JURY

COURT DECISION(S):

TRIAL COURT: FOR DEFENDANT
YEAR: 1968

REASON SUIT FAILED:
1. NEGLIGENCE OR CASE NOT PROVEN

145. KENDRICK V. UNITED STATES

ON SEPTEMBER 5, 1944, ISAIAH BUSH RECEIVED AN HONORABLE DISCHARGE FROM THE U.S. ARMY. HIS CERTIFICATE OF DISABILITY CONTAINED A DIAGNOSIS OF PSYCHOSIS, UNCLASSIFIED. FOR SOME TIME PRIOR TO DISCHARGE HIS ILLNESS HAD MANIFESTED ITSELF BY MUTENESS AND EXPLOSIVE PERIODS OF VIOLENT BEHAVIOR. ON SEPTEMBER 14 HE WAS ADMITTED TO THE VETERANS ADMINISTRATION FACILITY AT TUSKEGEE, ALABAMA, WHERE HE WAS DIAGNOSED AS PSYCHOTIC WITH A CONSTITUTIONALLY PSYCHOPATHIC STATE. A STAFF CONFERENCE DETERMINED THAT HIS CONDITION DID NOT RENDER HIM DANGEROUS TO HIMSELF OR TO OTHERS AND THE PATIENT WAS DISCHARGED ON JANUARY 6, 1945. SIX MONTHS LATER BUSH KILLED THE PLAINTIFF'S HUSBAND.

YEAR OF NEGLIGENT ACT: 1945

STATE IN WHICH NEGLIGENT ACT OCCURRED: ALABAMA

SETTING OF THE CASE: PUB. GEN. HOSP.

PLAINTIFF(S): 3RD PARTY, I

DEFENDANT(S):
1. FEDERAL GOV. &/OR OFFICIALS, ETC.

NEGLIGENT ACTIVITY:

TREATMENT: NOT APPLICABLE

DIAGNOSIS:

WHAT WAS DIAGNOSED:
1. MENTAL ILLNESS, INSTEAD OF SANITY
2. LACK OF DANGEROUSNESS

RESULT OF DIAGNOSIS:
1. IMPROPER RELEASE

CARE: NOT APPLICABLE

HARM CAUSED TO PLAINTIFF &/OR PATIENT:
1. NONSUICIDAL DEATH

TYPE OF ACTION BROUGHT:
1. NEGLIGENCE

HISTORY OF THE CASE:

TYPE OF COURT: FEDERAL

TRIER OF FACT: JUDGE;JURY PRESENT ?

COURT DECISION(S):

TRIAL COURT: FOR DEFENDANT
YEAR: 1949

REASON SUIT FAILED:
1. DEFENDANT(S) CANNOT BE SUED DUE TO: GOVERN. IMMUNITY

146. KENT V. WHITAKER

MRS. CAROL KENT WAS A WIDOW, FORTY-ONE YEARS OF AGE, WHO TAUGHT IN THE EATONVILLE PUBLIC SCHOOLS. ON THE MORNING IN QUESTION SHE ATTEMPTED SUICIDE IN HER BEDROOM, BUT WAS FOUND BY HER SON. SHE WAS TAKEN BY AMBULANCE TO PIERCE COUNTY HOSPITAL. AFTER A STOMACH LAVAGE AND OTHER EMERGENCY TREATMENT, MRS. KENT WAS PLACED IN A ROOM WITHOUT FURNITURE, EXCEPT FOR HER BED AND AN APPARATUS USED FOR INTRAVENOUS FEEDING, WHICH CONTAINED A LENGTH OF PLASTIC TUBING. MRS. KENT'S FAMILY ASKED TO REMAIN WITH HER, BUT THIS REQUEST WAS DENIED. THE HOSPITAL ATTENDANTS ASSURED THE FAMILY THAT SHE WOULD BE CLOSELY WATCHED. ON THE EVENING OF HER ADMISSION, MRS. KENT WAS FOUND IN HER LOCKED HOSPITAL ROOM STRANGLED TO DEATH BY THE PLASTIC TUBING. THE FAMILY SUED FOR WRONGFUL DEATH.

YEAR OF NEGLIGENT ACT: NOT SPECIFIED

STATE IN WHICH NEGLIGENT ACT OCCURRED: WASHINGTON

SETTING OF THE CASE: PUB. GEN. HOSP.

PLAINTIFF(S): PAT. & 3RD PTY., I

DEFENDANT(S):
1. NONPSYCHIAT.OR UNKNOWN TYPE PHYSICIAN(S)

NEGLIGENT ACTIVITY:

TREATMENT: NOT APPLICABLE

DIAGNOSIS:

WHAT WAS DIAGNOSED: NOT APPLICABLE

RESULT OF DIAGNOSIS: NOT APPLICABLE

CARE:
1. INADEQUATE SUPERVISION

HARM CAUSED TO PLAINTIFF &/OR PATIENT:
1. SUICIDE

TYPE OF ACTION BROUGHT:
1. NEGLIGENCE

HISTORY OF THE CASE:

TYPE OF COURT: STATE

TRIER OF FACT: JUDGE;JURY PRESENT ?

COURT DECISION(S):

TRIAL COURT: FOR PLAINTIFF
YEAR: NOT SPECIFIED
SUPREME COURT: FOR PLAINTIFF
YEAR: 1961

VERDICT AGAINST WHICH DEFENDANTS:
1. NONPSYCHIAT.OR UNKNOWN TYPE PHYSICIAN(S)

RECOVERY OR OTHER RELIEF GRANTED:
1. OTHER RECOVERY: NOT SPECIFIED

147. KLEBER V. STEVENS

LITTLE INFORMATION IS AVAILABLE FROM THE RECORD EXCEPT THAT MARIAN KLEBER CHARGED RALPH A. STEVENS AND ANTHONY PROFITA WITH FALSELY, FRAUDULENTLY, AND MALICIOUSLY COMPOSING TWO CERTIFICATES RESULTING IN HER EMERGENCY COMMITMENT TO KINGS PARK STATE HOSPITAL. THE PLAINTIFF STATED THAT THE CERTIFICATES WERE ILL-CONCEIVED AND BASED ON THE HEARSAY OF AN ALLEGEDLY VINDICTIVE HUSBAND.

YEAR OF NEGLIGENT ACT: NOT SPECIFIED

STATE IN WHICH NEGLIGENT ACT OCCURRED: NEW YORK

SETTING OF THE CASE: JUDICIAL PROCEEDING

PLAINTIFF(S): PATIENT(S) OR REP.

DEFENDANT(S):
1. NONPSYCHIAT.OR UNKNOWN TYPE PHYSICIAN(S)

NEGLIGENT ACTIVITY:

TREATMENT: NOT APPLICABLE

DIAGNOSIS:

WHAT WAS DIAGNOSED:
1. MENTAL ILLNESS, INSTEAD OF SANITY

RESULT OF DIAGNOSIS:
1. IMPROPER COMMITMENT

CARE: NOT APPLICABLE

HARM CAUSED TO PLAINTIFF &/OR PATIENT:
1. LOSS OF LIBERTY

TYPE OF ACTION BROUGHT:
1. NEGLIGENCE
2. FALSE IMPRISONMENT

HISTORY OF THE CASE:

TYPE OF COURT: STATE

TRIER OF FACT: JURY

COURT DECISION(S):

TRIAL COURT: FOR PLAINTIFF
YEAR: 1963
APPELLATE COURT: FOR PLAINTIFF
YEAR: 1964

VERDICT AGAINST WHICH DEFENDANTS:
1. NONPSYCHIAT.OR UNKNOWN TYPE PHYSICIAN(S)

RECOVERY OR OTHER RELIEF GRANTED:
1. $ 20000

148. KOSBERG V. WASHINGTON HOSPITAL CENTER

ROBERTA ANN CLARK WAS A NEWLY MARRIED, TWENTY-TWO-YEAR-OLD WOMAN, WHOSE MEDICAL PROBLEMS BEGAN WITH SYMPTOMS SUGGESTIVE OF PREGNANCY. SHE WAS SUCCESSIVELY TREATED BY THREE DOCTORS: A GENERAL PRACTITIONER, A PSYCHIATRIST, AND AN INTERNIST. THE GENERAL PRACTITIONER TREATED THE PATIENT FOR "MORNING SICKNESS" AND MALNUTRITION. WHEN SHE DID NOT IMPROVE SIGNIFICANTLY, HE REFERRED HER TO THE PSYCHIATRIST FOR TREATMENT OF A SUSPECTED EMOTIONAL PROBLEM. THE PSYCHIATRIST HOSPITALIZED THE PATIENT IN THE DEFENDANT HOSPITAL, GAVE HER ELECTRO-SHOCK TREATMENT, AND ADMINISTERED THORAZINE THROUGHOUT HER STAY. THE PATIENT'S CONDITION BECAME CRITICAL, AND THE INTERNIST, DR. SCHULMAN, WAS CALLED IN. HE ORDERED VARIOUS DRUGS FOR THE PATIENT, BUT SHE FAILED TO RESPOND AND DIED TWO DAYS AFTER RECEIVING THE ELECTRO-SHOCK THERAPY. THE ADMINISTRATOR OF THE ESTATE, ESTHER KOSBERG, BROUGHT SUIT ALLEGING THAT THE THERAPY HAD BEEN NEGLIGENTLY ADMINISTERED.

YEAR OF NEGLIGENT ACT: NOT SPECIFIED

STATE IN WHICH NEGLIGENT ACT OCCURRED: DISTRICT OF COLUMBIA

SETTING OF THE CASE: HOSPITAL

PLAINTIFF(S): PATIENT(S) OR REP.

DEFENDANT(S):
1. PSYCHIATRIST(S)
2. NONPSYCHIAT.OR UNKNOWN TYPE PHYSICIAN(S)
3. HOSPITAL &/OR OWNERS, ETC.

NEGLIGENT ACTIVITY:

TREATMENT:
1. NEGLIGENT ELECTROCONVULSIVE THERAPY

DIAGNOSIS:

WHAT WAS DIAGNOSED: NOT APPLICABLE

RESULT OF DIAGNOSIS: NOT APPLICABLE

CARE: NOT APPLICABLE

HARM CAUSED TO PLAINTIFF &/OR PATIENT:
1. NONSUICIDAL DEATH

TYPE OF ACTION BROUGHT:
1. NEGLIGENCE

HISTORY OF THE CASE:

TYPE OF COURT: FEDERAL

TRIER OF FACT: JUDGE;JURY PRESENT ?

COURT DECISION(S):

TRIAL COURT: FOR DEFENDANT
YEAR: NOT SPECIFIED
APPELLATE COURT: NONFINAL FOR PL.
YEAR: 1968

DEFENDANTS STILL INVOLVED IN SUIT:
1. PSYCHIATRIST(S)

149. KOWALSKI V. STATE

ON JANUARY 29, 1954, ARTHUR MORRIS WAS COMMITTED TO ISLIP STATE HOSPITAL WHERE HIS CONDITION WAS DIAGNOSED AS "PSYCHOSIS WITH PSYCHOPATHIC PERSONALITY." IN MAY THE PATIENT ATTEMPTED SUICIDE BY INFLICTING SUPERFICIAL CUTS ON HIS LEFT AND RIGHT FOREARMS. HE HAD A PREVIOUS HISTORY OF WRIST SLASHING. HOWEVER, HIS CONDITION GRADUALLY IMPROVED, AND ON JANUARY 29, 1955, HE WAS RELEASED IN THE CUSTODY OF HIS MOTHER. ONE MONTH LATER HE RETURNED TO THE HOSPITAL, WHERE HE AGAIN BEGAN TO MAKE PROGRESS. MORRIS COMMITTED SUICIDE ON AUGUST 10, 1955. THE ADMINISTRATOR OF HIS ESTATE BROUGHT SUIT AGAINST THE STATE FOR NEGLIGENCE, ALTHOUGH HE DID NOT ALLEGE ANY PARTICULARS.

YEAR OF NEGLIGENT ACT: 1955

STATE IN WHICH NEGLIGENT ACT OCCURRED: NEW YORK

SETTING OF THE CASE: PUB. MENT. HOSP.

PLAINTIFF(S): PATIENT(S) OR REP.

DEFENDANT(S):
1. STATE GOV. &/OR OFFICIALS, ETC.

NEGLIGENT ACTIVITY:

TREATMENT:
1. ? WHETHER TREAT.INV.

DIAGNOSIS:

WHAT WAS DIAGNOSED:
1. ? WHETHER DIAG.INV.

RESULT OF DIAGNOSIS: NOT APPLICABLE

CARE:
1. ? WHETHER CARE INV.

HARM CAUSED TO PLAINTIFF &/OR PATIENT:
1. SUICIDE

TYPE OF ACTION BROUGHT:
1. NEGLIGENCE

HISTORY OF THE CASE:

TYPE OF COURT: STATE

TRIER OF FACT: JUDGE,NO JURY

COURT DECISION(S):

TRIAL COURT: FOR DEFENDANT
YEAR: NOT SPECIFIED
APPELLATE COURT: FOR DEFENDANT
YEAR: 1958

REASON SUIT FAILED:
1. NEGLIGENCE OR CASE NOT PROVEN

150. KRAVITZ V. STATE

THE PLAINTIFFS ARE THE PARENTS OF DEBORAH ANN KRAVITZ, WHO DIED ON APRIL 4, 1967, AS THE RESULT OF A BRUTAL ASSAULT AT THE HANDS OF NICHOLAS WILLIAM TOCE. ON JANUARY 18, 1962, TOCE HAD BEEN COMMITTED TO ATASCADERO STATE HOSPITAL BY THE SUPERIOR COURT OF LOS ANGELES COUNTY FOR TWO SERIOUS ASSAULTS ON OTHERS. TOCE REMAINED AT ATASCADERO UNTIL AUGUST 1966, WHEN HE WAS TRANSFERRED TO METROPOLITAN STATE HOSPITAL. ON SEPTEMBER 8, 1966, METROPOLITAN'S SUPERINTENDENT AND MEDICAL DIRECTOR INFORMED THE COURT THAT TOCE WAS NO LONGER INSANE AND SHOULD BE RELEASED. ON JANUARY 12, 1967, A LOS ANGELES COURT ADOPTED THE REPORT AND TOCE WAS RELEASED. THE PLAINTIFFS BROUGHT SUIT CHARGING THE STATE AND CERTAIN PHYSICIANS WITH NEGLIGENTLY AND CARELESSLY PROVIDING THE SUPERIOR COURT WITH INCOMPLETE AND INACCURATE INFORMATION CONCERNING THE TESTING, EVALUATION, TREATMENT, AND PRESCRIPTION FOR SUPERVISION OF TOCE.

YEAR OF NEGLIGENT ACT: 1967

STATE IN WHICH NEGLIGENT ACT OCCURRED: CALIFORNIA

SETTING OF THE CASE: PUB. MENT. HOSP.

PLAINTIFF(S): 3RD PARTY, I

DEFENDANT(S):
1. STATE GOV. &/OR OFFICIALS, ETC.

NEGLIGENT ACTIVITY:

TREATMENT: NOT APPLICABLE

DIAGNOSIS:

WHAT WAS DIAGNOSED:
1. SANITY, INSTEAD OF MENTAL ILLNESS
2. LACK OF DANGEROUSNESS

RESULT OF DIAGNOSIS:
1. IMPROPER RELEASE

CARE: NOT APPLICABLE

HARM CAUSED TO PLAINTIFF &/OR PATIENT:
1. NONSUICIDAL DEATH

TYPE OF ACTION BROUGHT:
1. NEGLIGENCE

HISTORY OF THE CASE:

TYPE OF COURT: STATE

TRIER OF FACT: JUDGE;JURY PRESENT ?

COURT DECISION(S):

TRIAL COURT: FOR DEFENDANT
YEAR: NOT SPECIFIED
APPELLATE COURT: FOR DEFENDANT
YEAR: 1970

REASON SUIT FAILED:
1. NEGLIGENCE OR CASE NOT PROVEN
2. DEFENDANT(S) CANNOT BE SUED DUE TO: GOVERN. IMMUNITY

151. KUBAS V. STATE

STANLEY KUBAS WAS FIRST ADMITTED TO THE UTICA STATE HOSPITAL ON APRIL 27, 1939, UPON THE PETITION OF HIS BROTHER, JOSEPH. THIS PETITION STATED THAT, AMONG OTHER THINGS, STANLEY WAS DEPRESSED, HAD QUIT HIS JOB FOR UNKNOWN REASONS, AND DID NOT KNOW THAT HE DID PECULIAR THINGS. HE REMAINED AT THE INSTITUTION UNTIL JULY 29, 1939, WHEN HE WAS RELEASED ON PAROLE TO HIS FAMILY. LATE IN NOVEMBER OF 1940, STANLEY SHOT HIMSELF BELOW THE HEART. ONE MONTH LATER HE WAS AGAIN COMMITTED TO UTICA STATE. HIS MENTAL ILLNESS WAS DIAGNOSED AS DEMENTIA PRAECOX, SIMPLE TYPE. ON FEBRUARY 25, 1941, KUBAS WAS PLACED IN AN OPEN WARD. SEVEN MONTHS LATER, KUBAS WAS CONSIDERED FOR PAROLE, BUT HIS FAMILY DID NOT WANT HIM HOME. IN APRIL OF THE NEXT YEAR HE ESCAPED, BUT WAS APPREHENDED THE NEXT DAY. HE WAS AGAIN PLACED IN AN OPEN WARD. ON JULY 18, 1946, HE WAS GIVEN "EXTRAMURAL" PRIVILEGES, WHICH ALLOWED HIM TO GO UNACCOMPANIED TO THE MOVIES IN UTICA. IN DECEMBER, ON THE TWENTY-SECOND SUCH TRIP, HE OBTAINED A QUANTITY OF OIL OF WINTERGREEN, WHICH HE SWALLOWED INSIDE THE MOVIE THEATER. HE WAS RUSHED TO THE AMSTERDAM CITY HOSPITAL, WHERE HE DIED THAT NIGHT. HIS FAMILY BROUGHT SUIT, ALLEGING THAT THE HOSPITAL WAS NEGLIGENT IN TAKING PROPER CARE OF HIM.

YEAR OF NEGLIGENT ACT: 1946

STATE IN WHICH NEGLIGENT ACT OCCURRED: NEW YORK

SETTING OF THE CASE: PUB. MENT. HOSP.

PLAINTIFF(S): PATIENT(S) OR REP.

DEFENDANT(S):
1. STATE GOV. &/OR OFFICIALS, ETC.

NEGLIGENT ACTIVITY:

TREATMENT: NOT APPLICABLE

DIAGNOSIS:

WHAT WAS DIAGNOSED:
1. LACK OF SUICIDAL TENDENCIES

RESULT OF DIAGNOSIS:
1. IMPROPER CUSTODIAL CARE

CARE:
1. INADEQUATE SUPERVISION

HARM CAUSED TO PLAINTIFF &/OR PATIENT:
1. SUICIDE

TYPE OF ACTION BROUGHT:
1. NEGLIGENCE

HISTORY OF THE CASE:

TYPE OF COURT: STATE

TRIER OF FACT: JUDGE,NO JURY

COURT DECISION(S):

TRIAL COURT: FOR DEFENDANT
YEAR: 1949
APPELLATE COURT: FOR DEFENDANT
YEAR: 1951

REASON SUIT FAILED:
1. NEGLIGENCE OR CASE NOT PROVEN

152. LANDO V. STATE

ROSE LANDO, A MENTALLY DEFICIENT PATIENT AT KINGS PARK STATE HOSPITAL, HAD GAINED PRIVILEGES WHICH ALLOWED HER TO LEAVE HER WARD AS LONG AS SHE REMAINED ON HOSPITAL GROUNDS. ON THE EVENING OF AUGUST 10, 1971, SHE AND THREE OTHER PATIENTS SET OUT FOR A STROLL. AT ABOUT 7:30 P.M., THE OTHERS RETURNED WITHOUT MRS. LANDO. WHEN HER ABSENCE WAS DISCOVERED, THE HOSPITAL BEGAN AN UNSUCCESSFUL SEARCH TO FIND HER. ELEVEN DAYS LATER HER BADLY DECOMPOSED BODY WAS FOUND IN A WOODED AREA, FIFTY FEET FROM THE HOSPITAL PARKING LOT. HER FATHER CLAIMED THAT THE HOSPITAL DID NOT ENGAGE IN AN ADEQUATE SEARCH FOR HER.

YEAR OF NEGLIGENT ACT: 1971

STATE IN WHICH NEGLIGENT ACT OCCURRED: NEW YORK

SETTING OF THE CASE: PUB. MENT. HOSP.

PLAINTIFF(S): PAT. & 3RD PTY., I

DEFENDANT(S):
1. STATE GOV. &/OR OFFICIALS, ETC.

NEGLIGENT ACTIVITY:

TREATMENT: NOT APPLICABLE

DIAGNOSIS:

WHAT WAS DIAGNOSED: NOT APPLICABLE

RESULT OF DIAGNOSIS: NOT APPLICABLE

CARE:
1. FAILURE TO PROVIDE PROPER CUSTODIAL CARE

HARM CAUSED TO PLAINTIFF &/OR PATIENT:
1. NONSUICIDAL DEATH
2. EMOTIONAL DISTRESS

TYPE OF ACTION BROUGHT:
1. NEGLIGENCE
2. OTHER TORT(S): CONSC.PAIN & SUFFER.

HISTORY OF THE CASE:

TYPE OF COURT: STATE

TRIER OF FACT: JUDGE,NO JURY

COURT DECISION(S):

TRIAL COURT: FOR PLAINTIFF
YEAR: 1974
APPELLATE COURT: FOR DEFENDANT
YEAR: 1975
SUPREME COURT: FOR PLAINTIFF
YEAR: 1976

VERDICT AGAINST WHICH DEFENDANTS:
1. STATE GOV. &/OR OFFICIALS, ETC.

RECOVERY OR OTHER RELIEF GRANTED:
1. $ 5000

153. LAWRENCE V. STATE

AFTER SOME WEEKS OF BEING IN AN UPSET AND CONFUSED STATE OF MIND, DONALD LAWRENCE WAS COMMITTED TO ST. LAWRENCE STATE HOSPITAL ON MARCH 12, 1962. THE TWO PHYSICIANS WHO COMMITTED HIM DESCRIBED HIM AS DEPRESSED, DESTRUCTIVE, AND EXHIBITING SUICIDAL TENDENCIES, DELUSIONS AND HALLUCINATIONS. DIAGNOSIS UPON ADMISSION AND A SUBSEQUENT DIAGNOSIS ALSO AGREED. ON MARCH 19, HE WAS DIAGNOSED AS SCHIZOPHRENIC, PARANOID TYPE. HE WAS PLACED IN A MINIMUM SECURITY WARD, WHICH USED LESS BARS AND MORE TRANQUILIZERS THAN MAXIMUM SECURITY. SOON AFTER, BECAUSE HIS HISTORY AND X-RAYS INDICATED A POSSIBILITY OF ACTIVE TUBERCULOSIS, HE WAS TRANSFERRED TO A PRIVATE SECOND-FLOOR ROOM IN A MEDICAL PAVILION HE WAS NOT CLOSELY SUPERVISED, ALTHOUGH HIS VIOLENT AND SUICIDAL TENDENCIES WERE KNOWN. ON THE MORNING OF APRIL 5, HE JUMPED OUT OF HIS WINDOW AND WAS FOUND SEMI-CONSCIOUS AND INCOHERENT. EVIDENCE SHOWED THAT HE LANDED ON HIS HEAD. AS A RESULT OF HIS FALL, HE BECAME A PARAPLEGIC AND WAS TRANSFERRED TO A SERIES OF OTHER HOSPITALS. HE DIED FIVE MONTHS LATER. HIS WIFE BROUGHT SUIT AS THE ADMINISTRATOR OF HIS ESTATE FOR THE STATE'S NEGLIGENCE IN FAILING TO PROVIDE PROTECTIVE BARS ON THE WINDOWS AND IN PROVIDING INADEQUATE SUPERVISION.

YEAR OF NEGLIGENT ACT: 1962

STATE IN WHICH NEGLIGENT ACT OCCURRED: NEW YORK

SETTING OF THE CASE: PUB. MENT. HOSP.

PLAINTIFF(S): PATIENT(S) OR REP.

DEFENDANT(S):
1. HOSPITAL &/OR OWNERS, ETC.

NEGLIGENT ACTIVITY:

TREATMENT: NOT APPLICABLE

DIAGNOSIS:

WHAT WAS DIAGNOSED: NOT APPLICABLE

RESULT OF DIAGNOSIS: NOT APPLICABLE

CARE:
1. INADEQUATE SUPERVISION
2. FAILURE TO PROVIDE PROPER CUSTODIAL CARE

HARM CAUSED TO PLAINTIFF &/OR PATIENT:
1. SUICIDE

TYPE OF ACTION BROUGHT:
1. NEGLIGENCE

HISTORY OF THE CASE:

TYPE OF COURT: STATE

TRIER OF FACT: JUDGE,NO JURY

COURT DECISION(S):

TRIAL COURT: FOR PLAINTIFF
YEAR: 1964

VERDICT AGAINST WHICH DEFENDANTS: HOSPITAL &/OR OWNERS, ETC.

RECOVERY OR OTHER RELIEF GRANTED:
1. $ 40646

154. LEGION V. RICHARDSON

A CLASS ACTION SUIT WAS BROUGHT BY PLAINTIFFS ON BEHALF OF ONE MILLION MENTALLY ILL AMERICANS CONFINED IN PUBLIC INSTITUTIONS. THE MAIN THRUST OF THE CLAIM WAS THAT BOTH MEDICARE AND MEDICAID LEGISLATION DISCRIMINATED AGAINST BLACKS AND OTHER PATIENTS IN PUBLIC MENTAL INSTITUTIONS, RESULTING IN INADEQUATE TREATMENT.

YEAR OF NEGLIGENT ACT: NOT SPECIFIED, BUT OCCURRED OVER A SERIES OF YEARS

STATE IN WHICH NEGLIGENT ACT OCCURRED: NEW YORK

SETTING OF THE CASE: PUB. MENT. HOSP.

PLAINTIFF(S): PATIENT(S) OR REP.

DEFENDANT(S):
1. HOSPITAL &/OR OWNERS, ETC.
2. FEDERAL GOV. &/OR OFFICIALS, ETC.
3. STATE GOV. &/OR OFFICIALS, ETC.

NEGLIGENT ACTIVITY:

TREATMENT:
1. NO TREATMENT OR INADEQUATE TREATMENT

DIAGNOSIS:

WHAT WAS DIAGNOSED: NOT APPLICABLE

RESULT OF DIAGNOSIS: NOT APPLICABLE

CARE:
1. FAILURE TO PROVIDE PROPER CUSTODIAL CARE

HARM CAUSED TO PLAINTIFF &/OR PATIENT:
1. DEPRIVATION OF CONSTITUTIONAL RIGHTS
2. NO CHANCE FOR IMPR.

TYPE OF ACTION BROUGHT:
1. NEGLIGENCE
2. DEPRIVATION OF CONSTITUTIONAL RIGHTS: RIGHT TO TREATMENT
3. NONMONETARY RELIEF
4. OTHER ACTION, EXCLUDING TORT LAW: RACE DISCR-CL. ACT.

HISTORY OF THE CASE:

TYPE OF COURT: FEDERAL

TRIER OF FACT: JUDGE;JURY PRESENT ?

COURT DECISION(S):

TRIAL COURT: FOR DEFENDANT
YEAR: 1973
SUPREME COURT: FOR DEFENDANT
YEAR: 1974

REASON SUIT FAILED:
1. NEGLIGENCE OR CASE NOT PROVEN

155. LESTER V. AETNA CASUALTY & SURETY CO.

FEW BACKROUND FACTS ARE AVAILABLE IN THE REPORTED DECISION. THE MALPRACTICE SUIT WAS BROUGHT BY HARLAN F. LESTER AGAINST A PSYCHIATRIST WHO GAVE HIM ELECTRO-SHOCK THERAPY WITHOUT HIS CONSENT, BUT WITH HIS WIFE'S.

YEAR OF NEGLIGENT ACT: NOT SPECIFIED

STATE IN WHICH NEGLIGENT ACT OCCURRED: LOUISIANA

SETTING OF THE CASE: HOSPITAL

PLAINTIFF(S): 3RD PARTY, I

DEFENDANT(S):
1. INSURANCE COMPANY(S)

NEGLIGENT ACTIVITY:

TREATMENT:
1. NEGLIGENT ELECTROCONVULSIVE THERAPY

DIAGNOSIS:

WHAT WAS DIAGNOSED: NOT APPLICABLE

RESULT OF DIAGNOSIS: NOT APPLICABLE

CARE: NOT APPLICABLE

HARM CAUSED TO PLAINTIFF &/OR PATIENT:
1. NONSELF-INFLICTED INJURIES

TYPE OF ACTION BROUGHT:
1. NEGLIGENCE

HISTORY OF THE CASE:

TYPE OF COURT: FEDERAL

TRIER OF FACT: JURY

COURT DECISION(S):

TRIAL COURT: FOR DEFENDANT
YEAR: NOT SPECIFIED
APPELLATE COURT: FOR DEFENDANT
YEAR: 1957
SUPREME COURT: FOR DEFENDANT
YEAR: 1957

REASON SUIT FAILED:
1. NEGLIGENCE OR CASE NOT PROVEN

156. LEWANDOWSKI V. STATE

ON JUNE 22, 1968 THREE WOMEN WERE INJURED WHEN THE CAR THEY WERE DRIVING COLLIDED WITH AN AUTOMOBILE OPERATED BY ANDREW GRAVES. GRAVES HAD BEEN A PATIENT AT MARCY STATE HOSPITAL AS AN ACUTE ALCOHOLIC, AND THE PLAINTIFFS CLAIMED THAT THE STATE WAS NEGLIGENT IN RELEASING HIM WITHOUT TAKING AWAY HIS DRIVER'S LICENSE.

YEAR OF NEGLIGENT ACT: 1968

STATE IN WHICH NEGLIGENT ACT OCCURRED: NEW YORK

SETTING OF THE CASE: PUB. MENT. HOSP.

PLAINTIFF(S): 3RD PARTY, II

DEFENDANT(S):
1. STATE GOV. &/OR OFFICIALS, ETC.

NEGLIGENT ACTIVITY:

TREATMENT: NOT APPLICABLE

DIAGNOSIS:

WHAT WAS DIAGNOSED:
1. LACK OF DANGEROUSNESS

RESULT OF DIAGNOSIS:
1. IMPROPER RELEASE

CARE: NOT APPLICABLE

HARM CAUSED TO PLAINTIFF &/OR PATIENT:
1. NONSELF-INFLICTED INJURIES

TYPE OF ACTION BROUGHT:
1. NEGLIGENCE

HISTORY OF THE CASE:

TYPE OF COURT: STATE

TRIER OF FACT: JUDGE,NO JURY

COURT DECISION(S):

TRIAL COURT: FOR DEFENDANT
YEAR: 1971

REASON SUIT FAILED:
1. NO CAUSE OF ACTION STATED

157. LEXINGTON HOSPITAL V. WHITE

DAVID WHITE WAS ADMITTED TO WAYSIDE HOSPITAL, A PRIVATE SANITARIUM, ON MAY 12, 1949 FOR HIS PERIODIC EPILEPTIC ATTACKS, WHICH WERE GROWING MORE FREQUENT AND SEVERE. DURING THESE ATTACKS HE IMAGINED HE WAS IN A GERMAN PRISON WITH SPIES ALL AROUND HIM, AND ON THE SPUR OF THE MOMENT WOULD RUN OFF AND HIDE. UPON HIS ADMISSION, HIS WIFE AND BROTHER MADE THIS CLEAR TO THE ADMITTING AIDE, WHO SAID EVERYTHING WOULD BE TAKEN CARE OF. THEY STRESSED THAT HE SHOULD BE WATCHED CAREFULLY AND NOT BE ALLOWED TO ESCAPE. HE ESCAPED ON MAY 15, WENT TO HIS HOME, AND WAS RETURNED THAT NIGHT. THE FOLLOWING DAY, WHILE HE WAS LEFT UNATTENDED, WHITE WENT INTO A BATHROOM, SMASHED THROUGH THE UPPER UNBARRED PART OF THE WINDOW AND FELL TO A BRICK SIDEWALK TWO FLOORS BELOW, SUSTAINING SERIOUS INJURIES. WHITE SUED THE HOSPITAL FOR FAILING TO PROVIDE ADEQUATE SUPERVISION.

YEAR OF NEGLIGENT ACT: 1949

STATE IN WHICH NEGLIGENT ACT OCCURRED: KENTUCKY

SETTING OF THE CASE: PRIV. MENT. HOSP.

PLAINTIFF(S): PATIENT(S) OR REP.

DEFENDANT(S):
1. HOSPITAL &/OR OWNERS, ETC.

NEGLIGENT ACTIVITY:

TREATMENT: NOT APPLICABLE

DIAGNOSIS:

WHAT WAS DIAGNOSED: NOT APPLICABLE

RESULT OF DIAGNOSIS: NOT APPLICABLE

CARE:
1. INADEQUATE SUPERVISION

HARM CAUSED TO PLAINTIFF &/OR PATIENT:
1. NONSELF-INFLICTED INJURIES

TYPE OF ACTION BROUGHT:
1. NEGLIGENCE

HISTORY OF THE CASE:

TYPE OF COURT: STATE

TRIER OF FACT: JURY

COURT DECISION(S):

TRIAL COURT: FOR PLAINTIFF
YEAR: NOT SPECIFIED
SUPREME COURT: FOR PLAINTIFF
YEAR: 1952

VERDICT AGAINST WHICH DEFENDANTS:
1. HOSPITAL &/OR OWNERS, ETC.

RECOVERY OR OTHER RELIEF GRANTED:
1. $ 6964

158. LICHTENSTEIN V. MONTEFIORE HOSPITAL

GARY LICHTENSTEIN WAS A PATIENT ON AN OPEN WARD AT MONTEFIORE HOSPITAL'S PSYCHIATRIC UNIT. THE DOORS TO THIS PARTICULAR UNIT WERE NOT LOCKED, BUT A NURSE WAS AT THE DOOR TO MAKE SURE THAT ANYONE WHO LEFT HAD AUTHORIZATION TO DO SO. ON THE MORNING OF AUGUST 16, 1966, GARY WAS FOUND TO BE MISSING FROM THE UNIT. AT 4:30 P.M. THAT SAME DAY, HIS BODY WAS FOUND UNDER A SUBWAY TRAIN. HIS WIFE BROUGHT SUIT, ALLEGING THAT THE HOSPITAL WAS NEGLIGENT IN SUPERVISING HER HUSBAND. THE HOSPITAL ARGUED THAT ITS OPEN WARD POLICY CONSTITUTED ACCEPTED PRACTICE.

YEAR OF NEGLIGENT ACT: 1966

STATE IN WHICH NEGLIGENT ACT OCCURRED: NEW YORK

SETTING OF THE CASE: PRIV. GEN. HOSP.

PLAINTIFF(S): PATIENT(S) OR REP.

DEFENDANT(S):
1. NONPSYCHIAT.OR UNKNOWN TYPE PHYSICIAN(S)
2. HOSPITAL &/OR OWNERS, ETC.

NEGLIGENT ACTIVITY:

TREATMENT: NOT APPLICABLE

DIAGNOSIS:

WHAT WAS DIAGNOSED: NOT APPLICABLE

RESULT OF DIAGNOSIS: NOT APPLICABLE

CARE:
1. INADEQUATE SUPERVISION

HARM CAUSED TO PLAINTIFF &/OR PATIENT:
1. SUICIDE

TYPE OF ACTION BROUGHT:
1. NEGLIGENCE

HISTORY OF THE CASE:

TYPE OF COURT: STATE

TRIER OF FACT: JURY

COURT DECISION(S):

TRIAL COURT: FOR PLAINTIFF
YEAR: 1976
APPELLATE COURT: NONFINAL FOR DEF.
YEAR: 1977

DEFENDANTS STILL INVOLVED IN SUIT:
1. HOSPITAL &/OR OWNERS, ETC.

159. LINDER V. FOSTER

EUGENIA LINDER WAS COMMITTED TO AN ASYLUM FROM APRIL 5 TO DECEMBER 22, 1937 AS A RESULT OF AN ORDER BY DONALD BENNYHOFF, COURT COMMISSIONER OF HENNEPIN COUNTY. THIS ORDER WAS INSTIGATED BY HAZEL FOSTER, A SUPERVISOR OF PUBLIC RELIEF WITH THE CITY OF MINNEAPOLIS. MS. LINDER CONTENDED THAT THESE TWO PEOPLE HATED HER AND HAD INSTITUTED THE COMMITMENT PROCEEDING OUT OF MALICE. THE TWO DOCTORS APPOINTED BY BENNYHOFF TO EXAMINE HER FOUND HER TO BE INSANE, AND SHE INCLUDED THEM AS CO-CONSPIRATORS IN THE CASE.

YEAR OF NEGLIGENT ACT: 1937

STATE IN WHICH NEGLIGENT ACT OCCURRED: MINNESOTA

SETTING OF THE CASE: JUDICIAL PROCEEDING

PLAINTIFF(S): PATIENT(S) OR REP.

DEFENDANT(S):
1. NONPSYCHIAT.OR UNKNOWN TYPE PHYSICIAN(S)
2. MUNICIPAL GOV. &/OR OFFICIALS, ETC.
3. JUDICIARY &/OR CLERKS, ETC.

NEGLIGENT ACTIVITY:

TREATMENT: NOT APPLICABLE

DIAGNOSIS:

WHAT WAS DIAGNOSED:
1. MENTAL ILLNESS, INSTEAD OF SANITY

RESULT OF DIAGNOSIS:
1. IMPROPER COMMITMENT

CARE: NOT APPLICABLE

HARM CAUSED TO PLAINTIFF &/OR PATIENT:
1. LOSS OF CONSORTIUM

TYPE OF ACTION BROUGHT:
1. MALICIOUS PROSECUTION
2. OTHER ACTION, EXCLUDING TORT LAW: TYPE NOT SPECIFIED

HISTORY OF THE CASE:

TYPE OF COURT: STATE

TRIER OF FACT: JUDGE;JURY PRESENT ?

COURT DECISION(S):

TRIAL COURT: FOR DEFENDANT
YEAR: NOT SPECIFIED
SUPREME COURT: FOR DEFENDANT
YEAR: 1940

REASON SUIT FAILED:
1. DEFENDANT(S) CANNOT BE SUED DUE TO: JUDICIAL IMMUNITY

160. LOWEN V. HILTON

ROBERT LOWEN WAS CONFINED TO MOUNT AVY SANITARIUM FOR ABOUT A WEEK ON A PETITION TO THE COUNTY JUDGE SIGNED BY J. P. HILTON AND OTHERS. HILTON WAS A PSYCHIATRIST WHO HAD DIAGNOSED ROBERT AS HAVING A PARANOID THINKING DISORDER. CHARLES LOWEN, ROBERT'S BROTHER, ALSO SIGNED THE PETITION, WHICH RESULTED IN A HOLD-AND-TREAT ORDER ISSUED FOR ROBERT ON JUNE 7, 1954. ON JUNE 15, THE COUNTY ORDERED HIM DISCHARGED AS BEING SANE AND CAPABLE OF CARING FOR HIMSELF. ROBERT SUED HIS BROTHER'S ESTATE AND THE PSYCHIATRIST FOR WRONGFULLY COMMITTING HIM.

YEAR OF NEGLIGENT ACT: 1954

STATE IN WHICH NEGLIGENT ACT OCCURRED: COLORADO

SETTING OF THE CASE: JUDICIAL PROCEEDING

PLAINTIFF(S): PATIENT(S) OR REP.

DEFENDANT(S):
1. PSYCHIATRIST(S)

NEGLIGENT ACTIVITY:

TREATMENT: NOT APPLICABLE

DIAGNOSIS:

WHAT WAS DIAGNOSED:
1. MENTAL ILLNESS, INSTEAD OF SANITY

RESULT OF DIAGNOSIS:
1. IMPROPER COMMITMENT

CARE: NOT APPLICABLE

HARM CAUSED TO PLAINTIFF &/OR PATIENT:
1. NOT SPECIFIED

TYPE OF ACTION BROUGHT:
1. MALICIOUS PROSECUTION

HISTORY OF THE CASE:

TYPE OF COURT: STATE

TRIER OF FACT: JUDGE;JURY PRESENT ?

COURT DECISION(S):

TRIAL COURT: FOR DEFENDANT
YEAR: NOT SPECIFIED
SUPREME COURT: NONFINAL FOR PL.
YEAR: 1960

DEFENDANTS STILL INVOLVED IN SUIT:
1. PSYCHIATRIST(S)

161. LUCY WEBB HAYES NATIONAL TRAINING SCHOOL V. PEROTTI

WILLIAM PEROTTI, MARRIED AND THE FATHER OF TWO CHILDREN, HAD HAD NO RECORD OF MENTAL ILLNESS PRIOR TO 1963. IN THAT YEAR, HOWEVER, HE APPLIED FOR A TRANSFER, WHICH REQUIRED HIM TO TAKE A POLYGRAPH TEST. THE TEST MADE HIM EXTREMELY FEARFUL, CAUSING HIM TO LOSE TWENTY-FIVE POUNDS AND MAKING HIM UNABLE TO SLEEP. HIS PHYSICIAN SUGGESTED THAT PEROTTI VISIT A PSYCHIATRIST, WHO DIAGNOSED PARANOID DEPRESSION AND RECOMMENDED HOSPITALIZATION IN SIBLEY MEMORIAL HOSPITAL. THREE DAYS LATER HE WAS DISCHARGED AGAINST THE PSYCHIATRIST'S RECOMMENDATIONS, BUT HAVING SHOWN SOME IMPROVEMENT. THE FOLLOWING JANUARY, PEROTTI SUFFERED A RELAPSE AND WAS ADMITTED TO THE CLOSED WARD OF SIBLEY. THE DAY AFTER ADMITTANCE HE SLIPPED INTO AN ADJOINING OPEN WARD, ESCAPED INTO THE SOLARIUM, AND JUMPED THROUGH A WINDOW TO HIS DEATH.

YEAR OF NEGLIGENT ACT: 1964

STATE IN WHICH NEGLIGENT ACT OCCURRED: DISTRICT OF COLUMBIA

SETTING OF THE CASE: PRIV. MENT. HOSP.

PLAINTIFF(S): PATIENT(S) OR REP.

DEFENDANT(S):
1. HOSPITAL &/OR OWNERS, ETC.

NEGLIGENT ACTIVITY:

TREATMENT: NOT APPLICABLE

DIAGNOSIS:

WHAT WAS DIAGNOSED: NOT APPLICABLE

RESULT OF DIAGNOSIS: NOT APPLICABLE

CARE:
1. INADEQUATE SUPERVISION

HARM CAUSED TO PLAINTIFF &/OR PATIENT:
1. SUICIDE

TYPE OF ACTION BROUGHT:
1. NEGLIGENCE

HISTORY OF THE CASE:

TYPE OF COURT: FEDERAL

TRIER OF FACT: JURY

COURT DECISION(S):

TRIAL COURT: FOR PLAINTIFF
YEAR: NOT SPECIFIED
APPELLATE COURT: NONFINAL FOR DEF.
YEAR: 1969

DEFENDANTS STILL INVOLVED IN SUIT:
1. HOSPITAL &/OR OWNERS, ETC.

162. MABEN V. RANKIN

THE PLAINTIFF, DORIS MABEN, WAS EXAMINED BY ONE DR. RANKIN AT HER HUSBAND'S REQUEST. SHE CLAIMED THAT SHE WAS NOT MENTALLY ILL, BUT THAT SHE WAS EXTREMELY UPSET AT HER HUSBAND'S INFIDELITY AND OTHER OBJECTIONABLE CONDUCT. SHE WAS GIVEN AN INJECTION AGAINST HER WILL, AND THE NEXT THING SHE REMEMBERED WAS WAKING UP A WEEK LATER IN ST. JOHN'S HOSPITAL. SHE WAS DETAINED THERE AGAINST HER WILL FOR FIFTEEN DAYS.

YEAR OF NEGLIGENT ACT: NOT SPECIFIED

STATE IN WHICH NEGLIGENT ACT OCCURRED: CALIFORNIA

SETTING OF THE CASE: PRIV. MENT. HOSP.

PLAINTIFF(S): PATIENT(S) OR REP.

DEFENDANT(S):
1. PSYCHIATRIST(S)
2. HOSPITAL &/OR OWNERS, ETC.

NEGLIGENT ACTIVITY:

TREATMENT:
1. NEGLIGENT ELECTROCONVULSIVE THERAPY
2. FAILURE TO OBTAIN -OR LACK OF- CONSENT
3. NEG.ADMIN.OF DRUGS

DIAGNOSIS:

WHAT WAS DIAGNOSED:
1. MENTAL ILLNESS, INSTEAD OF SANITY

RESULT OF DIAGNOSIS:
1. IMPROPER TREATMENT PRESCRIBED
2. IMPROPER DRUG PRESCRIPTION
3. IMPROPER COMMITMENT

CARE: NOT APPLICABLE

HARM CAUSED TO PLAINTIFF &/OR PATIENT:
1. LOSS OF LIBERTY

TYPE OF ACTION BROUGHT:
1. ASSAULT AND BATTERY
2. FALSE IMPRISONMENT

HISTORY OF THE CASE:

TYPE OF COURT: STATE

TRIER OF FACT: JURY

COURT DECISION(S):

TRIAL COURT: FOR PLAINTIFF
YEAR: NOT SPECIFIED
SUPREME COURT: NONFINAL FOR DEF.
YEAR: 1961

DEFENDANTS STILL INVOLVED IN SUIT:
1. PSYCHIATRIST(S)
2. HOSPITAL &/OR OWNERS, ETC.

163. MCCABE V. STATE

SUFFERING FROM DEMENTIA PRAECOX, CATATONIC TYPE, JOHN MCCABE WAS ADMITTED TO ROCKLAND STATE HOSPITAL ON SEPTEMBER 25, 1942 WITH A HISTORY OF TWO PRIOR COMMITMENTS. FOLLOWING HIS COMMITMENT, HE WAS GIVEN A SERIES OF ELECTRO-SHOCK TREATMENTS AND IMPROVED MARKEDLY. HE WAS SUBSEQUENTLY ASSIGNED TO WORK ON THE HOSPITAL GROUNDS, WHICH WAS STANDARD PRACTICE AT ROCKLAND FOR A PATIENT IN HIS CONDITION. ON DECEMBER 15, THE CLAIMANT AND OTHER PATIENTS WERE LOADING COAL ONTO A CONVEYOR BELT, WHICH HE HAD DONE SEVERAL TIMES PREVIOUSLY. MCCABE PUT HIS HAND INTO A PARTLY COVERED GEAR BOX TO RETREIVE A PIECE OF COAL, WHICH RESULTED IN INJURY TO HIS RIGHT HAND. SEVERAL FINGERS WERE FRACTURED AND LACERATED AND PART OF SOME HAD TO BE AMPUTATED.

YEAR OF NEGLIGENT ACT: 1942

STATE IN WHICH NEGLIGENT ACT OCCURRED: NEW YORK

SETTING OF THE CASE: PUB. MENT. HOSP.

PLAINTIFF(S): PATIENT(S) OR REP.

DEFENDANT(S):
1. STATE GOV. &/OR OFFICIALS, ETC.

NEGLIGENT ACTIVITY:

TREATMENT: NOT APPLICABLE

DIAGNOSIS:

WHAT WAS DIAGNOSED: NOT APPLICABLE

RESULT OF DIAGNOSIS: NOT APPLICABLE

CARE:
1. INADEQUATE SUPERVISION

HARM CAUSED TO PLAINTIFF &/OR PATIENT:
1. NONSELF-INFLICTED INJURIES

TYPE OF ACTION BROUGHT:
1. NEGLIGENCE

HISTORY OF THE CASE:

TYPE OF COURT: STATE

TRIER OF FACT: JUDGE,NO JURY

COURT DECISION(S):

TRIAL COURT: FOR DEFENDANT
YEAR: 1947
APPELLATE COURT: FOR DEFENDANT
YEAR: 1948

REASON SUIT FAILED:
1. NEGLIGENCE OR CASE NOT PROVEN

164. MCCANDLESS V. STATE

JUNE MEREDITH MCCANDLESS WAS FIRST ADMITTED TO THE NEW YORK PSYCHIATRIC INSTITUTE AT THE AGE OF SEVENTEEN. FOR ABOUT THREE YEARS SHE WAS TREATED AT THE CENTER AND ALLOWED VISITS TO HER HOME. ON APRIL 22, 1952, AFTER SHE HAD BEEN TRANSFERRED TO A STATE HOSPITAL, A LOBOTOMY WAS PERFORMED, AND WHILE STILL RECOVERING FROM THE OPERATION, SHE ATTENDED A DANCE GIVEN BY THE HOSPITAL. MIDWAY THROUGH THE DANCE SHE AND ANOTHER PATIENT LEFT THE DANCE FLOOR THROUGH AN UNLOCKED AND UNGUARDED DOOR. THEY HAD SEXUAL INTERCOURSE IN A HALLWAY AND RETURNED TO THE DANCE. THEIR DEPARTURE, ABSENCE, AND RETURN WERE UNNOTICED. JUNE MEREDITH BECAME PREGNANT AS A RESULT. HER PREGNANCY WAS FIRST NOTED BY THE HOSPITAL NEARLY FIVE MONTHS LATER. THE DIRECTOR, THE ASSISTANT DIRECTOR, AND THE PSYCHIATRIST IN CHARGE AT THE MEDICAL-SURGICAL BUILDING DECIDED TO PERFORM AN "INTERRUPTION OF PREGNANCY." AS A RESULT OF THE OPERATION, THE PATIENT SUFFERED CONSIDERABLE PAIN, SUFFERING, AND MENTAL ANGUISH. THE PLAINTIFF CHARGED NEGLIGENCE IN ALLOWING THE SEXUAL INTERCOURSE TO OCCUR AND FOR THE SUFFERING RESULTING FROM THE UNAUTHORIZED ABORTION.

YEAR OF NEGLIGENT ACT: OCCURRED OVER A SERIES OF YEARS, ENDING IN 1953

STATE IN WHICH NEGLIGENT ACT OCCURRED: NEW YORK

SETTING OF THE CASE: PUB. MENT. HOSP.

PLAINTIFF(S): PATIENT(S) OR REP.

DEFENDANT(S):
1. STATE GOV. &/OR OFFICIALS, ETC.

NEGLIGENT ACTIVITY:

TREATMENT:
1. IMPROPER ABORTION

DIAGNOSIS:

WHAT WAS DIAGNOSED: NOT APPLICABLE

RESULT OF DIAGNOSIS: NOT APPLICABLE

CARE:
1. INADEQUATE SUPERVISION

HARM CAUSED TO PLAINTIFF &/OR PATIENT:
1. EMOTIONAL DISTRESS
2. SEXUAL OR MARITAL HARM
3. PREG.& ABORTION

TYPE OF ACTION BROUGHT:
1. NEGLIGENCE
2. ASSAULT

HISTORY OF THE CASE:

TYPE OF COURT: STATE

TRIER OF FACT: JUDGE,NO JURY

COURT DECISION(S):

TRIAL COURT: FOR PLAINTIFF
YEAR: 1956
APPELLATE COURT: FOR PLAINTIFF
YEAR: 1957
SUPREME COURT: FOR PLAINTIFF
YEAR: 1958

VERDICT AGAINST WHICH DEFENDANTS:
1. STATE GOV. &/OR OFFICIALS, ETC.

RECOVERY OR OTHER RELIEF GRANTED:
1. $ 2000

165. MCNEIL V. DIRECTOR, PATUXENT INSTITUTION

EDWARD MCNEIL WAS CONVICTED OF TWO ASSAULTS IN 1966, AND SENTENCED TO FIVE YEARS' IMPRISONMENT. THE SENTENCING COURT REFERRED MCNEIL TO PATUXENT INSTITUTION TO DETERMINE WHETHER MCNEIL SHOULD BE COMMITTED TO THE INSTITUTION FOR AN INDETERMINATE TERM UNDER THE MARYLAND DEFECTIVE DELINQUENCY LAW. SUCH A DETERMINATION WAS NEVER MADE, AND DESPITE THE FACT THAT MCNEIL'S ORIGINAL SENTENCE HAD EXPIRED, HIS CONFINEMENT CONTINUED. MCNEIL CLAIMED THAT WHEN HIS SENTENCE EXPIRED, THE STATE LOST ALL POWER TO HOLD HIM.

YEAR OF NEGLIGENT ACT: 1971

STATE IN WHICH NEGLIGENT ACT OCCURRED: MARYLAND

SETTING OF THE CASE: PUB. MENT. HOSP.

PLAINTIFF(S): PATIENT(S) OR REP.

DEFENDANT(S):
1. HOSPITAL &/OR OWNERS, ETC.

NEGLIGENT ACTIVITY:

TREATMENT: NOT APPLICABLE

DIAGNOSIS:

WHAT WAS DIAGNOSED:
1. FAILURE TO MAKE A DIAGNOSIS

RESULT OF DIAGNOSIS:
1. IMPROPER FAILURE TO RELEASE

CARE: NOT APPLICABLE

HARM CAUSED TO PLAINTIFF &/OR PATIENT:
1. DEPRIVATION OF CONSTITUTIONAL RIGHTS
2. LOSS OF LIBERTY

TYPE OF ACTION BROUGHT:
1. DEPRIVATION OF CONSTITUTIONAL RIGHTS: LOSS OF LIBERTY

HISTORY OF THE CASE:

TYPE OF COURT: STATE

TRIER OF FACT: JUDGE,NO JURY

COURT DECISION(S):

TRIAL COURT: FOR DEFENDANT
YEAR: NOT SPECIFIED
APPELLATE COURT: FOR DEFENDANT
YEAR: NOT SPECIFIED
U.S. SUPREME COURT (ON APPEAL FROM STATE COURT): FOR PLAINTIFF
YEAR: 1972

VERDICT AGAINST WHICH DEFENDANTS:
1. HOSPITAL &/OR OWNERS, ETC.

RECOVERY OR OTHER RELIEF GRANTED:
1. NONMONETARY RELIEF: INJ.OR OTHER EQ.REL.

166. MANIACI V. MARQUETTE UNIVERSITY

IN SEPTEMBER 1966, SARALEE MANIACI LEFT HER HOME IN WINDSOR, ONTARIO TO ATTEND SCHOOL AT MARQUETTE UNIVERSITY IN MILWAUKEE. SHE WAS SIXTEEN YEARS OLD AT THE TIME. IN HER MONTHS AT MARQUETTE, SARALEE BECAME VERY DISSATISFIED WITH HER COURSES, THE QUALITY OF EDUCATION, AND HER SOCIAL LIFE. ON NOVEMBER 2, SHE DECIDED TO LEAVE SCHOOL. SHE WITHDREW ALL OF HER FUNDS FROM THE STUDENT CREDIT BANK AND BOUGHT A TRAIN TICKET TO DETROIT. A REPRESENTATIVE OF THE STUDENT BANK NOTIFIED THE DEAN OF WOMEN'S OFFICE THAT SARALEE WAS LEAVING SCHOOL. SARALEE WAS TOLD BY THE HEAD RESIDENT AT HER DORMITORY TO REPORT TO THE DEAN OF WOMEN ON NOVEMBER 4. WHEN SARALEE DID NOT REPORT, THE DEAN VISITED SARALEE AND ATTEMPTED TO PERSUADE HER TO STAY. WHEN SARALEE REFUSED, THE DEAN CALLED IN THE STUDENT HEALTH PHYSICIAN, WHO CONFERRED WITH SARALEE FOR ABOUT TWO HOURS AND THEN DECIDED TO PLACE HER IN A MENTAL HOSPITAL. HER EMERGENCY DETENTION WAS ARRANGED, AND MILWAUKEE POLICE OFFICERS TOOK HER TO THE MILWAUKEE COUNTY GENERAL HOSPITAL. AFTER THE INTERCESSION OF HER FATHER, SARALEE WAS RELEASED THE NEXT MORNING.

YEAR OF NEGLIGENT ACT: 1966

STATE IN WHICH NEGLIGENT ACT OCCURRED: WISCONSIN

SETTING OF THE CASE: JUDICIAL PROCEEDING

PLAINTIFF(S): PATIENT(S) OR REP.

DEFENDANT(S):
1. NONPSYCHIAT.OR UNKNOWN TYPE PHYSICIAN(S)
2. HOSPITAL &/OR OWNERS, ETC.
3. EDUCATIONAL INST. &/OR DEANS, ETC.
4. NURSE(S)

NEGLIGENT ACTIVITY:

TREATMENT: NOT APPLICABLE

DIAGNOSIS:

WHAT WAS DIAGNOSED:
1. MENTAL ILLNESS, INSTEAD OF SANITY

RESULT OF DIAGNOSIS:
1. IMPROPER COMMITMENT

CARE: NOT APPLICABLE

HARM CAUSED TO PLAINTIFF &/OR PATIENT:
1. LOSS OF LIBERTY

TYPE OF ACTION BROUGHT:
1. FALSE IMPRISONMENT
2. MALICIOUS PROSECUTION

HISTORY OF THE CASE:

TYPE OF COURT: STATE

TRIER OF FACT: JURY

COURT DECISION(S):

TRIAL COURT: FOR PLAINTIFF
YEAR: NOT SPECIFIED
SUPREME COURT: NONFINAL FOR DEF.
YEAR: 1971

DEFENDANTS STILL INVOLVED IN SUIT:
1. NONPSYCHIAT.OR UNKNOWN TYPE PHYSICIAN(S)
2. HOSPITAL &/OR OWNERS, ETC.
3. EDUCATIONAL INST. &/OR DEANS, ETC.
4. NURSE(S)

167. MARKS V. ST. FRANCIS HOSPITAL

IN OCTOBER OF 1952, MARY MARGUERITE MARKS WAS HOSPITALIZED AT ST. FRANCIS HOSPITAL AND SCHOOL OF NURSING. SHE WAS PLACED UNDER THE CARE OF DR. STREET, A PSYCHIATRIST. ON NOVEMBER 10, MARY WAS ALLOWED TO LEAVE THE HOSPITAL UNATTENDED AND WAS KILLED SHORTLY THEREAFTER. THE CIRCUMSTANCES OF HER DEATH ARE NOT AVAILABLE IN THE REPORTED DECISION.

YEAR OF NEGLIGENT ACT: 1952

STATE IN WHICH NEGLIGENT ACT OCCURRED: KANSAS

SETTING OF THE CASE: PRIV. GEN. HOSP.

PLAINTIFF(S): 3RD PARTY, I

DEFENDANT(S):
1. HOSPITAL &/OR OWNERS, ETC.

NEGLIGENT ACTIVITY:

TREATMENT: NOT APPLICABLE

DIAGNOSIS:

WHAT WAS DIAGNOSED: NOT APPLICABLE

RESULT OF DIAGNOSIS: NOT APPLICABLE

CARE:
1. INADEQUATE SUPERVISION
2. FAILURE TO PROVIDE PROPER CUSTODIAL CARE

HARM CAUSED TO PLAINTIFF &/OR PATIENT:
1. SUIC.OR ACCID.DEATH

TYPE OF ACTION BROUGHT:
1. OTHER ACTION, EXCLUDING TORT LAW: TYPE NOT SPECIFIED

HISTORY OF THE CASE:

TYPE OF COURT: STATE

TRIER OF FACT: JUDGE;JURY PRESENT ?

COURT DECISION(S):

TRIAL COURT: FOR DEFENDANT
YEAR: NOT SPECIFIED
SUPREME COURT: FOR DEFENDANT
YEAR: 1956

REASON SUIT FAILED:
1. NO CAUSE OF ACTION STATED

168. MARTARELLA V. KELLEY

PLAINTIFFS BROUGHT A CLASS ACTION SUIT AGAINST NEW YORK STATE OFFICIALS AND OTHERS FOR VIOLATIONS OF THEIR CONSTITUTIONAL RIGHTS. THE PLAINTIFFS CONSISTED OF THOSE CHILDREN WHO WERE LABELED "PERSONS IN NEED OF SUPERVISION" BY THE STATE. THIS LABEL WAS APPLIED TO THOSE WHOSE CONDUCT REQUIRED INCARCERATION, ALTHOUGH NOT CRIMINAL IN CHARACTER OR LEGAL DESIGNATION. THE PLAINTIFFS PROTESTED THEIR DETENTION IN THE MAXIMUM SECURITY FACILITIES FOR JUVENILES AT SPOFFORD, MANIDA, AND ZEREGA. THEIR PROTEST WAS BASED ON THE LACK OF CARE AND TREATMENT PROVIDED, THE WOEFULLY INADEQUATE NATURE OF THE FACILITIES, AND THE FACT THAT THEY WERE INCARCERATED WITH JUVENILE DELINQUENTS. IT WAS MAINTAINED THAT SUCH DETENTION CONSTITUTED CRUEL AND UNUSUAL PUNISHMENT.

YEAR OF NEGLIGENT ACT: NOT SPECIFIED, BUT OCCURRED OVER A SERIES OF YEARS

STATE IN WHICH NEGLIGENT ACT OCCURRED: NEW YORK

SETTING OF THE CASE: PUB. MENT. HOSP.

PLAINTIFF(S): PATIENT(S) OR REP.

DEFENDANT(S):
1. MUNICIPAL GOV. &/OR OFFICIALS, ETC.
2. JUDICIARY &/OR CLERKS, ETC.
3. CORRECTIONAL INST.

NEGLIGENT ACTIVITY:

TREATMENT:
1. NO TREATMENT OR INADEQUATE TREATMENT

DIAGNOSIS:

WHAT WAS DIAGNOSED: NOT APPLICABLE

RESULT OF DIAGNOSIS: NOT APPLICABLE

CARE: NOT APPLICABLE

HARM CAUSED TO PLAINTIFF &/OR PATIENT:
1. EMOTIONAL DISTRESS
2. DEPRIVATION OF CONSTITUTIONAL RIGHTS
3. SEXUAL OR MARITAL HARM

TYPE OF ACTION BROUGHT:
1. NEGLIGENCE
2. FALSE IMPRISONMENT
3. DEPRIVATION OF CONSTITUTIONAL RIGHTS: CONST.RTS.IN GEN.
4. NONMONETARY RELIEF
5. OTHER ACTION, EXCLUDING TORT LAW: CLASS ACTION SUIT

HISTORY OF THE CASE:

TYPE OF COURT: FEDERAL

TRIER OF FACT: JUDGE,NO JURY

COURT DECISION(S):

TRIAL COURT: FOR PLAINTIFF
YEAR: 1972
APPELLATE COURT: FOR PLAINTIFF
YEAR: 1973

VERDICT AGAINST WHICH DEFENDANTS:
1. MUNICIPAL GOV. &/OR OFFICIALS, ETC.
2. JUDICIARY &/OR CLERKS, ETC.
3. CORRECTIONAL INST.

RECOVERY OR OTHER RELIEF GRANTED:
1. NONMONETARY RELIEF: INJ.OR OTHER EQ.REL.

169. MARTINDALE V. STATE

ON SEPTEMBER 11, 1933, JOSEPHINE E. MARTINDALE WAS ACCEPTED AS A PATIENT AT THE SYRACUSE PSYCHOPATHIC HOSPITAL. SHE WAS KNOWN TO POSSESS A PROPENSITY TO ESCAPE. ON THE MORNING OF OCTOBER 13, JOSEPHINE MANAGED TO AVOID NOTICE AND WENT FROM THE DAY ROOM TO THE TOILET ROOM. IN THE TOILET ROOM, SHE REMOVED A LUG WHICH HELD THE WINDOW SHUT. SHE THEN FELL OR JUMPED TO HER DEATH FROM THIS THIRD-FLOOR WINDOW.

YEAR OF NEGLIGENT ACT: 1933

STATE IN WHICH NEGLIGENT ACT OCCURRED: NEW YORK

SETTING OF THE CASE: PUB. MENT. HOSP.

PLAINTIFF(S): PATIENT(S) OR REP.

DEFENDANT(S):
1. STATE GOV. &/OR OFFICIALS, ETC.

NEGLIGENT ACTIVITY:

TREATMENT: NOT APPLICABLE

DIAGNOSIS:

WHAT WAS DIAGNOSED: NOT APPLICABLE

RESULT OF DIAGNOSIS: NOT APPLICABLE

CARE:
1. INADEQUATE SUPERVISION

HARM CAUSED TO PLAINTIFF &/OR PATIENT:
1. SUICIDE

TYPE OF ACTION BROUGHT:
1. NEGLIGENCE

HISTORY OF THE CASE:

TYPE OF COURT: STATE

TRIER OF FACT: JUDGE,NO JURY

COURT DECISION(S):

TRIAL COURT: FOR PLAINTIFF
YEAR: NOT SPECIFIED
APPELLATE COURT: FOR PLAINTIFF
YEAR: 1935
SUPREME COURT: FOR PLAINTIFF
YEAR: 1935

VERDICT AGAINST WHICH DEFENDANTS:
1. STATE GOV. &/OR OFFICIALS, ETC.

RECOVERY OR OTHER RELIEF GRANTED:
1. OTHER RECOVERY: NOT SPECIFIED

170. MAYER V. ALBANY MEDICAL CENTER HOSPITAL

JOYCE MAYER VISITED HER FATHER, WHO WAS A PATIENT IN THE PSYCHIATRIC WARD AT ALBANY MEDICAL CENTER HOSPITAL. WHILE VISITING HER FATHER, JOYCE WAS ASSAULTED BY ANOTHER PATIENT, RESULTING IN SERIOUS BODILY INJURY, FOR WHICH SHE CLAIMED THE HOSPITAL WAS RESPONSIBLE.

YEAR OF NEGLIGENT ACT: NOT SPECIFIED

STATE IN WHICH NEGLIGENT ACT OCCURRED: NEW YORK

SETTING OF THE CASE: PUB. MENT. HOSP.

PLAINTIFF(S): 3RD PARTY, II

DEFENDANT(S):
1. HOSPITAL &/OR OWNERS, ETC.

NEGLIGENT ACTIVITY:

TREATMENT: NOT APPLICABLE

DIAGNOSIS:

WHAT WAS DIAGNOSED: NOT APPLICABLE

RESULT OF DIAGNOSIS: NOT APPLICABLE

CARE:
1. INADEQUATE SUPERVISION

HARM CAUSED TO PLAINTIFF &/OR PATIENT:
1. NONSELF-INFLICTED INJURIES

TYPE OF ACTION BROUGHT:
1. NEGLIGENCE

HISTORY OF THE CASE:

TYPE OF COURT: STATE

TRIER OF FACT: JUDGE;JURY PRESENT ?

COURT DECISION(S):

TRIAL COURT: NONFINAL FOR DEF.
YEAR: 1971
APPELLATE COURT: NONFINAL FOR PL.
YEAR: 1971

DEFENDANTS STILL INVOLVED IN SUIT:
1. HOSPITAL &/OR OWNERS, ETC.

171. MEIER V. ROSS GENERAL HOSPITAL

ON JULY 5, 1962, KURT MEIER ATTEMPTED SUICIDE BY SLASHING HIS WRISTS. AFTER BEING TREATED FOR HIS PHYSICAL INJURIES, HIS FAMILY BROUGHT HIM TO ROSS GENERAL HOSPITAL. KURT WAS PLACED UNDER THE CARE OF DR. STUBBLEBINE, DIRECTOR OF THE HOSPITAL'S PSYCHIATRIC WING. ROSS GENERAL HOSPITAL HAD ADOPTED AN "OPEN DOOR" POLICY FOR ITS PSYCHIATRIC PATIENTS. THIS METHOD OF TREATMENT DE-EMPHASIZED PHYSICAL RESTRAINTS BY PROVIDING A "HOMELIKE" ATMOSPHERE FOR ITS PATIENTS. ON JULY 13, WHILE ALONE IN HIS ROOM, KURT MEIER PLUNGED TO HIS DEATH THROUGH AN OPEN SECOND-STORY WINDOW.

YEAR OF NEGLIGENT ACT: 1962

STATE IN WHICH NEGLIGENT ACT OCCURRED: CALIFORNIA

SETTING OF THE CASE: GENERAL HOSPITAL

PLAINTIFF(S): 3RD PARTY, I

DEFENDANT(S):
1. NONPSYCHIAT.OR UNKNOWN TYPE PHYSICIAN(S)
2. HOSPITAL &/OR OWNERS, ETC.

NEGLIGENT ACTIVITY:

TREATMENT: NOT APPLICABLE

DIAGNOSIS:

WHAT WAS DIAGNOSED: NOT APPLICABLE

RESULT OF DIAGNOSIS: NOT APPLICABLE

CARE:
1. INADEQUATE SUPERVISION

HARM CAUSED TO PLAINTIFF &/OR PATIENT:
1. SUICIDE

TYPE OF ACTION BROUGHT:
1. NEGLIGENCE

HISTORY OF THE CASE:

TYPE OF COURT: STATE

TRIER OF FACT: JURY

COURT DECISION(S):

TRIAL COURT: FOR DEFENDANT
YEAR: NOT SPECIFIED
SUPREME COURT: NONFINAL FOR PL.
YEAR: 1968

DEFENDANTS STILL INVOLVED IN SUIT:
1. NONPSYCHIAT.OR UNKNOWN TYPE PHYSICIAN(S)
2. HOSPITAL &/OR OWNERS, ETC.

172. MERCHANTS NATIONAL BANK V. UNITED STATES

ON JANUARY 17, 1965, ELOISE NEWGARD CALLED DR. MACK TRAYNOR AND THE REVEREND RICHARD FAUST TO HER HOME IN FARGO, NORTH DAKOTA BECAUSE OF THE BEHAVIOR OF HER HUSBAND, WILLIAM. THE LATTER WAS FOUND CLAD IN BOXER SHORTS AND A T-SHIRT AND PROCEEDED TO EXPOSE HIMSELF, WHILE THREATENING THE LIFE OF HIS WIFE AND STATING THAT HE WAS "GOING TO REPOPULATE THE WORLD." FAUST WAS ABLE TO GET WILLIAM TO ST. LUKE'S HOSPITAL IN FARGO BY LITERALLY MARCHING HIM THROUGH THE STREETS. EVENTUALLY HE WAS TRANSFERRED TO THE V.A. HOSPITAL IN FORT MEADE, SOUTH DAKOTA, WHERE HE WAS TREATED BY ONE DR. LINNELL. IN MAY, DR. LINNELL GRANTED WILLIAM PERMISSION TO VISIT FARGO FOR HIS UNCLE'S FUNERAL. ELOISE LEARNED OF HIS RELEASE AND ARRANGED TO HAVE WILLIAM TAKEN INTO CUSTODY AT THE BUS STOP AND RETURNED TO FORT MEADE. SEVERAL MONTHS LATER HE WAS PLACED ON A RANCH TO WORK AS A FARMHAND. THE OWNERS WERE TOLD ONLY THAT HE HAD SUFFERED A NERVOUS BREAKDOWN AND NEWGARD WAS FREE TO GO AS HE PLEASED. ON A WEEKEND OFF HE VISITED HIS PARENTS IN MAYVILLE, WHERE HE RAN INTO HIS WIFE. HIS ATTEMPT TO CONVINCE HER TO RETURN TO FARGO WITH HIM FAILED AND HE RETURNED TO THE RANCH. SHORTLY THEREAFTER HE OBTAINED A CAR AND DROVE TO HIS MOTHER-IN-LAW'S HOME IN DETROIT LAKES, MINNESOTA. ONCE THERE, HE ATTEMPTED TO RUN OVER HIS WIFE, AND EVENTUALLY SHOT HER TO DEATH.

YEAR OF NEGLIGENT ACT: 1965

STATE IN WHICH NEGLIGENT ACT OCCURRED: SOUTH DAKOTA

SETTING OF THE CASE: PUB. MENT. HOSP.

PLAINTIFF(S): 3RD PARTY, II

DEFENDANT(S):
1. FEDERAL GOV. &/OR OFFICIALS, ETC.

NEGLIGENT ACTIVITY:

TREATMENT: NOT APPLICABLE

DIAGNOSIS:

WHAT WAS DIAGNOSED:
1. SANITY, INSTEAD OF MENTAL ILLNESS
2. LACK OF DANGEROUSNESS

RESULT OF DIAGNOSIS:
1. IMPROPER RELEASE

CARE: NOT APPLICABLE

HARM CAUSED TO PLAINTIFF &/OR PATIENT:
1. NONSUICIDAL DEATH

TYPE OF ACTION BROUGHT:
1. NEGLIGENCE

HISTORY OF THE CASE:

TYPE OF COURT: FEDERAL

TRIER OF FACT: JUDGE,NO JURY

COURT DECISION(S):

TRIAL COURT: FOR PLAINTIFF
YEAR: 1967

VERDICT AGAINST WHICH DEFENDANTS:
1. FEDERAL GOV. &/OR OFFICIALS, ETC.

RECOVERY OR OTHER RELIEF GRANTED:
1. $200000
2. OTHER RECOVERY: COSTS

173. MEYNIER V. DE PAUL HOSPITAL

LOUISE MEYNIER WAS A SEVENTY-TWO-YEAR-OLD OUT-PATIENT OF DE PAUL HOSPITAL. BETWEEN AUGUST OF 1961 AND APRIL OF 1963, SHE HAD RECEIVED TWENTY ELECTRO-SHOCK TREATMENTS. ON APRIL 10, 1963, SHE RECEIVED TWO TREATMENTS OF 140 VOLTS EACH AND WAS KEPT IN THE RECOVERY ROOM FOR ABOUT ONE HOUR. WHEN SHE RECOVERED CONSCIOUSNESS, SHE WAS GIVEN COFFEE AND ASPIRIN. HER ATTENDANT WAS A THIRTEEN-YEAR VETERAN OF THIS TYPE OF HOSPITAL WORK. SHE ASSISTED LOUISE IN GETTING DRESSED AND HELPED HER OUT OF THE RECOVERY ROOM. HALFWAY DOWN A FLIGHT OF STAIRS MEYNIER SLIPPED AND FELL. THE FALL RESULTED IN THE FRACTURE OF HER LEFT ANKLE. LOUISE CHARGED THAT SHE SHOULD HAVE BEEN TAKEN FROM THE RECEPTION ROOM IN A WHEELCHAIR ALONG AN UNSTEPPED AND MORE DIRECT ROUTE THAT EXISTED.

YEAR OF NEGLIGENT ACT: 1963

STATE IN WHICH NEGLIGENT ACT OCCURRED: LOUISIANA

SETTING OF THE CASE: EDUCATIONAL INST.

PLAINTIFF(S): PATIENT(S) OR REP.

DEFENDANT(S):
1. PSYCHIATRIST(S)
2. HOSPITAL &/OR OWNERS, ETC.
3. INSURANCE COMPANY(S)

NEGLIGENT ACTIVITY:

TREATMENT: NOT APPLICABLE

DIAGNOSIS:

WHAT WAS DIAGNOSED: NOT APPLICABLE

RESULT OF DIAGNOSIS: NOT APPLICABLE

CARE:
1. INADEQUATE SUPERVISION

HARM CAUSED TO PLAINTIFF &/OR PATIENT:
1. NONSELF-INFLICTED INJURIES

TYPE OF ACTION BROUGHT:
1. NEGLIGENCE

HISTORY OF THE CASE:

TYPE OF COURT: STATE

TRIER OF FACT: ?, JUDGE OR JURY

COURT DECISION(S):

TRIAL COURT: FOR PLAINTIFF
YEAR: NOT SPECIFIED
APPELLATE COURT: FOR PLAINTIFF
YEAR: 1969

VERDICT AGAINST WHICH DEFENDANTS:
1. HOSPITAL &/OR OWNERS, ETC.
2. INSURANCE CO.

RECOVERY OR OTHER RELIEF GRANTED:
1. $ 4299
2. INTEREST

174. MEZULLO V. MALETZ

THE PLAINTIFF ALLEGED THAT THE DEFENDANT PHYSICIAN NEGLIGENTLY PERFORMED A MENTAL EXAMINATION OF HER, AS A RESULT OF WHICH SHE WAS COMMITTED TO A STATE INSTITUTION FOR THE INSANE. FURTHER DETAILS ARE UNAVAILABLE.

YEAR OF NEGLIGENT ACT: NOT SPECIFIED

STATE IN WHICH NEGLIGENT ACT OCCURRED: MASSACHUSETTS

SETTING OF THE CASE: JUDICIAL PROCEEDING

PLAINTIFF(S): PATIENT(S) OR REP.

DEFENDANT(S):
1. NONPSYCHIAT.OR UNKNOWN TYPE PHYSICIAN(S)

NEGLIGENT ACTIVITY:

TREATMENT: NOT APPLICABLE

DIAGNOSIS:

WHAT WAS DIAGNOSED:
1. MENTAL ILLNESS, INSTEAD OF SANITY

RESULT OF DIAGNOSIS:
1. IMPROPER COMMITMENT

CARE: NOT APPLICABLE

HARM CAUSED TO PLAINTIFF &/OR PATIENT:
1. LOSS OF LIBERTY

TYPE OF ACTION BROUGHT:
1. NEGLIGENCE

HISTORY OF THE CASE:

TYPE OF COURT: STATE

TRIER OF FACT: JUDGE;JURY PRESENT ?

COURT DECISION(S):

TRIAL COURT: FOR DEFENDANT
YEAR: NOT SPECIFIED
SUPREME COURT: FOR DEFENDANT
YEAR: 1954

REASON SUIT FAILED:
1. DEFENDANT(S) CANNOT BE SUED DUE TO: JUDICIAL IMMUNITY

175. MILANO V. STATE

A PATIENT AT ROCKLAND STATE HOSPITAL HAD BEEN DIAGNOSED AS HAVING A SCHIZOID PERSONALITY WITH AN I.Q. OF SIXTY-SEVEN. HIS FATHER WAS AN ALCOHOLIC AND POOR PROVIDER. HIS MOTHER WAS EMOTIONALLY INCAPABLE OF PROVIDING A STABLE HOME ENVIRONMENT FOR HER SON. THE PATIENT HAD A HISTORY OF SUICIDAL AND HOMICIDAL THREATS, AS WELL AS AGGRESSIVE BEHAVIOR TOWARD HIS MOTHER AND BROTHERS. NONETHELESS HE WAS GIVEN CONVALESCENT LEAVE IN MARCH, 1962. SEVERAL MONTHS LATER THE PATIENT SEXUALLY ASSAULTED AND STRANGLED A CHILD, RESULTING IN HIS DEATH.

YEAR OF NEGLIGENT ACT: 1962

STATE IN WHICH NEGLIGENT ACT OCCURRED: NEW YORK

SETTING OF THE CASE: PUB. MENT. HOSP.

PLAINTIFF(S): 3RD PARTY, II

DEFENDANT(S):
1. STATE GOV. &/OR OFFICIALS, ETC.

NEGLIGENT ACTIVITY:

TREATMENT: NOT APPLICABLE

DIAGNOSIS:

WHAT WAS DIAGNOSED:
1. LACK OF DANGEROUSNESS

RESULT OF DIAGNOSIS:
1. IMPROPER RELEASE

CARE:
1. INADEQUATE SUPERVISION
2. PREMATURE RELEASE

HARM CAUSED TO PLAINTIFF &/OR PATIENT:
1. NONSUICIDAL DEATH
2. SEXUAL OR MARITAL HARM

TYPE OF ACTION BROUGHT:
1. NEGLIGENCE

HISTORY OF THE CASE:

TYPE OF COURT: STATE

TRIER OF FACT: JUDGE,NO JURY

COURT DECISION(S):

TRIAL COURT: FOR DEFENDANT
YEAR: 1964

REASON SUIT FAILED:
1. NEGLIGENCE OR CASE NOT PROVEN

176. MILLARD V. CAMERON

ON SEPTEMBER 1, 1962, MAURICE MILLARD EXPOSED HIMSELF BEFORE SEVERAL PERSONS IN PUBLIC. HE WAS CHARGED WITH INDECENT EXPOSURE AND THE MUNICIPAL COURT ORDERED TWO PSYCHIATRISTS FROM THE DISTRICT OF COLUMBIA GENERAL HOSPITAL TO EXAMINE HIM. THE PSYCHIATRISTS CONCLUDED THAT HE WAS A SEXUAL PSYCHOPATH AS DEFINED UNDER THE SEXUAL PSYCHOPATH STATUTE, AND HE WAS PLACED IN ST. ELIZABETH'S HOSPITAL. THE PLAINTIFF INSTITUTED A HABEAS CORPUS PROCEEDING, CHARGING THAT HIS COMMITMENT WAS IMPROPER BECAUSE HE HAD BEEN GIVEN NO CHANCE TO DEFEND HIMSELF, TO EXAMINE OR CROSS-EXAMINE THE PSYCHIATRISTS, OR TO ENGAGE COUNSEL IN HIS BEHALF.

YEAR OF NEGLIGENT ACT: 1962

STATE IN WHICH NEGLIGENT ACT OCCURRED: DISTRICT OF COLUMBIA

SETTING OF THE CASE: JUDICIAL PROCEEDING

PLAINTIFF(S): PATIENT(S) OR REP.

DEFENDANT(S):
1. HOSPITAL &/OR OWNERS, ETC.

NEGLIGENT ACTIVITY:

TREATMENT: NOT APPLICABLE

DIAGNOSIS:

WHAT WAS DIAGNOSED:
1. MENTAL ILLNESS, INSTEAD OF SANITY
2. DANGEROUSNESS

RESULT OF DIAGNOSIS:
1. IMPROPER COMMITMENT

CARE: NOT APPLICABLE

HARM CAUSED TO PLAINTIFF &/OR PATIENT:
1. LOSS OF LIBERTY

TYPE OF ACTION BROUGHT:
1. DEPRIVATION OF CONSTITUTIONAL RIGHTS: LOSS OF LIBERTY
2. HABEAS CORPUS
3. NONMONETARY RELIEF

HISTORY OF THE CASE:

TYPE OF COURT: FEDERAL

TRIER OF FACT: JUDGE,NO JURY

COURT DECISION(S):

TRIAL COURT: FOR DEFENDANT
YEAR: NOT SPECIFIED
APPELLATE COURT: NONFINAL FOR PL.
YEAR: 1966
ON RETRIAL: FOR DEFENDANT
YEAR: NOT SPECIFIED
ON REAPPEAL TO APPELLATE COURT: FOR PLAINTIFF
YEAR: 1968

VERDICT AGAINST WHICH DEFENDANTS:
1. HOSPITAL &/OR OWNERS, ETC.

RECOVERY OR OTHER RELIEF GRANTED:
1. NONMONETARY RELIEF: INJ.OR OTHER EQ.REL.

177. MILLER V. DICKERT

WANNAMAKER MILLER BROUGHT SUIT AGAINST E. J. DICKERT AND V. W. RINEHART, TWO PRACTICING PHYSICIANS IN NEWBERRY COUNTY, FOR WRONGFULLY SIGNING A MEDICAL CERTIFICATE INDICATING THAT EACH HAD EXAMINED MILLER AND FOUND HIM DANGEROUS AND INCAPABLE OF CARING FOR HIMSELF. BECAUSE OF THIS CERTIFICATE, MILLER WAS INVOLUNTARILY COMMITTED TO THE SOUTH CAROLINA STATE HOSPITAL, WHERE HE WAS HELD FOR TWENTY-EIGHT DAYS.

YEAR OF NEGLIGENT ACT: 1969

STATE IN WHICH NEGLIGENT ACT OCCURRED: SOUTH CAROLINA

SETTING OF THE CASE: JUDICIAL PROCEEDING

PLAINTIFF(S): PATIENT(S) OR REP.

DEFENDANT(S):
1. NONPSYCHIAT.OR UNKNOWN TYPE PHYSICIAN(S)

NEGLIGENT ACTIVITY:

TREATMENT: NOT APPLICABLE

DIAGNOSIS:

WHAT WAS DIAGNOSED:
1. MENTAL ILLNESS, INSTEAD OF SANITY

RESULT OF DIAGNOSIS:
1. IMPROPER COMMITMENT

CARE: NOT APPLICABLE

HARM CAUSED TO PLAINTIFF &/OR PATIENT:
1. LOSS OF LIBERTY

TYPE OF ACTION BROUGHT:
1. FALSE IMPRISONMENT

HISTORY OF THE CASE:

TYPE OF COURT: STATE

TRIER OF FACT: JUDGE;JURY PRESENT ?

COURT DECISION(S):

TRIAL COURT: NONFINAL FOR PL.
YEAR: 1972
SUPREME COURT: FOR DEFENDANT
YEAR: 1972

REASON SUIT FAILED:
1. STATUTE OF LIMITATIONS BARRED SUIT

178. MILLER V. WEST

THE PLAINTIFF BROUGHT SUIT AGAINST TWO PHYSICIANS FOR FALSELY CERTIFYING TO THE MARYLAND HOSPITAL FOR THE INSANE THAT THE PLAINTIFF WAS PSYCHOTIC AND OTHERWISE MENTALLY DEFICIENT. THE PLAINTIFF WAS COMMITTED FOR NINE MONTHS BEFORE DISCHARGE, BUT ALLEGED THAT NEITHER PHYSICIAN HAD EVER EXAMINED HIM.

YEAR OF NEGLIGENT ACT: NOT SPECIFIED

STATE IN WHICH NEGLIGENT ACT OCCURRED: MARYLAND

SETTING OF THE CASE: JUDICIAL PROCEEDING

PLAINTIFF(S): PATIENT(S) OR REP.

DEFENDANT(S):
1. NONPSYCHIAT.OR UNKNOWN TYPE PHYSICIAN(S)

NEGLIGENT ACTIVITY:

TREATMENT: NOT APPLICABLE

DIAGNOSIS:

WHAT WAS DIAGNOSED:
1. MENTAL ILLNESS, INSTEAD OF SANITY

RESULT OF DIAGNOSIS:
1. IMPROPER COMMITMENT

CARE: NOT APPLICABLE

HARM CAUSED TO PLAINTIFF &/OR PATIENT:
1. LOSS OF LIBERTY

TYPE OF ACTION BROUGHT:
1. NEGLIGENCE
2. FALSE IMPRISONMENT

HISTORY OF THE CASE:

TYPE OF COURT: STATE

TRIER OF FACT: JUDGE;JURY PRESENT ?

COURT DECISION(S):

TRIAL COURT: FOR DEFENDANT
YEAR: NOT SPECIFIED
SUPREME COURT: FOR DEFENDANT
YEAR: 1933

REASON SUIT FAILED:
1. NEGLIGENCE OR CASE NOT PROVEN

179. MILLS V. SOCIETY OF THE NEW YORK HOSPITAL

THIS SUIT WAS BROUGHT BY THE PLAINTIFF TO RECOVER FOR THE DEATH OF HER INTESTATE, FREDERICK L. MILLS. MILLS HAD BEEN A PATIENT OF THE BLOOMINGDALE HOSPITAL FOR MENTAL DISEASES. THE DECEASED, ALONG WITH FOUR OTHER PATIENTS AND ONE PHYSICAL AIDE, HAD BEEN WALKING BY A PUBLIC HIGHWAY. HE SUDDENLY DARTED OUT ONTO THE HIGHWAY AND WAS KILLED BY A VEHICLE.

YEAR OF NEGLIGENT ACT: NOT SPECIFIED

STATE IN WHICH NEGLIGENT ACT OCCURRED: NEW YORK

SETTING OF THE CASE: PRIV. MENT. HOSP.

PLAINTIFF(S): PATIENT(S) OR REP.

DEFENDANT(S):
1. HOSPITAL &/OR OWNERS, ETC.

NEGLIGENT ACTIVITY:

TREATMENT: NOT APPLICABLE

DIAGNOSIS:

WHAT WAS DIAGNOSED:
1. SANITY, INSTEAD OF MENTAL ILLNESS

RESULT OF DIAGNOSIS:
1. IMPROPER CUSTODIAL CARE

CARE: NOT APPLICABLE

HARM CAUSED TO PLAINTIFF &/OR PATIENT:
1. SUICIDE

TYPE OF ACTION BROUGHT:
1. NEGLIGENCE
2. CONTRACT LAW: BREACH OF CONTRACT

HISTORY OF THE CASE:

TYPE OF COURT: STATE

TRIER OF FACT: JURY

COURT DECISION(S):

TRIAL COURT: FOR PLAINTIFF
YEAR: NOT SPECIFIED
APPELLATE COURT: FOR DEFENDANT
YEAR: 1934
SUPREME COURT: FOR DEFENDANT
YEAR: 1936

REASON SUIT FAILED:
1. NEGLIGENCE OR CASE NOT PROVEN

180. MITCHELL V. ROBINSON

WILLIAM MITCHELL AND DR. DE MOTT WERE SCHOOLMATES FROM BOYHOOD THROUGH COLLEGE. WHEN MITCHELL WAS BESET WITH EMOTIONAL PROBLEMS IN 1951, HE SOUGHT OUT DR. DE MOTT, WHO WAS THEN A SPECIALIST IN NEUROLOGY AND PSYCHIATRY. MITCHELL WAS DIAGNOSED AS HAVING PROCESS SCHIZOPHRENIA. HIS ILLNESS WAS CHARACTERIZED BY SERIOUS DEPRESSION AND SEVERE ANXIETY, COMPLICATED BY ALCOHOLISM. DR. DE MOTT AND HIS ASSOCIATES PRESCRIBED ELECTRO-SHOCK THERAPY FOR MITCHELL. ON OCTOBER 25, 1951, MITCHELL HAD HIS FIRST TREATMENT. PROGRESS WAS MADE UNTIL NOVEMBER 2, WHEN MITCHELL CAME IN DRUNK. THE TREATMENT BEGAN AGAIN ON NOVEMBER 4. ON NOVEMBER 7 HE EXPERIENCED A GRAND MAL SEIZURE, WHICH RESULTED IN A COMPRESSION FRACTURE OF THE FIFTH, SIXTH, AND SEVENTH DORSAL VERTEBRAE. THIS ACTION WAS INITIATED AGAINST THE PHYSICIAN PARTNERSHIP TO RECOVER DAMAGES FOR THOSE INJURIES.

YEAR OF NEGLIGENT ACT: 1951

STATE IN WHICH NEGLIGENT ACT OCCURRED: MISSOURI

SETTING OF THE CASE: PRIV. MENT. HOSP.

PLAINTIFF(S): PATIENT(S) OR REP.

DEFENDANT(S):
1. NONPSYCHIAT.OR UNKNOWN TYPE PHYSICIAN(S)

NEGLIGENT ACTIVITY:

TREATMENT:
1. NEGLIGENT INSULIN THERAPY

DIAGNOSIS:

WHAT WAS DIAGNOSED: NOT APPLICABLE

RESULT OF DIAGNOSIS: NOT APPLICABLE

CARE: NOT APPLICABLE

HARM CAUSED TO PLAINTIFF &/OR PATIENT:
1. NONSELF-INFLICTED INJURIES

TYPE OF ACTION BROUGHT:
1. NEGLIGENCE

HISTORY OF THE CASE:

TYPE OF COURT: STATE

TRIER OF FACT: JURY

COURT DECISION(S):

TRIAL COURT: FOR PLAINTIFF
YEAR: NOT SPECIFIED
SUPREME COURT: NONFINAL FOR DEF.
YEAR: 1960
ON RETRIAL: FOR DEFENDANT
YEAR: NOT SPECIFIED
ON REAPPEAL TO SUPREME COURT: FOR DEFENDANT
YEAR: 1962

REASON SUIT FAILED:
1. PATIENT HAD GIVEN INFORMED CONSENT

181. MOCHEN V. STATE

SEVENTEEN-YEAR-OLD GEORGE MOCHEN HAD SUFFERED FROM MENTAL PROBLEMS SINCE BIRTH. THESE HAD INCREASED IN SEVERITY SINCE AGE NINE, FROM WHICH TIME ON HE HAD BEEN A RESIDENT OF VARIOUS MENTAL INSTITUTIONS. IN NOVEMBER, 1967, HE WAS CONFINED TO BUFFALO STATE HOSPITAL FOR ATTACKING HIS PARENTS. TWO MONTHS LATER, AT MIDNIGHT HE AND A COHORT BROKE A METAL BAR GUARDING A WINDOW AND ATTEMPTED TO ESCAPE BY SLIDING DOWN KNOTTED SHEETS THIRTY OR FORTY FEET TO THE GROUND FROM A SECOND-STORY WINDOW. HIS FRIEND MADE IT, BUT HE SLIPPED AND FELL, CAUSING SERIOUS INJURY TO BOTH LEGS AND RENDERING HIM PERMANENTLY CRIPPLED. HIS ATTEMPTED ESCAPE WAS THE SECOND FROM BUFFALO STATE AND THE SIXTEENTH OVERALL ATTEMPT ON HIS RECORD. HIS GUARDIAN ALLEGED THAT THE STATE WAS NEGLIGENT IN ALLOWING HIM ACCESS TO BOTH THE WINDOW AND THE MATERIALS HE HAD USED TO CARRY OUT HIS ESCAPE ATTEMPT.

YEAR OF NEGLIGENT ACT: 1968

STATE IN WHICH NEGLIGENT ACT OCCURRED: NEW YORK

SETTING OF THE CASE: PUB. MENT. HOSP.

PLAINTIFF(S): PATIENT(S) OR REP.

DEFENDANT(S):
1. STATE GOV. &/OR OFFICIALS, ETC.

NEGLIGENT ACTIVITY:

TREATMENT: NOT APPLICABLE

DIAGNOSIS:

WHAT WAS DIAGNOSED: NOT APPLICABLE

RESULT OF DIAGNOSIS: NOT APPLICABLE

CARE:
1. INADEQUATE SUPERVISION

HARM CAUSED TO PLAINTIFF &/OR PATIENT:
1. SELF-INFLICTED INJURIES

TYPE OF ACTION BROUGHT:
1. NEGLIGENCE

HISTORY OF THE CASE:

TYPE OF COURT: STATE

TRIER OF FACT: JUDGE,NO JURY

COURT DECISION(S):

TRIAL COURT: FOR DEFENDANT
YEAR: NOT SPECIFIED
APPELLATE COURT: NONFINAL FOR PL.
YEAR: 1974
ON RETRIAL: FOR DEFENDANT
YEAR: NOT SPECIFIED
ON REAPPEAL TO APPELLATE COURT: FOR DEFENDANT
YEAR: 1977

REASON SUIT FAILED:
1. NEGLIGENCE OR CASE NOT PROVEN

182. MONTGOMERY COUNTY TRUST V. STATE

NO SPECIFIC FACTS ARE AVAILABLE FROM THE REPORTED CASE. THE CLAIM INVOLVED A SUIT FOR INJURIES SUSTAINED BY AN INCOMPETENT PATIENT IN A STATE HOSPITAL AT THE HANDS OF ANOTHER INCOMPETENT PATIENT.

YEAR OF NEGLIGENT ACT: NOT SPECIFIED

STATE IN WHICH NEGLIGENT ACT OCCURRED: NEW YORK

SETTING OF THE CASE: PUB. MENT. HOSP.

PLAINTIFF(S): PATIENT(S) OR REP.

DEFENDANT(S):
1. STATE GOV. &/OR OFFICIALS, ETC.

NEGLIGENT ACTIVITY:

TREATMENT: NOT APPLICABLE

DIAGNOSIS:

WHAT WAS DIAGNOSED: NOT APPLICABLE

RESULT OF DIAGNOSIS: NOT APPLICABLE

CARE:
1. INADEQUATE SUPERVISION

HARM CAUSED TO PLAINTIFF &/OR PATIENT:
1. NONSELF-INFLICTED INJURIES

TYPE OF ACTION BROUGHT:
1. OTHER ACTION, EXCLUDING TORT LAW: TYPE NOT SPECIFIED

HISTORY OF THE CASE:

TYPE OF COURT: STATE

TRIER OF FACT: JUDGE,NO JURY

COURT DECISION(S):

TRIAL COURT: NONFINAL FOR PL.
YEAR: 1953
APPELLATE COURT: NONFINAL FOR PL.
YEAR: 1954

DEFENDANTS STILL INVOLVED IN SUIT:
1. STATE GOV. &/OR OFFICIALS, ETC.

183. MORALES V. TURMAN

A CLASS ACTION SUIT WAS BROUGHT ON BEHALF OF THOSE INVOLUNTARILY COMMITTED TO THE CUSTODY OF THE TEXAS YOUTH COUNCIL AND CONFINED IN INSTITUTIONS UNDER THEIR JURISDICTION. THE PLAINTIFFS ALLEGED THAT THEIR CIVIL AND CONSTITUTIONAL RIGHTS WERE BEING VIOLATED AS A RESULT OF UNNECESSARY PHYSICAL ABUSE, THE REQUIREMENT OF PERFORMING NONFUNCTIONAL AND DEGRADING TASKS FOR HOURS, RACIAL SEGREGATION, THE USE OF SOLITARY CONFINEMENT AND OTHER FORMS OF TREATMENT, ALL OF WHICH AMOUNTED TO CRUEL AND UNUSUAL PUNISHMENT. ALSO, THEY CONTENDED THAT, BESIDES NOT RECEIVING ANY TREATMENT FOR THEIR VARIED PROBLEMS, THE CONDITIONS IMPOSED ON THEM WERE ACTUALLY MAKING THEIR ILLNESSES WORSE INSTEAD OF BETTER.

YEAR OF NEGLIGENT ACT: NOT SPECIFIED, BUT OCCURRED OVER A SERIES OF YEARS

STATE IN WHICH NEGLIGENT ACT OCCURRED: TEXAS

SETTING OF THE CASE: PUB. MENT. HOSP.

PLAINTIFF(S): PATIENT(S) OR REP.

DEFENDANT(S):
1. STATE GOV. &/OR OFFICIALS, ETC.
2. JUDICIARY &/OR CLERKS, ETC.

NEGLIGENT ACTIVITY:

TREATMENT:
1. NO TREATMENT OR INADEQUATE TREATMENT

DIAGNOSIS:

WHAT WAS DIAGNOSED: NOT APPLICABLE

RESULT OF DIAGNOSIS: NOT APPLICABLE

CARE: NOT APPLICABLE

HARM CAUSED TO PLAINTIFF &/OR PATIENT:
1. DEPRIVATION OF CONSTITUTIONAL RIGHTS

TYPE OF ACTION BROUGHT:
1. DEPRIVATION OF CONSTITUTIONAL RIGHTS: RIGHT TO TREATMENT
2. NONMONETARY RELIEF
3. OTHER ACTION, EXCLUDING TORT LAW: CLASS ACTION SUIT

HISTORY OF THE CASE:

TYPE OF COURT: FEDERAL

TRIER OF FACT: JUDGE,NO JURY

COURT DECISION(S):

TRIAL COURT: NONFINAL FOR PL.
YEAR: 1974
APPELLATE COURT: NONFINAL FOR DEF.
YEAR: 1976
SUPREME COURT: NONFINAL FOR PL.
YEAR: 1977

DEFENDANTS STILL INVOLVED IN SUIT:
1. STATE GOV. &/OR OFFICIALS, ETC.
2. JUDICIARY &/OR CLERKS, ETC.

184. MOREY V. KAISER FOUNDATION HOSPITALS

MS. MOREY WAS TOLD BY HER DOCTORS THAT THE MANY SYMPTOMS FROM WHICH SHE HAD BEEN SUFFERING HAD NO ORGANIC ETIOLOGY AND RECOMMENDED PSYCHIATRIC TREATMENT. A FIVE-WEEK IN-PATIENT HOSPITALIZATION AT A NEUROPSYCHIATRIC CENTER, HOWEVER, DID NOT RELIEVE HER SYMPTOMS. THREE YEARS LATER, A DOCTOR DIAGNOSED CHRONIC RIGHT MAXILLARY SINUSITIS WHICH WAS RELIEVED BY SURGERY. SOON AFTER A PULMONARY EMBOLISM AND ENDOMETRIOSIS WERE DIAGNOSED AND TREATED, FOLLOWED BY A TOTAL HYSTERECTOMY. SHE CLAIMED THAT THE DOCTORS WHO INITIALLY EXAMINED HER WERE NEGLIGENT IN NOT FINDING ANY ORGANIC PROBLEMS AND ARGUED THAT AT LEAST HER RIGHT MAXILLARY SINUSITIS OPERATION AND HYSTERECTOMY COULD HAVE BEEN AVOIDED, HAD THEY DIAGNOSED HER DISEASE EARLIER. THE DOCTORS CLAIMED THAT NO SYMPTOMS EXISTED AT THE TIME OF INITIAL DIAGNOSIS AND THAT THEY MUST HAVE DEVELOPED AFTER HER CONSULTATION WITH THEM.

YEAR OF NEGLIGENT ACT: NOT SPECIFIED

STATE IN WHICH NEGLIGENT ACT OCCURRED: CALIFORNIA

SETTING OF THE CASE: HOSPITAL

PLAINTIFF(S): PATIENT(S) OR REP.

DEFENDANT(S):
1. HOSPITAL &/OR OWNERS, ETC.

NEGLIGENT ACTIVITY:

TREATMENT: NOT APPLICABLE

DIAGNOSIS:

WHAT WAS DIAGNOSED:
1. MENT.ILL, INSTEAD OF PHYSICAL ILLNESS

RESULT OF DIAGNOSIS:
1. IMPROPER TREATMENT PRESCRIBED

CARE: NOT APPLICABLE

HARM CAUSED TO PLAINTIFF &/OR PATIENT:
1. EXACERB.OF PREV.CONDITION
2. ECONOMIC LOSS
3. LOSS OF HEALTH

TYPE OF ACTION BROUGHT:
1. NEGLIGENCE

HISTORY OF THE CASE:

TYPE OF COURT: STATE

TRIER OF FACT: JURY

COURT DECISION(S):

TRIAL COURT: FOR DEFENDANT
YEAR: 1973

REASON SUIT FAILED:
1. NEGLIGENCE OR CASE NOT PROVEN

185. MORGAN V. STATE

AT THE AGE OF FIFTY-SIX, JUDITH MORGAN WAS ARRESTED ON MAY 13, 1957, FOR STABBING ONE SAM SMITH, BELIEVING HIM TO BE A JUDGE WHO HAD DISMISSED A DAMAGE SUIT BROUGHT BY HER FOR $8 MILLION AGAINST SEVERAL STATE OFFICIALS AND JUDGES. SHE APPEARED IN COURT THE FOLLOWING DAY AND WAS COMMITTED TO KINGS COUNTY HOSPITAL FOR EXAMINATION AND OBSERVATION FOR A PERIOD NOT TO EXCEED SIXTY DAYS. BASED ON THE CERTIFICATES OF TWO PHYSICIANS AT KINGS COUNTY, SHE WAS LEGALLY DETERMINED TO BE A "MENTALLY ILL PERSON" AND ADMITTED TO CREEDMOOR STATE ON JUNE OF 1957. ON JANUARY 24, 1958, SHE WAS TRANSFERRED TO MATTEAWAN STATE HOSPITAL WHERE SHE STAYED FOR EIGHT YEARS. DURING THIS TIME SHE WAS SUBJECTED TO PHYSICAL ABUSE, STRAIT-JACKET TREATMENT, LOCKED IN A CELL SIX TIMES, AND DENIED BATHROOM PRIVILEGES FOR TWO AND A HALF DAYS WHILE STRAPPED TO A COT IN A STRAIT JACKET. MS. MORGAN CLAIMED THAT THIS CONSTITUTED CRUEL AND UNUSUAL PUNISHMENT.

YEAR OF NEGLIGENT ACT: OCCURRED OVER A SERIES OF YEARS, ENDING IN 1966

STATE IN WHICH NEGLIGENT ACT OCCURRED: NEW YORK

SETTING OF THE CASE: JUDICIAL PROCEEDING

PLAINTIFF(S): PATIENT(S) OR REP.

DEFENDANT(S):
1. STATE GOV. &/OR OFFICIALS, ETC.

NEGLIGENT ACTIVITY:

TREATMENT:
1. NO TREATMENT OR INADEQUATE TREATMENT

DIAGNOSIS:

WHAT WAS DIAGNOSED:
1. MENTAL ILLNESS, INSTEAD OF SANITY
2. INADEQUATE DIAGNOSIS

RESULT OF DIAGNOSIS:
1. IMPROPER COMMITMENT

CARE:
1. FAILURE TO PROVIDE PROPER CUSTODIAL CARE

HARM CAUSED TO PLAINTIFF &/OR PATIENT:
1. NONSELF-INFLICTED INJURIES
2. EXACERB.OF PREV.CONDITION
3. LOSS OF LIBERTY

TYPE OF ACTION BROUGHT:
1. NEGLIGENCE
2. ASSAULT
3. DEPRIVATION OF CONSTITUTIONAL RIGHTS: CONST.RTS.IN GEN.

HISTORY OF THE CASE:

TYPE OF COURT: STATE

TRIER OF FACT: JUDGE,NO JURY

COURT DECISION(S):

TRIAL COURT: FOR PLAINTIFF
YEAR: 1970
APPELLATE COURT: FOR DEFENDANT
YEAR: 1972
SUPREME COURT: FOR DEFENDANT
YEAR: 1974
U.S. SUPREME COURT (ON APPEAL FROM STATE COURT): FOR DEFENDANT
YEAR: 1974

REASON SUIT FAILED:
1. NEGLIGENCE OR CASE NOT PROVEN

186 MORRA V. STATE BOARD OF EXAMINERS OF PSYCHOLOGISTS

DR. MORRA, A PSYCHOLOGIST, HAD HIS LICENSE REVOKED BY THE BOARD OF EXAMINERS OF PSYCHOLOGISTS, WHO ALLEGED THAT HE WAS GUILTY OF UNETHICAL PROFESSIONAL PRACTICES. THE REVOCATION PROCEEDINGS BEGAN IN JULY 1971 WHEN THE BOARD HELD AN ELEVEN-HOUR HEARING BASED ON COMPLAINTS BY TWO PATIENTS OF THE PSYCHOLOGIST. BOTH OF THESE PATIENTS PRESENTED EVIDENCE THAT THE PSYCHOLOGIST HAD ATTEMPTED TO INDUCE THEM INTO SEXUAL INTIMACIES AND/OR INTERCOURSE. IN SEPTEMBER THE BOARD REVOKED THE PSYCHOLOGIST'S CERTIFICATE, BUT HE OBTAINED A STAY OF THE DECISION FROM THE DISTRICT COURT. THE STATE SUPREME COURT REVERSED THE STAY ORDER, AND THE PSYCHOLOGIST AGREED TO CEASE HIS PRIVATE PRACTICE.

YEAR OF NEGLIGENT ACT: 1970

STATE IN WHICH NEGLIGENT ACT OCCURRED: KANSAS

SETTING OF THE CASE: PRIVATE PRACTICE

PLAINTIFF(S): LICENSING BOARD

DEFENDANT(S):
1. PSYCHOLOGIST(S)

NEGLIGENT ACTIVITY:

TREATMENT:
1. SEXUAL ABUSE OR DISTURB.OF MARITAL REL.

DIAGNOSIS:

WHAT WAS DIAGNOSED: NOT APPLICABLE

RESULT OF DIAGNOSIS: NOT APPLICABLE

CARE: NOT APPLICABLE

HARM CAUSED TO PLAINTIFF &/OR PATIENT:
1. SEXUAL OR MARITAL HARM

TYPE OF ACTION BROUGHT:
1. NEGLIGENCE
2. ADMINISTRATIVE LAW: LIC.REV.PCDG.

HISTORY OF THE CASE:

TYPE OF COURT: STATE

TRIER OF FACT: JUDGE,NO JURY

COURT DECISION(S):

TRIAL COURT: FOR PLAINTIFF
YEAR: 1972
SUPREME COURT: FOR PLAINTIFF
YEAR: 1973

VERDICT AGAINST WHICH DEFENDANTS:
1. PSYCHOLOGIST(S)

RECOVERY OR OTHER RELIEF GRANTED:
1. NONMONETARY RELIEF: LOSS OF LICENSE

187. MORRIS V. ROUSOS

CHESTER MORRIS, A FORMER STUDENT AT THE UNIVERSITY OF TEXAS, BROUGHT SUIT AGAINST A UNIVERSITY PSYCHIATRIST AND HIS LIABILITY INSURER. IN THE SUIT HE ALLEGED THAT DR. ROUSOS HAD NEVER EXAMINED HIM DIRECTLY AND HAD IMPROPERLY DIAGNOSED HIS CONDITION, WHICH RESULTED IN HIS COMMITMENT TO AUSTIN STATE HOSPITAL. HE ALSO ALLEGED THAT A LETTER WRITTEN BY ROUSOS AND RETAINED IN THE UNIVERSITY FILES CONTAINED MALICIOUSLY FALSE INFORMATION, AS A RESULT OF WHICH MORRIS HAD DIFFICULTY IN GAINING EMPLOYMENT. THE LETTER CONTAINED A DESCRIPTION OF MORRIS'S CONDITION AND STATED THAT HE "WAS SUFFERING EITHER FROM A PRESENILE PSYCHOSIS OR AN EARLY CEREBRAL ARTERIOSCLEROTIC CHANGE."

YEAR OF NEGLIGENT ACT: 1950

STATE IN WHICH NEGLIGENT ACT OCCURRED: TEXAS

SETTING OF THE CASE: EDUCATIONAL INST.

PLAINTIFF(S): PATIENT(S) OR REP.

DEFENDANT(S):
1. PSYCHIATRIST(S)
2. INSURANCE COMPANY(S)

NEGLIGENT ACTIVITY:

TREATMENT: NOT APPLICABLE

DIAGNOSIS:

WHAT WAS DIAGNOSED:
1. MENTAL ILLNESS, INSTEAD OF SANITY

RESULT OF DIAGNOSIS:
1. IMPROPER CUSTODIAL CARE

CARE:
1. IMPROPER GIVING OF INFORMATION TO OTHERS

HARM CAUSED TO PLAINTIFF &/OR PATIENT:
1. ECONOMIC LOSS

TYPE OF ACTION BROUGHT:
1. OTHER ACTION, EXCLUDING TORT LAW: TYPE NOT SPECIFIED

HISTORY OF THE CASE:

TYPE OF COURT: STATE

TRIER OF FACT: JUDGE;JURY PRESENT ?

COURT DECISION(S):

TRIAL COURT: FOR DEFENDANT
YEAR: NOT SPECIFIED
APPELLATE COURT: FOR DEFENDANT
YEAR: 1966
U.S. SUPREME COURT (ON APPEAL FROM STATE COURT): FOR DEFENDANT
YEAR: 1966

REASON SUIT FAILED:
1. NEGLIGENCE OR CASE NOT PROVEN
2. NO CAUSE OF ACTION STATED

188. MORRIS V. UNIVERSITY OF TEXAS

CHESTER MORRIS, A FORMER STUDENT AT THE UNIVERSITY OF TEXAS, BROUGHT SUIT AGAINST THE UNIVERSITY FOR FALSE IMPRISONMENT CONNECTED WITH HIS COMMITMENT TO AUSTIN STATE HOSPITAL. ON THE INFORMATION OF ONE L. C. STROMQUIST THAT MORRIS WAS BELIEVED TO BE MENTALLY ILL, AN EXAMINATION WAS ORDERED BY THE STATE OF TEXAS AND CARRIED OUT BY TWO PHYSICIANS. THEY RECOMMENDED A NINETY-DAY COMMITMENT FOR OBSERVATION, AFTER WHICH MORRIS WAS TAKEN INTO CUSTODY.

YEAR OF NEGLIGENT ACT: 1956

STATE IN WHICH NEGLIGENT ACT OCCURRED: TEXAS

SETTING OF THE CASE: JUDICIAL PROCEEDING

PLAINTIFF(S): PATIENT(S) OR REP.

DEFENDANT(S):
1. NONPSYCHIAT.OR UNKNOWN TYPE PHYSICIAN(S)
2. STATE GOV. &/OR OFFICIALS, ETC.
3. EDUCATIONAL INST. &/OR DEANS, ETC.

NEGLIGENT ACTIVITY:

TREATMENT: NOT APPLICABLE

DIAGNOSIS:

WHAT WAS DIAGNOSED:
1. MENTAL ILLNESS, INSTEAD OF SANITY

RESULT OF DIAGNOSIS:
1. IMPROPER COMMITMENT

CARE: NOT APPLICABLE

HARM CAUSED TO PLAINTIFF &/OR PATIENT:
1. ECONOMIC LOSS

TYPE OF ACTION BROUGHT:
1. FALSE IMPRISONMENT

HISTORY OF THE CASE:

TYPE OF COURT: STATE

TRIER OF FACT: JUDGE;JURY PRESENT ?

COURT DECISION(S):

TRIAL COURT: FOR DEFENDANT
YEAR: 1960
APPELLATE COURT: FOR DEFENDANT
YEAR: 1961

REASON SUIT FAILED:
1. NEGLIGENCE OR CASE NOT PROVEN

189. MOSKOWITZ V. MCQUEEN

THE UNDERLYING SUIT HERE IS FOR NEGLIGENCE FOR THE AGGRAVATION OF A PRE-EXISTING PSYCHOSIS. IN THE INSTANT CASE, HOWEVER, THE DEFENDANT SUED FOR ACCESS TO THE PLAINTIFF'S HOSPITAL RECORDS. ALTHOUGH THE PLAINTIFF GAVE PERMISSION FOR SUCH ACCESS, THE HOSPITAL IN POSSESSION OF THEM REFUSED TO MAKE THEM AVAILABLE, STATING THAT THEY WERE PRIVILEGED COMMUNICATIONS.

YEAR OF NEGLIGENT ACT: NOT SPECIFIED

STATE IN WHICH NEGLIGENT ACT OCCURRED: NEW YORK

SETTING OF THE CASE: PRIVATE PRACTICE

PLAINTIFF(S): PATIENT(S) OR REP.

DEFENDANT(S):
1. NONPSYCHIAT.OR UNKNOWN TYPE PHYSICIAN(S)

NEGLIGENT ACTIVITY:

TREATMENT:
1. ? WHETHER TREAT.INV.

DIAGNOSIS:

WHAT WAS DIAGNOSED:
1. ? WHETHER DIAG.INV.

RESULT OF DIAGNOSIS: NOT APPLICABLE

CARE:
1. ? WHETHER CARE INV.

HARM CAUSED TO PLAINTIFF &/OR PATIENT:
1. EXACERB.OF PREV.CONDITION

TYPE OF ACTION BROUGHT:
1. NEGLIGENCE

HISTORY OF THE CASE:

TYPE OF COURT: STATE

TRIER OF FACT: JUDGE;JURY PRESENT ?

COURT DECISION(S):

TRIAL COURT: NONFINAL FOR DEF.
YEAR: 1963

DEFENDANTS STILL INVOLVED IN SUIT:
1. NONPSYCHIAT.OR UNKNOWN TYPE PHYSICIAN(S)

190. MOXON V. COUNTY OF KERN

FEW FACTS ARE AVAILABLE IN THE REPORTED CASE, EXCEPT THAT JOHN MOXON WAS A MENTAL PATIENT IN THE KERN COUNTY HOSPITAL WHERE HE WAS KILLED AT THE HANDS OF WILLIE WALKER, ANOTHER PATIENT SIMILARLY SITUATED. THE SUIT BROUGHT BY MRS. MOXON WAS FOR FAILING TO PROVIDE PROPER GUARDS OR SAFETY PROCEDURES TO PREVENT HARM TO HER DECEASED SPOUSE.

YEAR OF NEGLIGENT ACT: NOT SPECIFIED

STATE IN WHICH NEGLIGENT ACT OCCURRED: CALIFORNIA

SETTING OF THE CASE: PUB. MENT. HOSP.

PLAINTIFF(S): PATIENT(S) OR REP.

DEFENDANT(S):
1. COUNTY GOV. &/OR OFFICIALS, ETC.

NEGLIGENT ACTIVITY:

TREATMENT: NOT APPLICABLE

DIAGNOSIS:

WHAT WAS DIAGNOSED: NOT APPLICABLE

RESULT OF DIAGNOSIS: NOT APPLICABLE

CARE:
1. INADEQUATE SUPERVISION

HARM CAUSED TO PLAINTIFF &/OR PATIENT:
1. NONSUICIDAL DEATH

TYPE OF ACTION BROUGHT:
1. NEGLIGENCE
2. CONTRACT LAW: BREACH OF WARRANTY

HISTORY OF THE CASE:

TYPE OF COURT: STATE

TRIER OF FACT: ?, JUDGE OR JURY

COURT DECISION(S):

TRIAL COURT: FOR DEFENDANT
YEAR: NOT SPECIFIED
APPELLATE COURT: FOR DEFENDANT
YEAR: 1965
SUPREME COURT: FOR DEFENDANT
YEAR: 1965

REASON SUIT FAILED:
1. NO CAUSE OF ACTION STATED
2. DEFENDANT(S) CANNOT BE SUED DUE TO: GOVERN. IMMUNITY

191. MURRAY V. ST. MARY'S STATE HOSPITAL

ROSE MURRAY WAS SUFFERING FROM POST-PARTUM PSYCHOSIS FOLLOWING THE DELIVERY OF A CHILD AT ST. MARY'S HOSPITAL. ALTHOUGH AWARE OF HER CONDITION AND IRRATIONAL BEHAVIOR, THE HOSPITAL STAFF TOOK NO RESTRAINING MEASURES WHATSOEVER. MRS. MURRAY'S PRIVATE PHYSICIAN AND SPECIAL NURSE WERE IN THE ROOM WITH HER SHORTLY BEFORE THE OCCURRENCE. MRS. MURRAY ASKED IF A PHONE CALL COULD BE MADE FOR HER. WHILE THE NURSE WENT TO MAKE THE CALL AND THE DOCTOR'S BACK WAS TURNED, MRS. MURRAY JUMPED OUT OF A WINDOW TO HER DEATH. HER HUSBAND BROUGHT SUIT AGAINST THE HOSPITAL FOR FAILING TO ADEQUATELY SUPERVISE HER.

YEAR OF NEGLIGENT ACT: NOT SPECIFIED

STATE IN WHICH NEGLIGENT ACT OCCURRED: NEW YORK

SETTING OF THE CASE: PRIV. GEN. HOSP.

PLAINTIFF(S): PATIENT(S) OR REP.

DEFENDANT(S):
1. SOME OR ALL DEFENDANTS NOT SPECIFIED
2. HOSPITAL &/OR OWNERS, ETC.

NEGLIGENT ACTIVITY:

TREATMENT: NOT APPLICABLE

DIAGNOSIS:

WHAT WAS DIAGNOSED: NOT APPLICABLE

RESULT OF DIAGNOSIS: NOT APPLICABLE

CARE:
1. INADEQUATE SUPERVISION

HARM CAUSED TO PLAINTIFF &/OR PATIENT:
1. SUICIDE

TYPE OF ACTION BROUGHT:
1. NEGLIGENCE

HISTORY OF THE CASE:

TYPE OF COURT: STATE

TRIER OF FACT: JUDGE,UNINV.JURY

COURT DECISION(S):

TRIAL COURT: FOR DEFENDANT
YEAR: NOT SPECIFIED
APPELLATE COURT: NONFINAL FOR PL.
YEAR: 1952

DEFENDANTS S˜ILL INVOLVED IN SUIT:
1. HOSPITAL &/OR OWNERS, ETC.

192. NASON V. SUPERINTENDENT OF BRIDGEWATER STATE HOSPITAL

NASON WAS INDICTED FOR THE MURDER OF HIS WIFE ON SEPTEMBER 12, 1962, AFTER HAVING BEEN COMMITTED TO BRIDGEWATER STATE ON AUGUST 24, WHERE HE WAS TO STAY UNTIL HE WAS COMPETENT TO STAND TRIAL. DIAGNOSED AS SUFFERING FROM A CHRONIC SCHIZOPHRENIC REACTION WITH PARANOID FEATURES, THE DOCTORS FELT THAT WITH TREATMENT HE WOULD SOON BE ABLE TO GO TO COURT, BUT THIS DID NOT PROVE TO BE THE CASE. AT FIRST HE RECEIVED LITTLE TREATMENT, ALTHOUGH BY 1966 HE WAS RECEIVING DRUG THERAPY AND WAS SEEN ON A REGULAR BASIS. HIS PROGRESS, IF ANY, WAS DESCRIBED AS SLOW. NASON CLAIMED THAT IF ADEQUATE TREATMENT WAS NOT PROVIDED TO RECOVER TO THE POINT OF STANDING TRIAL, THE INDICTMENT AMOUNTED TO A LIFE SENTENCE. HE MAINTAINED THAT IF ADEQUATE TREATMENT WAS NOT PROVIDED IN A REASONABLE TIME, LEGALITY OF FURTHER INCARCERATION SHOULD BE PRESENTED TO THE COURTS.

YEAR OF NEGLIGENT ACT: OCCURRED OVER A SERIES OF YEARS, ENDING IN 1968

STATE IN WHICH NEGLIGENT ACT OCCURRED: MASSACHUSETTS

SETTING OF THE CASE: PUB. MENT. HOSP.

PLAINTIFF(S): PATIENT(S) OR REP.

DEFENDANT(S):
1. HOSPITAL &/OR OWNERS, ETC.

NEGLIGENT ACTIVITY:

TREATMENT:
1. NO TREATMENT OR INADEQUATE TREATMENT

DIAGNOSIS:

WHAT WAS DIAGNOSED: NOT APPLICABLE

RESULT OF DIAGNOSIS: NOT APPLICABLE

CARE: NOT APPLICABLE

HARM CAUSED TO PLAINTIFF &/OR PATIENT:
1. DEPRIVATION OF CONSTITUTIONAL RIGHTS
2. LOSS OF LIBERTY

TYPE OF ACTION BROUGHT:
1. DEPRIVATION OF CONSTITUTIONAL RIGHTS: RIGHT TO TREATMENT
2. HABEAS CORPUS
3. NONMONETARY RELIEF

HISTORY OF THE CASE:

TYPE OF COURT: STATE

TRIER OF FACT: JUDGE;JURY PRESENT ?

COURT DECISION(S):

SUPREME COURT: NONFINAL FOR PL.
YEAR: 1968

DEFENDANTS STILL INVOLVED IN SUIT:
1. HOSPITAL &/OR OWNERS, ETC.

193. NASTASI V. STATE

APPEARING WITHDRAWN, INCOHERENT AND IRRATIONAL, MURIEL BRUGEL WAS ADMITTED TO NASSAU COUNTY MEDICAL CENTER ON JANUARY 23, 1973. THE NEXT DAY SHE WAS TRANSFERRED TO NORTHEAST NASSAU PSYCHIATRIC HOSPITAL WHERE SHE WAS DIAGNOSED AS SUFFERING FROM A PSYCHOTIC DEPRESSION REACTION. ON FEBRUARY 15, SHE WAS TRANSFERRED TO KINGS PARK STATE HOSPITAL FROM WHERE HER FAMILY REMOVED HER TO A PRIVATE INSTITUTION. SHE DIED ON APRIL 2, 1973 FROM CANCER OF THE BRAIN. SUIT WAS BROUGHT BY MARILYN NASTASI, HER ADMINISTRATOR, ALLEGING THAT HER PHYSICIANS HAD FAILED TO DIAGNOSE PHYSICIAL ILLNESS.

YEAR OF NEGLIGENT ACT: 1973

STATE IN WHICH NEGLIGENT ACT OCCURRED: NEW YORK

SETTING OF THE CASE: PUB. MENT. HOSP.

PLAINTIFF(S): PATIENT(S) OR REP.

DEFENDANT(S):
1. STATE GOV. &/OR OFFICIALS, ETC.

NEGLIGENT ACTIVITY:

TREATMENT:
1. NO TREATMENT OR INADEQUATE TREATMENT

DIAGNOSIS:

WHAT WAS DIAGNOSED:
1. MENT.ILL, INSTEAD OF PHYSICAL ILLNESS

RESULT OF DIAGNOSIS:
1. IMPROPER TREATMENT PRESCRIBED

CARE: NOT APPLICABLE

HARM CAUSED TO PLAINTIFF &/OR PATIENT:
1. NONSUICIDAL DEATH

TYPE OF ACTION BROUGHT:
1. NEGLIGENCE

HISTORY OF THE CASE:

TYPE OF COURT: STATE

TRIER OF FACT: JUDGE,NO JURY

COURT DECISION(S):

TRIAL COURT: FOR DEFENDANT
YEAR: NOT SPECIFIED
APPELLATE COURT: FOR DEFENDANT
YEAR: 1976

REASON SUIT FAILED:
1. NEGLIGENCE OR CASE NOT PROVEN

194. NELSON V. HEYNE

A CLASS ACTION SUIT WAS BROUGHT AGAINST THE INDIANA BOYS SCHOOL ON BEHALF OF ITS MINOR INMATES SEEKING DECLARATORY AND INJUNCTIVE RELIEF WITH RESPECT TO ITS OPERATION. AMONG THOSE THINGS COMPLAINED OF WERE THE USE OF CORPORAL PUNISHMENT, THE USE OF TRANQUILIZING DRUGS WITHOUT ADEQUATE MEDICAL GUIDANCE OR PRESCRIPTION, AND A FAILURE TO PROVIDE ADEQUATE REHABILITATIVE TREATMENT.

YEAR OF NEGLIGENT ACT: NOT SPECIFIED

STATE IN WHICH NEGLIGENT ACT OCCURRED: INDIANA

SETTING OF THE CASE: CORRECTIONAL INST.

PLAINTIFF(S): PATIENT(S) OR REP.

DEFENDANT(S):
1. CORRECTIONAL INST.

NEGLIGENT ACTIVITY:

TREATMENT:
1. NO TREATMENT OR INADEQUATE TREATMENT
2. NEG.ADMIN.OF DRUGS

DIAGNOSIS:

WHAT WAS DIAGNOSED:
1. INADEQUATE DIAGNOSIS

RESULT OF DIAGNOSIS:
1. IMPROPER CUSTODIAL CARE

CARE: NOT APPLICABLE

HARM CAUSED TO PLAINTIFF &/OR PATIENT:
1. NONSELF-INFLICTED INJURIES
2. DEPRIVATION OF CONSTITUTIONAL RIGHTS

TYPE OF ACTION BROUGHT:
1. DEPRIVATION OF CONSTITUTIONAL RIGHTS: RIGHT TO TREATMENT
2. NONMONETARY RELIEF
3. OTHER ACTION, EXCLUDING TORT LAW: CLASS ACTION SUIT

HISTORY OF THE CASE:

TYPE OF COURT: FEDERAL

TRIER OF FACT: JUDGE,NO JURY

COURT DECISION(S):

TRIAL COURT: FOR PLAINTIFF
YEAR: 1972
APPELLATE COURT: FOR PLAINTIFF
YEAR: 1974
SUPREME COURT: FOR PLAINTIFF
YEAR: 1974

VERDICT AGAINST WHICH DEFENDANTS:
1. CORRECTIONAL INST.

RECOVERY OR OTHER RELIEF GRANTED:
1. NONMONETARY RELIEF: INJ.OR OTHER EQ.REL.

195. NEW YORK STATE ASSOCIATION FOR RETARDED CHILDREN V. ROCKEFELLER

THIS CLASS ACTION SUIT WAS BROUGHT ON BEHALF OF ALL RESIDENTS OF THE VARIOUS INSTITUTIONS FOR THE MENTALLY RETARDED IN NEW YORK STATE. IT SOUGHT EQUITABLE RELIEF RELATED TO THE TREATMENT AND CARE PROVIDED TO THE RESIDENTS, AND FOCUSED ON CONDITIONS AT THE WILLOWBROOK STATE SCHOOL FOR THE MENTALLY RETARDED. THE FIVE DAYS OF HEARINGS DEMONSTRATED THAT THE 1964 LEGISLATIVE RECOMMENDATIONS ON WILLOWBROOK HAD NOT BEEN SUFFICIENTLY HEEDED. OVERCROWDING, INADEQUATE STAFFING, AND INHUMANE CONDITIONS STILL PREDOMINATED. THE TESTIMONY OF PARENTS PLUS AFFIDAVITS OF OTHERS SHOWED FAILURE IN PROTECTING THE PHYSICAL SAFETY OF THE INMATES. THE PATIENTS TENDED TO DETERIORATE, RATHER THAN IMPROVE; 1,300 REPORTED INCIDENTS OF INJURY, PATIENT ASSAULTS, OR FIGHTS WERE REPORTED IN AN EIGHT-MONTH PERIOD IN 1972 ALONE. INJUNCTIVE RELIEF WAS SOUGHT TO IMPROVE BOTH THE QUALITY OF CARE AND TREATMENT AND THE PHYSICAL FACILITIES THEMSELVES.

YEAR OF NEGLIGENT ACT: NOT SPECIFIED, BUT OCCURRED OVER A SERIES OF YEARS

STATE IN WHICH NEGLIGENT ACT OCCURRED: NEW YORK

SETTING OF THE CASE: PUB. MENT. HOSP.

PLAINTIFF(S): PATIENT(S) OR REP.

DEFENDANT(S):
1. STATE GOV. &/OR OFFICIALS, ETC.

NEGLIGENT ACTIVITY:

TREATMENT:
1. NO TREATMENT OR INADEQUATE TREATMENT

DIAGNOSIS:

WHAT WAS DIAGNOSED: NOT APPLICABLE

RESULT OF DIAGNOSIS: NOT APPLICABLE

CARE:
1. INADEQUATE SUPERVISION
2. FAILURE TO PROVIDE PROPER CUSTODIAL CARE

HARM CAUSED TO PLAINTIFF &/OR PATIENT:
1. NONSELF-INFLICTED INJURIES
2. EXACERB.OF PREV.CONDITION
3. DEPRIVATION OF CONSTITUTIONAL RIGHTS

TYPE OF ACTION BROUGHT:
1. NEGLIGENCE
2. DEPRIVATION OF CONSTITUTIONAL RIGHTS: RIGHT TO TREATMENT
3. NONMONETARY RELIEF

HISTORY OF THE CASE:

TYPE OF COURT: FEDERAL

TRIER OF FACT: JUDGE,NO JURY

COURT DECISION(S):

TRIAL COURT: FOR PLAINTIFF
YEAR: 1973
TRIAL COURT: FOR PLAINTIFF
YEAR: 1975

VERDICT AGAINST WHICH DEFENDANTS:
1. STATE GOV. &/OR OFFICIALS, ETC.

RECOVERY OR OTHER RELIEF GRANTED:
1. NONMONETARY RELIEF: INJ.OR OTHER EQ.REL.

196. NICHOLSON V. HAN

MR. NICHOLSON AND HIS WIFE WERE EXPERIENCING MARITAL DIFFICULTIES. IN DECEMBER OF 1960 SHE INJURED HER FOOT AND WENT TO DR. MAOLIN HAN FOR TREATMENT. IN THE COURSE OF THIS TREATMENT, MR. NICHOLSON TALKED TO DR. HAN ABOUT THEIR MARITAL DIFFICULTIES. DR. HAN SUGGESTED THAT HE PROVIDE MRS. NICHOLSON WITH PSYCHIATRIC TREATMENT. MRS. NICHOLSON CONSULTED THE DEFENDANT AS PSYCHIATRIST AND MARRIAGE COUNSELOR FROM DECEMBER OF 1960 THROUGH 1962, AT WHICH POINT THE PATIENT'S MARITAL SITUATION HAD DETERIORATED TO THE POINT OF DIVORCE. TWO YEARS LATER THE PLAINTIFF SAW HIS EX-WIFE'S RECORD AT NORTHVILLE STATE HOSPITAL. IT ALLEGEDLY REVEALED THAT SHE HAD BEEN INTIMATE WITH DR. HAN.

YEAR OF NEGLIGENT ACT: 1961

STATE IN WHICH NEGLIGENT ACT OCCURRED: MICHIGAN

SETTING OF THE CASE: PRIVATE PRACTICE

PLAINTIFF(S): 3RD PARTY, I

DEFENDANT(S):
1. PSYCHIATRIST(S)

NEGLIGENT ACTIVITY:

TREATMENT:
1. SEXUAL ABUSE OR DISTURB.OF MARITAL REL.

DIAGNOSIS:

WHAT WAS DIAGNOSED: NOT APPLICABLE

RESULT OF DIAGNOSIS: NOT APPLICABLE

CARE: NOT APPLICABLE

HARM CAUSED TO PLAINTIFF &/OR PATIENT:
1. SEXUAL OR MARITAL HARM
2. ALIENATION OF AFFECTION

TYPE OF ACTION BROUGHT:
1. NEGLIGENCE
2. ASSAULT AND BATTERY
3. CONTRACT LAW: FRAUD-BREACH OF CON.

HISTORY OF THE CASE:

TYPE OF COURT: STATE

TRIER OF FACT: JUDGE;JURY PRESENT ?

COURT DECISION(S):

TRIAL COURT: FOR DEFENDANT
YEAR: NOT SPECIFIED
APPELLATE COURT: FOR DEFENDANT
YEAR: 1968

REASON SUIT FAILED:
1. NO CAUSE OF ACTION STATED

197. NOEL V. MENNINGER FOUNDATION

WILLIAM B. NOEL WAS FIRST PLACED IN ST. FRANCIS HOSPITAL DUE TO LACK OF SPACE AT THE DEFENDANT HOSPITAL. THE PATIENT WAS ADMITTED WITH PHYSICAL COMPLAINTS AND HAD NO NOTICEABLE MENTAL DISTURBANCES OR SUICIDAL OR HOMICIDAL TENDENCIES. HOWEVER, HIS DOCTORS SOON FELT THAT HE WOULD REQUIRE ELECTRO-SHOCK TREATMENTS BECAUSE NOEL COMPLAINED OF "GOING TO PIECES" AND WAS CONSIDERED A SUICIDAL RISK. AN ATTENDANT WAS CONSTANTLY AT THE SIDE OF THE SEVENTY-ONE-YEAR-OLD "SCRAWNY WISK OF A GRAY OLD MAN." NEVERTHELESS, THE PATIENT MADE SEVERAL SUICIDE ATTEMPTS, INCLUDING PLACING HIS HEAD IN A BUCKET OF WATER. ON APRIL 4, 1951, AT ABOUT 3:00 P.M., A HOSPITAL EMPLOYEE TOOK NOEL FOR A WALK ALONG A HEAVILY-TRAVELED STREET THAT BORDERED ST. FRANCIS HOSPITAL. AT ABOUT 4:00 P.M., THE PATIENT SUDDENLY DARTED INTO THE STREET AND WAS STRUCK BY A PICK-UP TRUCK. THE PATIENT BROUGHT SUIT AGAINST THE HOSPITAL AND OWNER OF THE TRUCK FOR THE INJURIES HE SUSTAINED.

YEAR OF NEGLIGENT ACT: 1951

STATE IN WHICH NEGLIGENT ACT OCCURRED: KANSAS

SETTING OF THE CASE: PRIV. MENT. HOSP.

PLAINTIFF(S): PATIENT(S) OR REP.

DEFENDANT(S):
1. HOSPITAL &/OR OWNERS, ETC.
2. LAYPERSON

NEGLIGENT ACTIVITY:

TREATMENT: NOT APPLICABLE

DIAGNOSIS:

WHAT WAS DIAGNOSED: NOT APPLICABLE

RESULT OF DIAGNOSIS: NOT APPLICABLE

CARE:
1. INADEQUATE SUPERVISION

HARM CAUSED TO PLAINTIFF &/OR PATIENT:
1. NONSELF-INFLICTED INJURIES

TYPE OF ACTION BROUGHT:
1. NEGLIGENCE

HISTORY OF THE CASE:

TYPE OF COURT: STATE

TRIER OF FACT: JUDGE;JURY PRESENT ?

COURT DECISION(S):

TRIAL COURT: FOR DEFENDANT
YEAR: NOT SPECIFIED
SUPREME COURT: NONFINAL FOR PL.
YEAR: 1956

DEFENDANTS STILL INVOLVED IN SUIT:
1. HOSPITAL &/OR OWNERS, ETC.

198. O'CONNOR V. DONALDSON

ON JANUARY 3, 1957, AT THE REQUEST OF HIS FATHER, WHO BELIEVED THAT HE WAS SUFFERING FROM DELUSIONS, KENNETH DONALDSON WAS COMMITTED TO THE FLORIDA STATE HOSPITAL. DONALDSON, A DIVORCED COLLEGE DROPOUT, WAS IN HIS EARLY FIFTIES AT THE TIME AND HIS PARENTS WERE UNABLE TO TAKE CARE OF HIM. HE WAS DIAGNOSED AS A PARANOID SCHIZOPHRENIC, BUT TOLD BY THE JUDGE THAT HE WOULD BE RELEASED SOON IF HE AGREED TO TAKE SOME NEW DRUGS FOR A FEW WEEKS. FOURTEEN AND A HALF YEARS LATER, AFTER PERSISTENT EFFORT, DONALDSON WAS FINALLY RELEASED. DURING THIS TIME HE RECEIVED LITTLE MORE THAN CUSTODIAL CARE. IN FACT, OVER ONE 8-YEAR PERIOD HE SPOKE TO A PSYCHIATRIST FOR NOT MORE THAN TWO HOURS--ABOUT FOURTEEN MINUTES A YEAR. EFFORTS BY VARIOUS ORGANIZATIONS AND FRIENDS TO HAVE HIM RELEASED MET WITH NO SUCCESS. HOSPITAL OFFICIALS ARGUED THAT HE WOULD BE UNABLE TO CARE FOR HIMSELF, AND CONTINUALLY RAISED REQUIREMENTS TO FRUSTRATE POTENTIAL HELPERS. AFTER HIS EVENTUAL RELEASE, DONALDSON CHARGED THAT THOSE IN AUTHORITY HAD BEEN KEEPING HIM CONFINED TO A MENTAL HOSPITAL WITHOUT PROVIDING TREATMENT AND DESPITE THE FACT THAT HE WAS NOT DANGEROUS TO HIMSELF OR OTHERS.

YEAR OF NEGLIGENT ACT: OCCURRED OVER A SERIES OF YEARS, ENDING IN 1971

STATE IN WHICH NEGLIGENT ACT OCCURRED: FLORIDA

SETTING OF THE CASE: PUB. MENT. HOSP.

PLAINTIFF(S): PATIENT(S) OR REP.

DEFENDANT(S):
1. NONPSYCHIAT.OR UNKNOWN TYPE PHYSICIAN(S)
2. HOSPITAL &/OR OWNERS, ETC.

NEGLIGENT ACTIVITY:

TREATMENT:
1. NO TREATMENT OR INADEQUATE TREATMENT

DIAGNOSIS:

WHAT WAS DIAGNOSED:
1. MENTAL ILLNESS, INSTEAD OF SANITY

RESULT OF DIAGNOSIS:
1. IMPROPER COMMITMENT
2. IMPROPER FAILURE TO RELEASE

CARE: NOT APPLICABLE

HARM CAUSED TO PLAINTIFF &/OR PATIENT:
1. DEPRIVATION OF CONSTITUTIONAL RIGHTS
2. LOSS OF LIBERTY

TYPE OF ACTION BROUGHT:
1. DEPRIVATION OF CONSTITUTIONAL RIGHTS: LOSS OF LIBERTY

HISTORY OF THE CASE:

TYPE OF COURT: FEDERAL

TRIER OF FACT: JURY

COURT DECISION(S):

TRIAL COURT: FOR PLAINTIFF
YEAR: NOT SPECIFIED
APPELLATE COURT: FOR PLAINTIFF
YEAR: 1974
SUPREME COURT: FOR PLAINTIFF
YEAR: 1975
ON REMAND TO APPELLATE COURT: FOR PLAINTIFF
YEAR: 1975
ON RETRIAL: FOR PLAINTIFF
YEAR: 1977

VERDICT AGAINST WHICH DEFENDANTS:
1. NONPSYCHIAT.OR UNKNOWN TYPE PHYSICIAN(S)

RECOVERY OR OTHER RELIEF GRANTED:
1. $ 20000
2. ATTORNEY FEES

199. OLEPA V. MAPLETOFF

WALTER OLEPA CHARGED THAT HE WAS COMMITTED TO WAYNE COUNTY GENERAL HOSPITAL FOR A PERIOD OF EIGHT DAYS WITHOUT CAUSE. FURTHER INFORMATION IS UNAVAILABLE.

YEAR OF NEGLIGENT ACT: 1962

STATE IN WHICH NEGLIGENT ACT OCCURRED: MICHIGAN

SETTING OF THE CASE: JUDICIAL PROCEEDING

PLAINTIFF(S): PATIENT(S) OR REP.

DEFENDANT(S):
1. NONPSYCHIAT.OR UNKNOWN TYPE PHYSICIAN(S)
2. JUDICIARY &/OR CLERKS, ETC.
3. PL'S.SPOUSE &/ MOTH.

NEGLIGENT ACTIVITY:

TREATMENT: NOT APPLICABLE

DIAGNOSIS:

WHAT WAS DIAGNOSED:
1. MENTAL ILLNESS, INSTEAD OF SANITY

RESULT OF DIAGNOSIS: NOT APPLICABLE

CARE: NOT APPLICABLE

HARM CAUSED TO PLAINTIFF &/OR PATIENT:
1. LOSS OF LIBERTY

TYPE OF ACTION BROUGHT:
1. OTHER TORT(S): WRONGFUL COMMITMENT

HISTORY OF THE CASE:

TYPE OF COURT: STATE

TRIER OF FACT: JUDGE;JURY PRESENT ?

COURT DECISION(S):

TRIAL COURT: FOR DEFENDANT
YEAR: NOT SPECIFIED
APPELLATE COURT: FOR DEFENDANT
YEAR: 1966

REASON SUIT FAILED:
1. NO CAUSE OF ACTION STATED
2. DEFENDANT(S) CANNOT BE SUED DUE TO: JUDICIAL IMMUNITY

200. OLIVER V. STATE

LOUIS OLIVER, JR., AGE FOURTEEN, ALLEGEDLY KILLED HIS TWO-YEAR-OLD BROTHER. HE WAS SENT TO MATTEAWAN STATE HOSPITAL IN NEW YORK AFTER BEING FOUND UNABLE TO STAND TRIAL BECAUSE OF INSANITY. HE REMAINED THERE FOR NINE YEARS, DURING WHICH TIME HE WAS GIVEN WORK AS A WAITER. AT AGE 15, CONTRARY TO STATE LABOR LAWS, HE WAS TRANSFERRED TO LAUNDRY WORK. THE MACHINE HE WAS ASSIGNED TO, WHICH WAS TOP-LOADING AND SPUN AT 1,000 REVOLUTIONS PER MINUTE, DID NOT MEET DEPARTMENT OF LABOR SAFETY STANDARDS. THE ONLY INSTRUCTION IN THE OPERATION OF THE MACHINE THAT LOUIS RECEIVED WAS FROM A FELLOW INMATE. ONE DAY HE SLIPPED AND HIS LEFT ARM CAUGHT IN THE FAST-SPINNING MACHINE. DOCTORS AMPUTATED HIS ARM MIDWAY BETWEEN THE SHOULDER AND THE ELBOW. AFTER HE WAS EVENTUALLY DECLARED SANE, HE WAS TRIED, CONVICTED, AND SENTENCED TO DEATH, BUT THE INDICTMENT WAS DISMISSED UPON APPEAL. OLIVER THEN BROUGHT SUIT AGAINST THE STATE FOR HIS EARLIER INJURIES.

YEAR OF NEGLIGENT ACT: 1946

STATE IN WHICH NEGLIGENT ACT OCCURRED: NEW YORK

SETTING OF THE CASE: PUB. MENT. HOSP.

PLAINTIFF(S): PATIENT(S) OR REP.

DEFENDANT(S):
1. STATE GOV. &/OR OFFICIALS, ETC.

NEGLIGENT ACTIVITY:

TREATMENT: NOT APPLICABLE

DIAGNOSIS:

WHAT WAS DIAGNOSED: NOT APPLICABLE

RESULT OF DIAGNOSIS: NOT APPLICABLE

CARE:
1. FAILURE TO PROVIDE PROPER CUSTODIAL CARE

HARM CAUSED TO PLAINTIFF &/OR PATIENT:
1. NONSELF-INFLICTED INJURIES
2. ECONOMIC LOSS

TYPE OF ACTION BROUGHT:
1. NEGLIGENCE

HISTORY OF THE CASE:

TYPE OF COURT: STATE

TRIER OF FACT: JUDGE,NO JURY

COURT DECISION(S):

TRIAL COURT: FOR PLAINTIFF
YEAR: 1959

VERDICT AGAINST WHICH DEFENDANTS:
1. STATE GOV. &/OR OFFICIALS, ETC.

RECOVERY OR OTHER RELIEF GRANTED:
1. $ 30000

201. O'NEIL V. STATE

JACQUELINE O'NEIL HAD A HISTORY OF MENTAL PROBLEMS. SHE BECAME ADDICTED TO BARBITURATES AS A RESULT OF THEIR PRESCRIPTION FOR HER CONDITION. HER DOCTOR DIAGNOSED HER AS SUFFERING FROM BARBITURATE POISONING AS A RESULT OF AN OVERDOSE OF NEMBUTAL, AND SUGGESTED THAT SHE BE HOSPITALIZED AT THE MANHATTAN GENERAL HOSPITAL TO BE SAFELY DETOXIFIED. SHE AND HER HUSBAND SET OUT TO FOLLOW THE DOCTOR'S ORDERS, BUT SHE INSISTED UPON GOING TO CREEDMOOR STATE HOSPITAL. SHE TOLD THE ADMITTING PHYSICIAN, AMONG OTHER THINGS, THAT SHE WAS TAKING NEMBUTAL. UNFORTUNATELY, HE DID NOT CHECK HER MEDICAL RECORDS FROM PREVIOUS STAYS AT CREEDMOOR OR SPEAK WITH HER PRIVATE DOCTOR OR HER HUSBAND. ACCORDING TO HER HUSBAND, ANY ONE OF THESE ACTIONS WOULD HAVE MADE THE DOCTOR AWARE OF HER BARBITURATE ADDICTION. AS A RESULT OF THE DOCTOR'S ALLEGED NEGLIGENCE IN DIAGNOSING EPILEPSY, JACQUELINE SUFFERED SEVERE WITHDRAWAL SYMPTOMS AND CONVULSIONS AND DIED FOUR DAYS LATER.

YEAR OF NEGLIGENT ACT: 1969

STATE IN WHICH NEGLIGENT ACT OCCURRED: NEW YORK

SETTING OF THE CASE: PUB. MENT. HOSP.

PLAINTIFF(S): PATIENT(S) OR REP.

DEFENDANT(S):
1. STATE GOV. &/OR OFFICIALS, ETC.

NEGLIGENT ACTIVITY:

TREATMENT: NOT APPLICABLE

DIAGNOSIS:

WHAT WAS DIAGNOSED:
1. PHYS.ILL, INSTEAD OF MENT.ILLNESS

RESULT OF DIAGNOSIS:
1. IMPROPER TREATMENT PRESCRIBED

CARE: NOT APPLICABLE

HARM CAUSED TO PLAINTIFF &/OR PATIENT:
1. NONSUICIDAL DEATH

TYPE OF ACTION BROUGHT:
1. NEGLIGENCE

HISTORY OF THE CASE:

TYPE OF COURT: STATE

TRIER OF FACT: JUDGE,NO JURY

COURT DECISION(S):

TRIAL COURT: FOR PLAINTIFF
YEAR: 1971

VERDICT AGAINST WHICH DEFENDANTS:
1. STATE GOV. &/OR OFFICIALS, ETC.

RECOVERY OR OTHER RELIEF GRANTED:
1. $ 5945
2. INTEREST

202. ORMAN V. STATE

THEODORE NEELY WAS A CATATONIC SCHIZOPHRENIC AT CENTRAL ISLIP HOSPITAL FOR SIXTEEN YEARS. DURING THOSE YEARS, THEODORE HAD UNDERGONE A LOBOTOMY, MEDICATION, AND OTHER THERAPY AS A PART OF HIS TREATMENT, BUT SHOWED LITTLE IMPROVEMENT. IN THE FIRST FEW YEARS HE WAS VIOLENT, BUT HE WAS LATER GIVEN THE RIGHT TO VISIT HIS PARENTS' HOME. WHILE ON ONE SUCH VISIT, THEODORE SHOT EDWARD ORMAN IN THE BACK AT A NEW YORK CITY SUBWAY. THE LOWER PORTION OF ORMAN'S BODY WAS PERMANENTLY PARALYZED, AND HE FILED SUIT, CHARGING THE HOSPITAL WITH NEGLIGENCE IN RELEASING THEODORE.

YEAR OF NEGLIGENT ACT: 1966

STATE IN WHICH NEGLIGENT ACT OCCURRED: NEW YORK

SETTING OF THE CASE: PUB. MENT. HOSP.

PLAINTIFF(S): 3RD PARTY, II

DEFENDANT(S):
1. STATE GOV. &/OR OFFICIALS, ETC.

NEGLIGENT ACTIVITY:

TREATMENT: NOT APPLICABLE

DIAGNOSIS:

WHAT WAS DIAGNOSED:
1. LACK OF DANGEROUSNESS
2. INADEQUATE DIAGNOSIS

RESULT OF DIAGNOSIS:
1. IMPROPER RELEASE

CARE:
1. INADEQUATE SUPERVISION
2. FAILURE TO PROVIDE PROPER CUSTODIAL CARE

HARM CAUSED TO PLAINTIFF &/OR PATIENT:
1. NONSELF-INFLICTED INJURIES

TYPE OF ACTION BROUGHT:
1. NEGLIGENCE

HISTORY OF THE CASE:

TYPE OF COURT: STATE

TRIER OF FACT: JUDGE,NO JURY

COURT DECISION(S):

TRIAL COURT: FOR DEFENDANT
YEAR: 1969
APPELLATE COURT: FOR DEFENDANT
YEAR: 1971
SUPREME COURT: FOR DEFENDANT
YEAR: 1971

REASON SUIT FAILED:
1. NEGLIGENCE OR CASE NOT PROVEN

203. O'ROURKE V. HALCYON REST

MAE O'ROURKE SUFFERED INJURIES DURING AN ELECTROSHOCK TREATMENT PRESCRIBED BY HER PRIVATE DOCTOR AND CARRIED OUT AT HALCYON REST OF NEW YORK BY ONE OF ITS PHYSICIANS. THE SPECIFIC NATURE AND CAUSE OF THE INJURIES ARE NOT MENTIONED IN THE COURT'S OPINION.

YEAR OF NEGLIGENT ACT: NOT SPECIFIED

STATE IN WHICH NEGLIGENT ACT OCCURRED: NEW YORK

SETTING OF THE CASE: PRIV. MENT. HOSP.

PLAINTIFF(S): PATIENT(S) OR REP.

DEFENDANT(S):
1. NONPSYCHIAT.OR UNKNOWN TYPE PHYSICIAN(S)
2. HOSPITAL &/OR OWNERS, ETC.

NEGLIGENT ACTIVITY:

TREATMENT:
1. NEGLIGENT ELECTROCONVULSIVE THERAPY

DIAGNOSIS:

WHAT WAS DIAGNOSED:
1. TYPE OF TREATMENT NEEDED

RESULT OF DIAGNOSIS:
1. IMPROPER TREATMENT PRESCRIBED

CARE: NOT APPLICABLE

HARM CAUSED TO PLAINTIFF &/OR PATIENT:
1. NONSELF-INFLICTED INJURIES

TYPE OF ACTION BROUGHT:
1. NEGLIGENCE

HISTORY OF THE CASE:

TYPE OF COURT: STATE

TRIER OF FACT: ?, JUDGE OR JURY

COURT DECISION(S):

TRIAL COURT: FOR PLAINTIFF
YEAR: NOT SPECIFIED
APPELLATE COURT: NONFINAL FOR DEF.
YEAR: 1953
SUPREME COURT: NONFINAL FOR DEF.
YEAR: 1954

DEFENDANTS STILL INVOLVED IN SUIT:
1. NONPSYCHIAT.OR UNKNOWN TYPE PHYSICIAN(S)
2. HOSPITAL &/OR OWNERS, ETC.

204. O'ROURKE V. O'ROURKE

EDWARD J. O'ROURKE WENT TO THE CORONER OF THE PARISH OF ORLEANS WITH HIS BROTHER. TOGETHER THEY TOLD HIM THAT THEIR SISTER, ANNA L. O'ROURKE, WAS INSANE. ON THE ORDER OF THE CORONER ANNA WAS THEREUPON TAKEN FROM HER HOME AT MIDNIGHT BY TWO POLICEMEN AND BROUGHT TO THE CITY HOSPITAL FOR MENTAL DISEASES IN NEW ORLEANS. SHE WAS RELEASED THE NEXT DAY TO HER SISTER-IN-LAW, AFTER A DIAGNOSIS OF UNDIFFERENTIATED PSYCHOSIS BY THE EXAMINING PHYSICIANS. ANNA FILED SUIT AGAINST ONE BROTHER (THE OTHER DIED BEFORE SHE FILED SUIT) AND THE CORONER, DR. C. GRENES COLE, CHARGING WRONGFUL SEIZURE AND COMMITMENT.

YEAR OF NEGLIGENT ACT: 1946

STATE IN WHICH NEGLIGENT ACT OCCURRED: LOUISIANA

SETTING OF THE CASE: JUDICIAL PROCEEDING

PLAINTIFF(S): PATIENT(S) OR REP.

DEFENDANT(S):
1. NONPSYCHIAT.OR UNKNOWN TYPE PHYSICIAN(S)
2. DEFENDANT'S SIBLING

NEGLIGENT ACTIVITY:

TREATMENT: NOT APPLICABLE

DIAGNOSIS:

WHAT WAS DIAGNOSED:
1. MENTAL ILLNESS, INSTEAD OF SANITY

RESULT OF DIAGNOSIS:
1. IMPROPER COMMITMENT

CARE: NOT APPLICABLE

HARM CAUSED TO PLAINTIFF &/OR PATIENT:
1. LOSS OF LIBERTY

TYPE OF ACTION BROUGHT:
1. FALSE IMPRISONMENT

HISTORY OF THE CASE:

TYPE OF COURT: STATE

TRIER OF FACT: ?, JUDGE OR JURY

COURT DECISION(S):

TRIAL COURT: FOR DEFENDANT
YEAR: NOT SPECIFIED
APPELLATE COURT: NONFINAL FOR PL.
YEAR: 1951
ON RETRIAL: FOR PLAINTIFF
YEAR: NOT SPECIFIED
ON REAPPEAL TO APPELLATE COURT: FOR PLAINTIFF
YEAR: 1953
ON REAPPEAL TO SUPREME COURT: FOR PLAINTIFF
YEAR: 1955

VERDICT AGAINST WHICH DEFENDANTS:
1. NONPSYCHIAT.OR UNKNOWN TYPE PHYSICIAN(S)
2. DEFENDANT'S SIBLING

RECOVERY OR OTHER RELIEF GRANTED:
1. $ 1000
2. OTHER RECOVERY: COSTS

205. PAPINI V. ALEXANDER SANITARIUM

JOSEPH HENRY PAPINI, A THIRTY-FIVE-YEAR-OLD HEMOPHILIAC, WAS A PATIENT IN THE ALEXANDER SANITARIUM, A PRIVATE SANITARIUM FOR NERVOUS DISEASES IN CALIFORNIA. HE WAS UNABLE TO WORK BECAUSE OF HIS ILLNESS. ONE DAY JOSEPH RAN SCREAMING FROM A LUNCHROOM WHERE HE HAD BEEN EATING WITH TWO FELLOW PATIENTS; HE WAS BLEEDING FROM A CUT ON THE NECK FROM WHICH HE EVENTUALLY DIED. HIS FAMILY FILED SUIT, CHARGING THAT THE HOSPITAL HAD BEEN NEGLIGENT IN NOT PROTECTING JOSEPH FROM ONE OF HIS LUNCHEON COMPANIONS WHO ALLEGEDLY ASSAULTED HIM WITH A FORK AND RAZOR BLADE.

YEAR OF NEGLIGENT ACT: 1933

STATE IN WHICH NEGLIGENT ACT OCCURRED: CALIFORNIA

SETTING OF THE CASE: PRIV. MENT. HOSP.

PLAINTIFF(S): 3RD PARTY, I

DEFENDANT(S):
1. SOME OR ALL DEFENDANTS NOT SPECIFIED
2. HOSPITAL &/OR OWNERS, ETC.

NEGLIGENT ACTIVITY:

TREATMENT: NOT APPLICABLE

DIAGNOSIS:

WHAT WAS DIAGNOSED: NOT APPLICABLE

RESULT OF DIAGNOSIS: NOT APPLICABLE

CARE:
1. INADEQUATE SUPERVISION

HARM CAUSED TO PLAINTIFF &/OR PATIENT:
1. NONSUICIDAL DEATH

TYPE OF ACTION BROUGHT:
1. NEGLIGENCE

HISTORY OF THE CASE:

TYPE OF COURT: STATE

TRIER OF FACT: ?, JUDGE OR JURY

COURT DECISION(S):

TRIAL COURT: FOR PLAINTIFF
YEAR: NOT SPECIFIED
APPELLATE COURT: FOR DEFENDANT
YEAR: 1936
SUPREME COURT: FOR DEFENDANT
YEAR: 1936

REASON SUIT FAILED:
1. NEGLIGENCE OR CASE NOT PROVEN

206. PARKER V. LOS ANGELES COUNTY

CLEOTUS LUCILLE PARKER WAS, AS THE COURT'S OPINION PUT IT, A "REFINED GENTLEWOMAN" WHO WAS CONFINED IN THE STATE MENTAL HOSPITAL IN PATTON, CALIFORNIA FOR SEVEN WEEKS AFTER BEING TEMPORARILY CONFINED IN THE LOS ANGELES COUNTY GENERAL HOSPITAL. THE HOSPITAL DIAGNOSED HER CONDITION AS UNQUESTIONABLY PARANOID, AND STATED THAT SHE WAS SUFFERING FROM EPILEPTIC SEIZURES. FILING SUIT WITHOUT LEGAL COUNSEL, CLEOTUS CHARGED THAT SHE SHOULD NOT HAVE BEEN COMMITTED.

YEAR OF NEGLIGENT ACT: 1936

STATE IN WHICH NEGLIGENT ACT OCCURRED: CALIFORNIA

SETTING OF THE CASE: JUDICIAL PROCEEDING

PLAINTIFF(S): PATIENT(S) OR REP

DEFENDANT(S):
1. STATE GOV. &/OR OFFICIALS, ETC.
2. COUNTY GOV. &/OR OFFICIALS, ETC.

NEGLIGENT ACTIVITY:

TREATMENT: NOT APPLICABLE

DIAGNOSIS:

WHAT WAS DIAGNOSED:
1. MENTAL ILLNESS, INSTEAD OF SANITY

RESULT OF DIAGNOSIS:
1. IMPROPER COMMITMENT

CARE: NOT APPLICABLE

HARM CAUSED TO PLAINTIFF &/OR PATIENT:
1. LOSS OF CONSORTIUM

TYPE OF ACTION BROUGHT:
1. NEGLIGENCE
2. FALSE IMPRISONMENT

HISTORY OF THE CASE:

TYPE OF COURT: STATE

TRIER OF FACT: JUDGE;JURY PRESENT ?

COURT DECISION(S):

TRIAL COURT: FOR DEFENDANT
YEAR: NOT SPECIFIED
APPELLATE COURT: FOR DEFENDANT
YEAR: 1944

REASON SUIT FAILED:
1. STATUTE OF LIMITATIONS BARRED SUIT
2. DEFENDANT(S) CANNOT BE SUED DUE TO: GOVERN. IMMUNITY

207. PAULEN V. SHINNICK

MRS. ANN PAULEN WAS A PATIENT AT THE HAVEN, A PRIVATE SANITARIUM IN MICHIGAN. THE STAFF WAS AWARE OF HER SUICIDAL TENDENCIES, AND SHE WAS PLACED IN A SPECIAL WARD WITH LOCKED WINDOW SCREENS USED ESPECIALLY FOR DEPRESSED PATIENTS. ONE AFTERNOON, ANN TOLD HER NURSE THAT SHE FELT FAINT. THE NURSE OPENED THE WINDOW, BUT BEFORE RELOCKING THE METAL SCREEN, STOOPED TO PICK UP A THIMBLE THAT ANN HAD DROPPED. ANN QUICKLY USED A CHAIR AS A STEP UP TO THE RADIATOR, THEN JUMPED OUT OF THE WINDOW, AND FELL THREE STORIES TO THE GROUND. THE NURSE CLUTCHED AT ANN'S SKIRT BUT WAS UNABLE TO PREVENT THE FALL, WHICH RESULTED IN BRUISES AND A FRACTURED WRIST. SHE AND HER HUSBAND FILED SUIT, CHARGING THE HAVEN WITH NEGLIGENCE IN NOT PROVIDING HER WITH SUFFICIENT PROTECTION FROM HERSELF.

YEAR OF NEGLIGENT ACT: 1937

STATE IN WHICH NEGLIGENT ACT OCCURRED: MICHIGAN

SETTING OF THE CASE: PRIV. MENT. HOSP.

PLAINTIFF(S): PATIENT(S) OR REP.

DEFENDANT(S):
1. HOSPITAL &/OR OWNERS, ETC.

NEGLIGENT ACTIVITY:

TREATMENT: NOT APPLICABLE

DIAGNOSIS:

WHAT WAS DIAGNOSED: NOT APPLICABLE

RESULT OF DIAGNOSIS: NOT APPLICABLE

CARE:
1. INADEQUATE SUPERVISION

HARM CAUSED TO PLAINTIFF &/OR PATIENT:
1. SELF-INFLICTED INJURIES

TYPE OF ACTION BROUGHT:
1. NEGLIGENCE

HISTORY OF THE CASE:

TYPE OF COURT: STATE

TRIER OF FACT: JURY

COURT DECISION(S):

TRIAL COURT: FOR PLAINTIFF
YEAR: NOT SPECIFIED
SUPREME COURT: FOR PLAINTIFF
YEAR: 1939

VERDICT AGAINST WHICH DEFENDANTS:
1. HOSPITAL &/OR OWNERS, ETC.

RECOVERY OR OTHER RELIEF GRANTED:
1. OTHER RECOVERY: NOT SPECIFIED

208. PENNELL V. CUMMINGS

LEMIRA C. PENNELL ALLEGED THAT SHE HAD WRONGFULLY BEEN COMMITTED ON THE EVIDENCE OF CERTIFICATES SIGNED BY FOUR PORTLAND PHYSICIANS. SHE CHARGED THAT SHE WAS DECLARED INSANE BECAUSE SHE TRIED TO GIVE THE PHYSICIANS GOOD ADVICE ABOUT VENTILATION, SEWERAGE, AND OTHER SANITARY MATTERS. SHE SAID, FURTHERMORE, THAT HER OPINIONS WERE SHARED BY SOME OF THE MOST RESPECTED MEN OF HER TIME.

YEAR OF NEGLIGENT ACT: NOT SPECIFIED

STATE IN WHICH NEGLIGENT ACT OCCURRED: MAINE

SETTING OF THE CASE: JUDICIAL PROCEEDING

PLAINTIFF(S): PATIENT(S) OR REP.

DEFENDANT(S):
1. NONPSYCHIAT.OR UNKNOWN TYPE PHYSICIAN(S)

NEGLIGENT ACTIVITY:

TREATMENT: NOT APPLICABLE

DIAGNOSIS:

WHAT WAS DIAGNOSED:
1. MENTAL ILLNESS, INSTEAD OF SANITY

RESULT OF DIAGNOSIS:
1. IMPROPER COMMITMENT

CARE: NOT APPLICABLE

HARM CAUSED TO PLAINTIFF &/OR PATIENT:
1. LOSS OF LIBERTY

TYPE OF ACTION BROUGHT:
1. NEGLIGENCE
2. OTHER TORT(S): WRONGFUL COMMITMENT

HISTORY OF THE CASE:

TYPE OF COURT: STATE

TRIER OF FACT: ?, JUDGE OR JURY

COURT DECISION(S):

TRIAL COURT: FOR DEFENDANT
YEAR: NOT SPECIFIED
SUPREME COURT: FOR DEFENDANT
YEAR: 1883

REASON SUIT FAILED:
1. NEGLIGENCE OR CASE NOT PROVEN
2. DEFENDANT(S) CANNOT BE SUED DUE TO: JUDICIAL IMMUNITY

209. PEOPLE V. BERNSTEIN

DR. WILLIAM G. BERNSTEIN WAS A PSYCHIATRIST AND NEUROLOGIST. MADELINE WAS A SIXTEEN-YEAR-OLD, UNMARRIED HIGH SCHOOL STUDENT WHO HAD BEEN SUSPENDED FROM SCHOOL AFTER HAVING SEXUAL INTERCOURSE WITH A FEW BOYS AT A PARTY. HER MOTHER BROUGHT HER TO DR. BERNSTEIN FOR TREATMENT. INITIALLY BERNSTEIN SIMPLY ASKED ABOUT HER PAST, BUT DURING ONE SESSION MADELINE BEGAN CRYING AND HE PUT HIS ARM AROUND HER AND KISSED HER ON THE FOREHEAD. IN MADELINE'S SUBSEQUENT VISITS THE SESSIONS BEGAN NORMALLY ENOUGH, BUT ABOUT FORTY-FIVE MINUTES INTO THE SESSION HE WOULD DRAW THE BLINDS AND JOIN HER ON THE COUCH, WHERE THEY KISSED AND FONDLED EACH OTHER. FINALLY, ONE SUCH ENCOUNTER LED TO SEXUAL INTERCOURSE. DR. BERNSTEIN WAS TRIED ON CRIMINAL CHARGES FOR STATUTORY RAPE.

YEAR OF NEGLIGENT ACT: 1957

STATE IN WHICH NEGLIGENT ACT OCCURRED: CALIFORNIA

SETTING OF THE CASE: PRIVATE PRACTICE

PLAINTIFF(S): STATE

DEFENDANT(S):
1. PSYCHIATRIST(S)

NEGLIGENT ACTIVITY:

TREATMENT:
1. SEXUAL ABUSE OR DISTURB.OF MARITAL REL.

DIAGNOSIS:

WHAT WAS DIAGNOSED: NOT APPLICABLE

RESULT OF DIAGNOSIS: NOT APPLICABLE

CARE: NOT APPLICABLE

HARM CAUSED TO PLAINTIFF &/OR PATIENT:
1. SEXUAL OR MARITAL HARM

TYPE OF ACTION BROUGHT:
1. CRIMINAL LAW: RAPE

HISTORY OF THE CASE:

TYPE OF COURT: STATE

TRIER OF FACT: JURY

COURT DECISION(S):

TRIAL COURT: FOR PLAINTIFF
YEAR: NOT SPECIFIED
APPELLATE COURT: FOR PLAINTIFF
YEAR: 1959

VERDICT AGAINST WHICH DEFENDANTS:
1. PSYCHIATRIST(S)

RECOVERY OR OTHER RELIEF GRANTED:
1. NONMONETARY RELIEF: CRIMINAL SENTENCE

210. PEOPLE V. LA VALLEE

ROBERT THOMAS SMITH WAS CONVICTED OF SECOND-DEGREE ASSAULT WITH INTENT TO COMMIT SODOMY AND SENTENCED TO ONE DAY TO LIFE. SMITH ALLEGED THAT HE HAD RECEIVED NO PSYCHIATRIC THERAPY, THERAPEUTIC CARE, OR OTHER TREATMENT DURING HIS PRISON SENTENCE, WHICH WAS IN ITS SIXTEENTH YEAR.

YEAR OF NEGLIGENT ACT: 1965

STATE IN WHICH NEGLIGENT ACT OCCURRED: NEW YORK

SETTING OF THE CASE: CORRECTIONAL INST.

PLAINTIFF(S): PATIENT(S) OR REP.

DEFENDANT(S):
1. STATE GOV. &/OR OFFICIALS, ETC.

NEGLIGENT ACTIVITY:

TREATMENT:
1. NO TREATMENT OR INADEQUATE TREATMENT

DIAGNOSIS:

WHAT WAS DIAGNOSED: NOT APPLICABLE

RESULT OF DIAGNOSIS: NOT APPLICABLE

CARE:
1. FAILURE TO PROVIDE PROPER CUSTODIAL CARE

HARM CAUSED TO PLAINTIFF &/OR PATIENT:
1. DEPRIVATION OF CONSTITUTIONAL RIGHTS
2. LOSS OF LIBERTY

TYPE OF ACTION BROUGHT:
1. DEPRIVATION OF CONSTITUTIONAL RIGHTS: CONST.RTS.IN GEN.

HISTORY OF THE CASE:

TYPE OF COURT: STATE

TRIER OF FACT: JUDGE,NO JURY

COURT DECISION(S):

TRIAL COURT: FOR DEFENDANT
YEAR: NOT SPECIFIED
APPELLATE COURT: NONFINAL FOR PL.
YEAR: 1968

DEFENDANTS STILL INVOLVED IN SUIT:

211. PEOPLE V. MCCAUGHAN

GRACE BELILL WAS A SEVENTY-ONE-YEAR-OLD PATIENT AT THE CALIFORNIA STATE HOSPITAL IN MODESTO. SHE SUFFERED FROM INVOLUTIONAL PSYCHOSIS WHICH OFTEN CAUSED HER TO REFUSE ANY FOOD GIVEN TO HER. HER HOSPITAL RECORDS INFORMED HER ATTENDANTS THAT SHE WAS TO BE SPOON FED IF NECESSARY. ON ONE OCCASION WHEN GRACE REFUSED TO EAT, AN ATTENDANT HELD A TOWEL OVER GRACE'S MOUTH AND NOSE, ANOTHER SAT ON HER LAP, AND VELVA IRENE MCCAUGHAN, THE THIRD ATTENDANT, PULLED GRACE'S HEAD BACK BY THE HAIR AND FED HER CREAMED POTATOES. AFTER THE THIRD SPOONFUL, GRACE COLLAPSED AND SUBSEQUENTLY DIED. THE CAUSE OF DEATH WAS DETERMINED TO BE ASPHYXIATION FROM THE REGURGITATED POTATOES. THE STATE BROUGHT CRIMINAL CHARGES AGAINST MCCAUGHAN FOR INVOLUNTARY MANSLAUGHTER.

YEAR OF NEGLIGENT ACT: 1955

STATE IN WHICH NEGLIGENT ACT OCCURRED: CALIFORNIA

SETTING OF THE CASE: PUB. MENT. HOSP.

PLAINTIFF(S): STATE

DEFENDANT(S):
1. PARAPROFESSIONAL, NONPRO.EMPLOYEE, ETC.

NEGLIGENT ACTIVITY:

TREATMENT: NOT APPLICABLE

DIAGNOSIS:

WHAT WAS DIAGNOSED: NOT APPLICABLE

RESULT OF DIAGNOSIS: NOT APPLICABLE

CARE:
1. FAILURE TO PROVIDE PROPER CUSTODIAL CARE

HARM CAUSED TO PLAINTIFF &/OR PATIENT:
1. NONSUICIDAL DEATH

TYPE OF ACTION BROUGHT:
1. CRIMINAL LAW: CRIMINAL NEGLIGENCE

HISTORY OF THE CASE:

TYPE OF COURT: STATE

TRIER OF FACT: JURY

COURT DECISION(S):

TRIAL COURT: FOR PLAINTIFF
YEAR: NOT SPECIFIED
APPELLATE COURT: FOR PLAINTIFF
YEAR: NOT SPECIFIED
SUPREME COURT: NONFINAL FOR DEF.
YEAR: 1957

DEFENDANTS STILL INVOLVED IN SUIT:
1. PARAPROFESSIONAL,NONPRO.EMPLOYEE, ETC.

212. PEOPLE V. WILKINS

ISIDORE KAGANOVITCH ALLEGEDLY SODOMIZED A TWELVE-YEAR-OLD BOY IN KINGS COUNTY, NEW YORK. HE PLEADED NOT GUILTY AND IN SEPTEMBER 1953 WAS SENT TO THE KINGS COUNTY MEDICAL CENTER FOR A PSYCHIATRIC EXAMINATION. HE WAS FOUND TO BE INSANE AND COMMITTED TO MATTEAWAN STATE HOSPITAL. IN FEBRUARY 1955 HE RETURNED FOR THE TRIAL AFTER BEING DECLARED SANE. HE PLEADED GUILTY TO ONE OF THE FIVE COUNTS, SECOND-DEGREE ASSAULT WITH THE INTENT TO COMMIT SODOMY, BUT WAS SENT BACK TO THE KINGS COUNTY HOSPITAL FOR FURTHER OBSERVATION AND, WITHOUT THE LEGALLY REQUIRED PSYCHIATRIC EXAMINATION, WAS FOUND SANE. HE WAS SENTENCED TO HARD LABOR, ONE DAY TO LIFE, AND SENT TO SING SING STATE PRISON IN OSSINING, FROM WHICH HE WAS TRANSFERRED TO ATTICA. KAGANOVITCH CHARGED THAT HE HAD RECEIVED NO PSYCHIATRIC TREATMENT, REHABILITATION, OR DIAGNOSIS, EXCEPT FOR HARD LABOR. THE STATE BROUGHT SUIT ON HIS BEHALF AGAINST WILKINS, THE ATTICA WARDEN WITH FAILING TO PROVIDE ADEQUATE DIAGNOSIS AND TREATMENT.

YEAR OF NEGLIGENT ACT: NOT SPECIFIED

STATE IN WHICH NEGLIGENT ACT OCCURRED: NEW YORK

SETTING OF THE CASE: PUB. MENT. HOSP.

PLAINTIFF(S): PATIENT(S) OR REP.

DEFENDANT(S):
1. NOPRF.ORG.PAT.,INS.

NEGLIGENT ACTIVITY:

TREATMENT:
1. NO TREATMENT OR INADEQUATE TREATMENT

DIAGNOSIS:

WHAT WAS DIAGNOSED:
1. INADEQUATE DIAGNOSIS

RESULT OF DIAGNOSIS:
1. IMPROPER COMMITMENT
2. IMPROPER FAILURE TO RELEASE

CARE: NOT APPLICABLE

HARM CAUSED TO PLAINTIFF &/OR PATIENT:
1. DEPRIVATION OF CONSTITUTIONAL RIGHTS
2. LOSS OF LIBERTY

TYPE OF ACTION BROUGHT:
1. DEPRIVATION OF CONSTITUTIONAL RIGHTS: CONST.RTS.IN GEN.
2. HABEAS CORPUS

HISTORY OF THE CASE:

TYPE OF COURT: STATE

TRIER OF FACT: JUDGE,NO JURY

COURT DECISION(S):

TRIAL COURT: FOR DEFENDANT
YEAR: NOT SPECIFIED
APPELLATE COURT: NONFINAL FOR PL.
YEAR: 1965

DEFENDANTS STILL INVOLVED IN SUIT:
1. NOPRF.ORG.PAT.,INS.

213. PETERS V. STATE

CHARLES HATZ, A UTICA STATE HOSPITAL PATIENT, ASSAULTED AND SHOT THERESA PETERS AFTER BEING RELEASED FROM UTICA. HE COMMITTED SUICIDE AND SHE BECAME PERMANENTLY CRIPPLED. THESE PROCEEDINGS WERE BROUGHT FOR THE PURPOSE OF OBTAINING HOSPITAL RECORDS TO SEE IF ANY CAUSE OF ACTION EXISTED WITH RESPECT TO THE ALLEGED NEGLIGENCE OF THE HOSPITAL IN PREMATURELY RELEASING HATZ.

YEAR OF NEGLIGENT ACT: 1959

STATE IN WHICH NEGLIGENT ACT OCCURRED: NEW YORK

SETTING OF THE CASE: PUB. MENT. HOSP.

PLAINTIFF(S): 3RD PARTY, II

DEFENDANT(S):
1. STATE GOV. &/OR OFFICIALS, ETC.

NEGLIGENT ACTIVITY:

TREATMENT: NOT APPLICABLE

DIAGNOSIS:

WHAT WAS DIAGNOSED:
1. LACK OF DANGEROUSNESS

RESULT OF DIAGNOSIS:
1. IMPROPER RELEASE

CARE: NOT APPLICABLE

HARM CAUSED TO PLAINTIFF &/OR PATIENT:
1. SUICIDE
2. NONSELF-INFLICTED INJURIES

TYPE OF ACTION BROUGHT:
1. NEGLIGENCE

HISTORY OF THE CASE:

TYPE OF COURT: STATE

TRIER OF FACT: JUDGE,NO JURY

COURT DECISION(S):

TRIAL COURT: NONFINAL FOR PL.
YEAR: 1964
APPELLATE COURT: NONFINAL FOR PL.
YEAR: 1964

DEFENDANTS STILL INVOLVED IN SUIT:
1. STATE GOV. &/OR OFFICIALS, ETC.

214. PETTIS V. STATE DEPARTMENT OF HOSPITALS

CECIL PETTIS SUFFERED FROM MENTAL PROBLEMS. AT THE URGINGS OF A SOCIAL WORKER, CECIL SOUGHT HELP. HE VOLUNTARILY ENTERED THE CENTRAL LOUISIANA STATE HOSPITAL IN PINEVILLE WHERE HE WAS COMMITTED, EXAMINED, AND TRANSFERRED TO THE INTENSIVE PSYCHIATRIC CARE WARD, SUFFERING FROM CHRONIC UNDIFFERENTIATED SCHIZOPHRENIA. AFTER TWO ELECTRO-SHOCK TREATMENTS DURING WHICH NO RELAXANT DRUGS WERE USED, CECIL COMPLAINED OF PAIN. TWO MORE TREATMENTS WERE GIVEN, BUT THE PHYSICIANS DID NOT EXAMINE CECIL BETWEEN TREATMENTS, NOR DID THEY READ THE NURSES' REPORTS. X-RAYS REVEALED THAT HE HAD SUSTAINED FRACTURES OF THREE VERTEBRAE, A SHOULDER BONE, AND PELVIS. AFTER TWO OPERATIONS CECIL STILL COMPLAINED OF PAIN IN HIS LEGS, LIMITATION OF MOVEMENT IN HIS ARMS, AND DIFFICULTY IN WALKING.

YEAR OF NEGLIGENT ACT: 1971

STATE IN WHICH NEGLIGENT ACT OCCURRED: LOUISIANA

SETTING OF THE CASE: PUB. MENT. HOSP.

PLAINTIFF(S): PATIENT(S) OR REP.

DEFENDANT(S):
1. PSYCHIATRIST(S)
2. NONPSYCHIAT.OR UNKNOWN TYPE PHYSICIAN(S)
3. HOSPITAL &/OR OWNERS, ETC.
4. STATE GOV. &/OR OFFICIALS, ETC.
5. INSURANCE COMPANY(S)

NEGLIGENT ACTIVITY:

TREATMENT:
1. NEGLIGENT ELECTROCONVULSIVE THERAPY

DIAGNOSIS:

WHAT WAS DIAGNOSED: NOT APPLICABLE

RESULT OF DIAGNOSIS: NOT APPLICABLE

CARE: NOT APPLICABLE

HARM CAUSED TO PLAINTIFF &/OR PATIENT:
1. NONSELF-INFLICTED INJURIES

TYPE OF ACTION BROUGHT:
1. NEGLIGENCE

HISTORY OF THE CASE:

TYPE OF COURT: STATE

TRIER OF FACT: JURY

COURT DECISION(S):

TRIAL COURT: FOR DEFENDANT
YEAR: 1973
APPELLATE COURT: NONFINAL FOR PL.
YEAR: 1973
ON RETRIAL: FOR DEFENDANT
YEAR: NOT SPECIFIED
ON REAPPEAL TO APPELLATE COURT: FOR PLAINTIFF
YEAR: 1976
ON REAPPEAL TO SUPREME COURT: FOR PLAINTIFF
YEAR: 1976
ON REMAND TO APPELLATE COURT: FOR PLAINTIFF
YEAR: 1976

VERDICT AGAINST WHICH DEFENDANTS:
1. PSYCHIATRIST(S)
2. NONPSYCHIAT.OR UNKNOWN TYPE PHYSICIAN(S)
3. HOSPITAL &/OR OWNERS, ETC.
4. STATE GOV. &/OR OFFICIALS, ETC.

RECOVERY OR OTHER RELIEF GRANTED:
1. $ 35000
2. INTEREST
3. OTHER RECOVERY: COSTS

215. PHILLIPS V. SINGLETARY

CECIL C. PHILLIPS PLEADED GUILTY TO RAPE CHARGES AND WAS SENTENCED TO TWENTY-FIVE YEARS IN PRISON. HE CHARGED THAT CLARENCE E. SINGLETARY, THE PRESIDING JUDGE, HIS LEGAL COUNSEL, AND THE DOCTOR WHO EXAMINED HIM, HAD DEPRIVED HIM OF HIS CONSTITUTIONAL RIGHTS AND CONSPIRED AGAINST HIM BY ALLOWING HIM TO PLEAD GUILTY TO THE CHARGES, DESPITE THE FACT THAT HE WAS UNDER THE INFLUENCE OF DRUGS AT THE TIME OF THE CRIME.

YEAR OF NEGLIGENT ACT: OCCURRED OVER A SERIES OF YEARS, ENDING IN 1972

STATE IN WHICH NEGLIGENT ACT OCCURRED: SOUTH CAROLINA

SETTING OF THE CASE: JUDICIAL PROCEEDING

PLAINTIFF(S): PATIENT(S) OR REP.

DEFENDANT(S):
1. NONPSYCHIAT.OR UNKNOWN TYPE PHYSICIAN(S)
2. LAWYER(S)
3. JUDICIARY &/OR CLERKS, ETC.

NEGLIGENT ACTIVITY:

TREATMENT: NOT APPLICABLE

DIAGNOSIS:

WHAT WAS DIAGNOSED:
1. SANITY, INSTEAD OF MENTAL ILLNESS

RESULT OF DIAGNOSIS:
1. NEG.DETERM.OF COMPETENCE TO STAND TRIAL

CARE: NOT APPLICABLE

HARM CAUSED TO PLAINTIFF &/OR PATIENT:
1. LOSS OF LIBERTY

TYPE OF ACTION BROUGHT:
1. DEPRIVATION OF CONSTITUTIONAL RIGHTS: CONST.RTS.IN GEN.

HISTORY OF THE CASE:

TYPE OF COURT: FEDERAL

TRIER OF FACT: JUDGE;JURY PRESENT ?

COURT DECISION(S):

TRIAL COURT: FOR DEFENDANT
YEAR: 1972

REASON SUIT FAILED:
1. NO CAUSE OF ACTION STATED
2. DEFENDANT(S) CANNOT BE SUED DUE TO: JUDICIAL IMMUNITY

216. PIETRUCHA V. GRANT HOSPITAL

ALBERT PIETRUCHA WAS A FORTY-TWO-YEAR-OLD POLISH CITIZEN WITH A WIFE AND SIX CHILDREN. HE ENTERED GRANT HOSPITAL TO BE TREATED FOR ACUTE SCHIZOPHRENIA. ALBERT HAD RECENTLY ATTEMPTED SUICIDE AND THE HOSPITAL WAS WARNED OF HIS CONTINUING SUICIDAL TENDENCIES. SHORTLY AFTER ADMISSION HE HANGED HIMSELF WITH A BELT AND HIS WIFE BROUGHT SUIT, ALLEGING NEGLIGENCE.

YEAR OF NEGLIGENT ACT: 1967

STATE IN WHICH NEGLIGENT ACT OCCURRED: ILLINOIS

SETTING OF THE CASE: PRIV. MENT. HOSP.

PLAINTIFF(S): PAT. & 3RD PTY., I

DEFENDANT(S):
1. HOSPITAL &/OR OWNERS, ETC.

NEGLIGENT ACTIVITY:

TREATMENT: NOT APPLICABLE

DIAGNOSIS:

WHAT WAS DIAGNOSED: NOT APPLICABLE

RESULT OF DIAGNOSIS: NOT APPLICABLE

CARE:
1. INADEQUATE SUPERVISION

HARM CAUSED TO PLAINTIFF &/OR PATIENT:
1. SUICIDE

TYPE OF ACTION BROUGHT:
1. NEGLIGENCE

HISTORY OF THE CASE:

TYPE OF COURT: FEDERAL

TRIER OF FACT: JURY

COURT DECISION(S):

TRIAL COURT: FOR DEFENDANT
YEAR: NOT SPECIFIED
APPELLATE COURT: NONFINAL FOR PL.
YEAR: 1971

DEFENDANTS STILL INVOLVED IN SUIT:
1. HOSPITAL &/OR OWNERS, ETC.

217. POWELL V. DUKE UNIVERSITY

ON DECEMBER 23, 1970, BOOKER T. POWELL APPEARED AT THE DUKE HOSPITAL EMERGENCY ROOM. HE SPOKE INCOHERENTLY AND WAS UNABLE TO EXPLAIN EXACTLY WHAT TYPE OF PRESCRIPTION HE WANTED. WHILE BEING EXAMINED BY A RESIDENT IN PSYCHIATRY, POWELL APPEARED INCREASINGLY HOSTILE, TENSE, AND AGGRESSIVE. HE REFUSED ANY EXAMINATION OR CALMING MEDICATION AND EXPLAINED THAT HE WAS SCHEDULED TO BE KILLED. HE ALLEGEDLY BECAME MORE HOSTILE AND THE RESIDENT HAD HIM PUT IN RESTRAINTS. THE RESIDENT THEN DECIDED THAT POWELL WAS DANGEROUS TO HIMSELF AND OTHERS AND MADE AN EMERGENCY COMMITMENT. POWELL WAS TAKEN TO UMSTEAD HOSPITAL AND KEPT THERE UNTIL JANUARY 1 AGAINST HIS WILL.

YEAR OF NEGLIGENT ACT: 1970

STATE IN WHICH NEGLIGENT ACT OCCURRED: NORTH CAROLINA

SETTING OF THE CASE: JUDICIAL PROCEEDING

PLAINTIFF(S): PATIENT(S) OR REP.

DEFENDANT(S):
1. NONPSYCHIAT.OR UNKNOWN TYPE PHYSICIAN(S)
2. HOSPITAL &/OR OWNERS, ETC.
3. EDUCATIONAL INST. &/OR DEANS, ETC.

NEGLIGENT ACTIVITY:

TREATMENT: NOT APPLICABLE

DIAGNOSIS:

WHAT WAS DIAGNOSED:
1. MENTAL ILLNESS, INSTEAD OF SANITY

RESULT OF DIAGNOSIS:
1. IMPROPER COMMITMENT

CARE: NOT APPLICABLE

HARM CAUSED TO PLAINTIFF &/OR PATIENT:
1. LOSS OF CONSORTIUM

TYPE OF ACTION BROUGHT:
1. NEGLIGENCE
2. FALSE IMPRISONMENT
3. DEPRIVATION OF CONSTITUTIONAL RIGHTS: LOSS OF LIBERTY
4. OTHER TORT(S): FALSE ARREST

HISTORY OF THE CASE:

TYPE OF COURT: STATE

TRIER OF FACT: JUDGE;JURY PRESENT ?

COURT DECISION(S):

TRIAL COURT: FOR DEFENDANT
YEAR: NOT SPECIFIED
APPELLATE COURT: FOR DEFENDANT
YEAR: 1973

REASON SUIT FAILED:
1. NEGLIGENCE OR CASE NOT PROVEN
2. DEFENDANT(S) CANNOT BE SUED DUE TO: JUDICIAL IMMUNITY

218. POWELL V. RISSER

NINETEEN-YEAR-OLD REYNOLD F. POWELL PLAYED THE TRUMPET AND TUNED AND REPAIRED PIANOS. SUFFERING FROM MANIC DEPRESSIVE PSYCHOSIS, POWELL WAS ADMITTED TO THE ALLENTOWN STATE HOSPITAL IN PENNSYLVANIA IN SEPTEMBER 1943. IN MAY 1946 POWELL ESCAPED AND WAS BROUGHT BACK BY THE POLICE IN A MANIC STATE. HE WAS VIOLENT AND THREATENED TO RUN AWAY AGAIN. DOCTOR RISSER DECIDED TO HAVE THE HOSPITAL NURSES GIVE POWELL WET PACK TREATMENTS. THREE SUCH TREATMENTS WERE ADMINISTERED. AFTER EACH OF THE FIRST TWO, RISSER FAILED TO CHECK POWELL'S CONDITION, AND DID NOT REALIZE THAT OVERLY TIGHT WRAPPING OF THE SHEETS HAD CUT OFF HIS CIRCULATION AND MADE POWELL'S HANDS SWELL TO ALMOST THREE TIMES THEIR NORMAL SIZE. POWELL SHOWED RISSER THE BLISTERS THAT HAD FORMED AND RISSER CUT SOME OF THEM OPEN WITH AN UNSTERILE PENKNIFE THAT HE PULLED OUT OF HIS POCKET. AS A RESULT OF THIS TREATMENT POWELL LOST 60 PERCENT OF THE USE OF HIS HANDS.

YEAR OF NEGLIGENT ACT: 1946

STATE IN WHICH NEGLIGENT ACT OCCURRED: PENNSYLVANIA

SETTING OF THE CASE: PUB. MENT. HOSP.

PLAINTIFF(S): PATIENT(S) OR REP.

DEFENDANT(S):
1. NONPSYCHIAT.OR UNKNOWN TYPE PHYSICIAN(S)

NEGLIGENT ACTIVITY:

TREATMENT:
1. NEG.APPL. OF WETPACK

DIAGNOSIS:

WHAT WAS DIAGNOSED: NOT APPLICABLE

RESULT OF DIAGNOSIS: NOT APPLICABLE

CARE: NOT APPLICABLE

HARM CAUSED TO PLAINTIFF &/OR PATIENT:
1. NONSELF-INFLICTED INJURIES

TYPE OF ACTION BROUGHT:
1. NEGLIGENCE
2. OTHER TORT(S): TRESPASS

HISTORY OF THE CASE:

TYPE OF COURT: STATE

TRIER OF FACT: JUDGE,UNINV.JURY

COURT DECISION(S):

TRIAL COURT: FOR PLAINTIFF
YEAR: 1948
SUPREME COURT: FOR DEFENDANT
YEAR: 1953

REASON SUIT FAILED:
1. NEGLIGENCE OR CASE NOT PROVEN

219. PULS V. ST. VINCENT HOSPITAL

MARY PULS, A FORTY-FOUR-YEAR-OLD MOTHER OF TWO, WAS ADMITTED TO THE PSYCHIATRIC WARD OF ST. VINCENT HOSPITAL IN GREEN BAY SUFFERING FROM A MODERATELY SEVERE ANXIETY REACTION BROUGHT ABOUT BY HOME PROBLEMS AND WORRIES ABOUT HER FAMILY. SHE WAS NOT CONFINED TO HER BED AND SHE WAS ALLOWED TO LEAVE THE HOSPITAL DURING THE DAY TO VISIT HER HOME OR GO SHOPPING. WHILE SHOPPING ONE DAY, MARY BECAME SEPARATED FROM THE FELLOW PATIENT SHE WAS WITH AND BECAME VERY TENSE. THAT NIGHT SHE SWALLOWED TOO MANY SLEEPING PILLS. NURSES OBSERVED THAT SHE WAS OVERLY DROWSY AT 1:30 A.M. BUT DID NOT CALL HER DOCTOR UNTIL 3:00 A.M. HE TOLD THE NURSE TO WATCH MARY AS CLOSELY AS POSSIBLE. SIX HOURS LATER MARY AROSE FROM BED AND FELL. SHE CLIMBED BACK ON THE BED, BUT ROLLED OFF THE OTHER SIDE. BY THE TIME THE NURSE CAME, MARY HAD FALLEN SEVERAL OTHER TIMES AND HAD INJURED HER BACK.

YEAR OF NEGLIGENT ACT: 1961

STATE IN WHICH NEGLIGENT ACT OCCURRED: WISCONSIN

SETTING OF THE CASE: PRIV. GEN. HOSP.

PLAINTIFF(S): PATIENT(S) OR REP.

DEFENDANT(S):
1. HOSPITAL &/OR OWNERS, ETC.

NEGLIGENT ACTIVITY:

TREATMENT: NOT APPLICABLE

DIAGNOSIS:

WHAT WAS DIAGNOSED: NOT APPLICABLE

RESULT OF DIAGNOSIS: NOT APPLICABLE

CARE:
1. INADEQUATE SUPERVISION

HARM CAUSED TO PLAINTIFF &/OR PATIENT:
1. NONSELF-INFLICTED INJURIES

TYPE OF ACTION BROUGHT:
1. NEGLIGENCE

HISTORY OF THE CASE:

TYPE OF COURT: STATE

TRIER OF FACT: JURY

COURT DECISION(S):

TRIAL COURT: FOR DEFENDANT
YEAR: 1966
SUPREME COURT: FOR DEFENDANT
YEAR: 1967

REASON SUIT FAILED:
1. NEGLIGENCE OR CASE NOT PROVEN

220. QUICK V. BENEDICTINE SISTERS HOSPITAL ASSOCIATION

WALTER G. QUICK WAS A PATIENT AT ST. MARY'S HOSPITAL IN DULUTH, MINNESOTA, WHERE HE RECEIVED ELECTRO-SHOCK TREATMENTS BECAUSE OF HIS MARKED PARANOID CONDITION. AFTER ONE SUCH TREATMENT, WALTER, IN A CONFUSED STATE, CLIMBED OVER THE SIDERAILS ON HIS BED AND FELL, FRACTURING HIS RIGHT SHOULDER. HE CHARGED THE HOSPITAL WITH NEGLIGENCE IN NOT PROVIDING ADEQUATE SUPERVISION.

YEAR OF NEGLIGENT ACT: 1955

STATE IN WHICH NEGLIGENT ACT OCCURRED: MINNESOTA

SETTING OF THE CASE: PRIV. MENT. HOSP.

PLAINTIFF(S): PATIENT(S) OR REP.

DEFENDANT(S):
1. HOSPITAL &/OR OWNERS, ETC.

NEGLIGENT ACTIVITY:

TREATMENT: NOT APPLICABLE

DIAGNOSIS:

WHAT WAS DIAGNOSED: NOT APPLICABLE

RESULT OF DIAGNOSIS: NOT APPLICABLE

CARE:
1. INADEQUATE SUPERVISION

HARM CAUSED TO PLAINTIFF &/OR PATIENT:
1. NONSELF-INFLICTED INJURIES

TYPE OF ACTION BROUGHT:
1. NEGLIGENCE

HISTORY OF THE CASE:

TYPE OF COURT: STATE

TRIER OF FACT: JUDGE,UNINV.JURY

COURT DECISION(S):

TRIAL COURT: FOR DEFENDANT
YEAR: NOT SPECIFIED
SUPREME COURT: NONFINAL FOR PL.
YEAR: 1960

DEFENDANTS STILL INVOLVED IN SUIT:
1. HOSPITAL &/OR OWNERS, ETC.

221. QUINLEY V. COCKE

EARL QUINLEY, A FIFTY-ONE-YEAR-OLD SECRETARY SUFFERING FROM A NERVOUS CONDITION BROUGHT ON BY PAIN FROM GALL BLADDER ATTACKS, ENTERED THE GARTLY-RAMSAY HOSPITAL OF MEMPHIS, TENNESSEE, FOR REST AND TREATMENT. HE UNDERWENT ELECTRO-SHOCK THERAPY TWICE. AFTER THE SECOND TREATMENT, QUINLEY FELT PAIN IN HIS RIGHT HIP AND THIGH AND COMPLAINED TO HIS DOCTOR, E. W. COCKE. NO X-RAYS WERE TAKEN UNTIL THREE DAYS LATER. THE PAIN WAS DUE TO A FRACTURED HIP SUSTAINED DURING THE ELECTRO-SHOCK TREATMENT.

YEAR OF NEGLIGENT ACT: 1942

STATE IN WHICH NEGLIGENT ACT OCCURRED: TENNESSEE

SETTING OF THE CASE: PRIV. MENT. HOSP.

PLAINTIFF(S): PATIENT(S) OR REP.

DEFENDANT(S):
1. PSYCHIATRIST(S)

NEGLIGENT ACTIVITY:

TREATMENT:
1. NEGLIGENT ELECTROCONVULSIVE THERAPY

DIAGNOSIS:

WHAT WAS DIAGNOSED: NOT APPLICABLE

RESULT OF DIAGNOSIS: NOT APPLICABLE

CARE: NOT APPLICABLE

HARM CAUSED TO PLAINTIFF &/OR PATIENT:
1. NONSELF-INFLICTED INJURIES

TYPE OF ACTION BROUGHT:
1. NEGLIGENCE

HISTORY OF THE CASE:

TYPE OF COURT: STATE

TRIER OF FACT: JUDGE,UNINV.JURY

COURT DECISION(S):

TRIAL COURT: FOR DEFENDANT
YEAR: NOT SPECIFIED
APPELLATE COURT: FOR DEFENDANT
YEAR: NOT SPECIFIED
SUPREME COURT: FOR DEFENDANT
YEAR: 1946

REASON SUIT FAILED:
1. NEGLIGENCE OR CASE NOT PROVEN

222. RENELLI V. DEPARTMENT OF MENTAL HYGIENE

ADRIENNE RENELLI WAS COMMITTED TO WILLOWBROOK STATE HOSPITAL BY HER PARENTS AT AGE TEN BECAUSE THEY BELIEVED SHE COULD BE PROVIDED WITH BETTER CARE THERE THAN AT HOME. DURING THE NEXT TWELVE YEARS ADRIENNE WAS NEGLECTED AND RECEIVED LITTLE MORE THAN CUSTODIAL CARE, AS A RESULT OF WHICH HER CONDITION DETERIORATED. WHEN SHE ENTERED THE HOSPITAL SHE WAS HAPPY, CHEERFUL, AND GENTLE, AND COULD DRESS HERSELF; BUT AFTER TWELVE YEARS SHE BECAME WITHDRAWN. CRANKY, BELLIGERENT, AND VIOLENT, AND WAS UNABLE TO DRESS HERSELF. THE UNDERSTAFFED AND OVERWORKED HOSPITAL REFUSED TO DEVELOP A PROGRAM BY WHICH ADRIENNE MIGHT BECOME TOILET-TRAINED, LEARN TO FEED HERSELF, OR PERFORM OTHER SIMPLE FUNCTIONS. THIS SUIT WAS AN EFFORT TO OBTAIN MORE THAN CUSTODIAL CARE FOR ADRIENNE AND DEMANDED TREATMENT THAT WOULD GIVE ADRIENNE A REALISTIC CHANCE OF IMPROVING.

YEAR OF NEGLIGENT ACT: 1972

STATE IN WHICH NEGLIGENT ACT OCCURRED: NEW YORK

SETTING OF THE CASE: PUB. MENT. HOSP.

PLAINTIFF(S): PATIENT(S) OR REP.

DEFENDANT(S):
1. STATE GOV. &/OR OFFICIALS, ETC.

NEGLIGENT ACTIVITY:

TREATMENT:
1. NO TREATMENT OR INADEQUATE TREATMENT

DIAGNOSIS:

WHAT WAS DIAGNOSED: NOT APPLICABLE

RESULT OF DIAGNOSIS: NOT APPLICABLE

CARE: NOT APPLICABLE

HARM CAUSED TO PLAINTIFF &/OR PATIENT:
1. DEPRIVATION OF CONSTITUTIONAL RIGHTS

TYPE OF ACTION BROUGHT:
1. DEPRIVATION OF CONSTITUTIONAL RIGHTS: RIGHT TO TREATMENT

HISTORY OF THE CASE:

TYPE OF COURT: STATE

TRIER OF FACT: JUDGE;JURY PRESENT ?

COURT DECISION(S):

TRIAL COURT: FOR PLAINTIFF
YEAR: 1973

VERDICT AGAINST WHICH DEFENDANTS:

RECOVERY OR OTHER RELIEF GRANTED:
1. NONMONETARY RELIEF: INJ.OR OTHER EQ.REL.

223. REYNOLDS V. NEILL

PERRY WAYNE REYNOLDS WAS INDICTED FOR MURDER WITH MALICE IN DALLAS COUNTY, TEXAS. A JURY FOUND PERRY INSANE AT THE TIME OF THE TRIAL AND AT THE TIME OF THE MURDER. HE WAS CRIMINALLY COMMITTED TO THE RUSK STATE MENTAL HOSPITAL UNTIL HE REGAINED HIS SANITY. REYNOLDS CHARGED THAT THE DIFFERENCES BETWEEN CIVIL AND CRIMINAL COMMITMENT PROCEEDINGS, TREATMENT, AND RELEASE PROCEDURES WERE UNCONSTITUTIONAL BECAUSE THEY VIOLATED HIS RIGHT TO EQUAL PROTECTION UNDER THE LAW. HE ALLEGED THAT THOSE CRIMINALLY COMMITTED RECEIVED POORER CARE AND HAD TO PASS THROUGH A MORE STRINGENT AND RIGOROUS RELEASE PROCEDURE.

YEAR OF NEGLIGENT ACT: NOT SPECIFIED, BUT OCCURRED OVER A SERIES OF YEARS

STATE IN WHICH NEGLIGENT ACT OCCURRED: TEXAS

SETTING OF THE CASE: PUB. MENT. HOSP.

PLAINTIFF(S): PATIENT(S) OR REP.

DEFENDANT(S):
1. HOSPITAL &/OR OWNERS, ETC.

NEGLIGENT ACTIVITY:

TREATMENT:
1. NO TREATMENT OR INADEQUATE TREATMENT

DIAGNOSIS:

WHAT WAS DIAGNOSED: NOT APPLICABLE

RESULT OF DIAGNOSIS: NOT APPLICABLE

CARE: NOT APPLICABLE

HARM CAUSED TO PLAINTIFF &/OR PATIENT:
1. DEPRIVATION OF CONSTITUTIONAL RIGHTS

TYPE OF ACTION BROUGHT:
1. DEPRIVATION OF CONSTITUTIONAL RIGHTS: CONST.RTS.IN GEN.
2. HABEAS CORPUS

HISTORY OF THE CASE:

TYPE OF COURT: FEDERAL

TRIER OF FACT: JUDGE,NO JURY

COURT DECISION(S):

TRIAL COURT: FOR PLAINTIFF
YEAR: 1974
SUPREME COURT: NONFINAL FOR DEF.
YEAR: 1975
ON RETRIAL: FOR PLAINTIFF
YEAR: 1975

VERDICT AGAINST WHICH DEFENDANTS:
1. HOSPITAL &/OR OWNERS, ETC.

RECOVERY OR OTHER RELIEF GRANTED:
1. NONMONETARY RELIEF: INJ.OR OTHER EQ.REL.

224. RHIVER V. RIETMAN

AT THE REQUEST OF PLAINTIFF'S WIFE, DR. H. JEROME RIETMAN FILED A REPORT STATING THAT LEWIS P. RHIVER WAS MENTALLY ILL AND SHOULD BE ADMITTED TO A STATE PSYCHIATRIC HOSPITAL. LEWIS HAD ALLEGEDLY BEEN IRRITABLE, HOSTILE, AND UNREASONABLE. IN ADDITION, HE HAD BEEN ABUSIVE AND MADE THREATS TO HIS WIFE AND SON AND HAD SOLD EXPENSIVE APPLIANCES AND A PIANO FOR MUCH LESS THAN THEY WERE WORTH. LEWIS WAS TEMPORARILY COMMITTED FOR TWO DAYS AND THEN RELEASED. HE CHARGED THE DOCTOR WITH NEGLIGENCE IN WRITING THE REPORT LEADING TO HIS COMMITMENT.

YEAR OF NEGLIGENT ACT: 1961

STATE IN WHICH NEGLIGENT ACT OCCURRED: INDIANA

SETTING OF THE CASE: JUDICIAL PROCEEDING

PLAINTIFF(S): PATIENT(S) OR REP.

DEFENDANT(S):
1. NONPSYCHIAT.OR UNKNOWN TYPE PHYSICIAN(S)

NEGLIGENT ACTIVITY:

TREATMENT: NOT APPLICABLE

DIAGNOSIS:

WHAT WAS DIAGNOSED:
1. MENTAL ILLNESS, INSTEAD OF SANITY

RESULT OF DIAGNOSIS:
1. IMPROPER COMMITMENT

CARE: NOT APPLICABLE

HARM CAUSED TO PLAINTIFF &/OR PATIENT:
1. LOSS OF LIBERTY

TYPE OF ACTION BROUGHT:
1. NEGLIGENCE

HISTORY OF THE CASE:

TYPE OF COURT: STATE

TRIER OF FACT: JUDGE;JURY PRESENT ?

COURT DECISION(S):

TRIAL COURT: FOR DEFENDANT
YEAR: NOT SPECIFIED
APPELLATE COURT: FOR DEFENDANT
YEAR: 1970

REASON SUIT FAILED:
1. NO CAUSE OF ACTION STATED
2. DEFENDANT(S) CANNOT BE SUED DUE TO: JUDICIAL IMMUNITY

225. RICE V. MERCY HOSPITAL

BETTY RICE HAD RECEIVED SHOCK TREATMENTS FOR MENTAL ILLNESS. SHE VOLUNTARILY ENTERED THE PSYCHIATRIC WARD OF MERCY HOSPITAL IN FLORIDA. SHE THEN DEMANDED TO BE RELEASED AND CONTINUED TO DEMAND THIS UNTIL HER RELEASE TWENTY-TWO DAYS LATER, DURING WHICH TIME SHE RECEIVED SEVERAL ELECTRO-SHOCK TREATMENTS. SHE ALLEGED THAT HER WRITTEN CONSENT WAS COERCED.

YEAR OF NEGLIGENT ACT: 1970

STATE IN WHICH NEGLIGENT ACT OCCURRED: FLORIDA

SETTING OF THE CASE: PUB. GEN. HOSP.

PLAINTIFF(S): PATIENT(S) OR REP.

DEFENDANT(S):
1. NONPSYCHIAT.OR UNKNOWN TYPE PHYSICIAN(S)
2. HOSPITAL &/OR OWNERS, ETC.

NEGLIGENT ACTIVITY:

TREATMENT:
1. NEGLIGENT ELECTROCONVULSIVE THERAPY
2. FAILURE TO OBTAIN -OR LACK OF- CONSENT

DIAGNOSIS:

WHAT WAS DIAGNOSED:
1. MENTAL ILLNESS, INSTEAD OF SANITY

RESULT OF DIAGNOSIS:
1. IMPROPER FAILURE TO RELEASE

CARE: NOT APPLICABLE

HARM CAUSED TO PLAINTIFF &/OR PATIENT: NOT APPLICABLE

TYPE OF ACTION BROUGHT:
1. NEGLIGENCE
2. ASSAULT AND BATTERY
3. FALSE IMPRISONMENT
4. CONTRACT LAW: BREACH OF CONTRACT

HISTORY OF THE CASE:

TYPE OF COURT: STATE

TRIER OF FACT: JURY

COURT DECISION(S):

TRIAL COURT: FOR DEFENDANT
YEAR: NOT SPECIFIED
APPELLATE COURT: NONFINAL FOR PL.
YEAR: NOT SPECIFIED
ON RETRIAL: FOR DEFENDANT
YEAR: NOT SPECIFIED
ON REAPPEAL TO APPELLATE COURT: FOR DEFENDANT
YEAR: 1975

REASON SUIT FAILED:
1. NEGLIGENCE OR CASE NOT PROVEN
2. PATIENT HAD GIVEN INFORMED CONSENT

226. ROBINSON V. STATE

LAWRENCE ROBINSON WAS A PATIENT AT ROCKLAND STATE HOSPITAL IN NEW YORK. ONE MORNING HE AND TWENTY-FOUR OTHER PATIENTS, ALL CLASSIFIED AS THE "MOST DISTURBED AND UNPREDICTABLE," WERE IN THE LAVATORY AREA. WITHOUT ANY ADVANCE NOTICE A FELLOW PATIENT, JAMES STRICKLAND, PUNCHED LAWRENCE AND FORCED HIM DOWN TO THE FLOOR WHERE HE CONTINUED ASSAULTING HIM. LAWRENCE SUFFERED FRACTURES TO BOTH THE LEFT AND RIGHT MANDIBLES AND PARTIAL FACIAL PARALYSIS, NECESSITATING THE WIRING OF HIS JAW. TREATMENT FOR THE ATTACK LASTED FIVE MONTHS, DURING WHICH TIME LAWRENCE SUFFERED MUCH PAIN. HE CHARGED THE HOSPITAL WITH INADEQUATE SUPERVISION IN FAILING TO PREVENT STRICKLAND'S ATTACK.

YEAR OF NEGLIGENT ACT: 1954

STATE IN WHICH NEGLIGENT ACT OCCURRED: NEW YORK

SETTING OF THE CASE: PUB. MENT. HOSP.

PLAINTIFF(S): PATIENT(S) OR REP.

DEFENDANT(S):
1. STATE GOV. &/OR OFFICIALS, ETC.

NEGLIGENT ACTIVITY:

TREATMENT: NOT APPLICABLE

DIAGNOSIS:

WHAT WAS DIAGNOSED: NOT APPLICABLE

RESULT OF DIAGNOSIS: NOT APPLICABLE

CARE:
1. INADEQUATE SUPERVISION

HARM CAUSED TO PLAINTIFF &/OR PATIENT:
1. NONSELF-INFLICTED INJURIES

TYPE OF ACTION BROUGHT:
1. NEGLIGENCE

HISTORY OF THE CASE:

TYPE OF COURT: STATE

TRIER OF FACT: JUDGE,NO JURY

COURT DECISION(S):

TRIAL COURT: FOR DEFENDANT
YEAR: 1959

REASON SUIT FAILED:
1. NEGLIGENCE OR CASE NOT PROVEN

227. ROGERS V. OKIN

THIS IS BOTH A CLASS ACTION SUIT AND A DEMAND FOR PERSONAL DAMAGES. SEVEN MENTAL PATIENTS FROM BOSTON STATE HOSPITAL CHARGED THAT THE HOSPITAL STAFF HAD COMMITTED ASSAULT AND BATTERY BY GIVING PATIENTS ANTI-PSYCHOTIC DRUGS AND PLACING THEM IN SECLUSION, OVER THEIR OBJECTIONS, IN NONEMERGENCY SITUATIONS. ONE OF THE MANY ALLEGED ABUSES INVOLVED PLACING A NONVIOLENT TEENAGE RETARDED GIRL IN SECLUSION FOR 2,000 HOURS, OFTEN FOR 24 HOURS A DAY. THESE AND OTHER ABUSES, SUCH AS PSYCHIATRIC DIAGNOSIS BY ATTENDANTS AND SOCIAL WORKERS RATHER THAN DOCTORS, WERE ALLEGED TO BE AT LEAST PARTIALLY DUE TO UNDERSTAFFING.

YEAR OF NEGLIGENT ACT: NOT SPECIFIED, BUT OCCURRED OVER A SERIES OF YEARS

STATE IN WHICH NEGLIGENT ACT OCCURRED: MASSACHUSETTS

SETTING OF THE CASE: PUB. MENT. HOSP.

PLAINTIFF(S): PATIENT(S) OR REP.

DEFENDANT(S):
1. PSYCHIATRIST(S)
2. PSYCHOLOGIST(S)

NEGLIGENT ACTIVITY:

TREATMENT:
1. FAILURE TO OBTAIN -OR LACK OF- CONSENT

DIAGNOSIS:

WHAT WAS DIAGNOSED: NOT APPLICABLE

RESULT OF DIAGNOSIS: NOT APPLICABLE

CARE: NOT APPLICABLE

HARM CAUSED TO PLAINTIFF &/OR PATIENT:
1. DEPRIVATION OF CONSTITUTIONAL RIGHTS

TYPE OF ACTION BROUGHT:
1. NEGLIGENCE
2. DEPRIVATION OF CONSTITUTIONAL RIGHTS: RT.TO REFUSE TREAT.

HISTORY OF THE CASE:

TYPE OF COURT: FEDERAL

TRIER OF FACT: JUDGE,NO JURY

COURT DECISION(S):

TRIAL COURT: NOT YET DECIDED
YEAR: NOT APPLICABLE

DEFENDANTS STILL INVOLVED IN SUIT:
1. PSYCHIATRIST(S)
2. PSYCHOLOGIST(S)

228. ROSARIO V. STATE

VICTOR ROSARIO WAS ARRESTED ON CHARGES OF UNLAWFUL POSSESSION OF A WEAPON AND ASSAULT. HE WAS GIVEN A PSYCHIATRIC EXAMINATION, JUDGED INSANE AND INCAPABLE OF STANDING TRIAL, AND WAS COMMITTED TO MATTEAWAN STATE HOSPITAL IN NEW YORK. WHILE IN MATTEAWAN, VICTOR INITIATED THREE HABEAS CORPUS PROCEEDINGS ON HIS OWN. ON EACH OCCASION HE WAS AGAIN JUDGED INSANE. EVENTUALLY HE WAS FOUND TO BE SANE AND IT TURNED OUT THAT HIS SANITY HAD NEVER BEEN LOST. PSYCHIATRISTS HAD SIMPLY DISMISSED SOME OF VICTOR'S STATEMENTS AS DELUSIONAL WITHOUT CHECKING TO SEE IF THEY WERE BASED ON FACT. THESE INCLUDED INSISTENCES THAT HIS WIFE'S LOVER HAD CUT VICTOR'S ARM, LET THE BLOOD FLOW INTO A GLASS, THEN DRANK THE BLOOD--ALL OF WHICH DID IN FACT OCCUR. VICTOR HAD HAD SEVERE PROBLEMS IN COMMUNICATING WITH THE HOSPITAL STAFF BECAUSE OF THE LACK OF SPANISH INTERPRETERS. DESPITE THE FACT THAT THE STAFF HAD ERRED, NEGLIGENCE WAS NOT FOUND BECAUSE IT INVOLVED AN ERROR IN PROFESSIONAL JUDGMENT.

YEAR OF NEGLIGENT ACT: OCCURRED OVER A SERIES OF YEARS, ENDING IN 1962

STATE IN WHICH NEGLIGENT ACT OCCURRED: NEW YORK

SETTING OF THE CASE: JUDICIAL PROCEEDING

PLAINTIFF(S): PATIENT(S) OR REP.

DEFENDANT(S):
1. STATE GOV. &/OR OFFICIALS, ETC.

NEGLIGENT ACTIVITY:

TREATMENT: NOT APPLICABLE

DIAGNOSIS:

WHAT WAS DIAGNOSED:
1. MENTAL ILLNESS, INSTEAD OF SANITY
2. INADEQUATE DIAGNOSIS

RESULT OF DIAGNOSIS:
1. IMPROPER COMMITMENT
2. IMPROPER FAILURE TO RELEASE

CARE: NOT APPLICABLE

HARM CAUSED TO PLAINTIFF &/OR PATIENT:
1. ECONOMIC LOSS
2. DEPRIVATION OF CONSTITUTIONAL RIGHTS
3. LOSS OF LIBERTY

TYPE OF ACTION BROUGHT:
1. NEGLIGENCE
2. FALSE IMPRISONMENT

HISTORY OF THE CASE:

TYPE OF COURT: STATE

TRIER OF FACT: JUDGE,NO JURY

COURT DECISION(S):

TRIAL COURT: FOR PLAINTIFF
YEAR: 1966
APPELLATE COURT: FOR DEFENDANT
YEAR: 1969
SUPREME COURT: FOR DEFENDANT
YEAR: 1975

REASON SUIT FAILED:
1. DEFENDANT(S) CANNOT BE SUED DUE TO: GOVERN. IMMUNITY

229. ROSENFELD V. COLEMAN

MR. ROSENFELD HAD SUFFERED FROM MIGRAINE HEADACHES AND NERVOUSNESS FOR A TEN-YEAR PERIOD. DR. COLEMAN, A NEUROPSYCHIATRIST IN EASTON, PENNSYLVANIA, PRESCRIBED DEMEROL, A SYNTHETIC NARCOTIC, AND INSTRUCTED ROSENFELD IN SELF-INJECTION. HE BECAME ADDICTED AND WAS SENT TO EASTERN HOSPITAL, WHERE HE UNDERWENT WITHDRAWAL FROM THE DRUG. COLEMAN, HOWEVER, GAVE IN TO HIS REQUESTS FOR THE DRUG AFTER HE HAD GONE THROUGH WITHDRAWAL. DURING THIS TIME ROSENFELD RECEIVED NO PSYCHIATRIC TREATMENT EXCEPT FOR HIS THREE INITIAL VISITS. ROSENFELD CHARGED DR. COLEMAN WITH MALPRACTICE IN VIOLATING A STATE LAW PROHIBITING THE PRESCRIPTION OF DRUGS TO KNOWN ADDICTS, UNLESS THE PURPOSE WAS TO CURE A PROBLEM OTHER THAN THE ADDICTION. UNDER THIS LAW A DOCTOR, NURSE OR OTHER RESPONSIBLE PERSON WAS REQUIRED TO ADMINISTER ANY SUCH DRUGS AND A DOCTOR MUST HAVE EXAMINED THE PATIENT BETWEEN EACH PRESCRIPTION. IN CONFLICTING TESTIMONY, ROSENFELD CLAIMED THAT HE HAD NEVER BEEN AN ADDICT BEFORE SEEING DR. COLEMAN, WHILE COLEMAN ARGUED THAT ROSENFELD HAD ADMITTED HE WAS AN ADDICT AT ONE OF HIS EARLY VISITS. COLEMAN ALLEGED THAT THE PURPOSE OF HIS THERAPY WAS TO GAIN ROSENFELD'S CONFIDENCE BY PRESCRIBING THE DEMEROL, THEN TO CURE HIM OF HIS "PSYCHOPATHIC CHARACTER DISORDER," AND FINALLY TO MAKE HIM UNDERSTAND WHY HE WAS AN ADDICT.

YEAR OF NEGLIGENT ACT: OCCURRED OVER A SERIES OF YEARS, ENDING IN 1957

STATE IN WHICH NEGLIGENT ACT OCCURRED: PENNSYLVANIA

SETTING OF THE CASE: PRIVATE PRACTICE

PLAINTIFF(S): PATIENT(S) OR REP.

DEFENDANT(S):
1. PSYCHIATRIST(S)

NEGLIGENT ACTIVITY:

TREATMENT:
1. NEG.ADMIN.OF DRUGS

DIAGNOSIS:

WHAT WAS DIAGNOSED: NOT APPLICABLE

RESULT OF DIAGNOSIS: NOT APPLICABLE

CARE: NOT APPLICABLE

HARM CAUSED TO PLAINTIFF &/OR PATIENT:
1. NONSELF-INFLICTED INJURIES
2. DRUG ADDICTION

TYPE OF ACTION BROUGHT:
1. NEGLIGENCE

HISTORY OF THE CASE:

TYPE OF COURT: STATE

TRIER OF FACT: JUDGE,UNINV.JURY

COURT DECISION(S):

TRIAL COURT: FOR DEFENDANT
YEAR: 1958
APPELLATE COURT: NONFINAL FOR PL.
YEAR: 1959

DEFENDANTS STILL INVOLVED IN SUIT:
1. PSYCHIATRIST(S)

230. ROSS V. LEONARD

DR. LEONARD ALLEGEDLY PERFORMED SEXUAL ACTIVITIES WITH THREE OF HIS FEMALE PATIENTS, WHO HAVE BROUGHT A FOUR MILLION DOLLAR MALPRACTICE SUIT AGAINST HIM FOR PRESCRIBING AN UNORTHODOX FORM OF THERAPY THAT CAUSED THEM MUCH PAIN AND MENTAL ANGUISH.

YEAR OF NEGLIGENT ACT: OCCURRED OVER A SERIES OF YEARS, ENDING IN 1977

STATE IN WHICH NEGLIGENT ACT OCCURRED: NEW YORK

SETTING OF THE CASE: PRIVATE PRACTICE

PLAINTIFF(S): PATIENT(S) OR REP.

DEFENDANT(S):
1. PSYCHIATRIST(S)

NEGLIGENT ACTIVITY:

TREATMENT:
1. SEXUAL ABUSE OR DISTURB.OF MARITAL REL.

DIAGNOSIS:

WHAT WAS DIAGNOSED: NOT APPLICABLE

RESULT OF DIAGNOSIS: NOT APPLICABLE

CARE: NOT APPLICABLE

HARM CAUSED TO PLAINTIFF &/OR PATIENT:
1. EMOTIONAL DISTRESS
2. SEXUAL OR MARITAL HARM

TYPE OF ACTION BROUGHT:
1. NEGLIGENCE

HISTORY OF THE CASE:

TYPE OF COURT: STATE

TRIER OF FACT: NOT YET DECIDED

COURT DECISION(S):

TRIAL COURT: NOT YET DECIDED
YEAR: NOT APPLICABLE

DEFENDANTS STILL INVOLVED IN SUIT:
1. PSYCHIATRIST(S)

231. ROSSING V. STATE

VICTOR F. ROSSING WAS A PATIENT AT GOWANDA STATE HOMEOPATHIC HOSPITAL AND SUFFERED FROM A MANIC DEPRESSIVE PSYCHOSIS OF THE MIXED TYPE. HE WAS A MEMBER OF THE DISTURBED WARD, WHERE ALL LOUD, MESSY, AND VIOLENT PATIENTS WERE ASSIGNED. ONE DAY VICTOR WAS ATTACKED WHILE SLEEPING ON A COT ON THE SUN PORCH. A HOMICIDAL, IRRITABLE FELLOW PATIENT SUFFERING FROM DEMENTIA PRAECOX, PARANOID TYPE, RIPPED THE ARM OFF OF A CHAIR AND BEGAN BEATING VICTOR ABOUT THE HEAD AND FACE WITH IT. VICTOR CHARGED THAT THE HOSPITAL WAS NEGLIGENT IN ONLY PROVIDING ONE ATTENDANT TO WATCH OVER FIFTY-SIX PATIENTS.

YEAR OF NEGLIGENT ACT: 1935

STATE IN WHICH NEGLIGENT ACT OCCURRED: NEW YORK

SETTING OF THE CASE: PUB. MENT. HOSP.

PLAINTIFF(S): PATIENT(S) OR REP.

DEFENDANT(S):
1. STATE GOV. &/OR OFFICIALS, ETC.

NEGLIGENT ACTIVITY:

TREATMENT: NOT APPLICABLE

DIAGNOSIS:

WHAT WAS DIAGNOSED: NOT APPLICABLE

RESULT OF DIAGNOSIS: NOT APPLICABLE

CARE:
1. INADEQUATE SUPERVISION

HARM CAUSED TO PLAINTIFF &/OR PATIENT:
1. NONSELF-INFLICTED INJURIES

TYPE OF ACTION BROUGHT:
1. NEGLIGENCE

HISTORY OF THE CASE:

TYPE OF COURT: STATE

TRIER OF FACT: JUDGE,NO JURY

COURT DECISION(S):

TRIAL COURT: FOR PLAINTIFF
YEAR: 1944

VERDICT AGAINST WHICH DEFENDANTS:
1. STATE GOV. &/OR OFFICIALS, ETC.

RECOVERY OR OTHER RELIEF GRANTED:
1. OTHER RECOVERY: NOT SPECIFIED

232. ROUSE V. CAMERON

EIGHTEEN-YEAR-OLD CHARLES C. ROUSE WAS ARRESTED FOR ILLEGAL POSSESSION OF A .45 CALIBER AUTOMATIC PISTOL AND A FEW HUNDRED ROUNDS OF AMMUNITION. HE WAS FOUND ABLE TO STAND TRIAL BY THE D.C. GENERAL HOSPITAL, ALTHOUGH SUFFERING FROM A PASSIVE-AGGRESSIVE PERSONALITY DISORDER. AT THE TRIAL CHARLES WAS FOUND INSANE, WITH HELP FROM HIS MOTHER'S TESTIMONY, AND COMMITTED TO ST. ELIZABETH'S HOSPITAL. AFTER FOUR AND A HALF YEARS THERE, CHARLES BROUGHT SUIT CHARGING THAT HE HAD BEEN SANE AT THE TIME OF THE TRIAL AND SANE THROUGHOUT HIS STAY AT ST. ELIZABETH'S. HE ALLEGED THAT HIS LAWYER HAD BEEN DISMISSED AT THE TIME OF THE TRIAL AND A NEW ONE HIRED, WITHOUT HIS KNOWLEDGE, WITH WHOM HE DID NOT SPEAK UNTIL MINUTES BEFORE THE TRIAL. IF CHARLES HAD BEEN FOUND GUILTY, NOT INSANE, AT HIS TRIAL, HE WOULD HAVE ONLY SERVED ONE YEAR IN JAIL.

YEAR OF NEGLIGENT ACT: 1962

STATE IN WHICH NEGLIGENT ACT OCCURRED: DISTRICT OF COLUMBIA

SETTING OF THE CASE: JUDICIAL PROCEEDING

PLAINTIFF(S): PATIENT(S) OR REP.

DEFENDANT(S):
1. HOSPITAL &/OR OWNERS, ETC.

NEGLIGENT ACTIVITY:

TREATMENT:
1. NO TREATMENT OR INADEQUATE TREATMENT

DIAGNOSIS:

WHAT WAS DIAGNOSED: NOT APPLICABLE

RESULT OF DIAGNOSIS: NOT APPLICABLE

CARE: NOT APPLICABLE

HARM CAUSED TO PLAINTIFF &/OR PATIENT:
1. DEPRIVATION OF CONSTITUTIONAL RIGHTS
2. LOSS OF LIBERTY

TYPE OF ACTION BROUGHT:
1. DEPRIVATION OF CONSTITUTIONAL RIGHTS: RIGHT TO TREATMENT
2. HABEAS CORPUS
3. NONMONETARY RELIEF

HISTORY OF THE CASE:

TYPE OF COURT: FEDERAL

TRIER OF FACT: JUDGE,NO JURY

COURT DECISION(S):

TRIAL COURT: FOR DEFENDANT
YEAR: NOT SPECIFIED
APPELLATE COURT: NONFINAL FOR PL.
YEAR: 1966
ON RETRIAL: FOR DEFENDANT
YEAR: NOT SPECIFIED
ON REAPPEAL TO APPELLATE COURT: FOR PLAINTIFF
YEAR: 1967

VERDICT AGAINST WHICH DEFENDANTS:
1. HOSPITAL &/OR OWNERS, ETC.

RECOVERY OR OTHER RELIEF GRANTED:
1. NONMONETARY RELIEF: INJ.OR OTHER EQ.REL.

233. ROUSE V. TWIN PINES SANITARIUM

PAUL ROUSE, A BARBER, BROKE HIS ANKLE WHILE DRINKING WITH HIS BROTHER. HE WAS TAKEN TO PARK SANITARIUM IN CALIFORNIA WHERE HIS ANKLE WAS PUT IN A CAST. DR. SNOW WHO TREATED HIM PRESCRIBED SLEEPING PILLS AND PARALDEHYDE FOR HIS NERVES, AND CODEINE FOR THE PAIN. HE CONTINUED TAKING THE SLEEPING PILLS AND PARALDEHYDE FOR ABOUT SEVEN MONTHS. ONCE DURING THAT PERIOD PAUL PASSED OUT IN HIS BARBERSHOP FROM THE MEDICATION. DR. SNOW REFUSED TO PRESCRIBE ANY MORE MEDICATION AND TOLD PAUL TO TAKE BROMIDES. PAUL OVER-DOSED ON THE NON-PRESCRIPTION BROMIDES AND WAS TAKEN TO TWIN PINES SANITARIUM. HE WAS COMMITTED BECAUSE OF CLEAR AND FIXED PSYCHOTIC SYMPTOMS AND DELUSIONS. HE CHARGED THAT DR. SNOW HAD COMMITTED MALPRACTICE IN SUGGESTING THAT HE TAKE BROMIDES AND IN HAVING HIM COMMITTED.

YEAR OF NEGLIGENT ACT: NOT SPECIFIED

STATE IN WHICH NEGLIGENT ACT OCCURRED: CALIFORNIA

SETTING OF THE CASE: JUD.PCDG.&PUB.HOSP.

PLAINTIFF(S): PATIENT(S) OR REP.

DEFENDANT(S):
1. NONPSYCHIAT.OR UNKNOWN TYPE PHYSICIAN(S)
2. HOSPITAL &/OR OWNERS, ETC.

NEGLIGENT ACTIVITY:

TREATMENT:
1. NEG.ADMIN.OF DRUGS

DIAGNOSIS:

WHAT WAS DIAGNOSED:
1. IMPROPER DRUG PRESCRIPTION

RESULT OF DIAGNOSIS:
1. IMPROPER DRUG PRESCRIPTION
2. IMPROPER COMMITMENT

CARE: NOT APPLICABLE

HARM CAUSED TO PLAINTIFF &/OR PATIENT:
1. NONSELF-INFLICTED INJURIES
2. LOSS OF CONSORTIUM

TYPE OF ACTION BROUGHT:
1. NEGLIGENCE
2. ASSAULT AND BATTERY
3. MALICIOUS PROSECUTION

HISTORY OF THE CASE:

TYPE OF COURT: STATE

TRIER OF FACT: JURY

COURT DECISION(S):

TRIAL COURT: FOR DEFENDANT
YEAR: NOT SPECIFIED
APPELLATE COURT: FOR DEFENDANT
YEAR: 1958

REASON SUIT FAILED:
1. NEGLIGENCE OR CASE NOT PROVEN
2. DEFENDANT(S) CANNOT BE SUED DUE TO: JUDICIAL IMMUNITY

234. ROY V. HARTOGS

JULIE ROY WENT TO SEE DR. RENATUS HARTOGS, A PSYCHIATRIST, IN MARCH OF 1969 TO TRY TO CURE HER SEXUAL PROBLEMS. AFTER ABOUT SIX MONTHS DR. HARTOGS PRESCRIBED SEXUAL RELATIONS AS PART OF HER TREATMENT; MORE SPECIFICALLY, THE DOCTOR CONVINCED JULIE TO HAVE SEXUAL RELATIONS WITH HIM. THIS TREATMENT LASTED THIRTEEN MONTHS. JULIE CHARGED DR. HARTOGS WITH MALPRACTICE IN PRESCRIBING AN UNORTHODOX, EMOTIONALLY DAMAGING FORM OF TREATMENT WHILE DISREGARDING THE STANDARD FORMS OF TREATMENT THAT MIGHT HAVE HELPED HER. AS PART OF HIS DEFENSE, DR. HARTOGS CLAIMED THAT HE HAD BEEN IMPOTENT SINCE 1965 BECAUSE OF A HYDROCELE, BUT THE COURT FOUND THAT HE HAD INDEED HAD SEXUAL INTERCOURSE WITH JULIE.

YEAR OF NEGLIGENT ACT: OCCURRED OVER A SERIES OF YEARS, ENDING IN 1970

STATE IN WHICH NEGLIGENT ACT OCCURRED: NEW YORK

SETTING OF THE CASE: PRIVATE PRACTICE

PLAINTIFF(S): PATIENT(S) OR REP.

DEFENDANT(S):
1. PSYCHIATRIST(S)

NEGLIGENT ACTIVITY:

TREATMENT:
1. SEXUAL ABUSE OR DISTURB.OF MARITAL REL.

DIAGNOSIS:

WHAT WAS DIAGNOSED: NOT APPLICABLE

RESULT OF DIAGNOSIS: NOT APPLICABLE

CARE: NOT APPLICABLE

HARM CAUSED TO PLAINTIFF &/OR PATIENT:
1. EMOTIONAL DISTRESS
2. SEXUAL OR MARITAL HARM

TYPE OF ACTION BROUGHT:
1. NEGLIGENCE
2. ASSAULT

HISTORY OF THE CASE:

TYPE OF COURT: STATE

TRIER OF FACT: JURY

COURT DECISION(S):

TRIAL COURT: FOR PLAINTIFF
YEAR: 1975
APPELLATE COURT: FOR PLAINTIFF
YEAR: 1976

VERDICT AGAINST WHICH DEFENDANTS:
1. PSYCHIATRIST(S)

RECOVERY OR OTHER RELIEF GRANTED:
1. $ 25000

235. RUFINO V. UNITED STATES

ORLANDO J. RUFINO, A VETERAN, DIED WHILE UNDERGOING INSULIN THERAPY AT THE VETERANS ADMINISTRATION HOSPITAL IN NEW YORK CITY. THE COURT'S OPINION IS UNCLEAR AS TO WHETHER THE PLAINTIFF, MARY C. RUFINO, HIS WIFE, WAS ALLEGING THAT HE DIED BECAUSE OF THE PRESCRIPTION OF AN IMPROPER FORM OF TREATMENT OR BECAUSE OF IMPROPER ADMINISTRATION OF THAT TREATMENT.

YEAR OF NEGLIGENT ACT: NOT SPECIFIED

STATE IN WHICH NEGLIGENT ACT OCCURRED: NEW YORK

SETTING OF THE CASE: PUB. GEN. HOSP.

PLAINTIFF(S): PATIENT(S) OR REP.

DEFENDANT(S):
1. FEDERAL GOV. &/OR OFFICIALS, ETC.

NEGLIGENT ACTIVITY:

TREATMENT:
1. NEGLIGENT INSULIN THERAPY

DIAGNOSIS:

WHAT WAS DIAGNOSED: NOT APPLICABLE

RESULT OF DIAGNOSIS: NOT APPLICABLE

CARE: NOT APPLICABLE

HARM CAUSED TO PLAINTIFF &/OR PATIENT:
1. NONSUICIDAL DEATH

TYPE OF ACTION BROUGHT:
1. NEGLIGENCE
2. ASSAULT

HISTORY OF THE CASE:

TYPE OF COURT: FEDERAL

TRIER OF FACT: JUDGE;JURY PRESENT ?

COURT DECISION(S):

TRIAL COURT: NONFINAL FOR PL.
YEAR: 1954

DEFENDANTS STILL INVOLVED IN SUIT:
1. FEDERAL GOV. &/OR OFFICIALS, ETC.

236. RUNYON V. REID

JOHN HUTCHINSON RUNYON WAS AN OUT-PATIENT AT THE TULSA PSYCHIATRIC FOUNDATION IN OKLAHOMA. HE WAS EXTREMELY INTELLIGENT, BUT SUFFERED FROM A MILD FORM OF SCHIZOPHRENIA. HE HAD BEEN ADMITTED TO A MENTAL HOSPITAL THREE SEPARATE TIMES, ONCE AFTER ATTEMPTING SUICIDE. AFTER NUMEROUS PRESCRIPTIONS OF ANTI-DEPRESSANT DRUGS AND TRANQUILIZERS, JOHN'S DOCTOR PRESCRIBED CARBRITAL, A SLEEPING PILL. AFTER EIGHT MONTHS OF TAKING CARBRITAL, JOHN WENT TO A DRUGGIST AND HAD A NON-REFILLABLE PRESCRIPTION OF SIXTY TABLETS FILLED. HE COMMITTED SUICIDE BY INGESTING MOST, IF NOT ALL, OF THE SIXTY PILLS IN A MATTER OF MINUTES. JOHN'S WIFE CHARGED THAT THE DOCTOR WAS NEGLIGENT IN PRESCRIBING THE PILLS AND THAT THE PHARMACIST WAS NEGLIGENT IN FILLING THE EXPIRED PRESCRIPTION.

YEAR OF NEGLIGENT ACT: 1964

STATE IN WHICH NEGLIGENT ACT OCCURRED: OKLAHOMA

SETTING OF THE CASE: PRIV. MENT. HOSP.

PLAINTIFF(S): 3RD PARTY, I

DEFENDANT(S):
1. PSYCHIATRIST(S)
2. NONPSYCHIAT.OR UNKNOWN TYPE PHYSICIAN(S)
3. HOSPITAL &/OR OWNERS, ETC.
4. PHARMACIST

NEGLIGENT ACTIVITY:

TREATMENT:
1. NEG.ADMIN.OF DRUGS

DIAGNOSIS:

WHAT WAS DIAGNOSED:
1. IMPROPER DRUG PRESCRIPTION

RESULT OF DIAGNOSIS:
1. IMPROPER DRUG PRESCRIPTION

CARE: NOT APPLICABLE

HARM CAUSED TO PLAINTIFF &/OR PATIENT:
1. SUICIDE

TYPE OF ACTION BROUGHT:
1. NEGLIGENCE

HISTORY OF THE CASE:

TYPE OF COURT: STATE

TRIER OF FACT: JUDGE;JURY PRESENT ?

COURT DECISION(S):

TRIAL COURT: FOR DEFENDANT
YEAR: NOT SPECIFIED
SUPREME COURT: FOR DEFENDANT
YEAR: 1973

REASON SUIT FAILED:
1. NEGLIGENCE OR CASE NOT PROVEN

237. ST. GEORGE V. STATE

ON FEBRUARY 23, 1947, SIXTEEN-YEAR-OLD WILLIAM JONES, A WAYWARD MINOR, WAS SENTENCED TO A THREE-YEAR TERM FOR DETENTION AND REHABILITATION. THREE PLACEMENTS OVER THE NEXT TWENTY-TWO MONTHS FOUND HIM AT THE VOCATIONAL INSTITUTION AT WEST COXSACKIE, WHERE ON DECEMBER 20, 1948 HE WAS DIAGNOSED AS PSYCHOTIC WITH A PSYCHOPATHIC PERSONALITY. TWO DAYS LATER, HE WAS COMMITTED TO MATTEAWAN STATE HOSPITAL WHERE HE REMAINED UNTIL MARCH 1, 1950, WHEN HIS SENTENCE EXPIRED. HE WAS RELEASED IN HIS MOTHER'S CUSTODY AND WENT TO LIVE AT HER HOME. DURING THE NEXT FIVE DAYS HE HAD CONSIDERABLE DIFFICULTY WITH ASSOCIATES AND PROBLEMS CONTROLLING HIS EMOTIONS, COUPLED WITH PARANOID THOUGHTS. HE EVEN HEADED BACK TO MATTEAWAN ONCE BUT TURNED BACK. FIVE DAYS AFTER HIS RELEASE HIS CONDITION DETERIORATED FURTHER. HE RAN INTO HIS MOTHER'S APARTMENT LOOKING FOR A WEAPON. FINDING NONE, HE RAN OUT AND INTO A RESTAURANT WHERE HE GRABBED A BREAD KNIFE. RUNNING DOWN THE STREET, KNIFE IN HAND, HE STABBED SEVEN PEOPLE, FOUR OF THEM FATALLY. ONE OF THEM WAS FRANK ST. GEORGE, THE PLAINTIFF'S LATE HUSBAND.

YEAR OF NEGLIGENT ACT: 1950

STATE IN WHICH NEGLIGENT ACT OCCURRED: NEW YORK

SETTING OF THE CASE: PUB. MENT. HOSP.

PLAINTIFF(S): 3RD PARTY, II

DEFENDANT(S):
1. STATE GOV. &/OR OFFICIALS, ETC.

NEGLIGENT ACTIVITY:

TREATMENT: NOT APPLICABLE

DIAGNOSIS:

WHAT WAS DIAGNOSED:
1. SANITY, INSTEAD OF MENTAL ILLNESS

RESULT OF DIAGNOSIS:
1. IMPROPER RELEASE

CARE: NOT APPLICABLE

HARM CAUSED TO PLAINTIFF &/OR PATIENT:
1. NONSUICIDAL DEATH

TYPE OF ACTION BROUGHT:
1. NEGLIGENCE

HISTORY OF THE CASE:

TYPE OF COURT: STATE

TRIER OF FACT: JUDGE,NO JURY

COURT DECISION(S):

TRIAL COURT: FOR PLAINTIFF
YEAR: NOT SPECIFIED
APPELLATE COURT: FOR DEFENDANT
YEAR: 1954
SUPREME COURT: FOR DEFENDANT
YEAR: 1954

REASON SUIT FAILED:
1. DEFENDANT(S) CANNOT BE SUED DUE TO: GOVERN. IMMUNITY

238. SALTER V. GRANT

IN AN EFFORT TO RESTORE HARMONY TO HIS MARRIAGE, GRANT HAD $7,500 WORTH OF THERAPY SESSIONS WITH DR. SALTER. THE LATTER SUED GRANT FOR THIS MONEY AND GRANT COUNTERSUED FOR $5,000, CLAIMING THAT HE HAD PAID THE FEES AND THAT SALTER'S TREATMENTS HAD AGGRAVATED HIS ESTRANGEMENT FROM HIS WIFE.

YEAR OF NEGLIGENT ACT: NOT SPECIFIED

STATE IN WHICH NEGLIGENT ACT OCCURRED: NEW YORK

SETTING OF THE CASE: PRIVATE PRACTICE

PLAINTIFF(S): PATIENT(S) OR REP.

DEFENDANT(S):
1. PSYCHIATRIST(S)

NEGLIGENT ACTIVITY:

TREATMENT:
1. NEGLIGENCE IN USE OF TECHNIQUE

DIAGNOSIS:

WHAT WAS DIAGNOSED: NOT APPLICABLE

RESULT OF DIAGNOSIS: NOT APPLICABLE

CARE: NOT APPLICABLE

HARM CAUSED TO PLAINTIFF &/OR PATIENT:
1. EXACERB.OF PREV.CONDITION
2. ALIENATION OF AFFECTION

TYPE OF ACTION BROUGHT:
1. OTHER ACTION, EXCLUDING TORT LAW: TYPE NOT SPECIFIED

HISTORY OF THE CASE:

TYPE OF COURT: STATE

TRIER OF FACT: NOT SPECIFIED

COURT DECISION(S):

TRIAL COURT: NOT SPECIFIED
YEAR: NOT APPLICABLE

DEFENDANTS STILL INVOLVED IN SUIT:
1. PSYCHIATRIST(S)

239. SAMONS V. MEYMANDI

KATHERINE SAMONS HAD A LONG HISTORY OF MENTAL ILLNESS AND HAD BEEN PREVIOUSLY INSTITUTIONALIZED FOR EIGHT YEARS AT ST. ELIZABETH'S HOSPITAL IN WASHINGTON, D.C. FOR SEVERAL DAYS SHE HAD BEEN PICKETING VARIOUS PUBLIC PLACES, INCLUDING THE MENTAL HEALTH CENTER AND THE HOSPITAL AUTHORITY WITH WHICH THE DEFENDANT WAS ASSOCIATED. ON MARCH 18, 1969, DR. MEYMANDI ATTEMPTED TO HAVE HER TAKEN INTO CUSTODY FOR AN EXAMINATION AS TO HER COMPETENCY. THESE PROCEEDINGS WERE DISMISSED BECAUSE THEY WERE NOT PROPERLY CARRIED OUT. THE NEXT DAY, HAVING RECEIVED THREATS FROM MS. SAMONS THAT SHE WOULD BLOW UP THE HOSPITAL, DR. MEYMANDI INSTITUTED EMERGENCY COMMITMENT PROCEEDINGS, WHICH RESULTED IN HER INCARCERATION AT DOROTHEA DIX HOSPITAL FROM MARCH 19 TO 31.

YEAR OF NEGLIGENT ACT: 1969

STATE IN WHICH NEGLIGENT ACT OCCURRED: NORTH CAROLINA

SETTING OF THE CASE: JUDICIAL PROCEEDING

PLAINTIFF(S): PATIENT(S) OR REP.

DEFENDANT(S):
1. PSYCHIATRIST(S)

NEGLIGENT ACTIVITY:

TREATMENT: NOT APPLICABLE

DIAGNOSIS:

WHAT WAS DIAGNOSED:
1. MENTAL ILLNESS, INSTEAD OF SANITY

RESULT OF DIAGNOSIS:
1. IMPROPER COMMITMENT

CARE: NOT APPLICABLE

HARM CAUSED TO PLAINTIFF &/OR PATIENT:
1. LOSS OF LIBERTY

TYPE OF ACTION BROUGHT:
1. FALSE IMPRISONMENT
2. OTHER TORT(S): ABUSE OF PROCESS

HISTORY OF THE CASE:

TYPE OF COURT: STATE

TRIER OF FACT: JURY

COURT DECISION(S):

TRIAL COURT: FOR PLAINTIFF
YEAR: NOT SPECIFIED
APPELLATE COURT: FOR PLAINTIFF
YEAR: 1970
SUPREME COURT: FOR PLAINTIFF
YEAR: 1971

VERDICT AGAINST WHICH DEFENDANTS:
1. PSYCHIATRIST(S)

RECOVERY OR OTHER RELIEF GRANTED:
1. OTHER RECOVERY: TO BE DETERM.ON RETR

240. SARON V. STATE

DIAGNOSED AS A SCHIZOPHRENIC, DAVID SARON VOLUNTARILY ENTERED A NEW YORK STATE HOSPITAL IN JUNE OF 1952. HE DIED IN THE HOSPITAL ON FEBRUARY 19, 1953 FROM ORGANIC BRAIN DAMAGE WHICH HIS WIDOW CLAIMS WAS CAUSED BY THE NEGLIGENCE OF THE HOSPITAL IN TREATING HIS DIABETES AND IN ADMINISTERING LETHAL AMOUNTS OF AN EXPERIMENTAL DRUG CALLED COMPOUND 100. FURTHER DETAILS FROM THE REPORTED CASE ARE UNAVAILABLE.

YEAR OF NEGLIGENT ACT: 1953

STATE IN WHICH NEGLIGENT ACT OCCURRED: NEW YORK

SETTING OF THE CASE: PUB. MENT. HOSP.

PLAINTIFF(S): PATIENT(S) OR REP.

DEFENDANT(S):
1. STATE GOV. &/OR OFFICIALS, ETC.

NEGLIGENT ACTIVITY:

TREATMENT:
1. NEG.ADMIN.OF DRUGS

DIAGNOSIS:

WHAT WAS DIAGNOSED:
1. IMPROPER DRUG PRESCRIPTION

RESULT OF DIAGNOSIS:
1. IMPROPER DRUG PRESCRIPTION

CARE: NOT APPLICABLE

HARM CAUSED TO PLAINTIFF &/OR PATIENT:
1. NONSELF-INFLICTED INJURIES
2. EMOTIONAL DISTRESS

TYPE OF ACTION BROUGHT:
1. NEGLIGENCE

HISTORY OF THE CASE:

TYPE OF COURT: STATE

TRIER OF FACT: JUDGE,NO JURY

COURT DECISION(S):

TRIAL COURT: FOR DEFENDANT
YEAR: NOT SPECIFIED
APPELLATE COURT: FOR DEFENDANT
YEAR: 1965

REASON SUIT FAILED:
1. NEGLIGENCE OR CASE NOT PROVEN

241. SAS V. STATE

PLAINTIFFS, INMATES OF MARYLAND'S PATUXENT INSTITUTION FOR DEFECTIVE DELINQUENTS, INITIATED A HABEAS CORPUS PROCEEDING TO HAVE MARYLAND'S DEFECTIVE DELINQUENT ACT, UNDER WHICH THEY WERE CONFINED, DECLARED UNCONSTITUTIONAL. THEY CLAIMED THAT THE ACT WAS DEFICIENT BECAUSE: (1) THE DEFINITION OF DEFECTIVE DELINQUENT WAS TOO VAGUE AND LIABLE TO SUBJECTIVE IMPRESSIONS; (2) THE EXAMINATION PROCEDURES DID NOT PROVIDE FOR NOTICE OR THE RIGHT TO COUNSEL; (3) THE STATE WAS NOT REQUIRED TO PROVE BEYOND A REASONABLE DOUBT THAT A YOUTH WAS A DEFECTIVE DELINQUENT; (4) HEARSAY EVIDENCE WAS ADMISSIBLE; (5) THE ACT PERMITTED CRUEL AND UNUSUAL PUNISHMENT; AND (6) PATUXENT INSTITUTION DID NOT HAVE THE PROPER FACILITIES TO INSTITUTE THE TREATMENT CONTEMPLATED BY THE ACT.

YEAR OF NEGLIGENT ACT: NOT SPECIFIED, BUT OCCURRED OVER A SERIES OF YEARS

STATE IN WHICH NEGLIGENT ACT OCCURRED: MARYLAND

SETTING OF THE CASE: JUD.PCDG.&PUB.HOSP.

PLAINTIFF(S): PATIENT(S) OR REP.

DEFENDANT(S):
1. STATE GOV. &/OR OFFICIALS, ETC.

NEGLIGENT ACTIVITY:

TREATMENT:
1. NO TREATMENT OR INADEQUATE TREATMENT

DIAGNOSIS:

WHAT WAS DIAGNOSED:
1. MENTAL ILLNESS, INSTEAD OF SANITY

RESULT OF DIAGNOSIS:
1. IMPROPER COMMITMENT

CARE: NOT APPLICABLE

HARM CAUSED TO PLAINTIFF &/OR PATIENT:
1. DEPRIVATION OF CONSTITUTIONAL RIGHTS
2. LOSS OF LIBERTY

TYPE OF ACTION BROUGHT:
1. DEPRIVATION OF CONSTITUTIONAL RIGHTS: CONST.RTS.IN GEN.
2. HABEAS CORPUS
3. NONMONETARY RELIEF

HISTORY OF THE CASE:

TYPE OF COURT: FEDERAL

TRIER OF FACT: JUDGE,NO JURY

COURT DECISION(S):

TRIAL COURT: FOR DEFENDANT
YEAR: NOT SPECIFIED
APPELLATE COURT: NONFINAL FOR PL.
YEAR: 1964
ON RETRIAL: FOR DEFENDANT
YEAR: 1969
ON REAPPEAL TO APPELLATE COURT: FOR DEFENDANT
YEAR: 1971
SUPREME COURT: FOR DEFENDANT
YEAR: 1972

REASON SUIT FAILED:
1. NEGLIGENCE OR CASE NOT PROVEN

242. SCHAFFER V. SPICER

BETTY SCHAFFER AND VIRGIL DORNBUSCH WERE DIVORCED ON JULY 16, 1965. FOR THE NEXT FOUR YEARS THERE WERE CONSTANT COURT BATTLES OVER THE CUSTODY OF THEIR THREE CHILDREN. ON JANUARY 23, 1969, WHILE THE CHILDREN WERE STILL WITH VIRGIL, BETTY WAS REQUIRED TO SHOW CAUSE WHY THE CHILDREN SHOULD NOT REMAIN WITH HIM. ATTACHED TO THESE PAPERS WAS AN EIGHT-PAGE AFFIDAVIT CONTAINING INFORMATION DIVULGED BY DR. SPICER, THE DEFENDANT IN THE PRESENT CASE. DR. SPICER HAD TREATED BETTY IN 1964 AND HAD GIVEN INFORMATION AS TO HER MENTAL HEALTH TO MR. DORNBUSCH'S ATTORNEY. HER THREE NERVOUS BREAKDOWNS AND HER STAY AT YANKTON STATE HOSPITAL WERE INCLUDED IN THE REPORT, AS WAS THE ELECTRO-SHOCK THERAPY ADMINISTERED BY THE DEFENDANT.

YEAR OF NEGLIGENT ACT: 1969

STATE IN WHICH NEGLIGENT ACT OCCURRED: SOUTH DAKOTA

SETTING OF THE CASE: JUDICIAL PROCEEDING

PLAINTIFF(S): PATIENT(S) OR REP.

DEFENDANT(S):
1. PSYCHIATRIST(S)

NEGLIGENT ACTIVITY:

TREATMENT: NOT APPLICABLE

DIAGNOSIS:

WHAT WAS DIAGNOSED:
1. MENTAL ILLNESS, INSTEAD OF SANITY

RESULT OF DIAGNOSIS:
1. IMPROPER DETERMINATION OF CUSTODY

CARE: NOT APPLICABLE

HARM CAUSED TO PLAINTIFF &/OR PATIENT:
1. INJURY TO REPUTATION

TYPE OF ACTION BROUGHT:
1. NEGLIGENCE
2. DEFAMATION OF CHARACTER: LIBEL AND SLANDER

HISTORY OF THE CASE:

TYPE OF COURT: STATE

TRIER OF FACT: ?, JUDGE OR JURY

COURT DECISION(S):

TRIAL COURT: FOR DEFENDANT
YEAR: NOT SPECIFIED
SUPREME COURT: NONFINAL FOR PL.
YEAR: 1974

DEFENDANTS STILL INVOLVED IN SUIT:
1. PSYCHIATRIST(S)

243. SCHANBARGER V. KELLOGG

DONALD SCHANBARGER WAS ARRESTED ON THE MORNING OF APRIL 30, 1968 BY ROBERT KELLOGG, A STATE TROOPER, FOR LOITERING. WHEN SCHANBARGER APPEARED IN COURT ON MAY 15, THE ASSISTANT DISTRICT ATTORNEY REQUESTED A PSYCHIATRIC EXAMINATION OF THE PLAINTIFF. HE WAS EXAMINED ON MAY 22, AND AT THE TRIAL HELD THEREAFTER HE WAS FOUND GUILTY AND CHARGED TEN DOLLARS. A SUBSEQUENT APPEAL FOUND THAT THE EVIDENCE ON WHICH HE WAS TRIED WAS INSUFFICIENT. THE JUDGMENT WAS REVERSED AND THE INFORMATION DISMISSED. THE PLAINTIFF CLAIMED THAT THE PSYCHIATRIC EXAMINATION CONSTITUTED A PERVERSION OF DUE PROCESS, AS WELL AS AN INVASION OF PRIVACY.

YEAR OF NEGLIGENT ACT: 1968

STATE IN WHICH NEGLIGENT ACT OCCURRED: NEW YORK

SETTING OF THE CASE: JUDICIAL PROCEEDING

PLAINTIFF(S): PATIENT(S) OR REP.

DEFENDANT(S):
1. NONPSYCHIAT.OR UNKNOWN TYPE PHYSICIAN(S)
2. JUDICIARY &/OR CLERKS, ETC.

NEGLIGENT ACTIVITY:

TREATMENT: NOT APPLICABLE

DIAGNOSIS:

WHAT WAS DIAGNOSED:
1. NEG.REC.TO TAKE PSYCHIATRIC EXAM

RESULT OF DIAGNOSIS:
1. UNKNOWN

CARE: NOT APPLICABLE

HARM CAUSED TO PLAINTIFF &/OR PATIENT:
1. NOT SPECIFIED

TYPE OF ACTION BROUGHT:
1. MALICIOUS PROSECUTION
2. OTHER TORT(S): PRIV.INV.-PROC.ABUSE

HISTORY OF THE CASE:

TYPE OF COURT: STATE

TRIER OF FACT: JUDGE;JURY PRESENT ?

COURT DECISION(S):

TRIAL COURT: FOR DEFENDANT
YEAR: NOT SPECIFIED
APPELLATE COURT: FOR DEFENDANT
YEAR: 1970
U.S. SUPREME COURT (ON APPEAL FROM STATE COURT): FOR DEFENDANT
YEAR: 1972

REASON SUIT FAILED:
1. DEFENDANT(S) CANNOT BE SUED DUE TO: JUDICIAL IMMUNITY

244. SCHWARTZ V. THIELE

AFTER HAVING BREAKFAST AT A LOS ANGELES RESTAURANT WITH HER SISTER, THE PLAINTIFF WALKED TO HER CAR IN THE PARKING LOT. THE DEFENDANT, AT THIS TIME A TOTAL STRANGER TO THE PLAINTIFF, INTRODUCED HIMSELF AND PURPORTED TO MAKE AN EXAMINATION AS TO HER MENTAL ILLNESS, WITHOUT HER KNOWLEDGE OR CONSENT. THE EXAM TOOK LESS THAN THREE MINUTES, INCLUDING A CALL TO HER ATTORNEY FROM WHOM SHE LEARNED THE DEFENDANT'S NAME. SUBSEQUENTLY, THE DEFENDANT WROTE A LETTER TO THE PSYCHIATRIC DEPARTMENT OF THE SUPREME COURT REQUESTING THAT SHE BE DETAINED. NO EXPLANATION IS GIVEN AS TO WHY THE PSYCHIATRIST SOUGHT HER COMMITMENT. MS. SCHWARTZ STAVED OFF THE COURT-APPOINTED DOCTORS AND HAD HER OWN PHYSICIAN EXAMINE HER. HE FOUND HER IN GOOD MENTAL HEALTH AND HIS LETTER TO THE COURT CAUSED THE DISMISSAL OF ALL PROCEEDINGS AGAINST HER. SHE THEREUPON BROUGHT SUIT AGAINST THE PSYCHIATRIST FOR INVASION OF PRIVACY.

YEAR OF NEGLIGENT ACT: 1962

STATE IN WHICH NEGLIGENT ACT OCCURRED: CALIFORNIA

SETTING OF THE CASE: JUDICIAL PROCEEDING

PLAINTIFF(S): PATIENT(S) OR REP.

DEFENDANT(S):
1. NONPSYCHIAT.OR UNKNOWN TYPE PHYSICIAN(S)

NEGLIGENT ACTIVITY:

TREATMENT: NOT APPLICABLE

DIAGNOSIS:

WHAT WAS DIAGNOSED:
1. MENTAL ILLNESS, INSTEAD OF SANITY

RESULT OF DIAGNOSIS:
1. IMPROPER COMMITMENT

CARE: NOT APPLICABLE

HARM CAUSED TO PLAINTIFF &/OR PATIENT:
1. EMOTIONAL DISTRESS
2. INJURY TO REPUTATION
3. INVASION OF PRIVACY

TYPE OF ACTION BROUGHT:
1. OTHER TORT(S): INVASION OF PRIVACY

HISTORY OF THE CASE:

TYPE OF COURT: STATE

TRIER OF FACT: JUDGE;JURY PRESENT ?

COURT DECISION(S):

TRIAL COURT: FOR DEFENDANT
YEAR: NOT SPECIFIED
APPELLATE COURT: FOR DEFENDANT
YEAR: 1966

REASON SUIT FAILED:
1. DEFENDANT(S) CANNOT BE SUED DUE TO: JUDICIAL IMMUNITY

245. SCHWENK V. STATE

AFTER SHOWING MUCH IMPROVEMENT DURING HIS STAY AT PILGRIM STATE HOSPITAL, ROBERT CANNON WAS RELEASED IN THE CUSTODY OF HIS SON LEROY AND PLACED ON CONVALESCENT CARE STATUS IN OCTOBER 1949. MR. CANNON HAD BEEN A PATIENT AT PILGRIM STATE SINCE MAY 18 WITH A DIAGNOSIS OF "CHRONIC ALCOHOLISM, EARLY SCHIZOPHRENIA," WHICH HE HAD RECEIVED IN 1946 WHILE A RESIDENT AT MEADOWBROOK HOSPITAL. BETWEEN OCTOBER 1949 AND MAY 1950, HE SEEMED TO BE MAKING A POSITIVE ADJUSTMENT. ON MAY 26, HOWEVER, AFTER DISEMBARKING FROM A BUS, HE FOLLOWED THE TWO PEOPLE AHEAD OF HIM AND FATALLY STABBED HERBERT SCHWENK, FOR WHICH HE WAS APPREHENDED AND COMMITTED TO MATTEAWAN STATE HOSPITAL. IT WAS DISCOVERED THAT HE HAD A LONG CRIMINAL RECORD AND A HISTORY OF ASSAULTIVE AND DANGEROUS PSYCHOTIC TENDENCIES, NONE OF WHICH WAS KNOWN TO THOSE WHO WERE RESPONSIBLE FOR HIS RELEASE.

YEAR OF NEGLIGENT ACT: 1950

STATE IN WHICH NEGLIGENT ACT OCCURRED: NEW YORK

SETTING OF THE CASE: PUB. MENT. HOSP.

PLAINTIFF(S): 3RD PARTY, II

DEFENDANT(S):
1. STATE GOV. &/OR OFFICIALS, ETC.

NEGLIGENT ACTIVITY:

TREATMENT: NOT APPLICABLE

DIAGNOSIS:

WHAT WAS DIAGNOSED:
1. LACK OF DANGEROUSNESS

RESULT OF DIAGNOSIS:
1. IMPROPER RELEASE

CARE:
1. INADEQUATE SUPERVISION
2. PREMATURE RELEASE

HARM CAUSED TO PLAINTIFF &/OR PATIENT:
1. NONSUICIDAL DEATH

TYPE OF ACTION BROUGHT:
1. NEGLIGENCE

HISTORY OF THE CASE:

TYPE OF COURT: STATE

TRIER OF FACT: JUDGE,NO JURY

COURT DECISION(S):

TRIAL COURT: FOR DEFENDANT
YEAR: 1953

REASON SUIT FAILED:
1. NEGLIGENCE OR CASE NOT PROVEN

246. SCOLAVINO V. STATE

MICHAEL SCOLAVINO AND JOHN BENTURIRA WERE INMATES AT HARLEM VALLEY HOSPITAL, OPERATED BY THE STATE OF NEW YORK FOR THE CARE AND TREATMENT OF THE MENTALLY ILL. BOTH WERE DIAGNOSED AS PSYCHOTIC AND FOR SOME YEARS HAD BEEN ON THE DISTURBED WARD FOR VIOLENT PATIENTS. ON MARCH 30, 1943, JOHN AND MICHAEL WERE IN THE RESTRAINT ROOM, WRAPPED IN RETAINING SHEETS, WHICH KEPT THEM COMPLETELY BOUND FROM NECK TO TOE. AT ABOUT 2 A.M., BENTURIRA ESCAPED FROM HIS RESTRAINTS AND BRUTALLY ATTACKED SCOLAVINO, WHO COULD NOT DEFEND HIMSELF. SCOLAVINO WAS RENDERED PERMANENTLY BLIND, SUFFERED A FRACTURED NOSE AND VARIOUS BRUISES. HOSPITAL RECORDS INDICATED THAT BENTURIRA HAD A KNOWN ASSAULTIVE DISPOSITION AND IN THE PAST HAD BEEN ABLE TO BREAK LOOSE FROM HIS RESTRAINING SHEETS.

YEAR OF NEGLIGENT ACT: 1943

STATE IN WHICH NEGLIGENT ACT OCCURRED: NEW YORK

SETTING OF THE CASE: PUB. MENT. HOSP.

PLAINTIFF(S): PATIENT(S) OR REP.

DEFENDANT(S):
1. STATE GOV. &/OR OFFICIALS, ETC.

NEGLIGENT ACTIVITY:

TREATMENT: NOT APPLICABLE

DIAGNOSIS:

WHAT WAS DIAGNOSED: NOT APPLICABLE

RESULT OF DIAGNOSIS: NOT APPLICABLE

CARE:
1. INADEQUATE SUPERVISION
2. FAILURE TO PROVIDE PROPER CUSTODIAL CARE

HARM CAUSED TO PLAINTIFF &/OR PATIENT:
1. NONSELF-INFLICTED INJURIES

TYPE OF ACTION BROUGHT:
1. NEGLIGENCE

HISTORY OF THE CASE:

TYPE OF COURT: STATE

TRIER OF FACT: JUDGE,NO JURY

COURT DECISION(S):

TRIAL COURT: FOR PLAINTIFF
YEAR: 1946
APPELLATE COURT: FOR PLAINTIFF
YEAR: 1946
SUPREME COURT: FOR PLAINTIFF
YEAR: 1947

VERDICT AGAINST WHICH DEFENDANTS:
1. STATE GOV. &/OR OFFICIALS, ETC.

RECOVERY OR OTHER RELIEF GRANTED:
1. $ 21137

247. SEALEY V. FINKELSTEIN

FEW FACTS ARE AVAILABLE FROM THE REPORTED CASE, EXCEPT THAT MS. STEIN, A SIXTY-TWO-YEAR-OLD PATIENT AT A FOREST HILLS, NEW YORK, NURSING HOME, ASSAULTED HER NURSE, DORIS SEALEY, CAUSING HER HARM. NURSE SEALEY CLAIMED THAT THE ADMITTING DOCTOR AND THE PATIENT'S DAUGHTER SHOULD HAVE WARNED HER OF MS. STEIN'S ASSAULTIVE NATURE.

YEAR OF NEGLIGENT ACT: 1957

STATE IN WHICH NEGLIGENT ACT OCCURRED: NEW YORK

SETTING OF THE CASE: NURSING HOME

PLAINTIFF(S): 3RD PARTY, II

DEFENDANT(S):
1. NONPSYCHIAT.OR UNKNOWN TYPE PHYSICIAN(S)
2. PATIENT'S DAUGHTER

NEGLIGENT ACTIVITY:

TREATMENT: NOT APPLICABLE

DIAGNOSIS:

WHAT WAS DIAGNOSED: NOT APPLICABLE

RESULT OF DIAGNOSIS: NOT APPLICABLE

CARE:
1. FAILURE TO WARN THIRD PARTIES

HARM CAUSED TO PLAINTIFF &/OR PATIENT:
1. NONSELF-INFLICTED INJURIES

TYPE OF ACTION BROUGHT:
1. NEGLIGENCE
2. ASSAULT

HISTORY OF THE CASE:

TYPE OF COURT: STATE

TRIER OF FACT: JUDGE;JURY PRESENT ?

COURT DECISION(S):

TRIAL COURT: FOR DEFENDANT
YEAR: 1960

REASON SUIT FAILED:
1. NEGLIGENCE OR CASE NOT PROVEN
2. NO CAUSE OF ACTION STATED

248. SEMLER V. PSYCHIATRIC INSTITUTE OF WASHINGTON

IN 1971 MR. GILREATH HAD BEEN ARRESTED FOR THE ABDUCTION OF A GIRL IN VIRGINIA. HE PLEADED GUILTY AND RECEIVED A TWENTY-YEAR SENTENCE, WHICH WAS SUSPENDED, CONDITIONAL ON HIS CONFINEMENT AND TREATMENT AT THE PSYCHIATRIC INSTITUTE. THE NEXT MONTH HE WAS ALLOWED TO GO HOME FOR THANKSGIVING, AND UNTIL 1973 HE CONTINUED TO RECEIVE WEEKEND PASSES AT THE DISCRETION OF THE PROBATION OFFICER. IN JULY OF THAT YEAR GILREATH SHOWED INTEREST IN MOVING TO OHIO TO WORK WITH HIS UNCLE, AND WAS GIVEN PERMISSION TO INVESTIGATE THIS POSSIBILITY. ASSUMING THAT GILREATH'S PROBATION WOULD BE TRANSFERRED TO AND ACCEPTED BY OHIO, HE WAS RELEASED FROM THE INSTITUTE ON AUGUST 29. WHEN HIS TRANSFER WAS REJECTED HE RETURNED HOME AS AN OUT-PATIENT. SHORTLY THEREAFTER GILREATH MURDERED NATALIA SEMLER, DAUGHTER OF THE PLAINTIFF.

YEAR OF NEGLIGENT ACT: 1973

STATE IN WHICH NEGLIGENT ACT OCCURRED: VIRGINIA

SETTING OF THE CASE: PRIV. MENT. HOSP.

PLAINTIFF(S): 3RD PARTY, II

DEFENDANT(S):
1. PSYCHIATRIST(S)
2. HOSPITAL &/OR OWNERS, ETC.
3. JUDICIARY &/OR CLERKS, ETC.

NEGLIGENT ACTIVITY:

TREATMENT: NOT APPLICABLE

DIAGNOSIS:

WHAT WAS DIAGNOSED:
1. LACK OF DANGEROUSNESS

RESULT OF DIAGNOSIS:
1. IMPROPER RELEASE

CARE: NOT APPLICABLE

HARM CAUSED TO PLAINTIFF &/OR PATIENT:
1. NONSUICIDAL DEATH

TYPE OF ACTION BROUGHT:
1. NEGLIGENCE

HISTORY OF THE CASE:

TYPE OF COURT: FEDERAL

TRIER OF FACT: JUDGE,NO JURY

COURT DECISION(S):

TRIAL COURT: FOR PLAINTIFF
YEAR: NOT SPECIFIED
APPELLATE COURT: FOR PLAINTIFF
YEAR: 1976
SUPREME COURT: FOR PLAINTIFF
YEAR: 1976

VERDICT AGAINST WHICH DEFENDANTS:
1. HOSPITAL &/OR OWNERS, ETC.
2. JUDICIARY &/OR CLERKS, ETC.

RECOVERY OR OTHER RELIEF GRANTED:
1. $ 25000

249. SEYMOUR V. LOFGREEN

FROM SEPTEMBER 1, 1964, THROUGH APRIL 25, 1967, BETTY SEYMOUR WAS UNDER THE CARE OF DR. VICTOR LOFGREEN, A GENERAL PRACTITIONER. SHE SUFFERED FROM HEADACHES, SWELLING OF THE STOMACH, EXTENSIVE SINUS DRAINAGE, MUCOUS COLITIS, SWEATING, NAUSEA AND LEG CRAMPS. AFTER THREE YEARS, DR. LOFGREEN COULD NOT FIND ANY PHYSICAL CAUSE FOR HER CONDITION, AS A RESULT OF WHICH HER FAMILY TOOK HER TO DR. E. H. TROWBRIDGE, JR., A PSYCHIATRIST, FOR A SECOND OPINION. HE IMMEDIATELY DIAGNOSED HER AS A SCHIZOPHRENIC WITH PARANOID TRENDS AND DEPRESSION, ADMITTED HER TO RESEARCH HOSPITAL IN KANSAS CITY AND BEGAN ELECTRO- AND INSULIN-SHOCK THERAPY. THE NEXT YEAR SHE WAS COMMITTED TO OSAWATOMIE STATE HOSPITAL FOR APPROXIMATELY SEVEN MONTHS. THIS SUIT FOR NEGLIGENCE WAS BROUGHT IN MARCH OF 1970, A YEAR AFTER HER RELEASE. IT CHARGED THAT BESIDES HIS FAILURE TO FIND A PHYSICAL CAUSE FOR HER PROBLEMS OR TO DIAGNOSE HER MENTAL ILLNESS, DR. LOFGREEN MISHANDLED THE TRANSFERENCE PHENOMENA. SPECIFICALLY BETTY ALLEGED THAT SHE LOVED DR. LOFGREEN AND CLAIMED THAT HE KNEW THIS, USING IT TO HIS SEXUAL ADVANTAGE.

YEAR OF NEGLIGENT ACT: OCCURRED OVER A SERIES OF YEARS, ENDING IN 1967

STATE IN WHICH NEGLIGENT ACT OCCURRED: KANSAS

SETTING OF THE CASE: PUB. MENT. HOSP.

PLAINTIFF(S): PATIENT(S) OR REP.

DEFENDANT(S):
1. NONPSYCHIAT.OR UNKNOWN TYPE PHYSICIAN(S)

NEGLIGENT ACTIVITY:

TREATMENT:
1. SEXUAL ABUSE OR DISTURB.OF MARITAL REL.
2. FAILURE TO CONSULT

DIAGNOSIS:

WHAT WAS DIAGNOSED:
1. SANITY, INSTEAD OF MENTAL ILLNESS
2. MENT.ILL, INSTEAD OF PHYSICAL ILLNESS
3. PHYS.ILL, INSTEAD OF MENT.ILLNESS

RESULT OF DIAGNOSIS:
1. IMPROPER TREATMENT PRESCRIBED

CARE: NOT APPLICABLE

HARM CAUSED TO PLAINTIFF &/OR PATIENT:
1. EMOTIONAL DISTRESS
2. EXACERB.OF PREV.CONDITION
3. ECONOMIC LOSS
4. SEXUAL OR MARITAL HARM
5. ALIENATION OF AFFECTION

TYPE OF ACTION BROUGHT:
1. NEGLIGENCE

HISTORY OF THE CASE:

TYPE OF COURT: STATE

TRIER OF FACT: JUDGE,UNINV.JURY

COURT DECISION(S):

TRIAL COURT: FOR DEFENDANT
YEAR: NOT SPECIFIED
SUPREME COURT: FOR DEFENDANT
YEAR: 1972

REASON SUIT FAILED:
1. STATUTE OF LIMITATIONS BARRED SUIT

250. SHATTUCK V. STATE

GEORGE SHATTUCK, A MENTAL DEFECTIVE CONFINED AT THE NEWARK STATE SCHOOL, SUFFERED FROM "NOSTALGIA." HIS LONGING FOR HOME MADE HIM ATTEMPT SEVERAL ESCAPES. HIS FIRST ESCAPE, THROUGH AN UNBLOCKED WINDOW, OCCURRED ON JANUARY 6, 1933, BUT LASTED ONLY A FEW DAYS. HIS SECOND OCCURRED ON FEBRUARY 23 DURING BITTER COLD WEATHER. SCANTILY DRESSED, HE ELUDED DETECTION UNTIL MARCH 13, WHEN HE WAS FOUND IN A BARN FROZEN AND UNCONSCIOUS. AS A RESULT OF HIS EXPOSURE TO THE ELEMENTS, BOTH OF HIS LEGS WERE AMPUTATED BELOW THE KNEES.

YEAR OF NEGLIGENT ACT: 1933

STATE IN WHICH NEGLIGENT ACT OCCURRED: NEW YORK

SETTING OF THE CASE: PUB. MENT. HOSP.

PLAINTIFF(S): PATIENT(S) OR REP.

DEFENDANT(S):
1. STATE GOV. &/OR OFFICIALS, ETC.

NEGLIGENT ACTIVITY:

TREATMENT: NOT APPLICABLE

DIAGNOSIS:

WHAT WAS DIAGNOSED: NOT APPLICABLE

RESULT OF DIAGNOSIS: NOT APPLICABLE

CARE:
1. INADEQUATE SUPERVISION

HARM CAUSED TO PLAINTIFF &/OR PATIENT:
1. NONSELF-INFLICTED INJURIES

TYPE OF ACTION BROUGHT:
1. NEGLIGENCE

HISTORY OF THE CASE:

TYPE OF COURT: STATE

TRIER OF FACT: JUDGE,NO JURY

COURT DECISION(S):

TRIAL COURT: FOR PLAINTIFF
YEAR: 1938
APPELLATE COURT: FOR PLAINTIFF
YEAR: 1938

VERDICT AGAINST WHICH DEFENDANTS:
1. STATE GOV. &/OR OFFICIALS, ETC.

RECOVERY OR OTHER RELIEF GRANTED:
1. OTHER RECOVERY: NOT SPECIFIED

251. SMART V. UNITED STATES

RALPH DUNGAN WAS A MENTAL PATIENT AT A V.A. HOSPITAL IN MARION, INDIANA. IN MAY OF 1951, THE HOSPITAL STAFF RECOMMENDED A NINETY-DAY TRIAL VISIT HOME, WHICH WAS LATER CANCELLED WHEN DUNGAN BECAME VIOLENT. BY AUGUST HE HAD IMPROVED TO THE POINT OF BEING ALLOWED GROUND PRIVILEGES, AND IN OCTOBER HIS FATHER REQUESTED HIS RELEASE. MR. DUNGAN SAID A JOB WOULD BE WAITING FOR RALPH IN PHOENIX AND THAT HE WOULD BE RESPONSIBLE FOR HIS CARE, TREATMENT, AND CONDUCT. A NINETY-DAY TRIAL VISIT WAS GRANTED. DUNGAN WAS GIVEN $141.23 AND SENT ON HIS WAY. DURING HIS TRIP, HE STOLE A CAR IN OKLAHOMA CITY AND INJURED SMART WHILE DRIVING RECKLESSLY.

YEAR OF NEGLIGENT ACT: 1951

STATE IN WHICH NEGLIGENT ACT OCCURRED: INDIANA

SETTING OF THE CASE: PUB. GEN. HOSP.

PLAINTIFF(S): 3RD PARTY, II

DEFENDANT(S):
1. FEDERAL GOV. &/OR OFFICIALS, ETC.

NEGLIGENT ACTIVITY:

TREATMENT: NOT APPLICABLE

DIAGNOSIS:

WHAT WAS DIAGNOSED:
1. LACK OF DANGEROUSNESS

RESULT OF DIAGNOSIS:
1. IMPROPER RELEASE

CARE: NOT APPLICABLE

HARM CAUSED TO PLAINTIFF &/OR PATIENT:
1. NONSELF-INFLICTED INJURIES

TYPE OF ACTION BROUGHT:
1. NEGLIGENCE

HISTORY OF THE CASE:

TYPE OF COURT: FEDERAL

TRIER OF FACT: JUDGE;JURY PRESENT ?

COURT DECISION(S):

TRIAL COURT: FOR DEFENDANT
YEAR: NOT SPECIFIED
APPELLATE COURT: FOR DEFENDANT
YEAR: 1953

REASON SUIT FAILED:
1. DEFENDANT(S) CANNOT BE SUED DUE TO: GOVERN. IMMUNITY

252. SPRINGER V. STEINER

THIS IS AN ACTION FOR FALSE IMPRISONMENT BROUGHT BY WINNIE SPRINGER FOR HER DETENTION IN THE OREGON STATE INSANE ASYLUM FROM JANUARY 15, 1915, TO MAY 31 OF THE SAME YEAR. SHE CLAIMED THAT SHE WAS TAKEN INTO CUSTODY, HANDCUFFED, CONVEYED THROUGH PUBLIC STREETS AND IMPRISONED WITH COMMON CRIMINALS WITHOUT ANY ORDER OR WARRANT. UPON BEING DELIVERED TO STEINER, THE SUPERINTENDENT OF THE ASYLUM, SHE WAS FOUND INSANE AND CONFINED FOR FOUR AND ONE-HALF MONTHS. SHE MAINTAINED THAT AT NO TIME WAS SHE INSANE.

YEAR OF NEGLIGENT ACT: 1915

STATE IN WHICH NEGLIGENT ACT OCCURRED: OREGON

SETTING OF THE CASE: JUDICIAL PROCEEDING

PLAINTIFF(S): PATIENT(S) OR REP

DEFENDANT(S):
1. NONPSYCHIAT.OR UNKNOWN TYPE PHYSICIAN(S)

NEGLIGENT ACTIVITY:

TREATMENT: NOT APPLICABLE

DIAGNOSIS:

WHAT WAS DIAGNOSED:
1. MENTAL ILLNESS, INSTEAD OF SANITY

RESULT OF DIAGNOSIS:
1. IMPROPER COMMITMENT

CARE: NOT APPLICABLE

HARM CAUSED TO PLAINTIFF &/OR PATIENT:
1. LOSS OF LIBERTY

TYPE OF ACTION BROUGHT:
1. FALSE IMPRISONMENT

HISTORY OF THE CASE:

TYPE OF COURT: STATE

TRIER OF FACT: JUDGE,UNINV.JURY

COURT DECISION(S):

TRIAL COURT: FOR PLAINTIFF
YEAR: NOT SPECIFIED
SUPREME COURT: FOR DEFENDANT
YEAR: 1919

REASON SUIT FAILED:
1. DEFENDANT(S) CANNOT BE SUED DUE TO: JUDICIAL IMMUNITY
2. NO BAD FAITH OR MAL.

253. STACHULAK V. COUGHLIN

A CLASS ACTION SUIT WAS BROUGHT BY FRANK STACHULAK, AND ALL THOSE SIMILARLY SITUATED, AGAINST THE ILLINOIS DIRECTOR OF CORRECTIONS FOR THEIR CONFINEMENT TO THE PSYCHIATRIC DIVISION OF THE DEPARTMENT OF CORRECTIONS UNDER THE SEXUALLY DANGEROUS PERSONS ACT. THEY ALLEGED THAT CONFINEMENT CONSTITUTED A VIOLATION OF DUE PROCESS IN THAT THE STATUTE DID NOT REQUIRE PROOF BEYOND A REASONABLE DOUBT; THAT THE LANGUAGE WAS TOO BROAD TO GUARANTEE EQUAL PROTECTION; THAT PLAINTIFFS WERE TREATED WORSE THAN CRIMINAL DEFENDANTS; AND THAT THEIR RIGHT TO TREATMENT WAS DENIED.

YEAR OF NEGLIGENT ACT: OCCURRED OVER A SERIES OF YEARS, ENDING IN 1973

STATE IN WHICH NEGLIGENT ACT OCCURRED: ILLINOIS

SETTING OF THE CASE: CORRECTIONAL INST.

PLAINTIFF(S): PATIENT(S) OR REP.

DEFENDANT(S):
1. CORRECTIONAL INST.

NEGLIGENT ACTIVITY:

TREATMENT:
1. NO TREATMENT OR INADEQUATE TREATMENT

DIAGNOSIS:

WHAT WAS DIAGNOSED:
1. MENTAL ILLNESS, INSTEAD OF SANITY
2. DANGEROUSNESS

RESULT OF DIAGNOSIS:
1. IMPROPER COMMITMENT

CARE: NOT APPLICABLE

HARM CAUSED TO PLAINTIFF &/OR PATIENT:
1. DEPRIVATION OF CONSTITUTIONAL RIGHTS
2. LOSS OF LIBERTY

TYPE OF ACTION BROUGHT:
1. DEPRIVATION OF CONSTITUTIONAL RIGHTS: CONST.RTS.IN GEN.
2. HABEAS CORPUS

HISTORY OF THE CASE:

TYPE OF COURT: FEDERAL

TRIER OF FACT: JUDGE,NO JURY

COURT DECISION(S):

TRIAL COURT: NONFINAL FOR PL.
YEAR: 1973

DEFENDANTS STILL INVOLVED IN SUIT:
1. CORRECTIONAL INST.

254. STALLMAN V. ROBINSON

FOUR DAYS AFTER ENTERING THE DEFENDANT'S SANITARIUM, RUBY STALLMAN, THE WIFE OF THE PLAINTIFF, COMMITTED SUICIDE BY HANGING HERSELF FROM A BATHROOM PIPE WITH STRIPS OF CLOTH FROM HER ROBE. THE ACTION WAS BY HER HUSBAND AGAINST THE OWNERS FOR NEGLIGENCE, ALLEGING THAT THEY KNEW OF HER SUICIDAL TENDENCIES AND THAT THEY ALSO KNEW SHE HAD TWICE PREVIOUSLY ATTEMPTED TO KILL HERSELF.

YEAR OF NEGLIGENT ACT: 1949

STATE IN WHICH NEGLIGENT ACT OCCURRED: MISSOURI

SETTING OF THE CASE: PRIV. MENT. HOSP.

PLAINTIFF(S): 3RD PARTY, I

DEFENDANT(S):
1. HOSPITAL &/OR OWNERS, ETC.

NEGLIGENT ACTIVITY:

TREATMENT: NOT APPLICABLE

DIAGNOSIS:

WHAT WAS DIAGNOSED: NOT APPLICABLE

RESULT OF DIAGNOSIS: NOT APPLICABLE

CARE:
1. INADEQUATE SUPERVISION

HARM CAUSED TO PLAINTIFF &/OR PATIENT:
1. SUICIDE

TYPE OF ACTION BROUGHT:
1. NEGLIGENCE

HISTORY OF THE CASE:

TYPE OF COURT: STATE

TRIER OF FACT: JURY

COURT DECISION(S):

TRIAL COURT: FOR PLAINTIFF
YEAR: NOT SPECIFIED
SUPREME COURT: FOR PLAINTIFF
YEAR: 1953

VERDICT AGAINST WHICH DEFENDANTS:
1. HOSPITAL &/OR OWNERS, ETC.

RECOVERY OR OTHER RELIEF GRANTED:
1. $ 9000

255. STANSFIELD V. GARDNER

WHILE PURSUING DOCTORAL STUDIES, CHARLES STANSFIELD SUFFERED A NERVOUS BREAKDOWN, WHICH RESULTED IN HIS TEMPORARY INSANITY. HE WAS DIAGNOSED AS SUFFERING FROM DEMENTIA PRAECOX, MANIC-DEPRESSIVE TYPE, AND ADMITTED TO THE DEFENDANT'S INSTITUTION IN AUGUST 1934. HE WAS GIVEN A ROOM AND A SPECIAL ASSISTANT, WHICH PUT A GREAT FINANCIAL BURDEN ON HIS FATHER. IN A FEW MONTHS, THE FATHER REQUESTED A PART-TIME INSTEAD OF A FULL-TIME ASSISTANT, TO WHICH THE DEFENDANT AGREED. IN FEBRUARY OF 1935, WHILE THE ATTENDANT WENT TO THE LAVATORY, CHARLES FELL OR JUMPED FROM THE SECOND-FLOOR LANDING TO THE FIRST FLOOR BELOW, SUFFERING MULTIPLE FRACTURES. THE HOSPITAL ALLEGEDLY DID NOT PROVIDE DUE MEDICAL ATTENTION FOR THESE INJURIES UNTIL SEVERAL DAYS LATER, DESPITE STANSFIELD'S COMPLAINTS OF PAIN.

YEAR OF NEGLIGENT ACT: 1935

STATE IN WHICH NEGLIGENT ACT OCCURRED: GEORGIA

SETTING OF THE CASE: PRIV. MENT. HOSP.

PLAINTIFF(S): PATIENT(S) OR REP.

DEFENDANT(S):
1. HOSPITAL &/OR OWNERS, ETC.

NEGLIGENT ACTIVITY:

TREATMENT: NOT APPLICABLE

DIAGNOSIS:

WHAT WAS DIAGNOSED: NOT APPLICABLE

RESULT OF DIAGNOSIS: NOT APPLICABLE

CARE:
1. INADEQUATE SUPERVISION

HARM CAUSED TO PLAINTIFF &/OR PATIENT:
1. NONSELF-INFLICTED INJURIES

TYPE OF ACTION BROUGHT:
1. NEGLIGENCE

HISTORY OF THE CASE:

TYPE OF COURT: STATE

TRIER OF FACT: JURY

COURT DECISION(S):

TRIAL COURT: FOR DEFENDANT
YEAR: NOT SPECIFIED
APPELLATE COURT: FOR DEFENDANT
YEAR: 1937

REASON SUIT FAILED:
1. NEGLIGENCE OR CASE NOT PROVEN

256. STEPHEN V. DREW

FEW DETAILS ARE AVAILABLE FROM THE REPORTED CASE. THE PLAINTIFF ALLEGED THAT ON FEBRUARY 4, 1972, OFFICIALS OF HAMPDEN-SYDNEY COLLEGE CAUSED HIM TO BE COMMITTED INVOLUNTARILY TO CENTRAL STATE HOSPITAL. HE FURTHER CLAIMED THAT THESE SAME DEFENDANTS CAUSED HIM TO BE TRANSFERRED TO WESTBROOK ON FEBRUARY 5, WHERE HE WAS DETAINED FOR THREE DAYS AGAINST HIS WILL. THOMAS STEPHEN CLAIMED THAT HE HAD NEVER BEEN MENTALLY ILL.

YEAR OF NEGLIGENT ACT: 1972

STATE IN WHICH NEGLIGENT ACT OCCURRED: VIRGINIA

SETTING OF THE CASE: JUDICIAL PROCEEDING

PLAINTIFF(S): PATIENT(S) OR REP.

DEFENDANT(S):
1. NONPSYCHIAT.OR UNKNOWN TYPE PHYSICIAN(S)
2. PSYCHOLOGIST(S)
3. HOSPITAL &/OR OWNERS, ETC.
4. JUDICIARY &/OR CLERKS, ETC.
5. EDUCATIONAL INST. &/OR DEANS, ETC.

NEGLIGENT ACTIVITY:

TREATMENT: NOT APPLICABLE

DIAGNOSIS:

WHAT WAS DIAGNOSED:
1. MENTAL ILLNESS, INSTEAD OF SANITY

RESULT OF DIAGNOSIS:
1. IMPROPER COMMITMENT
2. IMPROPER FAILURE TO RELEASE

CARE: NOT APPLICABLE

HARM CAUSED TO PLAINTIFF &/OR PATIENT:
1. LOSS OF LIBERTY
2. INJURY TO REPUTATION

TYPE OF ACTION BROUGHT:
1. NEGLIGENCE
2. MALICIOUS PROSECUTION
3. DEPRIVATION OF CONSTITUTIONAL RIGHTS: CONST.RTS.IN GEN.

HISTORY OF THE CASE:

TYPE OF COURT: FEDERAL

TRIER OF FACT: JUDGE,NO JURY

COURT DECISION(S):

TRIAL COURT: NONFINAL FOR PL.
YEAR: 1973

DEFENDANTS STILL INVOLVED IN SUIT:
1. NONPSYCHIAT.OR UNKNOWN TYPE PHYSICIAN(S)
2. PSYCHOLOGIST(S)
3. JUDICIARY &/OR CLERKS, ETC.
4. EDUCATIONAL INST. &/OR DEANS, ETC.

257. STONE V. PROCTOR

MR. STONE CLAIMED MALPRACTICE IN THE ADMINISTRATION OF ELECTRO-SHOCK THERAPY WHILE A PATIENT AT GRAYLYN HOSPITAL IN WINSTON-SALEM IN 1954. AFTER THE FIRST TREATMENT THE PATIENT SUFFERED SEVERE PAINS IN HIS LOWER BACK. NO X-RAYS WERE TAKEN AND FOUR MORE TREATMENTS WERE ADMINISTERED, THE LAST ON FEBRUARY 20. STONE WAS DISCHARGED ON THE 25TH AND TWO DAYS LATER VISITED A RADIOLOGIST, WHO FOUND A COMPRESSED FRACTURE OF THE NINTH VERTEBRA. DR. REGISTER, AN ORTHOPEDIC SURGEON, RECOMMENDED HOSPITAL TREATMENT, A TAYLOR BRACE AND CONFINEMENT IN BED FOR SIX WEEKS.

YEAR OF NEGLIGENT ACT: 1954

STATE IN WHICH NEGLIGENT ACT OCCURRED: NORTH CAROLINA

SETTING OF THE CASE: PRIVATE HOSPITAL

PLAINTIFF(S): PATIENT(S) OR REP.

DEFENDANT(S):
1. PSYCHIATRIST(S)

NEGLIGENT ACTIVITY:

TREATMENT:
1. NEGLIGENT ELECTROCONVULSIVE THERAPY

DIAGNOSIS:

WHAT WAS DIAGNOSED: NOT APPLICABLE

RESULT OF DIAGNOSIS: NOT APPLICABLE

CARE: NOT APPLICABLE

HARM CAUSED TO PLAINTIFF &/OR PATIENT:
1. NONSUICIDAL DEATH

TYPE OF ACTION BROUGHT:
1. NEGLIGENCE

HISTORY OF THE CASE:

TYPE OF COURT: STATE

TRIER OF FACT: JUDGE,UNINV.JURY

COURT DECISION(S):

TRIAL COURT: FOR DEFENDANT
YEAR: NOT SPECIFIED
SUPREME COURT: NONFINAL FOR PL.
YEAR: 1963

DEFENDANTS STILL INVOLVED IN SUIT:
1. PSYCHIATRIST(S)

258. STOVALL V. HARMS

EVELYN STOVALL'S FAMILY DOCTOR HAD RECENTLY PASSED AWAY. ACCORDINGLY, WHEN SHE WAS IN AN AUTO ACCIDENT ON FEBRUARY 2, 1970, HER ATTORNEY RECOMMENDED ONE ALBERT HARMS, THE DEFENDANT, TO TREAT HER. HE ADMITTED HER TO SHAWNEE MISSION HOSPITAL AND TREATED HER THERE UNTIL APRIL 9, 1970. SHE WAS RELEASED FROM THE HOSPITAL, STILL SUFFERING FROM ACUTE BACK STRAIN, SO DR. HARMS CALLED IN DR. WHITEHEAD, AN ORTHOPEDIC SPECIALIST, AND DR. ITURRALDE, A PSYCHIATRIST, FOR CONSULTATION. MS. STOVALL FIRST SAW DR. ITURRALDE ON APRIL 11, WITH SIX SUBSEQUENT VISITS. ON MAY 26 SHE HAD ANOTHER AUTO ACCIDENT. THE PLAINTIFF CLAIMED THAT DR. HARMS FAILED TO INFORM HER THAT DR. ITURRALDE WAS A PSYCHIATRIST. SHE FURTHER ALLEGED THAT ITURRALDE WAS NEGLIGENT IN NOT TELLING HER OF THE DANGERS OF DRIVING WHILE TAKING THE DRUGS HE HAD PRESCRIBED.

YEAR OF NEGLIGENT ACT: 1970

STATE IN WHICH NEGLIGENT ACT OCCURRED: KANSAS

SETTING OF THE CASE: PRIVATE PRACTICE

PLAINTIFF(S): PATIENT(S) OR REP.

DEFENDANT(S):
1. PSYCHIATRIST(S)
2. NONPSYCHIAT.OR UNKNOWN TYPE PHYSICIAN(S)

NEGLIGENT ACTIVITY:

TREATMENT:
1. FAILURE TO OBTAIN -OR LACK OF- CONSENT
2. NEG.ADMIN.OF DRUGS

DIAGNOSIS:

WHAT WAS DIAGNOSED: NOT APPLICABLE

RESULT OF DIAGNOSIS: NOT APPLICABLE

CARE: NOT APPLICABLE

HARM CAUSED TO PLAINTIFF &/OR PATIENT:
1. NONSELF-INFLICTED INJURIES

TYPE OF ACTION BROUGHT:
1. NEGLIGENCE

HISTORY OF THE CASE:

TYPE OF COURT: STATE

TRIER OF FACT: JUDGE;JURY PRESENT ?

COURT DECISION(S):

TRIAL COURT: NONFINAL FOR DEF.
YEAR: NOT SPECIFIED
SUPREME COURT: NONFINAL FOR DEF.
YEAR: 1974

DEFENDANTS STILL INVOLVED IN SUIT:
1. PSYCHIATRIST(S)

259. STOWERS V. ARDMORE ACRES HOSPITAL

CONTEMPLATING DIVORCE, MR. STOWERS ASKED DR. WOLODZKO TO HIS HOME TO DETERMINE HIS WIFE'S MENTAL CONDITION. SHE ALLEGED SHE DID NOT KNOW HE WAS A PSYCHIATRIST AND ENGAGED IN LIGHT CONVERSATION WITH HIM FOR A SHORT PERIOD OF TIME. SEVERAL DAYS LATER THEY BRIEFLY TALKED ON THE PHONE. ON THE BASIS OF THESE CONTACTS, DR. WOLODZKO DIAGNOSED MRS. STOWERS AS A PARANOID SCHIZOPHRENIC AND RECOMMENDED HOSPITALIZATION. SUBSEQUENTLY, HER HUSBAND OBTAINED A COURT ORDER AUTHORIZING DR. WOLODZKO TO HAVE HER COMMITTED. HE FORCIBLY TOOK HER TO ARDMORE ACRES, A PRIVATE MENTAL INSTITUTION, DESPITE THE FACT THAT THE COURT ORDER ALLOWED COMMITMENT ONLY TO A STATE HOSPITAL. AT ARDMORE ACRES THE PLAINTIFF REFUSED TO CONSENT TO TREATMENT, REFUSED MEDICATION, AND REFUSED TO EAT. THE DEFENDANT PSYCHIATRIST, NONETHELESS, ORDERED HER LOCKED IN A BARRED AND BARE ROOM FOR SIX DAYS AND DID NOT PERMIT HER ANY PHONE CALLS OR LETTERS. SHE WAS FORCIBLY ADMINISTERED SEVERAL TRANQUILIZERS. SHE EVENTUALLY MANAGED TO CONTACT HER LAWYER BY SUBTERFUGE TOWARD THE END OF HER STAY AND WAS DISCHARGED SHORTLY THEREAFTER.

YEAR OF NEGLIGENT ACT: 1964

STATE IN WHICH NEGLIGENT ACT OCCURRED: MICHIGAN

SETTING OF THE CASE: PRIV. MENT. HOSP.

PLAINTIFF(S): PATIENT(S) OR REP.

DEFENDANT(S):
1. PSYCHIATRIST(S)
2. HOSPITAL &/OR OWNERS, ETC.

NEGLIGENT ACTIVITY:

TREATMENT:
1. PHYSICAL ASSAULT
2. FAILURE TO OBTAIN -OR LACK OF- CONSENT

DIAGNOSIS:

WHAT WAS DIAGNOSED:
1. MENTAL ILLNESS, INSTEAD OF SANITY

RESULT OF DIAGNOSIS:
1. IMPROPER COMMITMENT

CARE: NOT APPLICABLE

HARM CAUSED TO PLAINTIFF &/OR PATIENT:
1. NONSELF-INFLICTED INJURIES
2. EMOTIONAL DISTRESS
3. LOSS OF LIBERTY

TYPE OF ACTION BROUGHT:
1. NEGLIGENCE
2. ASSAULT AND BATTERY
3. FALSE IMPRISONMENT

HISTORY OF THE CASE:

TYPE OF COURT: STATE

TRIER OF FACT: JURY

COURT DECISION(S):

TRIAL COURT: FOR PLAINTIFF
YEAR: NOT SPECIFIED
APPELLATE COURT: FOR PLAINTIFF
YEAR: 1969
SUPREME COURT: FOR PLAINTIFF
YEAR: 1971

VERDICT AGAINST WHICH DEFENDANTS:
1. PSYCHIATRIST(S)

RECOVERY OR OTHER RELIEF GRANTED:
1. $ 40000

260. SUHRE V. KOTT

JUST THE BAREST SKETCH IS AVAILABLE FROM THIS SIXTY-YEAR-OLD CASE. WILLIAM SUHRE CLAIMED MALICIOUS PROSECUTION AGAINST THE DEFENDANTS IN INITIATING LUNACY PROCEEDINGS AGAINST HIM. ON THE BASIS OF THIS PROCEEDING, HE WAS ARRESTED, BROUGHT BEFORE A JUSTICE OF THE PEACE, AND PLACED IN JAIL WITHOUT BOND. SUBSEQUENTLY, HE WAS BROUGHT BEFORE A SPECIAL COMMISSION, TRIED FOR LUNACY, AND DISCHARGED.

YEAR OF NEGLIGENT ACT: NOT SPECIFIED

STATE IN WHICH NEGLIGENT ACT OCCURRED: TEXAS

SETTING OF THE CASE: JUDICIAL PROCEEDING

PLAINTIFF(S): PATIENT(S) OR REP.

DEFENDANT(S):
1. SOME OR ALL DEFENDANTS NOT SPECIFIED

NEGLIGENT ACTIVITY:

TREATMENT: NOT APPLICABLE

DIAGNOSIS:

WHAT WAS DIAGNOSED:
1. MENTAL ILLNESS, INSTEAD OF SANITY

RESULT OF DIAGNOSIS:
1. IMPROPER COMMITMENT

CARE: NOT APPLICABLE

HARM CAUSED TO PLAINTIFF &/OR PATIENT:
1. LOSS OF LIBERTY
2. INJURY TO REPUTATION

TYPE OF ACTION BROUGHT:
1. MALICIOUS PROSECUTION

HISTORY OF THE CASE:

TYPE OF COURT: STATE

TRIER OF FACT: JUDGE;JURY PRESENT ?

COURT DECISION(S):

TRIAL COURT: FOR DEFENDANT
YEAR: NOT SPECIFIED
APPELLATE COURT: NONFINAL FOR PL.
YEAR: 1917

DEFENDANTS STILL INVOLVED IN SUIT:
1. TYPE NOT SPECIFIED

261. SURPRENANT V. STATE

ALLEN SURPRENANT, A VICTIM OF BOTH MENTAL AND PHYSIOLOGICAL CONGENITAL ILLNESSES, HAD SPENT MOST OF HIS SHORT LIFE IN INSTITUTIONS, WITH ONLY BRIEF AND INFREQUENT VISITS HOME. ON JANUARY 6, 1962, WHILE A PATIENT AT LETCHWORTH VILLAGE, A STATE INSTITUTION DESIGNED TO CARE FOR MENTALLY RETARDED CHILDREN, ALLEN SMASHED TWO UNBARRED AND UNSCREENED WINDOWS, CUTTING FLEXOR TENDONS AND A MEDIAN NERVE IN HIS RIGHT HAND. THESE SERIOUS LACERATIONS CAUSED PAIN AND SUFFERING, NECESSITATING AN AMPUTATION AND RESULTING IN AN IMPAIRED HANDGRASP. THIS TENDENCY FOR BREAKING GLASS HAD BEEN KNOWN TO THE ADMINISTRATORS AND STAFF OF THE HOSPITAL.

YEAR OF NEGLIGENT ACT: 1962

STATE IN WHICH NEGLIGENT ACT OCCURRED: NEW YORK

SETTING OF THE CASE: PUB. MENT. HOSP.

PLAINTIFF(S): PATIENT(S) OR REP.

DEFENDANT(S):
1. STATE GOV. &/OR OFFICIALS, ETC.

NEGLIGENT ACTIVITY:

TREATMENT: NOT APPLICABLE

DIAGNOSIS:

WHAT WAS DIAGNOSED: NOT APPLICABLE

RESULT OF DIAGNOSIS: NOT APPLICABLE

CARE:
1. INADEQUATE SUPERVISION

HARM CAUSED TO PLAINTIFF &/OR PATIENT:
1. SELF-INFLICTED INJURIES
2. ECONOMIC LOSS
3. LOSS OF COMPNNSHIP

TYPE OF ACTION BROUGHT:
1. NEGLIGENCE

HISTORY OF THE CASE:

TYPE OF COURT: STATE

TRIER OF FACT: JUDGE,NO JURY

COURT DECISION(S):

TRIAL COURT: FOR PLAINTIFF
YEAR: 1965

VERDICT AGAINST WHICH DEFENDANTS:
1. STATE GOV. &/OR OFFICIALS, ETC.

RECOVERY OR OTHER RELIEF GRANTED:
1. $ 21000

262. TAIG V. STATE

WHEN HE WAS ELEVEN, LOUIS SENSALE WAS DIAGNOSED AS A SCHIZOPHRENIC, PARANOID TYPE, AND ADMITTED TO ROCKLAND STATE HOSPITAL. HE REMAINED THERE FROM JULY 30, 1953 UNTIL JUNE 2, 1954. HIS CONDITION WAS CONSIDERED MUCH IMPROVED AND HE THEREFORE CONTINUED CONVALESCENT CARE AT THE BROOKLYN AFTER-CARE CLINIC, FROM WHICH HE WAS DISCHARGED ON JUNE 29, 1955. SEVERAL MONTHS LATER LOUIS, NOW THIRTEEN, ATTACKED FIFTEEN-YEAR-OLD JOAN TAIG. CLAIMANT'S MEDICAL WITNESS ARGUED THAT SENSALE HAD ACTUALLY EXHIBITED SIGNS OF RETROGRESSION PRIOR TO RELEASE AND SHOULD NOT HAVE BEEN DISCHARGED.

YEAR OF NEGLIGENT ACT: 1955

STATE IN WHICH NEGLIGENT ACT OCCURRED: NEW YORK

SETTING OF THE CASE: PUB. MENT. HOSP.

PLAINTIFF(S): 3RD PARTY, II

DEFENDANT(S):
1. STATE GOV. &/OR OFFICIALS, ETC.

NEGLIGENT ACTIVITY:

TREATMENT: NOT APPLICABLE

DIAGNOSIS:

WHAT WAS DIAGNOSED:
1. SANITY, INSTEAD OF MENTAL ILLNESS
2. LACK OF DANGEROUSNESS

RESULT OF DIAGNOSIS:
1. IMPROPER RELEASE

CARE: NOT APPLICABLE

HARM CAUSED TO PLAINTIFF &/OR PATIENT:
1. NONSELF-INFLICTED INJURIES

TYPE OF ACTION BROUGHT:
1. NEGLIGENCE

HISTORY OF THE CASE:

TYPE OF COURT: STATE

TRIER OF FACT: JUDGE,NO JURY

COURT DECISION(S):

TRIAL COURT: FOR DEFENDANT
YEAR: NOT SPECIFIED
APPELLATE COURT: FOR DEFENDANT
YEAR: 1963

REASON SUIT FAILED:
1. DEFENDANT(S) CANNOT BE SUED DUE TO: GOVERN. IMMUNITY

263. TARASOFF V. REGENTS OF THE UNIVERSITY OF CALIFORNIA

ON AUGUST 20, 1969, LAWRENCE MOORE, A CLINICAL PSYCHOLOGIST, INFORMED BERKELEY CAMPUS POLICE THAT PROSENJIT PODDAR, A STUDENT OF THE SCHOOL, WAS LIABLE TO HARM HIMSELF OR SOMEONE ELSE. PODDAR WAS A VOLUNTARY OUTPATIENT UNDERGOING THERAPY WITH DR. MOORE, AND HAD BEEN DIAGNOSED AS SUFFERING FROM "PARANOID SCHIZOPHRENIA REACTION, ACUTE AND SEVERE." TWO DAYS BEFORE, IN A THERAPY SESSION, HE HAD TOLD MOORE THAT HE WAS GOING TO KILL A WOMAN WHEN SHE RETURNED FROM BRAZIL. MOORE INFORMED THE CAMPUS POLICE CHIEF, WILLIAM BEALL, THAT HE WOULD ASSIGN A SEVENTY-TWO-HOUR EMERGENCY PSYCHIATRIC DETENTION ON PODDAR AND THAT THEY SHOULD PICK HIM UP AND DETAIN HIM. RESPONDING TO THIS, THE CAMPUS POLICE TOOK PODDAR INTO CUSTODY, BUT WERE SATISFIED THAT HE WAS SANE, RATIONAL AND HAD CHANGED HIS ATTITUDE ALTOGETHER. HE SAID HE WOULD TRY AND STAY AWAY FROM THE WOMAN AND THEY RELEASED HIM. AS A RESULT DR. HARVEY POWELSON, A PSYCHIATRIST AND MOORE'S SUPERIOR, CANCELLED ALL ORDERS REGARDING PODDAR AND THE RECORDS ON THIS MATTER WERE DESTROYED. ON OCTOBER 27, PODDAR CARRIED OUT HIS THREAT AND SHOT AND STABBED TATIANA TARASOFF TO DEATH.

YEAR OF NEGLIGENT ACT: 1969

STATE IN WHICH NEGLIGENT ACT OCCURRED: CALIFORNIA

SETTING OF THE CASE: PUB. MENT. HOSP.

PLAINTIFF(S): 3RD PARTY, II

DEFENDANT(S):
1. PSYCHIATRIST(S)
2. PSYCHOLOGIST(S)
3. HOSPITAL &/OR OWNERS, ETC.
4. EDUCATIONAL INST. &/OR DEANS, ETC.
5. POLICE

NEGLIGENT ACTIVITY:

TREATMENT: NOT APPLICABLE

DIAGNOSIS:

WHAT WAS DIAGNOSED:
1. SANITY, INSTEAD OF MENTAL ILLNESS
2. LACK OF DANGEROUSNESS

RESULT OF DIAGNOSIS:
1. IMPROPER CUSTODIAL CARE
2. IMPROPER FAILURE TO COMMIT

CARE:
1. FAILURE TO WARN THIRD PARTIES
2. FAILURE TO PROVIDE PROPER CUSTODIAL CARE

HARM CAUSED TO PLAINTIFF &/OR PATIENT:
1. NONSUICIDAL DEATH

TYPE OF ACTION BROUGHT:
1. NEGLIGENCE

HISTORY OF THE CASE:

TYPE OF COURT: STATE

TRIER OF FACT: JUDGE;JURY PRESENT ?

COURT DECISION(S):

TRIAL COURT: FOR DEFENDANT
YEAR: NOT SPECIFIED
APPELLATE COURT: FOR DEFENDANT
YEAR: 1973
SUPREME COURT: FOR DEFENDANT
YEAR: 1974
ON REAPPEAL TO SUPREME COURT: NONFINAL FOR PL.
YEAR: 1976

DEFENDANTS STILL INVOLVED IN SUIT:
1. PSYCHIATRIST(S)
2. PSYCHOLOGIST(S)
3. HOSPITAL &/OR OWNERS, ETC.
4. EDUCATIONAL INST. &/OR DEANS, ETC.

264. TAYLOR V. GLOTFELTY

FEW FACTS ARE AVAILABLE IN THE REPORTED CASE. WHEN THE PLAINTIFF WAS AN INMATE OF THE MEDICAL CENTER FOR FEDERAL PRISONERS AT SPRINGFIELD, MISSOURI, HE WAS DIAGNOSED AS SUFFERING FROM PARESIS, WHICH RESULTED IN HIS CONFINEMENT IN A WARD FOR THE INSANE. PLAINTIFF CLAIMED THAT THE DIAGNOSING PSYCHIATRIST MADE FALSE AND SLANDEROUS STATEMENTS TO MALICIOUSLY STIGMATIZE HIM. HE FURTHER ALLEGED THAT THE DEFENDANT HAD NEVER EXAMINED HIM.

YEAR OF NEGLIGENT ACT: NOT SPECIFIED

STATE IN WHICH NEGLIGENT ACT OCCURRED: MISSOURI

SETTING OF THE CASE: PUB. MENT. HOSP.

PLAINTIFF(S): PATIENT(S) OR REP.

DEFENDANT(S):
1. PSYCHIATRIST(S)

NEGLIGENT ACTIVITY:

TREATMENT: NOT APPLICABLE

DIAGNOSIS:

WHAT WAS DIAGNOSED:
1. MENTAL ILLNESS, INSTEAD OF SANITY

RESULT OF DIAGNOSIS:
1. IMPROPER COMMITMENT

CARE: NOT APPLICABLE

HARM CAUSED TO PLAINTIFF &/OR PATIENT:
1. LOSS OF LIBERTY
2. INJURY TO REPUTATION

TYPE OF ACTION BROUGHT:
1. DEFAMATION OF CHARACTER: LIBEL

HISTORY OF THE CASE:

TYPE OF COURT: FEDERAL

TRIER OF FACT: JUDGE;JURY PRESENT ?

COURT DECISION(S):

TRIAL COURT: FOR DEFENDANT
YEAR: NOT SPECIFIED
APPELLATE COURT: FOR DEFENDANT
YEAR: 1952

REASON SUIT FAILED:
1. DEFENDANT(S) CANNOT BE SUED DUE TO: GOVERN. IMMUNITY

265. TAYLOR V. STATE

PLAINTIFF CLAIMED THAT ALTHOUGH THE STATE KNEW THAT GARY SICKLER WAS A "CONVICTED FELON, A PRIOR SEXUAL OFFENDER, A DANGEROUS, IRRESPONSIBLE, VIOLENT, HOMICIDAL, (AND) PERVERTED INDIVIDUAL," HE WAS GRANTED PAROLE AND THEN ONLY LOOSELY SUPERVISED. WHILE ON PAROLE, HE STABBED KATHLEEN M. TAYLOR TO DEATH IN THE COURSE OF ATTEMPTED RAPE. KATHLEEN'S FATHER BROUGHT SUIT AGAINST THE STATE FOR ALLOWING SICKLER TO BE AT LARGE.

YEAR OF NEGLIGENT ACT: 1967

STATE IN WHICH NEGLIGENT ACT OCCURRED: NEW YORK

SETTING OF THE CASE: CORRECTIONAL INST.

PLAINTIFF(S): PATIENT(S) OR REP.

DEFENDANT(S):
1. STATE GOV. &/OR OFFICIALS, ETC.

NEGLIGENT ACTIVITY:

TREATMENT: NOT APPLICABLE

DIAGNOSIS:

WHAT WAS DIAGNOSED:
1. LACK OF DANGEROUSNESS

RESULT OF DIAGNOSIS:
1. IMPROPER RELEASE

CARE:
1. INADEQUATE SUPERVISION
2. PREMATURE RELEASE
3. FAILURE TO PROVIDE PROPER CUSTODIAL CARE

HARM CAUSED TO PLAINTIFF &/OR PATIENT:
1. NONSUICIDAL DEATH

TYPE OF ACTION BROUGHT:
1. NEGLIGENCE

HISTORY OF THE CASE:

TYPE OF COURT: STATE

TRIER OF FACT: JUDGE,NO JURY

COURT DECISION(S):

TRIAL COURT: NONFINAL FOR PL.
YEAR: NOT SPECIFIED
APPELLATE COURT: FOR DEFENDANT
YEAR: 1971
SUPREME COURT: FOR DEFENDANT
YEAR: 1974

REASON SUIT FAILED:
1. NEGLIGENCE OR CASE NOT PROVEN

266. THALL V. STATE

ANNE THALL HAD JUST COMPLETED HER SHOPPING AT A LONG ISLAND MALL AND WENT TO HER CAR IN THE PARKING LOT. AS SHE WAS ABOUT TO DEPART, A YOUTH APPEARED AND ASKED HER FOR HELP. WHEN SHE ATTEMPTED TO LOCK HER DOOR, HE PULLED IT OPEN AND STABBED HER WITH A KNIFE. DURING THEIR STRUGGLE SHE WAS ABLE TO SOUND THE HORN, WHICH FRIGHTENED THE YOUNG MAN AWAY. HER ASSAILANT WAS LATER IDENTIFIED AS ROBERT MARCIANO, A PATIENT AT THE NORTHEAST NASSAU PSYCHIATRIC HOSPITAL, WHO HAD RECENTLY ESCAPED. BESIDES RECEIVING STAB WOUNDS ON THE NECK AND HANDS, THALL ENTERED A STATE OF SHOCK AND WAS UNABLE TO RETURN HOME. SHE DEVELOPED A PHOBIA AGAINST COUNTRY LIVING, WHICH FORCED HER HUSBAND TO MOVE, AND SHE DEVELOPED A FIXATION ABOUT LOCKING DOORS. HER HUSBAND JOINED HER IN THIS SUIT AGAINST THE STATE FOR THE HARDSHIPS AND LOSS OF COMPANIONSHIP HE HAD TO ENDURE.

YEAR OF NEGLIGENT ACT: 1969

STATE IN WHICH NEGLIGENT ACT OCCURRED: NEW YORK

SETTING OF THE CASE: PUB. MENT. HOSP.

PLAINTIFF(S): 3RD PARTY, I & II

DEFENDANT(S):
1. STATE GOV. &/OR OFFICIALS, ETC.

NEGLIGENT ACTIVITY:

TREATMENT: NOT APPLICABLE

DIAGNOSIS:

WHAT WAS DIAGNOSED: NOT APPLICABLE

RESULT OF DIAGNOSIS: NOT APPLICABLE

CARE:
1. INADEQUATE SUPERVISION

HARM CAUSED TO PLAINTIFF &/OR PATIENT:
1. NONSELF-INFLICTED INJURIES
2. EMOTIONAL DISTRESS
3. LOSS OF CONSORTIUM

TYPE OF ACTION BROUGHT:
1. NEGLIGENCE

HISTORY OF THE CASE:

TYPE OF COURT: STATE

TRIER OF FACT: JUDGE,NO JURY

COURT DECISION(S):

TRIAL COURT: FOR PLAINTIFF
YEAR: 1972

VERDICT AGAINST WHICH DEFENDANTS:
1. STATE GOV. &/OR OFFICIALS, ETC.

RECOVERY OR OTHER RELIEF GRANTED:
1. $ 7790

267. TISINGER V. WOOLLEY

MRS. TISINGER WENT TO DR. WOOLLEY EARLY IN JULY OF 1946. TREATMENT CONTINUED THROUGH JULY, AND ON THE 27TH, SHE WAS ADMITTED TO EMORY UNIVERSITY HOSPITAL FOR EMOTIONAL PROBLEMS. EMORY WAS NOT A MENTAL HOSPITAL AND WAS NOT EQUIPPED FOR MRS. TISINGER'S SUICIDAL CONDITION. ON AUGUST 4, 1946, MRS. TISINGER FELL OR JUMPED TO HER DEATH FROM HER HOSPITAL ROOM WINDOW. SUIT WAS BROUGHT BY HER HUSBAND AND SON FOR HER WRONGFUL DEATH DUE TO THE NEGLIGENCE OF THE DOCTOR IN HAVING HER ADMITTED TO AN IMPROPER FACILITY FOR HER CONDITION AND THE NEGLIGENCE OF THE HOSPITAL IN KNOWING HER CONDITION AND ALLOWING HER TO REMAIN THERE, UNGUARDED AND NEAR AN UNSECURED WINDOW.

YEAR OF NEGLIGENT ACT: 1946

STATE IN WHICH NEGLIGENT ACT OCCURRED: GEORGIA

SETTING OF THE CASE: PRIV. GEN. HOSP.

PLAINTIFF(S): 3RD PARTY, I

DEFENDANT(S):
1. PSYCHIATRIST(S)
2. HOSPITAL &/OR OWNERS, ETC.

NEGLIGENT ACTIVITY:

TREATMENT: NOT APPLICABLE

DIAGNOSIS:

WHAT WAS DIAGNOSED:
1. LACK OF SUICIDAL TENDENCIES

RESULT OF DIAGNOSIS:
1. IMPROPER CUSTODIAL CARE

CARE: NOT APPLICABLE

HARM CAUSED TO PLAINTIFF &/OR PATIENT:
1. SUICIDE

TYPE OF ACTION BROUGHT:
1. NEGLIGENCE

HISTORY OF THE CASE:

TYPE OF COURT: STATE

TRIER OF FACT: JUDGE;JURY PRESENT ?

COURT DECISION(S):

TRIAL COURT: FOR DEFENDANT
YEAR: NOT SPECIFIED
APPELLATE COURT: FOR DEFENDANT
YEAR: 1948

REASON SUIT FAILED:
1. NEGLIGENCE OR CASE NOT PROVEN

268. TOBIAS V. MANHATTAN EYE & EAR HOSPITAL

WHILE A PATIENT AT MANHATTAN EYE & EAR HOSPITAL, AUDREY TOBIAS WAS TRANSFERRED TO BELLEVUE FOR A MENTAL EVALUATION. TOBIAS BROUGHT SUIT AGAINST THE HOSPITAL FOR THIS TRANSFER. NO FURTHER FACTS ARE AVAILABLE.

YEAR OF NEGLIGENT ACT: NOT SPECIFIED

STATE IN WHICH NEGLIGENT ACT OCCURRED: NEW YORK

SETTING OF THE CASE: PUB. GEN. HOSP.

PLAINTIFF(S): PATIENT(S) OR REP.

DEFENDANT(S):
1. PSYCHIATRIST(S)
2. HOSPITAL &/OR OWNERS, ETC.
3. MUNICIPAL GOV. &/OR OFFICIALS, ETC.

NEGLIGENT ACTIVITY:

TREATMENT: NOT APPLICABLE

DIAGNOSIS:

WHAT WAS DIAGNOSED:
1. TYPE OF CUSTODIAL CARE

RESULT OF DIAGNOSIS:
1. IMPROPER CUSTODIAL CARE

CARE: NOT APPLICABLE

HARM CAUSED TO PLAINTIFF &/OR PATIENT:
1. LOSS OF LIBERTY

TYPE OF ACTION BROUGHT:
1. NEGLIGENCE

HISTORY OF THE CASE:

TYPE OF COURT: STATE

TRIER OF FACT: JURY

COURT DECISION(S):

TRIAL COURT: FOR PLAINTIFF
YEAR: NOT SPECIFIED
APPELLATE COURT: FOR DEFENDANT
YEAR: 1967

REASON SUIT FAILED:
1. NEGLIGENCE OR CASE NOT PROVEN

269. TORRES V. STATE

MARIE TORRES SUSTAINED A BROKEN LEG AS THE RESULT OF AN ASSAULT BY ANOTHER PATIENT AT BROOKLYN STATE HOSPITAL. NO FURTHER FACTS ARE AVAILABLE IN THE REPORTED DECISIONS, SINCE THE CLAIM CONCERNS THE RIGHT TO PRETRIAL INVESTIGATION OF HOSPITAL RECORDS RELATING TO THE CASE.

YEAR OF NEGLIGENT ACT: 1955

STATE IN WHICH NEGLIGENT ACT OCCURRED: NEW YORK

SETTING OF THE CASE: PUB. MENT. HOSP.

PLAINTIFF(S): PATIENT(S) OR REP.

DEFENDANT(S):
1. STATE GOV. &/OR OFFICIALS, ETC.

NEGLIGENT ACTIVITY:

TREATMENT: NOT APPLICABLE

DIAGNOSIS:

WHAT WAS DIAGNOSED: NOT APPLICABLE

RESULT OF DIAGNOSIS: NOT APPLICABLE

CARE:
1. FAILURE TO PROVIDE PROPER CUSTODIAL CARE

HARM CAUSED TO PLAINTIFF &/OR PATIENT:
1. NONSELF-INFLICTED INJURIES

TYPE OF ACTION BROUGHT:
1. NEGLIGENCE

HISTORY OF THE CASE:

TYPE OF COURT: STATE

TRIER OF FACT: JUDGE,NO JURY

COURT DECISION(S):

TRIAL COURT: NONFINAL FOR PL.
YEAR: 1956
TRIAL COURT: NONFINAL FOR PL.
YEAR: 1958

DEFENDANTS STILL INVOLVED IN SUIT:
1. STATE GOV. &/OR OFFICIALS, ETC.

270. TRAPANI V. STATE

JOSEPHINE TRAPANI WAS ADMITTED TO A STATE HOSPITAL FOR THE MENTALLY ILL AS A CATATONIC SCHIZOPHRENIC. SHE HAD A RECORD OF PREVIOUS HOSPITALIZATIONS AND HAD THREATENED TO COMMIT SUICIDE WHEN THE OPPORTUNITY AROSE. NINE DAYS AFTER HER ADMISSION SHE WAS FOUND DEAD WITH A PLASTIC BAG SECURED AROUND HER HEAD. ON THE NIGHT OF HER SUICIDE SHE HAD GAINED PERMISSION TO MOVE HER MATTRESS TO A SMALL SIDEROOM TO ESCAPE THE SNORES OF OTHER PATIENTS. THIS ROOM WAS OUT OF SIGHT OF THE ATTENDANTS. WHEN SHE WAS FOUND IN THE MORNING SHE HAD BEEN DEAD FOR SOME HOURS. THE CLAIM AGAINST THE STATE WAS BASED ON NEGLIGENCE IN ALLOWING THE PATIENT TO SECURE THE PLASTIC BAG AND IN ALLOWING HER TO MOVE OUT OF VIEW OF THE ATTENDANTS.

YEAR OF NEGLIGENT ACT: NOT SPECIFIED

STATE IN WHICH NEGLIGENT ACT OCCURRED: NEW YORK

SETTING OF THE CASE: PUB. MENT. HOSP.

PLAINTIFF(S): PATIENT(S) OR REP.

DEFENDANT(S):
1. STATE GOV. &/OR OFFICIALS, ETC.

NEGLIGENT ACTIVITY:

TREATMENT: NOT APPLICABLE

DIAGNOSIS:

WHAT WAS DIAGNOSED: NOT APPLICABLE

RESULT OF DIAGNOSIS: NOT APPLICABLE

CARE:
1. INADEQUATE SUPERVISION

HARM CAUSED TO PLAINTIFF &/OR PATIENT:
1. SUICIDE

TYPE OF ACTION BROUGHT:
1. NEGLIGENCE

HISTORY OF THE CASE:

TYPE OF COURT: STATE

TRIER OF FACT: JUDGE,NO JURY

COURT DECISION(S):

TRIAL COURT: FOR DEFENDANT
YEAR: NOT SPECIFIED
APPELLATE COURT: FOR PLAINTIFF
YEAR: 1965

VERDICT AGAINST WHICH DEFENDANTS:
1. STATE GOV. &/OR OFFICIALS, ETC.

RECOVERY OR OTHER RELIEF GRANTED:
1. $ 9145
2. INTEREST
3. OTHER RECOVERY: COSTS

271. UNDERWOOD V. UNITED STATES

EDWARD F. DUNN WAS AN AIRMAN FIRST CLASS AT MAXWELL AIR FORCE BASE IN ALABAMA. HE HAD THREE CHILDREN, BUT HAD RECENTLY BEEN DIVORCED BY HIS WIFE. HIS COMMANDING OFFICER DECIDED TO SEND HIM FOR TREATMENT BECAUSE HE SEEMED DEPRESSED AND EMOTIONALLY ILL. DUNN WAS HOSPITALIZED AND RECEIVED A PSYCHIATRIC EXAMINATION. AT THAT TIME HIS WIFE INFORMED THE PSYCHIATRIST OF HER FORMER HUSBAND'S THREATS ON HER LIFE AND ASSAULTS ON HER. THE PSYCHIATRIST WAS TRANSFERRED AND FAILED TO TELL THE NEW PSYCHIATRIST ABOUT DUNN'S THREATS. DUNN WAS PUT BACK ON ACTIVE DUTY, TOOK A .45 CALIBER AUTOMATIC PISTOL, AND SHOT HIS FORMER WIFE. HER FATHER CHARGED THE GOVERNMENT WITH NEGLIGENCE BOTH IN ALLOWING DUNN TO RETURN TO DUTY AND IN ALLOWING HIM TO USE THE GUN, WHICH HE HAD OBTAINED BY THE FAILURE OF ANOTHER OFFICER TO FOLLOW PROPER PROCEDURES.

YEAR OF NEGLIGENT ACT: 1962

STATE IN WHICH NEGLIGENT ACT OCCURRED: ALABAMA

SETTING OF THE CASE: ARMED SERVICE

PLAINTIFF(S): 3RD PARTY, II

DEFENDANT(S):
1. FEDERAL GOV. &/OR OFFICIALS, ETC.

NEGLIGENT ACTIVITY:

TREATMENT: NOT APPLICABLE

DIAGNOSIS:

WHAT WAS DIAGNOSED:
1. LACK OF DANGEROUSNESS

RESULT OF DIAGNOSIS:
1. IMPROPER CUSTODIAL CARE
2. IMPROPER RELEASE

CARE:
1. PREMATURE RELEASE
2. FAILURE TO WARN THIRD PARTIES
3. FAILURE TO PROVIDE PROPER CUSTODIAL CARE

HARM CAUSED TO PLAINTIFF &/OR PATIENT:
1. NONSUICIDAL DEATH

TYPE OF ACTION BROUGHT:
1. NEGLIGENCE

HISTORY OF THE CASE:

TYPE OF COURT: FEDERAL

TRIER OF FACT: JUDGE,NO JURY

COURT DECISION(S):

TRIAL COURT: FOR DEFENDANT
YEAR: NOT SPECIFIED
APPELLATE COURT: FOR PLAINTIFF
YEAR: 1966

VERDICT AGAINST WHICH DEFENDANTS:
1. FEDERAL GOV. &/OR OFFICIALS, ETC.

RECOVERY OR OTHER RELIEF GRANTED:
1. OTHER RECOVERY: NOT SPECIFIED

272. UNITED STATES V. GRAY

MS. GRAY, A VETERAN WHO RECEIVED A MEDICAL DISCHARGE IN 1944, FOUND HERSELF IN AN ARMY HOSPITAL AT CAMP CARSON ON AUGUST 1, 1947. SHE HAD BEEN DIAGNOSED AS SUFFERING FROM A SEVERE DEPRESSIVE REACTION WITH SUICIDAL THOUGHTS AND INTENT. ON THE ABOVE DATE SHE OCCUPIED A SECOND-STORY ROOM AT THE HOSPITAL, KNOWING WHERE SHE WAS AND FULLY AWARE OF HER MENTAL CONDITION. SHORTLY THEREAFTER, SHE WAS FOUND BY THE GUARD OUTSIDE HER ROOM ATTEMPTING TO PUT GLASS IN HER MOUTH. THE GUARD PREVENTED HER FROM INJURING HERSELF, BUT SHE BECAME VERY AGITATED AND CRIED AT LENGTH. AFTER BEING LEFT ALONE ONCE AGAIN, SHE JUMPED OR FELL FROM HER UNGUARDED WINDOW, RESULTING IN A COMPLETE PARALYSIS OF HER BODY FROM THE CHEST AREA DOWNWARD. THE CLAIM AGAINST THE GOVERNMENT ALLEGED THAT THE EMPLOYEES AT THE HOSPITAL FAILED TO GIVE HER THE CARE AND ATTENTION NECESSARY FOR HER WELFARE. SPECIFICALLY, THE PLAINTIFF ARGUED THAT THE STATE SHOULD NOT HAVE LEFT HER ALONE OR PUT HER IN A ROOM WITH AN UNSECURED WINDOW, KNOWING OF HER SUICIDAL TENDENCIES.

YEAR OF NEGLIGENT ACT: 1947

STATE IN WHICH NEGLIGENT ACT OCCURRED: COLORADO

SETTING OF THE CASE: PUB. MENT. HOSP.

PLAINTIFF(S): PATIENT(S) OR REP.

DEFENDANT(S):
1. FEDERAL GOV. &/OR OFFICIALS, ETC.

NEGLIGENT ACTIVITY:

TREATMENT: NOT APPLICABLE

DIAGNOSIS:

WHAT WAS DIAGNOSED: NOT APPLICABLE

RESULT OF DIAGNOSIS: NOT APPLICABLE

CARE:
1. INADEQUATE SUPERVISION

HARM CAUSED TO PLAINTIFF &/OR PATIENT:
1. SELF-INFLICTED INJURIES

TYPE OF ACTION BROUGHT:
1. NEGLIGENCE

HISTORY OF THE CASE:

TYPE OF COURT: FEDERAL

TRIER OF FACT: JUDGE,NO JURY

COURT DECISION(S):

TRIAL COURT: FOR PLAINTIFF
YEAR: NOT SPECIFIED
APPELLATE COURT: FOR PLAINTIFF
YEAR: 1952

VERDICT AGAINST WHICH DEFENDANTS:
1. FEDERAL GOV. &/OR OFFICIALS, ETC.

RECOVERY OR OTHER RELIEF GRANTED:
1. OTHER RECOVERY: TO BE DETERM.ON RETR

273. UNITED STATES V. PARDUE

JAMES PARDUE BROUGHT A MOTION TO DISMISS AN INDICTMENT AGAINST HIM FOR THE ROBBERY OF A BANK. ON FEBRUARY 13, 1970, JAMES AND HIS BROTHER JOHN ALLEGEDLY ROBBED THE UNION SAVINGS BANK IN DANBURY, CONNECTICUT THROUGH THE USE OF THREE BOMBS PLANTED IN THE POLICE STATION, THE BANK, AND THEIR ABANDONED GETAWAY CAR. THE F.B.I. INVESTIGATION CAUGHT UP WITH THEM ON MARCH 7, 1970, AND BOTH PLEADED NOT GUILTY TO THE ROBBERY. FOUR DAYS LATER JAMES WAS DECLARED INSANE AND SHORTLY THEREAFTER HE WAS ADMITTED TO THE MEDICAL CENTER FOR FEDERAL PRISONERS AT SPRINGFIELD, MISSOURI. FOR THE NEXT TWO YEARS HE WAS SHUTTLED BACK AND FORTH AMONG SEVEN DIFFERENT INSTITUTIONS. EACH TIME DOCTORS BELIEVED HE HAD IMPROVED ENOUGH TO STAND TRIAL, BUT HE WOULD SUFFER RELAPSES, WHICH CAUSED HIM TO BE SENT TO OTHER INSTITUTIONS. IN THIS SUIT HE ARGUED THAT THE CHARGES AGAINST HIM SHOULD BE DISMISSED ON THE GROUNDS THAT HIS CONSTITUTIONAL RIGHT TO A SPEEDY TRIAL HAD BEEN VIOLATED, THAT HE WAS NOT GRANTED DUE PROCESS OF LAW, AND THAT HE WAS SUBJECTED TO CRUEL AND UNUSUAL PUNISHMENT. HE ALSO CLAIMED THAT HE WAS NOT PROVIDED WITH ADEQUATE TREATMENT.

YEAR OF NEGLIGENT ACT: OCCURRED OVER A SERIES OF YEARS, ENDING IN 1973

STATE IN WHICH NEGLIGENT ACT OCCURRED: CONNECTICUT

SETTING OF THE CASE: CORRECTIONAL INST.

PLAINTIFF(S): PATIENT(S) OR REP.

DEFENDANT(S):
1. FEDERAL GOV. &/OR OFFICIALS, ETC.

NEGLIGENT ACTIVITY:

TREATMENT:
1. NO TREATMENT OR INADEQUATE TREATMENT

DIAGNOSIS:

WHAT WAS DIAGNOSED: NOT APPLICABLE

RESULT OF DIAGNOSIS: NOT APPLICABLE

CARE: NOT APPLICABLE

HARM CAUSED TO PLAINTIFF &/OR PATIENT:
1. DEPRIVATION OF CONSTITUTIONAL RIGHTS
2. LOSS OF CONSORTIUM

TYPE OF ACTION BROUGHT:
1. DEPRIVATION OF CONSTITUTIONAL RIGHTS: RIGHT TO TREATMENT
2. CRIMINAL LAW: MOT.TO DISM.INDICT.

HISTORY OF THE CASE:

TYPE OF COURT: FEDERAL

TRIER OF FACT: JUDGE,NO JURY

COURT DECISION(S):

TRIAL COURT: FOR PLAINTIFF
YEAR: 1973

VERDICT AGAINST WHICH DEFENDANTS:
1. FEDERAL GOV. &/OR OFFICIALS, ETC.

RECOVERY OR OTHER RELIEF GRANTED:
1. NONMONETARY RELIEF: INJ.OR OTHER EQ.REL.

274. UNIVERSITY OF LOUISVILLE V. HAMMOCK

AUDIE HAMMOCK SUED THE UNIVERSITY OF LOUISVILLE FOR INJURIES RECEIVED WHILE SHE WAS A PATIENT AT THEIR HOSPITAL. ON THE DAY AFTER HER ADMISSION A PATIENT KNOWN AS DR. MEADOR WAS ADMITTED TO THE FLOOR BELOW WITH DELERIUM TREMENS. HE WAS A VERY POWERFUL MAN OF OVER 200 POUNDS, AND WAS PUT IN THE CUSTODY OF ONE FEMALE NURSE. AT ABOUT 10 P.M. ON THE SAME DAY HE BECAME UNCONTROLLABLE, ESCAPED FROM HIS ROOM, AND WALKED THROUGH THE HALLS OF THE BUILDING TALKING IN A LOUD VOICE AND UTTERING PROFANITIES AS HE WENT. HE CAME UPON AUDIE LYING IN HER BED AND TOOK HOLD OF HER, STRIKING HER, AND DRAGGING HER FROM BED. THREE PEOPLE FINALLY CONTAINED MEADOR AND RETURNED HIM TO HIS ROOM. PLAINTIFF CHARGED THAT THE UNIVERSITY WAS NEGLIGENT IN ALLOWING MEADOR TOE BE PLACED UNDER THE CONTROL OF A SINGLE FEMALE NURSE WHEN HIS UNCONTROLLABLE AND VIOLENT NATURE WAS KNOWN.

YEAR OF NEGLIGENT ACT: NOT SPECIFIED

STATE IN WHICH NEGLIGENT ACT OCCURRED: KENTUCKY

SETTING OF THE CASE: PRIV. GEN. HOSP.

PLAINTIFF(S): PATIENT(S) OR REP.

DEFENDANT(S):
1. EDUCATIONAL INST. &/OR DEANS, ETC.

NEGLIGENT ACTIVITY:

TREATMENT: NOT APPLICABLE

DIAGNOSIS:

WHAT WAS DIAGNOSED: NOT APPLICABLE

RESULT OF DIAGNOSIS: NOT APPLICABLE

CARE:
1. INADEQUATE SUPERVISION

HARM CAUSED TO PLAINTIFF &/OR PATIENT:
1. NONSELF-INFLICTED INJURIES
2. EXACERB.OF PREV.CONDITION

TYPE OF ACTION BROUGHT:
1. NEGLIGENCE

HISTORY OF THE CASE:

TYPE OF COURT: STATE

TRIER OF FACT: JURY

COURT DECISION(S):

TRIAL COURT: FOR PLAINTIFF
YEAR: NOT SPECIFIED
SUPREME COURT: FOR PLAINTIFF
YEAR: 1907

VERDICT AGAINST WHICH DEFENDANTS:
1. EDUCATIONAL INST. &/OR DEANS, ETC.

RECOVERY OR OTHER RELIEF GRANTED:
1. $ 1000

275. VAN BARNEVELD V. STATE

NO FACTS ARE AVAILABLE IN THE REPORTED DECISION, EXCEPT THAT VAN BARNEVELD WAS KILLED AS A RESULT OF A VICIOUS ASSAULT ON HIM BY ANOTHER PATIENT AT PILGRIM STATE HOSPITAL. HIS WIFE CLAIMED THAT THE STATE WAS NEGLIGENT IN FAILING TO PROVIDE PROPER CUSTODIAL CARE AND SUPERVISION.

YEAR OF NEGLIGENT ACT: NOT SPECIFIED

STATE IN WHICH NEGLIGENT ACT OCCURRED: NEW YORK

SETTING OF THE CASE: PUB. MENT. HOSP.

PLAINTIFF(S): PATIENT(S) OR REP.

DEFENDANT(S):
1. STATE GOV. &/OR OFFICIALS, ETC.

NEGLIGENT ACTIVITY:

TREATMENT: NOT APPLICABLE

DIAGNOSIS:

WHAT WAS DIAGNOSED: NOT APPLICABLE

RESULT OF DIAGNOSIS: NOT APPLICABLE

CARE:
1. INADEQUATE SUPERVISION

HARM CAUSED TO PLAINTIFF &/OR PATIENT:
1. NONSUICIDAL DEATH

TYPE OF ACTION BROUGHT:
1. NEGLIGENCE

HISTORY OF THE CASE:

TYPE OF COURT: STATE

TRIER OF FACT: JUDGE,NO JURY

COURT DECISION(S):

TRIAL COURT: FOR PLAINTIFF
YEAR: NOT SPECIFIED
APPELLATE COURT: FOR DEFENDANT
YEAR: 1970

REASON SUIT FAILED:
1. NEGLIGENCE OR CASE NOT PROVEN

276. VASSOLO V. COUNTY OF WESTCHESTER HALCYON REST HOSPITAL

AFTER AN ASSAULT ON HIS WIFE, SILVIO PROVENZANO WAS COMMITTED TO GRASSLANDS HOSPITAL AS A PARANOID SCHIZOPHRENIC. FOLLOWING AN UNSUCCESSFUL STAY, HE WAS TRANSFERRED TO HALCYON REST AT THE REQUEST OF HIS FAMILY SO HE COULD BE CLOSER TO HOME. AFTER FOUR UNEVENTFUL MONTHS, HE WAS RELEASED. HIS WIFE HAD CONTACTED JOSEPH VASSOLO, A HARRISON, NEW YORK LAWYER, WHEN SILVIO FAILED TO SUPPORT HER ACCORDING TO A COURT ORDER SHE HAD OBTAINED UPON HIS RELEASE. VASSOLO SET AN APPOINTMENT WITH PROVENZANO TO WORK OUT THE DETAILS OF PAYMENT. AT THIS MEETING PROVENZANO APPEARED NORMAL UNTIL HE SUDDENLY JUMPED UP ON VASSOLO'S DESK, BIT OFF THE END OF HIS NOSE, AND FLED. HE WAS LATER CONVICTED OF ASSAULT AND BATTERY AND SENTENCED TO THREE YEARS IN JAIL. CONCURRENTLY, VASSOLO BROUGHT THIS SUIT AGAINST HALCYON AND ONE OF ITS PSYCHIATRISTS FOR FAILURE TO PROPERLY CONFINE AND SUPERVISE A DANGEROUS MENTAL PATIENT.

YEAR OF NEGLIGENT ACT: NOT SPECIFIED

STATE IN WHICH NEGLIGENT ACT OCCURRED: NEW YORK

SETTING OF THE CASE: PUB.&PRIV.MEN.HOSP.

PLAINTIFF(S): 3RD PARTY, II

DEFENDANT(S):
1. PSYCHIATRIST(S)
2. HOSPITAL &/OR OWNERS, ETC.

NEGLIGENT ACTIVITY:

TREATMENT: NOT APPLICABLE

DIAGNOSIS:

WHAT WAS DIAGNOSED:
1. LACK OF DANGEROUSNESS

RESULT OF DIAGNOSIS:
1. IMPROPER CUSTODIAL CARE
2. IMPROPER RELEASE

CARE:
1. INADEQUATE SUPERVISION
2. FAILURE TO PROVIDE PROPER CUSTODIAL CARE

HARM CAUSED TO PLAINTIFF &/OR PATIENT:
1. NONSELF-INFLICTED INJURIES
2. EMOTIONAL DISTRESS
3. ECONOMIC LOSS

TYPE OF ACTION BROUGHT:
1. NEGLIGENCE

HISTORY OF THE CASE:

TYPE OF COURT: STATE

TRIER OF FACT: JURY

COURT DECISION(S):

TRIAL COURT: FOR PLAINTIFF
YEAR: 1966

VERDICT AGAINST WHICH DEFENDANTS:
1. PSYCHIATRIST(S)
2. HOSPITAL &/OR OWNERS, ETC.

RECOVERY OR OTHER RELIEF GRANTED:
1. $200000

277. VISTICA V. PRESBYTERIAN HOSPITAL AND MEDICAL CENTER

WHILE AT HOME ON AUGUST 5, 1961, LORRAINE VISTICA, A PERSON OF KNOWN SCHIZOPHRENIC PERSONALITY AND SUICIDAL TENDENCIES, STABBED HERSELF IN THE CHEST. AS A RESULT SHE WAS ADMITTED INTO THE DEFENDANT HOSPITAL AND EXAMINED BY DOCTOR CARTWRIGHT. HE NOTED HER SELF-DESTRUCTIVE TENDENCIES AND WARNED THE WARD PERSONNEL OF HER DISPOSITION. SHE BECAME A NIGHT PATIENT ON SEPTEMBER 8 BUT RETURNED TO FULL-TIME STATUS ON OCTOBER 19. AGAIN DOCTOR CARTWRIGHT ORDERED HOSPITAL PERSONNEL TO TAKE PRECAUTIONS AGAINST HER SUICIDAL AND ELOPEMENT TENDENCIES. TEN DAYS LATER LORRAINE'S MOTHER CAME TO VISIT. SHE FOUND HER IN THE SOLARIUM WITH THE FURNITURE ARRANGED IN A STEPLADDER CONFIGURATION TO ALLOW HER ACCESS TO AN OPEN TRANSOM ABOVE A LOCKED WINDOW. HER MOTHER TOLD DOCTOR CARTWRIGHT ABOUT THIS, AND HE SAID HE WOULD ORDER TWENTY-FOUR HOUR SURVEILLANCE. THE NEXT DAY LORRAINE AND DOCTOR CARTWRIGHT HAD A MEETING, DURING WHICH HE ASKED HER ABOUT THE FURNITURE IN THE SOLARIUM. SHE DENIED ANY PART OF IT, BUT BECAME TENSE AND ANGRY. THAT EVENING AT DINNER, SHE WAS LEFT ALONE FOR EIGHT MINUTES, DURING WHICH TIME THE WARD NURSE RECEIVED A CALL THAT A WOMAN'S BODY WAS LYING UNDER THE SOLARIUM WINDOW. LORRAINE WAS FOUND TO BE MISSING, THE SOLARIUM FURNITURE WAS ARRANGED AS BEFORE AND LORRAINE LAY DEAD ON THE PAVEMENT BELOW.

YEAR OF NEGLIGENT ACT: 1961

STATE IN WHICH NEGLIGENT ACT OCCURRED: CALIFORNIA

SETTING OF THE CASE: PRIV. GEN. HOSP.

PLAINTIFF(S): 3RD PARTY, I

DEFENDANT(S):
1. HOSPITAL &/OR OWNERS, ETC.

NEGLIGENT ACTIVITY:

TREATMENT: NOT APPLICABLE

DIAGNOSIS:

WHAT WAS DIAGNOSED: NOT APPLICABLE

RESULT OF DIAGNOSIS: NOT APPLICABLE

CARE:
1. INADEQUATE SUPERVISION

HARM CAUSED TO PLAINTIFF &/OR PATIENT:
1. SUICIDE

TYPE OF ACTION BROUGHT:
1. NEGLIGENCE

HISTORY OF THE CASE:

TYPE OF COURT: STATE

TRIER OF FACT: JURY

COURT DECISION(S):

TRIAL COURT: FOR DEFENDANT
YEAR: NOT SPECIFIED
SUPREME COURT: NONFINAL FOR PL.
YEAR: 1967

DEFENDANTS STILL INVOLVED IN SUIT:
1. HOSPITAL &/OR OWNERS, ETC.

278. VITELLO V. STATE

ON JUNE 12, 1935 ALPHONSE VITELLO WAS SENTENCED TO A MAXIMUM TERM OF FIVE YEARS FOR ROBBERY. HE REMAINED IN THE COUNTY JAIL UNTIL HE WAS TRANSFERRED TO SING SING PRISON. ON APRIL 17, 1937 HE WAS TRANSFERRED TO DANNEMORA STATE HOSPITAL, WHERE HE REMAINED FOR THIRTY YEARS, WHEN HE WAS COMMITTED TO CENTRAL ISLIP STATE HOSPITAL. ON MAY 20, 1966, HAVING SIGNED THE PROPER FORMS, HIS HOSPITALIZATION BECAME VOLUNTARY. HE BECAME AN "HONOR" PATIENT IN DECEMBER AND WAS RELEASED THE FOLLOWING MAY. HE ALLEGED THAT HIS COMMITMENT AMOUNTED TO IMPRISONMENT AND CONSTITUTED A VIOLATION OF HIS CIVIL AND CONSTITUTIONAL RIGHTS AFTER FEBRUARY 21, 1940, WHEN HIS ORIGINAL SENTENCE EXPIRED.

YEAR OF NEGLIGENT ACT: OCCURRED OVER A SERIES OF YEARS, ENDING IN 1967

STATE IN WHICH NEGLIGENT ACT OCCURRED: NEW YORK

SETTING OF THE CASE: PUB. MENT. HOSP.

PLAINTIFF(S): PATIENT(S) OR REP.

DEFENDANT(S):
1. STATE GOV. &/OR OFFICIALS, ETC.

NEGLIGENT ACTIVITY:

TREATMENT:
1. NO TREATMENT OR INADEQUATE TREATMENT

DIAGNOSIS:

WHAT WAS DIAGNOSED:
1. INADEQUATE DIAGNOSIS

RESULT OF DIAGNOSIS:
1. IMPROPER FAILURE TO RELEASE

CARE:
1. FAILURE TO PROVIDE PROPER CUSTODIAL CARE

HARM CAUSED TO PLAINTIFF &/OR PATIENT:
1. DEPRIVATION OF CONSTITUTIONAL RIGHTS
2. LOSS OF LIBERTY

TYPE OF ACTION BROUGHT:
1. NEGLIGENCE
2. FALSE IMPRISONMENT
3. DEPRIVATION OF CONSTITUTIONAL RIGHTS: CONST.RTS.IN GEN.

HISTORY OF THE CASE:

TYPE OF COURT: STATE

TRIER OF FACT: JUDGE,NO JURY

COURT DECISION(S):

TRIAL COURT: NONFINAL FOR PL.
YEAR: 1971
APPELLATE COURT: NONFINAL FOR PL.
YEAR: 1972

DEFENDANTS STILL INVOLVED IN SUIT:
1. STATE GOV. &/OR OFFICIALS, ETC.

279. VON EYE V. HAMMES

EVELYN VON EYE, A TWENTY-SIX-YEAR-OLD WIFE AND MOTHER OF THREE, BEGAN TO SHOW SIGNS OF MENTAL ILLNESS IN JULY OF 1954. THE FOLLOWING OCTOBER SHE CONSULTED WITH DR. E. M. HAMMES, SR. AND WAS ADMITTED TO THE PSYCHIATRIC WARD OF MOUNDS PARK HOSPITAL, WHERE SHE WAS DIAGNOSED AS A PARANOID SCHIZOPHRENIC. DURING HER FIRST SEVENTEEN DAYS AT THE HOSPITAL SHE WAS COOPERATIVE AND RELATIVELY STABLE. ON NOVEMBER 4, HOWEVER, SHE BECAME HOSTILE AND DISTURBED. HER DELUSIONS OF BEING WATCHED AND PERSECUTED BEGAN TO OVERCOME HER, AND HER BEHAVIOR BECAME MORE AND MORE BIZARRE. IN AN ATTEMPT TO ESCAPE, MRS. VON EYE LEFT HER ROOM ON THE MORNING OF NOVEMBER 8 AND WALKED TO AN ADJOINING OBSTETRIC WING THROUGH AN UNLOCKED DOOR. APPARENTLY NO NURSES WERE PRESENT EITHER ON THE FLOOR OR AT THE INTERSECTION OF THE TWO WINGS TO GUARD AGAINST HER ESCAPE. SHE ENTERED THE ROOM OF A MS. GLEWWE AND CLOSED THE DOOR BEHIND HER. HER FRANTIC BEHAVIOR CAUSED GLEWWE TO LEAVE THE ROOM IN SEARCH OF A NURSE. WHEN SHE RETURNED, MRS. VON EYE WAS ON THE WAY OUT THE WINDOW. SHE THEN SUED THE HOSPITAL AND DOCTORS FOR THE INJURIES SHE SUSTAINED AND WHICH SHE ALLEGED RESULTED FROM THEIR NEGLIGENCE IN ALLOWING HER TO ESCAPE FROM HER ROOM.

YEAR OF NEGLIGENT ACT: 1954

STATE IN WHICH NEGLIGENT ACT OCCURRED: MINNESOTA

SETTING OF THE CASE: PRIV. GEN. HOSP.

PLAINTIFF(S): PATIENT(S) OR REP.

DEFENDANT(S):
1. PSYCHIATRIST(S)
2. HOSPITAL &/OR OWNERS, ETC.

NEGLIGENT ACTIVITY:

TREATMENT: NOT APPLICABLE

DIAGNOSIS:

WHAT WAS DIAGNOSED: NOT APPLICABLE

RESULT OF DIAGNOSIS: NOT APPLICABLE

CARE:
1. INADEQUATE SUPERVISION

HARM CAUSED TO PLAINTIFF &/OR PATIENT:
1. SELF-INFLICTED INJURIES

TYPE OF ACTION BROUGHT:
1. NEGLIGENCE

HISTORY OF THE CASE:

TYPE OF COURT: FEDERAL

TRIER OF FACT: JURY

COURT DECISION(S):

TRIAL COURT: FOR PLAINTIFF
YEAR: 1956
APPELLATE COURT: FOR PLAINTIFF
YEAR: 1957

VERDICT AGAINST WHICH DEFENDANTS:
1. HOSPITAL &/OR OWNERS, ETC.

RECOVERY OR OTHER RELIEF GRANTED:
1. $ 39380

280. WARNER V. PACKER

FOR THE FIRST TEN YEARS OF THEIR MARRIAGE, THE WARNERS WERE CONSIDERED A HAPPY COUPLE. ABOUT 1900, MRS. WARNER BEGAN DETERIORATING. SHE THREATENED SUICIDE AND ASSAULTED HER HUSBAND, MAKING HIM SIGN UNUSUAL NONSENSICAL AGREEMENTS. SHE WAS CONVINCED THAT HE WAS ATTEMPTING TO DRIVE HER INSANE IN ORDER TO OBTAIN HER MONEY. IN 1904 MR. WARNER ASKED DRS. PACKER AND WILGUS TO EXAMINE HIS WIFE TO SEE IF THERE WAS SOME WAY TO HELP HER. THEY FOUND HER TO BE SUFFERING FROM MENTAL ILLNESS AND HAD HER CONFINED TO AN ASYLUM. MRS. WARNER BROUGHT SUIT, ALLEGING NEGLIGENCE ON THE PART OF THE EXAMINING DOCTORS IN FINDING HER INSANE.

YEAR OF NEGLIGENT ACT: 1904

STATE IN WHICH NEGLIGENT ACT OCCURRED: NEW YORK

SETTING OF THE CASE: JUDICIAL PROCEEDING

PLAINTIFF(S): PATIENT(S) OR REP.

DEFENDANT(S):
1. NONPSYCHIAT.OR UNKNOWN TYPE PHYSICIAN(S)

NEGLIGENT ACTIVITY:

TREATMENT: NOT APPLICABLE

DIAGNOSIS:

WHAT WAS DIAGNOSED:
1. MENTAL ILLNESS, INSTEAD OF SANITY

RESULT OF DIAGNOSIS:
1. IMPROPER COMMITMENT

CARE: NOT APPLICABLE

HARM CAUSED TO PLAINTIFF &/OR PATIENT:
1. LOSS OF LIBERTY

TYPE OF ACTION BROUGHT:
1. NEGLIGENCE

HISTORY OF THE CASE:

TYPE OF COURT: STATE

TRIER OF FACT: JURY

COURT DECISION(S):

TRIAL COURT: FOR PLAINTIFF
YEAR: 1907
APPELLATE COURT: NONFINAL FOR DEF.
YEAR: 1910

DEFENDANTS STILL INVOLVED IN SUIT:
1. NONPSYCHIAT.OR UNKNOWN TYPE PHYSICIAN(S)

281. WARNER V. STATE

THE CLAIMANT WAS COMMITTED TO MARCY STATE HOSPITAL ON THE BASIS OF THE SIGNATURE OF TWO QUALIFIED EXAMINERS IN LUNACY. DURING HIS DETENTION HE WAS GIVEN THREE ELECTRO-SHOCK TREATMENTS, WHICH RESULTED IN A FRACTURE OF HIS RIGHT SHOULDER AND AN INJURY TO HIS BACK. THE PLAINTIFF ARGUED THAT HIS COMMITMENT WAS UNLAWFUL, SLANDEROUS, AND AN INVASION OF HIS PERSONAL AND CIVIL RIGHTS. HE BROUGHT SUIT AGAINST THE HOSPITAL AND THE VARIOUS PHYSICIANS INVOLVED FOR THIS ALLEGEDLY WRONGFUL COMMITMENT AND FOR THE INJURIES HE SUSTAINED DURING HIS STAY.

YEAR OF NEGLIGENT ACT: 1944

STATE IN WHICH NEGLIGENT ACT OCCURRED: NEW YORK

SETTING OF THE CASE: JUD.PCDG.&PUB.HOSP.

PLAINTIFF(S): PATIENT(S) OR REP.

DEFENDANT(S):
1. STATE GOV. &/OR OFFICIALS, ETC.

NEGLIGENT ACTIVITY:

TREATMENT:
1. NEGLIGENT ELECTROCONVULSIVE THERAPY

DIAGNOSIS:

WHAT WAS DIAGNOSED:
1. MENTAL ILLNESS, INSTEAD OF SANITY

RESULT OF DIAGNOSIS:
1. IMPROPER COMMITMENT
2. IMPROPER FAILURE TO RELEASE

CARE: NOT APPLICABLE

HARM CAUSED TO PLAINTIFF &/OR PATIENT:
1. NONSELF-INFLICTED INJURIES
2. DEPRIVATION OF CONSTITUTIONAL RIGHTS
3. LOSS OF LIBERTY
4. INJURY TO REPUTATION

TYPE OF ACTION BROUGHT:
1. NEGLIGENCE
2. FALSE IMPRISONMENT
3. DEFAMATION OF CHARACTER: SLANDER
4. DEPRIVATION OF CONSTITUTIONAL RIGHTS: CONST.RTS.IN GEN.

HISTORY OF THE CASE:

TYPE OF COURT: STATE

TRIER OF FACT: JUDGE,NO JURY

COURT DECISION(S):

TRIAL COURT: FOR PLAINTIFF
YEAR: 1947
APPELLATE COURT: FOR DEFENDANT
YEAR: 1948
SUPREME COURT: FOR PLAINTIFF
YEAR: 1948

VERDICT AGAINST WHICH DEFENDANTS:
1. STATE GOV. &/OR OFFICIALS, ETC.

RECOVERY OR OTHER RELIEF GRANTED:
1. OTHER RECOVERY: TO BE DETERM.ON RETR

282. WEGLARZ V. STATE

ON NOVEMBER 21, 1963, POLICE FOUND THEODORE WEGLARZ IN THE NUDE YELLING AT PASSERS-BY FROM HIS BACKYARD. THEY TOOK HIM TO KINGS COUNTY HOSPITAL, FROM WHERE HE WAS COMMITTED TO PILGRIM STATE HOSPITAL AS A MENTALLY ILL PERSON ON DECEMBER 4. HE WAS PLACED ON A CLOSED WARD UNTIL JANUARY 6, 1964, WHEN HE WAS TRANSFERRED TO AN OPEN WARD. ON OR ABOUT JANUARY 13, 1964 HE DISAPPEARED. HIS BODY WAS FOUND ON MAY 11 IN A WOODED AREA ON THE HOSPITAL GROUNDS. THE AUTOPSY INDICATED SUICIDAL HANGING, AND PLAINTIFF BROUGHT SUIT FOR IMPROPER SUPERVISION, CARE, AND SURVEILLANCE.

YEAR OF NEGLIGENT ACT: 1964

STATE IN WHICH NEGLIGENT ACT OCCURRED: NEW YORK

SETTING OF THE CASE: PUB. MENT. HOSP.

PLAINTIFF(S): PATIENT(S) OR REP.

DEFENDANT(S):
1. STATE GOV. &/OR OFFICIALS, ETC.

NEGLIGENT ACTIVITY:

TREATMENT: NOT APPLICABLE

DIAGNOSIS:

WHAT WAS DIAGNOSED:
1. SANITY, INSTEAD OF MENTAL ILLNESS
2. LACK OF SUICIDAL TENDENCIES

RESULT OF DIAGNOSIS:
1. IMPROPER CUSTODIAL CARE

CARE: NOT APPLICABLE

HARM CAUSED TO PLAINTIFF &/OR PATIENT:
1. SUICIDE

TYPE OF ACTION BROUGHT:
1. NEGLIGENCE

HISTORY OF THE CASE:

TYPE OF COURT: STATE

TRIER OF FACT: JUDGE,NO JURY

COURT DECISION(S):

TRIAL COURT: FOR DEFENDANT
YEAR: NOT SPECIFIED
APPELLATE COURT: FOR DEFENDANT
YEAR: 1968

REASON SUIT FAILED:
1. DEFENDANT(S) CANNOT BE SUED DUE TO: GOVERN. IMMUNITY

283. WEIHS V. STATE

EDWARD BROWNING, AN INMATE OF KINGS PARK STATE HOSPITAL AND CONFINED TO WARD 16 FOR THE "WORST MALE INMATES," ESCAPED ON JULY 27, 1940 IN THE EARLY AFTERNOON. ABOUT THIS TIME MRS. WEIHS AND HER FOUR CHILDREN WERE WALKING NEAR THE HOSPITAL. SHE WAS APPROACHED FROM THE REAR AND STABBED TWICE IN THE BACK WITH A FOOT-LONG BUTCHER KNIFE. ALTHOUGH BROWNING ADMITTED HAVING A KNIFE AND BEING IN THE AREA AT THE TIME OF THE ASSAULT, HE DENIED THE ATTACK ON THE PLAINTIFF. HER INITIAL INABILITY TO IDENTIFY BROWNING SUGGESTED THAT HE MIGHT BE INNOCENT, BUT BOTH PLAINTIFF AND HER DAUGHTER WERE LATER ABLE TO IDENTIFY HIM. SHE BROUGHT SUIT AGAINST THE STATE FOR NEGLIGENCE IN ALLOWING BROWNING TO HAVE ACCESS TO A KNIFE ON HOSPITAL PROPERTY AND IN ALLOWING HIM TO ESCAPE.

YEAR OF NEGLIGENT ACT: 1940

STATE IN WHICH NEGLIGENT ACT OCCURRED: NEW YORK

SETTING OF THE CASE: PUB. MENT. HOSP.

PLAINTIFF(S): 3RD PARTY, II

DEFENDANT(S):
1. STATE GOV. &/OR OFFICIALS, ETC.

NEGLIGENT ACTIVITY:

TREATMENT: NOT APPLICABLE

DIAGNOSIS:

WHAT WAS DIAGNOSED: NOT APPLICABLE

RESULT OF DIAGNOSIS: NOT APPLICABLE

CARE:
1. INADEQUATE SUPERVISION

HARM CAUSED TO PLAINTIFF &/OR PATIENT:
1. NONSELF-INFLICTED INJURIES
2. EMOTIONAL DISTRESS

TYPE OF ACTION BROUGHT:
1. NEGLIGENCE

HISTORY OF THE CASE:

TYPE OF COURT: STATE

TRIER OF FACT: JUDGE,NO JURY

COURT DECISION(S):

TRIAL COURT: FOR PLAINTIFF
YEAR: 1943
APPELLATE COURT: FOR PLAINTIFF
YEAR: 1943

VERDICT AGAINST WHICH DEFENDANTS:
1. STATE GOV. &/OR OFFICIALS, ETC.

RECOVERY OR OTHER RELIEF GRANTED:
1. $ 1500

284. WEINSHENK V. KAISER FOUNDATION HOSPITALS

IN THIS NEGLIGENCE ACTION A PSYCHIATRIC RESIDENT EXAMINED WEINSHENK IN AN EMERGENCY ROOM AND DIAGNOSED HIM AS SUFFERING FROM VIRAL SORE THROAT AND HYSTERICAL REACTIONS. WEINSHENK TURNED OUT TO HAVE A STAPHYLOCOUCCAL INFECTION, WHICH CAUSED HIS DEATH. HIS FAMILY BROUGHT SUIT AGAINST THE HOSPITAL IN THE CALIFORNIA SUPERIOR COURT FOR NEGLIGENT DIAGNOSIS.

YEAR OF NEGLIGENT ACT: NOT SPECIFIED

STATE IN WHICH NEGLIGENT ACT OCCURRED: CALIFORNIA

SETTING OF THE CASE: PRIV. GEN. HOSP.

PLAINTIFF(S): 3RD PARTY, I

DEFENDANT(S):
1. SOME OR ALL DEFENDANTS NOT SPECIFIED
2. HOSPITAL &/OR OWNERS, ETC.

NEGLIGENT ACTIVITY:

TREATMENT: NOT APPLICABLE

DIAGNOSIS:

WHAT WAS DIAGNOSED:
1. MENT.ILL, INSTEAD OF PHYSICAL ILLNESS

RESULT OF DIAGNOSIS:
1. IMPROPER TREATMENT PRESCRIBED

CARE: NOT APPLICABLE

HARM CAUSED TO PLAINTIFF &/OR PATIENT:
1. NONSUICIDAL DEATH

TYPE OF ACTION BROUGHT:
1. NEGLIGENCE

HISTORY OF THE CASE:

TYPE OF COURT: STATE

TRIER OF FACT: ?, JUDGE OR JURY

COURT DECISION(S):

TRIAL COURT: FOR PLAINTIFF
YEAR: 1970

VERDICT AGAINST WHICH DEFENDANTS:
1. HOSPITAL &/OR OWNERS, ETC.

RECOVERY OR OTHER RELIEF GRANTED:
1. $250000

285. WELSCH V. LIKINS

A CLASS ACTION SUIT WAS BROUGHT BY SIX RETARDED PATIENTS OF VARIOUS MINNESOTA MENTAL HOSPITALS SEEKING DECLARATORY AND INJUNCTIVE RELIEF REGARDING THEIR RIGHT TO TREATMENT, IMPROVED CONDITIONS, AND ALTERNATIVE PLACEMENT FOR THEMSELVES AND ALL OTHERS SIMILARLY SITUATED. THE DEFENDANTS WERE PUBLIC OFFICIALS RESPONSIBLE FOR THE CARE AND CONDITIONS OF THE PLAINTIFFS. THE CONDITIONS COMPLAINED ABOUT INCLUDED THE EXCESSIVE USE OF SECLUSION, PHYSICAL RESTRAINTS, AND TRANQUILIZERS.

YEAR OF NEGLIGENT ACT: OCCURRED OVER A SERIES OF YEARS, ENDING IN 1971

STATE IN WHICH NEGLIGENT ACT OCCURRED: MINNESOTA

SETTING OF THE CASE: PUB. MENT. HOSP.

PLAINTIFF(S): PATIENT(S) OR REP.

DEFENDANT(S):
1. HOSPITAL &/OR OWNERS, ETC.
2. STATE GOV. &/OR OFFICIALS, ETC.

NEGLIGENT ACTIVITY:

TREATMENT:
1. NO TREATMENT OR INADEQUATE TREATMENT
2. NEG.ADMIN.OF DRUGS

DIAGNOSIS:

WHAT WAS DIAGNOSED: NOT APPLICABLE

RESULT OF DIAGNOSIS: NOT APPLICABLE

CARE:
1. FAILURE TO PROVIDE PROPER CUSTODIAL CARE

HARM CAUSED TO PLAINTIFF &/OR PATIENT:
1. DEPRIVATION OF CONSTITUTIONAL RIGHTS
2. LOSS OF LIBERTY

TYPE OF ACTION BROUGHT:
1. NEGLIGENCE
2. DEPRIVATION OF CONSTITUTIONAL RIGHTS: CONST.RTS.IN GEN.
3. NONMONETARY RELIEF
4. OTHER ACTION, EXCLUDING TORT LAW: CLASS ACTION SUIT

HISTORY OF THE CASE:

TYPE OF COURT: STATE

TRIER OF FACT: JUDGE,NO JURY

COURT DECISION(S):

TRIAL COURT: FOR PLAINTIFF
YEAR: 1974

VERDICT AGAINST WHICH DEFENDANTS:
1. HOSPITAL &/OR OWNERS, ETC.
2. STATE GOV. &/OR OFFICIALS, ETC.

RECOVERY OR OTHER RELIEF GRANTED:
1. NONMONETARY RELIEF: INJ.OR OTHER EQ.REL.

286. WENDOVER V. STATE

IN MAY OF 1963, CAROL ANN WENDOVER WAS ADMITTED TO THE HUDSON RIVER STATE HOSPITAL AT THE AGE OF SEVENTEEN AS A RESULT OF AN ATTEMPT TO SLASH HER WRISTS. ASIDE FROM HER MENTAL ILLNESS, SHE SUFFERED FROM A CONVULSIVE DISORDER WHICH WAS NOTED AND CONTROLLED THROUGH MEDICATION. EXCEPT FOR A TWO-MONTH STAY AT HOME, SHE WAS HOSPITALIZED CONTINUOUSLY. IN THE EARLY HOURS OF JANUARY 23, 1964, CAROL ANN WAS QUITE RESTLESS AND WAS, THEREFORE, CONSTANTLY CHECKED. AT 6:10 A.M. SHE SUFFERED A SEIZURE AND WAS FOUND WITH HER HEAD ON THE WINDOW SILL AND HER BODY OVER THE RADIATOR, WHICH WAS BURNING A PART OF HER BACK. A NURSE ATTEMPTED TO PULL HER OFF THE RADIATOR BUT CAROL ANN'S GREAT WEIGHT CAUSED HER TO SLIDE BETWEEN THE BED AND RADIATOR SO THAT MOST OF HER BACK AND ARMS WERE BEING BURNED. THE DIFFICULTY OF THE TASK WAS COMPOUNDED BECAUSE THE PATIENT HAD WET THE FLOOR AND TRACTION WAS AT A MINIMUM. OTHER NURSES WERE FINALLY ABLE TO PULL HER FROM THE RADIATOR, BUT SHE SUSTAINED SERIOUS BURNS, WHICH EVENTUALLY REQUIRED SKIN GRAFTING. PLAINTIFF SUED THE STATE FOR THESE PERMANENT INJURIES.

YEAR OF NEGLIGENT ACT: 1964

STATE IN WHICH NEGLIGENT ACT OCCURRED: NEW YORK

SETTING OF THE CASE: PUB. MENT. HOSP.

PLAINTIFF(S): PATIENT(S) OR REP.

DEFENDANT(S):
1. STATE GOV. &/OR OFFICIALS, ETC.

NEGLIGENT ACTIVITY:

TREATMENT: NOT APPLICABLE

DIAGNOSIS:

WHAT WAS DIAGNOSED: NOT APPLICABLE

RESULT OF DIAGNOSIS: NOT APPLICABLE

CARE:
1. INADEQUATE SUPERVISION

HARM CAUSED TO PLAINTIFF &/OR PATIENT:
1. NONSELF-INFLICTED INJURIES

TYPE OF ACTION BROUGHT:
1. NEGLIGENCE

HISTORY OF THE CASE:

TYPE OF COURT: STATE

TRIER OF FACT: JUDGE,NO JURY

COURT DECISION(S):

TRIAL COURT: FOR DEFENDANT
YEAR: 1970

REASON SUIT FAILED:
1. NEGLIGENCE OR CASE NOT PROVEN
2. DEFENDANT(S) CANNOT BE SUED DUE TO: GOVERN. IMMUNITY

287. WHALEY V. KIRBY

ON MAY 25, 1957, CLARENCE E. WHALEY STOOD ON A SIDEWALK AT 5TH AND BROADWAY IN SAN DIEGO WITH A SIGN PROTESTING THE DENIAL OF HIS CALIFORNIA DRIVERS INSTRUCTOR'S LICENSE. ON THIS SIGN WERE SLANDEROUS STATEMENTS AGAINST PEOPLE IN THE GOVERNMENT AND AN IMPUTATION OF UNCHASTITY AND WANTON SEXUAL ACTIVITY INVOLVING A YOUNG LADY EMPLOYEE OF THE DEPARTMENT OF MOTOR VEHICLES, STATING THAT SHE WAS INFECTED WITH A LOATHSOME VENEREAL DISEASE. OFFICER KIRBY AND OTHER OFFICERS PICKED WHALEY UP AND TOOK HIM TO A PSYCHIATRIC WARD. UPON ARRIVING AT THE HOSPITAL, WHALEY PUNCHED ONE OF THE OFFICERS IN THE FACE AND WAS STRAPPED DOWN FOR SOME HOURS. DRS. WIEND AND LENGYEL WERE INSTRUMENTAL IN HIS COMMITMENT TO PATTON STATE HOSPITAL. WHALEY SUED KIRBY AND THE PSYCHIATRISTS FOR FALSE IMPRISONMENT AND VIOLATION OF HIS CONSTITUTIONAL RIGHTS.

YEAR OF NEGLIGENT ACT: 1957

STATE IN WHICH NEGLIGENT ACT OCCURRED: CALIFORNIA

SETTING OF THE CASE: JUDICIAL PROCEEDING

PLAINTIFF(S): PATIENT(S) OR REP.

DEFENDANT(S):
1. NONPSYCHIAT.OR UNKNOWN TYPE PHYSICIAN(S)
2. JUDICIARY &/OR CLERKS, ETC.
3. POLICE

NEGLIGENT ACTIVITY:

TREATMENT: NOT APPLICABLE

DIAGNOSIS:

WHAT WAS DIAGNOSED:
1. MENTAL ILLNESS, INSTEAD OF SANITY

RESULT OF DIAGNOSIS:
1. IMPROPER COMMITMENT

CARE: NOT APPLICABLE

HARM CAUSED TO PLAINTIFF &/OR PATIENT:
1. DEPRIVATION OF CONSTITUTIONAL RIGHTS
2. LOSS OF LIBERTY

TYPE OF ACTION BROUGHT:
1. NEGLIGENCE
2. FALSE IMPRISONMENT
3. DEPRIVATION OF CONSTITUTIONAL RIGHTS: CONST.RTS.IN GEN.

HISTORY OF THE CASE:

TYPE OF COURT: STATE

TRIER OF FACT: JUDGE;JURY PRESENT ?

COURT DECISION(S):

TRIAL COURT: FOR DEFENDANT
YEAR: NOT SPECIFIED
APPELLATE COURT: FOR DEFENDANT
YEAR: 1962

REASON SUIT FAILED:
1. NO CAUSE OF ACTION STATED

288. WHITE V. UNITED STATES

WITH A LONG HISTORY OF SUICIDE ATTEMPTS AND SIX PREVIOUS HOSPITALIZATIONS SINCE 1948, DONALD MEEKS WAS TRANSFERRED TO ROANOKE VETERANS HOSPITAL ON AUGUST 27, 1959. HE WAS IMMEDIATELY PLACED ON OBSERVATION STATUS AND ON SEPTEMBER 15, TRANSFERRED TO PRIVILEGED STATUS, FOLLOWING A DECISION BY TWO DOCTORS. ON FRIDAY, OCTOBER 9, MEEKS CALLED DR. PARKS AND TOLD HIM HE WAS TENSE AND AFRAID AND REQUESTED TO BE ANCHORED TO HIS BED. DR. PARKS, UNAWARE OF HIS PAST SUICIDAL HISTORY, KEPT HIM ON PRIVILEGED STATUS AND INCREASED THE DOSAGE OF HIS TRANQUILIZERS. HE STATED THAT MEEKS DID NOT EXHIBIT SUICIDAL TENDENCIES. ON THE MORNING OF OCTOBER 10, MEEKS MET WITH DR. CROWGEY AND TOLD HIM OF HIS TENSENESS AND FEARS. CROWGEY ALSO ORDERED MORE SEDATIVES, BEING UNAWARE OF MEEKS'S SUICIDAL HISTORY. LATER THAT AFTERNOON MEEKS WAS FOUND ON THE RAILROAD TRACKS NEAR THE HOSPITAL, DEAD FROM INJURIES SUFFERED FROM BEING HIT BY A TRAIN. THE ADMINISTRATOR OF HIS ESTATE BROUGHT SUIT ALLEGING THAT THE V.A. HOSPITAL FAILED TO EXERCISE THE DEGREE OF CARE APPROPRIATE TO MEEKS'S MENTAL CONDITION.

YEAR OF NEGLIGENT ACT: 1959

STATE IN WHICH NEGLIGENT ACT OCCURRED: VIRGINIA

SETTING OF THE CASE: PUB. GEN. HOSP.

PLAINTIFF(S): PATIENT(S) OR REP.

DEFENDANT(S):
1. FEDERAL GOV. &/OR OFFICIALS, ETC.

NEGLIGENT ACTIVITY:

TREATMENT: NOT APPLICABLE

DIAGNOSIS:

WHAT WAS DIAGNOSED:
1. LACK OF SUICIDAL TENDENCIES

RESULT OF DIAGNOSIS:
1. IMPROPER TREATMENT PRESCRIBED
2. IMPROPER DRUG PRESCRIPTION

CARE: NOT APPLICABLE

HARM CAUSED TO PLAINTIFF &/OR PATIENT:
1. SUICIDE

TYPE OF ACTION BROUGHT:
1. NEGLIGENCE

HISTORY OF THE CASE:

TYPE OF COURT: FEDERAL

TRIER OF FACT: JUDGE;JURY PRESENT ?

COURT DECISION(S):

TRIAL COURT: FOR DEFENDANT
YEAR: NOT SPECIFIED
APPELLATE COURT: NONFINAL FOR PL.
YEAR: 1963
ON RETRIAL: FOR DEFENDANT
YEAR: 1965
ON REAPPEAL TO APPELLATE COURT: FOR DEFENDANT
YEAR: 1966

REASON SUIT FAILED:
1. NEGLIGENCE OR CASE NOT PROVEN

289. WHITESELL V. GREEN

THE PLAINTIFF, WHITESELL, AND HIS WIFE, CONSULTED A PSYCHOLOGIST FOR MARITAL COUNSELING. ONLY TWO WEEKS AFTER COUNSELING HAD ENDED THE PSYCHOLOGIST HAD AN AFFAIR WITH THE PLAINTIFF'S WIFE. WHITESELL CLAIMED THAT THIS CONSTITUTED A BREACH OF RESPONSIBILITY, WHILE THE PSYCHOLOGIST ARGUED THAT NO PROFESSIONAL RELATIONSHIP EXISTED AT THE TIME OF THE AFFAIR. THE JURY AWARDED WHITESELL $8,000 IN GENERAL DAMAGES AND $10,000 IN PUNITIVE DAMAGES.

YEAR OF NEGLIGENT ACT: NOT SPECIFIED

STATE IN WHICH NEGLIGENT ACT OCCURRED: HAWAII

SETTING OF THE CASE: PRIVATE PRACTICE

PLAINTIFF(S): 3RD PARTY, I

DEFENDANT(S):
1. PSYCHOLOGIST(S)

NEGLIGENT ACTIVITY:

TREATMENT:
1. SEXUAL ABUSE OR DISTURB.OF MARITAL REL.

DIAGNOSIS:

WHAT WAS DIAGNOSED: NOT APPLICABLE

RESULT OF DIAGNOSIS: NOT APPLICABLE

CARE: NOT APPLICABLE

HARM CAUSED TO PLAINTIFF &/OR PATIENT:
1. SEXUAL OR MARITAL HARM
2. LOSS OF CONSORTIUM
3. ALIENATION OF AFFECTION

TYPE OF ACTION BROUGHT:
1. NEGLIGENCE

HISTORY OF THE CASE:

TYPE OF COURT: STATE

TRIER OF FACT: JURY

COURT DECISION(S):

TRIAL COURT: FOR PLAINTIFF
YEAR: 1973

VERDICT AGAINST WHICH DEFENDANTS:
1. PSYCHOLOGIST(S)

RECOVERY OR OTHER RELIEF GRANTED:
1. $ 18000

290. WHITREE V. STATE

VICTOR WHITREE WAS ARRESTED ON MARCH 25, 1945, FOR STABBING ONE JOHN O'CONNOR IN NEW YORK CITY. HE WAS RELEASED ON BAIL ON APRIL 13, AND APPEARED IN COURT ON EIGHTEEN DIFFERENT OCCASIONS WITH A PLEA OF NOT GUILTY OF SECOND-DEGREE ASSAULT. ON NOVEMBER 15, 1946, HE FINALLY PLEADED GUILTY TO THIRD-DEGREE ASSAULT BECAUSE HE COULD NO LONGER AFFORD THE LAWYER OR LOSS OF TIME FROM WORK. HE WAS GIVEN A SUSPENDED SENTENCE ON DECEMBER 6 AND PLACED ON PROBATION. HE VIOLATED HIS PROBATION ON APRIL 7, 1947 AND WAS TAKEN INTO CUSTODY AND ORDERED TO BELLEVUE HOSPITAL FOR FORMAL PSYCHIATRIC EXAMINATION. HE WAS REPORTED INSANE BY AN EXAMINATION ON APRIL 29, AND ON MAY 15 WAS COMMITTED TO MATTEAWAN STATE HOSPITAL. THE LONGEST LEGAL EXTENT OF HIS CRIMINAL CONFINEMENT WOULD HAVE BEEN UNTIL MAY 19, 1949, BUT HE REMAINED AT MATTEAWAN FOR AN ADDITIONAL TWELVE YEARS AND FOUR MONTHS, IN SPITE OF FOURTEEN WRITS OF HABEAS CORPUS. DURING HIS CONFINEMENT AND ON NUMEROUS OCCASIONS HE WAS SUBJECTED TO BEATINGS, HAD HOT COFFEE POURED OVER HIM, WAS KICKED IN THE FACE, AND WAS EVEN BEATEN BY ATTENDANTS. AS A RESULT OF THIS TREATMENT HE SUSTAINED NUMEROUS FRACTURES AND FIRST-DEGREE BURNS, HAD RECURRING HEADACHES, DEVELOPED AN OSTEOARTHRITIC CONDITION, AND LOST SEVERAL OF HIS TEETH. HE CHARGED THE STATE WITH WRONGFUL INCARCERATION AND NEGLIGENCE AND SOUGHT DAMAGES FOR HIS LONG AND HARMFUL CONFINEMENT.

YEAR OF NEGLIGENT ACT: OCCURRED OVER A SERIES OF YEARS, ENDING IN 1961

STATE IN WHICH NEGLIGENT ACT OCCURRED: NEW YORK

SETTING OF THE CASE: PUB. MENT. HOSP.

PLAINTIFF(S): PATIENT(S) OR REP.

DEFENDANT(S):
1. STATE GOV. &/OR OFFICIALS, ETC.

NEGLIGENT ACTIVITY:

TREATMENT:
1. PHYSICAL ASSAULT
2. NO TREATMENT OR INADEQUATE TREATMENT
3. NEG.ADMIN.OF DRUGS

DIAGNOSIS:

WHAT WAS DIAGNOSED:
1. MENTAL ILLNESS, INSTEAD OF SANITY

RESULT OF DIAGNOSIS:
1. IMPROPER TREATMENT PRESCRIBED
2. IMPROPER DRUG PRESCRIPTION
3. IMPROPER FAILURE TO RELEASE

CARE:
1. FAILURE TO PROVIDE PROPER CUSTODIAL CARE

HARM CAUSED TO PLAINTIFF &/OR PATIENT:
1. NONSELF-INFLICTED INJURIES
2. EMOTIONAL DISTRESS
3. EXACERB.OF PREV.CONDITION
4. ECONOMIC LOSS

TYPE OF ACTION BROUGHT:
1. NEGLIGENCE

HISTORY OF THE CASE:

TYPE OF COURT: STATE

TRIER OF FACT: JUDGE,NO JURY

COURT DECISION(S):

TRIAL COURT: FOR PLAINTIFF
YEAR: 1968

VERDICT AGAINST WHICH DEFENDANTS:
1. STATE GOV. &/OR OFFICIALS, ETC.

RECOVERY OR OTHER RELIEF GRANTED:
1. $300000

291. WILLIAMS V. LE BAR

NO PARTICULARS ARE AVAILABLE IN THE REPORTED CASE EXCEPT THAT WILLIAMS BROUGHT AN ACTION AGAINST THE DOCTORS WHO CERTIFIED HIM OR HER AS INSANE. THE JUDGE FOUND THAT WILLIAMS WAS SANE AND THE DOCTORS WERE MISTAKEN, BUT HE ALSO FOUND THAT THE DOCTORS WERE NOT LIABLE FOR THEIR MISTAKES IN DIAGNOSING A "MYSTERIOUS DISEASE LIKE INSANITY."

YEAR OF NEGLIGENT ACT: NOT SPECIFIED

STATE IN WHICH NEGLIGENT ACT OCCURRED: PENNSYLVANIA

SETTING OF THE CASE: JUDICIAL PROCEEDING

PLAINTIFF(S): PATIENT(S) OR REP.

DEFENDANT(S):
1. NONPSYCHIAT.OR UNKNOWN TYPE PHYSICIAN(S)

NEGLIGENT ACTIVITY:

TREATMENT: NOT APPLICABLE

DIAGNOSIS:

WHAT WAS DIAGNOSED:
1. MENTAL ILLNESS, INSTEAD OF SANITY

RESULT OF DIAGNOSIS:
1. IMPROPER COMMITMENT

CARE: NOT APPLICABLE

HARM CAUSED TO PLAINTIFF &/OR PATIENT:
1. LOSS OF LIBERTY

TYPE OF ACTION BROUGHT:
1. NEGLIGENCE

HISTORY OF THE CASE:

TYPE OF COURT: STATE

TRIER OF FACT: JUDGE,NO JURY

COURT DECISION(S):

TRIAL COURT: FOR DEFENDANT
YEAR: NOT SPECIFIED
SUPREME COURT: FOR DEFENDANT
YEAR: 1891

REASON SUIT FAILED:
1. NEGLIGENCE OR CASE NOT PROVEN

292. WILLIAMS V. STATE

LORENE WILLIAMS WAS RAPED WHILE A PATIENT AT MANHATTAN STATE HOSPITAL AND GAVE BIRTH TO CHRISTINE. NO DETAILS ARE PROVIDED AS TO HOW THIS HAPPENED, BUT FRANK WILLIAMS BROUGHT SUIT AGAINST THE STATE ON BEHALF OF HIS WIFE FOR THE NEGLIGENT CARE AND PROTECTION SHE WAS GIVEN WHILE IN THE HOSPITAL. HE ALSO BROUGHT SUIT ON BEHALF OF CHRISTINE FOR "BEING CONCEIVED, BEING BORN, AND BEING BORN OUT OF WEDLOCK TO A MENTALLY DEFICIENT MOTHER," AND FOR BEING "DEPRIVED OF PROPERTY RIGHTS; DEPRIVED OF A NORMAL CHILDHOOD AND HOME LIFE; DEPRIVED OF PROPER PARENTAL CARE, SUPPORT AND REARING; CAUSED TO BEAR THE STIGMA OF ILLEGITIMACY AND (IN BEING OTHERWISE) GREATLY INJURED."

YEAR OF NEGLIGENT ACT: NOT SPECIFIED

STATE IN WHICH NEGLIGENT ACT OCCURRED: NEW YORK

SETTING OF THE CASE: PUB. MENT. HOSP.

PLAINTIFF(S): PAT. & 3RD PTY., I

DEFENDANT(S):
1. STATE GOV. &/OR OFFICIALS, ETC.

NEGLIGENT ACTIVITY:

TREATMENT: NOT APPLICABLE

DIAGNOSIS:

WHAT WAS DIAGNOSED: NOT APPLICABLE

RESULT OF DIAGNOSIS: NOT APPLICABLE

CARE:
1. INADEQUATE SUPERVISION
2. FAILURE TO PROVIDE PROPER CUSTODIAL CARE

HARM CAUSED TO PLAINTIFF &/OR PATIENT:
1. ECONOMIC LOSS
2. SEXUAL OR MARITAL HARM
3. INJURY TO REPUTATION
4. PREGNANCY

TYPE OF ACTION BROUGHT:
1. NEGLIGENCE

HISTORY OF THE CASE:

TYPE OF COURT: STATE

TRIER OF FACT: JUDGE,NO JURY

COURT DECISION(S):

TRIAL COURT: NONFINAL FOR PL.
YEAR: 1965
APPELLATE COURT: FOR DEFENDANT
YEAR: 1966
SUPREME COURT: FOR DEFENDANT
YEAR: 1966

REASON SUIT FAILED:
1. NO CAUSE OF ACTION STATED

293. WILLIS V. WESTERN HOSPITAL ASSOCIATION

CHARLEY WILLIS SEVERELY MANGLED HIS LEG ON OCTOBER 23, 1944. THE FORTY TO FIFTY-MILE RIDE TO OROFINO HOSPITAL WAS EXTREMELY PAINFUL FOR HIM AND HE REQUIRED IMMEDIATE ATTENTION ONCE AT THE HOSPITAL. HIS LEG HAD TO BE AMPUTATED AND THE OPERATION APPEARED TO BE SUCCESSFUL. THE NEXT DAY HE WAS SOMEWHAT COHERENT, UNDERSTOOD THE OPERATION AND THE NEED FOR AMPUTATION OF HIS LEG, AND SEEMED TO BE PROGRESSING. THE NEXT DAY, HOWEVER, HE BECAME RESTLESS, AND VOMITED ON SEVERAL OCCASIONS. HIS BROTHER FELT HE WAS NOT RECEIVING PROPER CARE. THE DOCTORS INFORMED HIS BROTHER THAT CHARLEY WOULD HAVE TO BE MOVED TO STATE HOSPITAL NORTH BECAUSE HE WAS MAKING TOO MUCH NOISE. ON THE ADVICE OF THE DEFENDANT DOCTORS, ESTHER SCHMIEL, A NURSE, SWORE TO AN INSANITY COMPLAINT, AND CHARLEY WAS TRANSFERRED. SHORTLY THEREAFTER HE DIED. HIS FAMILY BROUGHT SUIT AGAINST THE HOSPITAL FOR MEDICAL MALPRACTICE AND IMPROPER SURGERY, CARE, AND MOVEMENT OF THE PATIENT.

YEAR OF NEGLIGENT ACT: 1944

STATE IN WHICH NEGLIGENT ACT OCCURRED: IDAHO

SETTING OF THE CASE: JUD.PCDG.&PUB.HOSP.

PLAINTIFF(S): PATIENT(S) OR REP.

DEFENDANT(S):
1. NONPSYCHIAT.OR UNKNOWN TYPE PHYSICIAN(S)
2. HOSPITAL &/OR OWNERS, ETC.
3. NURSE(S)

NEGLIGENT ACTIVITY:

TREATMENT:
1. NEGLIGENT OPERATION

DIAGNOSIS:

WHAT WAS DIAGNOSED:
1. MENTAL ILLNESS, INSTEAD OF SANITY

RESULT OF DIAGNOSIS:
1. IMPROPER CUSTODIAL CARE
2. IMPROPER COMMITMENT

CARE:
1. FAILURE TO PROVIDE PROPER CUSTODIAL CARE

HARM CAUSED TO PLAINTIFF &/OR PATIENT:
1. NONSUICIDAL DEATH
2. EXACERB.OF PREV.CONDITION

TYPE OF ACTION BROUGHT:
1. NEGLIGENCE
2. CONTRACT LAW: BREACH OF CONTRACT

HISTORY OF THE CASE:

TYPE OF COURT: STATE

TRIER OF FACT: JUDGE,UNINV.JURY

COURT DECISION(S):

TRIAL COURT: FOR DEFENDANT
YEAR: NOT SPECIFIED
SUPREME COURT: FOR DEFENDANT
YEAR: 1947

REASON SUIT FAILED:
1. NEGLIGENCE OR CASE NOT PROVEN

294. WILSON V. LEHMAN

EXIE WILSON HAD, FOR MANY YEARS, SUFFERED FROM AMNESIA, WHICH REQUIRED REGULAR MEDICAL ATTENTION. SHE ALSO HAD DEPRESSIVE STATES BUT REFUSED PSYCHIATRIC HELP. FOLLOWING HER MOST RECENT HOSPITALIZATION IN APRIL OF 1960, DR. PEDIGO AGAIN SUGGESTED SHOCK TREATMENT, WHICH SHE AGAIN REFUSED, BUT SAID SHE WOULD DO IT IF SHE DID "NOT DO WELL." THE APPELLANT REENTERED THE HOSPITAL ON MAY 30 SAYING SHE WAS WILLING TO TRY ELECTRO-SHOCK THERAPY IF SHE COULD REMAIN ON THE MEDICAL FLOOR AND HAVE SOME SEDATIVES FOR HER PRETREATMENT ANXIETIES. DR. KASEY AGREED AND ADMINISTERED FIVE TREATMENTS AND SAID SHE NEEDED THREE OR FOUR MORE. DR. KASEY THEN WENT ON VACATION AND DR. LEHMAN TOOK CHARGE. HE MOVED HER TO THE PSYCHIATRIC FLOOR, GAVE HER SIX TREATMENTS AND DISCHARGED HER AT THE END OF JUNE. MRS. WILSON REMEMBERED NOTHING OF HER STAY IN THE HOSPITAL AND HER HUSBAND DID NOT GIVE CONSENT TO THE SHOCK TREATMENTS, ALTHOUGH HE DID NOTHING TO STOP THEM WHEN HE FOUND OUT. MRS. WILSON BROUGHT SUIT AGAINST DR. LEHMAN AND OTHERS FOR ADMINISTERING THESE TREATMENTS WITHOUT HER CONSENT.

YEAR OF NEGLIGENT ACT: 1960

STATE IN WHICH NEGLIGENT ACT OCCURRED: KENTUCKY

SETTING OF THE CASE: PRIV. GEN. HOSP.

PLAINTIFF(S): PATIENT(S) OR REP.

DEFENDANT(S):
1. PSYCHIATRIST(S)

NEGLIGENT ACTIVITY:

TREATMENT:
1. NEGLIGENT ELECTROCONVULSIVE THERAPY
2. FAILURE TO OBTAIN -OR LACK OF- CONSENT

DIAGNOSIS:

WHAT WAS DIAGNOSED: NOT APPLICABLE

RESULT OF DIAGNOSIS: NOT APPLICABLE

CARE: NOT APPLICABLE

HARM CAUSED TO PLAINTIFF &/OR PATIENT:
1. NONSELF-INFLICTED INJURIES

TYPE OF ACTION BROUGHT:
1. NEGLIGENCE

HISTORY OF THE CASE:

TYPE OF COURT: STATE

TRIER OF FACT: JUDGE,UNINV.JURY

COURT DECISION(S):

TRIAL COURT: FOR DEFENDANT
YEAR: NOT SPECIFIED
SUPREME COURT: FOR DEFENDANT
YEAR: 1964

REASON SUIT FAILED:
1. PATIENT HAD GIVEN INFORMED CONSENT

295. WOOD V. SAMARITAN INSTITUTION

FLORENCE WOOD HAD BEEN AN ALCOHOLIC FOR MANY YEARS, AND ON JANUARY 5, 1943 VOLUNTARILY ENTERED THE SAMARITAN INSTITUTION, WHICH WAS SPECIFICALLY FOCUSED ON THE CURE OF CHRONIC ALCOHOLISM. SHORTLY AFTER MIDNIGHT ON THE NEXT DAY, SHE WAS FOUND ON THE PAVEMENT BELOW HER WINDOW, HAVING SUFFERED SERIOUS INJURIES. DURING HER BRIEF STAY AT SAMARITAN BEFORE HER FALL, SHE WAS HIGHLY NERVOUS AND SOMETIMES DELUSIONAL. SHE DID NOT RECOGNIZE HER SISTER WHEN SHE CAME TO VISIT, AND A NURSE FOUND HER CLEANING THE HOSPITAL FLOOR, THINKING IT WAS HER KITCHEN. IN THE INSTANT SUIT SHE COMPLAINED THAT THE DEFENDANTS WERE NEGLIGENT IN FAILING TO GUARD HER AND PROPERLY BAR THE WINDOW FROM WHICH SHE JUMPED.

YEAR OF NEGLIGENT ACT: 1943

STATE IN WHICH NEGLIGENT ACT OCCURRED: CALIFORNIA

SETTING OF THE CASE: PRIV. MENT. HOSP.

PLAINTIFF(S): PATIENT(S) OR REP.

DEFENDANT(S):
1. HOSPITAL &/OR OWNERS, ETC.

NEGLIGENT ACTIVITY:

TREATMENT: NOT APPLICABLE

DIAGNOSIS:

WHAT WAS DIAGNOSED:
1. LACK OF DANGEROUSNESS

RESULT OF DIAGNOSIS:
1. IMPROPER CUSTODIAL CARE

CARE:
1. INADEQUATE SUPERVISION

HARM CAUSED TO PLAINTIFF &/OR PATIENT:
1. SELF-INFL.OR ACC.INJ

TYPE OF ACTION BROUGHT:
1. NEGLIGENCE

HISTORY OF THE CASE:

TYPE OF COURT: STATE

TRIER OF FACT: JUDGE,UNINV.JURY

COURT DECISION(S):

TRIAL COURT: FOR DEFENDANT
YEAR: NOT SPECIFIED
APPELLATE COURT: FOR DEFENDANT
YEAR: 1945
SUPREME COURT: NONFINAL FOR PL.
YEAR: 1945

DEFENDANTS STILL INVOLVED IN SUIT:
1. HOSPITAL &/OR OWNERS, ETC.

296. WOODRUFF V. SHORES

PLAINTIFF'S HUSBAND HAD FILED AN INFORMATION IN THE BUCHANAN COUNTY COURT ALLEGING THAT THE PLAINTIFF WAS INSANE. THE DEFENDANT, DR. E. M. SHORES, EXECUTED A CERTIFICATE THAT AGREED SHE WAS IN FACT INSANE. SHE WAS THEN COMMITTED TO A STATE HOSPITAL FOR APPROXIMATELY ONE MONTH, WHEN THE SUPERINTENDENT OF THE HOSPITAL PAROLED HER TO HER HUSBAND, WHO CONTINUED TO THREATEN HER WITH RE-INCARCERATION. IN THIS SUIT SHE ALLEGED THAT DR. SHORES HAD NEVER EXAMINED HER AND HAD FALSELY SIGNED THE COMMITMENT PAPERS.

YEAR OF NEGLIGENT ACT: 1944

STATE IN WHICH NEGLIGENT ACT OCCURRED: MISSOURI

SETTING OF THE CASE: JUDICIAL PROCEEDING

PLAINTIFF(S): PATIENT(S) OR REP.

DEFENDANT(S):
1. NONPSYCHIAT.OR UNKNOWN TYPE PHYSICIAN(S)

NEGLIGENT ACTIVITY:

TREATMENT: NOT APPLICABLE

DIAGNOSIS:

WHAT WAS DIAGNOSED:
1. MENTAL ILLNESS, INSTEAD OF SANITY

RESULT OF DIAGNOSIS:
1. IMPROPER COMMITMENT

CARE: NOT APPLICABLE

HARM CAUSED TO PLAINTIFF &/OR PATIENT:
1. EMOTIONAL DISTRESS
2. LOSS OF LIBERTY

TYPE OF ACTION BROUGHT:
1. NEGLIGENCE

HISTORY OF THE CASE:

TYPE OF COURT: STATE

TRIER OF FACT: JUDGE;JURY PRESENT ?

COURT DECISION(S):

TRIAL COURT: FOR DEFENDANT
YEAR: NOT SPECIFIED
SUPREME COURT: FOR DEFENDANT
YEAR: 1945

REASON SUIT FAILED:
1. STATUTE OF LIMITATIONS BARRED SUIT

297. WOODS, V. BRUMLOP

ON THE ADVICE OF HER PHYSICIAN, BEULAH WOODS SAW DR. BRUMLOP FOR PSYCHIATRIC TREATMENT. DR. BRUMLOP ADVISED ELECTRO-SHOCK THERAPY AT NEW MEXICO MENTAL HOSPITAL. PLAINTIFF ENTERED THE HOSPITAL AND HAD THE TREATMENT UNDER DR. GONZALES. SHE CLAIMED THAT DURING THIS TREATMENT SHE SUSTAINED A COMPRESSION FRACTURE OF HER SPINE WHICH RESULTED IN A LOSS OF HEARING. SHE SUED DR. BRUMLOP FOR FAILING TO INFORM HER OF THE RISK AND FOR FALSELY CLAIMING THAT THE TREATMENT WAS SAFE.

YEAR OF NEGLIGENT ACT: NOT SPECIFIED

STATE IN WHICH NEGLIGENT ACT OCCURRED: NEW MEXICO

SETTING OF THE CASE: PUB. MENT. HOSP.

PLAINTIFF(S): PATIENT(S) OR REP.

DEFENDANT(S):
1. PSYCHIATRIST(S)

NEGLIGENT ACTIVITY:

TREATMENT:
1. NEGLIGENT ELECTROCONVULSIVE THERAPY
2. FAILURE TO OBTAIN -OR LACK OF- CONSENT

DIAGNOSIS:

WHAT WAS DIAGNOSED: NOT APPLICABLE

RESULT OF DIAGNOSIS: NOT APPLICABLE

CARE: NOT APPLICABLE

HARM CAUSED TO PLAINTIFF &/OR PATIENT:
1. NONSELF-INFLICTED INJURIES

TYPE OF ACTION BROUGHT:
1. NEGLIGENCE

HISTORY OF THE CASE:

TYPE OF COURT: STATE

TRIER OF FACT: JURY

COURT DECISION(S):

TRIAL COURT: FOR PLAINTIFF
YEAR: NOT SPECIFIED
SUPREME COURT: NONFINAL FOR DEF.
YEAR: 1962

DEFENDANTS STILL INVOLVED IN SUIT:
1. PSYCHIATRIST(S)

298. WRIGHT V. STATE

ON THE EVENING OF FEBRUARY 6, 1964, RONALD WRIGHT BECAME DISTRAUGHT AND SET ON TAKING HIS OWN LIFE. HIS MOTHER FOUND HIM HOLDING A SYRINGE CONTAINING 100 CC OF INSULIN, WHICH HE THREATENED TO INJECT INTO HIMSELF. BECAUSE RONALD HAD HAD A HISTORY OF SUICIDE ATTEMPTS, MRS. WRIGHT TOOK THE SYRINGE AND CALLED HER HUSBAND, WHO CALLED THE FAMILY PHYSICIAN AND THEN THE POLICE. HE WAS ADMITTED TO THE SYRACUSE PSYCHIATRIC HOSPITAL, WHERE HIS CONDITION VARIED GREATLY. HE ESCAPED SEVERAL TIMES, BUT AT OTHER TIMES WAS COOPERATIVE. ONE NIGHT RONALD RETURNED FROM A PASS WITH ALCOHOL ON HIS BREATH AND BLOOD ON HIS RIGHT HAND. WHILE ON WARD ROUNDS, DR. NEWTON WAS CONFRONTED BY RONALD ASKING TO BE DISCHARGED. DR. NEWTON QUIETED HIM AND SENT HIM BACK TO HIS ROOM. AT MIDNIGHT HE AGAIN DEMANDED TO BE DISCHARGED. HE PACKED HIS BAGS AND TRIED TO LEAVE VIA THE ELEVATOR BUT WAS BROUGHT BACK. HE THEN SAID HE WOULD LEAVE THROUGH A WINDOW ELEVATOR BUT WAS BROUGHT BACK. HE THEN SAID HE WOULD LEAVE THROUGH A WINDOW, WHICH HE OPENED. DR. NEWTON INFORMED RONALD HE COULD BE RELEASED THE FOLLOWING DAY. RONALD RETURNED TO HIS ROOM AND SAT ON HIS WINDOW SILL WITH HIS PACKED SUITCASE. RONALD'S REQUEST TO CLOSE HIS DOOR WAS GRANTED DESPITE HIS RECORD OF SUICIDE ATTEMPTS. THE NURSE WAS INSTRUCTED TO WATCH HIM THROUGH THE KEYHOLE. SHORTLY THEREAFTER A NURSE WENT TO THE NEXT ROOM AND LOOKED ACROSS TO SEE RONALD HANGING FROM THE SILL. HE FELL BEFORE ANYONE COULD REACH HIM, RESULTING IN A 50 PERCENT FRACTURE OF HIS VERTEBRAE.

YEAR OF NEGLIGENT ACT: 1964

STATE IN WHICH NEGLIGENT ACT OCCURRED: NEW YORK

SETTING OF THE CASE: PUB. MENT. HOSP.

PLAINTIFF(S): PATIENT(S) OR REP.

DEFENDANT(S):
1. STATE GOV. &/OR OFFICIALS, ETC.

NEGLIGENT ACTIVITY:

TREATMENT: NOT APPLICABLE

DIAGNOSIS:

WHAT WAS DIAGNOSED:
1. TYPE OF CUSTODIAL CARE

RESULT OF DIAGNOSIS:
1. IMPROPER CUSTODIAL CARE

CARE:
1. FAILURE TO PROVIDE PROPER CUSTODIAL CARE

HARM CAUSED TO PLAINTIFF &/OR PATIENT:
1. SELF-INFLICTED INJURIES

TYPE OF ACTION BROUGHT:
1. NEGLIGENCE

HISTORY OF THE CASE:

TYPE OF COURT: STATE

TRIER OF FACT: JUDGE,NO JURY

COURT DECISION(S):

TRIAL COURT: FOR DEFENDANT
YEAR: 1967
APPELLATE COURT: FOR PLAINTIFF
YEAR: 1969

VERDICT AGAINST WHICH DEFENDANTS:
1. STATE GOV. &/OR OFFICIALS, ETC.

RECOVERY OR OTHER RELIEF GRANTED:
1. OTHER RECOVERY: TO BE DETERM.ON RETR

299. WYATT V. STICKNEY

THIS CLASS ACTION SUIT WAS FILED ON BEHALF OF PATIENTS AT BRYCE HOSPITAL IN TUSCALOOSA, ALABAMA AND ELSEWHERE WHO WERE INVOLUNTARILY COMMITTED THROUGH NON-CRIMINAL PROCEDURES. THE DEFENDANTS WERE OFFICIALS IN THE ALABAMA STATE GOVERNMENT AND COURT OFFICIALS INVOLVED IN THE COMMITMENT OF PATIENTS AND THE MAINTENANCE OF THE ALABAMA STATE HOSPITALS. PLAINTIFFS SOUGHT INJUNCTIVE RELIEF, DECLARING THAT THE FACILITIES DID NOT AFFORD THEM THE OPPORTUNITY FOR ADEQUATE TREATMENT.

YEAR OF NEGLIGENT ACT: OCCURRED OVER A SERIES OF YEARS, ENDING IN 1970

STATE IN WHICH NEGLIGENT ACT OCCURRED: ALABAMA

SETTING OF THE CASE: PUB. MENT. HOSP.

PLAINTIFF(S): PATIENT(S) OR REP.

DEFENDANT(S):
1. STATE GOV. &/OR OFFICIALS, ETC.
2. JUDICIARY &/OR CLERKS, ETC.

NEGLIGENT ACTIVITY:

TREATMENT:
1. NO TREATMENT OR INADEQUATE TREATMENT

DIAGNOSIS:

WHAT WAS DIAGNOSED: NOT APPLICABLE

RESULT OF DIAGNOSIS: NOT APPLICABLE

CARE: NOT APPLICABLE

HARM CAUSED TO PLAINTIFF &/OR PATIENT:
1. DEPRIVATION OF CONSTITUTIONAL RIGHTS

TYPE OF ACTION BROUGHT:
1. NEGLIGENCE
2. DEPRIVATION OF CONSTITUTIONAL RIGHTS: RIGHT TO TREATMENT
3. OTHER ACTION, EXCLUDING TORT LAW: CLASS ACTION SUIT

HISTORY OF THE CASE:

TYPE OF COURT: FEDERAL

TRIER OF FACT: JUDGE,NO JURY

COURT DECISION(S):

TRIAL COURT: NONFINAL FOR PL.
YEAR: 1971
TRIAL COURT: NONFINAL FOR PL.
YEAR: 1971
TRIAL COURT: FOR PLAINTIFF
YEAR: 1972
APPELLATE COURT: FOR PLAINTIFF
YEAR: 1974

VERDICT AGAINST WHICH DEFENDANTS:
1. STATE GOV. &/OR OFFICIALS, ETC.

RECOVERY OR OTHER RELIEF GRANTED:
1. NONMONETARY RELIEF: INJ.OR OTHER EQ.REL.

300. ZIPKIN V. FREEMAN

AT THE TIME OF THE SUIT DR. FREEMAN WAS A PRACTICING PSYCHIATRIST IN COLUMBIA, MISSOURI. ON APRIL 18, 1959, ADA ZIPKIN CAME TO HIM FOR DIARRHEA AND HEADACHES. THE TREATMENT CONTINUED UNTIL 1961 AND PROVED TO BE VERY BIZARRE. PRIOR TO HER REFERRAL TO DR. FREEMAN BY HER FAMILY PHYSICIAN, ADA WAS AN ACTIVE PTA AND CHURCH MEMBER, WAS CONSIDERED A GOOD MOTHER AND WIFE, AND HAD MANY FRIENDS. AFTER TWO MONTHS OF TREATMENT WITH DR. FREEMAN, HER SYMPTOMS WERE "COMPLETELY GONE." HOWEVER, FREEMAN SAID THAT SHE SHOULD CONTINUE TO GET AT THE ROOT OF HER PROBLEM AND BE COMPLETELY CURED. AS TREATMENT CONTINUED MRS. ZIPKIN'S AFFECTIONS BECAME COMPLETELY TRANSFERRED FROM HER HUSBAND AND FAMILY TO HER DOCTOR. HER INVOLVEMENT WITH FREEMAN INCREASED UNTIL "THERAPY" INCLUDED NUDE BATHING PARTIES, WEEKEND TRIPS, AND INVESTING IN HIS BUSINESS ADVENTURES. HIS ADVICE INCLUDED A RECOMMENDATION THAT SHE DIVORCE HER HUSBAND. AS A RESULT OF HER TREATMENT MRS. ZIPKIN GAVE UP HER FRIENDS AND COMMUNITY COMMITMENTS. SHE MOVED IN ABOVE DR. FREEMAN AND LATER GAVE HIM $14,000 TOWARD A FARM INVESTMENT. SHE MOVED TO THE FARM AND PAID $100/MONTH RENT TO FREEMAN TO STAY THERE. EVENTUALLY SHE REALIZED THAT DR. FREEMAN HAD DESTROYED HER LIFE, AND SHE BROUGHT SUIT AGAINST HIM.

YEAR OF NEGLIGENT ACT: OCCURRED OVER A SERIES OF YEARS, ENDING IN 1961

STATE IN WHICH NEGLIGENT ACT OCCURRED: MISSOURI

SETTING OF THE CASE: PRIVATE PRACTICE

PLAINTIFF(S): PATIENT(S) OR REP.

DEFENDANT(S):
1. PSYCHIATRIST(S)
2. INSURANCE COMPANY(S)

NEGLIGENT ACTIVITY:

TREATMENT:
1. SEXUAL ABUSE OR DISTURB.OF MARITAL REL.
2. NEG.TRANSFER.OR CTRT

DIAGNOSIS:

WHAT WAS DIAGNOSED: NOT APPLICABLE

RESULT OF DIAGNOSIS: NOT APPLICABLE

CARE: NOT APPLICABLE

HARM CAUSED TO PLAINTIFF &/OR PATIENT:
1. EMOTIONAL DISTRESS
2. EXACERB.OF PREV.CONDITION
3. ECONOMIC LOSS
4. SEXUAL OR MARITAL HARM

TYPE OF ACTION BROUGHT:
1. NEGLIGENCE
2. CONTRACT LAW: GARNISHMENT

HISTORY OF THE CASE:

TYPE OF COURT: STATE

TRIER OF FACT: JURY

COURT DECISION(S):

TRIAL COURT: FOR PLAINTIFF
YEAR: NOT SPECIFIED
SUPREME COURT: FOR PLAINTIFF
YEAR: 1968

VERDICT AGAINST WHICH DEFENDANTS:
1. PSYCHIATRIST(S)
2. INSURANCE CO.

RECOVERY OR OTHER RELIEF GRANTED:
1. $ 5000
2. INTEREST

Appendix B

List of Cases, by Study Variables

In order to provide easy access to those cases involving specific study variables, the following list of variables has been provided, along with their associated cases. The order of variables follows the form of the synopsis. Thus, the first variable is the state in which the negligent act occurred, and all cases occurring in each of the states are listed. This variable is followed by the setting, plaintiffs, defendants, negligent activities (in treatment, diagnosis, and care), harm caused, type of action brought, type of court, trier of fact, verdict for whom, special doctrines, types and amounts of recovery, reason suit failed, and level of court. Each of these variables is described more fully in the introduction to Appendix A.

TABLE OF CASES

1. A.A. V STATE
2. ABRAHAM V ZASLOW
3. ADAMS V RICKS
4. ADAMS V STATE
5. AIKEN V CLARY
6. ANCLOTE M.F.V WILK.
7. ANNIS V DONAHUE
8. ANONYMOUS V STATE
9. ARL. HTS.V DEADERICK
10. AVEY V ST.FRAN.HOSP.
11. AYERS V RUSSELL
12. BACON V BACON
13. BAKER V ORLOWSKY
14. BAKER V U.S.
15. BANGS V STATE
16. BARTLETT V WEIMER
17. BEAUMONT V MORGAN
18. BECKHAM V CLINE
19. BELLANDI V PARK SAN.
20. BELLOWS V STATE
21. BENCOMO V MORGAN
22. BENJAMIN V HAVENS
23. BENNETT V STATE
24. BERRY V MOENCH
25. BETTS V STATE
26. BLAUER V STATE
27. BLITZ V BOOG
28. BOGUST V IVERSON
29. BOLAND V STATE
30. BOOE V HALL
31. BORKER V N.T.L.
32. BOYKIN V STATE
33. BRADSHAW V STATE
34. BRANDT V BRANDT
35. BRIGANTE V STATE
36. BROWN V MOORE
37. BURKES V CALLION
38. BURKS V ROSS
39. BURNHAM V D.P.HEALTH
40. BYRNE V KYSAR
41. CALLAHAN V STATE
42. CAMERON V STATE
43. CAMPBELL V GLENWOOD
44. CARLINO V STATE
45. CASTIGLIONE V STATE
46. CASTILLO V U.S.
47. CAWTHON V COFFER
48. CENTENO V CITY OF NY
49. CHRISTY V SALITERMAN
50. CHUDY V CHUDY
51. CLARK V GERACI
52. COLLINS V BENSINGER
53. COLLINS V HAND
54. COLLINS V STATE
55. COL.ST.BD. V WEILER
56. COMMONWEALTH V PAGE
57. CONSTANT V HOWE
58. COOPER V BD.MED.EX.
59. CORCORAN V JERREL
60. CTY.OF L.A.V SUP.CT.
61. COX V STATE
62. CROCCO V HARRIS
63. CURLEY V STATE
64. DABKOWSKI V DAVIS
65. DALEY V STATE
66. DANIELS V FINNEY
67. DARNELL V CAMERON
68. DAVIS V WATKINS
69. DEMARTINI V ALEX.SAN
70. DENNISON V STATE
71. DI FIORE V STATE
72. DI GIOVANNI V PESSEL
73. DILLMAN V HELLMAN
74. DIMIT.V CHI.W.M.HOSP
75. DINNERSTEIN V U.S.
76. DOE V ROE
77. DOTY V STATE
78. DOUGHERTY V SNYDER
79. DOWLY V STATE
80. DUGAN V U.S.
81. DUNBAR V GREENLAW
82. DUNN V STATE
83. DUZYNSKI V NOSAL
84. EABY V U.S.
85. EANES V U.S.
86. EDDINGS V PENN.
87. EISELE V MALONE
88. EVANUIK V U.PITT.
89. EXCEL.INS.CO.V STATE
90. FAIR V UNITED STATES
91. FARBER V OLKON
92. FATUCK V HILL.HOSP.
93. FEITELBERG V STATE
94. FERNANDEZ V BARUCH
95. FINKEL V STATE
96. FISCHER V CITY ELM.
97. FORDE V CTY.L.A.
98. FOSTER V STATE
99. FOWLE V FOWLE
100. FOWLER V NRWYS. SAN.
101. FOXLUGER V STATE
102. FREACH V COMMONWEAL
103. FRIEDLAND V U.S.
104. GSPERINI V MNGINELLI
105. GERBA V NEUROL.HOSP.
106. GIOIA V STATE
107. GOULD V STATE
108. GRANT V N.T.L.
109. GREGORY V ROBINSON
110. GRIES V L.I. HOME
111. GROCE V MYERS
112. GUZY V GUZY
113. HAMMER V POLSKY
114. HAMMER V ROSEN
115. HARRIS HOSP. V POPE
116. HAWLEY V STATE
117. HEBEL V HINSDALE SAN
118. HEIFETZ V PHIL.HOSP.
119. HENDLER V STATE
120. HENDRY V U.S.
121. HERNAND V. ST.OF CAL
122. HERNAND V ST.OF N.Y.
123. HICKS V U.S.
124. HIGGINS V STATE
125. HIRSH V STATE
126. HOMERE V STATE
127. HOUGH V OGDEN
128. HUNGERFORD V U.S.
129. HUNT V KING COUNTY
130. IN RE ANONYMOUS
131. IN RE MADDOX
132. IN RE PIERRE ESTATE
133. IN RE WARRINGTON
134. JACKSON V INDIANA
135. JAMES V TURNER
136. JOBSON V HENNE
137. JOHNSON V GREER
138. JOHNSON V METH. HOSP
139. JOHNSON V U.S.
140. JOHNSTON V RODIS
141. JOYCE V FERRAZZI
142. KATZ V STATE
143. KEATING V KELLER
144. KELLY V STATE
145. KENDRICK V U.S.
146. KENT V WHITAKER
147. KLEBER V STEVENS
148. KOSBERG V WASH. HOSP
149. KOWALSKI V STATE
150. KRAVITZ V STATE
151. KUBAS V STATE
152. LANDO V STATE
153. LAWRENCE V STATE
154. LEGION V RICHARDSON
155. LESTER V AETNA
156. LEWANDOWSKI V STATE
157. LEXINGTON HOS V WHIT
158. LICHT. V MONT. HOSP.
159. LINDER V FOSTER
160. LOWEN V HILTON
161. LUCY HAYES V PEROTTI
162. MABEN V RANKIN
163. MCCABE V STATE
164. MCCANDLESS V STATE
165. MCNEIL V DIRECTOR
166. MANIACI V MARQUET.U.
167. MARKS V ST FRAN HOSP
168. MARTARELLA V KELLEY
169. MARTINDALE V STATE
170. MAYER V ALBANY HOSP.
171. MEIER V ROSS HOSP.
172. MERCHANTS BANK V US
173. MEYNIER V DE PAUL
174. MEZULLO V MALETZ
175. MILANO V STATE
176. MILLARD V CAMERON
177. MILLER V DICKERT
178. MILLER V WEST
179. MILLS V SOC.NY. HOSP
180. MITCHELL V ROBINSON
181. MOCHEN V STATE
182. MONTGOM.CTY.TR.V ST.
183. MORALES V TURMAN
184. MOREY V KAISER FOUND
185. MORGAN V STATE
186. MORRA V ST.BD.PSYCH.
187. MORRIS V ROUSOS
188. MORRIS V U. TEXAS
189. MOSKOWITZ V MCQUEEN

TABLE OF CASES (CONT.)

190. MOXON V CTY.OF KERN
191. MURRAY V ST.MARY'S
192. NASON V SUPER.OF BR.
193. NASTASI V STATE
194. NELSON V HEYNE
195. NYSA V ROCKEFELLER
196. NICHOLSON V HAN
197. NOEL V MENNING.FOUND
198. O'CONNOR V DONALDSON
199. OLEPA V MAPLETOFF
200. OLIVER V STATE
201. O'NEIL V STATE
202. ORMAN V STATE
203. O'ROURKE V HALCYON
204. O'ROURKE V O'ROURKE
205. PAPINI V ALEX.SAN.
206. PARKER V LA COUNTY
207. PAULEN V SHINNICK
208. PENNELL V CUMMINGS
209. PEOPLE V BERNSTEIN
210. PEOPLE V LA VALLEE
211. PEOPLE V MCCAUGHAN
212. PEOPLE V WILKINS
213. PETERS V STATE
214. PETTIS V ST.DEPT.HOS
215. PHILLIPS V SINGLETAR
216. PIETRUCHA V GRANT HO
217. POWELL V DUKE UNIV.
218. POWELL V RISSER
219. PULS V ST.VINC.HOSP.
220. QUICK V BEN.SIS.HOS.
221. QUINLEY V COCKE
222. RENELLI V DEPT.OF MH
223. REYNOLDS V NEILL
224. RHIVER V RIETMAN
225. RICE V MERCY HOSP.
226. ROBINSON V STATE
227. ROGERS V OKIN
228. ROSARIO V STATE
229. ROSENFELD V COLEMAN
230. ROSS V LEONARD
231. ROSSING V STATE
232. ROUSE V CAMERON
233. ROUSE V TWIN PINES
234. ROY V HARTOGS
235. RUFINO V U.S.
236. RUNYON V REID
237. ST. GEORGE V STATE
238. SALTER V GRANT
239. SAMONS V MEYMANDI
240. SARON V STATE
241. SAS V STATE
242. SCHAFFER V SPICER
243. SCHANBARGER V KELLOG
244. SCHWARTZ V THIELE
245. SCHWENK V STATE
246. SCOLAVINO V STATE
247. SEALEY V FINKELSTEIN
248. SEMLER V PSY.INS.WA.
249. SEYMOUR V LOFGREEN
250. SHATTUCK V STATE
251. SMART V U.S.
252. SPRINGER V STEINER
253. STACHULAK V COUGHLIN
254. STALLMAN V ROBINSON
255. STANSFIELD V GARDNER
256. STEPHEN V DREW
257. STONE V PROCTOR
258. STOVALL V HARMS
259. STOWERS V ARD.HOSP.
260. SUHRE V KOTT
261. SURPRENANT V STATE
262. TAIG V STATE
263. TARASOFF V REG.U.CA.
264. TAYLOR V GLOTFELTY
265. TAYLOR V STATE
266. THALL V STATE
267. TISINGER V WOOLLEY
268. TOBIAS V MANHAT.E&E
269. TORRES V STATE
270. TRAPANI V STATE
271. UNDERWOOD V U.S.
272. UNITED STATES V GRAY
273. U.S. V PARDUE
274. U.LOUISVILLE V HAM.
275. VAN BARNEVELD V ST.
276. VASSOLO V CTY.HOSP.
277. VISTICA V PRES. HOSP
278. VITELLO V STATE
279. VON EYE V HAMMES
280. WARNER V PACKER
281. WARNER V STATE
282. WEGLARZ V STATE
283. WEIHS V STATE
284. WEINSHENK V KAISER
285. WELSCH V LIKINS
286. WENDOVER V STATE
287. WHALEY V KIRBY
288. WHITE V U.S.
289. WHITESELL V GREEN
290. WHITREE V STATE
291. WILLIAMS V LE BAR
292. WILLIAMS V STATE
293. WILLIS V WEST.HOSP.
294. WILSON V LEHMAN
295. WOOD V SAMARITAN INS
296. WOODRUFF V SHORES
297. WOODS V BRUMLOP
298. WRIGHT V STATE
299. WYATT V STICKNEY
300. ZIPKIN V FREEMAN

STATE IN WHICH NEGLIGENT ACT OCCURRED

ALABAMA
KENDRICK V U.S.
UNDERWOOD V U.S.
WYATT V STICKNEY
TOTAL: 3

ALASKA
TOTAL: 0

ARIZONA
TOTAL: 0

ARKANSAS
CHUDY V CHUDY
TOTAL: 1

CALIFORNIA
ABRAHAM V ZASLOW
BELLANDI V PARK SAN.
BURKES V CALLION
COOPER V BD.MED.EX.
CTY.OF L.A.V SUP.CT.
CROCCO V HARRIS
DEMARTINI V ALEX.SAN
FARBER V OLKON
FORDE V CTY.L.A.
HERNAND V. ST.OF CAL
KRAVITZ V STATE
MABEN V RANKIN
MEIER V ROSS HOSP.
MOREY V KAISER FOUND
MOXON V CTY.OF KERN
PAPINI V ALEX.SAN.
PARKER V LA COUNTY
PEOPLE V BERNSTEIN
PEOPLE V MCCAUGHAN
ROUSE V TWIN PINES
SCHWARTZ V THIELE
TARASOFF V REG.U.CA.
VISTICA V PRES. HOSP
WEINSHENK V KAISER
WHALEY V KIRBY
WOOD V SAMARITAN INS
TOTAL: 26

COLORADO
COL.ST.BD. V WEILER
LOWEN V HILTON
UNITED STATES V GRAY
TOTAL: 3

CONNECTICUT
DINNERSTEIN V U.S.
U.S. V PARDUE
TOTAL: 2

DELAWARE
TOTAL: 0

DISTRICT OF COLUMBIA
DARNELL V CAMERON
DUGAN V U.S.
EABY V U.S.
HICKS V U.S.
JOHNSTON V RODIS
KOSBERG V WASH. HOSP
LUCY HAYES V PEROTTI
MILLARD V CAMERON
ROUSE V CAMERON
TOTAL: 9

FLORIDA
ANCLOTE M.F.V WILK.
BECKHAM V CLINE
BENCOMO V MORGAN
CAWTHON V COFFER
DILLMAN V HELLMAN
O'CONNOR V DONALDSON
RICE V MERCY HOSP.
TOTAL: 7

GEORGIA
ADAMS V RICKS
BURNHAM V D.P.HEALTH
JOHNSON V U.S.
STANSFIELD V GARDNER
TISINGER V WOOLLEY
TOTAL: 5

HAWAII
WHITESELL V GREEN
TOTAL: 1

IDAHO
WILLIS V WEST.HOSP.
TOTAL: 1

ILLINOIS
BRANDT V BRANDT
BYRNE V KYSAR
COLLINS V BENSINGER
DIMIT.V CHI.W.M.HOSP
DUZYNSKI V NOSAL
HEBEL V HINSDALE SAN
PIETRUCHA V GRANT HO
STACHULAK V COUGHLIN
TOTAL: 8

INDIANA
FOWLER V NRWYS. SAN.
JACKSON V INDIANA
NELSON V HEYNE
RHIVER V RIETMAN
SMART V U.S.
TOTAL: 5

IOWA
BAKER V U.S.
CORCORAN V JERREL
TOTAL: 2

KANSAS
AVEY V ST.FRAN.HOSP.
MARKS V ST FRAN HOSP
MORRA V ST.BD.PSYCH.
NOEL V MENNING.FOUND
SEYMOUR V LOFGREEN
STOVALL V HARMS
TOTAL: 6

KENTUCKY
LEXINGTON HOS V WHIT
U.LOUISVILLE V HAM.
WILSON V LEHMAN
TOTAL: 3

LOUISIANA
KEATING V KELLER
LESTER V AETNA
MEYNIER V DE PAUL
O'ROURKE V O'ROURKE
PETTIS V ST.DEPT.HOS
TOTAL: 5

MAINE
DUNBAR V GREENLAW
PENNELL V CUMMINGS
TOTAL: 2

MARYLAND
MCNEIL V DIRECTOR
MILLER V WEST
SAS V STATE
TOTAL: 3

MASSACHUSETTS
ANNIS V DONAHUE
BEAUMONT V MORGAN
COMMONWEALTH V PAGE
FRIEDLAND V U.S.
JOYCE V FERRAZZI
MEZULLO V MALETZ
NASON V SUPER.OF BR.
ROGERS V OKIN
TOTAL: 8

STATES IN WHICH NEGLIGENT ACTS OCCURRED (CONT.)

MICHIGAN
BURKS V ROSS
DABKOWSKI V DAVIS
IN RE MADDOX
NICHOLSON V HAN
OLEPA V MAPLETOFF
PAULEN V SHINNICK
STOWERS V ARD.HOSP.
TOTAL: 7

MINNESOTA
CAMPBELL V GLENWOOD
CHRISTY V SALITERMAN
LINDER V FOSTER
QUICK V BEN.SIS.HOS.
VON EYE V HAMMES
WELSCH V LIKINS
TOTAL: 6

MISSISSIPPI
BACON V BACON
TOTAL: 1

MISSOURI
AIKEN V CLARY
DOUGHERTY V SNYDER
GERBA V NEUROL.HOSP.
GREGORY V ROBINSON
MITCHELL V ROBINSON
STALLMAN V ROBINSON
TAYLOR V GLOTFELTY
WOODRUFF V SHORES
ZIPKIN V FREEMAN
TOTAL: 9

MONTANA
TOTAL: 0

NEBRASKA
TOTAL: 0

NEVADA
TOTAL: 0

NEW HAMPSHIRE
GRANT V N.T.L.
TOTAL: 1

NEW JERSEY
DI GIOVANNI V PESSEL
FERNANDEZ V BARUCH
HOUGH V OGDEN
TOTAL: 3

NEW MEXICO
CASTILLO V U.S.
WOODS V BRUMLOP
TOTAL: 2

NEW YORK
A.A. V STATE
ANONYMOUS V STATE
AYERS V RUSSELL
BANGS V STATE
BELLOWS V STATE
BENNETT V STATE
BETTS V STATE
BLAUER V STATE
BLITZ V BOOG
BOLAND V STATE
BORKER V N.T.L.
BOYKIN V STATE
BRADSHAW V STATE
BRIGANTE V STATE
CALLAHAN V STATE
CAMERON V STATE
CARLINO V STATE
CASTIGLIONE V STATE
CENTENO V CITY OF NY
CLARK V GERACI
COLLINS V STATE
COX V STATE
CURLEY V STATE
DALEY V STATE
DENNISON V STATE
DI FIORE V STATE
DOE V ROE
DOTY V STATE
DOWLY V STATE
DUNN V STATE
EISELE V MALONE
EXCEL.INS.CO.V STATE
FATUCK V HILL.HOSP.
FEITELBERG V STATE
FINKEL V STATE
FISCHER V CITY ELM.
FOSTER V STATE
FOXLUGER V STATE
GSPERINI V MNGINELLI
GIOIA V STATE
GOULD V STATE
GRIES V L.I. HOME
GUZY V GUZY
HAMMER V POLSKY
HAMMER V ROSEN
HAWLEY V STATE
HENDLER V STATE
HENDRY V U.S.
HERNAND V ST.OF N.Y.
HIGGINS V STATE
HIRSH V STATE
HOMERE V STATE
IN RE ANONYMOUS
IN RE PIERRE ESTATE
IN RE WARRINGTON
JOBSON V HENNE
JOHNSON V METH. HOSP
KATZ V STATE
KELLY V STATE
KLEBER V STEVENS
KOWALSKI V STATE
KUBAS V STATE
LANDO V STATE
LAWRENCE V STATE
LEGION V RICHARDSON
LEWANDOWSKI V STATE
LICHT. V MONT. HOSP.
MCCABE V STATE
MCCANDLESS V STATE
MARTARELLA V KELLEY
MARTINDALE V STATE
MAYER V ALBANY HOSP.
MILANO V STATE
MILLS V SOC.NY. HOSP
MOCHEN V STATE
MONTGOM.CTY.TR.V ST.
MORGAN V STATE
MOSKOWITZ V MCQUEEN
MURRAY V ST.MARY'S
NASTASI V STATE
NYSA V ROCKEFELLER
OLIVER V STATE
O'NEIL V STATE
ORMAN V STATE
O'ROURKE V HALCYON
PEOPLE V LA VALLEE
PEOPLE V WILKINS
PETERS V STATE
RENELLI V DEPT.OF MH
ROBINSON V STATE
ROSARIO V STATE
ROSS V LEONARD
ROSSING V STATE
ROY V HARTOGS
RUFINO V U.S.
ST. GEORGE V STATE
SALTER V GRANT
SARON V STATE
SCHANBARGER V KELLOG
SCHWENK V STATE
SCOLAVINO V STATE
SEALEY V FINKELSTEIN
SHATTUCK V STATE
SURPRENANT V STATE
TAIG V STATE
TAYLOR V STATE
THALL V STATE
TOBIAS V MANHAT.E&E
TORRES V STATE
TRAPANI V STATE
VAN BARNEVELD V ST.
VASSOLO V CTY.HOSP.
VITELLO V STATE
WARNER V PACKER
WARNER V STATE
WEGLARZ V STATE
WEIHS V STATE
WENDOVER V STATE
WHITREE V STATE
WILLIAMS V STATE
WRIGHT V STATE
TOTAL: 121

STATES IN WHICH NEGLIGENT ACTS OCCURRED (CONT.)

NORTH CAROLINA
BOOE V HALL
FOWLE V FOWLE
GROCE V MYERS
POWELL V DUKE UNIV.
SAMONS V MEYMANDI
STONE V PROCTOR
TOTAL: 6

NORTH DAKOTA
TOTAL: 0

OHIO
BAKER V ORLOWSKY
BARTLETT V WEIMER
DAVIS V WATKINS
TOTAL: 3

OKLAHOMA
RUNYON V REID
TOTAL: 1

OREGON
SPRINGER V STEINER
TOTAL: 1

PENNSYLVANIA
BROWN V MOORE
COLLINS V HAND
EDDINGS V PENN.
EVANUIK V U.PITT.
FREACH V COMMONWEAL
HEIFETZ V PHIL.HOSP.
POWELL V RISSER
ROSENFELD V COLEMAN
WILLIAMS V LE BAR
TOTAL: 9

RHODE ISLAND
TOTAL: 0

SOUTH CAROLINA
MILLER V DICKERT
PHILLIPS V SINGLETAR
TOTAL: 2

SOUTH DAKOTA
MERCHANTS BANK V US
SCHAFFER V SPICER
TOTAL: 2

TENNESSEE
JAMES V TURNER
QUINLEY V COCKE
TOTAL: 2

TEXAS
ARL. HTS.V DEADERICK
CONSTANT V HOWE
DANIELS V FINNEY
FAIR V UNITED STATES
HARRIS HOSP. V POPE
JOHNSON V GREER
MORALES V TURMAN
MORRIS V ROUSOS
MORRIS V U. TEXAS
REYNOLDS V NEILL
SUHRE V KOTT
TOTAL: 11

UTAH
BERRY V MOENCH
TOTAL: 1

VERMONT
TOTAL: 0

VIRGINIA
EANES V U.S.
SEMLER V PSY.INS.WA.
STEPHEN V DREW

WHITE V U.S.
TOTAL: 4

WASHINGTON
ADAMS V STATE
BENJAMIN V HAVENS
HUNGERFORD V U.S.
HUNT V KING COUNTY
KENT V WHITAKER
TOTAL: 5

WEST VIRGINIA
TOTAL: 0

WISCONSIN
BOGUST V IVERSON
MANIACI V MARQUET.U.
PULS V ST.VINC.HOSP.
TOTAL: 3

WYOMING
TOTAL: 0

SETTINGS IN WHICH NEGLIGENT ACTS OCCURRED

PUB. MENT. HOSP.
A.A. V STATE
ADAMS V STATE
ANONYMOUS V STATE
BENNETT V STATE
BETTS V STATE
BLAUER V STATE
BOYKIN V STATE
BRADSHAW V STATE
BRANDT V BRANDT
BRIGANTE V STATE
BURNHAM V D.P.HEALTH
CALLAHAN V STATE
CAMERON V STATE
CARLINO V STATE
CASTIGLIONE V STATE
CENTENO V CITY OF NY
COLLINS V STATE
CONSTANT V HOWE
COX V STATE
CURLEY V STATE
DALEY V STATE
DARNELL V CAMERON
DAVIS V WATKINS
DENNISON V STATE
DI FIORE V STATE
DOTY V STATE
DOWLY V STATE
DUGAN V U.S.
DUNN V STATE
EABY V U.S.
EANES V U.S.
EXCEL.INS.CO.V STATE
FARBER V OLKON
FEITELBERG V STATE
FINKEL V STATE
FOXLUGER V STATE
FREACH V COMMONWEAL
GIOIA V STATE
GOULD V STATE
HEIFETZ V PHIL.HOSP.
HERNAND V. ST.OF CAL
HERNAND V ST.OF N.Y.
HICKS V U.S.
HIGGINS V STATE
HIRSH V STATE
HOMERE V STATE
IN RE PIERRE ESTATE
IN RE WARRINGTON
JACKSON V INDIANA
JOBSON V HENNE

SETTINGS IN WHICH NEGLIGENT ACTS OCCURRED (CONT.)

MENTAL HOSPITALS (CONT.)
JOHNSON V U.S.
KATZ V STATE
KOWALSKI V STATE
KRAVITZ V STATE
KUBAS V STATE
LANDO V STATE
LAWRENCE V STATE
LEGION V RICHARDSON
LEWANDOWSKI V STATE
MCCABE V STATE
MCCANDLESS V STATE
MCNEIL V DIRECTOR
MARTARELLA V KELLEY
MARTINDALE V STATE
MAYER V ALBANY HOSP.
MERCHANTS BANK V US
MILANO V STATE
MOCHEN V STATE
MONTGOM.CTY.TR.V ST.
MORALES V TURMAN
MOXON V CTY.OF KERN
NASON V SUPER.OF BR.
NASTASI V STATE
NYSA V ROCKEFELLER
O'CONNOR V DONALDSON
OLIVER V STATE
O'NEIL V STATE
ORMAN V STATE
PEOPLE V MCCAUGHAN
PEOPLE V WILKINS
PETERS V STATE
PETTIS V ST.DEPT.HOS
POWELL V RISSER
RENELLI V DEPT.OF MH
REYNOLDS V NEILL
ROBINSON V STATE
ROGERS V OKIN
ROSSING V STATE
ST. GEORGE V STATE
SARON V STATE
SCHWENK V STATE
SCOLAVINO V STATE
SEYMOUR V LOFGREEN
SHATTUCK V STATE
SURPRENANT V STATE
TAIG V STATE
TARASOFF V REG.U.CA.
TAYLOR V GLOTFELTY
THALL V STATE
TORRES V STATE
TRAPANI V STATE
UNITED STATES V GRAY
VAN BARNEVELD V ST.
VITELLO V STATE
WEGLARZ V STATE
WEIHS V STATE
WELSCH V LIKINS
WENDOVER V STATE
WHITREE V STATE
WILLIAMS V STATE
WOODS V BRUMLOP
WRIGHT V STATE
WYATT V STICKNEY
TOTAL: 113

PRIV. MENT. HOSP.
ADAMS V RICKS
ANCLOTE M.F.V WILK.
ARL. HTS.V DEADERICK
BELLANDI V PARK SAN.
BROWN V MOORE
CAMPBELL V GLENWOOD
CHRISTY V SALITERMAN
COLLINS V HAND
DEMARTINI V ALEX.SAN
EISELE V MALONE
EVANUIK V U.PITT.
FOWLER V NRWYS. SAN.
GREGORY V ROBINSON
GRIES V L.I. HOME
HEBEL V HINSDALE SAN
JAMES V TURNER
LEXINGTON HOS V WHIT
LUCY HAYES V PEROTTI
MABEN V RANKIN
MILLS V SOC.NY. HOSP
MITCHELL V ROBINSON
NOEL V MENNING.FOUND
O'ROURKE V HALCYON
PAPINI V ALEX.SAN.
PAULEN V SHINNICK
PIETRUCHA V GRANT HO
QUICK V BEN.SIS.HOS.
QUINLEY V COCKE
RUNYON V REID
SEMLER V PSY.INS.WA.
STALLMAN V ROBINSON
STANSFIELD V GARDNER
STOWERS V ARD.HOSP.
WOOD V SAMARITAN INS
TOTAL: 34

PUB. GEN. HOSP.
BAKER V U.S.
BLITZ V BOOG
BURKS V ROSS
CASTILLO V U.S.
CTY.OF L.A.V SUP.CT.
DINNERSTEIN V U.S.
FERNANDEZ V BARUCH
FRIEDLAND V U.S.
HUNGERFORD V U.S.
HUNT V KING COUNTY
KENDRICK V U.S.
KENT V WHITAKER
RICE V MERCY HOSP.
RUFINO V U.S.
SMART V U.S.
TOBIAS V MANHAT.E&E
WHITE V U.S.
TOTAL: 17

PRIV. GEN. HOSP.
AVEY V ST.FRAN.HOSP.
BENJAMIN V HAVENS
GERBA V NEUROL.HOSP.
LICHT. V MONT. HOSP.
MARKS V ST FRAN HOSP
MURRAY V ST.MARY'S
PULS V ST.VINC.HOSP.
TISINGER V WOOLLEY
U.LOUISVILLE V HAM.
VISTICA V PRES. HOSP
VON EYE V HAMMES
WEINSHENK V KAISER
WILSON V LEHMAN
TOTAL: 13

GENERAL HOSPITAL
MEIER V ROSS HOSP.
TOTAL: 1

MENTAL HOSPITAL
DILLMAN V HELLMAN
JOHNSON V GREER
TOTAL: 2

HOSPITAL
DIMIT.V CHI.W.M.HOSP
FATUCK V HILL.HOSP.
HARRIS HOSP. V POPE
KOSBERG V WASH. HOSP
LESTER V AETNA
MOREY V KAISER FOUND
TOTAL: 6

PUBLIC HOSPITAL
FORDE V CTY.L.A.
TOTAL: 1

PRIVATE HOSPITAL
GROCE V MYERS
JOHNSON V METH. HOSP
STONE V PROCTOR
TOTAL: 3

PUB.&PRIV.MEN.HOSP.
VASSOLO V CTY.HOSP.
TOTAL: 1

JUD.PCDG.&PUB.HOSP.
ROUSE V TWIN PINES
SAS V STATE
WARNER V STATE
WILLIS V WEST.HOSP.
TOTAL: 4

SETTINGS IN WHICH NEGLIGENT ACTS OCCURRED (CONT.)

NURSING HOME
- SEALEY V FINKELSTEIN
- TOTAL: 1

FARM
- HAWLEY V STATE
- HENDLER V STATE
- TOTAL: 2

CORRECTIONAL INST.
- BELLOWS V STATE
- COLLINS V BENSINGER
- FISCHER V CITY ELM.
- NELSON V HEYNE
- PEOPLE V LA VALLEE
- STACHULAK V COUGHLIN
- TAYLOR V STATE
- U.S. V PARDUE
- TOTAL: 8

JUDICIAL PROCEEDING
- AYERS V RUSSELL
- BACON V BACON
- BAKER V ORLOWSKY
- BANGS V STATE
- BARTLETT V WEIMER
- BEAUMONT V MORGAN
- BECKHAM V CLINE
- BENCOMO V MORGAN
- BOLAND V STATE
- BOOE V HALL
- BURKES V CALLION
- BYRNE V KYSAR
- CAWTHON V COFFER
- CHUDY V CHUDY
- COMMONWEALTH V PAGE
- CORCORAN V JERREL
- DABKOWSKI V DAVIS
- DANIELS V FINNEY
- DI GIOVANNI V PESSEL
- DOUGHERTY V SNYDER
- DUNBAR V GREENLAW
- DUZYNSKI V NOSAL
- EDDINGS V PENN.
- FOWLE V FOWLE
- GUZY V GUZY
- HAMMER V POLSKY
- HOUGH V OGDEN
- IN RE ANONYMOUS
- IN RE MADDOX
- JOYCE V FERRAZZI
- KEATING V KELLER
- KELLY V STATE
- KLEBER V STEVENS
- LINDER V FOSTER
- LOWEN V HILTON
- MANIACI V MARQUET.U.
- MEZULLO V MALETZ
- MILLARD V CAMERON
- MILLER V DICKERT
- MILLER V WEST
- MORGAN V STATE
- MORRIS V U. TEXAS
- OLEPA V MAPLETOFF
- O'ROURKE V O'ROURKE
- PARKER V LA COUNTY
- PENNELL V CUMMINGS
- PHILLIPS V SINGLETAR
- POWELL V DUKE UNIV.
- RHIVER V RIETMAN
- ROSARIO V STATE
- ROUSE V CAMERON
- SAMONS V MEYMANDI
- SCHAFFER V SPICER
- SCHANBARGER V KELLOG
- SCHWARTZ V THIELE
- SPRINGER V STEINER
- STEPHEN V DREW
- SUHRE V KOTT
- WARNER V PACKER
- WHALEY V KIRBY
- WILLIAMS V LE BAR
- WOODRUFF V SHORES
- TOTAL: 62

PRIVATE PRACTICE
- ABRAHAM V ZASLOW
- AIKEN V CLARY
- BERRY V MOENCH
- CLARK V GERACI
- COL.ST.BD. V WEILER
- COOPER V BD.MED.EX.
- CROCCO V HARRIS
- DOE V ROE
- GSPERINI V MNGINELLI
- HAMMER V ROSEN
- MORRA V ST.BD.PSYCH.
- MOSKOWITZ V MCQUEEN
- NICHOLSON V HAN
- PEOPLE V BERNSTEIN
- ROSENFELD V COLEMAN
- ROSS V LEONARD
- ROY V HARTOGS
- SALTER V GRANT
- STOVALL V HARMS
- WHITESELL V GREEN
- ZIPKIN V FREEMAN
- TOTAL: 21

ENCOUNTER GROUP
- ANNIS V DONAHUE
- BORKER V N.T.L.
- GRANT V N.T.L.
- TOTAL: 3

EDUCATIONAL INST.
- BOGUST V IVERSON
- FOSTER V STATE
- MEYNIER V DE PAUL
- MORRIS V ROUSOS
- TOTAL: 4

ARMED SERVICE
- FAIR V UNITED STATES
- HENDRY V U.S.
- UNDERWOOD V U.S.
- TOTAL: 3

TYPE NOT SPECIFIED
- JOHNSTON V RODIS
- TOTAL: 1

PLAINTIFF(S)

PATIENT(S) OR REP.
- A.A. V STATE
- ABRAHAM V ZASLOW
- ADAMS V RICKS
- AIKEN V CLARY
- ANNIS V DONAHUE
- ANONYMOUS V STATE
- AVEY V ST.FRAN.HOSP.
- AYERS V RUSSELL
- BACON V BACON
- BAKER V ORLOWSKY
- BANGS V STATE
- BARTLETT V WEIMER
- BEAUMONT V MORGAN
- BECKHAM V CLINE
- BELLOWS V STATE
- BENCOMO V MORGAN
- BENNETT V STATE
- BERRY V MOENCH
- BETTS V STATE
- BLAUER V STATE
- BLITZ V BOOG
- BOLAND V STATE
- BOOE V HALL
- BORKER V N.T.L.
- BOYKIN V STATE
- BRADSHAW V STATE
- BRANDT V BRANDT
- BRIGANTE V STATE
- BROWN V MOORE

PLAINTIFFS (CONT.)

BURKES V CALLION
BURKS V ROSS
BURNHAM V D.P.HEALTH
BYRNE V KYSAR
CALLAHAN V STATE
CAMPBELL V GLENWOOD
CARLINO V STATE
CASTIGLIONE V STATE
CASTILLO V U.S.
CAWTHON V COFFER
CENTENO V CITY OF NY
CHRISTY V SALITERMAN
CHUDY V CHUDY
CLARK V GERACI
COLLINS V BENSINGER
COLLINS V HAND
COMMONWEALTH V PAGE
CONSTANT V HOWE
CORCORAN V JERREL
CTY.OF L.A.V SUP.CT.
COX V STATE
CROCCO V HARRIS
CURLEY V STATE
DABKOWSKI V DAVIS
DALEY V STATE
DANIELS V FINNEY
DARNELL V CAMERON
DAVIS V WATKINS
DEMARTINI V ALEX.SAN
DENNISON V STATE
DI FIORE V STATE
DI GIOVANNI V PESSEL
DILLMAN V HELLMAN
DIMIT.V CHI.W.M.HOSP
DINNERSTEIN V U.S.
DOE V ROE
DOTY V STATE
DOUGHERTY V SNYDER
DOWLY V STATE
DUGAN V U.S.
DUNBAR V GREENLAW
DUZYNSKI V NOSAL
EABY V U.S.
EDDINGS V PENN.
EISELE V MALONE
FARBER V OLKON
FEITELBERG V STATE
FISCHER V CITY ELM.
FORDE V CTY.L.A.
FOSTER V STATE
FOWLE V FOWLE
FOWLER V NRWYS. SAN.
FRIEDLAND V U.S.
GIOIA V STATE
GOULD V STATE
GRANT V N.T.L.
GREGORY V ROBINSON
GRIES V L.I. HOME
GROCE V MYERS
GUZY V GUZY
HAMMER V POLSKY
HAWLEY V STATE
HEBEL V HINSDALE SAN
HENDLER V STATE
HENDRY V U.S.
HERNAND V ST.OF N.Y.
HIRSH V STATE
HOUGH V OGDEN
HUNGERFORD V U.S.
IN RE ANONYMOUS
IN RE MADDOX
IN RE PIERRE ESTATE
IN RE WARRINGTON
JACKSON V INDIANA
JOBSON V HENNE
JOHNSON V GREER
JOHNSON V METH. HOSP
JOHNSTON V RODIS
JOYCE V FERRAZZI
KATZ V STATE
KEATING V KELLER
KELLY V STATE
KLEBER V STEVENS
KOSBERG V WASH. HOSP
KOWALSKI V STATE
KUBAS V STATE
LAWRENCE V STATE
LEGION V RICHARDSON
LEXINGTON HOS V WHIT
LICHT. V MONT. HOSP.
LINDER V FOSTER
LOWEN V HILTON
LUCY HAYES V PEROTTI
MABEN V RANKIN
MCCABE V STATE
MCCANDLESS V STATE
MCNEIL V DIRECTOR
MANIACI V MARQUET.U.
MARTARELLA V KELLEY
MARTINDALE V STATE
MEYNIER V DE PAUL
MEZULLO V MALETZ
MILLARD V CAMERON
MILLER V DICKERT
MILLER V WEST
MILLS V SOC.NY. HOSP
MITCHELL V ROBINSON
MOCHEN V STATE
MONTGOM.CTY.TR.V ST.
MORALES V TURMAN
MOREY V KAISER FOUND
MORGAN V STATE
MORRIS V ROUSOS
MORRIS V U. TEXAS
MOSKOWITZ V MCQUEEN
MOXON V CTY.OF KERN
MURRAY V ST.MARY'S
NASON V SUPER.OF BR.
NASTASI V STATE
NELSON V HEYNE
NYSA V ROCKEFELLER
NOEL V MENNING.FOUND
O'CONNOR V DONALDSON
OLEPA V MAPLETOFF
OLIVER V STATE
O'NEIL V STATE
O'ROURKE V HALCYON
O'ROURKE V O'ROURKE
PARKER V LA COUNTY
PAULEN V SHINNICK
PENNELL V CUMMINGS
PEOPLE V LA VALLEE
PEOPLE V WILKINS
PETTIS V ST.DEPT.HOS
PHILLIPS V SINGLETAR
POWELL V DUKE UNIV.
POWELL V RISSER
PULS V ST.VINC.HOSP.
QUICK V BEN.SIS.HOS.
QUINLEY V COCKE
RENELLI V DEPT.OF MH
REYNOLDS V NEILL
RHIVER V RIETMAN
RICE V MERCY HOSP.
ROBINSON V STATE
ROGERS V OKIN
ROSARIO V STATE
ROSENFELD V COLEMAN
ROSS V LEONARD
ROSSING V STATE
ROUSE V CAMERON
ROUSE V TWIN PINES
ROY V HARTOGS
RUFINO V U.S.
SALTER V GRANT
SAMONS V MEYMANDI
SARON V STATE
SAS V STATE
SCHAFFER V SPICER
SCHANBARGER V KELLOG
SCHWARTZ V THIELE
SCOLAVINO V STATE
SEYMOUR V LOFGREEN
SHATTUCK V STATE
SPRINGER V STEINER
STACHULAK V COUGHLIN
STANSFIELD V GARDNER
STEPHEN V DREW
STONE V PROCTOR
STOVALL V HARMS
STOWERS V ARD.HOSP.
SUHRE V KOTT
SURPRENANT V STATE
TAYLOR V GLOTFELTY
TAYLOR V STATE
TOBIAS V MANHAT.E&E
TORRES V STATE
TRAPANI V STATE
UNITED STATES V GRAY
U.S. V PARDUE
U.LOUISVILLE V HAM.
VAN BARNEVELD V ST.
VITELLO V STATE
VON EYE V HAMMES
WARNER V PACKER
WARNER V STATE
WEGLARZ V STATE
WELSCH V LIKINS
WENDOVER V STATE

PLAINTIFFS (CONT.)

WHALEY V KIRBY
WHITE V U.S.
WHITREE V STATE
WILLIAMS V LE BAR
WILLIS V WEST.HOSP.
WILSON V LEHMAN
WOOD V SAMARITAN INS
WOODRUFF V SHORES
WOODS V BRUMLOP
WRIGHT V STATE
WYATT V STICKNEY
ZIPKIN V FREEMAN
TOTAL: 230

PAT. & 3RD PTY., I
BAKER V U.S.
BENJAMIN V HAVENS
FERNANDEZ V BARUCH
FOXLUGER V STATE
GSPERINI V MNGINELLI
GERBA V NEUROL.HOSP.
HAMMER V ROSEN
HARRIS HOSP. V POPE
HUNT V KING COUNTY
KENT V WHITAKER
LANDO V STATE
PIETRUCHA V GRANT HO
WILLIAMS V STATE
TOTAL: 13

3RD PARTY, I
ADAMS V STATE
ANCLOTE M.F.V WILK.
ARL. HTS.V DEADERICK
BELLANDI V PARK SAN.
BOGUST V IVERSON
DUNN V STATE
FATUCK V HILL.HOSP.
KENDRICK V U.S.
KRAVITZ V STATE
LESTER V AETNA
MARKS V ST FRAN HOSP
MEIER V ROSS HOSP.
NICHOLSON V HAN
PAPINI V ALEX.SAN.
RUNYON V REID
STALLMAN V ROBINSON
TISINGER V WOOLLEY
VISTICA V PRES. HOSP
WEINSHENK V KAISER
WHITESELL V GREEN
TOTAL: 20

3RD PARTY, II
CAMERON V STATE
COLLINS V STATE
EANES V U.S.
EVANUIK V U.PITT.
EXCEL.INS.CO.V STATE
FAIR V UNITED STATES
FINKEL V STATE
FREACH V COMMONWEAL
HEIFETZ V PHIL.HOSP.
HERNAND V. ST.OF CAL
HIGGINS V STATE
HOMERE V STATE
JAMES V TURNER
LEWANDOWSKI V STATE
MAYER V ALBANY HOSP.
MERCHANTS BANK V US
MILANO V STATE
ORMAN V STATE
PETERS V STATE
ST. GEORGE V STATE
SCHWENK V STATE
SEALEY V FINKELSTEIN
SEMLER V PSY.INS.WA.
SMART V U.S.
TAIG V STATE
TARASOFF V REG.U.CA.
UNDERWOOD V U.S.
VASSOLO V CTY.HOSP.
WEIHS V STATE
TOTAL: 29

3RD PARTY, I & II
HICKS V U.S.
JOHNSON V U.S.
THALL V STATE
TOTAL: 3

STATE
PEOPLE V BERNSTEIN
PEOPLE V MCCAUGHAN
TOTAL: 2

LICENSING BOARD
COL.ST.BD. V WEILER
COOPER V BD.MED.EX.
MORRA V ST.BD.PSYCH.
TOTAL: 3

DEFENDANTS

NONPSYCHIAT.OR UNKNOWN TYPE PHYSICIAN(S)
AYERS V RUSSELL
BACON V BACON
BAKER V ORLOWSKY
BARTLETT V WEIMER
BEAUMONT V MORGAN
BECKHAM V CLINE
BELLANDI V PARK SAN.
BENCOMO V MORGAN
BOOE V HALL
BRANDT V BRANDT
BROWN V MOORE
BURKS V ROSS
BYRNE V KYSAR
CAMPBELL V GLENWOOD
CHUDY V CHUDY
CLARK V GERACI
COL.ST.BD. V WEILER
CONSTANT V HOWE
CORCORAN V JERREL
DABKOWSKI V DAVIS
DI GIOVANNI V PESSEL
DIMIT.V CHI.W.M.HOSP
DUNBAR V GREENLAW
DUZYNSKI V NOSAL
EDDINGS V PENN.
FOWLE V FOWLE
FOWLER V NRWYS. SAN.
FREACH V COMMONWEAL
GREGORY V ROBINSON
GROCE V MYERS
GUZY V GUZY
HAMMER V POLSKY
HOUGH V OGDEN
JAMES V TURNER
JOYCE V FERRAZZI
KEATING V KELLER
KENT V WHITAKER
KLEBER V STEVENS
KOSBERG V WASH. HOSP
LICHT. V MONT. HOSP.
LINDER V FOSTER
MANIACI V MARQUET.U.
MEIER V ROSS HOSP.
MEZULLO V MALETZ
MILLER V DICKERT
MILLER V WEST
MITCHELL V ROBINSON
MORRIS V U. TEXAS
MOSKOWITZ V MCQUEEN
O'CONNOR V DONALDSON
OLEPA V MAPLETOFF
O'ROURKE V HALCYON
O'ROURKE V O'ROURKE
PENNELL V CUMMINGS
PETTIS V ST.DEPT.HOS
PHILLIPS V SINGLETAR
POWELL V DUKE UNIV.
POWELL V RISSER

DEFENDANTS (CONT.)

RHIVER V RIETMAN
RICE V MERCY HOSP.
ROUSE V TWIN PINES
RUNYON V REID
SCHANBARGER V KELLOG
SCHWARTZ V THIELE
SEALEY V FINKELSTEIN
SEYMOUR V LOFGREEN
SPRINGER V STEINER
STEPHEN V DREW
STOVALL V HARMS
WARNER V PACKER
WHALEY V KIRBY
WILLIAMS V LE BAR
WILLIS V WEST.HOSP.
WOODRUFF V SHORES
TOTAL: 74

PSYCHIATRIST(S)
AIKEN V CLARY
BEAUMONT V MORGAN
BENJAMIN V HAVENS
BERRY V MOENCH
BLITZ V BOOG
BURKES V CALLION
BURKS V ROSS
CAWTHON V COFFER
COLLINS V HAND
CROCCO V HARRIS
DANIELS V FINNEY
DILLMAN V HELLMAN
DOE V ROE
EISELE V MALONE
FARBER V OLKON
FERNANDEZ V BARUCH
GSPERINI V MNGINELLI
HAMMER V ROSEN
HEIFETZ V PHIL.HOSP.
JOBSON V HENNE
JOHNSTON V RODIS
KOSBERG V WASH. HOSP
LOWEN V HILTON
MABEN V RANKIN
MEYNIER V DE PAUL
MORRIS V ROUSOS
NICHOLSON V HAN
PEOPLE V BERNSTEIN
PETTIS V ST.DEPT.HOS
QUINLEY V COCKE
ROGERS V OKIN
ROSENFELD V COLEMAN
ROSS V LEONARD
ROY V HARTOGS
RUNYON V REID
SALTER V GRANT
SAMONS V MEYMANDI
SCHAFFER V SPICER
SEMLER V PSY.INS.WA.
STONE V PROCTOR
STOVALL V HARMS
STOWERS V ARD.HOSP.
TARASOFF V REG.U.CA.
TAYLOR V GLOTFELTY
TISINGER V WOOLLEY
TOBIAS V MANHAT.E&E
VASSOLO V CTY.HOSP.
VON EYE V HAMMES
WILSON V LEHMAN
WOODS V BRUMLOP
ZIPKIN V FREEMAN
TOTAL: 51

PSYCHOLOGIST(S)
ABRAHAM V ZASLOW
COOPER V BD.MED.EX.
MORRA V ST.BD.PSYCH.
ROGERS V OKIN
STEPHEN V DREW
TARASOFF V REG.U.CA.
WHITESELL V GREEN
TOTAL: 7

SOCIAL WORKER(S)
TOTAL: 0

NURSE(S)
BELLANDI V PARK SAN.
BROWN V MOORE
BURKS V ROSS
FARBER V OLKON
MANIACI V MARQUET.U.
WILLIS V WEST.HOSP.
TOTAL: 6

LAWYER(S)
BYRNE V KYSAR
CHRISTY V SALITERMAN
PHILLIPS V SINGLETAR
TOTAL: 3

PHARMACIST
RUNYON V REID
TOTAL: 1

PARAPROFESSIONAL,
NONPRO.EMPLOYEE, ETC.
BURKS V ROSS
FOWLER V NRWYS. SAN.
FREACH V COMMONWEAL
PEOPLE V MCCAUGHAN
TOTAL: 4

ENCOUNT.GRP.LEADER
ANNIS V DONAHUE
TOTAL: 1

STATE GOVERNMENT
A.A. V STATE
ADAMS V STATE
ANONYMOUS V STATE
BANGS V STATE
BELLOWS V STATE
BENNETT V STATE
BETTS V STATE
BLAUER V STATE
BOLAND V STATE
BRADSHAW V STATE
BRIGANTE V STATE
BURNHAM V D.P.HEALTH
CALLAHAN V STATE
CAMERON V STATE
CARLINO V STATE
CASTIGLIONE V STATE
COLLINS V STATE
COMMONWEALTH V PAGE
COX V STATE
CURLEY V STATE
DALEY V STATE
DENNISON V STATE
DI FIORE V STATE
DOTY V STATE
DOWLY V STATE
DUNN V STATE
EDDINGS V PENN.
EXCEL.INS.CO.V STATE
FEITELBERG V STATE
FINKEL V STATE
FOSTER V STATE
FOXLUGER V STATE
FREACH V COMMONWEAL
GIOIA V STATE
GOULD V STATE
HAWLEY V STATE
HENDLER V STATE
HERNAND V. ST.OF CAL
HERNAND V ST.OF N.Y.
HIGGINS V STATE
HIRSH V STATE
HOMERE V STATE
IN RE MADDOX
IN RE PIERRE ESTATE
JACKSON V INDIANA
KATZ V STATE
KELLY V STATE
KOWALSKI V STATE
KRAVITZ V STATE
KUBAS V STATE
LANDO V STATE
LEGION V RICHARDSON
LEWANDOWSKI V STATE
MCCABE V STATE
MCCANDLESS V STATE
MARTINDALE V STATE
MILANO V STATE
MOCHEN V STATE
MONTGOM.CTY.TR.V ST.
MORALES V TURMAN
MORGAN V STATE
MORRIS V U. TEXAS

DEFENDANTS (CONT.)

STATE GOVERNMENT (CONT.)
NASTASI V STATE
NYSA V ROCKEFELLER
OLIVER V STATE
O'NEIL V STATE
ORMAN V STATE
PARKER V LA COUNTY
PEOPLE V LA VALLEE
PETERS V STATE
PETTIS V ST.DEPT.HOS
RENELLI V DEPT.OF MH
ROBINSON V STATE
ROSARIO V STATE
ROSSING V STATE
ST. GEORGE V STATE
SARON V STATE
SAS V STATE
SCHWENK V STATE
SCOLAVINO V STATE
SHATTUCK V STATE
SURPRENANT V STATE
TAIG V STATE
TAYLOR V STATE
THALL V STATE
TORRES V STATE
TRAPANI V STATE
VAN BARNEVELD V ST.
VITELLO V STATE
WARNER V STATE
WEGLARZ V STATE
WEIHS V STATE
WELSCH V LIKINS
WENDOVER V STATE
WHITREE V STATE
WILLIAMS V STATE
WRIGHT V STATE
WYATT V STICKNEY
TOTAL: 98

FEDERAL GOVERNMENT
BAKER V U.S.
BLITZ V BOOG
CASTILLO V U.S.
DINNERSTEIN V U.S.
DUGAN V U.S.
EABY V U.S.
EANES V U.S.
FAIR V UNITED STATES
FRIEDLAND V U.S.
HENDRY V U.S.
HICKS V U.S.
HUNGERFORD V U.S.
JOHNSON V U.S.
KENDRICK V U.S.
LEGION V RICHARDSON
MERCHANTS BANK V US
RUFINO V U.S.
SMART V U.S.
UNDERWOOD V U.S.
UNITED STATES V GRAY
U.S. V PARDUE
WHITE V U.S.
TOTAL: 22

MUNICIPAL GOVERNMENT
AYERS V RUSSELL
CENTENO V CITY OF NY
EDDINGS V PENN.
FISCHER V CITY ELM.
FREACH V COMMONWEAL
HUNT V KING COUNTY
JOYCE V FERRAZZI
LINDER V FOSTER
MARTARELLA V KELLEY
TOBIAS V MANHAT.E&E
TOTAL: 10

COUNTY GOVERNMENT
BOOE V HALL
CONSTANT V HOWE
CTY.OF L.A.V SUP.CT.
FISCHER V CITY ELM.
FORDE V CTY.L.A.
MOXON V CTY.OF KERN
PARKER V LA COUNTY
TOTAL: 7

HOSPITALS
ADAMS V RICKS
ANCLOTE M.F.V WILK.
ARL. HTS.V DEADERICK
AVEY V ST.FRAN.HOSP.
BELLANDI V PARK SAN.
BENJAMIN V HAVENS
BOYKIN V STATE
BROWN V MOORE
BURKS V ROSS
CAMPBELL V GLENWOOD
CONSTANT V HOWE
DARNELL V CAMERON
DAVIS V WATKINS
DEMARTINI V ALEX.SAN
DI GIOVANNI V PESSEL
DIMIT.V CHI.W.M.HOSP
EISELE V MALONE
EVANUIK V U.PITT.
FARBER V OLKON
FATUCK V HILL.HOSP.
FOWLER V NRWYS. SAN.
FREACH V COMMONWEAL
GERBA V NEUROL.HOSP.
GRIES V L.I. HOME
HARRIS HOSP. V POPE
HEBEL V HINSDALE SAN
HEIFETZ V PHIL.HOSP.
IN RE ANONYMOUS
IN RE WARRINGTON
JOBSON V HENNE
JOHNSON V GREER
JOHNSON V METH. HOSP
JOYCE V FERRAZZI
KOSBERG V WASH. HOSP
LAWRENCE V STATE
LEGION V RICHARDSON
LEXINGTON HOS V WHIT
LICHT. V MONT. HOSP.
LUCY HAYES V PEROTTI
MABEN V RANKIN
MCNEIL V DIRECTOR
MANIACI V MARQUET.U.
MARKS V ST FRAN HOSP
MAYER V ALBANY HOSP.
MEIER V ROSS HOSP.
MEYNIER V DE PAUL
MILLARD V CAMERON
MILLS V SOC.NY. HOSP
MOREY V KAISER FOUND
MURRAY V ST.MARY'S
NASON V SUPER.OF BR.
NOEL V MENNING.FOUND
O'CONNOR V DONALDSON
O'ROURKE V HALCYON
PAPINI V ALEX.SAN.
PAULEN V SHINNICK
PETTIS V ST.DEPT.HOS
PIETRUCHA V GRANT HO
POWELL V DUKE UNIV.
PULS V ST.VINC.HOSP.
QUICK V BEN.SIS.HOS.
REYNOLDS V NEILL
RICE V MERCY HOSP.
ROUSE V CAMERON
ROUSE V TWIN PINES
RUNYON V REID
SEMLER V PSY.INS.WA.
STALLMAN V ROBINSON
STANSFIELD V GARDNER
STEPHEN V DREW
STOWERS V ARD.HOSP.
TARASOFF V REG.U.CA.
TISINGER V WOOLLEY
TOBIAS V MANHAT.E&E
VASSOLO V CTY.HOSP.
VISTICA V PRES. HOSP
VON EYE V HAMMES
WEINSHENK V KAISER
WELSCH V LIKINS
WILLIS V WEST.HOSP.
WOOD V SAMARITAN INS
TOTAL: 81

EDUCATIONAL INSTITUTIONS
ANNIS V DONAHUE
BOGUST V IVERSON
MANIACI V MARQUET.U.
MORRIS V U. TEXAS
POWELL V DUKE UNIV.
STEPHEN V DREW
TARASOFF V REG.U.CA.
U.LOUISVILLE V HAM.
TOTAL: 8

GROWTH CENTER
BORKER V N.T.L.
GRANT V N.T.L.
TOTAL: 2

DEFENDANTS (CONT.)

JUDICIARY &/OR CLERKS, ETC.
BOOE V HALL
BURKES V CALLION
BYRNE V KYSAR
DUZYNSKI V NOSAL
FREACH V COMMONWEAL
LINDER V FOSTER
MARTARELLA V KELLEY
MORALES V TURMAN
OLEPA V MAPLETOFF
PHILLIPS V SINGLETAR
SCHANBARGER V KELLOG
SEMLER V PSY.INS.WA.
STEPHEN V DREW
WHALEY V KIRBY
WYATT V STICKNEY
TOTAL: 15

CORRECTIONAL INST.
COLLINS V BENSINGER
MARTARELLA V KELLEY
NELSON V HEYNE
STACHULAK V COUGHLIN
TOTAL: 4

POLICE
JOYCE V FERRAZZI
TARASOFF V REG.U.CA.
WHALEY V KIRBY
TOTAL: 3

INSURANCE COMPANY(S)
LESTER V AETNA
MEYNIER V DE PAUL
MORRIS V ROUSOS
PETTIS V ST.DEPT.HOS
ZIPKIN V FREEMAN
TOTAL: 5

LAYPERSON
CAWTHON V COFFER
DUZYNSKI V NOSAL
NOEL V MENNING.FOUND
TOTAL: 3

COMMIT.PCDGS.INIT.
DOUGHERTY V SNYDER
TOTAL: 1

PATIENT(S) OR REP.
EVANUIK V U.PITT.
TOTAL: 1

NOPRF.ORG.PAT.,INS.
FREACH V COMMONWEAL
PEOPLE V WILKINS
TOTAL: 2

DEFENDANT'S SIBLING
O'ROURKE V O'ROURKE
TOTAL: 1

PATIENT'S DAUGHTER
SEALEY V FINKELSTEIN
TOTAL: 1

DEFENDANT'S SPOUSE
BENJAMIN V HAVENS
TOTAL: 1

PL'S.SPOUSE &/ MOTH.
BOOE V HALL
BRANDT V BRANDT
GUZY V GUZY
OLEPA V MAPLETOFF
TOTAL: 4

SOME OR ALL DEFENDANTS NOT SPECIFIED
DEMARTINI V ALEX.SAN
MURRAY V ST.MARY'S
PAPINI V ALEX.SAN.
SUHRE V KOTT
WEINSHENK V KAISER
TOTAL: 5

NEGLIGENT ACTIVITIES: IN TREATMENT

SEXUAL ABUSE OR DISTURB. OF MARITAL REL.
ANCLOTE M.F.V WILK.
COL.ST.BD. V WEILER
COOPER V BD.MED.EX.
CROCCO V HARRIS
MORRA V ST.BD.PSYCH.
NICHOLSON V HAN
PEOPLE V BERNSTEIN
ROSS V LEONARD
ROY V HARTOGS
SEYMOUR V LOFGREEN
WHITESELL V GREEN
ZIPKIN V FREEMAN
TOTAL: 12

PHYSICAL ASSAULT
ABRAHAM V ZASLOW
BELLANDI V PARK SAN.
HAMMER V ROSEN
STOWERS V ARD.HOSP.
WHITREE V STATE
TOTAL: 5

NEGLIGENT INSULIN THERAPY
MITCHELL V ROBINSON
RUFINO V U.S.
TOTAL: 2

NEGLIGENT ELECTROCONVULSIVE THERAPY
ADAMS V RICKS
COLLINS V HAND
EISELE V MALONE
FARBER V OLKON
FOXLUGER V STATE
JOHNSTON V RODIS
KOSBERG V WASH. HOSP
LESTER V AETNA
MABEN V RANKIN
O'ROURKE V HALCYON
PETTIS V ST.DEPT.HOS
QUINLEY V COCKE
RICE V MERCY HOSP.
STONE V PROCTOR
WARNER V STATE
WILSON V LEHMAN
WOODS V BRUMLOP
TOTAL: 17

NEG.ADMIN.OF DRUGS
CROCCO V HARRIS
FISCHER V CITY ELM.
JOHNSON V GREER
JOHNSON V U.S.
MABEN V RANKIN
NELSON V HEYNE
ROSENFELD V COLEMAN
ROUSE V TWIN PINES
RUNYON V REID
SARON V STATE
STOVALL V HARMS
WELSCH V LIKINS
WHITREE V STATE
TOTAL: 13

FAILURE TO OBTAIN -OR LACK OF- CONSENT
AIKEN V CLARY
ANONYMOUS V STATE
BLITZ V BOOG
MABEN V RANKIN
RICE V MERCY HOSP.
ROGERS V OKIN

NEGLIGENT ACTIVITIES: IN TREATMENT (CONT.)

STOVALL V HARMS
STOWERS V ARD.HOSP.
WILSON V LEHMAN
WOODS V BRUMLOP
TOTAL: 10

NO TREATMENT OR INADEQUATE TREATMENT
BELLOWS V STATE
BURNHAM V D.P.HEALTH
COLLINS V BENSINGER
COMMONWEALTH V PAGE
DAVIS V WATKINS
FREACH V COMMONWEAL
GSPERINI V MNGINELLI
HUNGERFORD V U.S.
IN RE ANONYMOUS
IN RE MADDOX
JACKSON V INDIANA
JOHNSON V U.S.
LEGION V RICHARDSON
MARTARELLA V KELLEY
MORALES V TURMAN
MORGAN V STATE
NASON V SUPER.OF BR.
NASTASI V STATE
NELSON V HEYNE
NYSA V ROCKEFELLER
O'CONNOR V DONALDSON
PEOPLE V LA VALLEE
PEOPLE V WILKINS
RENELLI V DEPT.OF MH
REYNOLDS V NEILL
ROUSE V CAMERON
SAS V STATE
STACHULAK V COUGHLIN
U.S. V PARDUE
VITELLO V STATE
WELSCH V LIKINS
WHITREE V STATE
WYATT V STICKNEY
TOTAL: 33

NEGLIGENCE IN USE OF TECHNIQUE
ABRAHAM V ZASLOW
ANNIS V DONAHUE
BELLANDI V PARK SAN.
BLAUER V STATE
BROWN V MOORE
GRANT V N.T.L.
HAMMER V ROSEN
JOBSON V HENNE
JOHNSON V U.S.
SALTER V GRANT
TOTAL: 10

NEG.TRANSFER.OR CTRT
ANCLOTE M.F.V WILK.
ZIPKIN V FREEMAN
TOTAL: 2

UNSPEC.NEG.TREAT
BANGS V STATE
BOLAND V STATE
BORKER V N.T.L.
JOHNSON V METH. HOSP
TOTAL: 4

? WHETHER TREAT.INV.
BRADSHAW V STATE
IN RE WARRINGTON
KOWALSKI V STATE
MOSKOWITZ V MCQUEEN
TOTAL: 4

FAILURE TO CONSULT
GSPERINI V MNGINELLI
SEYMOUR V LOFGREEN
TOTAL: 2

IMPROPER ABORTION
MCCANDLESS V STATE
TOTAL: 1

NEG.APPL. OF WETPACK
POWELL V RISSER
TOTAL: 1

NEGLIGENT OPERATION
WILLIS V WEST.HOSP.
TOTAL: 1

NEGLIGENT ACTIVITIES: IN DIAGNOSIS - WHAT WAS DIAGNOSED

SANITY, INSTEAD OF MENTAL ILLNESS
BURKES V CALLION
CAMERON V STATE
CHRISTY V SALITERMAN
HIGGINS V STATE
KRAVITZ V STATE
MERCHANTS BANK V US
MILLS V SOC.NY. HOSP
PHILLIPS V SINGLETAR
ST. GEORGE V STATE
SEYMOUR V LOFGREEN
TAIG V STATE
TARASOFF V REG.U.CA.
WEGLARZ V STATE
TOTAL: 13

MENT.ILL, INSTEAD OF PHYSICAL ILLNESS
BLITZ V BOOG
BROWN V MOORE
HUNGERFORD V U.S.
MOREY V KAISER FOUND
NASTASI V STATE
SEYMOUR V LOFGREEN
WEINSHENK V KAISER
TOTAL: 7

PHYS.ILL, INSTEAD OF MENT.ILLNESS
O'NEIL V STATE
SEYMOUR V LOFGREEN
TOTAL: 2

TYPE OF MENTAL ILLNESS
HENDRY V U.S.
TOTAL: 1

SUICIDAL TENDENCIES
TOTAL: 0

LACK OF SUICIDAL TENDENCIES
BAKER V U.S.
BOGUST V IVERSON
DILLMAN V HELLMAN
FERNANDEZ V BARUCH
IN RE PIERRE ESTATE
JOHNSON V U.S.
KATZ V STATE
KUBAS V STATE
TISINGER V WOOLLEY
WEGLARZ V STATE
WHITE V U.S.
TOTAL: 11

MENTAL ILLNESS, INSTEAD OF SANITY
AYERS V RUSSELL
BACON V BACON
BAKER V ORLOWSKY
BANGS V STATE
BARTLETT V WEIMER

NEGLIGENT ACTIVITIES: IN DIAGNOSIS - WHAT WAS DIAGNOSED (CONT.)

BEAUMONT V MORGAN
BECKHAM V CLINE
BENCOMO V MORGAN
BOLAND V STATE
BOOE V HALL
BRANDT V BRANDT
BYRNE V KYSAR
CAWTHON V COFFER
CHUDY V CHUDY
CORCORAN V JERREL
DABKOWSKI V DAVIS
DANIELS V FINNEY
DARNELL V CAMERON
DENNISON V STATE
DI GIOVANNI V PESSEL
DOUGHERTY V SNYDER
DUNBAR V GREENLAW
DUZYNSKI V NOSAL
EDDINGS V PENN.
FOWLE V FOWLE
GUZY V GUZY
HAMMER V POLSKY
HOUGH V OGDEN
JACKSON V INDIANA
JOHNSON V GREER
JOYCE V FERRAZZI
KEATING V KELLER
KELLY V STATE
KENDRICK V U.S.
KLEBER V STEVENS
LINDER V FOSTER
LOWEN V HILTON
MABEN V RANKIN
MANIACI V MARQUET.U.
MEZULLO V MALETZ
MILLARD V CAMERON
MILLER V DICKERT
MILLER V WEST
MORGAN V STATE
MORRIS V ROUSOS
MORRIS V U. TEXAS
O'CONNOR V DONALDSON
OLEPA V MAPLETOFF
O'ROURKE V O'ROURKE
PARKER V LA COUNTY
PENNELL V CUMMINGS
POWELL V DUKE UNIV.
RHIVER V RIETMAN
RICE V MERCY HOSP.
ROSARIO V STATE
SAMONS V MEYMANDI
SAS V STATE
SCHAFFER V SPICER
SCHWARTZ V THIELE
SPRINGER V STEINER
STACHULAK V COUGHLIN
STEPHEN V DREW
STOWERS V ARD.HOSP.
SUHRE V KOTT
TAYLOR V GLOTFELTY
WARNER V PACKER
WARNER V STATE
WHALEY V KIRBY
WHITREE V STATE
WILLIAMS V LE BAR
WILLIS V WEST.HOSP.
WOODRUFF V SHORES
TOTAL: 72

DANGEROUSNESS
COMMONWEALTH V PAGE
DARNELL V CAMERON
DOUGHERTY V SNYDER
IN RE ANONYMOUS
IN RE MADDOX
KELLY V STATE
MILLARD V CAMERON
STACHULAK V COUGHLIN
TOTAL: 8

LACK OF DANGEROUSNESS
CENTENO V CITY OF NY
EANES V U.S.
FAIR V UNITED STATES
FREACH V COMMONWEAL
HEIFETZ V PHIL.HOSP.
HICKS V U.S.
HIGGINS V STATE
HOMERE V STATE
JOHNSON V U.S.
KENDRICK V U.S.
KRAVITZ V STATE
LEWANDOWSKI V STATE
MERCHANTS BANK V US
MILANO V STATE
ORMAN V STATE
PETERS V STATE
SCHWENK V STATE
SEMLER V PSY.INS.WA.
SMART V U.S.
TAIG V STATE
TARASOFF V REG.U.CA.
TAYLOR V STATE
UNDERWOOD V U.S.
VASSOLO V CTY.HOSP.
WOOD V SAMARITAN INS
TOTAL: 25

IMPROPER DRUG PRESCRIPTION
CAMPBELL V GLENWOOD
CHRISTY V SALITERMAN
COOPER V BD.MED.EX.
FISCHER V CITY ELM.
ROUSE V TWIN PINES
RUNYON V REID
SARON V STATE
TOTAL: 7

TYPE OF TREATMENT NEEDED
CASTILLO V U.S.
CENTENO V CITY OF NY
CHRISTY V SALITERMAN
COLLINS V HAND
O'ROURKE V HALCYON
TOTAL: 5

TYPE OF CUSTODIAL CARE
ARL. HTS.V DEADERICK
BENJAMIN V HAVENS
CAMPBELL V GLENWOOD
CHRISTY V SALITERMAN
FORDE V CTY.L.A.
TOBIAS V MANHAT.E&E
WRIGHT V STATE
TOTAL: 7

UNFITNESS FOR DUTY
HENDRY V U.S.
TOTAL: 1

NEG.REC.TO TAKE PSYCHIATRIC EXAM
BENCOMO V MORGAN
SCHANBARGER V KELLOG
TOTAL: 2

FAILURE TO MAKE A DIAGNOSIS
BELLOWS V STATE
HIGGINS V STATE
KEATING V KELLER
MCNEIL V DIRECTOR
TOTAL: 4

INADEQUATE DIAGNOSIS
BURNHAM V D.P.HEALTH
MORGAN V STATE
NELSON V HEYNE
ORMAN V STATE
PEOPLE V WILKINS
ROSARIO V STATE
VITELLO V STATE
TOTAL: 7

OTHER NEGLIGENT DIAGNOSIS

? WHETHER DIAG.INV.
BRADSHAW V STATE
IN RE WARRINGTON
KOWALSKI V STATE
MOSKOWITZ V MCQUEEN
TOTAL: 4

NEGLIGENT ACTIVITIES: IN DIAGNOSIS - RESULTS OF DIAGNOSES

IMPROPER RELEASE
CAMERON V STATE
CENTENO V CITY OF NY
CHRISTY V SALITERMAN
EANES V U.S.
FAIR V UNITED STATES
FERNANDEZ V BARUCH
FREACH V COMMONWEAL
HEIFETZ V PHIL.HOSP.
HICKS V U.S.
HOMERE V STATE
JOHNSON V U.S.
KENDRICK V U.S.
KRAVITZ V STATE
LEWANDOWSKI V STATE
MERCHANTS BANK V US
MILANO V STATE
ORMAN V STATE
PETERS V STATE
ST. GEORGE V STATE
SCHWENK V STATE
SEMLER V PSY.INS.WA.
SMART V U.S.
TAIG V STATE
TAYLOR V STATE
UNDERWOOD V U.S.
VASSOLO V CTY.HOSP.
TOTAL: 26

IMPROPER CUSTODIAL CARE
ARL. HTS.V DEADERICK
BAKER V U.S.
BENJAMIN V HAVENS
BOGUST V IVERSON
BROWN V MOORE
CAMPBELL V GLENWOOD
CHRISTY V SALITERMAN
DILLMAN V HELLMAN
HIGGINS V STATE
IN RE ANONYMOUS
IN RE MADDOX
IN RE PIERRE ESTATE
KATZ V STATE
KUBAS V STATE
MILLS V SOC.NY. HOSP
MORRIS V ROUSOS
NELSON V HEYNE
TARASOFF V REG.U.CA.
TISINGER V WOOLLEY
TOBIAS V MANHAT.E&E
UNDERWOOD V U.S.
VASSOLO V CTY.HOSP.
WEGLARZ V STATE
WILLIS V WEST.HOSP.
WOOD V SAMARITAN INS
WRIGHT V STATE
TOTAL: 26

IMPROPER COMMITMENT
AYERS V RUSSELL
BACON V BACON
BAKER V ORLOWSKY
BANGS V STATE
BARTLETT V WEIMER
BEAUMONT V MORGAN
BECKHAM V CLINE
BENCOMO V MORGAN
BOLAND V STATE
BOOE V HALL
BRANDT V BRANDT
BURKES V CALLION
BYRNE V KYSAR
CAWTHON V COFFER
CHUDY V CHUDY
COMMONWEALTH V PAGE
CORCORAN V JERREL
DABKOWSKI V DAVIS
DANIELS V FINNEY
DARNELL V CAMERON
DENNISON V STATE
DI GIOVANNI V PESSEL
DOUGHERTY V SNYDER
DUNBAR V GREENLAW
DUZYNSKI V NOSAL
EDDINGS V PENN.
FORDE V CTY.L.A.
FOWLE V FOWLE
GUZY V GUZY
HOUGH V OGDEN
JACKSON V INDIANA
JOYCE V FERRAZZI
KEATING V KELLER
KELLY V STATE
KLEBER V STEVENS
LINDER V FOSTER
LOWEN V HILTON
MABEN V RANKIN
MANIACI V MARQUET.U.
MEZULLO V MALETZ
MILLARD V CAMERON
MILLER V DICKERT
MILLER V WEST
MORGAN V STATE
MORRIS V U. TEXAS
O'CONNOR V DONALDSON
O'ROURKE V O'ROURKE
PARKER V LA COUNTY
PENNELL V CUMMINGS
PEOPLE V WILKINS
POWELL V DUKE UNIV.
RHIVER V RIETMAN
ROSARIO V STATE
ROUSE V TWIN PINES
SAMONS V MEYMANDI
SAS V STATE
SCHWARTZ V THIELE
SPRINGER V STEINER
STACHULAK V COUGHLIN
STEPHEN V DREW
STOWERS V ARD.HOSP.
SUHRE V KOTT
TAYLOR V GLOTFELTY
WARNER V PACKER
WARNER V STATE
WHALEY V KIRBY
WILLIAMS V LE BAR
WILLIS V WEST.HOSP.
WOODRUFF V SHORES
TOTAL: 69

IMPROPER FAILURE TO COMMIT
TARASOFF V REG.U.CA.
TOTAL: 1

IMPROPER TREATMENT PRESCRIBED
BLITZ V BOOG
BOGUST V IVERSON
BROWN V MOORE
BURNHAM V D.P.HEALTH
CASTILLO V U.S.
CENTENO V CITY OF NY
CHRISTY V SALITERMAN
COLLINS V HAND
HUNGERFORD V U.S.
MABEN V RANKIN
MOREY V KAISER FOUND
NASTASI V STATE
O'NEIL V STATE
O'ROURKE V HALCYON
SEYMOUR V LOFGREEN
WEINSHENK V KAISER
WHITE V U.S.
WHITREE V STATE
TOTAL: 18

IMPROPER DRUG PRESCRIPTION
CAMPBELL V GLENWOOD
CHRISTY V SALITERMAN
COOPER V BD.MED.EX.
FISCHER V CITY ELM.
MABEN V RANKIN
ROUSE V TWIN PINES
RUNYON V REID
SARON V STATE
WHITE V U.S.
WHITREE V STATE
TOTAL: 10

IMPROPER FAILURE TO RELEASE
BEAUMONT V MORGAN
BELLOWS V STATE
DARNELL V CAMERON
DENNISON V STATE
JACKSON V INDIANA
JOHNSON V GREER
MCNEIL V DIRECTOR
O'CONNOR V DONALDSON
PEOPLE V WILKINS
RICE V MERCY HOSP.
ROSARIO V STATE
STEPHEN V DREW
VITELLO V STATE
WARNER V STATE
WHITREE V STATE
TOTAL: 15

NEGLIGENT ACTIVITIES: IN DIAGNOSIS - RESULTS OF DIAGNOSES (CONT.)

IMPROPER DETERMINATION OF CUSTODY
- HAMMER V POLSKY
- SCHAFFER V SPICER
- TOTAL: 2

NEG. DETERM.OF UNFITNESS FOR DUTY
- HENDRY V U.S.
- TOTAL: 1

NEG.DETERM.OF COMPETENCE TO STAND TRIAL
- PHILLIPS V SINGLETAR
- TOTAL: 1

UNKNOWN
- SCHANBARGER V KELLOG
- TOTAL: 1

NEGLIGENT ACTIVITIES: IN CARE

FAILURE TO PROVIDE PROPER CUSTODIAL CARE
- A.A. V STATE
- BENNETT V STATE
- BURNHAM V D.P.HEALTH
- CALLAHAN V STATE
- CAMPBELL V GLENWOOD
- GROCE V MYERS
- HAWLEY V STATE
- HENDLER V STATE
- HERNAND V. ST.OF CAL
- JOHNSON V METH. HOSP
- LANDO V STATE
- LAWRENCE V STATE
- LEGION V RICHARDSON
- MARKS V ST FRAN HOSP
- MORGAN V STATE
- NYSA V ROCKEFELLER
- OLIVER V STATE
- ORMAN V STATE
- PEOPLE V LA VALLEE
- PEOPLE V MCCAUGHAN
- SCOLAVINO V STATE
- TARASOFF V REG.U.CA.
- TAYLOR V STATE
- TORRES V STATE
- UNDERWOOD V U.S.
- VASSOLO V CTY.HOSP.
- VITELLO V STATE
- WELSCH V LIKINS
- WHITREE V STATE
- WILLIAMS V STATE
- WILLIS V WEST.HOSP.
- WRIGHT V STATE
- TOTAL: 32

PREMATURE RELEASE
- CAMERON V STATE
- FAIR V UNITED STATES
- FERNANDEZ V BARUCH
- HERNAND V. ST.OF CAL
- JOHNSON V U.S.
- MILANO V STATE
- SCHWENK V STATE
- TAYLOR V STATE
- UNDERWOOD V U.S.
- TOTAL: 9

FAILURE TO RELEASE
- JOHNSON V GREER
- TOTAL: 1

FAILURE TO WARN THIRD PARTIES
- BOGUST V IVERSON
- FAIR V UNITED STATES
- FERNANDEZ V BARUCH
- SEALEY V FINKELSTEIN
- TARASOFF V REG.U.CA.
- UNDERWOOD V U.S.
- TOTAL: 6

IMPROPER GIVING OF INFORMATION TO OTHERS
- BERRY V MOENCH
- CLARK V GERACI
- DOE V ROE
- GSPERINI V MNGINELLI
- HAMMER V POLSKY
- MORRIS V ROUSOS
- TOTAL: 6

INADEQUATE SUPERVISION
- A.A. V STATE
- ADAMS V RICKS
- ADAMS V STATE
- ARL. HTS.V DEADERICK
- AVEY V ST.FRAN.HOSP.
- BAKER V U.S.
- BENJAMIN V HAVENS
- BETTS V STATE
- BOGUST V IVERSON
- BOYKIN V STATE
- BRIGANTE V STATE
- BROWN V MOORE
- BURKS V ROSS
- CALLAHAN V STATE
- CARLINO V STATE
- CASTIGLIONE V STATE
- CASTILLO V U.S.
- COLLINS V STATE
- CONSTANT V HOWE
- CTY.OF L.A.V SUP.CT.
- COX V STATE
- CURLEY V STATE
- DALEY V STATE
- DEMARTINI V ALEX.SAN
- DI FIORE V STATE
- DILLMAN V HELLMAN
- DIMIT.V CHI.W.M.HOSP
- DINNERSTEIN V U.S.
- DOTY V STATE
- DOWLY V STATE
- DUGAN V U.S.
- DUNN V STATE
- EABY V U.S.
- EVANUIK V U.PITT.
- EXCEL.INS.CO.V STATE
- FATUCK V HILL.HOSP.
- FEITELBERG V STATE
- FINKEL V STATE
- FISCHER V CITY ELM.
- FORDE V CTY.L.A.
- FOSTER V STATE
- FOWLER V NRWYS. SAN.
- FRIEDLAND V U.S.
- GERBA V NEUROL.HOSP.
- GIOIA V STATE
- GOULD V STATE
- GREGORY V ROBINSON
- GRIES V L.I. HOME
- HARRIS HOSP. V POPE
- HAWLEY V STATE
- HEBEL V HINSDALE SAN
- HENDLER V STATE
- HERNAND V ST.OF N.Y.
- HIGGINS V STATE
- HIRSH V STATE
- HUNT V KING COUNTY
- IN RE PIERRE ESTATE
- JAMES V TURNER
- JOHNSON V U.S.
- KENT V WHITAKER
- KUBAS V STATE
- LAWRENCE V STATE
- LEXINGTON HOS V WHIT
- LICHT. V MONT. HOSP.
- LUCY HAYES V PEROTTI
- MCCABE V STATE
- MCCANDLESS V STATE

NEGLIGENT ACTIVITIES: IN CARE (CONT.)

MARKS V ST FRAN HOSP
MARTINDALE V STATE
MAYER V ALBANY HOSP.
MEIER V ROSS HOSP.
MEYNIER V DE PAUL
MILANO V STATE
MOCHEN V STATE
MONTGOM.CTY.TR.V ST.
MOXON V CTY.OF KERN
MURRAY V ST.MARY'S
NYSA V ROCKEFELLER
NOEL V MENNING.FOUND
ORMAN V STATE
PAPINI V ALEX.SAN.
PAULEN V SHINNICK
PIETRUCHA V GRANT HO
PULS V ST.VINC.HOSP.
QUICK V BEN.SIS.HOS.
ROBINSON V STATE
ROSSING V STATE
SCHWENK V STATE
SCOLAVINO V STATE
SHATTUCK V STATE
STALLMAN V ROBINSON
STANSFIELD V GARDNER
SURPRENANT V STATE
TAYLOR V STATE
THALL V STATE
TRAPANI V STATE
UNITED STATES V GRAY
U.LOUISVILLE V HAM.
VAN BARNEVELD V ST.
VASSOLO V CTY.HOSP.
VISTICA V PRES. HOSP
VON EYE V HAMMES
WEIHS V STATE
WENDOVER V STATE
WILLIAMS V STATE
WOOD V SAMARITAN INS
TOTAL: 106

OTHER NEGLIGENT CARE

? WHETHER CARE INV.
BRADSHAW V STATE
IN RE WARRINGTON
KOWALSKI V STATE
MOSKOWITZ V MCQUEEN
TOTAL: 4

HARM CAUSED TO PLAINTIFFS AND/OR PATIENTS

SUICIDE
ANCLOTE M.F.V WILK.
BOGUST V IVERSON
BORKER V N.T.L.
CENTENO V CITY OF NY
COLLINS V STATE
DIMIT.V CHI.W.M.HOSP
DINNERSTEIN V U.S.
FAIR V UNITED STATES
FATUCK V HILL.HOSP.
FERNANDEZ V BARUCH
FOWLER V NRWYS. SAN.
FRIEDLAND V U.S.
GIOIA V STATE
GRIES V L.I. HOME
HIRSH V STATE
IN RE PIERRE ESTATE
JAMES V TURNER
JOHNSON V U.S.
KATZ V STATE
KENT V WHITAKER
KOWALSKI V STATE
KUBAS V STATE
LAWRENCE V STATE
LICHT. V MONT. HOSP.
LUCY HAYES V PEROTTI
MARTINDALE V STATE
MEIER V ROSS HOSP.
MILLS V SOC.NY. HOSP
MURRAY V ST.MARY'S
PETERS V STATE
PIETRUCHA V GRANT HO
RUNYON V REID
STALLMAN V ROBINSON
TISINGER V WOOLLEY
TRAPANI V STATE
VISTICA V PRES. HOSP
WEGLARZ V STATE
WHITE V U.S.
TOTAL: 38

NONSUICIDAL DEATH
ARL. HTS.V DEADERICK
BELLANDI V PARK SAN.
BLAUER V STATE
BROWN V MOORE
BURKS V ROSS
CASTILLO V U.S.
DALEY V STATE
DOWLY V STATE
DUGAN V U.S.
DUNN V STATE
EVANUIK V U.PITT.
FAIR V UNITED STATES
FINKEL V STATE
FREACH V COMMONWEAL
GOULD V STATE
HEBEL V HINSDALE SAN
HERNAND V. ST.OF CAL
HICKS V U.S.
KENDRICK V U.S.
KOSBERG V WASH. HOSP
KRAVITZ V STATE
LANDO V STATE
MERCHANTS BANK V US
MILANO V STATE
MOXON V CTY.OF KERN
NASTASI V STATE
O'NEIL V STATE
PAPINI V ALEX.SAN.
PEOPLE V MCCAUGHAN
RUFINO V U.S.
ST. GEORGE V STATE
SCHWENK V STATE
SEMLER V PSY.INS.WA.
STONE V PROCTOR
TARASOFF V REG.U.CA.
TAYLOR V STATE
UNDERWOOD V U.S.
VAN BARNEVELD V ST.
WEINSHENK V KAISER
WILLIS V WEST.HOSP.
TOTAL: 40

SELF-INFLICTED INJURIES
ADAMS V STATE
BAKER V U.S.
DEMARTINI V ALEX.SAN
DILLMAN V HELLMAN
FORDE V CTY.L.A.
GERBA V NEUROL.HOSP.
GREGORY V ROBINSON
HARRIS HOSP. V POPE
HUNT V KING COUNTY
MOCHEN V STATE
PAULEN V SHINNICK
SURPRENANT V STATE
UNITED STATES V GRAY
VON EYE V HAMMES
WRIGHT V STATE
TOTAL: 15

ECONOMIC LOSS
ANCLOTE M.F.V WILK.
CAWTHON V COFFER
CLARK V GERACI
DENNISON V STATE
DUZYNSKI V NOSAL
EXCEL.INS.CO.V STATE
GSPERINI V MNGINELLI
GERBA V NEUROL.HOSP.
HAMMER V ROSEN
HEIFETZ V PHIL.HOSP.
HENDRY V U.S.
KELLY V STATE
MOREY V KAISER FOUND
MORRIS V ROUSOS
MORRIS V U. TEXAS
OLIVER V STATE

HARM CAUSED TO PLAINTIFFS AND/OR PATIENTS (CONT.)

ROSARIO V STATE
SEYMOUR V LOFGREEN
SURPRENANT V STATE
VASSOLO V CTY.HOSP.
WHITREE V STATE
WILLIAMS V STATE
ZIPKIN V FREEMAN
TOTAL: 23

NONSELF-INFLICTED INJURIES
ABRAHAM V ZASLOW
ADAMS V RICKS
AIKEN V CLARY
ANNIS V DONAHUE
BENJAMIN V HAVENS
BENNETT V STATE
BETTS V STATE
BOYKIN V STATE
CALLAHAN V STATE
CAMERON V STATE
CASTIGLIONE V STATE
CHRISTY V SALITERMAN
COLLINS V HAND
CONSTANT V HOWE
CTY.OF L.A.V SUP.CT.
COX V STATE
CURLEY V STATE
DI FIORE V STATE
DOTY V STATE
EABY V U.S.
EANES V U.S.
EISELE V MALONE
FARBER V OLKON
FEITELBERG V STATE
FISCHER V CITY ELM.
FOSTER V STATE
FOXLUGER V STATE
GRANT V N.T.L.
GROCE V MYERS
HAMMER V ROSEN
HAWLEY V STATE
HENDLER V STATE
HERNAND V ST.OF N.Y.
HIGGINS V STATE
HOMERE V STATE
IN RE WARRINGTON
JOHNSON V GREER
JOHNSON V METH. HOSP
JOHNSON V U.S.
JOHNSTON V RODIS
LESTER V AETNA
LEWANDOWSKI V STATE
LEXINGTON HOS V WHIT
MCCABE V STATE
MAYER V ALBANY HOSP.
MEYNIER V DE PAUL
MITCHELL V ROBINSON
MONTGOM.CTY.TR.V ST.
MORGAN V STATE
NELSON V HEYNE
NYSA V ROCKEFELLER
NOEL V MENNING.FOUND
OLIVER V STATE
ORMAN V STATE
O'ROURKE V HALCYON
PETERS V STATE
PETTIS V ST.DEPT.HOS
POWELL V RISSER
PULS V ST.VINC.HOSP.
QUICK V BEN.SIS.HOS.
QUINLEY V COCKE
ROBINSON V STATE
ROSENFELD V COLEMAN
ROSSING V STATE
ROUSE V TWIN PINES
SARON V STATE
SCOLAVINO V STATE
SEALEY V FINKELSTEIN
SHATTUCK V STATE
SMART V U.S.
STANSFIELD V GARDNER
STOVALL V HARMS
STOWERS V ARD.HOSP.
TAIG V STATE
THALL V STATE
TORRES V STATE
U.LOUISVILLE V HAM.
VASSOLO V CTY.HOSP.
WARNER V STATE
WEIHS V STATE
WENDOVER V STATE
WHITREE V STATE
WILSON V LEHMAN
WOODS V BRUMLOP
TOTAL: 84

SELF-INFL.OR ACC.INJ
AVEY V ST.FRAN.HOSP.
CARLINO V STATE
WOOD V SAMARITAN INS
TOTAL: 3

SUIC.OR ACCID.DEATH
BRIGANTE V STATE
MARKS V ST FRAN HOSP
TOTAL: 2

SEXUAL OR MARITAL HARM
A.A. V STATE
ANCLOTE M.F.V WILK.
COL.ST.BD. V WEILER
COOPER V BD.MED.EX.
CROCCO V HARRIS
FREACH V COMMONWEAL
MCCANDLESS V STATE
MARTARELLA V KELLEY
MILANO V STATE
MORRA V ST.BD.PSYCH.
NICHOLSON V HAN
PEOPLE V BERNSTEIN
ROSS V LEONARD
ROY V HARTOGS
SEYMOUR V LOFGREEN
WHITESELL V GREEN
WILLIAMS V STATE
ZIPKIN V FREEMAN
TOTAL: 18

PREG.& ABORTION
MCCANDLESS V STATE
TOTAL: 1

DEPRIVATION OF CONSTITUTIONAL RIGHTS
BELLOWS V STATE
BURKES V CALLION
BURNHAM V D.P.HEALTH
BYRNE V KYSAR
CAMPBELL V GLENWOOD
COLLINS V BENSINGER
COMMONWEALTH V PAGE
DAVIS V WATKINS
DENNISON V STATE
EDDINGS V PENN.
IN RE ANONYMOUS
IN RE MADDOX
JACKSON V INDIANA
JOBSON V HENNE
JOHNSON V GREER
JOYCE V FERRAZZI
LEGION V RICHARDSON
MCNEIL V DIRECTOR
MARTARELLA V KELLEY
MORALES V TURMAN
NASON V SUPER.OF BR.
NELSON V HEYNE
NYSA V ROCKEFELLER
O'CONNOR V DONALDSON
PEOPLE V LA VALLEE
PEOPLE V WILKINS
RENELLI V DEPT.OF MH
REYNOLDS V NEILL
ROGERS V OKIN
ROSARIO V STATE
ROUSE V CAMERON
SAS V STATE
STACHULAK V COUGHLIN
U.S. V PARDUE
VITELLO V STATE
WARNER V STATE
WELSCH V LIKINS
WHALEY V KIRBY
WYATT V STICKNEY
TOTAL: 39

LOSS OF LIBERTY
BARTLETT V WEIMER
BEAUMONT V MORGAN
BECKHAM V CLINE
BLITZ V BOOG
BURKES V CALLION
CHUDY V CHUDY

HARM CAUSED TO PLAINTIFFS AND/OR PATIENTS (CONT.)

COMMONWEALTH V PAGE
DENNISON V STATE
JACKSON V INDIANA
JOHNSON V GREER
KLEBER V STEVENS
MABEN V RANKIN
MCNEIL V DIRECTOR
MANIACI V MARQUET.U.
MEZULLO V MALETZ
MILLARD V CAMERON
MILLER V DICKERT
MILLER V WEST
MORGAN V STATE
NASON V SUPER.OF BR.
O'CONNOR V DONALDSON
OLEPA V MAPLETOFF
O'ROURKE V O'ROURKE
PENNELL V CUMMINGS
PEOPLE V LA VALLEE
PEOPLE V WILKINS
PHILLIPS V SINGLETAR
RHIVER V RIETMAN
ROSARIO V STATE
ROUSE V CAMERON
SAMONS V MEYMANDI
SAS V STATE
SPRINGER V STEINER
STACHULAK V COUGHLIN
STEPHEN V DREW
STOWERS V ARD.HOSP.
SUHRE V KOTT
TAYLOR V GLOTFELTY
TOBIAS V MANHAT.E&E
VITELLO V STATE
WARNER V PACKER
WARNER V STATE
WELSCH V LIKINS
WHALEY V KIRBY
WILLIAMS V LE BAR
WOODRUFF V SHORES
TOTAL: 46

NOT SPECIFIED
ANONYMOUS V STATE
AYERS V RUSSELL
BAKER V ORLOWSKY
BANGS V STATE
BOLAND V STATE
BOOE V HALL
BRADSHAW V STATE
BRANDT V BRANDT
CORCORAN V JERREL
CROCCO V HARRIS
DABKOWSKI V DAVIS
DANIELS V FINNEY
DARNELL V CAMERON
DI GIOVANNI V PESSEL
DOUGHERTY V SNYDER
DUNBAR V GREENLAW
FOWLE V FOWLE
GUZY V GUZY
HAMMER V POLSKY
HOUGH V OGDEN
HUNGERFORD V U.S.
KEATING V KELLER
LOWEN V HILTON
SCHANBARGER V KELLOG
TOTAL: 24

PREGNANCY
WILLIAMS V STATE
TOTAL: 1

LOSS OF COMPNNSHIP
SURPRENANT V STATE
TOTAL: 1

LOSS OF CONSORTIUM
ADAMS V STATE
GERBA V NEUROL.HOSP.
LINDER V FOSTER
PARKER V LA COUNTY
POWELL V DUKE UNIV.
ROUSE V TWIN PINES
THALL V STATE
U.S. V PARDUE
WHITESELL V GREEN
TOTAL: 9

ALIENATION OF AFFECTION
NICHOLSON V HAN
SALTER V GRANT
SEYMOUR V LOFGREEN
WHITESELL V GREEN
TOTAL: 4

EMOTIONAL DISTRESS
A.A. V STATE
ADAMS V RICKS
ANCLOTE M.F.V WILK.
BACON V BACON
BENCOMO V MORGAN
CAWTHON V COFFER
CHRISTY V SALITERMAN
CHUDY V CHUDY
EISELE V MALONE
GOULD V STATE
GRANT V N.T.L.
HAMMER V ROSEN
HENDRY V U.S.
KELLY V STATE
LANDO V STATE
MCCANDLESS V STATE
MARTARELLA V KELLEY
ROSS V LEONARD
ROY V HARTOGS
SARON V STATE
SCHWARTZ V THIELE
SEYMOUR V LOFGREEN
STOWERS V ARD.HOSP.
THALL V STATE
VASSOLO V CTY.HOSP.
WEIHS V STATE
WHITREE V STATE
WOODRUFF V SHORES
ZIPKIN V FREEMAN
TOTAL: 29

INVASION OF PRIVACY
DOE V ROE
SCHWARTZ V THIELE
TOTAL: 2

INJURY TO REPUTATION
BACON V BACON
BERRY V MOENCH
CHUDY V CHUDY
GSPERINI V MNGINELLI
SCHAFFER V SPICER
SCHWARTZ V THIELE
STEPHEN V DREW
SUHRE V KOTT
TAYLOR V GLOTFELTY
WARNER V STATE
WILLIAMS V STATE
TOTAL: 11

LOSS OF HEALTH
CAWTHON V COFFER
MOREY V KAISER FOUND
TOTAL: 2

DRUG ADDICTION
ROSENFELD V COLEMAN
TOTAL: 1

EXACERB.OF PREV.CONDITION
A.A. V STATE
ABRAHAM V ZASLOW
MOREY V KAISER FOUND
MORGAN V STATE
MOSKOWITZ V MCQUEEN
NYSA V ROCKEFELLER
SALTER V GRANT
SEYMOUR V LOFGREEN
U.LOUISVILLE V HAM.
WHITREE V STATE
WILLIS V WEST.HOSP.
ZIPKIN V FREEMAN
TOTAL: 12

INSANITY
JOHNSON V METH. HOSP
TOTAL: 1

NO CHANCE FOR IMPR.
LEGION V RICHARDSON
TOTAL: 1

TYPES OF ACTIONS BROUGHT

NEGLIGENCE
A.A. V STATE
ABRAHAM V ZASLOW
ADAMS V RICKS
ADAMS V STATE
AIKEN V CLARY
ANCLOTE M.F.V WILK.
ANNIS V DONAHUE
ARL. HTS.V DEADERICK
AVEY V ST.FRAN.HOSP.
AYERS V RUSSELL
BAKER V U.S.
BANGS V STATE
BECKHAM V CLINE
BELLANDI V PARK SAN.
BELLOWS V STATE
BENJAMIN V HAVENS
BENNETT V STATE
BETTS V STATE
BLAUER V STATE
BLITZ V BOOG
BOGUST V IVERSON
BOLAND V STATE
BORKER V N.T.L.
BOYKIN V STATE
BRIGANTE V STATE
BROWN V MOORE
BURKS V ROSS
CALLAHAN V STATE
CAMERON V STATE
CARLINO V STATE
CASTIGLIONE V STATE
CASTILLO V U.S.
CAWTHON V COFFER
CENTENO V CITY OF NY
CHRISTY V SALITERMAN
CLARK V GERACI
COLLINS V BENSINGER
COLLINS V HAND
COLLINS V STATE
CONSTANT V HOWE
CTY.OF L.A.V SUP.CT.
COX V STATE
CURLEY V STATE
DALEY V STATE
DANIELS V FINNEY
DEMARTINI V ALEX.SAN
DI FIORE V STATE
DI GIOVANNI V PESSEL
DILLMAN V HELLMAN
DIMIT.V CHI.W.M.HOSP
DINNERSTEIN V U.S.
DOTY V STATE
DOWLY V STATE
DUGAN V U.S.
DUNBAR V GREENLAW
DUNN V STATE
DUZYNSKI V NOSAL
EABY V U.S.
EANES V U.S.
EDDINGS V PENN.
EISELE V MALONE
EVANUIK V U.PITT.
EXCEL.INS.CO.V STATE
FAIR V UNITED STATES
FARBER V OLKON
FATUCK V HILL.HOSP.
FEITELBERG V STATE
FERNANDEZ V BARUCH
FINKEL V STATE
FISCHER V CITY ELM.
FORDE V CTY.L.A.
FOSTER V STATE
FOWLE V FOWLE
FOWLER V NRWYS. SAN.
FOXLUGER V STATE
FREACH V COMMONWEAL
FRIEDLAND V U.S.
GSPERINI V MNGINELLI
GERBA V NEUROL.HOSP.
GIOIA V STATE
GOULD V STATE
GRANT V N.T.L.
GREGORY V ROBINSON
GRIES V L.I. HOME
GROCE V MYERS
HAMMER V POLSKY
HAMMER V ROSEN
HARRIS HOSP. V POPE
HAWLEY V STATE
HEBEL V HINSDALE SAN
HEIFETZ V PHIL.HOSP.
HENDLER V STATE
HENDRY V U.S.
HERNAND V. ST.OF CAL
HERNAND V ST.OF N.Y.
HICKS V U.S.
HIRSH V STATE
HOMERE V STATE
HUNGERFORD V U.S.
HUNT V KING COUNTY
IN RE PIERRE ESTATE
JAMES V TURNER
JOHNSON V METH. HOSP
JOHNSON V U.S.
JOHNSTON V RODIS
KATZ V STATE
KEATING V KELLER
KELLY V STATE
KENDRICK V U.S.
KENT V WHITAKER
KLEBER V STEVENS
KOSBERG V WASH. HOSP
KOWALSKI V STATE
KRAVITZ V STATE
KUBAS V STATE
LANDO V STATE
LAWRENCE V STATE
LEGION V RICHARDSON
LESTER V AETNA
LEWANDOWSKI V STATE
LEXINGTON HOS V WHIT
LICHT. V MONT. HOSP.
LUCY HAYES V PEROTTI
MCCABE V STATE
MCCANDLESS V STATE
MARTARELLA V KELLEY
MARTINDALE V STATE
MAYER V ALBANY HOSP.
MEIER V ROSS HOSP.
MERCHANTS BANK V US
MEYNIER V DE PAUL
MEZULLO V MALETZ
MILANO V STATE
MILLER V WEST
MILLS V SOC.NY. HOSP
MITCHELL V ROBINSON
MOCHEN V STATE
MOREY V KAISER FOUND
MORGAN V STATE
MORRA V ST.BD.PSYCH.
MOSKOWITZ V MCQUEEN
MOXON V CTY.OF KERN
MURRAY V ST.MARY'S
NASTASI V STATE
NYSA V ROCKEFELLER
NICHOLSON V HAN
NOEL V MENNING.FOUND
OLIVER V STATE
O'NEIL V STATE
ORMAN V STATE
O'ROURKE V HALCYON
PAPINI V ALEX.SAN.
PARKER V LA COUNTY
PAULEN V SHINNICK
PENNELL V CUMMINGS
PETERS V STATE
PETTIS V ST.DEPT.HOS
PIETRUCHA V GRANT HO
POWELL V DUKE UNIV.
POWELL V RISSER
PULS V ST.VINC.HOSP.
QUICK V BEN.SIS.HOS.
QUINLEY V COCKE
RHIVER V RIETMAN
RICE V MERCY HOSP.
ROBINSON V STATE
ROGERS V OKIN
ROSARIO V STATE
ROSENFELD V COLEMAN
ROSS V LEONARD
ROSSING V STATE
ROUSE V TWIN PINES
ROY V HARTOGS
RUFINO V U.S.
RUNYON V REID
ST. GEORGE V STATE
SARON V STATE
SCHAFFER V SPICER
SCHWENK V STATE
SCOLAVINO V STATE
SEALEY V FINKELSTEIN
SEMLER V PSY.INS.WA.
SEYMOUR V LOFGREEN
SHATTUCK V STATE
SMART V U.S.
STALLMAN V ROBINSON
STANSFIELD V GARDNER
STEPHEN V DREW

TYPES OF ACTIONS BROUGHT (CONT.)

NEGLIGENCE (CONT.)
STONE V PROCTOR
STOVALL V HARMS
STOWERS V ARD.HOSP.
SURPRENANT V STATE
TAIG V STATE
TARASOFF V REG.U.CA.
TAYLOR V STATE
THALL V STATE
TISINGER V WOOLLEY
TOBIAS V MANHAT.E&E
TORRES V STATE
TRAPANI V STATE
UNDERWOOD V U.S.
UNITED STATES V GRAY
U.LOUISVILLE V HAM.
VAN BARNEVELD V ST.
VASSOLO V CTY.HOSP.
VISTICA V PRES. HOSP
VITELLO V STATE
VON EYE V HAMMES
WARNER V PACKER
WARNER V STATE
WEGLARZ V STATE
WEIHS V STATE
WEINSHENK V KAISER
WELSCH V LIKINS
WENDOVER V STATE
WHALEY V KIRBY
WHITE V U.S.
WHITESELL V GREEN
WHITREE V STATE
WILLIAMS V LE BAR
WILLIAMS V STATE
WILLIS V WEST.HOSP.
WILSON V LEHMAN
WOOD V SAMARITAN INS
WOODRUFF V SHORES
WOODS V BRUMLOP
WRIGHT V STATE
WYATT V STICKNEY
ZIPKIN V FREEMAN
TOTAL: 229

MALICIOUS PROSECUTION
BACON V BACON
BANGS V STATE
BARTLETT V WEIMER
BENCOMO V MORGAN
BOOE V HALL
BRANDT V BRANDT
CHUDY V CHUDY
DANIELS V FINNEY
LINDER V FOSTER
LOWEN V HILTON
MANIACI V MARQUET.U.
ROUSE V TWIN PINES
SCHANBARGER V KELLOG
STEPHEN V DREW
SUHRE V KOTT
TOTAL: 15

ASSAULT
FREACH V COMMONWEAL
HIGGINS V STATE
MCCANDLESS V STATE
MORGAN V STATE
ROY V HARTOGS
RUFINO V U.S.
SEALEY V FINKELSTEIN
TOTAL: 7

ASSAULT AND BATTERY
ANNIS V DONAHUE
ANONYMOUS V STATE
CAMPBELL V GLENWOOD
DABKOWSKI V DAVIS
FARBER V OLKON
MABEN V RANKIN
NICHOLSON V HAN
RICE V MERCY HOSP.
ROUSE V TWIN PINES
STOWERS V ARD.HOSP.
TOTAL: 10

FALSE IMPRISONMENT
BACON V BACON
BANGS V STATE
BECKHAM V CLINE
BLITZ V BOOG
BOLAND V STATE
BOOE V HALL
CAMPBELL V GLENWOOD
DABKOWSKI V DAVIS
DENNISON V STATE
DI GIOVANNI V PESSEL
DOUGHERTY V SNYDER
GUZY V GUZY
JOHNSON V GREER
KELLY V STATE
KLEBER V STEVENS
MABEN V RANKIN
MANIACI V MARQUET.U.
MARTARELLA V KELLEY
MILLER V DICKERT
MILLER V WEST
MORRIS V U. TEXAS
O'ROURKE V O'ROURKE
PARKER V LA COUNTY
POWELL V DUKE UNIV.
RICE V MERCY HOSP.
ROSARIO V STATE
SAMONS V MEYMANDI
SPRINGER V STEINER
STOWERS V ARD.HOSP.
VITELLO V STATE
WARNER V STATE
WHALEY V KIRBY
TOTAL: 32

MISREPRESENTATION
GRANT V N.T.L.
TOTAL: 1

DEFAMATION OF CHARACTER

TYPE NOT SPECIFIED
BACON V BACON
TOTAL: 1

LIBEL
BERRY V MOENCH
CORCORAN V JERREL
FOWLE V FOWLE
GSPERINI V MNGINELLI
HAMMER V POLSKY
TAYLOR V GLOTFELTY
TOTAL: 6

SLANDER
WARNER V STATE
TOTAL: 1

LIBEL AND SLANDER
BARTLETT V WEIMER
BENCOMO V MORGAN
SCHAFFER V SPICER
TOTAL: 3

DEPRIVATION OF
CONSTITUTIONAL RIGHTS

RIGHT TO TREATMENT
BURNHAM V D.P.HEALTH
COLLINS V BENSINGER
COMMONWEALTH V PAGE
DAVIS V WATKINS
DUZYNSKI V NOSAL
IN RE ANONYMOUS
IN RE MADDOX
JACKSON V INDIANA
JOBSON V HENNE
LEGION V RICHARDSON
MORALES V TURMAN
NASON V SUPER.OF BR.
NELSON V HEYNE
NYSA V ROCKEFELLER
RENELLI V DEPT.OF MH
ROUSE V CAMERON
U.S. V PARDUE
WYATT V STICKNEY
TOTAL: 18

LOSS OF LIBERTY
BARTLETT V WEIMER
BEAUMONT V MORGAN
BURKES V CALLION
BYRNE V KYSAR
DENNISON V STATE
MCNEIL V DIRECTOR
MILLARD V CAMERON
O'CONNOR V DONALDSON
POWELL V DUKE UNIV.
TOTAL: 9

TYPES OF ACTIONS BROUGHT (CONT.)

CONST.RTS.IN GEN.
CAMPBELL V GLENWOOD
EDDINGS V PENN.
JOHNSON V GREER
JOYCE V FERRAZZI
MARTARELLA V KELLEY
MORGAN V STATE
PEOPLE V LA VALLEE
PEOPLE V WILKINS
PHILLIPS V SINGLETAR
REYNOLDS V NEILL
SAS V STATE
STACHULAK V COUGHLIN
STEPHEN V DREW
VITELLO V STATE
WARNER V STATE
WELSCH V LIKINS
WHALEY V KIRBY
TOTAL: 17

RT.TO REFUSE TREAT.
ROGERS V OKIN
TOTAL: 1

OTHER TORT(S)

ABUSE OF PROCESS
BOOE V HALL
SAMONS V MEYMANDI
TOTAL: 2

MAL.INFL.OF EMOT.DIS
BENCOMO V MORGAN
TOTAL: 1

WRONGFUL COMMITMENT
BAKER V ORLOWSKY
BANGS V STATE
BARTLETT V WEIMER
BRANDT V BRANDT
DUZYNSKI V NOSAL
FOWLE V FOWLE
HOUGH V OGDEN
OLEPA V MAPLETOFF
PENNELL V CUMMINGS
TOTAL: 9

PRIMA FACIE TORT
CLARK V GERACI
HAMMER V POLSKY
TOTAL: 2

FAIL.TO DO STAT.DUTY
COLLINS V BENSINGER
TOTAL: 1

INVASION OF PRIVACY
DOE V ROE
SCHWARTZ V THIELE
TOTAL: 2

INVOLUNT. SERVITUDE
JOBSON V HENNE
TOTAL: 1

FALSE ARREST
KELLY V STATE
POWELL V DUKE UNIV.
TOTAL: 2

CONSC.PAIN & SUFFER.
LANDO V STATE
TOTAL: 1

TRESPASS
POWELL V RISSER
TOTAL: 1

PRIV.INV.-PROC.ABUSE
SCHANBARGER V KELLOG
TOTAL: 1

CONTRACT LAW

BREACH OF CONTRACT
ANCLOTE M.F.V WILK.
CHRISTY V SALITERMAN
GSPERINI V MNGINELLI
MILLS V SOC.NY. HOSP
RICE V MERCY HOSP.
WILLIS V WEST.HOSP.
TOTAL: 6

FRAUD
TOTAL: 0

BREACH OF WARRANTY
JOHNSTON V RODIS
MOXON V CTY.OF KERN
TOTAL: 2

INS.CLAIM PAYMENT
TOTAL: 0

GARNISHMENT
ZIPKIN V FREEMAN
TOTAL: 1

FRAUD-BREACH OF CON.
HAMMER V ROSEN
NICHOLSON V HAN
TOTAL: 2

CRIMINAL LAW

RAPE
PEOPLE V BERNSTEIN
TOTAL: 1

ASSAULT & BATTERY
TOTAL: 0

CRIMINAL NEGLIGENCE
PEOPLE V MCCAUGHAN
TOTAL: 1

MOT.TO DISM.INDICT.
U.S. V PARDUE
TOTAL: 1

ADMINISTRATIVE LAW

LIC.REV.PCDG.
COL.ST.BD. V WEILER
COOPER V BD.MED.EX.
MORRA V ST.BD.PSYCH.
TOTAL: 3

OTHER ACTION,
EXCLUDING TORT LAW

BREACH OF CONFIDENCE
DOE V ROE
TOTAL: 1

RACE DISCR-CL. ACT.
LEGION V RICHARDSON
TOTAL: 1

ACT.NOT YET BROUGHT
BRADSHAW V STATE
TOTAL: 1

TYPE NOT SPECIFIED
CROCCO V HARRIS
LINDER V FOSTER
MARKS V ST FRAN HOSP
MONTGOM.CTY.TR.V ST.
MORRIS V ROUSOS
SALTER V GRANT
TOTAL: 6

TYPES OF ACTIONS BROUGHT (CONT.)

CLASS ACTION SUIT
BURNHAM V D.P.HEALTH
MARTARELLA V KELLEY
MORALES V TURMAN
NELSON V HEYNE
WELSCH V LIKINS
WYATT V STICKNEY
TOTAL: 6

HABEAS CORPUS
DARNELL V CAMERON
IN RE MADDOX
MILLARD V CAMERON
NASON V SUPER.OF BR.
PEOPLE V WILKINS
REYNOLDS V NEILL
ROUSE V CAMERON
SAS V STATE
STACHULAK V COUGHLIN
TOTAL: 9

NONMONETARY RELIEF
BURNHAM V D.P.HEALTH
DAVIS V WATKINS
IN RE ANONYMOUS
IN RE WARRINGTON
LEGION V RICHARDSON
MARTARELLA V KELLEY
MILLARD V CAMERON
MORALES V TURMAN
NASON V SUPER.OF BR.
NELSON V HEYNE
NYSA V ROCKEFELLER
ROUSE V CAMERON
SAS V STATE
WELSCH V LIKINS
TOTAL: 14

JUDICIAL HISTORY: TYPES OF COURTS

FEDERAL
BAKER V U.S.
BARTLETT V WEIMER
BEAUMONT V MORGAN
BLITZ V BOOG
BORKER V N.T.L.
BROWN V MOORE
BURKES V CALLION
BURKS V ROSS
BURNHAM V D.P.HEALTH
BYRNE V KYSAR
CAMPBELL V GLENWOOD
CASTILLO V U.S.
COLLINS V BENSINGER
DARNELL V CAMERON
DAVIS V WATKINS
DINNERSTEIN V U.S.
DUGAN V U.S.
DUZYNSKI V NOSAL
EABY V U.S.
EANES V U.S.
EDDINGS V PENN.
FAIR V UNITED STATES
FRIEDLAND V U.S.
GRANT V N.T.L.
HENDRY V U.S.
HICKS V U.S.
HUNGERFORD V U.S.
JOBSON V HENNE
JOHNSON V GREER
JOHNSON V U.S.
JOHNSTON V RODIS
JOYCE V FERRAZZI
KENDRICK V U.S.
KOSBERG V WASH. HOSP
LEGION V RICHARDSON
LESTER V AETNA
LUCY HAYES V PEROTTI
MARTARELLA V KELLEY
MERCHANTS BANK V US
MILLARD V CAMERON
MORALES V TURMAN
NELSON V HEYNE
NYSA V ROCKEFELLER
O'CONNOR V DONALDSON
PIETRUCHA V GRANT HO
PHILLIPS V SINGLETAR
REYNOLDS V NEILL
ROGERS V OKIN
ROUSE V CAMERON
RUFINO V U.S.
SAS V STATE
SEMLER V PSY.INS.WA.
SMART V U.S.
STACHULAK V COUGHLIN
STEPHEN V DREW
TAYLOR V GLOTFELTY
UNDERWOOD V U.S.
UNITED STATES V GRAY
U.S. V PARDUE
VON EYE V HAMMES
WHITE V U.S.
WYATT V STICKNEY
TOTAL: 62

STATE
A.A. V STATE
ABRAHAM V ZASLOW
ADAMS V RICKS
ADAMS V STATE
AIKEN V CLARY
ANCLOTE M.F.V WILK.
ANNIS V DONAHUE
ANONYMOUS V STATE
ARL. HTS.V DEADERICK
AVEY V ST.FRAN.HOSP.
AYERS V RUSSELL
BACON V BACON
BAKER V ORLOWSKY
BANGS V STATE
BECKHAM V CLINE
BELLANDI V PARK SAN.
BELLOWS V STATE
BENCOMO V MORGAN
BENJAMIN V HAVENS
BENNETT V STATE
BERRY V MOENCH
BETTS V STATE
BLAUER V STATE
BOGUST V IVERSON
BOLAND V STATE
BOOE V HALL
BOYKIN V STATE
BRADSHAW V STATE
BRANDT V BRANDT
BRIGANTE V STATE
CALLAHAN V STATE
CAMERON V STATE
CARLINO V STATE
CASTIGLIONE V STATE
CAWTHON V COFFER
CENTENO V CITY OF NY
CHRISTY V SALITERMAN
CHUDY V CHUDY
CLARK V GERACI
COLLINS V HAND
COLLINS V STATE
COL.ST.BD. V WEILER
COMMONWEALTH V PAGE
CONSTANT V HOWE
COOPER V BD.MED.EX.
CORCORAN V JERREL
CTY.OF L.A.V SUP.CT.
COX V STATE
CROCCO V HARRIS
CURLEY V STATE
DABKOWSKI V DAVIS
DALEY V STATE
DANIELS V FINNEY
DEMARTINI V ALEX.SAN
DENNISON V STATE
DI FIORE V STATE
DI GIOVANNI V PESSEL
DILLMAN V HELLMAN
DIMIT.V CHI.W.M.HOSP
DOE V ROE
DOTY V STATE
DOUGHERTY V SNYDER

JUDICIAL HISTORY: TYPES OF COURTS (CONT.)

STATE (CONT.)
DOWLY V STATE
DUNBAR V GREENLAW
DUNN V STATE
EISELE V MALONE
EVANUIK V U.PITT.
EXCEL.INS.CO.V STATE
FARBER V OLKON
FATUCK V HILL.HOSP.
FEITELBERG V STATE
FERNANDEZ V BARUCH
FINKEL V STATE
FISCHER V CITY ELM.
FORDE V CTY.L.A.
FOSTER V STATE
FOWLE V FOWLE
FOWLER V NRWYS. SAN.
FOXLUGER V STATE
FREACH V COMMONWEAL
GSPERINI V MNGINELLI
GERBA V NEUROL.HOSP.
GIOIA V STATE
GOULD V STATE
GREGORY V ROBINSON
GRIES V L.I. HOME
GROCE V MYERS
GUZY V GUZY
HAMMER V POLSKY
HAMMER V ROSEN
HARRIS HOSP. V POPE
HAWLEY V STATE
HEBEL V HINSDALE SAN
HEIFETZ V PHIL.HOSP.
HENDLER V STATE
HERNAND V. ST.OF CAL
HERNAND V ST.OF N.Y.
HIGGINS V STATE
HIRSH V STATE
HOMERE V STATE
HOUGH V OGDEN
HUNT V KING COUNTY
IN RE ANONYMOUS
IN RE MADDOX
IN RE PIERRE ESTATE
IN RE WARRINGTON
JACKSON V INDIANA
JAMES V TURNER
JOHNSON V METH. HOSP
KATZ V STATE
KEATING V KELLER
KELLY V STATE
KENT V WHITAKER
KLEBER V STEVENS
KOWALSKI V STATE
KRAVITZ V STATE
KUBAS V STATE
LANDO V STATE
LAWRENCE V STATE
LEWANDOWSKI V STATE
LEXINGTON HOS V WHIT
LICHT. V MONT. HOSP.
LINDER V FOSTER
LOWEN V HILTON
MABEN V RANKIN
MCCABE V STATE
MCCANDLESS V STATE
MCNEIL V DIRECTOR
MANIACI V MARQUET.U.
MARKS V ST FRAN HOSP
MARTINDALE V STATE
MAYER V ALBANY HOSP.
MEIER V ROSS HOSP.
MEYNIER V DE PAUL
MEZULLO V MALETZ
MILANO V STATE
MILLER V DICKERT
MILLER V WEST
MILLS V SOC.NY. HOSP
MITCHELL V ROBINSON
MOCHEN V STATE
MONTGOM.CTY.TR.V ST.
MOREY V KAISER FOUND
MORGAN V STATE
MORRA V ST.BD.PSYCH.
MORRIS V ROUSOS
MORRIS V U. TEXAS
MOSKOWITZ V MCQUEEN
MOXON V CTY.OF KERN
MURRAY V ST.MARY'S
NASON V SUPER.OF BR.
NASTASI V STATE
NICHOLSON V HAN
NOEL V MENNING.FOUND
OLEPA V MAPLETOFF
OLIVER V STATE
O'NEIL V STATE
ORMAN V STATE
O'ROURKE V HALCYON
O'ROURKE V O'ROURKE
PAPINI V ALEX.SAN.
PARKER V LA COUNTY
PAULEN V SHINNICK
PENNELL V CUMMINGS
PEOPLE V BERNSTEIN
PEOPLE V LA VALLEE
PEOPLE V MCCAUGHAN
PEOPLE V WILKINS
PETERS V STATE
PETTIS V ST.DEPT.HOS
POWELL V DUKE UNIV.
POWELL V RISSER
PULS V ST.VINC.HOSP.
QUICK V BEN.SIS.HOS.
QUINLEY V COCKE
RENELLI V DEPT.OF MH
RHIVER V RIETMAN
RICE V MERCY HOSP.
ROBINSON V STATE
ROSARIO V STATE
ROSENFELD V COLEMAN
ROSS V LEONARD
ROSSING V STATE
ROUSE V TWIN PINES
ROY V HARTOGS
RUNYON V REID
ST. GEORGE V STATE
SALTER V GRANT
SAMONS V MEYMANDI
SARON V STATE
SCHAFFER V SPICER
SCHANBARGER V KELLOG
SCHWARTZ V THIELE
SCHWENK V STATE
SCOLAVINO V STATE
SEALEY V FINKELSTEIN
SEYMOUR V LOFGREEN
SHATTUCK V STATE
SPRINGER V STEINER
STALLMAN V ROBINSON
STANSFIELD V GARDNER
STONE V PROCTOR
STOVALL V HARMS
STOWERS V ARD.HOSP.
SUHRE V KOTT
SURPRENANT V STATE
TAIG V STATE
TARASOFF V REG.U.CA.
TAYLOR V STATE
THALL V STATE
TISINGER V WOOLLEY
TOBIAS V MANHAT.E&E
TORRES V STATE
TRAPANI V STATE
U.LOUISVILLE V HAM.
VAN BARNEVELD V ST.
VASSOLO V CTY.HOSP.
VISTICA V PRES. HOSP
VITELLO V STATE
WARNER V PACKER
WARNER V STATE
WEGLARZ V STATE
WEIHS V STATE
WEINSHENK V KAISER
WELSCH V LIKINS
WENDOVER V STATE
WHALEY V KIRBY
WHITESELL V GREEN
WHITREE V STATE
WILLIAMS V LE BAR
WILLIAMS V STATE
WILLIS V WEST.HOSP.
WILSON V LEHMAN
WOOD V SAMARITAN INS
WOODRUFF V SHORES
WOODS V BRUMLOP
WRIGHT V STATE
ZIPKIN V FREEMAN
TOTAL: 238

JUDICIAL HISTORY: TRIERS OF FACTS

JURY
ABRAHAM V ZASLOW
ADAMS V STATE
AIKEN V CLARY
ANCLOTE M.F.V WILK.
ARL. HTS.V DEADERICK
AVEY V ST.FRAN.HOSP.
BACON V BACON
BEAUMONT V MORGAN
BELLANDI V PARK SAN.
BENJAMIN V HAVENS
BERRY V MOENCH
BROWN V MOORE
CHRISTY V SALITERMAN
COLLINS V HAND
CONSTANT V HOWE
DEMARTINI V ALEX.SAN
DI GIOVANNI V PESSEL
DOUGHERTY V SNYDER
EISELE V MALONE
EVANUIK V U.PITT.
FARBER V OLKON
FATUCK V HILL.HOSP.
FERNANDEZ V BARUCH
HAMMER V ROSEN
HARRIS HOSP. V POPE
HOUGH V OGDEN
HUNT V KING COUNTY
JOHNSON V GREER
KLEBER V STEVENS
LESTER V AETNA
LEXINGTON HOS V WHIT
LICHT. V MONT. HOSP.
LUCY HAYES V PEROTTI
MABEN V RANKIN
MANIACI V MARQUET.U.
MEIER V ROSS HOSP.
MILLS V SOC.NY. HOSP
MITCHELL V ROBINSON
MOREY V KAISER FOUND
O'CONNOR V DONALDSON
PAULEN V SHINNICK
PEOPLE V BERNSTEIN
PEOPLE V MCCAUGHAN
PETTIS V ST.DEPT.HOS
PIETRUCHA V GRANT HO
PULS V ST.VINC.HOSP.
RICE V MERCY HOSP.
ROUSE V TWIN PINES
ROY V HARTOGS
SAMONS V MEYMANDI
STALLMAN V ROBINSON
STANSFIELD V GARDNER
STOWERS V ARD.HOSP.
TOBIAS V MANHAT.E&E
U.LOUISVILLE V HAM.
VASSOLO V CTY.HOSP.
VISTICA V PRES. HOSP
VON EYE V HAMMES
WARNER V PACKER
WHITESELL V GREEN
WOODS V BRUMLOP
ZIPKIN V FREEMAN
TOTAL: 62

JUDGE,NO JURY
A.A. V STATE
ANONYMOUS V STATE
BAKER V ORLOWSKY
BAKER V U.S.
BANGS V STATE
BELLOWS V STATE
BENNETT V STATE
BETTS V STATE
BLAUER V STATE
BOLAND V STATE
BOYKIN V STATE
BRADSHAW V STATE
BRIGANTE V STATE
BURNHAM V D.P.HEALTH
CALLAHAN V STATE
CAMERON V STATE
CARLINO V STATE
CASTIGLIONE V STATE
CASTILLO V U.S.
COLLINS V BENSINGER
COLLINS V STATE
COMMONWEALTH V PAGE
COOPER V BD.MED.EX.
COX V STATE
CURLEY V STATE
DALEY V STATE
DARNELL V CAMERON
DAVIS V WATKINS
DENNISON V STATE
DI FIORE V STATE
DOE V ROE
DOTY V STATE
DOWLY V STATE
DUNN V STATE
EABY V U.S.
EANES V U.S.
EXCEL.INS.CO.V STATE
FEITELBERG V STATE
FINKEL V STATE
FOSTER V STATE
FOXLUGER V STATE
FREACH V COMMONWEAL
GIOIA V STATE
GOULD V STATE
HAWLEY V STATE
HENDLER V STATE
HERNAND V ST.OF N.Y.
HIGGINS V STATE
HIRSH V STATE
HOMERE V STATE
IN RE ANONYMOUS
IN RE MADDOX
IN RE PIERRE ESTATE
IN RE WARRINGTON
JACKSON V INDIANA
JOHNSON V U.S.
KATZ V STATE
KELLY V STATE
KOWALSKI V STATE
KUBAS V STATE
LANDO V STATE
LAWRENCE V STATE
LEWANDOWSKI V STATE
MCCABE V STATE
MCCANDLESS V STATE
MCNEIL V DIRECTOR
MARTARELLA V KELLEY
MARTINDALE V STATE
MERCHANTS BANK V US
MILANO V STATE
MILLARD V CAMERON
MOCHEN V STATE
MONTGOM.CTY.TR.V ST.
MORALES V TURMAN
MORGAN V STATE
MORRA V ST.BD.PSYCH.
NASTASI V STATE
NELSON V HEYNE
NYSA V ROCKEFELLER
OLIVER V STATE
O'NEIL V STATE
ORMAN V STATE
PEOPLE V LA VALLEE
PEOPLE V WILKINS
PETERS V STATE
REYNOLDS V NEILL
ROBINSON V STATE
ROGERS V OKIN
ROSARIO V STATE
ROSSING V STATE
ROUSE V CAMERON
ST. GEORGE V STATE
SARON V STATE
SAS V STATE
SCHWENK V STATE
SCOLAVINO V STATE
SEMLER V PSY.INS.WA.
SHATTUCK V STATE
STACHULAK V COUGHLIN
STEPHEN V DREW
SURPRENANT V STATE
TAIG V STATE
TAYLOR V STATE
THALL V STATE
TORRES V STATE
TRAPANI V STATE
UNDERWOOD V U.S.
UNITED STATES V GRAY
U.S. V PARDUE
VAN BARNEVELD V ST.
VITELLO V STATE
WARNER V STATE
WEGLARZ V STATE
WEIHS V STATE
WELSCH V LIKINS
WENDOVER V STATE
WHITREE V STATE
WILLIAMS V LE BAR
WILLIAMS V STATE
WRIGHT V STATE
WYATT V STICKNEY
TOTAL: 121

JUDICIAL HISTORY: TRIERS OF FACTS (CONT.)

JUDGE,UNINV.JURY
BRANDT V BRANDT
CENTENO V CITY OF NY
DANIELS V FINNEY
FOWLER V NRWYS. SAN.
GREGORY V ROBINSON
GRIES V L.I. HOME
GROCE V MYERS
HEBEL V HINSDALE SAN
JAMES V TURNER
JOBSON V HENNE
JOHNSTON V RODIS
MURRAY V ST.MARY'S
POWELL V RISSER
QUICK V BEN.SIS.HOS.
QUINLEY V COCKE
ROSENFELD V COLEMAN
SEYMOUR V LOFGREEN
SPRINGER V STEINER
STONE V PROCTOR
WILLIS V WEST.HOSP.
WILSON V LEHMAN
WOOD V SAMARITAN INS
TOTAL: 22

JUDGE;JURY PRESENT ?
ADAMS V RICKS
AYERS V RUSSELL
BARTLETT V WEIMER
BECKHAM V CLINE
BENCOMO V MORGAN
BLITZ V BOOG
BOGUST V IVERSON
BOOE V HALL
BURKES V CALLION
BURKS V ROSS
BYRNE V KYSAR
CAMPBELL V GLENWOOD
CAWTHON V COFFER
CHUDY V CHUDY
CLARK V GERACI
COL.ST.BD. V WEILER
CORCORAN V JERREL
CTY.OF L.A.V SUP.CT.
DILLMAN V HELLMAN
DIMIT.V CHI.W.M.HOSP
DUGAN V U.S.
DUZYNSKI V NOSAL
EDDINGS V PENN.
FISCHER V CITY ELM.
FORDE V CTY.L.A.
FOWLE V FOWLE
FRIEDLAND V U.S.
GSFERINI V MNGINELLI
GERBA V NEUROL.HOSP.
GUZY V GUZY
HAMMER V POLSKY
HEIFETZ V PHIL.HOSP.
HENDRY V U.S.
HERNAND V. ST.OF CAL
HICKS V U.S.
HUNGERFORD V U.S.
JOHNSON V METH. HOSP
JOYCE V FERRAZZI
KENDRICK V U.S.
KENT V WHITAKER
KOSBERG V WASH. HOSP
KRAVITZ V STATE
LEGION V RICHARDSON
LINDER V FOSTER
LOWEN V HILTON
MARKS V ST FRAN HOSP
MAYER V ALBANY HOSP.
MEZULLO V MALETZ
MILLER V DICKERT
MILLER V WEST
MORRIS V ROUSOS
MORRIS V U. TEXAS
MOSKOWITZ V MCQUEEN
NASON V SUPER.OF BR.
NICHOLSON V HAN
NOEL V MENNING.FOUND
OLEPA V MAPLETOFF
PARKER V LA COUNTY
PHILLIPS V SINGLETAR
POWELL V DUKE UNIV.
RENELLI V DEPT.OF MH
RHIVER V RIETMAN
RUFINO V U.S.
RUNYON V REID
SCHANBARGER V KELLOG
SCHWARTZ V THIELE
SEALEY V FINKELSTEIN
SMART V U.S.
STOVALL V HARMS
SUHRE V KOTT
TARASOFF V REG.U.CA.
TAYLOR V GLOTFELTY
TISINGER V WOOLLEY
WHALEY V KIRBY
WHITE V U.S.
WOODRUFF V SHORES
TOTAL: 76

?, JUDGE OR JURY
DABKOWSKI V DAVIS
DINNERSTEIN V U.S.
DUNBAR V GREENLAW
FAIR V UNITED STATES
KEATING V KELLER
MEYNIER V DE PAUL
MOXON V CTY.OF KERN
O'ROURKE V HALCYON
O'ROURKE V O'ROURKE
PAPINI V ALEX.SAN.
PENNELL V CUMMINGS
SCHAFFER V SPICER
WEINSHENK V KAISER
TOTAL: 13

SETTLED OUT OF COURT
ANNIS V DONAHUE
BORKER V N.T.L.
CROCCO V HARRIS
GRANT V N.T.L.
TOTAL: 4

NOT YET DECIDED
ROSS V LEONARD
SALTER V GRANT
TOTAL: 2

JUDICIAL HISTORY: VERDICTS FOR WHOM

VERDICT FOR PLAINTIFF
A.A. V STATE
ABRAHAM V ZASLOW
ADAMS V STATE
ANCLOTE M.F.V WILK.
ANNIS V DONAHUE
ARL. HTS.V DEADERICK
BACON V BACON
BELLANDI V PARK SAN.
BENNETT V STATE
BLAUER V STATE
BORKER V N.T.L.
BROWN V MOORE
BURNHAM V D.P.HEALTH
CALLAHAN V STATE
CHRISTY V SALITERMAN
COLLINS V STATE
COMMONWEALTH V PAGE
COOPER V BD.MED.EX.
COX V STATE
CROCCO V HARRIS
CURLEY V STATE
DALEY V STATE
DAVIS V WATKINS
DINNERSTEIN V U.S.
DOE V ROE
DOTY V STATE
DOWLY V STATE
EVANUIK V U.PITT.
FATUCK V HILL.HOSP.
FINKEL V STATE
FOSTER V STATE
GIOIA V STATE

JUDICIAL HISTORY: VERDICTS FOR WHOM (CONT.)

GOULD V STATE
GRANT V N.T.L.
HENDLER V STATE
HICKS V U.S.
HOMERE V STATE
HOUGH V OGDEN
HUNT V KING COUNTY
IN RE ANONYMOUS
IN RE MADDOX
KEATING V KELLER
KENT V WHITAKER
KLEBER V STEVENS
LANDO V STATE
LAWRENCE V STATE
LEXINGTON HOS V WHIT
MCCANDLESS V STATE
MCNEIL V DIRECTOR
MARTARELLA V KELLEY
MARTINDALE V STATE
MERCHANTS BANK V US
MEYNIER V DE PAUL
MILLARD V CAMERON
MORRA V ST.BD.PSYCH.
NELSON V HEYNE
NYSA V ROCKEFELLER
O'CONNOR V DONALDSON
OLIVER V STATE
O'NEIL V STATE
O'ROURKE V O'ROURKE
PAULEN V SHINNICK
PEOPLE V BERNSTEIN
PETTIS V ST.DEPT.HOS
RENELLI V DEPT.OF MH
REYNOLDS V NEILL
ROSSING V STATE
ROUSE V CAMERON
ROY V HARTOGS
SAMONS V MEYMANDI
SCOLAVINO V STATE
SEMLER V PSY.INS.WA.
SHATTUCK V STATE
STALLMAN V ROBINSON
STOWERS V ARD.HOSP.
SURPRENANT V STATE
THALL V STATE
TRAPANI V STATE
UNDERWOOD V U.S.
UNITED STATES V GRAY
U.S. V PARDUE
U.LOUISVILLE V HAM.
VASSOLO V CTY.HOSP.
VON EYE V HAMMES
WARNER V STATE
WEIHS V STATE
WEINSHENK V KAISER
WELSCH V LIKINS
WHITESELL V GREEN
WHITREE V STATE
WRIGHT V STATE
WYATT V STICKNEY
ZIPKIN V FREEMAN
TOTAL: 93

VERDICT FOR THE DEFENDANT

ANONYMOUS V STATE
BAKER V ORLOWSKY
BAKER V U.S.
BANGS V STATE
BARTLETT V WEIMER
BEAUMONT V MORGAN
BELLOWS V STATE
BENCOMO V MORGAN
BETTS V STATE
BLITZ V BOOG
BOGUST V IVERSON
BRANDT V BRANDT
BRIGANTE V STATE
BURKES V CALLION
BYRNE V KYSAR
CAMERON V STATE
CAMPBELL V GLENWOOD
CARLINO V STATE
CASTIGLIONE V STATE
CASTILLO V U.S.
CAWTHON V COFFER
CENTENO V CITY OF NY
CLARK V GERACI
COLLINS V BENSINGER
COLLINS V HAND
COL.ST.BD. V WEILER
CONSTANT V HOWE
CORCORAN V JERREL
CTY.OF L.A.V SUP.CT.
DABKOWSKI V DAVIS
DANIELS V FINNEY
DEMARTINI V ALEX.SAN
DENNISON V STATE
DI FIORE V STATE
DI GIOVANNI V PESSEL
DILLMAN V HELLMAN
DIMIT.V CHI.W.M.HOSP
DOUGHERTY V SNYDER
DUGAN V U.S.
DUNBAR V GREENLAW
DUNN V STATE
DUZYNSKI V NOSAL
EABY V U.S.
EANES V U.S.
EXCEL.INS.CO.V STATE
FARBER V OLKON
FEITELBERG V STATE
FERNANDEZ V BARUCH
FORDE V CTY.L.A.
FOWLE V FOWLE
FOXLUGER V STATE
GERBA V NEUROL.HOSP
GREGORY V ROBINSON
GUZY V GUZY
HARRIS HOSP. V POPE
HAWLEY V STATE
HEBEL V HINSDALE SAN
HEIFETZ V PHIL.HOSP.
HENDRY V U.S.
HERNAND V. ST.OF CAL
HERNAND V ST.OF N.Y.
HIGGINS V STATE
HIRSH V STATE
IN RE PIERRE ESTATE
JAMES V TURNER
JOHNSON V U.S.
JOYCE V FERRAZZI
KATZ V STATE
KELLY V STATE
KENDRICK V U.S.
KOWALSKI V STATE
KRAVITZ V STATE
KUBAS V STATE
LEGION V RICHARDSON
LESTER V AETNA
LEWANDOWSKI V STATE
LINDER V FOSTER
MCCABE V STATE
MARKS V ST FRAN HOSP
MEZULLO V MALETZ
MILANO V STATE
MILLER V DICKERT
MILLER V WEST
MILLS V SOC.NY. HOSP
MITCHELL V ROBINSON
MOCHEN V STATE
MOREY V KAISER FOUND
MORGAN V STATE
MORRIS V ROUSOS
MORRIS V U. TEXAS
MOXON V CTY.OF KERN
NASTASI V STATE
NICHOLSON V HAN
OLEPA V MAPLETOFF
ORMAN V STATE
PAPINI V ALEX.SAN.
PARKER V LA COUNTY
PENNELL V CUMMINGS
PHILLIPS V SINGLETAR
POWELL V DUKE UNIV.
POWELL V RISSER
PULS V ST.VINC.HOSP.
QUINLEY V COCKE
RHIVER V RIETMAN
RICE V MERCY HOSP.
ROBINSON V STATE
ROSARIO V STATE
ROUSE V TWIN PINES
RUNYON V REID
ST. GEORGE V STATE
SARON V STATE
SAS V STATE
SCHANBARGER V KELLOG
SCHWARTZ V THIELE
SCHWENK V STATE
SEALEY V FINKELSTEIN
SEYMOUR V LOFGREEN
SMART V U.S.
SPRINGER V STEINER
STANSFIELD V GARDNER
TAIG V STATE
TAYLOR V GLOTFELTY
TAYLOR V STATE
TISINGER V WOOLLEY
TOBIAS V MANHAT.E&E

JUDICIAL HISTORY: VERDICTS FOR WHOM (CONT.)

VAN BARNEVELD V ST.
WEGLARZ V STATE
WENDOVER V STATE
WHALEY V KIRBY
WHITE V U.S.
WILLIAMS V LE BAR
WILLIAMS V STATE
WILLIS V WEST.HOSP.
WILSON V LEHMAN
WOODRUFF V SHORES
TOTAL: 135

NONFINAL DECISION

IN FAVOR OF DEF.
EISELE V MALONE
LICHT. V MONT. HOSP.
LUCY HAYES V PEROTTI
MABEN V RANKIN
MANIACI V MARQUET.U.
O'ROURKE V HALCYON
PEOPLE V MCCAUGHAN
STOVALL V HARMS
WARNER V PACKER
WOODS V BRUMLOP
TOTAL: 10

IN FAVOR OF PLAINT.
ADAMS V RICKS
AIKEN V CLARY
AVEY V ST.FRAN.HOSP.
AYERS V RUSSELL
BECKHAM V CLINE
BENJAMIN V HAVENS
BERRY V MOENCH
BOLAND V STATE
BOOE V HALL
BOYKIN V STATE
BRADSHAW V STATE
BURKS V ROSS
CHUDY V CHUDY
DARNELL V CAMERON
EDDINGS V PENN.
FAIR V UNITED STATES
FISCHER V CITY ELM.
FOWLER V NRWYS. SAN.
FREACH V COMMONWEAL
FRIEDLAND V U.S.
GSPERINI V MNGINELLI
GRIES V L.I. HOME
GROCE V MYERS
HAMMER V POLSKY
HAMMER V ROSEN
HUNGERFORD V U.S.
IN RE WARRINGTON
JACKSON V INDIANA
JOBSON V HENNE
JOHNSON V GREER
JOHNSON V METH. HOSP
JOHNSTON V RODIS
KOSBERG V WASH. HOSP
LOWEN V HILTON
MAYER V ALBANY HOSP.
MEIER V ROSS HOSP.
MONTGOM.CTY.TR.V ST.
MORALES V TURMAN
MOSKOWITZ V MCQUEEN
MURRAY V ST.MARY'S
NASON V SUPER.OF BR.
NOEL V MENNING.FOUND
PEOPLE V LA VALLEE
PEOPLE V WILKINS
PETERS V STATE
PIETRUCHA V GRANT HO
QUICK V BEN.SIS.HOS.
ROSENFELD V COLEMAN
RUFINO V U.S.
SCHAFFER V SPICER
STACHULAK V COUGHLIN
STEPHEN V DREW
STONE V PROCTOR
SUHRE V KOTT
TARASOFF V REG.U.CA.
TORRES V STATE
VISTICA V PRES. HOSP
VITELLO V STATE
WOOD V SAMARITAN INS
TOTAL: 59

NOT YET DECIDED
ROGERS V OKIN
ROSS V LEONARD
SALTER V GRANT
TOTAL: 3

JUDICIAL HISTORY: SPECIAL DOCTRINES

RES IPSA LOQUITUR
BAKER V U.S.
BRIGANTE V STATE
DEMARTINI V ALEX.SAN
FARBER V OLKON
JOHNSTON V RODIS
LICHT. V MONT. HOSP.
MEIER V ROSS HOSP.
PIETRUCHA V GRANT HO
PULS V ST.VINC.HOSP.
QUINLEY V COCKE
STANSFIELD V GARDNER
VISTICA V PRES. HOSP
WENDOVER V STATE
WOOD V SAMARITAN INS
TOTAL: 14

DOC-PAT.PRIV.PREVENTED INFO.DISCLOSURE
BERRY V MOENCH
MILANO V STATE
SCHAFFER V SPICER
TOTAL: 3

LOCALITY RULE
AVEY V ST.FRAN.HOSP.
CHRISTY V SALITERMAN
ROSENFELD V COLEMAN
SUHRE V KOTT
TOTAL: 4

THERAPIST GUARANTEED CURE
COL.ST.BD. V WEILER
TOTAL: 1

STATUTE OF LIMITATIONS
BOLAND V STATE
GERBA V NEUROL.HOSP.
HUNGERFORD V U.S.
JOHNSON V METH. HOSP
MILLER V DICKERT
PARKER V LA COUNTY
SEYMOUR V LOFGREEN
VITELLO V STATE
WARNER V STATE
WOODRUFF V SHORES
TOTAL: 10

PATIENT GAVE INFORMED CONSENT
AIKEN V CLARY
ANONYMOUS V STATE
FARBER V OLKON
MITCHELL V ROBINSON
RICE V MERCY HOSP.
WILSON V LEHMAN
WOODS V BRUMLOP
TOTAL: 7

CONTRIBUTORY NEGLIGENCE
GOULD V STATE
HUNT V KING COUNTY
MOCHEN V STATE
MONTGOM.CTY.TR.V ST.
MOXON V CTY.OF KERN
TOTAL: 5

DEF.ACTED UNDER COLOR OF STATE LAW
JOYCE V FERRAZZI
OLEPA V MAPLETOFF
TOTAL: 2

JUDICIAL HISTORY: SPECIAL DOCTRINES (CONT.)

IMMUNITY

GOVERN. IMMUNITY
BELLOWS V STATE
BLITZ V BOOG
BURKS V ROSS
CTY.OF L.A.V SUP.CT.
FAIR V UNITED STATES
FISCHER V CITY ELM.
FORDE V CTY.L.A.
FREACH V COMMONWEAL
HAWLEY V STATE
HEIFETZ V PHIL.HOSP.
HENDRY V U.S.
HERNAND V. ST.OF CAL
HICKS V U.S.
HIGGINS V STATE
HUNGERFORD V U.S.
JOBSON V HENNE
KENDRICK V U.S.
KRAVITZ V STATE
MERCHANTS BANK V US
MOXON V CTY.OF KERN
PARKER V LA COUNTY
RUFINO V U.S.
ST. GEORGE V STATE
SEMLER V PSY.INS.WA.
SMART V U.S.
TAIG V STATE
TARASOFF V REG.U.CA.
TAYLOR V GLOTFELTY
UNDERWOOD V U.S.
WEGLARZ V STATE
WENDOVER V STATE
TOTAL: 31

JUDICIAL IMMUNITY
BAKER V ORLOWSKY
BARTLETT V WEIMER
BECKHAM V CLINE
BENCOMO V MORGAN
BYRNE V KYSAR
CAMPBELL V GLENWOOD
CAWTHON V COFFER
CHUDY V CHUDY
CORCORAN V JERREL
DABKOWSKI V DAVIS
DENNISON V STATE
DUNBAR V GREENLAW
DUZYNSKI V NOSAL
FOWLE V FOWLE
LINDER V FOSTER
LOWEN V HILTON
MEZULLO V MALETZ
MORGAN V STATE
OLEPA V MAPLETOFF
PENNELL V CUMMINGS
PHILLIPS V SINGLETAR
POWELL V DUKE UNIV.
RHIVER V RIETMAN
ROUSE V TWIN PINES
SCHANBARGER V KELLOG
SCHWARTZ V THIELE
SPRINGER V STEINER
STEPHEN V DREW
STOWERS V ARD.HOSP.
TOTAL: 29

CHARITABLE IMMUNITY
U.LOUISVILLE V HAM.
TOTAL: 1

RESPONDEAT SUPERIOR
BROWN V MOORE
COLLINS V HAND
CTY.OF L.A.V SUP.CT.
KENT V WHITAKER
MILLS V SOC.NY. HOSP
RUFINO V U.S.
STOVALL V HARMS
TOTAL: 7

NEGLIGENCE PER SE
CASTILLO V U.S.
ROSENFELD V COLEMAN
TOTAL: 2

OTHER SPECIAL DOCTRINES INVOKED

HOSP.INFO.IS PRIV.
BRADSHAW V STATE
MOSKOWITZ V MCQUEEN
TOTAL: 2

JUDICIAL HISTORY: TYPES AND AMOUNTS OF RECOVERIES

NONMONETARY RELIEF

INJ.OR OTHER EQ.REL.
BURNHAM V D.P.HEALTH
COMMONWEALTH V PAGE
DAVIS V WATKINS
DOE V ROE
IN RE ANONYMOUS
IN RE MADDOX
MCNEIL V DIRECTOR
MARTARELLA V KELLEY
MILLARD V CAMERON
NASON V SUPER.OF BR.
NELSON V HEYNE
NYSA V ROCKEFELLER
RENELLI V DEPT.OF MH
REYNOLDS V NEILL
ROUSE V CAMERON
STACHULAK V COUGHLIN
U.S. V PARDUE
WELSCH V LIKINS
WYATT V STICKNEY
TOTAL: 19

TO BE DETERM.ON RETR
DALEY V STATE
SAMONS V MEYMANDI
UNITED STATES V GRAY
WARNER V STATE
WRIGHT V STATE
TOTAL: 5

NOT SPECIFIED
DINNERSTEIN V U.S.
DOWLY V STATE
EVANUIK V U.PITT.
HOMERE V STATE
HUNT V KING COUNTY
KENT V WHITAKER
MARTINDALE V STATE
PAULEN V SHINNICK
ROSSING V STATE
SHATTUCK V STATE
UNDERWOOD V U.S.
TOTAL: 11

LOSS OF LICENSE
COOPER V BD.MED.EX.
MORRA V ST.BD.PSYCH.
TOTAL: 2

CRIMINAL SENTENCE
PEOPLE V BERNSTEIN
TOTAL: 1

OTHER RECOVERY

ATTORNEY FEES
O'CONNOR V DONALDSON
TOTAL: 1

INTEREST
MEYNIER V DE PAUL
O'NEIL V STATE
PETTIS V ST.DEPT.HOS
TRAPANI V STATE
ZIPKIN V FREEMAN
TOTAL: 5

COSTS
MERCHANTS BANK V US
O'ROURKE V O'ROURKE
PETTIS V ST.DEPT.HOS
TRAPANI V STATE
TOTAL: 4

JUDICIAL HISTORY: TYPES AND AMOUNTS OF RECOVERIES (CONT.)

AMOUNT OF RECOVERY

A.A. V STATE	($ 90000)	KLEBER V STEVENS	($ 20000)
ABRAHAM V ZASLOW	($170000)	LANDO V STATE	($ 5000)
ADAMS V STATE	($275000)	LAWRENCE V STATE	($ 40646)
ANCLOTE M.F.V WILK.	($ 28600)	LEXINGTON HOS V WHIT	($ 6964)
ANNIS V DONAHUE	($ 2500)	MCCANDLESS V STATE	($ 2000)
ARL. HTS.V DEADERICK	($ 5000)	MERCHANTS BANK V US	($200000)
BACON V BACON	($ 1500)	MEYNIER V DE PAUL	($ 4299)
BELLANDI V PARK SAN.	($ 15000)	O'CONNOR V DONALDSON	($ 20000)
BENNETT V STATE	($ 10000)	OLIVER V STATE	($ 30000)
BLAUER V STATE	($ 18000)	O'NEIL V STATE	($ 5945)
BORKER V N.T.L.	($ 50000)	O'ROURKE V O'ROURKE	($ 1000)
BROWN V MOORE	($ 60000)	PETTIS V ST.DEPT.HOS	($ 35000)
CALLAHAN V STATE	($ 25220)	ROY V HARTOGS	($ 25000)
CHRISTY V SALITERMAN	($103530)	SCOLAVINO V STATE	($ 21137)
COLLINS V STATE	($ 8492)	SEMLER V PSY.INS.WA.	($ 25000)
COX V STATE	($ 9647)	STALLMAN V ROBINSON	($ 9000)
CROCCO V HARRIS	($ 50000)	STOWERS V ARD.HOSP.	($ 40000)
CURLEY V STATE	($ 6000)	SURFRENANT V STATE	($ 21000)
DOTY V STATE	($ 30000)	THALL V STATE	($ 7790)
FATUCK V HILL.HOSP.	($ 30000)	TRAPANI V STATE	($ 9145)
FINKEL V STATE	($ 70997)	U.LOUISVILLE V HAM.	($ 1000)
FOSTER V STATE	($ 14000)	VASSOLO V CTY.HOSP.	($200000)
GIOIA V STATE	($ 41124)	VON EYE V HAMMES	($ 39380)
GOULD V STATE	($ 6320)	WEIHS V STATE	($ 1500)
GRANT V N.T.L.	($ 7500)	WEINSHENK V KAISER	($250000)
HENDLER V STATE	($ 15000)	WHITESELL V GREEN	($ 18000)
HICKS V U.S.	($100000)	WHITREE V STATE	($300000)
HOUGH V OGDEN	($ 3000)	ZIFKIN V FREEMAN	($ 5000)
KEATING V KELLER	($ 3500)		

TOTAL: 57

JUDICIAL HISTORY: REASONS SUITS FAILED

DEFENDANT(S) CANNOT BE SUED DUE TO

GOVERN. IMMUNITY
- BELLOWS V STATE
- BLITZ V BOOG
- CTY.OF L.A.V SUP.CT.
- FORDE V CTY.L.A.
- HAWLEY V STATE
- HEIFETZ V PHIL.HOSP.
- HENDRY V U.S.
- HERNAND V. ST.OF CAL
- HIGGINS V STATE
- KENDRICK V U.S.
- KRAVITZ V STATE
- MOXON V CTY.OF KERN
- PARKER V LA COUNTY
- ROSARIO V STATE
- ST. GEORGE V STATE
- SMART V U.S.
- TAIG V STATE
- TAYLOR V GLOTFELTY
- WEGLARZ V STATE
- WENDOVER V STATE

TOTAL: 20

JUDICIAL IMMUNITY
- BAKER V ORLOWSKY
- BARTLETT V WEIMER
- BENCOMO V MORGAN
- BURKES V CALLION
- BYRNE V KYSAR
- CAMPBELL V GLENWOOD
- CAWTHON V COFFER
- CORCORAN V JERREL
- DABKOWSKI V DAVIS
- DENNISON V STATE
- DUNBAR V GREENLAW
- DUZYNSKI V NOSAL
- FOWLE V FOWLE
- LINDER V FOSTER
- MEZULLO V MALETZ
- OLEPA V MAPLETOFF
- PENNELL V CUMMINGS
- PHILLIPS V SINGLETAR
- POWELL V DUKE UNIV.
- RHIVER V RIETMAN
- ROUSE V TWIN PINES
- SCHANBARGER V KELLOG
- SCHWARTZ V THIELE
- SPRINGER V STEINER

TOTAL: 24

NEGLIGENCE OR CASE NOT PROVEN
- BAKER V U.S.
- BANGS V STATE
- BEAUMONT V MORGAN
- BENCOMO V MORGAN
- BETTS V STATE
- BOGUST V IVERSON
- BRIGANTE V STATE
- BYRNE V KYSAR
- CAMERON V STATE

JUDICIAL HISTORY: REASONS SUITS FAILED (CONT.)

CARLINO V STATE
CASTIGLIONE V STATE
CASTILLO V U.S.
CENTENO V CITY OF NY
CLARK V GERACI
COLLINS V HAND
COL.ST.BD. V WEILER
CONSTANT V HOWE
DANIELS V FINNEY
DEMARTINI V ALEX.SAN
DENNISON V STATE
DI FIORE V STATE
DI GIOVANNI V PESSEL
DILLMAN V HELLMAN
DIMIT.V CHI.W.M.HOSP
DUGAN V U.S.
DUNN V STATE
EABY V U.S.
EANES V U.S.
EXCEL.INS.CO.V STATE
FARBER V OLKON
FEITELBERG V STATE
FERNANDEZ V BARUCH
FOXLUGER V STATE
GREGORY V ROBINSON
HARRIS HOSP. V POPE
HENDRY V U.S.
HERNAND V ST.OF N.Y.
HIRSH V STATE
IN RE PIERRE ESTATE
JAMES V TURNER
JOHNSON V U.S.
KATZ V STATE
KELLY V STATE
KOWALSKI V STATE
KRAVITZ V STATE
KUBAS V STATE
LEGION V RICHARDSON
LESTER V AETNA
MCCABE V STATE
MILANO V STATE
MILLER V WEST
MILLS V SOC.NY. HOSP
MOCHEN V STATE
MOREY V KAISER FOUND
MORGAN V STATE
MORRIS V ROUSOS
MORRIS V U. TEXAS
NASTASI V STATE
ORMAN V STATE
PAPINI V ALEX.SAN.
PENNELL V CUMMINGS
POWELL V DUKE UNIV.
POWELL V RISSER
PULS V ST.VINC.HOSP.
QUINLEY V COCKE
RICE V MERCY HOSP.
ROBINSON V STATE
ROUSE V TWIN PINES
RUNYON V REID
SARON V STATE
SAS V STATE
SCHWENK V STATE
SEALEY V FINKELSTEIN
STANSFIELD V GARDNER
TAYLOR V STATE
TISINGER V WOOLLEY
TOBIAS V MANHAT.E&E
VAN BARNEVELD V ST.
WENDOVER V STATE
WHITE V U.S.
WILLIAMS V LE BAR
WILLIS V WEST.HOSP.
TOTAL: 82

NO CAUSE OF ACTION STATED
BRANDT V BRANDT
CAWTHON V COFFER
COLLINS V BENSINGER
DUZYNSKI V NOSAL
GUZY V GUZY
HEBEL V HINSDALE SAN
JOYCE V FERRAZZI
LEWANDOWSKI V STATE
MARKS V ST FRAN HOSP
MORRIS V ROUSOS
MOXON V CTY.OF KERN
NICHOLSON V HAN
OLEPA V MAPLETOFF
PHILLIPS V SINGLETAR
RHIVER V RIETMAN
SEALEY V FINKELSTEIN
WHALEY V KIRBY
WILLIAMS V STATE
TOTAL: 18

PATIENT HAD GIVEN INFORMED CONSENT
ANONYMOUS V STATE
MITCHELL V ROBINSON
RICE V MERCY HOSP.
WILSON V LEHMAN
TOTAL: 4

STATUTE OF LIMITATIONS BARRED SUIT
GERBA V NEUROL.HOSP.
MILLER V DICKERT
PARKER V LA COUNTY
SEYMOUR V LOFGREEN
WOODRUFF V SHORES
TOTAL: 5

OTHER REASON SUIT FAILED

NO BAD FAITH OR MAL.
DOUGHERTY V SNYDER
SPRINGER V STEINER
TOTAL: 2

JUDICIAL HISTORY: LEVELS OF COURTS

CASES NEVER AT TRIAL LEVEL
ANNIS V DONAHUE
BORKER V N.T.L.
COMMONWEALTH V PAGE
CROCCO V HARRIS
GRANT V N.T.L.
NASON V SUPER.OF BR.
ROGERS V OKIN
ROSS V LEONARD
SALTER V GRANT
TOTAL: 9

SETTLED OUT OF COURT
ANNIS V DONAHUE
BORKER V N.T.L.
CROCCO V HARRIS
GRANT V N.T.L.
TOTAL: 4

NOT YET DECIDED
ROGERS V OKIN
ROSS V LEONARD
SALTER V GRANT
TOTAL: 3

APPELLATE
ADAMS V RICKS
ANCLOTE M.F.V WILK.
ANONYMOUS V STATE
ARL. HTS.V DEADERICK
AYERS V RUSSELL
BAKER V ORLOWSKY
BAKER V U.S.
BANGS V STATE
BARTLETT V WEIMER
BEAUMONT V MORGAN
BELLOWS V STATE
BENCOMO V MORGAN
BLITZ V BOOG
BOLAND V STATE
BOOE V HALL
BOYKIN V STATE
BRADSHAW V STATE

JUDICIAL HISTORY: LEVELS OF COURTS (CONT.)

BRANDT V BRANDT
BROWN V MOORE
BURKES V CALLION
BURKS V ROSS
BURNHAM V D.P.HEALTH
BYRNE V KYSAR
CALLAHAN V STATE
CAMERON V STATE
CARLINO V STATE
CASTIGLIONE V STATE
CASTILLO V U.S.
CAWTHON V COFFER
CENTENO V CITY OF NY
COLLINS V BENSINGER
COLLINS V STATE
CONSTANT V HOWE
COOPER V BD.MED.EX.
CTY.OF L.A.V SUP.CT.
COX V STATE
CURLEY V STATE
DALEY V STATE
DANIELS V FINNEY
DARNELL V CAMERON
DEMARTINI V ALEX.SAN
DENNISON V STATE
DI FIORE V STATE
DI GIOVANNI V PESSEL
DILLMAN V HELLMAN
DIMIT.V CHI.W.M.HOSP
DINNERSTEIN V U.S.
DOE V ROE
DOUGHERTY V SNYDER
DUNN V STATE
DUZYNSKI V NOSAL
EANES V U.S.
EISELE V MALONE
EVANUIK V U.PITT.
EXCEL.INS.CO.V STATE
FAIR V UNITED STATES
FATUCK V HILL.HOSP.
FEITELBERG V STATE
FERNANDEZ V BARUCH
FORDE V CTY.L.A.
FOWLER V NRWYS. SAN.
GIOIA V STATE
GRIES V L.I. HOME
GUZY V GUZY
HAMMER V ROSEN
HARRIS HOSP. V POPE
HAWLEY V STATE
HEBEL V HINSDALE SAN
HENDRY V U.S.
HERNAND V. ST.OF CAL
HERNAND V ST.OF N.Y.
HICKS V U.S.
HIGGINS V STATE
HIRSH V STATE
HOMERE V STATE
HUNGERFORD V U.S.
HUNT V KING COUNTY
IN RE ANONYMOUS
IN RE PIERRE ESTATE
IN RE WARRINGTON
JAMES V TURNER
JOBSON V HENNE
JOHNSON V GREER
JOHNSON V METH. HOSP
JOHNSTON V RODIS
JOYCE V FERRAZZI
KEATING V KELLER
KLEBER V STEVENS
KOSBERG V WASH. HOSP
KOWALSKI V STATE
KRAVITZ V STATE
KUBAS V STATE
LANDO V STATE
LESTER V AETNA
LICHT. V MONT. HOSP.
LUCY HAYES V PEROTTI
MCCABE V STATE
MCCANDLESS V STATE
MCNEIL V DIRECTOR
MARTARELLA V KELLEY
MARTINDALE V STATE
MAYER V ALBANY HOSP.
MEYNIER V DE PAUL
MILLARD V CAMERON
MILLS V SOC.NY. HOSP
MOCHEN V STATE
MONTGOM.CTY.TR.V ST.
MORALES V TURMAN
MORGAN V STATE
MORRIS V ROUSOS
MORRIS V U. TEXAS
MOXON V CTY.OF KERN
MURRAY V ST.MARY'S
NASTASI V STATE
NELSON V HEYNE
NICHOLSON V HAN
O'CONNOR V DONALDSON
OLEPA V MAPLETOFF
ORMAN V STATE
O'ROURKE V HALCYON
O'ROURKE V O'ROURKE
PAPINI V ALEX.SAN.
PARKER V LA COUNTY
PEOPLE V BERNSTEIN
PEOPLE V LA VALLEE
PEOPLE V MCCAUGHAN
PEOPLE V WILKINS
PETERS V STATE
PETTIS V ST.DEPT.HOS
PIETRUCHA V GRANT HO
POWELL V DUKE UNIV.
QUINLEY V COCKE
RHIVER V RIETMAN
RICE V MERCY HOSP.
ROSARIO V STATE
ROSENFELD V COLEMAN
ROUSE V CAMERON
ROUSE V TWIN PINES
ROY V HARTOGS
ST. GEORGE V STATE
SAMONS V MEYMANDI
SARON V STATE
SAS V STATE
SCHANBARGER V KELLOG
SCHWARTZ V THIELE
SCOLAVINO V STATE
SEMLER V PSY.INS.WA.
SHATTUCK V STATE
SMART V U.S.
STANSFIELD V GARDNER
STOWERS V ARD.HOSP.
SUHRE V KOTT
TAIG V STATE
TARASOFF V REG.U.CA.
TAYLOR V GLOTFELTY
TAYLOR V STATE
TISINGER V WOOLLEY
TOBIAS V MANHAT.E&E
TRAPANI V STATE
UNDERWOOD V U.S.
UNITED STATES V GRAY
VAN BARNEVELD V ST.
VITELLO V STATE
VON EYE V HAMMES
WARNER V PACKER
WARNER V STATE
WEGLARZ V STATE
WEIHS V STATE
WHALEY V KIRBY
WHITE V U.S.
WILLIAMS V STATE
WOOD V SAMARITAN INS
WRIGHT V STATE
WYATT V STICKNEY
TOTAL: 174

SUPREME COURT
ADAMS V STATE
AIKEN V CLARY
AVEY V ST.FRAN.HOSP.
BACON V BACON
BEAUMONT V MORGAN
BECKHAM V CLINE
BELLANDI V PARK SAN.
BENJAMIN V HAVENS
BERRY V MOENCH
BLITZ V BOOG
BOGUST V IVERSON
BOLAND V STATE
BURKES V CALLION
BYRNE V KYSAR
CAMERON V STATE
CENTENO V CITY OF NY
CHRISTY V SALITERMAN
CHUDY V CHUDY
COLLINS V BENSINGER
COLLINS V HAND
COLLINS V STATE
COL.ST.BD. V WEILER
COMMONWEALTH V PAGE
CONSTANT V HOWE
CORCORAN V JERREL
CTY.OF L.A.V SUP.CT.
DABKOWSKI V DAVIS
DALEY V STATE

JUDICIAL HISTORY: LEVELS OF COURTS (CONT.)

DENNISON V STATE
DI GIOVANNI V PESSEL
DOE V ROE
DUNBAR V GREENLAW
EXCEL.INS.CO.V STATE
FARBER V OLKON
FATUCK V HILL.HOSP.
FERNANDEZ V BARUCH
FOWLE V FOWLE
FREACH V COMMONWEAL
GERBA V NEUROL.HOSP.
GREGORY V ROBINSON
GROCE V MYERS
HAMMER V ROSEN
HAWLEY V STATE
HIRSH V STATE
HOUGH V OGDEN
IN RE ANONYMOUS
IN RE MADDOX
IN RE WARRINGTON
JACKSON V INDIANA
JAMES V TURNER
KENT V WHITAKER
LANDO V STATE
LEGION V RICHARDSON
LESTER V AETNA
LEXINGTON HOS V WHIT
LINDER V FOSTER
LOWEN V HILTON
MABEN V RANKIN
MCCANDLESS V STATE
MANIACI V MARQUET.U.
MARKS V ST FRAN HOSP
MARTINDALE V STATE
MEIER V ROSS HOSP.
MEZULLO V MALETZ
MILLER V DICKERT
MILLER V WEST
MILLS V SOC.NY. HOSP
MITCHELL V ROBINSON
MORALES V TURMAN
MORGAN V STATE
MORRA V ST.BD.PSYCH.
MOXON V CTY.OF KERN
NASON V SUPER.OF BR.
NELSON V HEYNE
NOEL V MENNING.FOUND
O'CONNOR V DONALDSON
ORMAN V STATE
O'ROURKE V HALCYON
PAPINI V ALEX.SAN.
PAULEN V SHINNICK
PENNELL V CUMMINGS
PEOPLE V MCCAUGHAN
POWELL V RISSER
PULS V ST.VINC.HOSP.
QUICK V BEN.SIS.HOS.
QUINLEY V COCKE
REYNOLDS V NEILL
ROSARIO V STATE
RUNYON V REID
ST. GEORGE V STATE
SAMONS V MEYMANDI
SAS V STATE
SCHAFFER V SPICER
SCOLAVINO V STATE
SEMLER V PSY.INS.WA.
SEYMOUR V LOFGREEN
SPRINGER V STEINER
STALLMAN V ROBINSON
STONE V PROCTOR
STOVALL V HARMS
STOWERS V ARD.HOSP.
TARASOFF V REG.U.CA.
TAYLOR V STATE
U.LOUISVILLE V HAM.
VISTICA V PRES. HOSP
WARNER V STATE
WILLIAMS V LE BAR
WILLIAMS V STATE
WILLIS V WEST.HOSP.
WILSON V LEHMAN
WOOD V SAMARITAN INS
WOODRUFF V SHORES
WOODS V BRUMLOP
ZIPKIN V FREEMAN
TOTAL: 114

US SUP.CT. FR. STATE
DENNISON V STATE
JACKSON V INDIANA
MCNEIL V DIRECTOR
MORGAN V STATE
MORRIS V ROUSOS
SCHANBARGER V KELLOG
TOTAL: 6

RETRIAL
COX V STATE
DUNN V STATE
GIOIA V STATE
MILLARD V CAMERON
MITCHELL V ROBINSON
MOCHEN V STATE
O'CONNOR V DONALDSON
O'ROURKE V O'ROURKE
PETTIS V ST.DEPT.HOS
REYNOLDS V NEILL
RICE V MERCY HOSP.
ROUSE V CAMERON
SAS V STATE
WHITE V U.S.
TOTAL: 14

REAPPEAL TO APP.
GIOIA V STATE
MILLARD V CAMERON
MOCHEN V STATE
O'ROURKE V O'ROURKE
PETTIS V ST.DEPT.HOS
RICE V MERCY HOSP.
ROUSE V CAMERON
SAS V STATE
WHITE V U.S.
TOTAL: 9

REAPPEAL TO S.C.
DUNN V STATE
MITCHELL V ROBINSON
O'ROURKE V O'ROURKE
PETTIS V ST.DEPT.HOS
TARASOFF V REG.U.CA.
TOTAL: 5

REMANDED TO APP.CT.
O'CONNOR V DONALDSON
PETTIS V ST.DEPT.HOS
TOTAL: 2

Appendix C

Correlations of Study Variables with Verdict, Year of Final Decisions, and Other Variables

The following forty-six tables provide the basic correlations essential for a meaningful analysis of malpractice trends in the field of psychotherapy. Two basic correlations comprise the bulk of the tables. In the first, whether the verdict was for the plaintiff, defendant, or was nonfinal is correlated with different study variables. This provides information on what types of suits are most or least likely to succeed, although causal inferences are not thereby demonstrated. The second common correlation gives the degree of correlation of different variables with the decade in which the last court decision took place. Analyzing changes in the number of suits per decade gives an excellent picture of the trends that are occurring in psychotherapeutic malpractice suits.

In addition, other tables provide information on the reasons suits failed, the amount of recovery, the amount of time involved in the judicial process, and how different variables correlated with size of recovery. Each of these variables is explained in the introduction to Appendix A, and an analysis of the tables is presented in Chapter 3.

A word of explanation is necessary on reading the tables. The majority have boxes that contain a number with three percentages immediately below. The number is the number of cases in which the variable occurs. The percentage listed immediately below the number is the row percentage; it indicates the degree to which a variable has occurred within a certain time frame or the degree to which such a variable results in a decision for plaintiff or defendant. In Table 13, for instance, one sees that between 1960 and 1969 there were three cases involving sex between therapist and client, which is 25 percent of all cases involving this variable. In the period 1970-1977, seven instances occurred, which comprise 58.3 percent of all cases involving sexual abuse as the negligent treatment alleged.

The third figure is the column percentage. It tells how often a specific variable occurs in a given time period in comparison with other variables, or how frequently such a variable will result in a specific verdict in relation to other variables. In Table 14, for instance, one sees that sexual abuse occurred a total of twelve times, eight of which resulted in verdicts for the plaintiff, which represents 66.7 percent (row percentage) of all cases involving sexual abuse, and 17.8 percent (column percentage) of all verdicts for plaintiff. This latter percentage means that other forms of negligent treatment constituted 77.2 percent of all cases.

The last percentage provided in the box gives the extent to which a certain variable occurs in relation to all the variables in the table. In Table 14, for instance, sexual abuse cases decided in favor of the plaintiff represent 6.8 percent of all cases involving some form of negligent treatment. The row and column totals contain only one percentage, which is the number of cases for a particular variable divided by the total number of cases in which any variable in the table occurs. In Table 14 this tells one that sexual abuse occurred twelve times, which was 10.3 percent of all cases involving negligent treatment, while in the bottom row one sees that forty-five cases were decided for plaintiff, which constitutes 38.5 percent of all decided cases.

EXAMPLE:

Row Percentage

Column Percentage

Table 3. Final Decisions Correlated with Region of Country

Region of Country	*Verdict for Whom* *Plaintiff*	*Defendant*	*Nonfinal for Plaintiff*	*Nonfinal for Defendant*	*Not Yet Decided*	*Totals*
New York	42 34.7% 45.2% 14.0%	51 42.1% 37.8% 17.0%	22 18.2% 37.3% 7.3%	4 3.3 40.0% 1.3%	2 1.7% 66.7% 0.7%	121 40.3%
California	6 23.1% 6.5% 2.0%	14 53.8% 10.4% 4.7%	4 15.4% 6.8% 1.3%	2 7.7% 20.0% 0.7%	— — — —	26 8.7%
All Other States	45 29.4% 48.4% 15.0%	70 45.8% 51.9% 23.3%	33 21.6% 55.9% 11.0%	4 2.6% 40.0% 1.3%	1 0.7% 33.3% 0.3%	153 51.0%
Totals	93 31.0%	135 45.0%	59 19.7%	10 3.3%	3 1.0%	300 100%

Total Percentage

4 indicates that there were four cases involving a nonfinal decision for the defendant in states other than New York and California, which constitute 2.6 percent of the 153 cases involving these other states, 40.0 percent of the ten cases involving nonfinal decisions for the defendant, and 1.3 percent of the total number of cases (300).

Table 1. Results of Suits Correlated with Year of Final Decision

	Year of Final Decision						
Verdict for Whom	*Unspecified*	*1850–1949*	*1950–1959*	*1960–1969*	*1970–1977*	*Not Yet Decided*	*Total*
Plaintiff	2	17	13	23	38	0	93
	2.2%	18.3%	14.0%	24.7%	40.9%	—	31.0%
	100.0%	34.7%	26.5%	23.2%	38.8%	—	
	0.7%	5.7%	4.3%	7.7%	12.7%	—	
Defendant	0	23	20	51	41	0	135
	—	17.0%	14.8%	37.8%	30.4%	—	45.0%
	—	46.9%	40.8%	51.5%	41.8%	—	
	—	7.7%	6.7%	17.0%	13.7%	—	
Nonfinal for Plaintiff	0	8	13	22	16	0	59
	—	13.6%	22.0%	37.3%	27.1%	—	19.7%
	—	16.3%	26.5%	22.2%	16.3%	—	
	—	2.7%	4.3%	7.3%	5.3%	—	
Nonfinal for Defendant	0	1	3	3	3	0	10
	—	10.0%	30.0%	30.0%	30.0%	—	3.3%
	—	2.0%	6.1%	3.0%	3.1%	—	
	—	0.3%	1.0%	1.0%	1.0%	—	
Not Yet Decided	0	0	0	0	0	3	3
	—	—	—	—	—	100.0%	1.0%
	—	—	—	—	—	100.0%	
	—	—	—	—	—	1.0%	
Totals	2	49	49	99	98	3	300
	0.7%	16.3%	16.3%	33.0%	32.7%	1.0%	100%

Table 2. Results of Suits Correlated with Year of Initial Decision

	Year of Initial Decision						
Verdict for Whom	*Unspecified*	*1850–1949*	*1950–1959*	*1960–1969*	*1970–1977*	*Not Yet Decided*	*Total*
Plaintiff	48	11	8	18	24	0	109
	44.0%	10.1%	7.3%	16.5%	22.0%	—	36.3%
	28.9%	61.1%	38.1%	40.0%	51.1%	—	
	16.0%	3.7%	2.7%	6.0%	8.0%	—	
Defendant	113	6	8	18	13	0	158
	71.5%	3.8%	5.1%	11.4%	8.2%	—	52.7%
	68.1%	33.3%	38.1%	40.0%	27.7%	—	
	37.7%	2.0%	2.7%	6.0%	4.3%	—	
Nonfinal for Plaintiff	4	1	5	8	9	0	27
	14.8%	3.7%	18.5%	29.6%	33.3%	—	9.0%
	2.4%	5.6%	23.8%	17.8%	19.1%	—	
	1.3%	0.3%	1.7%	2.7%	3.0%	—	
Nonfinal for Defendant	1	0	0	1	1	0	3
	33.3%	—	—	33.3%	33.3%	—	1.0%
	0.6%	—	—	2.2%	2.1%	—	
	0.3%	—	—	0.3%	0.3%	—	
Not Yet Decided	0	0	0	0	0	3	3
	—	—	—	—	—	100.0%	1.0%
	—	—	—	—	—	100.0%	
	—	—	—	—	—	1.0%	
Totals	166	18	21	45	47	3	300
	55.3%	6.0%	7.0%	15.0%	15.7%	1.0%	100%

Table 3. Final Decisions Correlated with Region of Country

	Verdict for Whom					
Region of Country	*Plaintiff*	*Defendant*	*Nonfinal for Plaintiff*	*Nonfinal for Defendant*	*Not Yet Decided*	*Totals*
New York	42	51	22	4	2	121
	34.7%	42.1%	18.2%	3.3	1.7%	
	45.2%	37.8%	37.3%	40.0%	66.7%	40.3%
	14.0%	17.0%	7.3%	1.3%	0.7%	
California	6	14	4	2	—	26
	23.1%	53.8%	15.4%	7.7%	—	
	6.5%	10.4%	6.8%	20.0%	—	8.7%
	2.0%	4.7%	1.3%	0.7%	—	
All Other States	45	70	33	4	1	153
	29.4%	45.8%	21.6%	2.6%	0.7%	
	48.4%	51.9%	55.9%	40.0%	33.3%	51.0%
	15.0%	23.3%	11.0%	1.3%	0.3%	
Totals	93	135	59	10	3	300
	31.0%	45.0%	19.7%	3.3%	1.0%	100%

Table 4. Initial Decisions Correlated with Region of Country

	Verdict for Whom					
Region of Country	*Plaintiff*	*Defendant*	*Nonfinal for Plaintiff*	*Nonfinal for Defendant*	*Not Yet Decided*	*Totals*
New York	54	47	16	2	2	121
	44.6%	38.8%	13.2%	1.7%	1.7%	
	49.5%	29.7%	59.3%	66.7%	66.7%	40.3%
	18.0%	15.7%	5.3%	0.7%	0.7%	
California	9	16	1	—	—	26
	34.6%	61.5%	3.8%	—	—	
	8.3%	10.1%	3.7%	—	—	8.7%
	3.0%	5.3%	0.3%	—	—	
All Other States	46	95	10	1	1	153
	30.1%	62.1%	6.5%	0.7%	0.7%	
	42.2%	60.1%	37.0%	33.3%	33.3%	51.0%
	15.3%	31.7%	3.3%	0.3%	0.3%	
Totals	109	158	27	3	3	300
	36.3%	52.7%	9.0%	1.0%	1.0%	100%

Table 5. Changes over Time in Type of Setting

Setting	*Year of Final Decision* *Unspecified*	*1850–1949*	*1950–1959*	*1960–1969*	*1970–1977*	*Not Yet Decided*	*Totals*
Judicial Proceeding	— — — —	17 25.8% 33.3% 5.6%	8 12.1% 16.0% 2.6%	18 27.3% 18.2% 5.9%	23 34.8% 23.2% 7.6%	— — — —	66 21.7%
All Hospitals*	— — — —	33 16.8% 64.7% 10.9%	37 18.9% 74.0% 12.2%	65 33.2% 65.7% 21.4%	60 30.6% 60.6% 19.7%	1 0.5% 33.3% 0.3%	196 64.5%
Mental Hospitals*	— — — —	27 18.0% 52.9% 8.8%	30 20.0% 60.0% 9.9%	44 29.3% 44.4% 14.5%	48 32.0% 48.5% 15.8%	1 0.7% 33.3% 0.3%	150 49.3%
General Hospitals*	— — — —	3 9.7% 5.9% 1.0%	5 16.1% 10.0% 1.6%	16 51.6% 16.2% 5.3%	7 22.6% 7.1% 2.3%	— — — —	31 10.2%
Public Hospitals*	— — — —	19 14.0% 37.3% 6.3%	25 18.4% 50.0% 8.2%	45 33.1% 45.5% 14.8%	46 33.8% 46.5% 15.1%	1 0.7% 33.3% 0.3%	136 44.7%
Private Hospitals*	— — — —	14 27.5% 27.5% 4.6%	11 21.6% 22.0% 3.6%	17 33.3% 17.2% 5.6%	9 17.6% 9.1% 3.0%	— — — —	51 16.8%
Private Practice	— — — —	1 4.8% 2.0% 0.3%	3 14.3% 6.0% 1.0%	7 33.3% 7.1% 2.3%	8 38.1% 8.1% 2.6%	2 9.5% 66.7% 0.7%	21 6.9%
Encounter Groups	2 66.7% 100% 0.7%	— — — —	— — — —	— — — —	1 33.3% 1.0% 0.3%	— — — —	3 1.0%
Other Settings**	— — — —	— — — —	2 11.1% 4.0% 0.6%	9 50.0% 9.1% 3.0%	7 38.9% 7.1% 2.3%	— — — —	18 5.9%
Totals	2 0.6%	51* 16.8%	50* 16.4%	99* 32.6%	99* 32.6%	3* 1.0%	304 100%

*The subcategories for hospitals are not included in the column totals for number of decisions within a certain time frame. In addition, the sum of the subcategories may be more than the total number for all hospitals because a hospital may be both a public hospital and a general hospital, or a private hospital and a mental hospital, etc., in which case it would be listed twice.

**Includes Armed Services, Correctional Institutions, Farms, and Types Not Specified

Table 6. Results of Suits Correlated with Type of Setting

Type of Setting	*Verdict for Whom*					
	Plaintiff	*Defendant*	*Nonfinal for Plaintiff*	*Nonfinal for Defendant*	*Not Yet Decided*	*Totals*
Judicial Proceeding	12	41	11	2	—	66
	18.2%	62.1%	16.7%	3.0%	—	21.7%
	12.8%	29.7%	18.6%	20.0%	—	
	3.9%	13.5%	3.6%	0.7%	—	
All Hospitals*	64	87	37	7	1	196
	32.7%	44.4%	18.9%	3.6%	0.5%	64.5%
	68.1%	63.0%	62.7%	70.0%	33.3%	
	21.1%	28.6%	12.2%	2.3%	0.3%	
Mental hospitals*	56	63	24	6	1	150
	37.3%	42.0%	16.0%	4.0%	0.7%	49.3%
	60.0%	45.7%	40.7%	60.0%	33.3%	
	10.4%	20.7%	7.9%	2.0%	0.3%	
General hospitals*	6	15	9	1	—	31
	19.4%	48.4%	29.0%	3.2%	—	10.2%
	6.4%	10.9%	15.3%	10.0%	—	
	2.0%	4.9%	3.0%	0.3%	—	
Public hospitals*	49	64	20	2	1	136
	36.0%	47.1%	14.7%	1.5%	0.7%	44.7%
	52.1%	46.4%	33.9%	20.0%	33.3%	
	16.1%	21.1%	6.6%	0.7%	0.3%	
Private hospitals	15	17	14	5	—	51
	29.4%	33.3%	27.5%	9.8%	—	16.8%
	16.0%	12.3%	23.7%	50.0%	—	
	4.9%	5.6%	4.6%	1.6%	—	
Private Practice	9	3	6	1	2	21
	42.9%	14.3%	28.6%	4.8%	9.5%	6.9%
	9.6%	2.2%	10.2%	10.0%	66.7%	
	3.0%	1.0%	2.0%	0.3%	0.7%	
Encounter Groups	3	—	—	—	—	3
	100%	—	—	—	—	1.0%
	3.2%	—	—	—	—	
	1.0%	—	—	—	—	
Other Settings**	6	7	5	—	—	18
	33.3%	38.9%	27.8%	—	—	5.9%
	6.4%	5.1%	8.5%	—	—	
	2.0%	2.3%	1.6%	—	—	
	94*	138*	59*	10*	3*	304
Totals	30.9%	45.4%	19.4%	3.3%	1.0%	100%

*The subcategories for hospitals are not included in the column totals for the number of verdicts for plaintiff, defendant, etc. In addition, the sum of the subcategories may be more than the total number for all hospitals because a hospital may be both a public hospital and a general hospital, or a private hospital and a mental hospital, etc., in which case it would be multiply listed.

**Includes Armed Services, Correctional Institutions, Farms, and Types Not Specified

Table 7. Changes over Time in Type of Plaintiffs

	Year of Final Decision						
Plaintiff	*Unspecified*	*1850–1949*	*1950–1959*	*1960–1969*	*1970–1977*	*Not Yet Decided*	*Totals*
Patient or Representative	2 0.8% 100.0% .6%	41 16.9% 82.0% 13.0%	40 16.5% 81.6% 12.7%	82 33.7% 76.6% 25.9%	75 30.9% 71.4% 23.7%	3 1.2% 100.0% 0.9%	243 76.9%
Third Party Injured by Harm to Patient	0 — — —	6 16.7% 12.0% 1.9%	3 8.3% 6.1% .9%	13 36.1% 12.1% 4.1%	14 38.9% 13.3% 4.4%	0 — — —	36 11.4%
Third Party Injured by Patient	0 — — —	3 9.4% 6.0% 0.9%	4 12.5% 8.2% 1.3%	11 34.4% 10.3% 3.5%	14 43.8 13.3 4.4%	0 — — —	32 10.1%
State or Licensing Board	0 — — —	0 — — —	2 40.0% 4.1% 0.6%	1 20.0% 0.9% 0.3%	2 40.0% 1.9% 0.6%	0 — — —	5 1.6%
Totals	2 0.6%	50 15.8%	49 15.5%	107 33.9%	105 33.2%	3 0.9%	316 100%

Table 8. Results of Suits Correlated with Type of Plaintiff

	Verdict for Whom					
Plaintiff	*Plaintiff*	*Defendant*	*Nonfinal for Defendant*	*Nonfinal for Defendant*	*Not Yet Decided*	*Totals*
Patient or Representative	71 29.2% 72.4% 22.5%	108 44.4% 76.1% 34.2%	52 21.4% 82.5% 16.5%	9 3.7% 90.0% 2.8%	3 1.2% 100.0% 0.9%	243 76.9%
Third Party Injured by Harm to Patient	13 36.1% 13.3% 4.1%	17 47.2% 12.0% 5.4%	6 16.7% 9.5% 1.9%	0 — — —	0 — — —	36 11.4%
Third Party Injured by Patient	11 34.4% 11.2% 3.5%	16 50.0% 11.3% 5.1%	5 15.6% 7.9% 1.6%	0 — — —	0 — — —	32 10.1%
State or Licensing Board	3 60.0% 3.1% .9%	1 20.0% 0.7% 0.3%	0 — — —	1 20.0% 10.0% 0.3%	0 — — —	5 1.6%
Totals	98 31.0%	142 44.9%	63 19.9%	10 3.2%	3 0.9%	316 100%

Table 9. Changes over Time in Sex of Person Harmed

	Year of Final Decision						
Sex of Person Harmed	*Unspecified*	*1850–1949*	*1950–1959*	*1960–1969*	*1970–1977*	*Not Yet Decided*	*Totals*
Female	1 0.9% 50.0% 0.3%	22 18.8% 44.9% 7.3%	15 12.8% 30.6% 5.0%	39 33.3% 39.4% 13.0%	39 33.3% 39.8% 13.0%	1 0.9% 33.3% 0.3%	117 39.0%
Male	0 — — —	26 16.0% 53.1% 8.7%	29 17.9% 59.2% 9.7%	59 36.4% 59.6% 19.7%	47 29.0% 48.0% 15.7%	1 0.6% 33.3% 0.3%	162 54.0%
Unknown or Not Applicable	1 4.8% 50.0% 0.3%	1 4.8% 2.0% 0.3%	5 23.8% 10.2% 1.7%	1 4.8% 1.0% 0.3%	12 57.1% 12.2% 4.0%	1 4.8% 33.3% 0.3%	21 7.0%
Totals	2 0.7%	49 16.3%	49 16.3%	99 33.0%	98 32.7%	3 1.0%	300 100.0%

Table 10. Results of Suits Correlated with Sex of Person Harmed

	Verdict for Whom					
Sex of Person Harmed	*Plaintiff*	*Defendant*	*Nonfinal for Plaintiff*	*Nonfinal for Defendant*	*Not Yet Decided*	*Totals*
Female	39 33.3% 41.9% 13.0%	52 44.4% 38.5% 17.3%	19 16.2% 32.2% 6.3%	6 5.1% 60.0% 2.0%	1 0.9% 33.3% 0.3%	117 39.0%
Male	45 27.8% 48.4% 15.0%	77 47.5% 57.0% 25.7%	36 22.2% 61.0% 12.0%	3 1.9% 30.0% 1.0%	1 0.6% 33.3% 0.3%	162 54.0%
Unknown or Not Applicable	9 42.9% 9.7% 3.0%	6 28.6% 4.4% 2.0%	4 19.0% 6.8% 1.3%	1 4.8% 10.0% 0.3%	1 4.8% 33.3% 0.3%	21 7.0%
Totals	93 31.0%	135 45.0%	59 19.7%	10 3.3%	3 1.0%	300 100.0%

Table 11 Changes over Time in Type of Defendants Initially Sued

	Year of Final Decision						
Defendant	*Unspecified*	*1850–1949*	*1950–1959*	*1960–1969*	*1970–1977*	*Not Yet Decided*	*Totals*
Practitioners	—	21	18	44	40	3	126
	—	16.7%	14.3%	34.9%	31.7%	2.4%	31.9%
	—	36.2%	31.0%	33.3%	28.2%	100%	
	—	5.3%	4.6%	11.1%	10.1%	0.8%	
Hospitals	—	11	15	25	30	—	81
	—	13.6%	18.5%	30.9%	37.0%	—	20.5%
	—	19.0%	25.9%	18.9%	21.1%	—	
	—	2.8%	3.8%	6.3%	7.6%	—	
All Government*	—	20	21	45	46	—	132
	—	15.2%	15.9%	34.1%	34.8%	—	33.4%
	—	34.5%	36.2%	34.1%	32.4%	—	
	—	5.1%	5.3%	11.4%	11.6%	—	
Federal*	—	1	5	10	6	—	22
	—	4.5%	22.7%	45.5%	27.3%	—	5.6%
	—	1.7%	8.6%	7.6%	4.2%	—	
	—	0.3%	1.3%	2.5%	1.5%	—	
State*	—	17	16	30	35	—	98
	—	17.3%	16.3%	30.6%	35.7%	—	24.8%
	—	29.3%	27.6%	22.7%	24.6%	—	
	—	4.3%	4.1%	7.6%	8.9%	—	
County*	—	1	—	3	3	—	7
	—	14.3%	—	42.9%	42.9%	—	1.8%
	—	1.7%	—	2.3%	2.1%	—	
	—	0.3%	—	0.8%	0.8%	—	
Municipal*	—	2	—	2	6	—	10
	—	20%	—	20%	60%	—	2.5%
	—	3.4%	—	1.5%	4.2%	—	
	—	0.5%	—	0.5%	1.5%	—	
Judiciary	—	1	—	4	10	—	15
	—	6.7%	—	26.7%	66.7%	—	3.8%
	—	1.7%	—	3.0%	7.0%	—	
	—	0.3%	—	1.0%	2.5%	—	
Educational Institutions	—	1	—	2	5	—	8
	—	12.5%	—	25.0%	62.5%	—	2.0%
	—	1.7%	—	1.5%	3.5%	—	
	—	0.3%	—	0.5%	1.3%	—	
Other**	2	4	4	12	11	—	33
	6.5%	12.9%	12.9%	32.3%	35.5%	—	8.4%
	100%	6.9%	6.9%	9.1%	7.7%	—	
	0.5%	1.0%	1.0%	3.0%	2.8%	—	
Totals	2	58	58	132	142	3	395
	0.5%	14.7%	14.7%	33.4%	35.9%	0.8%	100%

*The various branches of government, which are listed as subcategories, are not included in the column totals for number of decisions within a certain time frame. The sum of the subcategories is not necessarily the total number for all government because a suit may involve more than one branch of government, in which case it would be multiply listed.

**Includes paraprofessionals, nonprofessionals, insurance companies, encounter group leaders, nurses, relatives, growth centers, police, nonprofit organizations, and types not specified.

Table 12. Results of Suits Correlated with Defendant Initially Sued

	Verdict for Whom					
Defendant	*Plaintiff*	*Defendant*	*Nonfinal for Plaintiff*	*Nonfinal for Defendant*	*Not Yet Decided*	*Totals*
Practitioners	27 21.4% 23.5% 6.8%	61 48.4% 34.5% 15.4%	26 20.6% 31.0% 6.6%	9 7.1% 56.3% 2.3%	3 2.4% 100% 0.8%	126 31.9%
Hospitals	25 30.9% 21.7% 6.3%	25 30.9% 14.1% 6.3%	25 30.9% 29.8% 6.3%	6 7.4% 37.5% 1.5%	— — — —	81 20.5%
All Government*	48 36.4% 41.7% 12.2%	66 50.0% 31.3% 16.7%	18 13.6% 21.4% 4.6%	— — — —	— — — —	132 33.4%
Federal*	6 27.3% 5.2% 1.5%	12 54.5% 6.8% 3.0%	4 18.2% 4.8% 1.0%	— — — —	— — — —	22 5.6%
State*	40 40.8% 34.8% 10.1%	47 48.0% 26.6% 11.9%	11 11.2% 13.1% 2.8%	— — — —	— — — —	98 26.0%
County*	— — — —	5 71.4% 2.8% 1.3%	2 28.6% 2.4% 0.5%	— — — —	— — — —	7 1.8%
Municipal*	2 20% 1.7% 0.5%	4 40% 2.3% 1.0%	4 40% 4.8% 1.0%	— — — —	— — — —	10 2.5%
Judiciary	3 20% 2.6% 0.8%	8 53.3% 4.5% 2.0%	4 26.7% 4.8% 1.0%	— — — —	— — — —	15 3.8%
Educational Institutions	2 25% 1.7% 0.5%	3 37.5% 1.7% 0.8%	2 25.0% 2.4% 0.5%	1 12.5% 6.3% 0.3%	— — — —	8 2.0%
Others**	10 30.3% 8.7% 2.5%	14 42.4% 7.9% 3.5%	9 27.3% 10.7% 2.3%	— — — —	— — — —	33 8.4%
Totals	115 29.1%	177 44.8%	84 21.2%	16 4.1%	3 0.8%	395 100%

*The subcategories for government are not included in the column totals for the number of verdicts for plaintiff, defendant, etc. The sum of the subcategories may be more than the total number for all branches of government because a suit may involve both the federal and state government, or state and municipal government, etc, in which case it would be multiply listed.

**Includes paraprofessionals, nonprofessionals, insurance companies, encounter group leaders, nurses, relatives, growth centers, police, nonprofit organizations, and types not specified.

Table 13. Changes over Time in Allegations of Negligent Treatment

	Year of Decision						
Allegation	*Unspecified*	*1850–1949*	*1950–1959*	*1960–1969*	*1970–1977*	*Not Yet Decided*	*Totals*
Sexual	—	—	1	3	7	1	12
Involvement	—	—	8.3%	25.0%	58.3%	8.3%	10.3%
	—	—	5.3%	9.1%	13.2%	33.3%	
	—	—	0.9%	2.6%	6.0%	0.9%	
Physical	—	1	—	2	2	—	5
Assault	—	20.0%	—	40.0%	40.0%	—	4.3%
	—	14.3%	—	6.1%	3.8%	—	
	—	0.9%	—	1.7%	1.7%	—	
Negligent	—	—	2	3	8	—	13
Administration	—	—	15.4%	23.1%	61.5%	—	11.1%
of Drugs	—	—	10.5%	9.1%	15.1%	—	
(excluding insulin)	—	—	1.7%	2.6%	6.8%	—	
Negligent	—	—	1	1	—	—	2
Insulin	—	—	50.0%	50.0%	—	—	1.7%
Therapy	—	—	5.3%	3.0%	—	—	
	—	—	0.9%	0.9%	—	—	
Negligent	—	2	6	7	2	—	17
Electro-	—	11.8%	35.3%	41.2%	11.8%	—	14.5%
Convulsive	—	28.6%	31.6%	21.2%	3.8%	—	
Therapy	—	1.7%	5.1%	6.0%	1.7%	—	
Failure to	—	—	—	6	3	1	10
Obtain	—	—	—	60.0%	30.0%	10.0%	8.5%
Informed	—	—	—	18.2%	5.7%	33.3%	
Consent	—	—	—	5.1%	2.6%	0.9%	
No Treatment	—	1	2	6	24	—	33
or Inadequate	—	3.0%	6.1%	18.2%	72.7%	—	28.2%
Treatment	—	14.3%	10.5%	18.2%	45.3%	—	
	—	0.9%	1.7%	5.1%	20.5%	—	
Other*	2	3	7	5	7	1	25
	8.0%	12.0%	28.0%	20.0%	28.0%	4.0%	21.4%
	100%	42.9%	36.8%	15.2%	13.2%	33.3%	
	1.7%	2.6%	6.0%	4.3%	6.0%	0.9%	
Totals	2	7	19	33	53	3	117
	1.7%	6.0%	16.2%	28.2%	45.3%	2.6%	100%

*Includes negligence in use of technique, negligent handling of the transference or countertransference relationship, failure to consult another therapist, negligent abortion, negligent application of wetpack, negligent operation, unspecified negligent treatment, and four cases in which a question exists as to whether negligent treatment was involved.

Table 14. Results of Suits Correlated with Type of Negligent Treatment Alleged

	Verdict for Whom					
Allegation	*Plaintiff*	*Defendant*	*Nonfinal for Plaintiff*	*Nonfinal for Defendant*	*Not Yet Decided*	*Totals*
Sexual	8	3	—	—	1	12
Involvement	66.7%	25.0%	—	—	8.3%	10.3%
	17.8%	9.4%	—	—	33.3%	
	6.8%	2.6%	—	—	0.9%	
Physical	4	—	1	—	—	5
Assault	80.0%	—	20.0%	—	—	4.3%
	8.9%	—	3.6%	—	—	
	3.4%	—	0.9%	—	—	
Negligent	4	4	3	2	—	13
Administration	30.8%	30.8%	23.1%	15.4%	—	11.1%
of Drugs	8.9%	12.5%	10.7%	22.2%	—	
(excluding insulin)	3.4%	3.4%	2.6%	1.7%	—	
Negligent	—	1	1	—	—	2
Insulin	—	50.0%	50.0%	—	—	1.7%
Therapy	—	3.1%	3.6%	—	—	
	—	0.9%	0.9%	—	—	
Negligent	2	7	4	4	—	17
Electro-	11.8%	41.2%	23.5%	23.5%	—	14.5%
Convulsive	4.4%	21.9%	14.3%	44.4%	—	
Therapy	1.7%	6.0%	3.4%	3.4%	—	
Failure to	1	4	1	3	1	10
Obtain	10.0%	40.0%	10.0%	30.0%	10.0%	8.5%
Informed	2.2%	12.5%	3.6%	33.3%	33.3%	
Consent	0.9%	3.4%	0.9%	2.6%	0.9%	
No Treatment	16	7	10	—	—	33
or Inadequate	48.5%	21.2%	30.3%	—	—	28.2%
Treatment	35.6%	21.9%	35.7%	—	—	
	13.7%	6.0%	8.5%	—	—	
Other*	10	6	8	—	1	25
	40.0%	24.0%	32.0%	—	4.0%	21.4%
	22.2%	18.8%	28.6%	—	33.3%	
	8.5%	5.1%	6.8%	—	0.9%	
Totals	45	32	28	9	3	117
	38.5%	27.4%	23.9%	7.7%	2.6%	100%

*Includes negligence in use of technique, negligent handling of the transference or countertransference relationship, failure to consult another therapist, negligent abortion, negligent application of wetpack, negligent operation, unspecified negligent treatment, and four cases in which a question exists as to whether negligent treatment was involved.

Table 15. Changes Over Time in What Was Alleged to Be Negligently Diagnosed

	Year of Decision						
What Was Diagnosed	*Unspecified*	*1850–1949*	*1950–1959*	*1960–1969*	*1970–1977*	*Not Yet Decided*	*Totals*
Mental Illness,	—	19	6	21	26	—	72
Instead of Sanity	—	26.3%	8.3%	29.2%	36.1%	—	40.9%
	—	79.2%	28.6%	36.8%	35.1%	—	
	—	10.8%	3.4%	11.9%	14.8%		
Sanity, Instead	—	1	1	4	7	—	13
of Mental	—	7.7%	7.7%	30.8%	53.8%	—	7.4%
Illness	—	4.2%	4.8%	7.0%	9.5%	—	
	—	0.6%	0.6%	2.3%	4.0%	—	
Mental Illness,	—	—	1	2	4	—	7
Instead of	—	—	14.3%	28.6%	57.1%	—	4.0%
Physical	—	—	4.8%	3.5%	5.4%	—	
Illness	—	—	0.6%	1.1%	2.3%	—	
Physical Illness,	—	—	—	—	2	—	2
Instead of	—	—	—	—	100%	—	1.1%
Mental Illness	—	—	—	—	2.7%	—	
	—	—	—	—	1.1%	—	
Dangerousness	—	1	2	3	2	—	8
	—	12.5%	25.0%	37.5%	25.0%	—	4.5%
	—	4.2%	9.5%	5.3%	2.7%	—	
	—	0.6%	1.1%	1.7%	1.1%	—	
Lack of	—	2	3	8	12	—	25
Dangerousness	—	8.0%	12.0%	32.0%	48.0%	—	14.2%
	—	8.3%	14.3%	14.0%	16.2%	—	
	—	1.1%	1.7%	4.5%	6.8%	—	
Lack of	—	1	2	6	2	—	11
Suicidal	—	9.1%	18.2%	54.5%	18.2%	—	6.3%
Tendencies	—	4.2%	9.5%	10.5%	2.7%	—	
	—	0.6%	1.1%	3.4%	1.1%	—	
Type of	—	—	1	1	3	—	5
Treatment	—	—	20.0%	20.0%	60.0%	—	2.8%
Needed	—	—	4.8%	1.8%	4.1%	—	
(excluding drugs)	—	—	0.6%	0.6%	1.7%	—	
Type of	—	—	1	2	4	—	7
Drugs Needed	—	—	14.3%	28.6%	57.1%	—	4.0%
	—	—	4.8%	3.5%	5.4%	—	
	—	—	0.6%	1.1%	2.3%	—	
Type of	—	—	1	4	2	—	7
Care Needed	—	—	14.3%	57.1%	28.6%	—	4.0%
	—	—	4.8%	7.0%	2.7%	—	
	—	—	0.6%	2.3%	1.1%	—	
Other*	—	—	3	6	10	—	19
	—	—	15.8%	31.6%	52.6%	—	10.8%
	—	—	14.3%	10.5%	13.5%	—	
	—	—	1.7%	3.4%	5.7%		
Totals	0	24	21	57	74	0	176
	—	13.6%	11.9%	32.4%	42.0%	—	100%

*Includes unfitness for duty, failure to make a diagnosis when one was called for, negligent recommendation to take a psychiatric examination when one was not called for, inadequate diagnosis, negligent diagnosis of what type of mental illness a person had, and four cases in which a question exists as to whether negligent diagnosis was involved.

Table 16. Results of Suits Correlated with What Was Alleged to Be Negligently Diagnosed

	Verdict for Whom					
What Was Diagnosed	*Plaintiff*	*Defendant*	*Nonfinal for Plaintiff*	*Nonfinal for Defendant*	*Not Yet Decided*	*Totals*
Mental Illness,	11	43	15	3	—	72
Instead of	15.3%	59.7%	20.8%	4.2%	—	40.9%
Sanity	30.6%	41.0%	46.9%	100%	—	
	6.3%	24.4%	8.5%	1.7%	—	
Sanity, Instead	2	10	1	—	—	13
of Mental	15.4%	76.9%	7.7%	—	—	7.4%
Illness	5.6%	9.5%	3.1%	—	—	
	1.1%	5.7%	0.6%	—	—	
Mental Illness,	2	4	1	—	—	7
Instead of	28.6%	57.1%	14.3%	—	—	4.0%
Physical	5.6%	3.8%	3.1%	—	—	
Illness	1.1%	2.3%	0.6%	—	—	
Physical Illness,	1	1	—	—	—	2
Instead of	50.0%	50%	—	—	—	1.1%
Mental Illness	2.8%	1.0%	—	—	—	
	0.6%	0.6%	—	—	—	
Dangerousness	4	2	2	—	—	8
	50.0%	25.0%	25.0%	—	—	4.5%
	11.1%	1.9%	6.3%	—	—	
	2.3%	1.1%	1.1%	—	—	
Lack of	6	14	5	—	—	25
Dangerousness	24.0%	56.0%	20.0%	—	—	14.2%
	16.7%	13.3%	15.6%	—	—	
	3.4%	8.0%	2.8%			
Lack of Suicidal	—	11	—	—	—	11
Tendencies	—	100%	—	—	—	6.3%
	—	10.5%	—	—	—	
	—	6.3%	—	—	—	
Type of	1	3	1	—	—	5
Treatment	20.0%	60.0%	20.0%	—	—	2.8%
Needed	2.8%	2.9%	3.1%	—	—	
(excluding drugs)	0.6%	1.7%	0.6%	—	—	
Type of	2	4	1	—	—	7
Drugs Needed	28.6%	57.1%	14.3%	—	—	4.0%
	5.6%	3.8%	3.1%	—	—	
	1.1%	2.3%	0.6%	—	—	
Type of	3	3	1	—	—	7
Care Needed	42.9%	42.9%	14.3%	—	—	4.0%
	8.3%	2.9%	3.1%	—	—	
	1.7%	1.7%	0.6%	—	—	
Other*	4	10	5	—	—	19
	21.1%	52.6%	26.3%	—	—	10.8%
	11.1%	9.5%	15.6%	—	—	
	2.3%	5.7%	2.8%	—	—	
Totals	36	105	32	3	0	176
	20.5%	59.7%	18.2%	1.7%	—	100%

*Includes unfitness for duty, failure to make a diagnosis when one was called for, negligent recommendation to take a psychiatric examination when one was not called for, inadequate diagnosis, negligent diagnosis of what type of mental illness a person had, and four cases in which a question exists as to whether negligent diagnosis was involved.

Table 17. Changes over Time in Results of Allegedly Negligent Diagnoses

	Year of Final Decision						
Result of Diagnosis	*Unspecified*	*1850–1949*	*1950–1959*	*1960–1969*	*1970–1977*	*Not Yet Decided*	*Totals*
Improper Treatment (excluding drugs)	—	—	2	7	9	—	18
	—	—	11.1%	38.9%	50.0%	—	10.5%
	—	—	10.5%	12.5%	12.7%	—	
	—	—	1.2%	4.1%	5.3%	—	
Improper Prescription of Drugs	—	—	1	5	4	—	10
	—	—	10.0%	50.0%	40.0%	—	5.8%
	—	—	5.3%	8.9%	5.6%	—	
	—	—	0.6%	2.9%	2.3%	—	
Improper Care	—	5	4	12	5	—	26
	—	19.2%	15.4%	46.2%	19.2%	—	15.2%
	—	20.0%	21.1%	21.5%	7.0%	—	
	—	2.9%	2.3%	7.0%	2.9%	—	
Improper Commitment	—	18	8	19	25	—	70
	—	25.7%	11.4%	27.1%	35.7%	—	40.9%
	—	72.0%	42.1%	33.9%	35.2%	—	
	—	10.5%	4.7%	11.1%	14.6%	—	
Improper Failure to Commit	—	—	—	—	1	—	1
	—	—	—	—	100%	—	0.6%
	—	—	—	—	1.4%	—	
	—	—	—	—	0.6%		
Improper Release	—	1	4	8	13	—	26
	—	3.8%	15.4%	30.8%	50.0%	—	15.2%
	—	4.0%	21.1%	14.3%	18.3%	—	
	—	0.6%	2.3%	4.7%	7.6%	—	
Improper Failure to Release	—	1	—	3	11	—	15
	—	6.7%	—	20.0%	73.3%	—	8.8%
	—	4.0%	—	5.4%	15.5%	—	
	—	0.6%	—	1.8%	6.4%	—	
Other*	—	—	—	2	3	—	5
	—	—	—	40.0%	60.0%	—	2.9%
	—	—	—	3.6%	4.2%	—	
	—	—	—	1.2%	1.8%	—	
Totals	0	25	19	56	71	0	171
	—	14.6%	11.1%	32.7%	41.5%	—	100%

*Includes negligent determination of competence to stand trial, improper determination of custody, negligent determination of unfitness for duty, and one case in which the result of diagnosis is unknown.

Table 18. Results of Suits Correlated with Results of Allegedly Negligent Diagnoses

	Verdict for Whom					
Result of Diagnosis	*Plaintiff*	*Defendant*	*Nonfinal for Plaintiff*	*Nonfinal for Defendant*	*Not Yet Decided*	*Totals*
Improper	6	9	1	2	—	18
Treatment	33.3%	50.0%	5.6%	11.1%	—	10.5%
(excluding	15.0%	9.5%	3.3%	33.3%	—	
drugs)	3.5%	5.3%	0.6%	1.2%	—	
Improper	3	5	1	1	—	10
Prescription	30.0%	50.0%	10.0%	10.0%	—	5.8%
of Drugs	7.5%	5.3%	3.3%	16.7%	—	
	1.8%	2.9%	0.6%	0.6%	—	
Improper	9	14	3	—	—	26
Care	34.6%	53.8%	11.5%	—	—	15.2%
	22.5%	14.7%	10%	—	—	
	5.3%	8.2%	1.8%	—	—	
Improper	11	43	13	3	—	70
Commitment	15.7%	61.4%	18.6%	4.3%	—	40.9%
	27.5%	45.3%	43.3%	50.0%	—	
	6.4%	25.1%	7.5%	1.8%	—	
Improper	—	—	1	—	—	1
Failure to	—	—	100%	—	—	0.6%
Commit	—	—	3.3%	—	—	
	—	—	0.6%	—	—	
Improper	7	16	3	—	—	26
Release	26.9%	61.5%	11.5%	—	—	15.2%
	17.5%	16.8%	10%	—	—	
	4.1%	9.4%	1.8%	—	—	
Improper	4	5	6	—	—	15
Failure to	26.7%	33.3%	40.0%	—	—	8.8%
Release	10%	5.3%	20%	—	—	
	2.3%	2.9%	3.5%	—	—	
Other*	—	3	2	—	—	5
	—	60.0%	40.0%	—	—	2.9%
	—	3.2%	6.7%	—	—	
	—	1.8%	1.2%	—	—	
Totals	40	95	30	6	0	171
	23.4%	55.6%	17.5%	3.5%	—	100%

*Includes negligent determination of competence to stand trial, improper determination of custody, negligent determination of unfitness for duty, and one case in which the result of diagnosis is unknown.

Table 19. Changes over Time in Allegations of Negligent Care

	Year of Final Decision						
Care	*Unspecified*	*1850–1949*	*1950–1959*	*1960–1969*	*1970–1977*	*Not Yet Decided*	*Totals*
Inadequate Supervision	—	24	20	39	23	—	106
	—	22.6%	18.9%	36.8%	21.7%	—	65.4%
	—	82.8%	66.7%	62.9%	56.1%	—	
	—	14.8%	12.3%	24.1%	14.2%	—	
Failure to Provide Proper Care	—	4	3	12	11	—	30
	—	13.3%	10.0%	40.0%	36.7%	—	18.5%
	—	13.8%	10%	19.4%	26.8%	—	
	—	2.5%	1.9%	7.4%	6.8%	—	
Premature Release	—	—	2	3	4	—	9
	—	—	22.2%	33.3%	44.4%	—	5.6%
	—	—	6.7%	4.8%	9.8%	—	
	—	—	1.2%	1.9%	2.5%	—	
Failure to Warn Third Parties	—	—	1	4	1	—	6
	—	—	16.7%	66.7%	16.7%	—	3.7%
	—	—	0.3%	6.5%	2.4%		
	—	—	0.6%	2.5%	0.6%	—	
Improper Giving of Information to Others	—	1	1	3	1	—	6
	—	16.7%	16.7%	50.0%	16.7%	—	3.7%
	—	3.4%	3.3%	4.8%	2.4%	—	
	—	0.6%	0.6%	1.9%	0.6%	—	
Other*	—	—	3	1	1	—	5
	—	—	60.0%	20.0%	20.0%	—	3.1%
	—	—	10%	1.6%	2.4%	—	
	—	—	1.9%	0.6%	0.6%	—	
Totals	0	29	30	62	41	0	162
		17.9%	18.5%	38.3%	25.3%	—	100%

*Includes failure to release, and four cases in which a question exists as to whether negligent care was involved.

Table 20. Results of Suits Correlated with Type of Negligent Care Alleged

	Verdict for Whom					
Care	*Plaintiff*	*Defendant*	*Nonfinal for Plaintiff*	*Nonfinal for Defendant*	*Not Yet Decided*	*Totals*
Inadequate	40	46	18	2	—	106
Supervision	37.7%	43.4%	17.0%	1.9%	—	65.4%
	70.2%	67.6%	52.9%	66.7%	—	
	24.7%	28.4%	11.1%	1.2%	—	
Failure to	14	9	6	1	—	30
Provide	46.7%	30.0%	20.0%	3.3%	—	18.5%
Proper	24.6%	13.2%	17.6%	33.3%	—	
Care	8.6%	5.6%	3.7%	0.6%	—	
Premature	1	7	1	—	—	9
Release	11.1%	77.8%	11.1%	—	—	5.6%
	1.8%	10.3%	2.9%	—	—	
	0.6%	4.3%	0.6%	—	—	
Failure to	1	3	2	—	—	6
Warn	16.7%	50.0%	33.3%	—	—	3.7%
Third	1.8%	4.4%	5.9%	—	—	
Parties	0.6%	1.9%	1.2%			
Improper	1	2	3	—	—	6
Giving of	16.7%	33.3%	50.0%	—	—	3.7%
Information	1.8%	2.9%	8.8%	—	—	
to Others	0.6%	1.2%	1.9%	—	—	
Other*	—	1	4	—	—	5
	—	20.0%	80.0%	—	—	3.1%
	—	1.5%	11.8%	—	—	
	—	0.6%	2.5%	—	—	
Totals	57	68	34	3	0	162
	35.2%	42.0%	21.0%	1.9%	—	100%

*Includes failure to release, and four cases in which a question exists as to whether negligent care was involved.

Table 21. Changes over Time in Type of Harm Caused

	Year of Final Decision						
Harm Caused	*Unspeci-fied*	*1850–2949*	*1950–1959*	*1960–1969*	*1970–1977*	*Not Yet Decided*	*Totals*
Suicide	1	6	6	17	8	—	38
	2.6%	15.8%	15.8%	44.7%	21.1%	—	9.4%
	33.3%	10.0%	10.2%	12.8%	5.5%	—	
	0.2%	1.5%	1.5%	4.2%	2.0%	—	
Accidental	—	8	9	7	16	—	40
Death	—	20.0%	22.5%	17.5%	40.0%	—	9.9%
	—	13.3%	15.2%	5.3%	11.1%	—	
	—	2.0%	2.2%	1.7%	4.0%	—	
Self-inflicted	—	1	2	7	5	—	15
Injuries	—	6.7%	13.3%	46.7%	33.3%	—	3.7%
	—	1.6%	3.9%	5.3%	3.5%	—	
	—	0.2%	0.5%	1.7%	1.2%	—	
Accidental							
Injuries	1	14	20	29	20	—	84
	1.2%	16.7%	23.8%	34.5%	23.8%	—	20.8%
	33.3%	23.3%	33.9%	21.8%	13.9%	—	
	0.2%	3.5%	5.0%	7.2%	5.0%	—	
Sexual or	—	—	2	6	9	1	18
Marital Harm	—	—	11.1%	33.3%	50.0%	5.6%	4.4%
	—	—	3.4%	4.5%	6.2%	20.0%	
	—	—	0.5%	1.5%	2.2%	0.2%	
Emotional	1	4	3	11	9	1	29
Distress	3.4%	13.8%	10.3%	37.9%	31.0%	3.4%	7.2%
	33.3%	6.7%	5.1%	8.3%	6.2%	20.0%	
	0.2%	1.0%	0.7%	2.7%	2.2%	0.2%	
Exacerbation of	—	2	—	4	5	1	12
Previous Condition	—	16.7%	—	33.3%	41.7%	8.3%	3.0%
	—	3.3%	—	3.0%	3.5%	20.0%	
	—	0.5%	—	1.0%	1.2%	0.2%	
Economic	—	2	1	13	7	—	23
Loss	—	8.7%	4.3%	56.5%	30.4%	—	5.7%
	—	3.3%	1.7%	9.8%	4.9%	—	
	—	0.5%	0.2%	3.2%	1.7%	—	
Loss of	—	9	5	12	20	—	46
Liberty	—	19.6%	10.9%	26.1%	43.5%	—	11.4%
	—	15.0%	8.5%	9.0%	13.9%	—	
	—	2.2%	1.2%	3.0%	5.0%	—	
Deprivation of	—	1	2	9	26	1	39
Constitutional	—	2.6%	5.1%	23.1%	66.7%	2.6%	9.6%
Rights	—	1.6%	3.4%	6.7%	18.0%	20.0%	
	—	0.2%	0.5%	2.2%	6.4%	0.2%	
Other*	—	13	9	18	19	1	60
	—	21.7%	15.0%	30.0%	31.7%	1.7%	14.9%
	—	21.7%	15.2%	13.5%	13.2%	20.0%	
	—	3.2%	2.2%	4.4%	4.7%	0.2%	
Totals	3	60	59	133	144	5	404
	0.7%	14.8%	14.6%	32.9%	35.6%	1.2%	100%

*Includes exacerbation of previous condition, loss of consortium, injury to reputation, alienation of affection, loss of health, invasion of privacy, insanity, no chance for improvement, pregnancy and abortion, drug addiction, loss of companionship, three cases in which it is unknown whether the injury was accidental or self-inflicted, two cases in which it is unknown whether death was accidental or a suicide, and twenty-four instances in which the type of harm was not specified.

Table 22. Results of Suits Correlated with Type of Harm Caused

Harm Caused	Verdict for Whom: Plaintiff	Defendant	Nonfinal for Plaintiff	Nonfinal for Defendant	Not Yet Decided	Totals
Suicide	11	16	9	2	—	38
	28.9%	42.1%	23.7%	5.3%	—	9.4%
	7.8%	9.6%	11.3%	18.2%	—	
	2.7%	4.0%	2.2%	0.5%	—	
Accidental Death	16	16	7	1	—	40
	40.0%	40.0%	17.5%	2.5%	—	10.0%
	11.3%	9.6%	8.8%	9.1%	—	
	4.0%	4.0%	1.7%	0.2%		
Self-inflicted Injury	7	8	—	—	—	15
	46.7%	53.3%	—	—	—	3.7%
	5.0%	4.8%	—	—	—	
	1.7%	2.0%	—	—	—	
Accidental Injury	28	34	18	4	—	84
	33.3%	40.5%	21.4%	4.8%	—	20.8%
	19.9%	20.4%	22.5%	36.4%	—	
	6.9%	8.4%	4.5%	1.0%		
Sexual Abuse	11	5	1	—	1	18
	61.1%	27.8%	5.6%	—	5.6%	4.5%
	7.8%	3.0%	1.3%	—	20.0%	
	2.7%	1.2%	0.2%	—	0.2%	
Emotional Distress	16	8	3	1	1	29
	55.2%	27.6%	10.3%	3.4%	3.4%	7.2%
	11.3%	4.8%	3.8%	9.1%	20.0%	
	4.0%	2.0%	0.7%	0.2%	.2%	
Exacerbation of Previous Condition	6	4	1	—	1	12
	50.0%	33.3%	8.3%	—	8.3%	3.0%
	4.3%	2.4%	1.3%	—	20.0%	
	1.5%	1.0%	0.2%	—	0.2%	
Economic Loss	6	15	2	—	—	23
	26.1%	65.2%	8.7%	—	—	5.7%
	4.3%	9.0%	2.5%	—	—	
	1.5%	3.7%	0.5%	—	—	
Loss of Liberty	11	21	11	3	—	46
	23.9%	45.7%	23.9%	6.5%	—	11.4%
	7.8%	12.6%	13.8%	27.3%	—	
	2.7%	5.2%	2.7%	0.7%	—	
Deprivation of Constitutional Rights	17	11	10	—	1	39
	43.6%	28.2%	25.6%	—	2.6%	9.7%
	12.1%	6.6%	12.5%	—	20.0%	
	4.2%	2.7%	2.5%	—	0.2%	
Other*	12	29	18	—	1	60
	20.0%	48.3%	30.0%	—	1.7%	14.9%
	8.5%	17.4%	22.5%	—	20.0%	
	3.0%	7.2%	4.5%	—	0.2%	
Totals	141	167	80	11	5	404
	34.9%	41.3%	19.8%	2.7%	1.2%	100%

*Includes exacerbation of previous condition, loss of consortium, injury to reputation, alienation of affection, loss of health, invasion of privacy, insanity, no chance for improvement, pregnancy, abortion, drug addiction, loss of companionship, three cases in which it is unknown whether the injury was accidental or self-inflicted, two cases in which it is unknown whether death was accidental or a suicide, and twenty-four instances in which the type of harm was not specified.

Table 23. Changes over Time in Type of Action Brought

	Year of Decision						
Action Brought	*Unspecified*	*1850–1949*	*1950–1959*	*1960–1969*	*1970–1977*	*Not Yet Decided*	*Totals*
Negligence	2	41	37	76	71	2	229
	0.9%	17.9%	16.2%	33.2%	31.0%	0.9%	57.5%
	66.7%	64.1%	62.7%	61.3%	49.3%	50.0%	
	0.5%	10.3%	9.3%	19.1%	17.8%	0.5%	
Assault	—	—	4	7	6	—	17
and/or	—	—	23.5%	41.2%	35.3%	—	4.3%
Battery	—	—	6.8%	5.6%	4.2%	—	
	—	—	1.0%	1.8%	1.5%	—	
False	—	7	1	9	15	—	32
Imprisonment	—	21.9%	3.1%	28.1%	46.9%	—	8.0%
	—	10.9%	1.7%	7.3%	10.4%	—	
	—	1.8%	0.2%	2.3%	3.8%	—	
Malicious	—	4	3	3	5	—	15
Prosecution	—	26.7%	20.0%	20.0%	33.3%	—	3.8%
	—	6.2%	5.1%	2.4%	3.5%	—	
	—	1.0%	0.7%	0.7%	1.3%	—	
Defamation	—	4	3	3	1	—	11
of	—	36.4%	27.3%	27.3%	9.1%	—	2.8%
Character	—	6.2%	5.1%	2.4%	0.7%	—	
	—	1.0%	0.7%	0.7%	0.2%	—	
Deprivation	—	1	3	11	29	1	45
of	—	2.2%	6.7%	24.4%	64.4%	2.2%	11.3%
Consitutional	—	1.6%	5.1%	8.9%	20.1%	25.0%	
Rights	—	0.2%	0.7%	2.8%	7.3%	0.2%	
Contract	—	3	1	4	3	—	11
Law	—	27.3%	9.1%	36.4%	27.3%	—	2.8%
	—	4.5%	1.7%	3.2%	2.1%	—	
	—	0.8%	0.2%	1.0%	0.7%	—	
Criminal	—	—	2	—	1	—	3
Law	—	—	66.7%	—	33.3%	—	0.7%
	—	—	3.4%	—	0.7%	—	
	—	—	0.5%	—	0.2%	—	
Administrative	—	—	—	1	2	—	3
Law	—	—	—	33.3%	66.7%	—	0.7%
	—	—	—	0.8%	1.4%	—	
	—	—	—	0.2%	0.5%	—	
Other*	1	4	5	10	11	1	32
	3.1%	12.5%	15.6%	31.3%	34.4%	3.1%	8.0%
	33.3%	6.2%	8.5%	8.1%	7.6%	25.0%	
	0.2%	1.0%	1.3%	2.5%	2.8%	0.2%	
Totals	3	64	59	124	144	4	398
	0.7%	16.1%	14.8%	31.4%	36.2%	1.0%	100%

*Includes misrepresentation, abuse of process, malicious infliction of emotional distress, prima facie tort, failure to do one's statutory duty, invasion of privacy, involuntary servitude, false arrest, conscious pain and suffering, trespass, breach of confidence, racial discrimination, six cases in which the type of action brought was not specified, and one case where no action was yet brought.

Table 24. Results of Suits Correlated with Type of Action Brought

	Verdict for Whom					
Action Brought	*Plaintiff*	*Defendant*	*Nonfinal for Plaintiff*	*Nonfinal for Defendant*	*Not Yet Decided*	*Totals*
Negligence	72	106	42	7	2	229
	31.4%	46.3%	18.3%	3.1%	0.9%	57.5%
	61.5%	56.4%	54.5%	58.3%	50.0%	
	18.1%	26.6%	10.5%	1.8%	0.5%	
Assault	4	10	2	1	—	17
and/or	23.5%	58.8%	11.8%	5.9%	—	4.3%
Battery	3.4%	5.3%	2.6%	8.3%	—	
	1.0%	2.5%	0.5%	0.3%	—	
False	7	18	5	2	—	32
Imrpisonment	21.9%	56.3%	15.6%	6.3%	—	8.0%
	6.0%	9.6%	6.5%	16.7%	—	
	1.8%	4.5%	1.3%	0.5%	—	
Malicious	1	8	5	1	—	15
Prosecution	6.7%	53.3%	33.3%	6.7%	—	3.8%
	0.8%	4.2%	6.5%	8.3%	—	
	0.3%	2.0%	1.3%	0.3%	—	
Defamation	2	5	4	—	—	11
of Character	18.2%	45.5%	36.4%	—	—	2.8%
	1.7%	2.7%	5.2%	—	—	
	0.5%	1.3%	1.0%	—	—	
Deprivation of	18	15	11	—	1	45
Constitutional	40.0%	33.3%	24.4%	—	2.2%	11.3%
Rights	15.4%	8.0%	14.3%	—	25.0%	
	4.9%	3.8%	2.8%	—	0.3%	
Contract	3	5	3	—	—	11
Law	27.3%	45.5%	27.3%	—	—	2.8%
	2.6%	2.7%	3.9%	—	—	
	0.7%	1.3%	0.7%	—	—	
Criminal	2	—	—	1	—	3
Law	66.7%	—	—	33.3%	—	0.7%
	1.7%	—	—	8.3%	—	
	0.5%	—	—	0.3%	—	
Administrative	2	1	—	—	—	3
Law	66.7%	33.3%	—	—	—	0.7%
	1.7%	0.5%	—	—	—	
	0.5%	0.3%	—	—	—	
Other*	6	20	5	—	1	32
	18.8%	62.5%	15.6%	—	3.1%	8.0%
	5.1%	10.6%	6.5%	—	25.0%	
	1.5%	5.0%	1.3%	—	0.3%	
Totals	117	188	77	12	4	398
	29.4%	47.2%	19.3%	3.0%	1.0%	100%

*Includes misrepresentation, abuse of process, malicious infliction of emotional distress, prima facie tort, failure to do one's statutory duty, invasion of privacy, involuntary servitude, false arrest, conscious pain and suffering, trespass, breach of confidence, racial discrimination, six cases in which the type of action brought was not specified, and one case where no action was yet brought.

Table 25. Changes over Time in Number of Habeas Corpus Petitions, Class Actions, and Suits for Equitable Relief

	Year of Final Decision						
Type of Suit	*Unspecified*	*1850–1949*	*1950–1959*	*1960–1969*	*1970–1977*	*Not Yet Decided*	*Totals*
Habeas	—	—	1	5	3	—	9
Corpus	—	—	11.1%	55.6%	33.3%	—	100%
Equitable	—	—	1	3	10	—	14
Relief	—	—	7.1%	21.4%	71.4%	—	100%
Class	—	—	—	—	6	—	6
Actions	—	—	—	—	100%	—	100%

Table 26. Results of Habeas Corpus Petitions, Class Actions, and Suits for Equitable Relief

	Verdict for Whom					
Type of Suit	*Plaintiff*	*Defendant*	*Nonfinal for Plaintiff*	*Nonfinal for Defendant*	*Not Yet Decided*	*Totals*
Habeas	4	1	4	—	—	9
Corpus	44.4%	11.1%	44.4%	—	—	100%
Equitable	9	2	3	—	—	14
Relief	64.3%	14.3%	21.4%	—	—	100%
Class	5	—	1	—	—	6
Actions	83.3%	—	16.7%	—	—	100%

Table 27. Changes over Time in Number of State and Federal Suits

	Year of Final Decision						
Type of of Court	*Unspecified*	*1850–1949*	*1950–1959*	*1960–1969*	*1970–1977*	*Not Yet Decided*	*Totals*
State	—	48	38	79	71	2	238
	—	20.1%	16.0%	33.2%	29.8%	0.8%	79.3%
	—	98.0%	77.6%	79.8%	72.4%	66.7%	
	—	16.0%	12.7%	26.3%	23.7%	0.6%	
Federal	2	1	11	20	27	1	62
	3.2%	1.6%	17.7%	32.3%	43.5%	1.6%	20.7%
	100%	2.0%	22.4%	20.2%	27.5%	33.3%	
	0.6%	0.3%	3.7%	6.7%	9.0%	0.3%	
Total	2	49	49	99	98	3	300
	0.7%	16.3%	16.3%	33.0%	32.7%	1.0%	100%

Table 28. Results of Suits Correlated with Whether Court Was State or Federal

	Verdict for Whom					
Type of of Court	*Plaintiff*	*Defendant*	*Nonfinal for Plaintiff*	*Nonfinal for Defendant*	*Not Yet Decided*	*Totals*
State	72 30.3% 77.4% 24.0%	111 46.6% 82.2% 37.0%	44 18.5% 74.6% 14.7%	9 3.8% 90.0% 3.0%	2 0.8% 66.7% 0.7%	238 79.3%
Federal	21 33.9% 22.6% 7.0%	24 38.7% 17.8% 8.0%	15 24.2% 25.4% 5.0%	1 1.6% 10.0% 0.3%	1 1.6% 33.3% 0.3%	62 20.7%
Totals	93 31.0%	135 45.0%	59 19.7%	10 3.3%	3 1.0%	300 100%

Table 29. Changes over Time in Trier of Fact

	Year of Final Decision						
	Unspecified	*1850–1949*	*1950–1959*	*1960–1969*	*1970–1977*	*Not Yet Decided*	*Totals*
Judge	— — — —	37 16.9% 75.5% 12.3%	34 15.5% 69.4% 11.3%	76 34.7% 76.8% 25.3%	71 32.4% 72.4% 23.7%	1 0.5% 33.3% 0.3%	219 73.0%
Judge, No Jury	— — — —	17 14.0% 34.7% 5.7%	19 15.7% 38.8% 6.3%	38 31.4% 38.4% 12.7%	46 38.0% 46.9% 15.3%	1 0.8% 33.3% 0.3%	121 40.3%
Judge, Uninvolved Jury	— — — —	9 40.9% 18.4% 3.0%	6 27.3% 12.2% 2.0%	5 22.7% 5.1% 1.7%	2 9.1% 2.0% 0.7%	— — — —	22 7.3%
Judge; Unknown whether jury present	— — — —	11 14.5% 22.4% 3.7%	9 11.8% 18.4% 3.0%	33 43.4% 33.3% 11.0%	23 30.3% 23.5% 7.7%	— — — —	76 25.3%
Jury	— — — —	10 16.1% 20.4% 3.3%	11 17.7% 22.4% 3.7%	20 32.3% 20.2% 6.7%	21 33.9% 21.4% 7.0%	— — — —	62 20.7%
Unknown whether Judge or Jury Decided Case	— — — —	2 15.4% 4.1% 0.7%	4 30.8% 8.2% 1.3%	3 23.1% 3.0% 1.0%	4 30.8% 4.1% 1.3%	— — — —	13 4.3%
Settled out of Court	2 50.0% 100% 0.7%	— — — —	— — — —	— — — —	2 50.0% 2.0% 0.7%	— — — —	4 1.3%
Not Yet Decided	— — — —	— — — —	— — — —	— — — —	— — — —	2 100% 66.7% 0.7%	2 0.7%
Totals	2 0.7%	49 16.3%	49 16.3%	99 33.0%	98 32.7%	3 1.0%	300 100%

Table 30. Results of Suits Correlated with Trier of Fact

	Verdict for Whom					
Trier of Fact	*Plaintiff*	*Defendant*	*Nonfinal for Plaintiff*	*Nonfinal for Defendant*	*Not Yet Decided*	*Totals*
Judge	57. 26.0% 61.3% 19.0%	112 51.1% 83.0% 37.3%	48 21.9% 81.4% 16.0%	1 0.5% 10.0% 0.3%	1 0.5% 33.3% 0.3%	219 73.0%
Judge, No Jury	54 44.6% 58.1% 18.0%	50 41.3% 37.0% 16.7%	16 13.2% 27.1% 5.3%	— — — —	1 0.8% 33.3% 0.3%	121 40.3%
Judge, Uninvolved Jury	— — — —	12 54.5% 8.9% 4.0%	10 45.5% 16.9% 3.3%	— — — —	— — — —	22 7.3%
Judge; Unknown whether Jury Present	3 3.9% 3.2% 1.0%	50 65.8% 37.0% 16.7%	22 28.9% 37.3% 7.3%	1 1.3% 10.0% 0.3%	— — — —	76 25.3%
Jury	27 43.5% 29.0% 9.0%	18 29.0% 13.3% 6.0%	9 14.5% 15.3% 3.0%	8 12.9% 80.0% 2.7%	— — — —	62 20.7%
Unknown whether Judge or Jury Decided Case	5 38.5% 5.4% 1.7%	5 38.5% 3.7% 1.7%	2 15.4% 3.4% 0.7%	1 7.7% 10.0% 0.3%	— — — —	13 4.3%
Settled out of Court	4 100% 4.3% 1.3%	— — — —	— — — —	— — — —	— — — —	4 1.3%
Not Yet Decided	— — — —	— — — —	— — — —	— — — —	2 100% 66.7% 0.7%	2 0.7%
Total	93 31.0%	135 45.0%	59 19.7%	10 3.3%	3 1.0%	300 100%

Table 31. Changes over Time in Level of Court

	Year of Final Decision						
Level of of Court	*Unspecified*	*1850–1949*	*1950–1959*	*1960–1969*	*1970–1977*	*Not Yet Decided*	*Totals*
Trial Court	164	18	20	44	45	—	291
	56.4%	6.2%	6.9%	15.1%	15.5%	—	46.8%
	90.6%	26.5%	27.8%	30.8%	29.0%	—	
	26.4%	2.9%	3.2%	7.1%	7.2%	—	
Appellate	7	25	32	53	57	—	174
Court	4.0%	14.4%	18.4%	30.5%	32.8%	—	28.0%
	3.9%	36.8%	44.4%	37.1%	36.8%	—	
	1.1%	4.0%	5.1%	8.5%	9.2%	—	
Supreme	—	25	17	37	35	—	114
Court	—	21.9%	14.9%	32.5%	30.7%	—	18.3%
	—	36.8%	23.6%	25.9%	22.6%	—	
	—	4.0%	2.7%	5.9%	5.6%	—	
U.S. Supreme	—	—	—	1	5	—	6
Court on Appeal	—	—	—	16.7%	83.3%	—	1.0%
from State	—	—	—	0.7%	3.2%	—	
Court	—	—	—	0.2%	0.8%	—	
Courts in	8	—	3	8	11	—	30
Remanded	26.7%	—	10.0%	26.7%	36.7%	—	4.8%
Decisions	4.4%	—	4.2%	5.6%	7.1%	—	
	1.3%	—	0.5%	1.3%	1.8%	—	
Retrial	8	—	1	3	2	—	14
	57.1%	—	7.1%	21.4%	14.3%	—	2.2%
	4.4%	—	1.4%	2.0%	1.3%	—	
	1.3%	—	0.2%	0.5%	0.3%	—	
Reappeal to	—	—	1	4	4	—	9
Appellate	—	—	11.1%	44.4%	44.4%	—	1.4%
Court	—	—	1.4%	2.8%	2.6%	—	
	—	—	0.2%	0.6%	0.6%	—	
Reappeal to	—	—	1	1	3	—	5
Supreme	—	—	20.0%	20.0%	60.0%	—	0.8%
Court	—	—	1.4%	0.7%	1.9%	—	
	—	—	0.2%	0.2%	0.5%	—	
Appellate	—	—	—	—	2	—	2
Court on	—	—	—	—	100%	—	0.3%
Remand	—	—	—	—	1.3%	—	
	—	—	—	—	0.3%	—	
Settled out	2	—	—	—	2	—	4
of Court	50.0%	—	—	—	50.0%	—	0.6%
	1.1%	—	—	—	1.3%	—	
	0.3%	—	—	—	0.3%	—	
Not Yet	—	—	—	—	—	3	3
Decided	—	—	—	—	—	100%	0.5%
	—	—	—	—	—	100%	
	—	—	—	—	—	0.5%	
Totals	181	68	72	143	155	3	622
	29.1%	10.9%	11.6%	23.0%	24.9%	0.5%	100%

Table 32. Results of Suits at Various Levels of Court

	Verdict for Whom					
Level of Court	*Plaintiff*	*Defendant*	*Nonfinal for Plaintiff*	*Nonfinal for Defendant*	*Not Yet Decided*	*Totals*
All Trial	105	158	25	3	—	291
Courts	36.1%	54.3%	8.6%	1.0%	—	46.8%
	53.0%	50.0%	29.4%	15.0%	—	
	16.9%	25.4%	4.0%	0.5%	—	
Final	26	20	10	—	—	56
Decisions	46.4%	35.7%	17.9%	—	—	9.0%
	13.1%	6.3%	11.8%	—	—	
	4.2%	3.2%	1.6%	—	—	
Appealed	79	138	15	3	—	235
Decisions	33.6%	58.7%	6.4%	1.3%	—	37.8%
	39.9%	43.7%	17.6%	15.0%	—	
	12.7%	22.2%	2.4%	0.4%	—	
Appellate	45	83	37	9	—	174
Court	25.9%	47.7%	21.3%	5.2%	—	28.0%
	22.7%	26.3%	43.5%	45.0%	—	
	7.2%	13.3%	5.9%	1.4%	—	
Supreme	29	56	21	8	—	114
Court	25.4%	49.1%	18.4%	7.0%	—	18.3%
	14.6%	17.7%	24.7%	40.0%	—	
	4.7%	9.0%	3.4%	1.3%	—	
U.S. Supreme	1	4	1	—	—	6
Court on	16.7%	66.7%	16.7%	—	—	1.0%
Appeal from	0.5%	1.3%	1.2%	—	—	
State Courts	0.2%	0.6%	0.2%	—	—	
Courts in	14	15	1	—	—	30
Remanded	46.7%	50.0%	3.3%	—	—	4.8%
Decisions	7.1%	4.7%	1.2%	—	—	
	2.2%	2.4%	0.2%	—	—	
Retrial	5	9	—	—	—	14
	35.7%	64.3%	—	—	—	2.2%
	2.5%	2.8%	—	—	—	
	0.8%	1.4%	—	—	—	
Reappeal to	5	4	—	—	—	9
Appellate	55.5%	44.4%	—	—	—	1.4%
Court	2.5%	1.3%	—	—	—	
	0.8%	0.6%	—	—	—	
Reappeal to	2	2	1	—	—	5
Supreme	40.0%	40.0%	20.0%	—	—	0.8%
Court	1.0%	0.6%	1.2%	—	—	
	0.3%	0.3%	0.2%	—	—	
Appellate	2	—	—	—	—	2
Court on	100%	—	—	—	—	0.3%
Remand	1.0%	—	—	—	—	
	0.3%	—	—	—	—	
Settled out	4	—	—	—	—	4
of Court	100%	—	—	—	—	0.6%
	2.0%	—	—	—	—	
	0.3%	—	—	—	—	
Not Yet	—	—	—	—	3	5
Decided	—	—	—	—	100%	0.5%
	—	—	—	—	100%	
	—	—	—	—	0.5%	
Totals	198	316	85	20	3	622
	31.8%	50.8%	13.7%	3.2%	0.5%	100%

Table 33. Results of Suits Correlated with Level of Court in Final Decision

	Verdict for Whom					
Level of of Court	*Plaintiff*	*Defendant*	*Nonfinal for Plaintiff*	*Nonfinal for Defendant*	*Not Yet Decided*	*Totals*
Not Yet Decided	— — — —	— — — —	— — — —	— — — —	3 100% 100% 1.0%	3 1.0%
Trial Court	26 46.4% 28.0% 8.7%	20 35.7% 14.8% 6.7%	10 17.9% 16.9% 3.3%	— — — —	— — — —	56 18.7%
Appellate Court	26 23.6% 28.0% 8.7%	54 49.1% 40.0% 18.0%	26 23.6% 44.1% 8.7%	4 3.6% 40.0% 1.3%	— — — —	110 36.7%
Supreme Court	28 26.2% 30.1% 9.3%	52 48.6% 38.5% 17.3%	21 19.6% 35.6% 7.0%	6 5.6% 60.0% 2.0%	— — —	107 35.7%
U.S. Supreme Court on Appeal from State Court	1 16.7% 1.1% 0.3%	4 66.7% 3.0% 1.3%	1 16.7% 1.7% 0.3%	— — — —	— — — —	6 2.0%
Courts in Remanded Decisions	8 57.1% 8.6% 2.7%	5 35.7% 5.4% 1.7%	1 7.1% 1.7% 0.3%	— — — —	— — — —	14 4.7%
Retrial	3 100% 3.2% 1.0%	— — — —	— — — —	— — — —	— — — —	3 1.0%
Reappeal to Appellate Court	2 33.3% 2.2% 0.7%	4 66.7% 3.0% 1.3%	— — — —	— — — —	— — — —	6 2.0%
Reappeal to Supreme Court	2 50.0% 2.2% 0.7%	1 25.0% 0.7% 0.3%	1 25.0% 1.7% 0.3%	— — — —	— — — —	4 1.3%
Appellate Court on Remand	1 100% 1.1% 0.3%	— — — —	— — — —	— — — —	— — — —	1 0.3%
Settled out of Court	4 100% 4.3% 1.3%	— — — —	— — — —	— — — —	— — — —	4 1.3%
Totals	93 31.0%	135 45.0%	59 19.7%	10 3.3%	3 1.0%	300 100%

Table 34. Results of Suits Correlated with Level of Court in Final Decisions, But Excluding All Unappealed Decisions.

	Verdict for Whom					
Level of Court	*Plaintiff*	*Defendant*	*Nonfinal for Plaintiff*	*Nonfinal for Defendant*	*Not Yet Decided*	*Totals*
Trial	1	—	1	—	—	2
Court	50.0%	—	50.0%	—	—	0.8%
	1.6%	—	2.0%	—	—	
	0.4%	—	0.4%	—	—	
Appellate	26	54	26	4	—	110
Court	23.6%	49.1%	23.6%	3.6%	—	46.4%
	41.3%	47.0%	53.1%	40.0%	—	
	11.0%	22.8%	11.0%	1.7%	—	
Supreme	27	52	20	6	-	105
Court	25.7%	49.5%	19.0%	5.7%	—	44.3%
	42.9%	45.2%	40.8%	60.0%	—	
	11.4%	21.9%	8.4%	2.5%		
U.S. Supreme	1	4	1	—	—	6
Court on	16.7%	66.7%	16.7%	—	—	2.5%
Appeal from	1.6%	3.5%	2.0%	—	—	
State Court	0.4%	1.7%	0.4%	—	—	
Courts in	8	5	1	—	—	14
Remanded	57.1%	35.7%	7.1%	—	—	5.9%
Decisions	12.7%	4.3%	2.0%	—	—	
	3.4%	2.1%	0.4%	—	—	
Retrial	3	—	—	—	—	3
	100%	—	—	—	—	1.3%
	4.8%	—	—	—	—	
	1.3%	—	—	—	—	
Reappeal to	2	4	—	—	—	6
Appellate	33.3%	66.7%	—	—	—	2.5%
Court	3.2%	3.5%	—	—	—	
	0.8%	1.7%	—	—	—	
Reappeal to	2	1	1	—	—	4
Supreme	50.0%	25.0%	25.0%	—	—	1.7%
Court	3.2%	0.9%	2.0%	—	—	
	0.8%	0.4%	0.4%	—	—	
Appellate	1	—	—	—	—	
Court on	100%	—	—	—	—	
Remand	1.6%	—	—	—	—	
	0.4%	—	—	—	—	
Totals	63	115	49	10	0	237
	26.6%	48.5%	20.7%	4.2%	—	100%

Table 35. Reasons for Failure of Suits

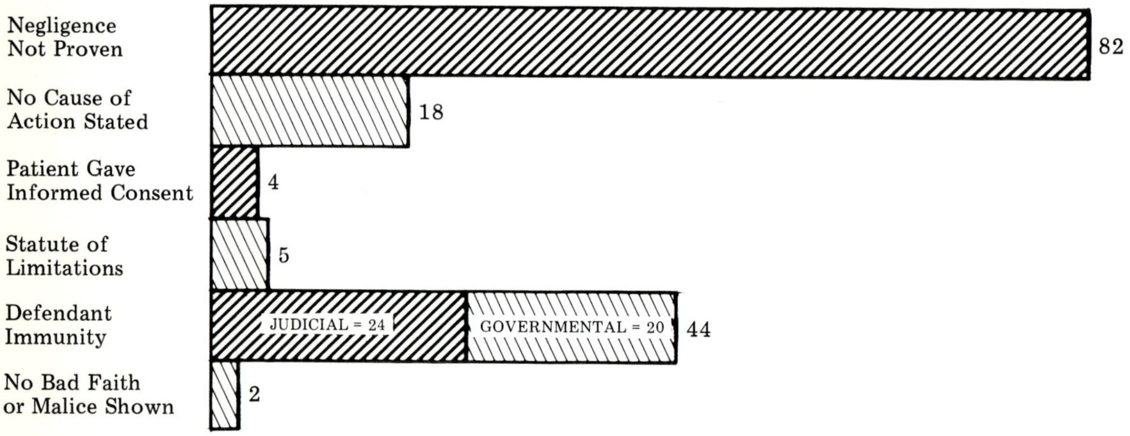

Table 36. Changes over Time in Reasons for Failure of Suits

	Year of Final Decision						
Reason Suit Failed	*Unspecified*	*1850–1949*	*1950–1959*	*1960–1969*	*1970–1977*	*Not Yet Decided*	*Totals*
Negligence	—	15	12	29	26	—	82
Not	—	18.3%	14.6%	35.4%	31.7%	—	52.9%
Proven	—	57.7%	57.1%	49.2%	53.1%	—	
	—	9.7%	7.7%	18.7%	16.8%	—	
No Cause	—	1	2	10	5	—	18
of Action	—	5.6%	11.1%	55.6%	27.8%	—	11.6%
Stated	—	3.8%	9.5%	16.9%	10.2%	—	
	—	0.6%	1.3%	6.5%	3.2%	—	
Patient Gave	—	—	—	3	1	—	4
Informed	—	—	—	75.0%	25.0%	—	2.6%
Consent	—	—	—	5.1%	2.0%	—	
	—	—	—	1.9%	0.6%	—	
Statute of	—	2	—	1	2	—	5
Limitations	—	40.0%	—	20.0%	40.0%	—	3.2%
Barred Suit	—	7.7%	—	1.7%	4.1%	—	
	—	1.3%	—	0.6%	1.3%	—	
Defendant	—	6	7	16	15	—	44
Immunity	—	13.6%	15.9%	36.4%	34.1%	—	28.4%
	—	23.1%	33.3%	27.1%	30.6%	—	
	—	3.9%	4.5%	10.3%	9.7%	—	
No Bad	—	2	—	—	—	—	2
Faith or	—	100%	—	—	—	—	1.3%
Malice	—	7.7%	—	—	—	—	
Shown	—	1.3%	—	—	—	—	
Totals	0	26	21	59	49	0	155
	—	16.8%	13.5%	38.1%	31.6%	—	100%

Table 37. Final Decisions Granting Monetary Awards, by Amount and Including Mean, Median, and Modal Recoveries

Case	*Award*
Whitree v. State	$300,000
Adams v. State	275,000
Weinshenk v. Kaiser	250,000
Merchants Bank v. US	200,000
Vassolo v. Cty. Hosp.	200,000
Abraham v. Zaslow	170,000
Christy v. Saliterman	103,530
Hicks v. U.S.	100,000
A.A. v. State	90,000
Finkel v. State	70,997
Brown v. Moore	60,000
Borker v. N.T.L.	50,000
Crocco v. Harris	50,000
Gioia v. State	41,124
Lawrence v. State	40,646
Stowers v. Ard. Hosp.	40,000
Von Eye v. Hammes	39,380
Pettis v. St. Dept. Hos	35,000
Doty v. State	30,000
Fatuck v. Hill. Hosp.	30,000
Oliver v. State	30,000
Anclote M.F. v. Wilk.	28,600
Callahan v. State	25,220
Roy v. Hartogs	25,000
Semler v. Psy. Ins. Wa.	25,000
Scolavino v. State	21,137
Surprenant v. State	21,000
Kleber v. Stevens	20,000
O'Connor v. Donaldson	20,000
Blauer v. State	18,000
Whitesell v. Green	18,000
Bellandi v. Park San.	15,000
Hendler v. State	15,000
Foster v. State	14,000
Bennett v. State	10,000
Cox v. State	9,647
Trapani v. State	9,145
Stallman v. Robinson	9,000
Collins v. State	8,492
Thall v. State	7,790
Grant v. N.T.L.	7,500
Lexington Hos v. Whit	6,964
Gould v. State	6,320
Curley v. State	6,000
O'Neil v. State	5,945
Arl. Hts. v. Deaderick	5,000
Lando v. State	5,000
Zipkin v. Freeman	5,000
Meynier v. De Paul	4,299
Keating v. Keller	3,500
Hough v. Ogden	3,000
Annis v. Donahue	2,500
McCandless v. State	2,000
Bacon v. Bacon	1,500
Weihs v. State	1,500
O'Rourke v. O'Rourke	1,000
U. Louisvill v. Ham.	1,000
Mean $45,504	
Median $20,000	
Mode $30,000 & $5,000	

Table 38. Size of Recovery Correlated with Study Variables

		*Percentage of Suits at Varying Levels of Recovery**								
Category	*Variable*	*$50,000 and Up (N = 13) 1*	*$25,000–$50,000 (N = 12) 2*	*$25,000 and Up (N = 25) 3 = 1 + 2*	*$1–$25,000 (N = 32) 4*	*$1 and Up (N = 57) 5 = 3 + 4*	*Cases for Plaintiff but No Recovery (N = 36) 6*	*Cases for Plaintiff as % of Total Verdicts for Plaintiff (N = 93) and as % of All Cases in Which Variable Occurs 7 = 5 + 6*	*All Cases in Which Variable Occurs (N = 300)*	*Mean Amount of Recovery*
Reported Decisions	Reported Decisions	61.5% (8)	100% (12)	80.0% (20)	87.5% (28)	84.2% (48)	100% (36)	90.3% 28.9% (84)	97.0% (291)	$ 38,078
	Unreported Decisions or Settled out of Court	38.5% (5)	— (0)	20.0% (5)	12.5% (4)	15.8% (9)	— (0)	9.7% 100% (9)	3.0% (9)	$ 85,111
Region	New York	38.5% (5)	58.3% (7)	48.0% (12)	53.1% (17)	50.9% (29)	36.1% (13)	45.2% 34.7% (42)	40.3% (121)	$ 38,413
	California	23.1% (3)	— (0)	12.0% (3)	3.1% (1)	7.0% (4)	5.6% (2)	6.5% 23.1% (6)	8.7% (26)	$121,250
	Other States	38.5% (5)	41.7% (5)	40.0% (10)	43.8% (14)	42.1% (24)	58.3% (21)	31.6% 29.4% (45)	51.0% (153)	$ 41,449
Setting	All Hospitals	76.9% (10)	91.7% (11)	84.0% (21)	62.5% (20)	71.9% (41)	63.9% (23)	68.8% 32.7% (64)	65.3% (196)	$ 53,742
	Public Hospitals	53.8% (7)	50.0% (6)	52.0% (13)	46.9% (15)	49.1% (28)	58.3% (21)	52.7% 36.0% (49)	45.3% (136)	$ 56,784
	Mental Hospitals	69.2% (9)	75.0% (9)	72.0% (18)	59.4% (19)	64.9% (37)	52.8% (19)	60.2% 37.3% (56)	50.0% (150)	$ 50,893

	Encounter Groups	7.7% (1)	— (0)	4.0% (1)	6.3% (2)	5.3% (3)	— (0)	3.2% 100% (3)	1.0% (3)	$ 20,000
	Private Practice	15.4% (2)	8.3% (1)	12.0% (3)	6.3% (2)	8.8% (5)	11.1% (4)	9.7% 42.9% (9)	7.0% (21)	$ 53,600
	Judicial Proceedings	— (0)	— (0)	— (0)	15.6% (5)	8.8% (5)	19.4% (7)	12.9% 18.2% (12)	22.0% (66)	$ 5,800
	Other Settings	— (0)	— (0)	— (0)	9.4% (3)	5.3% (3)	8.3% (3)	6.5% 33.3% (6)	6.0% (18)	$ 11,100
Plaintiff	Patients (or Reps.)	53.8% (7)	75.0% (9)	64.0% (16)	78.1% (25)	71.9% (41)	83.3% (30)	76.3% 29.2% (71)	81.0% (243)	$ 32,911
	Persons Injured by Harm to Patient	23.1% (3)	16.7% (2)	20.0% (5)	18.8% (6)	19.3% (11)	5.6% (2)	14.0% 36.1% (13)	12.0% (36)	$ 67,581
	Persons Injured by Patient	30.8% (4)	8.3% (1)	20.0% (5)	9.4% (3)	14.0% (5)	8.3% (3)	11.9% 34.4% (11)	10.7% (32)	$ 76,722
	States or Licensing Boards	— (0)	— (0)	— (0)	— (0)	— (0)	8.3% (3)	3.2% 60.0% (3)	1.7% (5)	—
Defendant Initially Sued	Practitioners	38.5% (5)	41.7% (5)	40.0% (10)	34.4% (11)	36.8% (21)	16.7% (6)	29.0% 21.4% (27)	42.0% (126)	$ 40,081
	Hospitals	23.1% (3)	58.3% (7)	40.0% (10)	18.8% (6)	28.1% (16)	25.0% (9)	26.9% 30.9% (25)	27.0% (81)	$ 50,556
	State Government	30.8% (4)	41.7% (5)	36.0% (9)	50.0% (16)	43.9% (25)	41.7% (15)	43.0% 40.8% (40)	32.7% (98)	$ 42,333
	Federal Government	15.4% (2)	— (0)	8.0% (2)	— (0)	3.5% (2)	11.1% (4)	6.5% 27.3% (6)	7.3% (22)	$150,000
	Educational Institutions	— (0)	— (0)	— (0)	6.3% (2)	3.5% (2)	— (0)	2.2% 25.0% (2)	2.7% (8)	$ 1,750

Table 38. continued

Category	*Variable*	*Percentage of Suits at Varying Levels of Recovery** *\$50,000 and Up (N = 13) 1*	*\$25,000–\$50,000 (N = 12) 2*	*\$25,000 and Up (N = 25) 3 = 1 + 2*	*\$1–\$25,000 (N = 32) 4*	*\$1 and Up (N = 57) 5 = 3 + 4*	*Cases for Plaintiff but No Recovery (N = 36) 6*	*Cases for Plaintiff as % of Total Verdicts for Plaintiff (N = 93) and as % of All Cases in Which Variable Occurs 7 = 5 + 6*	*All Cases in Which Variable Occurs (N = 300)*	*Mean Amount of Recovery*
	Other Defendants	23.1% (3)	16.7% (2)	20.0% (5)	15.6% (5)	17.5% (10)	69.4% (25)	37.6% 50.0% (35)	20.0% *(60)	\$ 45,280
Negligent Treatment	Sexual Involvement	7.7% (1)	16.7% (2)	12.0% (3)	6.3% (2)	8.8% (5)	8.3% (3)	8.6% 66.7% (8)	4.0% (12)	\$ 25,320
	Physical Assault	15.4% (2)	8.3% (1)	12.0% (3)	3.1% (1)	7.0% (4)	— (0)	4.3% 80.0% (4)	1.7% (5)	\$131,250
	Negligent Administration of Drugs	15.4% (2)	— (0)	8.0% (2)	— (0)	3.5% (2)	5.6% (2)	4.3% 30.8% (4)	4.3% (13)	\$170,000
	No Treatment or Inadequate Treatment	7.7% (1)	— (0)	4.0% (1)	3.1% (1)	3.5% (2)	38.9% (14)	17.2% 48.5% (16)	11.0% (33)	\$160,000
	Other Treatment	23.1% (3)	25.0% (3)	24.0% (6)	18.8% (6)	21.0% (12)	2.8% (1)	14.0% 24.1% (13)	18.0% (54)	\$ 23,933
	Mental Illness, Instead of Sanity	7.7% (1)	8.3% (1)	8.0% (2)	18.8% (6)	14.0% (8)	8.3% (3)	11.9% 15.3% (11)	24.0% (72)	\$ 48,625
	Sanity, Instead of Mental Illness	15.4% (2)	— (0)	8.0% (2)	— (0)	3.5% (2)	— (0)	2.2% 15.4% (2)	4.3% (13)	\$151,765

What Was Diagnosed	Lack of Dangerousness	23.1% (3)	8.3% (1)	16.0% (4)	— (0)	7.0% (4)	5.6% (2)	6.5% 24.0% (6)	8.3% (25)	$131,250
	Lack of Suicidal Tendencies	— (0)	— (0)	— (0)	— (0)	— (0)	— (0)	— — (0)	3.7% (11)	—
	Mental or Physical Illness, Instead of Opposite	15.4% (2)	— (0)	8.0% (2)	3.1% (1)	5.3% (3)	— (0)	3.2% 33.3% (3)	3.0% (9)	$105,315
	Other Diagnosis	7.7% (1)	— (0)	4.0% (1)	6.2% (2)	5.3% (3)	30.6% (11)	15.1% 30.4% (14)	15.3% (46)	$ 37,343
Result of Diagnosis	Improper Commitment	— (0)	8.3% (1)	4.0% (1)	18.8% (6)	12.3% (7)	11.1% (4)	11.9% 15.7% (11)	23.3% (70)	$ 12,714
	Improper Care	23.1% (3)	— (0)	12.0% (3)	3.1% (1)	7.0% (4)	13.9% (5)	9.7% 34.6% (9)	8.7% (26)	$ 92,133
	Improper Release	30.8% (4)	8.3% (1)	20.0% (5)	— (0)	8.8% (5)	5.6% (2)	7.5% 26.9% (7)	8.7% (26)	$125,706
	Improper Treatment	30.8% (4)	— (0)	16.0% (4)	3.1% (1)	8.8% (5)	2.8% (1)	6.5% 33.3% (6)	6.0% (18)	$143,895
	Other Result	15.4% (2)	— (0)	8.0% (2)	3.1% (1)	5.3% (3)	11.1% (4)	7.5% 22.6% (7)	10.3% (31)	$141,177
Care	Failure to Provide Proper Care	23.1% (3)	25.0% (3)	24.0% (6)	12.5% (4)	17.5% (10)	11.1% (4)	15.1% 46.7% (14)	10.0% (30)	$ 73,700
	Inadequate Supervision	38.5% (5)	50.0% (6)	44.0% (11)	53.1% (17)	49.1% (28)	33.3% (12)	43.0% 37.7% (40)	35.3% (106)	$ 37,524
	Premature Release	— (0)	— (0)	— (0)	— (0)	— (0)	2.8% (1)	1.1% 11.1% (1)	3.0% (9)	—
	Other Type of Care	— (0)	— (0)	— (0)	— (0)	— (0)	5.6% (2)	2.2% 11.8% (2)	5.7% *(17)	—

Table 38. continued

Category	Variable	*Percentage of Suits at Varying Levels of Recovery**								
		$50,000 and Up (N = 13) 1	*$25,000–$50,000 (N = 12)* 2	*$25,000 and Up (N = 25)* 3 = 1 + 2	*$1–$25,000 (N = 32)* 4	*$1 and Up (N = 57)* 5 = 3 + 4	*Cases for Plaintiff but No Recovery (N = 36)* 6	*Cases for Plaintiff as % of Total Verdicts for Plaintiff (N = 93) and as % of All Cases in Which Variable Occurs* 7 = 5 + 6	*All Cases in Which Variable Occurs (N = 300)*	*Mean Amount of Recovery*
Harm Caused	Suicide	7.7% (1)	33.3% (4)	20.0% (5)	9.4% (3)	14.0% (8)	8.3% (3)	11.9% 28.9% (11)	12.7% (38)	$ 27,126
	Accidental Death	38.5% (5)	8.3% (1)	24.0% (6)	18.8% (6)	21.1% (12)	11.1% (4)	17.2% 40.0% (16)	13.3% (40)	$ 63,429
	Non-self-Inflicted Injuries	30.8% (4)	41.7% (5)	36.0% (9)	40.6% (13)	38.6% (22)	16.7% (6)	30.1% 33.3% (28)	28.0% (84)	$ 47,332
	Self-inflicted Injuries	7.7% (1)	8.3% (1)	8.0% (2)	3.1% (1)	5.3% (3)	11.1% (4)	7.5% 46.7% (7)	5.0% (15)	$111,839
	Sexual or Marital Harm	15.4% (2)	16.7% (2)	16.0% (4)	9.4% (3)	12.3% (7)	11.1% (4)	11.9% 61.1% (11)	6.0% (18)	$ 31,229
	Emotional Distress	30.8% (4)	25.0% (3)	28.0% (7)	25.0% (8)	26.3% (15)	2.8% (1)	17.2% 55.2% (16)	9.7% (29)	$ 54,916
	Economic Loss	15.4% (2)	16.7% (2)	16.0% (4)	6.2% (2)	10.5% (6)	— (0)	6.5% 26.1% (6)	7.7% (23)	$ 97,433
	Other Harm	38.5% (5)	8.3% (1)	24.0% (6)	37.5% (12)	31.6% (18)	**	66.7% 39.5% (62)	52.3% (157)	$ 57,155

Type of Legal Action	Negligence	92.3% (12)	100% (12)	96.0% (24)	87.5% (28)	91.2% (52)	55.6% (20)	77.4% 31.4% (72)	76.3% (229)	$ 48,428
	Other Legal Action	15.4% (2)	16.7% (2)	16.0% (4)	31.3% (10)	24.6% (14)	86.1% (31)	48.4% 26.6% (45)	56.3% (169)	$ 23,836
Type of Court	State	69.2% (9)	83.3% (10)	76.0% (19)	93.8% (30)	86.0% (49)	63.9% (23)	77.4% 30.3% (72)	79.3% (238)	$ 42,691
	Federal	30.8% (4)	16.7% (2)	24.0% (6)	6.3% (2)	14.0% (8)	36.1% (13)	22.6% 33.9% (21)	20.7% (62)	$ 62,735
Trier of Fact	Judge	38.5% (5)	50.0% (6)	44.0% (11)	50.0% (16)	47.4% (27)	83.3% (30)	61.3% 26.0% (57)	73.0% (219)	$ 41,258
	Jury	38.5% (5)	50.0% (6)	44.0% (11)	34.4% (11)	38.6% (22)	13.9% (5)	29.0% 43.5% (27)	20.7% (62)	$ 50,499
	Unknown	7.7% (1)	— (0)	4.0% (1)	9.4% (3)	7.0% (4)	2.8% (1)	5.4% 38.5% (5)	4.3% (13)	$ 64,700
	Settled out of Court or Not Yet Decided	15.4% (2)	— (0)	8.0% (2)	6.3% (2)	7.0% (4)	— (0)	4.3% 66.7% (4)	2.0% (6)	$ 27,500
Time	Mean Years from Negligent Act to Final Decision	5.8	5.2	5.5	5.3	5.4	—	—	—	4.8
	Mean Number of Court Decisions	1.3	2.4	1.9	2.1	2.0	—	—	—	2.1

*The percentages given represent the number of cases in a given cell divided by the number of cases at that level of recovery, except for the last two columns. In the second to last column, two percentages are given: one is based on the total verdicts for plaintiff, the other is based on the total number of times the variable occurs. The last column is based on the total number of cases reviewed (300).

**The SPSS program did not provide ready access to this data.

Table 39. Study Variables, by Rank Order of Mean Amount of Recovery

Variable	
1. *Negligent Treatment:* Negligent Administration of Drugs	$170,000
2. *Negligent Treatment:* No Treatment or Inadequate Treatment	$160,000
3. *What Was Diagnosed:* Sanity, Instead of Mental Illness	$151,765
4. *Defendant Initially Sued:* Federal Government	$150,000
5. *Result of Diagnosis:* Improper Treatment	$143,895
6. *Result of Diagnosis:* Other Result	$141,177
7. *Negligent Treatment:* Physical Assault	$131,250
8. *What Was Diagnosed:* Lack of Dangerousness	$131,250
9. *Result of Diagnosis:* Improper Release	$125,706
10. *Region:* California	$121,250
11. *Harm Caused:* Self-Inflicted Injury	$111,839
12. *What Was Diagnosed:* Mental or Physical Illness, Instead of Opposite	$105,315
13. *Harm Caused:* Economic Loss	$ 97,433
14. *Result of Diagnosis:* Improper Care	$ 92,133
15. *Reported Decisions:* Unreported Decisions or Settled Out of Court	$ 85,111
16. *Plaintiff:* Persons Injured by Patient	$ 76,722
17. *Care:* Failure to Provide Proper Care	$ 73,700
18. *Plaintiff:* Persons Injured by Harm to Patient	$ 67,581
19. *Trier of Fact:* Unknown	$ 64,700
20. *Harm Caused:* Accidental Death	$ 63,439
21. *Type of Court:* Federal	$ 62,735
22. *Harm Caused:* Other Harm	$ 57,155
23. *Setting:* Public Hospitals	$ 56,784
24. *Harm Caused:* Emotional Distress	$ 54,916
25. *Setting:* All Hospitals	$ 53,742
26. *Setting:* Private Practice	$ 53,600
27. *Setting:* Mental Hospitals	$ 50,893
28. *Defendant:* Initially Sued: Hospitals	$ 50,556
29. *Trier of Fact:* Jury	$ 50,499
30. *What Was Diagnosed:* Mental Illness, Instead of Sanity	$ 48,625
31. *Type of Legal Action:* Negligence	$ 48,428
32. *Harm Caused:* Non-Self Inflicted Injuries	$ 47,332
33. *Defendant Initially Sued:* Other Defendants	$ 45,280
34. *Type of Court:* State	$ 42,691
35. *Defendant Initially Sued:* State Government	$ 42,333
36. *Region:* Other States	$ 41,449
37. *Trier of Fact:* Judge	$ 41,258
38. *Defendant Initially Sued:* Practioners	$ 40,081
39. *Region:* New York	$ 38,413
40. *Reported Decisions:* Reported Decisions	$ 38,078
41. *Care:* Inadequate Supervision	$ 37,524
42. *What Was Diagnosed:* Other Diagnosis	$ 37,343
43. *Plaintiff:* Patients (or Repres.)	$ 32,911
44. *Harm Caused:* Sexual or Marital Harm	$ 31,299
45. *Trier of Fact:* Settled Out of Court or Not Yet Decided	$ 27,500
46. *Harm Caused:* Suicide	$ 27,126
47. *Negligent Treatment:* Sexual Involvement	$ 25,320
48. *Negligent Treatment:* Other Treatment	$ 23,933
49. *Type of Legal Action:* Other Legal Action	$ 23,836
50. *Setting:* Encounter Groups	$ 20,000
51. *Result of Diagnosis:* Improper Commitment	$ 12,714
52. *Setting:* Other Settings	$ 11,100
53. *Setting:* Judicial Proceedings	$ 5,800
54. *Defendant Initially Sued:* Educational Institutions	$ 1,750
55. *Plaintiff:* States or Licensing Boards	—
56. *What Was Diagnosed:* Lack of Suicidal Tendencies	—
57. *Care:* Premature Release	—
58. *Care:* Other Type of Care	—
Overall:	
1. Negligent Diagnosis (N = 20) — $82,275	
2. Negligent Treatment (N = 25) — $64,352	
3. Negligent Care (N = 38) — $47,044	

Table 40. Changes over Time in Size of Recoveries

	Year of Final Decision					
Size of Recovery	*Unspecified*	*1850–1949*	*1950–1959*	*1960–1969*	*1970–1977*	*Totals*
Less than $50,000	1	10	8	12	13	44
	2.3%	22.7%	18.2%	27.3%	29.5%	77.2%
	50.0%	100%	88.9%	66.7%	72.2%	
	1.8%	17.5%	14.0%	21.1%	22.8%	
Greater than or Equal to $50,000	1	0	1	6	5	13
	7.7%	—	7.7%	46.2%	38.5%	22.8%
	50.0%	—	11.1%	33.3%	27.8%	
	1.8%	—	1.8%	10.5%	8.8%	
Totals	2	10	9	18	18	57
	3.5%	17.5%	15.8%	31.6%	31.6%	100%

Table 41. Number of Years from Time Negligent Act Occurred to Final Decision.

No. Years	*Absolute Freq.*	*Relative Freq. (%)*	*Cum. Freq. (%)*
0	5	2.3%	2.3%
1	10	4.6	6.9
2	34	15.7	22.6
3	30	13.8	36.4
4	27	12.4	48.8
5	44	20.3	69.1
6	22	10.1	79.3
7	13	6.0	85.3
8	7	3.2	88.5
9	10	4.6	93.1
10	5	2.3	95.4
11	3	1.4	96.8
12	2	0.9	97.7
13	3	1.4	99.1
16	1	0.5	99.5
21	1	0.5	100.0
Totals	217	100.0%	—

Statistics

Mean	4.829	Std. Error	0.203	Median	4.557
Mode	5.000	Std. Deviation	2.988	Variance	8.929
Kurtosis	4.083	Skewness	1.460	Range	21.000
Minimum	0.0	Maximum	21.000		

Table 42. Number of Years from Time Negligent Act Occurred to Time of Trial.

Years	*Absolute Freq.*	*Relative Freq. (%)*	*Cum Freq. (%)*
0	8	8.2%	8.2%
1	7	7.2	15.5
2	22	22.7	38.1
3	21	21.6	59.8
4	13	13.4	73.2
5	11	11.3	84.5
6	6	6.2	90.7
7	3	3.1	93.8
9	1	1.0	94.8
10	1	1.0	95.9
11	1	1.0	96.9
12	1	1.0	97.9
13	1	1.0	99.0
19	1	1.0	100.0
Totals	97	100.0%	—

Statistics

Mean	3.629	Std. Error	0.298	Median	3.048
Mode	2.000	Std. Deviation	2.938	Variance	8.632
Kurtosis	7.678	Skewness	2.247	Range	19.000
Minimum	0.0	Maximum	19.000		

Table 43. Number of Years from Time of Trial to Final Decision

Years	*Absolute Freq.*	*Relative Freq. (%)*	*Cum. Freq. (%)*
0	10	13.7%	13.7%
1	32	43.8	57.5
2	15	20.5	78.1
3	7	9.6	87.7
4	5	6.8	94.5
5	1	1.4	95.9
7	2	2.7	98.6
9	1	1.4	100.0
Totals	73	100.0%	—

Statistics

Mean	1.795	Std. Error	0.197	Median	1.328
Mode	1.000	Std. Deviation	1.683	Variance	2.832
Kurtosis	4.825	Skewness	1.985	Range	9.000
Minimum	0.0	Maximum	9.000		

Table 44. Year of Negligent Act

	1940–1949	*1950–1959*	*1960–1969*	*1970–1977*	*Not Specified*
1850–1899	Beckham v. Cline	A.A. v. State	Adams v. State	Booe v. Hall	Abraham v. Zaslow
Ayers v. Russell	Betts v. State	Anonymous v. State	Aiken v. Clary	Burnham v. D. P. Health	Adams v. Ricks
Total 1	Brigante v. State	Benjamin v. Havens	Anclote M. F. v. Wilk.	Castillo v. U.S.	Bacon v. Bacon
1900–1909	Brown v. Moore	Berry v. Moench	Annis v. Donahue	Collins v. Bensinger	Bangs v. State
Warner v. Packer	Callahan v. State	Blauer v. State	Avey v. St. Fran. Hosp.	Davis v. Watkins	Bartlett v. Weimer
Total 1	Cox v. State	Bogust v. Iverson	Baker v. Orlowsky	Doe v. Roe	Bencomo v. Morgan
1910–1919	Daley v. State	Boykin v. State	Baker v. U.S.	Fischer v. City Elm.	Borker v. N.T.L.
Corcoran v. Jerrel	Dowly v. State	Castiglione v. State	Beaumong v. Morgan	Forde v. Cty. L.A.	Bradshaw v. State
Hough v. Ogden	Farber v. Olkon	Centeno v. City of NY	Bellows v. State	Freach v. Commonweal	Burkes v. Callion
Springer v. Steiner	Foster v. State	Collins v. Hand	Bennett v. State	Harris Hosp. v. Pope	Byrne v. Kysar
Total 3	Groce v. Myers	Collins v. State	Blitz v. Boog	Homere v. State	Campbell v. Glenwood
1920–1929	In Re Pierre Estate	Commonwealth v. Page	Boland v. State	In Re Anonymous	Cawthon v. Coffer
Arl. Hts. v. Deaderick	In Re Warrington	Daniels v. Finney	Burks v. Ross	Johnson v. U.S.	Clark v. Geraci
Bellandi v. Park San.	Kendrick v. U.S.	Dimit. v. Chi. W.M. Hosp.	Cameron v. State	Lando v. State	Col. St. Bed. v. Weiler
Curley v. State	Kubas v. State	Doty v. State	Carlino v. State	McNeil v. Director	Cooper v. Bd. Med. Ex.
Total 3	Lexington Hosp. v. Whit.	Dugan v. U.S.	Christy v. Saliterman	Morra v. St. Bd. Psych.	Dabkowski v. Davis
1930–1939	McCabe v. State	Fair v. U.S.	Chudy v. Chudy	Nastasi v. State	Demartini v. Alex. San.
Brandt v. Brandt	Oliver v. State	Finkel v. State	Constant v. Howe	O'Connor v. Donaldson	Di Fiore v. State
Excel. Ins. Co. v. State	O'Rourke v. O'Rourke	Foxluger v. State	Cty. of L.A. v. Sup. Ct.	Pettis v. St. Dept. Hos	Dillman v. Hellman
Fowler v. Nrwys. San.	Powell v. Risser	Gregory v. Robinson	Darnell v. Cameron	Phillips v. Singletar	Dougherty v. Snyder
James v. Turner	Quinley v. Cocke	Hammer v. Rosen	Dennison v. State	Powell v. Duke Univ.	Dunbar v. Greenlaw
Linder v. Foster	Scolavino v. State	Hawley v. State	Di Giovanni v. Pessel	Renelli v. Dept. of MH	Eaby v. U.S.
Martindale v. State	Stallman v. Robinson	Hendler v. State	Dinnerstein v. U.S.	Rice v. Mercy Hosp.	Eddings v. Penn.
Papini v. Alex. San.	Tisinger v. Woolley	Hirsh v. State	Dunn v. State	Ross v. Leonard	Eisele v. Malone
Parker v. La County	United States v. Gray	Hungerford v. U.S.	Duzynski v. Nosal	Roy v. Hartogs	Evanuik v. U. Pitt.
Paulen v. Shinnick	Warner v. State	Johnson v. Meth. Hosp.	Eanes v. U.S.	Semler v. Psy. Ins. Wa.	Feitelberg v. State
Rossing v. State	Weihs v. State	Kowalski v. State	Fatuck v. Hill. Hosp.	Stachulak v. Coughlin	Friedland v. U.S.
Shattuck v. State	Willis v. West. Hosp.	Lowen v. Hilton	Fernandez v. Baruch	Stephen v. Drew	Gsperini v. Mnginelli
Stansfield v. Gardner	Wood v. Samaritan Ins.	McCandless v. State	Fowle v. Fowle	Stovall v. Harms	Gioia v. State
Total: 12	Woodruff v. Shores	Marks v. St. Fran Hosp.	Gerba v. Neurol. Hosp.	U.S. v. Pardue	Gould v. State
	Total: 30	Mitchell v. Robinson	Grant v. N.T.L.	Welsch v. Likins	Gries v. L.I. Home
		Morris v. Rousos	Hendry v. U.S.	Wyatt v. Stickney	Guzy v. Guzy
		Morris v. U. Texas	Hernand v. St. of Cal.	Total: 32	Hammer v. Polsky
		Noel v. Menning. Found.	Harnand v. St. of N.Y.		Hebel v. Hinsdale San.
		People v. Bernstein	Hicks v. U.S.		Heifetz v. Phil. Hosp.
		People v. McCaughan	Higgins v. State		In Re Maddox
		Peters v. State	Hunt v. King County		Jackson v. Indiana
		Quick v. Ben. Sis. Hosp.	Jobson v. Henne		Johnson v. Greer
		Robinson v. State	Katz v. State		Johnston v. Rodis
		Rosenfeld v. Coleman	Keating v. Keller		Joyce v. Ferrazzi
		St. George v. State	Kelly v. State		Kent v. Whitakers
		Saron v. State	Kravitz v. State		Kleber v. Stevens
		Schwenk v. State	Lawrence v. State		Kosberg v. Wash. Hosp.
		Sealey v. Finkelstein	Levandowski v. State		Lester v. Aetna
		Smart v. U.S.	Licht. v. Mont. Hosp.		Maben v. Rankin
		Stone v. Proctor	Lucy Hayes v. Perotti		Mayer v. Albany Hosp.
		Taig v. State	Maniaci v. Marquet. U.		Mezullo v. Maletz
		Torres v. State	Meier v. Ross Hosp.		Miller v. West
		Von Eye v. Hammes	Merchants Bank v. U.S.		Mills v. Soc. N.Y. Hosp.
		Whaley v. Kirby	Meynier v. De Paul		Montgom. Cty. Tr. v. State

(continued)

Table 44. continued

1940–1949	1950–1959	1960–1969	1970–1977	Not Specified
	White v. U.S.	Milano v. State		Morey v. Kaiser Found.
	Total: 51	Millard v. Cameron		Moskowitz v. McQueen
		Miller v. Dickert		Moxon v. Cty. of Kern
		Mochen v. State		Murray v. St. Mary's
		Morgan v. State		Nelson v. Heyne
		Nason v. Super. of Br.		O'Rourke v. Halcyon
		Nicholson v. Han		Pennell v. Cummings
		Olepa v. Mapletoff		People v. Wilkins
		O'Neil v. State		Rouse v. Twin Pines
		Orman v. State		Rufino v. U.S.
		People v. La Vallee		Salter v. Grant
		Pietrucha v. Grant Hosp.		Suhre v. Kott
		Puls v. St. Vinc. Hosp.		Taylor v. Glotfelty
		Rhiver v. Rietman		Tobias v. Manhat. E&E
		Rosario v. State		Trapani v. State
		Rouse v. Cameron		U. Louisville v. Ham.
		Runyon v. Reid		Van Barneveld v. St.
		Samons v. Meymandi		Vassolo v. Cty. Hosp.
		Schaffer v. Spicer		Weinshenk v. Kaiser
		Schanbarger v. Kellog		Whitesell v. Green
		Schwartz v. Thiele		Williams v. Le Bar
		Seymour v. Lofgreen		Williams v. State
		Stowers v. Ard. Hosp.		Woods v. Brumlop
		Surprenant v. State		Total 73
		Tarasoff v. Reg. U. Cal.		Occurred over Period
		Taylor v. State		Yrs., but Unspecified
		Thall v. State		Crocco v. Harris
		Underwood v. U.S.		Legion v. Richardson
		Vistica v. Pres. Hosp.		Martarella v. Kelley
		Vitello v. State		Morales v. Turman
		Weglarz v. State		NYSA v. Rockefeller
		Wendover v. State		Reynolds v. Neill
		Whitree v. State		Rogers v. Okin
		Wilson v. Lehman		Sas v. State
		Wright v. State		Total: 8
		Zipkin v. Freeman		
		Total: 86		

Table 45. Year of Final Decision

1850–1949	*1950–1959*	*1960–1969*	*1970–1977*	*Not Yet Decided*
Arl. Hts. v. Deaderick	Adams v. Ricks	A.A. v. State	Abraham v. Zaslow	Rogers v. Okin
Ayers v. Russell	Bartlett v. Weimer	Adams v. State	Anclote M.F. v. Wilk.	Ross v. Leonard
Bacon v. Bacon	Berry v. Moench	Aiken v. Clary	Annis v. Donahue	Salter v. Grant
Beckham v. Cline	Blauer v. State	Anonymous v. State	Baker v. Orlowsky	Total: 3
Betts v. State	Boykin v. State	Avey v. St. Fran. Hosp.	Bangs v. State	Unspecified
Brandt v. Brandt	Bradshaw v. State	Baker v. U.S.	Beaumong v. Morgan	Borker v. N.T.L.
Brigante v. State	Brown v. Moore	Bencomo v. Morgan	Bellows v. State	Grant v. N.T.L.
Callahan v. State	Commonwealth v. Page	Benjamin v. Havens	Boland v. State	Total: 2
Corcoran v. Jerrel	Cox v. State	Blitz v. Boog	Booe v. Hall	
Curley v. State	Daniels v. Finney	Bogust v. Iverson	Burkes v. Callion	
Daley v. State	Dugan v. U.S.	Byrne v. Kysar	Burks v. Ross	
Di Fiore v. State	Dunbar v. Greenlaw	Campbell v. Glenwood	Burnham v. D.P. Health	
Dougherty v. Snyder	Eisele v. Malone	Carlino v. State	Cameron v. State	
Dowly v. State	Fair v. U.S.	Castiglione v. State	Castillo v. U.S.	
Excel. Ins. Co. v. State	Farber v. Olkon	Chudy v. Chudy	Cawthon v. Coffer	
Fowler v. Nrwys. San.	Feitelberg v. State	Clark v. Geraci	Centeno v. City of N.Y.	
Gsperini v. Mnginelli	Hebel v. Hinsdale San.	Collins v. Hand	Christy v. Saliterman	
Gould v. State	In Re Maddox	Collins v. State	Collins v. Bensinger	
Gries v. L.I. Home	In Re Pierre Estate	Col. St. Bd. v. Weiler	Cooper v. Bd. med. ex.	
Groce v. Myers	In Re Warrington	Constant v. Howe	Crocco v. Harris	
Hough v. Ogden	Johnston v. Rodis	Cty. of L.A. v. Sup. Ct.	Davis v. Watkins	
James v. Turner	Kowalski v. State	Dabkowski v. Davis	Dennison v. State	
Kendrick v. U.S.	Kubas v. State	Darnell v. Cameron	Di Giovanni v. Pessel	
Linder v. Foster	Lester v. Aetna	Demartini v. Alex. San.	Dillman v. Hellman	
McCabe v. State	Lexington Hosp. v. Whit	Dimit. v. Chi. W.M. Hosp.	Dinnerstein v. U.S.	
Martindale v. State	McCandless v. State	Doty v. State	Doe v. Roe	
Miller v. West	Marks v. St. Fran Hosp.	Duzynski v. Nosal	Dunn v. State	
Mills v. Soc. N.Y. Hosp.	Mezullo v. Maletz	Eaby v. U.S.	Eddings v. Penn.	
Papini v. Alex. San.	Montgom. Cty. Tr. v. St.	Eanes v. U.S.	Evanuik v. U. Pitt.	
Parker v. La. County	Murray v. St. Mary's	Fernandez v. Baruch	Fatuck v. Hill. Hosp.	
Paulen v. Shinnick	Noel v. Menning. Found.	Finkel v. State	Fischer v. City Elm.	
Pennell v. Cummings	Oliver v. State	Foster v. State	Forde v. Cty. L.A.	
Quinley v. Cocke	O'Rourke v. Halcyon	Fowle v. Fowle	Freach v. Commonweal	
Rossing v. State	O'Rourke v. O'Rourke	Foxluger v. State	Harris Hosp. v. Pope	
Scolavino v. State	People v. Bernstein	Friedland v. U.S.	Heifetz v. Phil. Hosp.	
Shattuck v. State	People v. McCaughan	Gerba v. Neurol. Hosp.	Hernand v. St. of Cal.	
Springer v. Steiner	Powell v. Risser	Gioia v. State	Hernand v. St. of N.Y.	
Stansfield v. Gardner	Robinson v. State	Gregory v. Robinson	Hicks v. U.S.	
Suhre v. Kott	Rosenfeld v. Coleman	Guzy v. Guzy	Homere v. State	
Tisinger v. Woolley	Rouse v. Twin Pines	Hammer v. Polsky	Hunt v. King County	
U. Louisville v. Ham.	Rufino v. U.S.	Hammer v. Rosen	In Re Anonymous	
Warner v. Packer	Rufino v. U.S.	Hawley v. State	Jackson v. Indiana	

(continued)

Table 45. continued

1850–1949	*1950–1959*	*1960–1969*	*1970–1977*	*Not Yet Decided*
Weihs v. State	St. George v. State	Hendler v. State	Johnson v. Greer	
Williams v. Le Bar	Schwenk v. State	Hendry v. U.S.	Johnson v. U.S.	
Willis v. West. Hosp.	Smart v. U.S.	Higgins v. State	Keating v. Keller	
Wood v. Samaritan Ins.	Stallman v. Robinson	Hirsh v. State	Kravitz v. State	
Woodruff v. Shores	Taylor v. Glotfelty	Hungerford v. U.S.	Lando v. State	
Total: 49	Torres v. State	Jobson v. Henne	Legion v. Richardson	
	United States v. Gray	Johnson v. Meth. Hosp.	Levandowski v. State	
	Von Eye v. Hammes	Joyce v. Ferrazzi	Licht v. Mont. Hosp.	
	Total: 49	Katz v. State	McNeil v. Director	
		Kelly v. State	Maniaci v. Marquet. U.	
		Kent v. Whitakers	Martarella v. Kelley	
		Kleber v. Stevens	Mayer v. Albany Hosp.	
		Kosberg v. Wash. Hosp.	Miller v. Dickert	
		Lawrence v. State	Mochen v. State	
		Lowen v. Hilton	Morales v. Turman	
		Lucy Hayes v. Perotti	Morey v. Kaiser Found	
		Maben v. Rankin	Morgan v. State	
		Meier Ross Gen Hosp.	Morra v. St. Bd. Psych.	
		Merchants Bank v. U.S.	Nastasi v. State	
		Meynier v. De Paul	Nelson v. Heyne	
		Milano v. State	NYSA v. Rockefeller	
		Millard v. Cameron	O'Connor v. Donaldson	
		Mitchel v. Robinson	O'Neill v. State	
		Morris v. Rousos	Orman v. State	
		Morris v. U. Texas	Phillips v. Singletar	
		Moskowitz v. McQueen	Pietrucha v. Grant Ho.	
		Moxon v. Cty. of Kern	Powell v. Duke Univ.	
		Nason v. Super. of Br.	Renelli v. Dept. of M.H.	
		Nicholson v. Han	Reynolds v. Neill	
		Olepa v. Mapletoff	Rhiver v. Rietman	
		People v. La Vallee	Rice v. Mercy Hosp.	
		People v. Wilkins	Rosario v. State	
		Peters v. State	Roy v. Hartogs	
		Puls v. St. Vinc. Hosp.	Runyon v. Reid	
		Quick v. Ben. Sis. Hosp.	Samons v. Meymandi	
		Rouse v. Cameron	Sas v. State	
		Saron v. State	Schaffer v. Spicer	
		Schwartz v. Thiele	Schanbarger v. Kellog	
		Sealey v. Finkelstein	Semler v. Psy. Ins. Wa.	
		Stone v. Proctor	Seymour v. Lofgreen	
		Surprenant v. State	Stachulak v. Coughlin	
		Taig v. State	Stephen v. Drew	

Tobias v. Manhat. E&E	Stovall v. Harms
Trapani v. State	Stowers v. Ard. Hosp.
Underwood v. U.S.	Tarasoff v. Reg. U. Ca.
Vassolo v. Cty. Hosp.	Taylor v. State
Vistica v. Pres. Hosp.	Thall v. State
Weglarz v. State	U.S. v. Pardue
Whaley v. Kirby	Van Barneveld v. State
White v. U.S.	Vitello v. State
Whitree v. State	Weinshenk v. Kaiser
Williams v. State	Welsch v. Likins
Wilson v. Lehman	Wendover v. State
Woods v. Brumlop	Whitesell v. Green
Wright v. State	Wyatt v. Stickney
Zipkin v. Freeman	Total: 98
Total: 99	

Table 46. Number of Suits per State

0	*1*	*2*	*3*	*4–6*	*7–9*	*10 +*
Alaska	Arkansas	Connecticut	Alabama	Georgia (5)	D.C. (9)	California (26)
Arizona	Hawaii	Iowa	Colorado	Indiana (5)	Florida (7)	New York (121)
Delaware	Idaho	Maine	Kentucky	Kansas (6)	Illinois (8)	Texas (11)
Montana	Mississippi	New Mexico	Maryland	Louisiana (5)	Massachusetts (8)	Total: 3
Nebraska	New Hamp.	South Carolina	New Jersey	Minnesota (6)	Michigan (7)	
Nevada	Oklahoma	South Dakota	Ohio	North Carolina (6)	Missouri (9)	
North Dakota	Oregon	Tennessee	Wisconsin	Virginia (4)	Pennsylvania (9)	
Rhode Island	Utah	Total: 7	Total: 7	Washington (6)	Total: 7	
Vermont	Total: 8			Total: 8		
West Virginia						
Wyoming						
Total: 11						

Appendix D

Legal Citations and Related References

This appendix contains the legal citations to the 300 cases reviewed, citations to other cases involving therapeutic malpractice, foreign cases, and other legal cases referred to in the text. Because the case name may be reversed in other reference works—depending on the level of court reached at the time—a defendant table of cases has been provided. Where available, secondary source material commenting upon or reporting cases has been included.

MALPRACTICE CASES INVOLVING PSYCHOTHERAPY.

A.A. v. State, 43 Misc. 2d 1004, 252 N.Y.S.2d 800 (Ct. Cl. 1964).

Abraham v. Zaslow, No. 245862 (Cal. Super. Ct., June 30, 1972).

Related Cases and References

"Psychologist Faces Malpractice Charges," *APA Monitor*, September-October 1972, at 16.

"Rage Reduction Therapy Pioneer Battles to Keep California License," *APA Monitor*, March 1973, at 5.

Slovenko, R. *Psychiatry and Law.* Boston: Little, Brown, 1973.

Zaslow v. Board of Medical Examiners, No. D-1330 (Cal. Super. Ct. Sept. 24, 1972).

Zaslow v. Board of Medical Examiners, No. 655-667 (Cal. Super. Ct. Dec. 4, 1972).

Adams v. Ricks, 91 Ga. App. 494, 86 S.E.2d 329 (1955).

Adams v. State, 71 Wash. 2d 414, 429 P.2d 109 (1967).

Aiken v. Clary, 396 S.W.2d 668 (Mo. 1965).

Anclote Manor Foundation v. Wilkinson, 263 So. 2d 256 (Fla. Dist. Ct. App. 1972).

Annis v. Donahue, No. 303295 (D. Mass., filed 1969).

Related Cases and References

Hogan, D.B., "The Regulation of Human Relations Training: An Examination of Some Assumptions and Some Recommendations." Unpublished third-year manuscript, Harvard Law School, Cambridge, 1972.

Penn, M.R. "The Application of Tort Doctrines to the Encounter or Sensitivity Movement." Unpublished manuscript, Harvard Law School, Cambridge, Mass., 1971.

Anonymous v. State, 17 App. Div. 2d 495, 236 N.Y.S.2d 88 (1963).

Arlington Heights Sanitarium v. Deaderick, 272 S.W. 497 (Tex. Ct. App. 1925).

Avey v. St. Francis Hospital, 201 Kan. 687, 442 P.2d 1013 (1968).
Ayers v. Russell, 50 Hun. 292, 3 N.Y.S. 338 (Sup. Ct. 1888).
Bacon v. Bacon, 76 Miss. 468, 24 So. 968 (1899).
Baker v. Orlowsky, 28 Ohio App. 2d 188, 275 N.E.2d 342 (1971).
Baker v. United States, 226 F. Supp. 129 (S.D. Iowa 1964), *aff'd*, 343 F.2d 222 (8th Cir. 1965).
Bangs v. State, 41 App. Div. 2d 988, 343 N.Y.S.2d 976 (1973).
Bartlett v. Weimer, 268 F.2d 860 (7th Cir. 1959).
Beaumont v. Morgan, 427 F.2d 667 (1st Cir. 1970), *cert. denied mem.*, 400 U.S. 882 (1970).

Related Cases and References

Beaumont v. Segal, 362 Mass. 30, 283 N.E.2d 858 (1972).

Beckham v. Cline, 151 Fla. 481, 10 So. 2d 419 (1942).
Bellandi v. Park Sanitarium Association, 214 Cal. 472, 6 P.2d 508 (1931).
Bellows v. State, 37 App. Div. 2d 342, 325 N.Y.S.2d 225 (1971).
Bencomo v. Morgan, 210 So. 2d 236 (Fla. Dist. Ct. App. 1968).
Benjamin v. Havens, Inc., 60 Wash. 2d 196, 373 P.2d 109 (1962).
Bennett v. State, 59 Misc. 2d 306, 299 N.Y.S.2d 288 (Ct. Cl. 1969).
Berry v. Moench, 8 Utah 2d 191, 331 P.2d 814 (1958).
Betts v. State, 54 N.Y.S.2d 475 (Ct. Cl. 1945).
Blauer v. State, No. 31824 (N.Y. Ct. Cl., June 17, 1955).

Related Cases and References

Barrett v. State, 85 Misc. 2d 456, 378 N.Y.S.2d 946 (Ct. Cl. 1976).

Blitz v. Boog, 328 F.2d 596 (2d Cir. 1964), *cert. denied mem.*, 379 U.S. 855 (1964).
Bogust v. Iverson, 10 Wis. 2d 129, 102 N.W.2d 228 (1960).
Boland v. State, 61 Misc. 2d 802, 306 N.Y.S.2d 508 (Ct. Cl. 1969), *rev'd*, 35 App. Div. 2d 855, 315 N.Y.S.2d 216 (1970), *orig. j. reinstated*, 30 N.Y.2d 337, 333 N.Y.S.2d 410, 284 N.E.2d 569 (1972).
Booe v. Hall, 24 N.C. App. 276, 210 S.E.2d 293 (1974).
Borker v. NTL Institute, No. 69-4793 (U.S.D.C., S.D.N.Y., filed Nov. 3, 1969).

Related Cases and References

Information on this case was provided by NTL's legal counsel, Allan Mendelsohn, personal communication, May 3, 1974.
Aetna Ins. Co. v. NTL Institute, No. 1992-70 (S.D.N.Y., filed July 2, 1970).
Penn, M.R. "The Application of Tort Doctrines to the Encounter or Sensitivity Movement." Unpublished manuscript, Harvard Law School, Cambridge, Mass., 1971, pp. 48–49.

Boykin v. State, 13 Misc. 2d 1037, 179 N.Y.S.2d 197 (Ct. Cl. 1958), *aff'd.* 7 App. Div. 2d. 819, 180 N.Y.S.2d 884 (1958).
Bradshaw v. State, 5 App. Div. 2d 511, 173 N.Y.S.2d 406 (1958).
Brandt v. Brandt, 286 Ill. App. 151, 3 N.E.2d 96 (1936).
Brigante v. State, 33 N.Y.S.2d 354 (Ct. Cl. 1942).
Brown v. Moore, 143 F. Supp. 816 (W.D. Pa. 1956), *aff'd*, 247 F.2d 711 (3d Cir. 1957).
Burkes v. Callion, 433 F.2d 318 (9th Cir. 1970), *cert. denied mem.*, 403 U.S. 908 (1971).
Burks v. Ross, 438 F.2d 230 (6th Cir. 1971).
Burnham v. Department of Public Health, 349 F. Supp. 1335 (N.D. Ga. 1972), *rev'd*, 503 F.2d 1319 (5th Cir. 1974).
Byrne v. Kysar, 347 F.2d 734 (7th Cir. 1965), *cert. denied mem.*, 383 U.S. 913 (1966); *rehearing denied mem.*, 384 U.S. 914 (1966), 384 U.S. 994 (1966).
Callahan v. State, 179 Misc. 781, 40 N.Y.S.2d 109 (Ct. Cl. 1943), *aff'd*, 266 App. Div. 1054, 46 N.Y.S.2d 104 (1943).
Cameron v. State, 37 App. Div. 2d 46, 322 N.Y.S.2d 562 (1971), *aff'd.*, 30 N.Y.2d 596, 331 N.Y.S.2d 30 (1972).
Campbell v. Glenwood Hills Hospital, 224 F. Supp. 27 (D. Minn. 1963).

Carlino v. State, 30 App. Div. 2d 987, 294 N.Y.S.2d 30 (1968).

Castiglione v. State, 25 App. Div. 2d 895, 269 N.Y.S.2d 248 (1966).

Castillo v. United States, 552 F.2d 1385 (10th Cir. 1977).

Cawthon v. Coffer, 264 So. 2d 873 (Fla. Dist. Ct. App. 1972).

Centeno v. City of New York, 48 App. Div. 2d 812, 369 N.Y.S.2d 710 (1975), *aff'd*, 40 N.Y.2d 932, 389 N.Y.S.2d 837, 358 N.E.2d 527 (1976).

Christy v. Saliterman, 288 Minn. 144, 179 N.W.2d 288 (1970).

Chudy v. Chudy, 243 Ark. 332, 420 S.W.2d 401 (1967).

Clark v. Geraci, 29 Misc. 2d 791, 208 N.Y.S.2d 564 (Sup. Ct., Trial Term, 1960).

Collins v. Bensinger, 374 F. Supp. 273 (N.D. Ill. 1974), *aff'd*, 506 F.2d 1405 (7th Cir. 1974), *cert. denied mem.* 422 U.S. 1058 (1975).

Collins v. Hand, 431 Pa. 378, 246 A.2d 398 (1968).

Collins v. State, 23 App. Div. 2d 898, 258 N.Y.S.2d 938 (1965), *aff'd*, 17 N.Y.2d 542, 268 N.Y.S.2d 314 (1966).

Colorado State Board of Medical Examiners v. Weiler, 157 Colo. 244, 402 P.2d 606 (1965).

Related Cases and References

Colorado State Board of Medical Examiners v. Weiler, 15 A.L.R.3d 1171; Annot., 15 A.L.R.3d 1179, 1181 (§ 3).

Commonwealth v. Page, 339 Mass. 313, 159 N.E.2d 82 (1959).

Constant v. Howe, 436 S.W.2d 115 (Tex. 1968).

Cooper v. Board of Medical Examiners, 49 Cal. App. 3d 931, 123 Cal. Rptr. 563 (1975).

Related Cases and References

Cooper v. Board of Medical Examiners, No. D-1329 (Cal. Super. Ct. Dec. 15, 1972).

Cooper v. Board of Medical Examiners, No. M-6038 (Cal. Super. Ct. Dec. 20, 1973).

Glenn, R.D. "Standard of Care in Administering Non-traditional Psychotherapy," 7 *University of California, Davis Law Review* 56-83 (1974).

Corcoran v. Jerrel, 185 Iowa 532, 170 N.W. 776 (1919).

County of Los Angeles v. Superior Court, 43 Cal. Rptr. 392 (Dist. Ct. App. 1965), *vacated*, 62 Cal. 2d839, 44 Cal. Rptr. 796, 402 P.2d 868 (1965).

Cox v. State, 202 Misc. 870, 113 N.Y.S.2d 342 (Ct. Cl. 1952), *rev'd*, 282 App. Div. 815, 122 N.Y.S.2d 589 (1953), *judgment on retrial sub. nom.*, McGrath v. State, 207 Misc. 639, 139 N.Y.S.2d 801 (Ct. Cl. 1954).

Crocco v. Harris, Seattle *Times*, October 24, 1974, p. H4.

Curley v. State, 148 Misc. 336, 265 N.Y.S. 762 (Ct. Cl. 1933), *aff'd sub nom.*, Luke v. State, 253 App. Div. 783, 1 N.Y.S.2d 19 (1937).

Dabkowski v. Davis, 364 Mich. 429, 111 N.W.2d 68 (1961).

Daley v. State, 273 App. Div. 552, 78 N.Y.S.2d 584 (1948), *aff'd*, 298 N.Y. 880, 84 N.E.2d 801 (1949).

Daniels v. Finney, 262 S.W.2d 431 (Tex. Ct. App. 1953).

Darnell v. Cameron, 348 F.2d 64 (D.C. Cir. 1965).

Davis v. Watkins, 384 F. Supp. 1196 (N.D. Ohio 1974).

DeMartini v. Alexander Sanitarium, 192 Cal. App. 2d 442, 13 Cal. Rptr. 564 (1961).

Dennison v. State, 49 Misc. 2d 933, 267 N.Y.S.2d 920 (Ct. Cl. 1966), *rev'd and dismissed*, 28 App. Div. 2d 608, 280 N.Y.S.2d 31 (1967), *reversal aff'd*, 23 N.Y.2d 996, 298 N.Y.S.2d 1002, 246 N.E.2d 760 (1969), *modified*, 25 N.Y.2d 904, 304 N.Y.S.2d 596, 252 N.E.2d 129 (1969), *cert. denied*, 397 U.S. 923 (1970).

Di Fiore v. State, 275 App. Div. 885, 88 N.Y.S.2d 815 (1949).

Di Giovanni v. Pessel, 104 N.J. Super. 550, 250 A.2d 756 (App. Div. 1969), *modified*, 55 N.J. 188, 260 A.2d 510 (1970).

Dillmann v. Hellman, 283 So.2d 388 (Fla. Dist. Ct. App. 1973).

Dimitrijevic v. Chicago Wesley Memorial Hospital, 92 Ill. App. 2d 251, 236 N.E.2d 309 (1968).

Dinnerstein v. United States, 486 F.2d 34 (2d Cir. 1973).

Doe v. Roe, 42 App. Div. 2d 559, 345 N.Y.S.2d 560 (1973), *aff'd*, 33 N.Y.2d 902, 352 N.Y.S.2d 626 (1973), *modified*, 34 N.Y.2d 562, 354 N.Y.S.2d 941, 310 N.E.2d 562 (1974).
Doty v. State, 33 Misc. 2d 330, 226 N.Y.S.2d 901 (Ct. Cl. 1961).
Dougherty v. Snyder, 97 Mo. App. 495, 71 S.W. 463 (1903).
Dowly v. State, 190 Misc. 16, 68 N.Y.S.2d 573 (Ct. Cl. 1947).
Dugan v. United States, 147 F. Supp. 674 (D.C. Cir. 1956).
Dunbar v. Greenlaw, 152 Me. 270, 128 A.2d 218 (1956).
Dunn v. State, 34 App. Div. 2d 267, 312 N.Y.S.2d 61 (1970), *rev'd*, 29 N.Y.2d 313, 327 N.Y.S.2d 622, 277 N.E.2d 647 (1971).
Duzynski v. Nosal, 324 F.2d 924 (7th Cir. 1963).
Eaby v. United States, 298 F. Supp. 959 (D.D.C. 1969).
Eanes v. United States, 280 F. Supp. 143 (E.D. Va. 1968), *aff'd*, 407 F.2d 823 (4th Cir. 1969).
Eddings v. Pennsylvania, 311 F. Supp. 944 (E.D. Pa. 1970).
Eisele v. Malone, 2 App. Div. 2d 550, 157 N.Y.S.2d 155 (1956).
Evanuik v. University of Pittsburgh Western Psychiatric Institute, 234 Pa. Super. Ct. 287, 338 A.2d 636 (1975).
Excelsior Insurance Co. v. State, 178 Misc. 1079, 37 N.Y.S.2d 378 (Ct. Cl. 1942), *rev'd*, 269 App. Div. 464, 57 N.Y.S.2d 60 (1945), *reversal modified*, 270 App. Div. 1058, 64 N.Y.S.2d 174 (1946), *orig. j. reinstated*, 297 N.Y. 40, 169 N.E.2d 553 (1946).
Fair v. United States, 234 F.2d 288 (5th Cir. 1956).
Farber v. Olkon, 40 Cal.2d 503, 254 P.2d 520 (1953).
Fatuck v. Hillside Hospital, 45 App. Div. 2d 708, 356 N.Y.S.2d 105 (1974), *aff'd*, 36 N.Y.2d 736, 368 N.Y.S.2d 161 (1975).
Feitelberg v. State, 284 App. Div. 1086, 136 N.Y.S.2d 78 (1954).
Fernandez v. Baruch, 96 N.J. Super. 125, 232 A.2d 661 (App. Div. 1967), *rev'd*, 52 N.J. 127, 244 A.2d 109 (1968).
Finkel v. State, 37 Misc. 2d 757, 237 N.Y.S.2d 66 (Ct. Cl. 1962).
Fischer v. City of Elmira, 75 Misc. 2d 510, 347 N.Y.S.2d 770 (Ct. Cl. 1973).
Forde v. County of Los Angeles, 64 Cal. App. 3d 477, 134 Cal. Rptr. 549 (1977).
Foster v. State, 26 Misc. 2d 426, 210 N.Y.S.2d 956 (Ct. Cl. 1961).
Fowle v. Fowle, 255 N.C. 720, 122 S.E.2d 722 (1961).
Fowler v. Norways Sanitorium, 112 Ind. App. 347, 42 N.E.2d 415 (1942).
Foxluger v. State, 23 Misc.2d 933, 203 N.Y.S.2d 985 (Ct. Cl. 1960).
Freach v. Commonwealth, 354 A.2d 908, 23 Pa. Commonw. Ct. 546 (1976), *modified*, 370 A.2d 1163 (Pa. 1977).
Friedland v. United States, 209 F. Supp. 684 (D. Mass. 1962).
Gasperini v. Manginelli, 196 Misc. 547, 92 N.Y.S.2d 575 (Sup. Ct. 1949).
Gerba v. Neurological Hospital Association, 416 S.W.2d 126 (Mo. 1967).
Gioia v. State, 38 Misc. 2d 833, 238 N.Y.S.2d 758 (Ct. Cl. 1963), *rev'd*, 22 App. Div. 2d 181, 254 N.Y.S.2d 384 (1964).
Gould v. State, 181 Misc. 884, 46 N.Y.S.2d 313 (Ct. Cl. 1944).
Grant v. NTL Institute, No. 3505-70 (U.S.D.C., D.C. Cir., filed 1970).

Related Cases and References

Penn, M.R. "The Application of Tort Doctrines to the Encounter or Sensitivity Movement." Unpublished manuscript, Harvard Law School, Cambridge, Mass., 1971.
Ungar, S.J. "$500,000 Tag on Sensitivity," *New York Post*, December 4, 1970, at 39.
Further information on this suit was provided by NTL's former president, Vlad Dupre, personal communication, May 1, 1974; and by its legal counsel, Allan Mendelsohn, personal communication, May 3, 1974.

Gregory v. Robinson, 338 S.W.2d 88 (Mo. 1960).
Gries v. Long Island Home, 274 App. Div. 938, 83 N.Y.S.2d 728 (1948).
Groce v. Myers, 224 N.C. 165, 29 S.E.2d 553 (1944).

Guzy v. Guzy, 11 App. Div. 2d 1047, 206 N.Y.S.2d 355 (1960).
Hammer v. Polsky, 36 Misc. 2d 482, 233 N.Y.S.2d 110 (Sup. Ct. 1962).
Hammer v. Rosen, 7 App. Div. 2d 216, 181 N.Y.S.2d 805 (1959), *modified*, 7 N.Y.2d 376, 198 N.Y.S.2d 65 (1960).
Harris Hospital v. Pope, 520 S.W.2d 813 (Tex. Ct. App. 1975).
Hawley v. State, 41 Misc. 2d 275, 245 N.Y.S.2d 677 (Ct. Cl. 1963), *aff'd*, 22 App. Div. 2d 357, 256 N.Y.S.2d 269 (1965), *rev'd*, 16 N.Y.2d 809, 263 N.Y.S.2d 6 (1965).
Hebel v. Hinsdale Sanitarium, 2 Ill. App. 2d 527, 119 N.E.2d 506 (1954).
Heifetz v. Philadelphia State Hospital, 22 Pa. Commonw. Ct. 325, 348 A.2d 455 (1975).
Hendler v. State, 33 Misc. 2d 171, 225 N.Y.S.2d 878 (Ct. Cl. 1962).
Hendry v. United States, 280 F. Supp. 27 (S.D.N.Y. 1968), *aff'd*, 418 F.2d 774 (2d Cir. 1969).
Hernandez v. State of California, 11 Cal. App. 3d 895, 90 Cal. Rptr. 205 (1970).
Hernandez v. State of New York, 46 App. Div. 2d 1712, 360 N.Y.S.2d 314 (1974).
Hicks v. United States, 511 F.2d 407 (D.C. Cir. 1975).
Higgins v. State, 24 App. Div. 2d 147, 265 N.Y.S.2d 254 (1965).
Hirsh v. State, 18 Misc. 2d 360, 183 N.Y.S.2d 175 (Ct. Cl. 1959), *aff'd*, 9 App. Div. 2d 1006, 194 N.Y.S.2d 935 (1959), *aff'd on rehearing*, 8 N.Y.2d 125, 202 N.Y.S.2d 296, 168 N.E.2d 372 (1960).
Homere v. State, 79 Misc. 2d 972, 361 N.Y.S.2d 820 (Ct. Cl. 1974), *aff'd*, 48 App. Div. 2d 422, 370 N.Y.S.2d 246 (1975).
Hough v. Ogden, 4 N.J. Misc. 455, 133 A. 73 (1926).
Hungerford v. United States, 307 F.2d 99 (9th Cir. 1962).
Hunt v. King County, 4 Wash. App. 14, 481 P.2d 593 (1971).
In re Anonymous, 69 Misc. 2d 181, 329 N.Y.S.2d 542 (Sup. Ct. 1972), *rev'd*, 39 App. Div. 410, 334 N.Y.S.2d 738 (1972); *orig. decision reinstated sub. nom.*, Kesselbrenner v. Anonymous, 33 N.Y.2d 161, 350 N.Y.S.2d 889, 305 N.E.2d 903 (1973).
In re Maddox, 351 Mich. 358, 88 N.W.2d 470 (1958).
In re Pierre's Estate, 207 Misc. 726, 139 N.Y.S.2d 825 (Ct. Cl. 1955), *rev'd*, 286 App. Div. 573, 146 N.Y.S.2d 81 (1955).
In re Warrington, 277 App. Div. 1076, 100 N.Y.S.2d 655 (1950), *aff'd*, 303 N.Y. 129, 100 N.E.2d 170 (1951).
Jackson v. Indiana, 406 U.S. 715 (1972).
James v. Turner, 184 Tenn. 563, 201 S.W.2d 691 (1942).
Jobson v. Henne, 355 F.2d 129 (2nd Cir. 1966).
Johnson v. Greer, 477 F.2d 101 (5th Cir. 1973).
Johnson v. Methodist Hospital, 14 App. Div. 2d 912, 218 N.Y.S.2d 568 (1961).
Johnson v. United States, 409 F. Supp. 1283 (S.D. Cal. 1976).
Johnston v. Rodis, 151 F. Supp. 345 (D.D.C. 1957), *rev'd*, 251 F.2d 917 (D.C. Cir. 1958).
Joyce v. Ferrazzi, 323 F.2d 931 (1st Cir. 1963).
Katz v. State, 46 Misc. 2d 61, 258 N.Y.S.2d 912 (Ct. Cl. 1965).
Keating v. Keller, 242 So. 2d 892 (La. Ct. App. 1970).
Kelly v. State, 57 Misc. 2d 466, 293 N.Y.S.2d 208 (Ct. Cl. 1968).
Kendrick v. United States, 82 F. Supp. 430 (N.D. Ala. 1949).
Kent v. Whitaker, 58 Wash. 2d 569, 364 P.2d 556 (1961).
Kleber v. Stevens, 39 Misc. 2d 712, 241 N.Y.S.2d 497 (Sup. Ct. 1963), *aff'd*, 20 App. Div. 2d 896, 249 N.Y.S.2d 668 (1964).
Kosberg v. Washington Hospital Center, 394 F.2d 947 (D.C. Cir. 1968).
Kowalski v. State, 7 App. Div. 2d 762, 179 N.Y.S.2d 925 (1958).
Kravitz v. State, 8 Cal. App. 3d 301, 87 Cal Rptr. 352 (1970).
Kubas v. State, 198 Misc. 130, 96 N.Y.S.2d 408 (Ct. Cl. 1949), *aff'd*, 278 App. Div. 887, 104 N.Y.S.2d 856 (1951).
Lando v. State, 47 App. Div. 2d 972, 366 N.Y.S.2d 679 (1975), *modified*, 39 N.Y.2d 803, 385 N.Y.S.2d 759, 351 N.E.2d 426 (1976).
Lawrence v. State, 44 Misc. 2d 756, 255 N.Y.S.2d 129 (Ct. Cl. 1964).

Legion v. Richardson, 354 F. Supp. 456 (S.D.N.Y. 1972), *aff'd*, 414 U.S. 1058 (1974).
Lester v. Aetna Casualty & Surety Co., 240 F.2d 676 (5th Cir. 1957), *cert. denied*, 354 U.S. 923 (1957).
Lewandowski v. State, 65 Misc. 2d 511, 318 N.Y.S.2d 83 (Ct. Cl. 1971).
Lexington Hospital v. White, 245 S.W.2d 927 (Ky. 1952).
Lichtenstein v. Montefiore Hospital, 56 App. Div. 2d 281, 392 N.Y.S.2d 18 (1977).
Linder v. Foster, 209 Minn. 43, 295 N.W. 299 (1940).
Lowen v. Hilton, 142 Colo. 200, 351 P.2d 881 (1960).
Lucy Webb Hayes National Training School v. Perotti, 419 F.2d 704 (D.C. Cir. 1969).
Maben v. Rankin, 55 Cal. 2d 139, 10 Cal. Rptr. 353, 358 P.2d 681.
McCabe v. State, 190 Misc. 11, 73 N.Y.S.2d 441 (Ct. Cl. 1947), *aff'd*, 273 App. Div. 1048, 78 N.Y.S.2d 687 (1948).
McCandless v. State, 6 Misc. 2d 391, 166 N.Y.S.2d 272 (Ct. Cl. 1956), *modified*, 3 App. Div. 2d 600, 162 N.Y.S.2d 570 (1957), *judgment on appeal aff'd*, 4 N.Y.2d 797, 173 N.Y.S.2d 30, 149 N.E.2d 529 (1958).
McNeil v. Director, Patuxent Institution, 407 U.S. 245 (1972).
Maniaci v. Marquette University, 50 Wisc. 2d 287, 184 N.W.2d 168 (1971).
Marks v. St. Francis Hospital, 179 Kan. 268, 294 P.2d 258 (1956).
Martarella v. Kelley, 349 F. Supp. 575 (S.D.N.Y. 1972), *enforced*, 359 F. Supp. 478 (S.D.N.Y. 1973).
Martindale v. State, 244 App. Div. 877, 281 N.Y.S. 686 (1935), *aff'd*, 269 N.Y. 554, 2 N.Y.S.2d 356, 199 N.E. 667 (1935).
Mayer v. Albany Medical Center Hospital, 37 App. Div. 2d 1011, 325 N.Y.S.2d 517 (1971).
Meier v. Ross General Hospital, 69 Cal. 2d 420, 71 Cal. Rptr. 903, 445 P.2d 519 (1968).
Merchants National Bank v. United States, 272 F. Supp. 409 (D.N.D. 1967).
Meynier v. De Paul Hospital, 218 So. 2d 98 (La. Ct. App. 1969).
Mezullo v. Maletz, 331 Mass. 233, 118 N.E.2d 356 (1954).
Milano v. State, 44 Misc. 2d 290, 253 N.Y.S.2d 662 (Ct. Cl. 1964).
Millard v. Cameron, 125 U.S. App. D.C. 383, 373 F.2d 468 (1966).
Miller v. Dickert, 259 S.C. 1, 190 S.E.2d 459 (1972).
Miller v. West, 165 Md. 245, 167 A. 696 (1933).
Mills v. Society of the New York Hospital, 242 App. Div. 245, 274 N.Y.S. 233 (1934), *aff'd*, 270 N.Y. 594, 1 N.E.2d 346 (1936).
Mitchell v. Robinson, 334 S.W.2d 11 (Mo. 1960), *judgment on remand aff'd*, 360 S.W.2d 673 (1962).
Mochen v. State, 43 App. Div. 2d 484, 352 N.Y.S.2d 290 (1974), *judgment on remand aff'd*, 57 App. Div. 2d 719 (1977).
Montgomery County Trust Co. v. State, 283 App. Div. 1008, 130 N.Y.S.2d 796 (1954).
Morales v. Turman, 383 F. Supp. 53 (E.D. Tex. 1974), *vacated*, 535 F.2d 864 (5th Cir. 1976), *judgment reinstated*, 97 S. Ct. 1189 (1977), *rehearing denied*, 97 S. Ct. 1690 (1977).
Related Cases and References
Morales v. Turman, 364 F. Supp. 166 (E.D. Tex. 1973).
Morey v. Kaiser Foundation Hospitals, No. 240601 (Cal. Super. Ct. Nov. 9, 1972).
Morgan v. State, 65 Misc. 2d 978, 319 N.Y.S.2d 151 (Ct. Cl. 1970), *aff'd in part and rev'd in part*, 40 App. Div. 2d 891, 333 N.Y.S.2d 536 (1972), *judgment on appeal aff'd*, 34 N.Y.2d 709, 313 N.E.2d 340 (1974), *cert. denied mem.*, 419 U.S. 1013 (1974).
Morra v. State Board of Examiners of Psychologists, 212 Kan. 103, 510 P.2d 614 (1973).
Morris v. Rousos, 397 S.W.2d 504 (Tex. Ct. App. 1965), *cert. denied*, 385 U.S. 869 (1966).
Morris v. University of Texas, 348 S.W.2d 644 (Tex. Ct. App. 1961).
Moskowitz v. McQueen, 38 Misc. 2d 1053, 236 N.Y.S.2d 919 (Sup. Ct. 1963).

Moxon v. County of Kern, 233 Cal. App. 2d 393, 43 Cal. Rptr. 481 (1965).
Murray v. St. Mary's Hospital, 280 App. Div. 803, 113 N.Y.S.2d 104 (1952).
Nason v. Superintendent of Bridgewater State Hospital, 353 Mass. 604, 233 N.E.2d 908 (1968).
Nastasi v. State, 55 App. Div. 2d 724, 389 N.Y.S.2d 175 (1976).
Nelson v. Heyne, 355 F. Supp. 451 (N.D. Ind. 1972), *aff'd*, 491 F.2d 352 (7th Cir. 1974), *cert. denied*, 417 U.S. 976 (1974).
New York State Association for Retarded Children v. Rockefeller, 357 F. Supp. 752 (E.D.N.Y. 1973), *modified*, 393 F. Supp. 715 (E.D.N.Y. 1975).
Nicholson v. Han, 12 Mich. App. 35, 162 N.W.2d 313 (1968).
Noel v. Menninger Foundation, 180 Kan. 23, 299 P.2d 38 (1956).
O'Connor v. Donaldson, 493 F.2d 507 (5th Cir. 1974), *vacated*, 422 U.S. 563 (1975).
Related Cases and References
"O'Connor v. Donaldson," 3 *Mental Health Law Project* 5 (1977).
Olepa v. Mapletoff, 2 Mich. App. 734, 141 N.W.2d 350 (1966).
Oliver v. State, 17 Misc. 2d 1018, 186 N.Y.S.2d 151 (Ct. Cl. 1959).
O'Neil v. State, 66 Misc. 2d 936, 323 N.Y.S.2d 56 (Ct. Cl. 1971).
Orman v. State, 59 Misc. 2d 337, 299 N.Y.S.2d 510 (Ct. Cl. 1969), *aff'd*, 37 App. Div. 2d 674, 322 N.Y.S.2d 914 (1971), *appeal dismissed*, 29 N.Y.2d 668, 324 N.Y.S.2d 958 (1971).
O'Rourke v. Halcyon Rest, 281 App. Div. 838, 118 N.Y.S.2d 693 (1953), *aff'd*, 306 N.Y. 692, 117 N.E.2d 639 (1954).
O'Rourke v. O'Rourke, 69 So. 2d 567 (La. App. 1953), *modified*, 79 So. 2d 87 (La. 1955).
Papini v. Alexander Sanitarium, 12 Cal. App. 2d 249, 55 P.2d 270 (1936).
Parker v. Los Angeles County, 62 Cal. App. 2d 130, 144 P.2d 70 (1944).
Paulen v. Shinnick, 291 Mich. 288, 289 N.W. 162 (1939).
Pennell v. Cummings, 75 Me. 163 (1883).
People v. Bernstein, 171 Cal. App. 2d 279, 340 P.2d 299 (1959).
Related Cases and References
Bernstein v. Board of Medical Examiners, 204 Cal. App. 2d 378, 22 Cal. Rptr. 419 (1962).
People v. La Vallee, 29 App. Div. 2d 248, 287 N.Y.S.2d 601 (1968).
People v. McCaughan, 306 P.2d 61 (1957), *vacated*, 49 Cal. 2d 409, 317 P.2d 974 (1957).
People v. Wilkins, 23 App. Div. 2d 178, 259 N.Y.S.2d 462 (1965).
Peters v. State, 41 Misc. 2d 980, 247 N.Y.S.2d 811 (Ct. Cl. 1964), *aff'd*, 22 App. Div. 2d 764 (1964).
Pettis v. State Department of Hospitals, 281 So. 2d 881 (La. Ct. App. 1973), *judgment on remand modified*, 336 So. 2d 521 (La. Ct. App. 1976), *rev'd*, 339 So. 2d 855 (La. 1976), *judgment on remand*, 340 So. 2d 1108 (La. Ct. App. 1976).
Phillips v. Singletary, 350 F. Supp. 297 (D.S.C. 1972).
Pietrucha v. Grant Hospital, 447 F.2d 1029 (7th Cir. 1971).
Powell v. Duke University, 18 N.C. App. 736, 197 S.E.2d 910 (1973).
Powell v. Risser, 375 Pa. 60, 99 A.2d 454 (1953).
Puls v. St. Vincent Hospital, 36 Wis. 2d 679, 154 N.W.2d 308 (1967).
Quick v. Benedictine Sisters Hospital Association, 257 Minn. 470, 102 N.W.2d 36 (1960).
Quinley v. Cocke, 183 Tenn. 428, 192 S.W.2d 992 (1946).
Renelli v. Department of Mental Hygiene, 73 Misc. 2d 261, 340 N.Y.S.2d 498 (Sup. Ct. 1973).
Reynolds v. Neill, 381 F. Supp. 1374 (N.D. Tex. 1974), *vacated sub nom.*, Sheldon v. Reynolds, 422 U.S. 1050 (1975), *orig. j. reaff'd*, 404 F. Supp. 1004 (N.D. Tex. 1975).
Rhiver v. Rietman, 148 Ind. App. 266, 265 N.E.2d 245 (1970).
Rice v. Mercy Hospital, 318 So. 2d 436 (Fla. Dist. Ct. App. 1975).
Robinson v. State, 17 Misc. 2d 775, 187 N.Y.S.2d 257 (Ct. Cl. 1959).
Rogers v. Okin, No. 75-1610-T (D. Mass., filed Apr. 5, 1975).

Related Cases and References

Bruzelius, N.J. "Mental Patient's Rights Versus Doctor's Duty," Boston *Globe*, December 5, 1977.

Rosario v. State, 51 Misc. 2d 790, 274 N.Y.S.2d 81 (Ct. Cl. 1966), *rev'd*, 33 App. Div. 2d 122, 305 N.Y.S.2d 574 (1969), *reversal aff'd*, 36 N.Y.2d 901, 372 N.Y.S.2d 647 (1975).

Rosenfeld v. Coleman, 19 Pa. D. & C.2d 635, 35 N.W. 206 (1959).

Ross v. Leonard, *New York Times*, November 27, 1977.

Rossing v. State, 47 N.Y.S.2d 262 (Ct. Cl. 1944).

Rouse v. Cameron, 387 F.2d 241 (D.C. Cir. 1967).

Rouse v. Twin Pines Sanitarium, 162 Cal. App. 2d 639, 328 P.2d 536 (1958).

Roy v. Hartogs, 81 Misc. 2d 350, 366 N.Y.S.2d 297 (Civ. Ct. 1975), *modified*, 85 Misc. 2d 891, 381 N.Y.S.2d 587 (App. Term 1976).

Related Cases and References

Hartogs v. Employers Mutual Liability Insurance Co., 89 Misc. 2d 468, 391 N.Y.S.2d 962 (Sup. Ct. 1977).

"Love Thy Analyst," *Time*, March 24, 1975, at 76.

Freeman, L., and Roy, J. *Betrayal*. New York: Stein and Day, 1976.

Rufino v. United States, 126 F. Supp. 132 (S.D.N.Y. 1954).

Runyon v. Reid, 510 P.2d 943 (Okla. 1973).

St. George v. State, 283 App. Div. 245, 127 N.Y.S.2d 147 (1954), *aff'd*, 308 N.Y. 681, 124 N.E.2d 320 (1954).

Salter v. Grant, *Parade Magazine*, May 3, 1970, at 2.

Samons v. Meymandi, 9 N.C. App. 490, 177 S.E.2d 209 (1970), *cert. denied*, 277 N.C. 458, 178 S.E.2d 225 (1971).

Saron v. State, 24 App. Div. 2d 771, 263 N.Y.S.2d 591 (1965).

Sas v. State, 334 F.2d 506 (4th Cir. 1964), *judgment on remand*, 295 F. Supp. 389 (D. Md. 1969), *remanded judgment aff'd sub nom.*, Tippett v. State, 436 F.2d 1153 (4th Cir. 1971), *cert. dismissed sub nom.*, Murel v. Baltimore City Criminal Court, 407 U.S. 355 (1972).

Schaffer v. Spicer, 215 N.W.2d 134 (S.D. 1974).

Schanbarger v. Kellogg, 35 App. Div. 2d 902, 315 N.Y.S.2d 1013 (1970), *cert. denied*, 405 U.S. 919 (1972).

Schwartz v. Thiele, 242 Cal. App. 2d 799, 51 Cal. Rptr. 767 (1966).

Schwenk v. State, 205 Misc. 407, 129 N.Y.S.2d 92 (Ct. Cl. 1953).

Scolavino v. State, 187 Misc. 253, 62 N.Y.S.2d 17 (Ct. Cl. 1946), *modified*, 271 App. Div. 618, 67 N.Y.S.2d 202 (1946), *modification aff'd*, 297 N.Y. 460, 74 N.E.2d 174 (1947).

Sealey v. Finkelstein, 206 N.Y.S.2d 512 (Sup. Ct. 1960).

Semler v. Psychiatric Institute of Washington, 538 F.2d 121 (4th Cir. 1976), *cert. denied mem. sub nom.*, Folliard v. Semler, 429 U.S. 827 (1976).

Seymour v. Lofgreen, 209 Kan. 72, 495 P.2d 969 (1972).

Shattuck v. State, 166 Misc. 271, 2 N.Y.S.2d 353 (Ct. Cl. 1938), *aff'd*, 254 App. Div. 926, 5 N.Y.S.2d 812 (1938).

Smart v. United States, 207 F.2d 841 (10th Cir. 1953).

Springer v. Steiner, 91 Or. 100, 178 P. 592 (1919).

Stachulak v. Coughlin, 364 F. Supp. 686 (N.D. Ill. 1973).

Stallman v. Robinson, 364 Mo. 275, 260 S.W.2d 743 (1953).

Stansfield v. Gardner, 56 Ga. App. 634, 193 S.E. 375 (1937).

Stephen v. Drew, 359 F. Supp. 746 (D.C.E.D. Va. 1973).

Stone v. Proctor, 259 N.C. 633, 131 S.E.2d 297 (1963).

Stovall v. Harms, 214 Kan. 835, 522 P.2d 353 (1974).

Stowers v. Ardmore Acres Hospital, 19 Mich. App. 115, 172 N.W.2d 497 (1969), *aff'd sub nom.*, Stowers v. Wolodsko, 386 Mich. 119, 191 N.W.2d 355 (1971).

Suhre v. Kott, 193 S.W. 417 (Tex. Ct. App. 1917).
Surprenant v. State, 46 Misc. 2d 190, 259 N.Y.S.2d 306 (Ct. Cl. 1965).
Taig v. State, 19 App. Div. 2d 183, 241 N.Y.S.2d 495 (1963).
Tarasoff v. Regents of the University of California, 33 Cal. 3d 275, 108 Cal. Rptr. 878 (1973), *aff'd*, 529 P.2d 553, 118 Cal. Rptr. 129 (1974), *vacated after rehearing*, 551 P.2d 334, 131 Cal. Rptr. 14 (1976).
Taylor v. Glotfelty, 201 F.2d 51 (6th Cir. 1952).
Taylor v. State, 36 App. Div. 2d 878, 320 N.Y.S.2d 343 (1971), *aff'd*, 33 N.Y.2d 937, 353 N.Y.S.2d 727, 309 N.E.2d 131 (1974).
Thall v. State, 69 Misc. 2d 382, 329 N.Y.S.2d 837 (Ct. Cl. 1972).
Tisinger v. Woolley, 50 S.E.2d 122 (Ga. Ct. App. 1948).
Tobias v. Manhattan Eye & Ear Hospital, 28 App. Div. 2d 972, 283 N.Y.S.2d 398 (1967).
Torres v. State, 14 Misc. 2d 246, 179 N.Y.S.2d 201 (Ct. Cl. 1958).
Trapani v. State, 23 App. Div. 2d 709, 257 N.Y.S.2d 224 (1965).
Underwood v. United States, 356 F.2d 92 (5th Cir. 1966).
United States v. Gray, 199 F.2d 239 (10th Cir. 1952).
United States v. Pardue, 354 F. Supp. 1377 (D. Conn. 1973).
University of Louisville v. Hammock, 127 Ky. 564, 106 S.W. 219 (1907).
Van Barneveld v. State, 35 App. Div. 2d 900, 315 N.Y.S.2d 764 (1970).
Vassolo v. County of Westchester Halcyon Rest Hospital, *Medical World News*, October 14, 1966, at 170-71.
Vistica v. Presbyterian Hospital & Medical Center, 67 Cal. 2d 465, 62 Cal. Rptr. 577, 432 P.2d 193 (1967).
Vitello v. State, 66 Misc. 2d 582, 321 N.Y.S.2d 787 (Ct. Cl. 1971), *aff'd*, 39 App. Div. 2d 792, 332 N.Y.S.2d 289 (1972).
Von Eye v. Hammes, 147 F. Supp. 174 (D.C. Minn. 1956), *aff'd sub nom.*, Mounds Park Hospital v. Von Eye, 245 F.2d 756 (8th Cir. 1957).
Warner v. Packer, 139 App. Div. 207, 123 N.Y.S. 725 (1910).
Warner v. State, 189 Misc. 51, 68 N.Y.S.2d 60 (Ct. Cl. 1947), *rev'd*, 272 App. Div. 954, 71 N.Y.S.2d 559 (1947), *orig. j. reinstated with new trial on damages only*, 297 N.Y. 395, 79 N.E. 2d 459 (1948).
Weglarz v. State, 31 App. Div. 2d 595, 295 N.Y.S.2d 152 (1968).
Weihs v. State, 40 N.Y.S.2d 283 (Ct. Cl. 1943), *aff'd*, 267 App. Div. 233, 45 N.Y.S.2d 542 (1943).
Weinshenk v. Kaiser Foundation Hospitals, No. 400278 (Cal. Super. Ct. 1970).
Welsch v. Likins, 373 F. Supp. 487 (D. Minn. 1974).
Wendover v. State, 63 Misc. 2d 368, 313 N.Y.S.2d 287 (Ct. Cl. 1970).
Whaley v. Kirby, 208 Cal. App. 332, 25 Cal. Rptr. 50 (1962).
Related Cases and References
Whaley v. Jansen, 208 Cal. App. 2d 222, 25 Cal. Rptr. 184 (1962).
White v. United States, 244 F. Supp. 127 (D.C.E.D. Va. 1965), *aff'd*, 359 F.2d 989 (4th Cir. 1966).
Whitesell v. Green, No. 38745 (Hawaii Dist. Ct. Nov. 19, 1973).
Whitree v. State, 56 Misc. 2d 693, 290 N.Y.S.2d 486 (Ct. Cl. 1968).
Williams v. Le Bar, 141 Pa. 149, 21 A. 525 (1891).
Williams v. State, 46 Misc. 2d 824, 260 N.Y.S.2d 953 (Ct. Cl. 1965), *rev'd*, 25 App. Div. 2d 907, 269 N.Y.S.2d 786 (1966), *reversal aff'd*, 18 N.Y.2d 481, 276 N.Y.S.2d 885 (1966).
Willis v. Western Hospital Association, 67 Idaho 435, 182 P.2d 950 (1947).
Wilson V. Lehman, 379 S.W.2d 478 (Ky. 1964).
Wood v. Samaritan Institution, 156 P.2d 470 (Cal. Dist. Ct. App. 1945), *rev'd*, 26 Cal. 2d 847, 161 P.2d 556 (1945).
Woodruff v. Shores, 354 Mo. 742, 190 S.W.2d 994 (1945).
Woods v. Brumlop, 71 N.M. 221, 377 P.2d 520 (1962).

Wright v. State, 53 Misc. 2d 521, 279 N.Y.S.2d 215 (Ct. Cl. 1967), *rev'd*, 31 App. Div. 2d 421, 300 N.Y.S.2d 153 (1969).
Wyatt v. Stickney, 325 F. Supp. 781 (M.D. Ala. 1971), *enforced in* 344 F. Supp. 373 (M.D. Ala. 1972), *enforcement aff'd in part, modified in part sub nom.*, Wyatt v. Aderholt, 503 F.2d 1305 (5th Cir. 1974).
Zipkin V. Freeman, 436 S.W.2d 753 (Mo. 1968).

CASES, BY DEFENDANT

United States, Johnson v.
United States, Kendrick v.
United States, Merchants National Bank v.
United States, Rufino v.
United States, Smart v.
United States, Underwood v.
United States, White v.
University of Pittsburgh Western Psychiatric Institute, Evanuik v.
University of Texas, Morris v.
Washington Hospital Center, Kosberg v.
Watkins, Davis v.
Weiler, Colorado State Board of Medical Examiners v.
Weimer, Bartlett v.
West, Miller v.
Western Hospital Association, Willis v.
Whitaker, Kent v.
White, Lexington Hospital v.
Wilkins, People v.
Wilkinson, Anclote Manor Foundation v.
Woolley, Tisinger v.
Zaslow, Abraham v.

ADDITIONAL CASES INVOLVING THE MALPRACTICE OF PSYCHOTHERAPISTS

Austin W. Jones Co. v. State, 122 Me. 214, 119 A. 577 (1923).
Dixon v. Weinberger, 405 F. Supp. 974 (D.D.C. 1975).
Emergy v. Littlejohn, 83 Wash. 334, 145 P. 423 (1915).
Geis v. Mark, Boston *Globe* (*New England Magazine*), January 1, 1978, at 8.
Joachim v. State, 180 Misc. 963, 43 N.Y.S.2d 167 (Ct. Cl. 1943).
Jones v. State, 267 App. Div. 254, 45 N.Y.S.2d 404 (1943).
Nelson v. Hudspeth, No. J75-40(R) (S.D. Miss.).
Related Cases and References
"Nelson v. Hudspeth." 3 *Mental Health Law Project* 8 (1977).
Pernetti v. State, 44 Misc. 2d 582, 254 N.Y.S.2d 332 (Ct. Cl. 1964).
Torrey V. Riverside Sanitarium, 163 Wis. 71, 157 N.W. 552 (1916).
Wouri v. Rosser, No. 75-80 (S.D. Me., filed Aug. 12, 1975).
Related Cases and References
"*Wouri v. Rosser.*" *3 Mental Health Law Project* 5-6 (1977).

FOREIGN CASES INVOLVING THE MALPRACTICE OF PSYCHOTHERAPISTS

Bolam v. Friern Hospital Management Committee, [1957] 1 W.L.R. 582, 2 All. E.R. 118 (Q.B.).
Furniss v. Fitchett, [1958] N.Z.L.R. 396 (1958).
Hall v. Semple, [1862] 3 F. & F. 337, 176 Eng. Rep. 151 (Q.B.).
Landau v. Werner, 105 Sol. J. 257 (Q.B. Mar. 7, 1961), *aff'd*, 105 Sol. J. 1008 (C.A. Nov. 22, 1961).

OTHER CASES REFERRED TO IN TEXT

Brune v. Belinkoff, 354 Mass. 102, 235 N.E.2d 793 (1968).
Cross v. Guthrey, 2 Root 90 (Conn. 1794).

Force v. Gregory, 63 Conn. 167, 27 A. 1116 (1893).
Lanphier v. Phipos, 8 Carrington and Payne's 475, 173 Eng. Rep. 581 (1832).
Nelson v. Dahl, 174 Minn. 574, 219 N.W. 941 (1928).
Scott v. London & St. Katherine Docks Co., 3 Hurlestone and Gordon's 596, 159 Eng. Rep. 665 (Exch. Ch. 1865).
Slater v. Baker & Stapleton, 2 Wils, 359, 95 Eng. Rep. 860 (K.B. 1767).

Bibliography

MALPRACTICE IN PSYCHOTHERAPY: LAW REVIEW ARTICLES AND BOOKS

American Law Reports 2d. "Civil Liability for Death by Suicide." *American Law Reports 2d*, 1950, v. 11, pp. 751-802.

American Law Reports 2d. "Intercourse Accomplished under Pretext of Medical Treatment as Rape." *American Law Reports 2d*, 1960, v. 70, pp. 824-29.

American Law Reports 2d. "Liability of Drugless Practitioner or Healer for Malpractice." *American Law Reports 2d*, 1951, v. 19, pp. 1188-224.

American Law Reports 2d. "Malpractice Liability with Respect to Diagnosis and Treatment of Mental Disease." *American Law Reports 2d*, 1965, v. 99, pp. 599-627.

American Law Reports 3d. "Civil Liability of Doctor or Psychologist for Having Sexual Relationship with Patient." *American Law Reports 3d*, 1970, v. 33, pp. 1393-96.

American Law Reports 3d. "Improper or Immoral Conduct toward Female Patient as Ground for Disciplinary Measure against Physician or Dentist." *American Law Reports*, 1967, v. 15, pp. 1179-82.

Beresford, H.R. "Professional Liability of Psychiatrists." *Defense Law Journal*, 1972, v. 21, pp. 123-67.

Cassidy, P.S. "The Liability of Psychiatrists for Malpractice." *University of Pittsburgh Law Review*, 1974, v. 36, pp. 108-37.

Dawidoff, D.J. "The Malpractice of Psychiatrists." *Duke Law Journal*, 1966, v. 1966, pp. 696-716.

Dawidoff, D.J. *The Malpractice of Psychiatrists: Malpractice in Psychoanalysis, Psychotherapy and Psychiatry.* Springfield, Ill.: Charles C. Thomas, 1973.

Fink, V.M. "Medical Malpractice: The Liability of Psychiatrists." *Notre Dame Lawyer*, 1973, v. 48, pp. 693-708.

Glenn, R.D. "Standard of Care in Administering Non-traditional Psychotherapy." *University of California, Davis Law Review*, 1974, v. 7, pp. 56-83.

Harris, M. "Tort Liability of the Psychotherapist." *University of San Francisco Law Review*, 1973, v. 8, pp. 405-36.

Heller, M.S. "Some Comments to Lawyers on the Practice of Psychiatry." *Temple Law Quarterly*, 1957, v. 30, pp. 401-7.

Kennedy, C.A. "Injuries Precipitated by Psychotherapy: Liability without Fault as a Basis for Recovery." *South Dakota Law Review*, 1975, v. 20, pp. 401-17.

Leroy, D.H. "The Potential Criminal Liability of Human Sex Clinics and Their Patients." *St. Louis University Law Journal*, 1972, v. 16, pp. 586-603.

Love, G.H., Jr., and Yanity, G. J. "Psychotherapy and the Law." *Medical Trial Technique Quarterly*, 1974, v. 20, pp. 405-29.

Merrill, R.A. "Compensation for Prescription Drug Injuries." *Virginia Law Review*, 1973, v. 59, pp. 1-120.

Messinger, S. "Malpractice Suits—The Psychiatrist's Turn." *Journal of Legal Medicine*, 1975, v. 3(4), pp. 31-39.

Morse, H.N. "The Tort Liability of the Psychiatrist." *Buffalo Law Review*, 1966-67, v. 16, pp. 649-87.

Perr, I.N. "Legal Aspects of Sexual Therapies." *Journal of Legal Medicine*, 1975, v. 3(1), pp. 33-38.

Rothblatt, H.B., and Leroy, D.H. "Avoiding Psychiatric Malpractice," *California Western Law Review*, 1973, v. 9, pp. 260-72.

Sauer, J.G. "Psychiatric Malpractice—A Survey." *Washburn Law Journal*, 1972, v. 11, pp. 461-70.

Saxe, D.B. "Psychiatric Treatment and Malpractice." *Medico-Legal Journal*, 1969, v. 37, pp. 187-96.

Stone, A.A. "The *Tarasoff* Decisions: Suing Psychotherapists to Safeguard Society." *Harvard Law Review*, 1976, v. 90, pp. 358-78.

Tarshis, C.B. "Liability for Psychotherapy." *Faculty of Law Review* (University of Toronto), 1972, v. 30, pp. 75-92.

MALPRACTICE IN PSYCHOTHERAPY: OTHER REFERENCES

APA Monitor. "Psychologist Faces Malpractice Charges." *APA Monitor*, September-October 1972, p. 16.

APA Monitor. "Rage Reduction Therapy Pioneer Battles to Keep California License." *APA Monitor*, March 1973, p. 5.

Appleton, W.S. "Legal Problems in Psychiatric Drug Prescription." *American Journal of Psychiatry*, 1968, v. 124, pp. 877-82.

Behavior Today, "Malpractice-Insurance Problems for Psychologists." *Behavior Today*, March 8, 1976, pp. 4-5.

Behavior Today. "Malpractice Insurance and the Psychotherapists." *Behavior Today*, January 17, 1977, pp. 2-4.

Bellamy, W.A. "Malpractice in Psychiatry." *Diseases of the Nervous System*, 1965, v. 26, pp. 312-20.

Bellamy, W.A. "Malpractice Risks Confronting the Psychiatrist: A Nationwide Fifteen-year Study of Appellate Court Cases, 1946 to 1961." *American Joural of Psychiatry*, 1962, v. 118, pp. 769-80.

British Medical Journal. "Negligent Psychiatric Treatment." *British Medical Journal*, March 18, 1961, pp. 835-36.

Brownfain, J.J. "The APA Professional Liability Insurance Program." *American Psychologist*, 1971, v. 26, pp, 648-52.

Dawidoff, D.J. "Some Suggestions to Psychiatrists for Avoiding Legal Jeopardy." *Archives of General Psychiatry*, 1973, v. 29, pp. 699-701.

Freeman, L., and Roy, J. *Betrayal*. New York: Stein and Day, 1976.

Garcetti, G., and Suarez, J.M. "The Liability of Psychiatric Hospitals for the Acts of Their Patients." *American Journal of Psychiatry*, 1968, v. 124, pp. 961-68.

Hamilton, J.M. "Malpractice from the Private Practice and Institutional Psychiatric Viewpoint." *Maryland State Medical Journal*, 1970, v. 19, pp. 69-74.

Layne, B. "Excessive Prescription of Amphetamines: Who Enforces Ethical Norms?" Case Study No. 14. Mimeographed. Kennedy Interfaculty Program in Medical Ethics, Harvard University, Cambrdige, Mass., undated.

Penn, M.R. "The Application of Tort Doctrines to the Encounter or Sensitivity Movement." Unpublished manuscript, Harvard Law School, Cambridge, Mass., 1971.

Perr, I.N. "Liability of Hospital and Psychiatrist in Suicide." *American Journal of Psychiatry*, 1965, v. 122, pp. 631-38.

Roston, R.A., and Sherrer, C.W. "Malpractice: What's New?" *Professional Psychology*, 1973, v. 4, pp. 270-76.

Sadusk, J.F., and Waterson, R. "Professional Liability—A Statistical Study of Professional Liability Claims in California." *California Medicine*, 1957, v. 87, pp. 192-99.

Schneider, C. "Beyond *Roy v. Hartogs:* Liability of Psychiatrists for Sexual Relationships with Former Patients." Unpublished Third-Year Paper, Harvard Law School, Cambridge, Mass., 1976.

Slawson, P.F. "Psychiatric Malpractice: A Regional Incidence Study." *American Journal of Psychiatry*, 1970, v. 126, pp. 1302-5.

Slawson, P.F.; Flinn, D.E.; and Schwartz, D.A. "Legal Responsibility for Suicide." *Psychiatric Quarterly*, 1974, v. 48, pp. 50-64.

Slovenko, R. "The Impact of the Law on Psychiatric Practice." *Career Directions*, 1976, v. 5, pp. 33-44.

Slovenko, R. *Psychiatry and Law*. Boston: Little, Brown, 1973.

Stone, A.A. "The Legal Implications of Sexual Activity between Psychiatrist and Patient." *American Journal of Psychiatry*, 1976, v. 133, pp. 1138-41.

Trent, C.L. "Early Claims Experience with the A.P.A. Professional Liability Program." Unpublished manuscript, undated.

Trent, C.L., and Muhl, W.P. "Professional Liability Insurance and the American Psychiatrist." *American Journal of Psychiatry*, 1975, v. 132, pp. 1312-14.

Tryon, W.W. "Behavior Modification Therapy and the Law." *Professional Psychology*, 1976, v. 7, pp. 468-74.

White, A.E., and Gross, R.B. "Professional Liability Insurance and the Psychologist." *Professional Psychology*, 1975, v. 6, pp. 267-71.

RIGHT TO TREATMENT

American Psychiatric Association, Commission on Judicial Action. "Amicus Curiae Brief in the Donaldson Case." *American Journal of Psychiatry*, 1975, v. 132, pp. 109-15.

Bazelon, D.L. "Implementing the Right to Treatment." *University of Chicago Law Review*, 1969, v. 36, pp. 742-54.

Catholic Lawyer, "Adequate Psychiatric Treatment—A Constitutional Right?" *Catholic Lawyer*, 1973, v. 19, pp. 322-45.

Chambers, D.L. "Alternatives to Civil Commitment of the Mentally Ill: Practical Guides and Constitutional Imperatives." *Michigan Law Review*, 1972, v. 70, pp. 1107-200.

Flaschner, F.N. "Legal Rigthts of the Mentally Handicapped: A Judge's Viewpoint." *American Bar Association Journal*, 1974, v. 30, pp. 1370-75.

Fordham Urban Law Journal. "Civil Rights—Right to Treatment—Neither Due Process Nor Equal Protection Clause of the Fourteenth Amendment Guarantees the 'Right to Treatment' for Mentally Retarded Children Confined in a State Institution through Noncriminal Procedures." *Fordham Urban Law Journal*, 1974, v. 2, pp. 363-75.

Harvard Law Review. "*Wyatt v. Stickney* and the Right of Civilly Committed Mental Patients to Adequate Treatment." *Harvard Law Review*, 1973, v. 86, pp. 1282-306.

Kenney, H. "Civil Rights: The Federal Courts and the 'Right to Treatment' under 42 U.S.C. § 1983 (1970)." *Oklahoma Law Review*, 1974, v. 27, pp. 238-43.

Kopolow, L.E. "A Review of Major Implications of the *O'Connor v. Donaldson* Decision." *American Journal of Psychiatry*, 1976, v. 133, pp. 379-83.

Schwitzgebel, R.K. "The Right to Effective Mental Treatment." *California Law Review*, 1974, v. 62, pp. 936-56.

Schwitzgebel, R.K. "Right to Treatment for the Mentally Disabled: The Need for Realistic Standards and Objective Criteria." *Harvard Civil Rights-Civil Liberties Law Review*, 1973, v. 8, pp. 513-35.

Stone, A.A. "Overview: The Right to Treatment—Comments on the Law and Its Impact." *American Journal of Psychiatry*, 1975, v. 132, pp. 1125-34.

Stone, A.A. "Recent Mental Health Litigation: A Critical Perspective." *American Journal of Psychiatry*, 1977, v. 134, pp. 273-79.

Stone, A.A. "The Right to Treatment and the Medical Establishment." *Bulletin of the American Academy of Psychiatry and the Law*, 1974, v. 2, pp. 159-67.

University of Colorado Law Review. "The Supreme Court Sidesteps the Right to Treatment Question." *University of Colorado Law Review*, 1976, v. 47, pp. 299-323.

Virginia Law Review. "The Nascent Right to Treatment." *Virginia Law Review*, 1967, v. 53, pp. 1134-60.

BASIC TEXTS ON MALPRACTICE LAW

Ficarra, B. *Surgical and Allied Malpractice.* Springfield, Ill.: C.C. Thomas, 1968.

Holder, A.R. *Medical Malpractice Law.* New York: John Wiley, 1975.

Louisell, D.W., and Williams, H. *Medical Malpractice.* 2 vols. New York: Matthew Bander, 1973 and 1975.

Morris, R.C., and Moritz, A. *Doctor and Patient and the Law.* 5th ed. St. Louis, Mo.: Mosby, 1971.

Prosser, W.L. *Handbook of the Law of Torts.* 3rd ed. St. Paul, Minn.: West Publishing Co., Hornbook Series, 1964.

IMPACT OF MALPRACTICE SUITS GENERALLY, AND RECOMMENDATIONS FOR CHANGE

Aitken, W.A. "Medical Malpractice: The Alleged 'Crisis' in Perspective." *Western State University Law Review*, 1975, v. 3, pp. 27-39.

Bernzweig, E.P. "Lawsuits: A Symptom, Not a Cause." *Trial*, February-March 1970, pp. 14-15, 22.

Brook, R.H.; Brutoco, R.L.; and Williams, K.N. "The Relationship between Medical Malpractice and Quality of Care." In Duke Law Journal, *Medical Malpractice.* Cambridge, Mass.: Ballinger Publishing Co., 1977, pp. 19-53. (Reprint of January 1975 issue.)

Havighurst, C.C., and Tancredi, L.R. "'Medical Adversity Insurance'—A No-Fault Approach to Medical Malpractice and Quality Assurance." *Insurance Law Journal*, 1974 (no. 613), pp. 69-100.

Hullverson, T.C. "Medical Malpractice and Screening Panels." *Journal of the Missouri Bar*, 1975, v. 31, pp. 458-70.

King, J.Y. "A Critique of the Report of HEW's Medical Malpractice Commission." *Journal of Legal Medicine*, 1974, v. 2(2), pp. 39-44.

McDonald, D., ed. *Medical Malpractice: A Discussion of Alternative Compensation and Quality Control Systems.* Santa Barbara, Calif.: Center for the Study of Democratic Institutions, 1971.

Mechanic, D. "Some Social Aspects of the Medical Malpractice Dilemma." In Duke

Law Journal, *Medical Malpractice.* Cambridge, Mass.: Ballinger Publishing Co., 1977, pp. 1-18. (Reprint of January 1975 issue).

Miike, L.H. "Public Policy Directions in Medical Malpractice." *Journal of Legal Medicine,* 1976, v. 4(4), pp. 9-13.

O'Connell, J. *Ending Insult to Injury: No-Fault Insurance for Products and Services.* Urbana, Ill.: University of Illinois Press, 1975.

U.S. Congress. Senate. Committee on Government Operations. Subcommittee on Executive Reorganization. *Medical Malpractice: The Patient Versus the Physician.* 91st Cong., 1st sess., November 20, 1969. Washington, D.C.: U.S. Government Printing Office, 1969.

U.S. Department of Health, Education, and Welfare (DHEW). *Medical Malpractice: Report of the Secretary's Commission on Medical Malpractice.* DHEW Publication No. OS 73-88. Washington, D.C.: U.S. Government Printing Office, 1973.

U.S. Department of Health, Education, and Welfare. *Medical Malpractice: Report of the Secretary's Commission on Medical Malpractice: Appendix.* DHEW Publication No. OS 73-89. Washington, D.C.: U.S. Government Printing Office, 1973.

OTHER REFERENCES

Boston Globe, "Physician, Heal Thyself." (Editorial.) *Boston Globe,* August 24, 1975.

Brophy, J.J. "Suicide Attempts with Psychotherapeutic Drugs." *Archives of General Psychiatry,* 1967, v. 17, pp. 652-57.

Curran, W.J. "Professional Negligence—Some General Comments." *Vanderbilt Law Review,* 1959, v. 12, pp. 535-47.

Curran, W.J., and Shapiro, E.D. *Law, Medicine, and Forensic Science.* Boston: Little, Brown, 1970.

Dörken, H. and Associates. *The Professional Psychologist Today: New Developments in Law, Health Insurance, and Health Practice.* San Francisco: Jossey-Bass, 1976.

Garceau, O. "The Morals of Medicine." *Annals of the American Academy of Political and Social Science,* 1966, v. 363, pp. 60-69.

Grunebaum, H.; Nadelson, C.C.; and Macht, L.B. "Sexual Activity with the Psychiatrist: A District Branch Dilemma." Unpublished manuscript draft, undated.

Henahan, J.F. "Malpractice." *Atlantic Monthly,* April 1976, pp. 6, 11-12, 14, 16, 18.

Knapp, T.A., and Huff, R.L. "Emerging Trends in the Physician's Duty to Disclose: An Update of *Canterbury v. Spence.*" *Journal of Legal Medicine,* 1975, v. 3(1), pp. 41-45.

McCleery, R.S.; Keelty, L.T.; Lam, M.; Phillips, R.E.; and Quirin, T.M. *One Life—One Physician: An Inquiry into the Medical Profession's Performance in Self-Regulation.* A Report to the Center for Study of Responsive Law. Washington, D.C.: Public Affairs Press, 1971.

McCoid, A.H. "The Care Required of Medical Practitioners." *Vanderbilt Law Review,* 1959, v. 12, pp. 549-632.

Magruder, C. "Mental and Emotional Disturbance in the Law of Torts." *Harvard Law Review,* 1936, v. 49, pp. 1033-67.

Minnesota Law Review. "Overcoming the 'Conspiracy of Silence.'" *Minnesota Law Review.* 1961, v. 45, pp. 119-55.

New England Law Review. "Helling v. Carey: Landmark or Exception in Medical Malpractice? Compliance with the Medical Standard of Care May Not Protect the Specialist from Liability." *New England Law Review,* 1975, v. 11, pp. 301-12.

Proehl, P.O. "Tort Liability of Teachers." *Vanderbilt Law Review,* 1959, v. 12, pp. 723-54.

Sandor, A.A. "The History of Professional Liability Suits in the United States." *Journal of the American Medical Association,* 1957, v. 163, pp. 459-66.

Smith, H.W., and Solomon, H.C. "Traumatic Neuroses in Court." *Virginia Law Review*, 1943, v. 30, pp. 87-175.

Symonds, A. "Machismo at Its Worst." *Psychistric News*, 1977, v. 12(4), p.2.

Time Magazine. "Suing the Doctor." *Time Magazine*, July 15, 1974, p. 78.

Wharton, L. "Medical Malpractice—Compliance with Professional Standards Does Not Necessarily Absolve Ophthalmologist from Liability for Negligence in Failing to Diagnose and Treat Glaucoma." *Texas Tech Law Review*, 1974, v. 6, pp. 279-84.

References*

Bellamy, W.A. 1965. "Malpractice in Psychiatry." *Diseases of the Nervous System*, v. 26, pp. 312-20.

Bellamy, W.A. 1962. "Malpractice Risks Confronting the Psychiatrist: A Nationwide Fifteen-year Study of Appellate Court Cases, 1946 to 1961." *American Journal of Psychiatry*, v. 118, pp. 769-80.

Brook, R.H.; Brutoco, R.L.; and Williams, K.N. 1977. "The Relationship between Medical Malpractice and Quality of Care." In Duke Law Journal, *Medical Malpractice*. Cambridge, Mass.: Ballinger Publishing Co., pp. 19-53. (Reprint of January 1975 issue.)

Brownfain, J.J. 1971. "The APA Professional Liability Insurance Program." *American Psychologist*, v. 26, pp. 648-52.

Cassidy, P.S. 1974. "The Liability of Psychiatrists for Malpractice." *University of Pittsburgh Law Review*, v. 36, pp. 108-37.

Curran, W.J. 1959. "Professional Negligence—Some General Comments." *Vanderbilt Law Review*, v. 12, pp. 535-47.

Dawidoff, D.J. 1973. *The Malpractice of Psychiatrists: Malpractice in Psychoanalysis, Psychotherapy and Psychiatry*. Springfield, Ill.: Charles C. Thomas.

Dawidoff, D.J. 1966. "The Malpractice of Psychiatrists." *Duke Law Journal*, 1966, v. 1966, pp. 696-716.

Dörken, H. and Associates. 1976. *The Professional Psychologist Today: New Developments in Law, Health Insurance, and Health Practice*. San Francisco: Jossey-Bass.

Ficarra, B. 1968. *Surgical and Allied Malpractice*. Springfield, Ill.: C.C. Thomas.

Fink, V.M. 1973. "Medical Malpractice: The Liability of Psychiatrists." *Notre Dame Lawyer*, v. 48, pp. 693-708.

Frank, J.D. 1973. *Persuasion and Healing: A Comparative Study of Psychotherapy*. Rev. ed. Baltimore, Md.: Johns Hopkins Press.

Heller, M.S. 1957. "Some Comments to Lawyers on the Practice of Psychiatry." *Temple Law Quarterly*, v. 30, pp. 401-7.

Holder, A.R. 1975. *Medical Malpractice Law*. New York: John Wiley.

Kett, J.F. 1968. *The Formation of the American Medical Profession, 1780-1860*. New Haven, Conn.: Yale University Press.

Louisell, D.W., and Williams, H. 1973. *Medical Malpractice*. Vol. 1. New York: Matthew Bender.

Louisell, D.W., and Williams, H. 1975. *Medical Malpractice*. Vol 2. New York: Matthew Bender.

*Legal cases are contained in Appendix D.

Magruder, C. 1936. "Mental and Emotional Disturbance in the Law of Torts." *Harvard Law Review*, v. 49, pp. 1033-67.

Mechanic, D. 1977. "Some Social Aspects of the Medical Malpractice Dilemma." In Duke Law Journal, *Medical Malpractice.* Cambridge, Mass.: Ballinger Publishing Co., pp. 1-18.

Minnesota Law Review. 1961. "Overcoming the 'Conspiracy of Silence.'" *Minnesota Law Review*, v. 45, pp. 119-55.

Pope, Alexander. 1754. "Who Shall Decide When Doctors Disagree?" In *Moral Essays.* Glasgow: R. Urie.

Prosser, W.L. 1964. *Handbook of the Law of Torts.* 3rd ed. St. Paul, Minn.: West Publishing Co., Hornbook Series.

Rothblatt, H.B., and Leroy, D.H. 1973. "Avoiding Psychiatric Malpractice." *California Western Law Review*, v. 9, pp. 260-72.

Sadusk, J.F., and Waterson, R. 1957. "Professional Liability—A Statistical Study of Professional Liability Claims in California." *California Medicine*, v. 87, pp. 192-99.

Sandor, A.A. 1957. "The History of Professional Liability Suits in the United States." *Journal of the American Medical Association*, v. 163, pp. 459-66.

Saxe, D.B. 1969. "Psychiatric Treatment and Malpractice." *Medico-Legal Journal*, v. 37, pp. 187-96.

Slawson, P.F. 1970. "Psychiatric Malpractice: A Regional Incidence Study." *American Journal of Psychiatry*, v. 126, pp. 1302-5.

Stone, A.A. 1977. "Recent Mental Health Litigation: A Critical Perspective." *American Journal of Psychiatry*, v. 134, pp. 273-79.

Stone, A.A. 1976. "The *Tarasoff* Decisions: Suing Psychotherapists to Safeguard Society." *Harvard Law Review*, v. 90, pp. 358-78.

Stone, A.A. 1975. "Overview: The Right to Treatment—Comments on the Law and Its Impact." *American Journal of Psychiatry*, v. 132, pp. 1125-34.

Stone, A.A. 1970. "The Quest of the Counterculture." *International Journal of Psychiatry*, v. 9, pp. 219-26.

Trent, C.L. Undated. "Early Claims Experience with the A.P.A. Professional Liability Program." Unpublished manuscript.

U.S. Department of Health, Education, and Welfare. 1973. *Medical Malpractice: Report of the Secretary's Commission on Medical Malpractice.* (DHEW Publication No. OS 73-88.) Washington, D.C.: U.S. Government Printing Office.

U.S. Department of Health, Education, and Welfare. 1973a. *Medical Malpractice: Report of the Secretary's Commission on Medical Malpractice: Appendix.* (DHEW Publication No. OS 73-89.) Washington, D.C.: U.S. Government Printing Office.

White, A.E., and Gross, R.B. 1975. "Professional Liability Insurance and the Psychologist." *Professional Psychology*, v. 6, pp. 267-71.

Wigmore, J.H. 1961. *Evidence in Trials at Common Law.* (Rev. ed.) Boston: Little, Brown.

Glossary of Abbreviations and Symbols

Cases Never at Trial Level Includes cases settled out of court, those not yet decided, and those begun at the supreme court level.

Commit. Pcdgs. Init. Initiator of mental hospital commitment proceedings.

Consc. Pain & Suffer. Conscious pain and suffering.

Const. Rts. in Gen. Constitutional rights in general.

Correctional Inst. Correctional institution.

Doc-Pat. Priv. Prevented Info. Disclosure The doctor-patient relationship as establishing a privilege preventing information disclosure.

Encounter. Grp. Leader Encounter group leader.

Exacerb. of Prev. Condition Exacerbation of a person's previous condition.

Fail. to do Stat. Duty Failure to do one's statutory duty.

Failure to Consult Failure to properly consult another therapist.

Fraud-Breach of Con. Fraud and breach of contract.

Govern. Immunity Governmental immunity barred suit.

Hosp. Infor. is Priv. Hospital information is privileged.

Ins. Claim Payment Insurance claim payment.

Involunt. Servitude Involuntary servitude, peonage, and/or slavery.

Jud. Pcdg. & Pub. Hosp. Judicial proceeding and public hospital.

Judge; Jury Present? Decision made by judge, but unknown whether jury was present.

Judge, no jury Decision made by judge with no jury present.

Judge, Uninv. Jury Decision made by judge, although jury was present.

Jury Decision made by jury.

Lic. Rev. Pcdg. License revocation proceeding.

Loss of Compnship Loss of companionship.

Mal. Infl. of Emot. Dis Malicious infliction of emotional distress.

Ment. Ill, Instead of Physical Illness Mental illness, instead of physical illness.

Mot. to Dism. Indict. Motion to dismiss indictment.

Neg. Admin. of Drugs Negligent administration of drugs.

Neg. Appl. of Wetpack Negligent application of wetpacks.

Neg. Determ. of Competence to Stand Trial Negligent determination of a person's competence to stand trial.

Neg. Determ. of Type of Sentence Negligent determination of type of sentence.

Neg. Determ. of Unfitness for Duty Negligent determination that person was unfit for duty.

Neg. Rec. to take Psychiatric Exam Negligent recommendation to take a psychiatric examination.

Neg. Transfer. or Ctrt. Negligent handling of the transference or countertransference relationship.

No bad faith or Mal. No bad faith or malice demonstrated.

No Chance for Impr. No chance for improvement.

Nonprof. Org. Pat., Ins. Nonprofit organization, patient, and correctional institution.

Nonpsychiat. or Unknown Type Physician(s) Nonpsychiatrist(s) or unknown type of physician(s).

Pat. & 3rd Pty., I Patient and third party injured by harm to patient.

Patient(s) or Rep. Patient(s) or representative(s).

Phys. Ill, Instead of Ment. Illness Physical illness, instead of mental illness.

Pl's. Spouse &/ Moth. Plaintiff's spouse and/or mother.

Preg. & Abortion Pregnancy and abortion.

Priv. Gen. Hosp. Private general hospital.

Priv. Inv.-Proc. Abuse Invasion of privacy and abuse of process.

Priv. Ment. Hosp. Private mental hospital.

Pub. & Priv. Men. Hosp. Public and private mental hospital.

Pub. Gen. Hosp. Public general hospital.

Pub. Ment. Hosp. Public mental hospital.

?, Judge or Jury A question exists as to whether the decision was made by a judge or jury.

? Whether Care Inv. A question exists as to whether care is involved.

? Whether Diag. Inv. A question exists as to whether diagnosis is involved.

? Whether Treat. Inv. A question exists as to whether negligent treatment was involved.

Race Discr-Cl. Act. Racial discrimination suit and class action.

Reappeal to App. Includes all cases remanded to a lower court and reappealed to the appellate court level.

Reappeal to S.C. Includes all cases remanded to a lower court and reappealed to the supreme court either directly or after reappeal to an appellate-level court.

Remanded to App. Ct. Includes cases remanded from the supreme court to an appellate court, instead of for retrial.

Respondeat Superior The doctrine that those responsible for another's behavior are equally liable for that person's acts.

Rt. to Refuse Treat. Right to refuse treatment.

Self-infl. or Acc. Inj Self-inflicted injuries or accidental injuries, but unknown which one.

Sexual Abuse or Disturb or Marital Rel. Sexual abuse or disturbance of the marital relationship.

State of Limitations The statute of limitations operating as a bar to suit.

Suic. or Accid. Death Suicide or accidental death, but unknown which one.

3rd Party, I Third party injured by harm to patient.

3rd Party, I & II Third party injured by patient and third party injured by harm to patient.

To be Determ. on Retr Damages to be determined on retrial.

US Sup. Ct. fr. State Includes only those U.S. Supreme Court cases on appeal from state courts.

Unspec. Neg. Treat The type of negligent treatment was unspecified.

About the Author

After graduating from Yale University in 1965, Dan Hogan was a Peace Corps volunteer in rural community development in Lesotho, Africa. He subsequently obtained a master's degree in education from Boston University and in 1972 received his law degree from Harvard Law School. Since then he has been a consultant in the small-group field, with the main focus of his work on T-groups and the training of small-group leaders. In this capacity he has been an Associate of McBer and Company in Boston and has been a consultant to various government and nongovernment agencies, including the Department of Health, Education, and Welfare and the Office of Minority Business Enterprise.

Hogan's major current interest is the development and regulation of the mental health profession. He is also extremely interested in the role of the professions in society and in establishing sound mechanisms for determining professional competence. Hogan serves on the Board of Directors of the National Center for the Study of Professions, the International Association of Applied Social Scientists, and the New England Training Institute. For the past three years he has been a Research Fellow in the Department of Psychology and Social Relations at Harvard University, where he is currently completing his Ph.D. in Social Psychology.